MW01628160

Livio Pestilli

Bernini and His World

Sculpture and Sculptors in Early Modern Rome

LUND HUMPHRIES

First published in 2022 by Lund Humphries

Lund Humphries
Office 3, Book House
261A City Road
London EC1V 1JX
UK

www.lundhumphries.com

ISBN: 978-1-84822-549-7

A Cataloguing-in-Publication record for this book is available from the British Library.

Front cover:
Gian Lorenzo Bernini, *Apollo and Daphne* (detail), 1625, marble, height 243 cm (95 11⁄16 in), Galleria Borghese, Rome. © Luciano Romano. Courtesy of Borghese Gallery, Rome.

Back cover:
Ottavio Leoni, *Portrait of Gian Lorenzo Bernini*, 1622, engraving, 14.1 × 11 cm (5 9⁄16 × 4 5⁄16 in), Royal Collection Trust, Windsor Castle. Royal Collection Trust/© Her Majesty Queen Elizabeth II 2021.

Copy edited by Pamela Bertram
Designed by Jacqui Cornish
Proofread by Patrick Cole
Cover design by Mark Thomson
Set in Adobe Caslon Pro
Printed in China

Contents

Acknowledgments

My heartfelt thanks to all those individuals who helped on various aspects and phases of this book. I would like to express my sincere gratitude to Roberta Bartoli, Mario Bevilacqua, Francesca Cappelletti, Giorgio Capriotti, Sonia Cardenas, Lorenza D'Alessandro, Dario Del Puppo, Ursula Verena Fischer Pace, Giuseppe Greco Luciani, Kristina Hermann Fiore, Stephen D. Marth, Daniele Martini, Heather Minor, Jennifer Montagu, Francesca Nicoli, Mitchell A. Polin, Francesca Persegati, Louise Rice, Ingrid D. Rowland, Jennifer Thompson, Simona Turriziani, Xena Wang and Pietro Zander.

Special thanks to The Cesare Barbieri Endowment for Italian Studies (Hartford, Connecticut) and Trinity College (Hartford and Rome) for their generous subsidies that helped cover publication costs and to Federico Pestilli for his advice and assistance on photographic matters. I would also like to acknowledge my indebtedness to Erika Gaffney at Lund Humphries for her continued support of my projects through the years, as well as to William E. Wallace and Wendy Imperial for their valuable comments and suggestions on an early version of the text. Most of all, I wish to thank Steven F. Ostrow, whose knowledge of Bernini studies, advice, critique and recommendations throughout the gestation of the book were instrumental to the successful completion of the same.

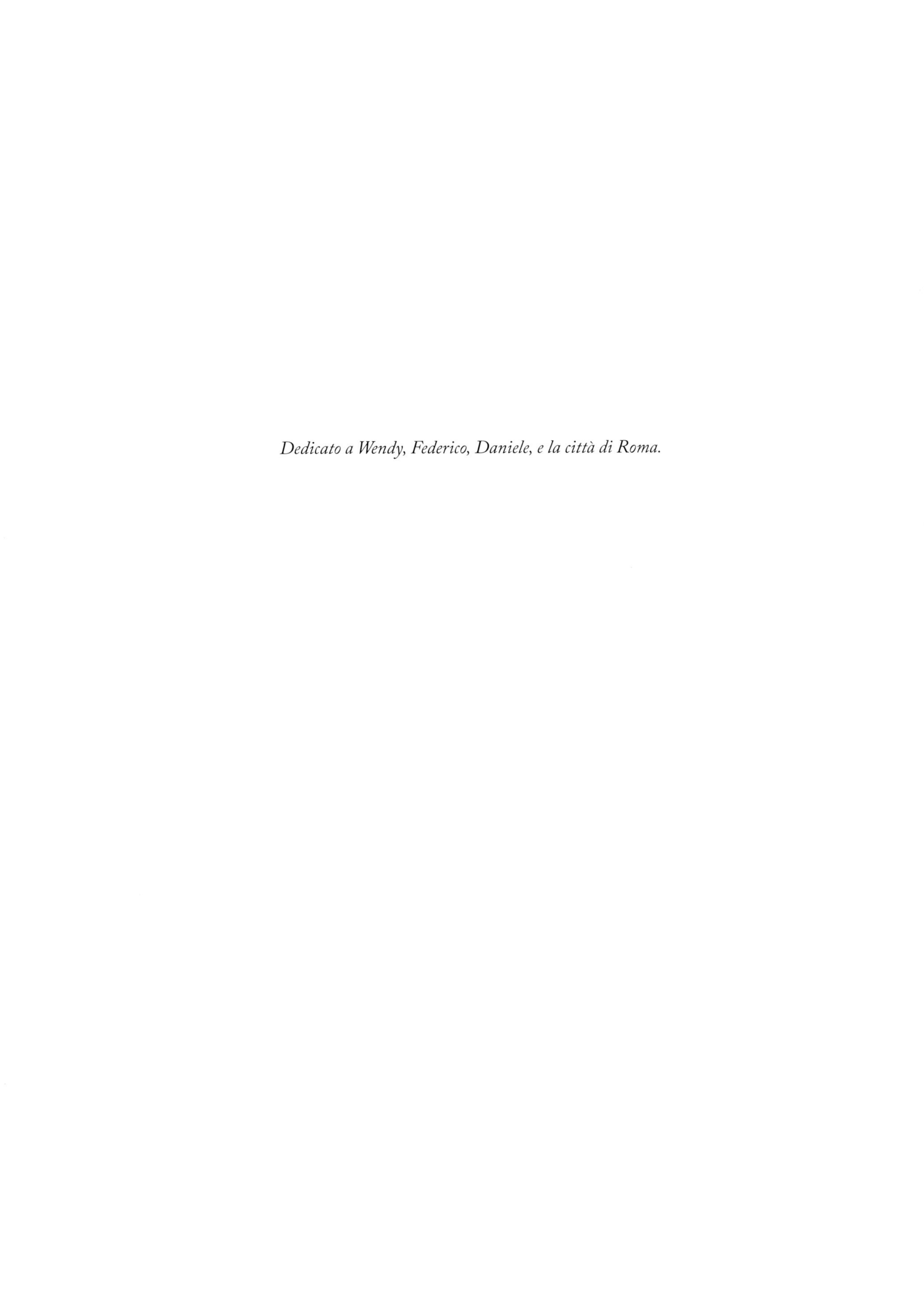

Dedicato a Wendy, Federico, Daniele, e la città di Roma.

Preface

An astounding feature of seventeenth- and early eighteenth-century Roman art is the plethora of sculptural works that fill the city's numerous churches and museums. A visit to a single venue in the Eternal City is sufficient evidence of the sculptors' copious output during this period: the church of Sant'Agnese in Agone. Even the 'accidental tourist' who walks into what was basically the Pamphili family private chapel in Piazza Navona cannot be but struck by the fact that all seven altars in this house of prayer are graced with sculptures rather than paintings. But a jaunt to any other church in the heart of the Holy City by the discerning art lover will only reinforce the perception that the sculptors working at that time had vast employment opportunities. Indeed, echoing Cassiodorus' advice to the city's prefect to hire an architect for the preservation of Rome's statues – 'an artificial population almost equal to its natural one' – Leopoldo Cicognara noted in his history of Italian sculpture how 'a population of statues decorated all of these sacred edifices'.[1] In fact, during this period, scores of marble workers from different parts of Italy and north of the Alps were attracted to Rome in search of work and fame. None, however, was so successful in giving his personal artistic imprint to the city as did Gian Lorenzo Bernini.[2] As the recipient of the most important papal and private commissions, Bernini astounded his contemporaries by prodigious carving skills that allowed him to quickly rise to the top of his professional and social pyramid. Looking at any of his sculptures, one can easily understand why already during his lifetime he was considered the new Michelangelo. Of course, there were other contemporary sculptors who produced great works of art, but it would not be inaccurate to claim that Baroque Rome is ultimately 'Bernini's Rome'.

In the course of the last century, numerous books and articles have been devoted to the great artist that have reclaimed his proper role in the history of western art. After the Neoclassical infatuation with Greek art and the caustic censure voiced from the mid-eighteenth to the early nineteenth century by critics such as Winckelmann, Fernow, Milizia and Cicognara, a new phase in Bernini studies was initiated by the publication of Stanislao Fraschetti's *Il Bernini: la sua vita, la sua opera, il suo tempo* (1900). Despite the passage of time, this volume remains a valuable source and a model of significant archival research by Adolfo Venturi's incredibly prolific protégé who tragically died at the young age of twenty-seven. However, no two scholars in the twentieth century did more for the revival of interest in Bernini and Baroque art than Rudolf Wittkower and Irving Lavin. Starting with the coedited study with Heinrich Brauer of Bernini's drawings, *Die Zeichnungen des Gianlorenzo Bernini* (1931), followed by the standard (to this day) anthology *Art and Architecture in Italy 1600–1750* (1958), and the even more valuable *Gian Lorenzo Bernini: The Sculptor of the Roman Baroque* (1955), Wittkower single-handedly brought about a fundamental reassessment of the most creative genius of seventeenth-century Italy. But what Wittkower initiated, Lavin consolidated. The latter's profuse output of influential Bernini studies that stretch across the second half of the twentieth century are too numerous to mention, but they may now be conveniently consulted in the two-volume set *Visible Spirit: The Art of Gian Lorenzo Bernini* (2007–9). Nevertheless, Lavin's *Bernini and the Unity of the Visual Arts* (1980) merits special mention as the one work that left his most important mark on the subject. In fact, this publication and Wittkower's *Art and Architecture in Italy 1600–1750* have proven so fundamental to Bernini studies that they were recently included in a small, exclusive list of essential readings on Baroque art.[3] The work of these two 'giants' has influenced many scholars who, in turn, have enriched our understanding of Bernini and the Baroque. Enumerating them would generate a very long list of doubtful expediency in this context. Suffice it to say that a quick glance at any online library catalogue will give an indication of the extensive body of scholarly writing that has been generated.[4] The present study represents a contribution to these ongoing efforts.

Even though sculpture is the common denominator of this book, the impetus to write it arose from a desire to study the artist and the context in which he worked through different 'lenses'. Thus, while loosely retaining a chronological progression that follows the artist from 'the cradle to the grave', I have chosen to treat the subject typologically; that is, I have concentrated on themes that, by taking Bernini as their starting point, shed a light on the wider artistic context. However, it should be clear from the outset that the book is not just about Bernini, nor is it limited to subjects and events that relate strictly to his lifetime. Rather, it is a study that looks at social and anthropological themes that expand our horizon on the subject; it looks to the past as well as to the period following Bernini's death to better understand his world, the mythopoeic efforts of his biographers, and the influence he exerted on other artists.

Thus, in the first chapter, '*Berninus Neapolitan[us] sculptor*', I choose to address a socio-anthropological bias present in seventeenth-century Italy that helps us understand why Bernini, though born in Naples, preferred to refer to himself as a Florentine or a Roman. Besides the artist's personal and artistic reasons for claiming allegiance to Florence or Rome, the study reveals how deep-seated geographical and ethnic biases vis-à-vis southerners, in general, and Neapolitans, in particular, were prevalent not just on Italian soil, but in Europe at large, and further assesses to what extent Bernini was truly a '*Neapolitanus sculptor*'.

In Chapter 2, 'Of Sculptors and Cobblers', I focus on the basic psychological change in approach to sculpture that evolved from the sixteenth to the seventeenth centuries. Given the deference artists and intellectuals had towards the classical tradition and their misconceived notion that in antiquity the sculptors' ultimate challenge was represented by a marble sculpture executed out of one marble block (*ex uno lapide*), the chapter considers the socio-artistic background that led to the acceptance of what became a 'trademark' of Baroque sculpture: figures composed of multiple blocks. In the light of Renaissance prejudices with regard to those sculptors who, in restoring fragments of ancient statues, 'patched' them by the addition of the missing parts so as to make them 'whole', or who, in the execution of their own sculptures, added pieces to the core of the statue, this chapter raises the question as to why these artists were derogatorily labeled as 'cobblers'. Paradoxically, it is argued, it was only when marble carvers became 'cobblers' that the new Baroque sculptural style came into its own.

In Chapter 3, 'Tall Tales', the attention is shifted from sculptures to the literary tradition. While analyses of artists' biographies from antiquity to the Renaissance have been 'mined' for more than factual information, at least since the publication of Ernst Kris and Otto Kurz's *Legend, Myth, and Magic in the Image of the Artist*, a similar line of investigation with regard to seventeenth- and eighteenth-century sources has been relatively scarce. It was not until recently that the most significant collection of essays on the subject with regard to Bernini was finally published. Edited by Maarten Delbeke, Evonne Levy, and Steven F. Ostrow, *Bernini's Biographies: Critical Essays* (2006) is a landmark in such inquiries that finally brought attention to the subtle ways in which Filippo Baldinucci's and Domenico Bernini's biographies, in the wake of Vasari's *Lives*, spun stories that reveal the authors' multiple agendas. This chapter of my book sheds further light on a number of anecdotes narrated by the two authors that I believe needed further elucidation and are exposed for what they are: anecdotal fabrications.

Chapter 4 is the 'sibling' of the previous chapter but it is fully devoted to a leitmotif present in biographies of artists that has received insufficient consideration in contemporary studies. 'Biographies, Garments, and Bernini's "*Abito . . . grosso, e rozzo*" in Perspective' traces the way in which sartorial details – which in antiquity were occasionally employed to distinguish artists with a claim to higher manual ability and social status – by the Renaissance and the Baroque had become a fixed feature and a crowning aspect of the artists' *Lives*. Frequently used as signs of the artists' compliance with societal mores, garments were also employed to extol or denigrate an individual and indicate an artist's specific profession or morality. It is through the inquiry of the historical significance vestments acquired through the ages that the biographers' single mention of Bernini's attire – his sculptor's 'heavy rough garment' – may be fully appreciated.

'Pride and Prejudice: Paris–Rome', the subject of Chapter 5, seeks to investigate the dynamics generated by the juxtaposition of artists of different nationalities when working within the same context. Thus, by taking Bernini's negative experience in Paris, vis-à-vis French artists and critics as a starting point, this chapter looks at the way foreign artists were conversely regarded and treated in Rome from the sixteenth through the early eighteenth century. Proceeding from more general to specific assessments of circumstances in which potential tensions between Italian and foreign artists – and sculptors in particular – could have surfaced, this section of the book focuses on the transnational character of the Eternal City that made it a unique artistic laboratory in early modern Europe. To corroborate the analysis, the chapter further looks at three 'case studies' and epistolary documentation from a historical juncture when Rome gradually ceded the scepter to Paris as the leading European artistic center. The ancillary theme of this chapter is a consideration of Rome's acclaimed cosmopolitanism in the 'tug-of-war' with Paris over artistic and cultural supremacy.

The sixth and final chapter, 'Bernini's Shadow', considers the persistent influence Bernini had on generations of sculptors and art lovers through much of the eighteenth century. Contrary to a traditional belief that Gian Lorenzo Bernini's critical fortune waned by the turn of the century, through the analysis of epistolary and institutional records – such as those of the Académie de France and the Accademia di San Luca – as well as the visual, artistic production of the period, this chapter provides ample proof that such an interpretation is the result of strabismic hindsight. For Bernini's compositional innovations and personal carving style left their mark on future generations of artists right to the end of the eighteenth century and are readily verifiable by visiting many Roman churches.

It is hoped that the kaleidoscopic approach here employed will contribute, for those familiar with the subject, to a heightened understanding of Bernini and his world, and, for readers less conversant with the artist, to a greater interest in one of the most outstanding periods in early modern sculpture. Simply stated, this volume represents another 'brick in the wall' of the common house that unites, under one roof, art lovers of Baroque Rome and its most representative artist.

I

'Berninus Neapolitan[us] sculptor'

'To honor the unworthy is to ruin him and discredit Honor itself . . . A Prince's whim cannot elevate one without creating enemies not only among the nobles, who feel offended in their dignity, but also among the lower classes, who enviously see him advance while previously they walked apace.'[1] The sentiment, expressed by Giovanni Pietro De' Crescenzi Romani in his *Treatise on Nobility*, may not reflect the initial attitude fellow artists had towards Gian Lorenzo Bernini when in 1621, at the age of twenty-three, Gregory XV (1621–3) knighted him 'soldier in the army of Christ under the title of Saint Augustine'[2] in recognition of the three portraits he had executed of the Ludovisi Pope (fig.1.1).[3] However, it echoes perfectly well some artists' feelings as Bernini quickly made his ascent to the top of the profession as the undisputed protagonist and envied 'king maker' of papal projects.[4] Indeed, soon after his sculptural tours de force for Cardinal Scipione Borghese – the *Aeneas, Anchises and Ascanius Fleeing Troy*, *Pluto and Proserpina*, *David*, and *Apollo and Daphne* were executed between 1619 and 1625 – things changed as Gian Lorenzo began working for the popes (seven of them by the end of his life);[5] a new condition that sustained his meteoric rise to fame and increased his artistic clout in the Holy City. One gets a glimpse of the professional jealousy his overarching control of official projects must have instigated from Giovanni Battista Passeri – never sympathetic towards the artist – who blames Bernini's egotism for this state of affairs. With a mythological flair, Passeri wrote: '[Bernini,] that Dragon, vigilant custodian of the Hesperian gardens, to ensure that others not steal the golden apples of the pontifical graces, vomited poison everywhere, and always sowed the most

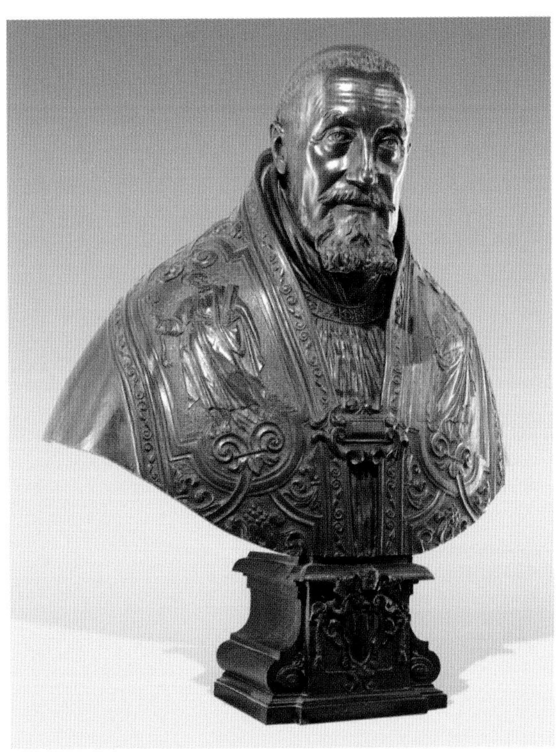

1.1 Gian Lorenzo Bernini, *Gregory XV*, 1621–2, bronze, 78 × 66 cm (30 11⁄16 × 26 in), Jacquemart-André Museum, Paris

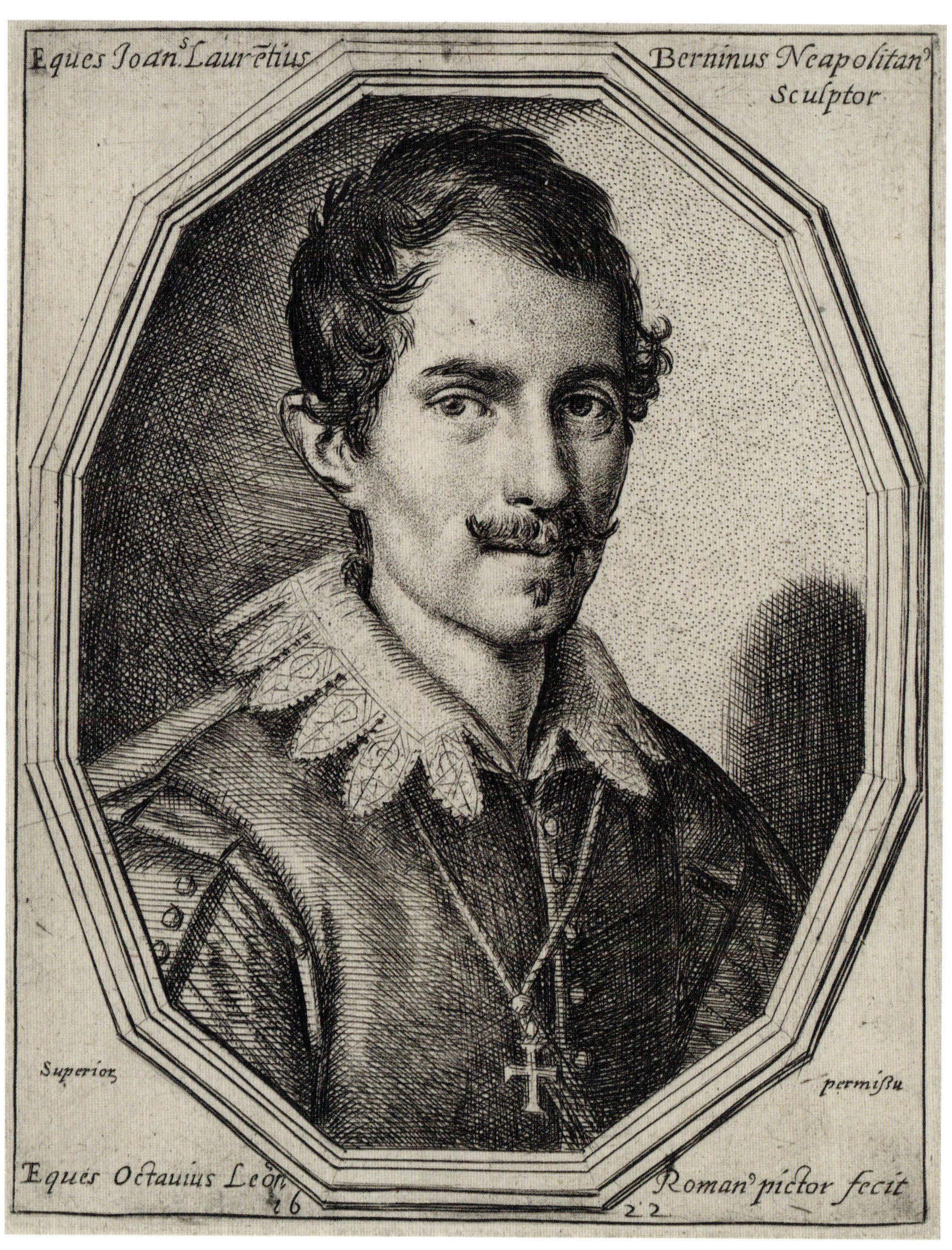

1.2 Ottavio Leoni, *Portrait of Gian Lorenzo Bernini*, 1622, engraving, 14.1 × 11 cm (5 9/16 × 4 5/16 in), Royal Collection Trust, Windsor Castle

pungent thorns of aversion on the path that led to the attainment of significant [papal] favors.'[6]

Bernini's social promotion was announced in a brief dated 30 June 1621, just five months after Pope Gregory XV had been raised to the throne of Peter. Commemorating the event in 1622, Ottavio Leoni executed an engraving of the sculptor's portrait in which the young man exudes all of the justifiable pride and alertness that anyone familiar with Bernini's biography would expect (fig.1.2).[7] Besides depicting the papal gold chain and cross on his chest – purposely transferring it from the proper left in the original drawing to proper right of center so as to give it greater relevance – and incising Bernini's new title in the upper left corner of the print (*Eques Joan[ne]s Laure[n]tius*), on the opposite side Ottavio Leoni specified his friend's national identity: '*Berninus Neapolitan[us] sculptor*'.[8] In fact, Bernini was born in Naples on 7 December 1598, from a Neapolitan mother, Angelica Galante, and a Florentine father, the sculptor Pietro Bernini, who had moved to Rome in 1606 when Gian Lorenzo was barely eight years old.[9] Given the prominence the engraving gives to this declaration of ennoblement and national affiliation, one must assume that at that time the now *Cavaliere* Bernini was proud of his Neapolitan roots. Yet, this must not always have been the case. For, as subsequent events and documents in the artist's life reveal, Bernini tended to distance himself from his native city. The following pages investigate to what extent Bernini associated with his Neapolitan roots by placing him in the larger context of regional prejudices and artistic trends present in early modern Italy.[10]

* * *

Since Italy did not become a nation-state until the nineteenth century, it is unsurprising that regionalism or *campanilismo*[11] – depending on context also chauvinism or parochialism – should have been more strongly felt in the Renaissance and Baroque periods than after unification.[12] At that time it was not unusual for patrons, writers or artists to declare their nationality on edifices, books, artifacts or any place where self-worth could be proclaimed and notoriety increased. Thus, just as Pope Paul II flaunted his Venetian origins above the windows of Palazzo Venezia (fig.1.3),

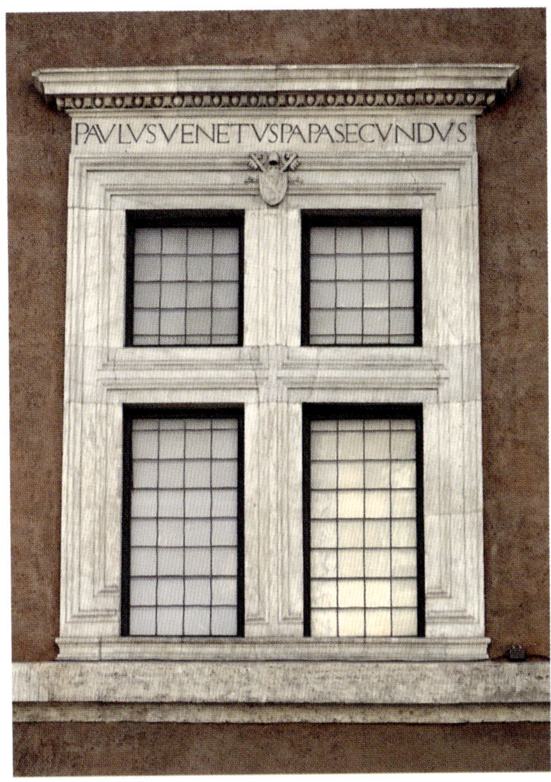

1.3 Palazzo Venezia, detail, *c.*1466–7, Rome

and Francesco Maria Torrigio declared his Roman citizenship on the cover page of his book on Rome's architectural treasures (fig.1.4),[13] so too did the young Michelangelo, when completing his Rome *Pietà*, proudly declare his Florentine nationality by signing the sculpture across the Madonna's sash 'MICHAEL•ANGELUS•BONAROTUS•

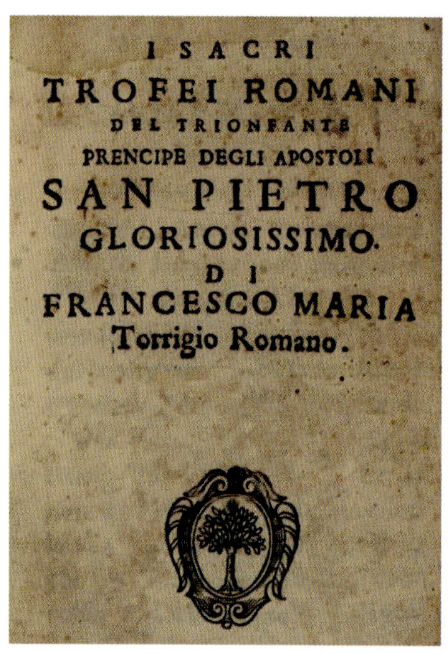

I SACRI
TROFEI ROMANI
DEL TRIONFANTE
PRENCIPE DEGLI APOSTOLI
SAN PIETRO
GLORIOSISSIMO.
DI
FRANCESCO MARIA
Torrigio Romano.

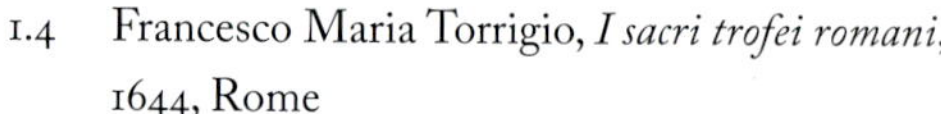

1.4 Francesco Maria Torrigio, *I sacri trofei romani*, 1644, Rome

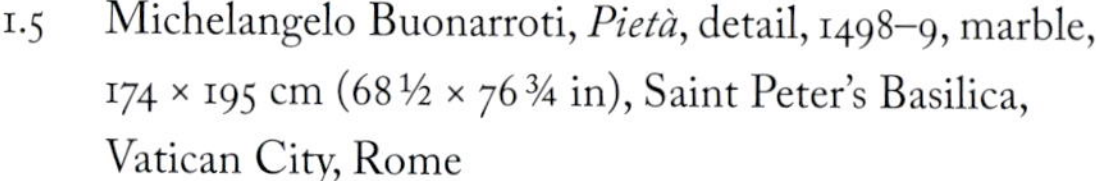

1.5 Michelangelo Buonarroti, *Pietà*, detail, 1498–9, marble, 174 × 195 cm (68 ½ × 76 ¾ in), Saint Peter's Basilica, Vatican City, Rome

1.6 Gian Lorenzo Bernini (workshop), *Saint Veronica*, 1627, third full-scale model for the Veronica niche, drawing, pen and wash, The Albertina Museum, Vienna

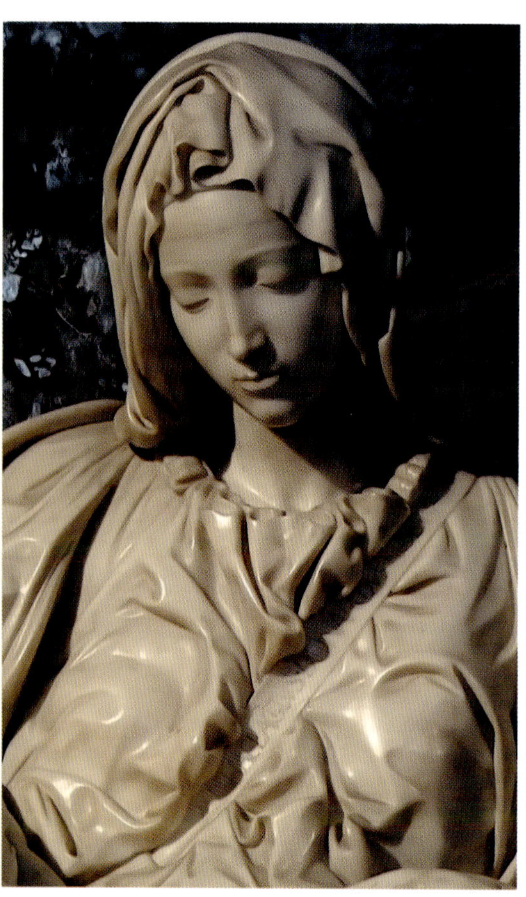

FLORENT[INUS]•FACIEBA[T]'[14] (fig.1.5). Therefore, the proclamation of Bernini's Neapolitan roots in Leoni's engraving can be seen as following a well-established tradition.

In their 'Prolegomena to Bernini's Biographies', Maarten Delbeke, Evonne Levy, and Steven F. Ostrow review the ways in which Filippo Baldinucci and Domenico Bernini treated this topic and point out that 'while Bernini considered himself variably Florentine or Neapolitan, Baldinucci's Bernini is Florentine (though born in Naples), whereas Domenico has no distinct regional bias, reporting his Neapolitan origins but effectively making him a Roman'.[15] Given the sculptor's place of birth, his father's Florentine nationality, his having lived most of his life in Rome and having been granted Roman citizenship on 24 August 1630,[16] it is reasonable to find him listed variably under one or more of the three rubrics. Nevertheless, it is significant that, as his reputation increased, he preferred thinking of himself primarily as a Florentine or a Roman.[17]

Three documents that evince Bernini's proclivity are a 1627 annotation to his wooden model proposal for the niche and altar for the relic of Saint Veronica's *sudarium* in Saint Peter's (fig.1.6), the ledger which

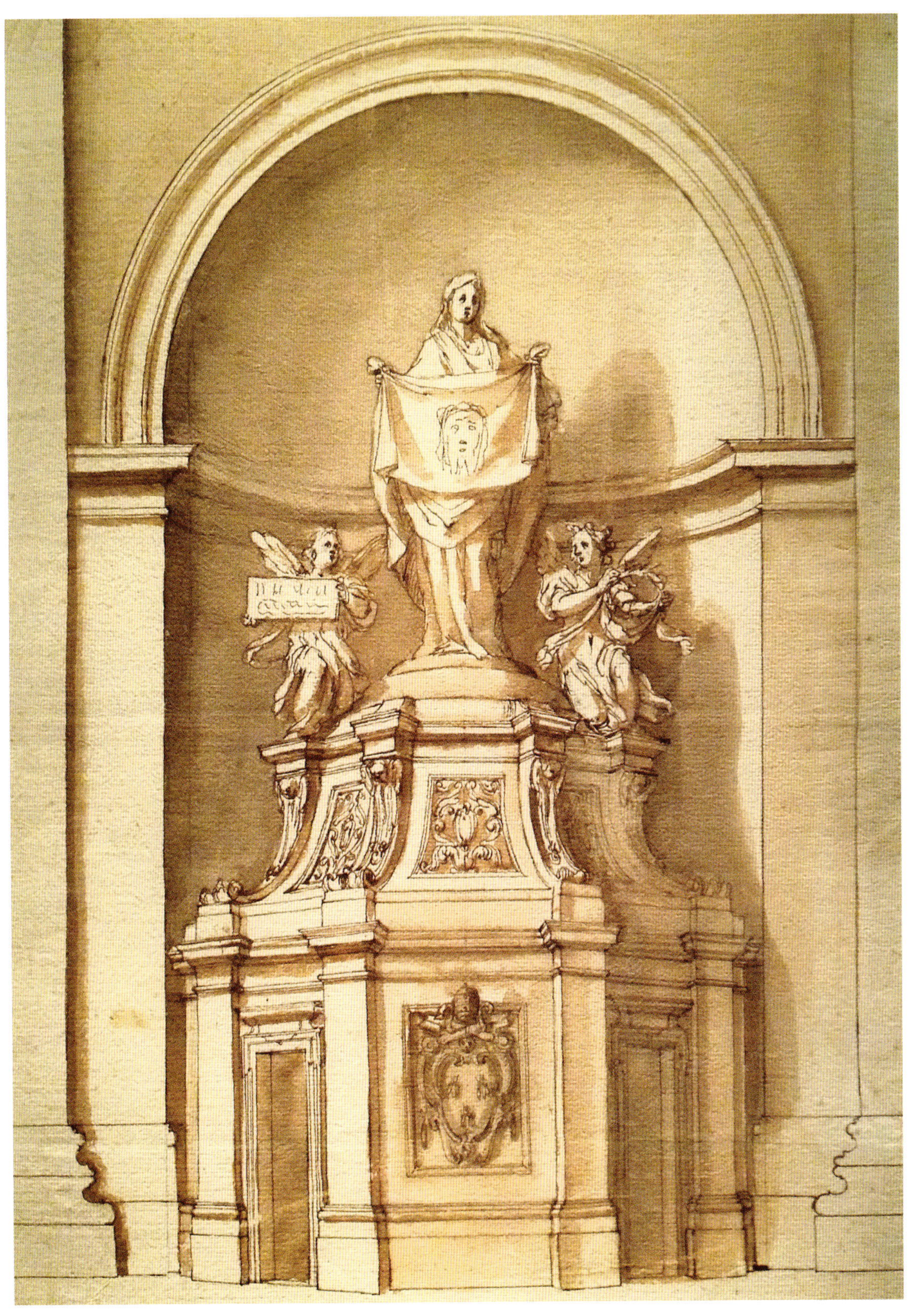

1.7 Annotation correcting Bernini's alleged Florentine nationality, Biblioteca Apostolica Vaticana, Archivio Capitolare di San Pietro, H71, fol. 162v.

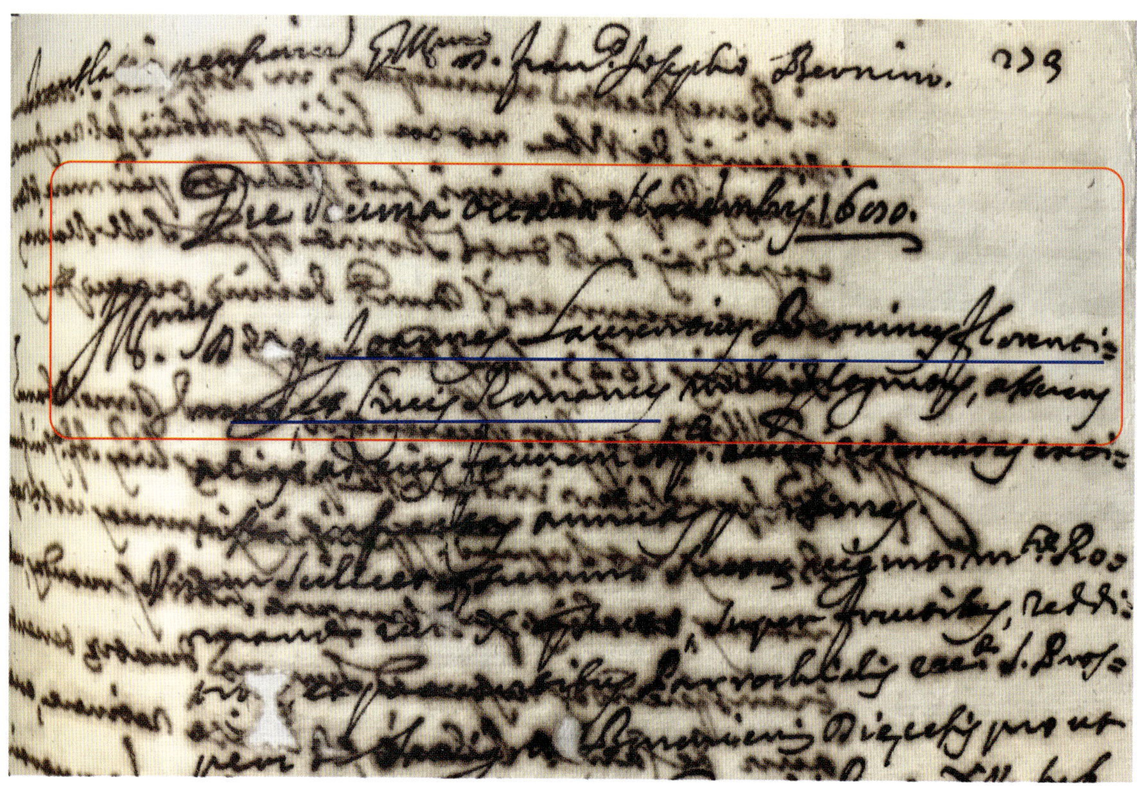

1.8 Gian Lorenzo Bernini's *Testament*, detail, 18 November 1680, Archivio di Stato di Roma (ASR), Notai AC 4245, pp. 273r.–275v., 300r.–301v.

records his nomination as the new architect of Saint Peter's Basilica in 1629, and the artist's last will and testament. In the first case, in a register recording the payment to both the carpenter and painter who executed the model, the designer of the project is labeled as '*inventore Equite Io. Laurentio Bernino ~~Florentino~~ Neapolitano*' (fig.1.7) with a line crossing out the word *Florentino* and the correct nationality, *Neapolitano*, subsequently written above it.[18] In the second occurrence, five days after Carlo Maderno's passing, on 5 February 1629 Bernini '*the Florentine*' was nominated as the new architect of the basilica.[19] In the third instance, the notary who penned the document on 18 November 1680, just ten days before Bernini's passing, referred to him as 'florentinus et civis romanus',[20] with no mention of his Neapolitan roots (fig.1.8). One obvious reason for this change of heart was that, since throughout his life he had been seen as the new Michelangelo, by stressing his paternal, Tuscan lineage, Bernini reinforced his Florentine artistic pedigree.[21] But there may be more to this desire of distancing himself from his southern origins than one might expect. It is probably not coincidental, for example, that Giovanni Battista Passeri, the Roman biographer of those artists who had worked and died in the Eternal City between 1643 and 1673,[22] in his *Life* of Andra Camassei made the cutting remark 'Bernini the Neapolitan, or, as he would have it, the Florentine' ('Cav.re Gio. Lorenzo Bernini Napoletano, o Fiorentino come egli vuole').[23] Indeed, evidence that in time Bernini chose to distance himself from his place of birth is corroborated by another document: Fioravante Martinelli's unpublished guidebook *Roma ornata dall'Architettura, Pittura e Scultura* (*c.*1658–60). In listing the papal architects who had been responsible for work on the new Saint Peter's Basilica, Martinelli wrote: 'after Maderno's death, came Cavalier Giovanni Lorenzo Bernini; a Florentine, as Baglione records'. The manuscript, however, was given by Martinelli to his friend Francesco Borromini for some editing and the latter diligently placed a number of glosses at the margins of the guidebook to complement or correct his friend's claims. Thus, after changing Martinelli's full stop at the end of the cited sentence to a semicolon, Borromini added: 'mà la verità è che è nato in Napoli' ('but the truth is that he was born in Naples')[24] (fig.1.9). Coming from Bernini's great antagonist, who was born in the northern Italian town of Bissone on Lake Lugano, it is clear that this editorial gloss was meant as a disparaging amendment.[25]

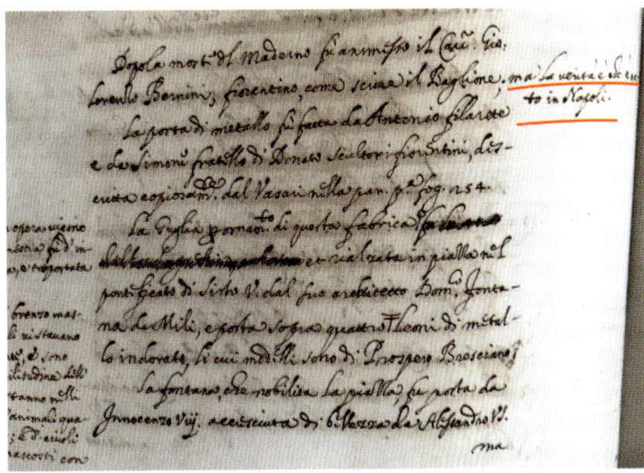

1.9 Fioravante Martinelli, *Roma ornata dall'Architettura, Pittura e Scultura*, *c.*1658–60 with Francesco Borromini's annotation specifying that Bernini was born in Naples. Biblioteca Casanatense, Ms. 4984, Rome

As these documents demonstrate, Bernini's personal claims to a Florentine 'ethnicity' are actually inversely related to Michelangelo's, who had no such 'identity crisis' later in life and could even feign insouciance on this topic. For, as related by Flaminio Vacca in his *Memoirs*, when asked by a judge as to where he came from, rather than proudly asserting his nationality in the first person, Michelangelo responded 'dicono che sono fiorentino' ('they say that I am a Florentine').[26] Nevertheless, the cited examples not only allow a glimpse into Bernini's preferred national and professional identity, but also alert us to the existence of a regional bias that 'northerners' – from Rome to London and Vienna – had of Naples and its inhabitants. Thus, it will be useful to review how Naples was perceived by non-Neapolitans, consider what constituted *napoletanità* in the eyes of others, understand how outsiders viewed Neapolitan artists at that time, and, ultimately, question to what extent Bernini could be truly considered *Neapolitanus*.

* * *

Four individuals whose views permit a better grasp of how the sons and daughters of Parthenope were perceived by foreigners at this time are the aforementioned Giovanni Battista Passeri (*c.*1610–79), the Spanish Viceroy in Naples, Pedro Antonio de Aragón (1666–71), Lorenzo Casoni, the apostolic nuncio to Naples from 1690 to 1702, and the Austrian Viceroy Count Harrach (1728–33). In describing Salvator Rosa's peculiar personality in his biography of the artist, Passeri claimed that Rosa's vainglorious character was a disposition common to all those who were born in the shadow of Vesuvius. In Passeri's view, Rosa's narcissism and vanity were not just ascribable to the painter's personal character. Rather, 'these qualities were typical national traits that he could not eradicate, since they were inherited from the local climate'.[27] Similarly, Viceroy Pedro Antonio de Aragón, who in 1668 had begun a radical attempt to eliminate brigandage in the Kingdom of Naples, believed banditry was an inevitable evil in this part of the world 'since it is connatural to the character of this nation' ('por ser natural en el genio de la nacion').[28] The apostolic nuncio Monsignor Casoni, instead, harped on the Neapolitans' moral character. In a letter dated 14 June 1701, reporting on the Neapolitans' ill-concealed support of the Austrians' cause against the Spanish Viceregency during the War of the Spanish Succession, he stated that, despite the mistreatment the Neapolitans received at the hands of the Spanish viceroy, 'no one would ever dare move a finger unless the Austrians were just about ready to enter the Kingdom, for courage does not abide in this country'.[29] Finally, Viceroy Aloys Thomas Raimund von Harrach, on his part, felt that prior to his implementation of changes in its judicial system, Naples had been 'a jungle of thieves and assassins' and characterised its population as 'indolent and cowardly'.[30]

Thus, in the eyes of some influential foreigners, excessive pride and lawlessness, if not violence altogether, were traits associated with the Neapolitans. These were commonplaces, of course, that would only be further propagated in the eighteenth century with regard to local artists by the biographer Bernardo De Dominici. Along with other fabrications, Bernardo De Dominici is responsible for disseminating the fable associated with the 'Compagnia della Morte'.[31] Initiated by the painter Aniello Falcone to avenge the killing of a relative and one of his assistants by Spanish soldiers, this motley crew was supposedly made up primarily of artists, among whom were Domenico Gargiulo (i.e., Micco Spadaro), Cesare and Francesco Fracanzano, Andrea and Nicola Vaccaro, and, of course, Salvator Rosa himself.[32] Thus, it comes as no shock if well into the nineteenth century Salvator Rosa's Irish biographer, Lady (Sidney) Morgan, claimed that Francesco Fracanzano, Rosa's brother-in-law, 'like most young Neapolitan painters of his time was a turbulent and factious character, vain and self-opinionated'.[33] However, if the Compagnia della Morte was fiction, the aggressive and intimidating hospitality Neapolitan artists carefully orchestrated for foreign colleagues who came to their city to undertake important commissions was real. The cabal that was mounted against artists such as Guido Reni and Domenichino, which drove them out of town and, in the latter's case, possibly to his death, was proof enough to foreigners that Neapolitan artists could be all too envious of and threatening to outsiders.[34] As Malvasia noted in the life of Guido Reni, 'those people', that is, the Neapolitans, were 'not too friendly to foreigners and conspired . . . against any Master who was not one of their number'.[35]

Vanity, envy, violence, and irascibility, of course, are only a few of the perceived characteristics of the Neapolitans. Typically, however, what distinguished – one might say almost 'branded' – the national identity was a sort of *discordia concors*; a unity of opposites that is intimately related to the location of the city itself, nestled as it is between the amenable, paradisiacal, prolific nature surrounding the Bay of Naples and the threatening, infernal, devastating character of Vesuvius. Goethe called it 'The Terrible beside the Beautiful' and claimed 'the Neapolitan would certainly be a different creature if he did not feel himself wedged between God and the Devil'.[36] Thus, if Horace referred to Naples as '*otiosa*' ('care free') and in March 1495, Charles VIII, after conquering Naples, claimed that it only needed Adam and Eve to make it the perfect reification of the Garden of Eden, Athanasius Kircher, after climbing to the top of Vesuvius during his tour of southern Italy in 1637–8, looking into the crater observed: 'It was just like hell, only lacking the demons to complete the picture!'[37] Of course, if Adam and Eve had long been absent from the Neapolitan context, many had already found the perfect substitutes for the demons. Indeed, it gave rise to one of the long-lasting commonplaces about Naples. In a letter to Alessandro Corvino in 1539, Bernardino Daniello quipped: 'Naples is a paradise inhabited by devils.'[38] The devils, of course, were the *lazzaroni*, the poorest members of society who, half undressed and unshod, lived and begged by the thousands in the streets of Naples. Thus, if for many visitors the city and its surrounding area were blessed by a beautifully copious nature, the very mild climate and land that generated such fertility were, in their mind, also responsible for the kind of slothful, lazy personality of its inhabitants, most typically represented by the unemployed *lazzaroni* who wiled away their time in total inactivity. As Joseph Addison pointed out in his *Remarks on Several Parts of Italy* of 1761, the Neapolitans were notorious for leading a life of laziness and pleasure as a result of the mild climate 'that relaxes the fibres of their bodies, and disposes the people to such indolent humour'.[39]

In the eyes of the established order, of course, indolence and inactivity could only degenerate into a riotous, explosive behavior. This impression was certainly consolidated in the mind of contemporaries after the fishmonger Masaniello headed the famous revolt against the Spanish crown in 1647.[40] In a report on the political, economic, and civil state of the Kingdom of Naples, the Genoese Pietro Mattia Doria reported in 1709 that 'if maliciousness makes them [the Neapolitans] inclined to plot, their all-too-fervid temperament makes them impervious to secrecy and stability. Thus, since sudden revolts are the result of unleashed, violent emotions, these are to be feared especially in the Neapolitans as this is their specific defect: a particular inclination . . . towards violence.'[41]

As this brief excursus makes clear, in the collective imagination of foreigners, *napoletanità* was a combination of often conflicting attributes best encapsulated in Lord Shaftesbury's pithy reformulation of these commonplaces: 'Never were a more ingenious and more dissolute people both at once.'[42] For outsiders, and especially the Romans and the Florentines who got to know him while he lived in their cities, Salvator Rosa was probably the very embodiment of such cliches.[43] In artistic terms, however, what was it that differentiated artists in this region from those of other centers?

The Roman, Giovanni Battista Passeri, again, is the best guide to understand what was perceived as a major divide between Campanian artists and those who worked in the hegemonic Tuscan-Roman tradition. At the outset of Salvator Rosa's biography, Passeri specifies: 'Neapolitan painters are not too prone to apply themselves to drawing, but are wont to handle brushes prematurely to, as they say, "pittare".'[44] Besides underscoring with a supercilious, condescending tone the infinitive form of the verb 'to paint' employed by southerners (*pittare* or *pintare* instead of the Tuscan/Roman *dipignere* or *dipingere*),[45] this statement underscores both the Neapolitans' impatience and unwillingness – their 'laziness' one might say – to go through the laborious training process that focused on *disegno* as the Roman and Florentine schools taught, and a disregard for the meticulously planned and well-wrought painting.

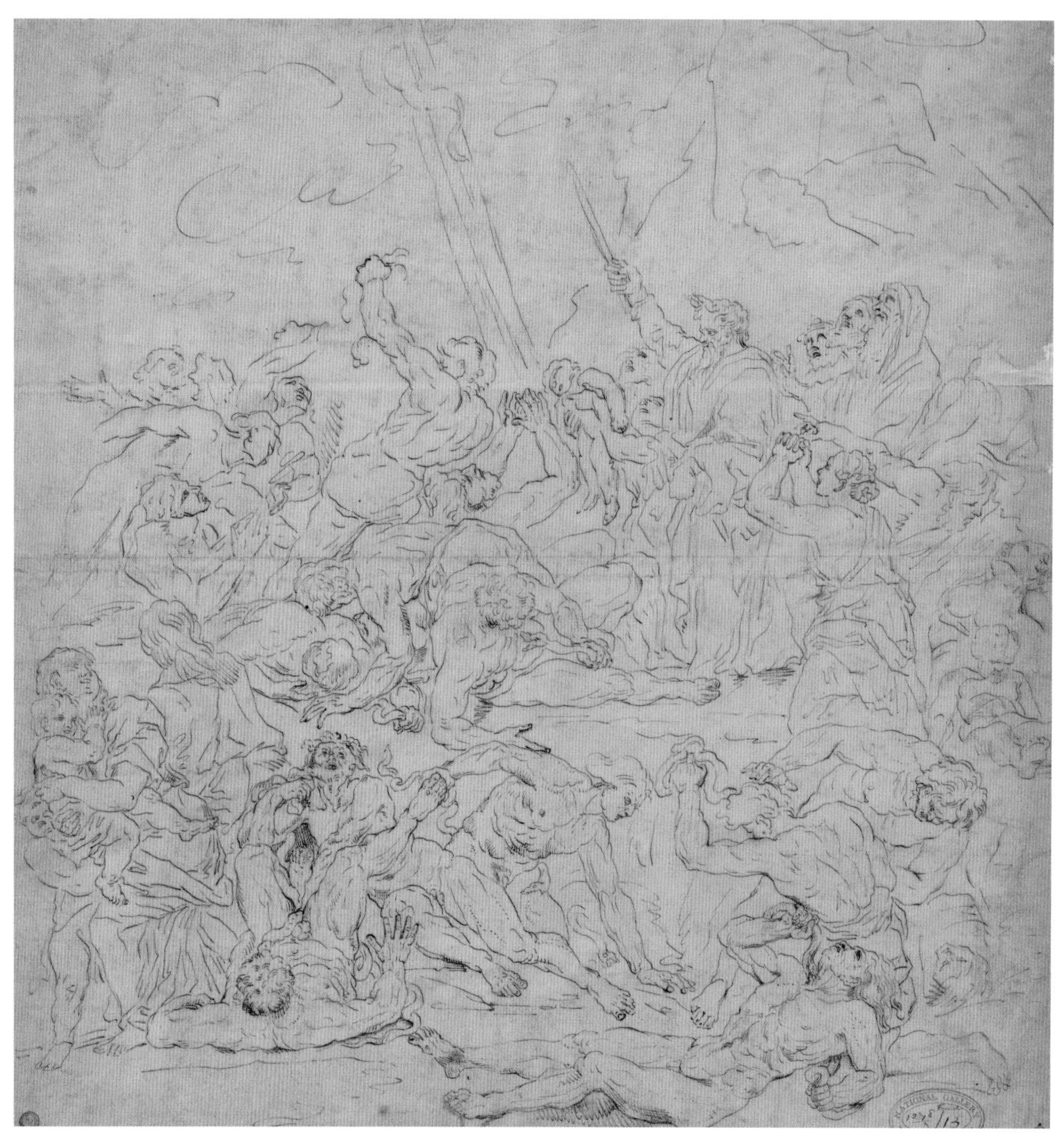

1.10 Raymond la Fage, *Moses and the Brazen Serpent*, pen and brown ink over pencil, 52.5 × 43.5 cm (20½ × 17⅛ in), National Gallery of Victoria, Melbourne. Felton Bequest, 1923

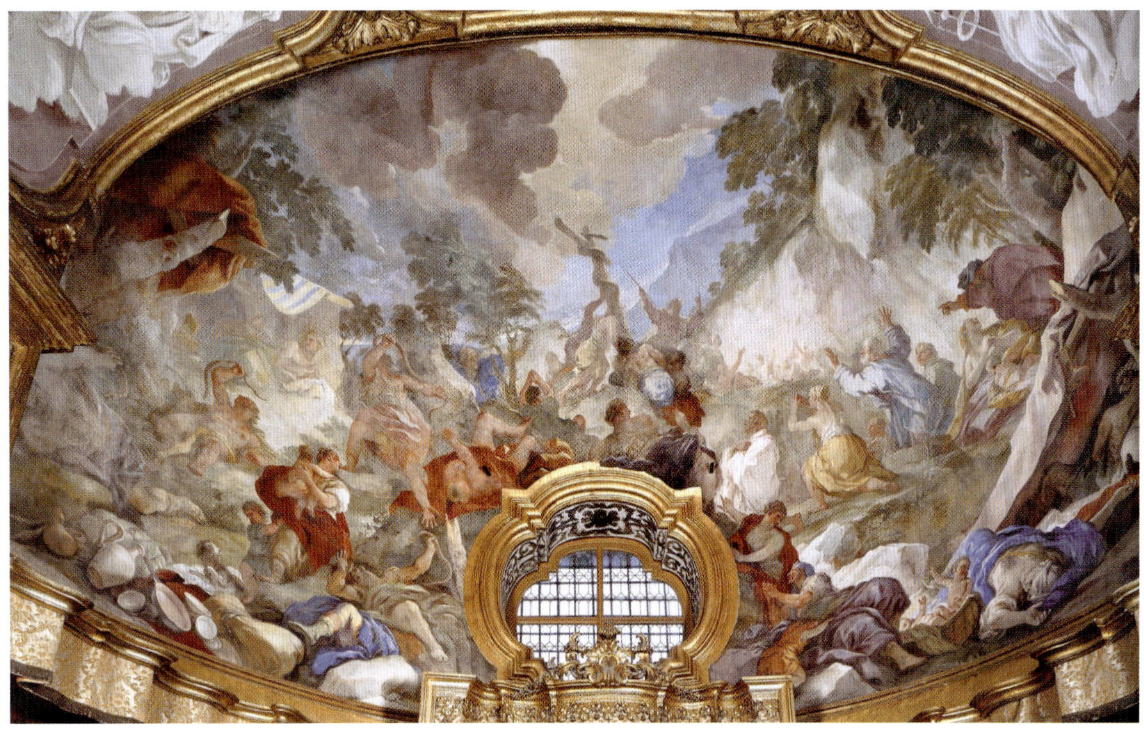

1.11 Luca Giordano, *Moses and the Brazen Serpent*, 1704, fresco, Cappella del Tesoro, Museo Nazionale di San Martino, Naples

In truth, this opinion not only seems to perfectly fit the stereotypical, indolent yet 'fiery temper of the Neapolitans', as Addison claimed;[46] it also lays bare the Neapolitans' lack of draftsmanship that was taken by outsiders to be their Achilles' heel. In fact, this view stung the Neapolitan cognoscenti so much that Bernardo De Dominici, in his *Vite de' pittori, scultori ed architetti napoletani* (1742–5), felt obliged to counter such claims by describing at length how his idol, Francesco Solimena, trained his students in a very thorough and painstaking drawing process.[47] However, since this critique of the Neapolitan school of painting in the eyes of De Dominici must have been true to some extent, he found no better way of counteracting such allegations than by relating an exchange that supposedly occurred between the talented French draftsman, Raymond la Fage (1652/1656–84), and Naples' most celebrated son, Luca Giordano, who, because of the rapidity with which he executed his paintings, was nicknamed 'Luca fa presto'.[48] According to the biographer, when the French artist, who attempted to demonstrate the superiority of drawing over painting, failed in his application of colors over his own under-drawing of a picture of *Moses and the Brazen Serpent* (fig.1.10), Giordano retorted by saying: 'My dear Monsù [*Monsieur*], see how much difference there is between a painter and a draftsman. For anyone who applies himself [to the task] may draw well, but not everyone is able to paint well. [Therefore] I would much rather be Luca Giordano than Monsù la Fage and all of the draftsmen in the world'[49] (fig.1.11). De Dominici blamed this lacuna in the training of Neapolitan artists on the lack of classical statuary in Naples from which they could have learned 'the perfection of measurements and the nobility of the parts of ancient statues . . . necessary in the making of an excellent painter'.[50] Nonetheless, De Dominici's defense of Neapolitan artists propagated exactly the kind of cliches that foreigners were likely to disseminate about Campanian artists, for he adds, 'if the Neapolitans were to follow such practice [of drawing after classical statuary], it would cool off that fire, which gave birth to such great, magnificent works as, for example, one sees in Luca Giordano'.[51] Indeed, according to Giovan Pietro Bellori, Neapolitan artists attempted to discredit Domenichino, who had been called to Naples to decorate the dome of the Cappella del Tesoro in the Cathedral of Naples, by claiming that 'by belaboring his work too much he detracted from the grace of his figures'.[52]

It is no surprise, then, that Passeri claimed 'he [Salvator Rosa] used to speak of Paolo Veronese more than anyone else, and [claimed he] had a natural empathy for the Venetians' style. However, he was not too fond of Raphael because the Neapolitan school of painting considered him stiff, hard as a rock, dry and not attracted by him.'[53] Despite the fact that modern studies have now shown how this commonplace about the Neapolitans' lack of interest in drawing is certainly inaccurate,[54] it would seem that for them the function of the graphic medium was more a means to an end than an end in itself.[55]

As argued by Andrea Zezza, this Tuscan-Roman critique of the Neapolitans' lack of *disegno* goes back to a fourteenth- and fifteenth-century invective perpetuated by authors such as Cino da Pistoia, Poggio Bracciolini, and Cristoforo Landino against the Neapolitan nobility, but it spilled into the art historical discourse when, in Vasari's *Lives* of Giotto, Polidoro, and Marco Calabrese, the Neapolitan nobles were accused of being fickle, disloyal, ignorant, lazy, and of not producing individuals predisposed to the arts.[56] Vasari's diatribe, however, reached its peak in a passage added to the 1568 edition of his life of Giovanni da Nola where he dismisses the Neapolitan as a capable sculptor but branded his work as having been executed 'con buona pratica, ma non con molto disegno' ('with skill but not much design').[57]

The ultimate response to Vasari's *Lives* and his cliches about Neapolitan artists was provided in a number of ways by Bernardo De Dominici's biographies. If, on the one hand, Vasari remained silent about Campanian artists (such as failing to include in his opus the life of Colantonio whose invention of oil painting the Neapolitans vaunted with great national pride) or garnished their biographies with insinuating, slandering remarks (in Marco Calabrese's *Life*, Vasari expresses his surprise for this outstanding artist since he was born in a region that did not generate good painters),[58] De Dominici, on the other hand, retaliated by relying on another trick of the biographers' trade: he transcribed Filippo Baldinucci's life of Bernini verbatim and included it among his own biographies. By so doing, De Dominici provided greater acclaim for Neapolitan artists by including among the locals an undisputed international giant. The biographer's attempt, however, must not have made much headway since even a non-Italian observer, such as Jérôme Lalande, who in listing Neapolitan artists of merit in his guidebook *Voyage d'un François en Italie, fait dans les Années 1765 & 1766*, merely mentions Bernini's name, only to note that he spent most of his life in Rome, thus implying that he could not really be considered a Neapolitan artist.[59]

Plausibly, since later in life Bernini chose to distance himself from his Neapolitan roots, had he been alive at the time of De Dominici's publication, he would have had mixed feelings about the tribute that the Neapolitan biographer paid him. Indeed, this was because on the social and artistic levels Neapolitans were seen by northerners as inferior to them. For Bernini – who according to Baldinucci 'was most singular in the arts he pursued because he possessed in high measure skill in drawing' and who drew inspiration from Raphael rather than finding him 'stiff, hard as a rock, dry' like Salvator Rosa claimed – there was little to be gained by associating himself with his southern origins. In fact, echoing Jean-Jacques Bouchard's statement in his *Voyage dans le Royaume de Naples* (1632), who claimed that there was no one more vain and concerned with appearances and superficialities than the Neapolitan nobility,[60] in conversing with Paul Fréart de Chantelou – the Frenchman who kept a diary of Bernini's visit to Paris – about the superiority of *disegno* over *colorito*, Bernini supposedly criticised his former countrymen, stating that 'in Naples . . . only trifles and gilding are appreciated'.[61]

It is abundantly evident by now that not infrequently those individuals who looked at Naples, its inhabitants, and its art through northern lenses – so to speak – ultimately suffered from what one might call a superiority complex; that is, they often saw a charming, lively society that, however, on many levels they considered inferior to theirs. By the eighteenth century this age-old prejudice found its theoretical, anthropological justification in Montesquieu's *De l'esprit des loix* (1748–9)[62] where the author juxtaposed the vigor and strength of northern people to the passive indolence of the southerners.[63] In a chapter 'On the laws in their relation to the nature of the climate' he wrote:

> Cold air contracts the extremities of the body's surface fibers; this increases their spring and favors the return of blood from the extremities to the heart. It shortens these same fibers; therefore, it increases their strength in this way too. Hot air, by contrast, relaxes these extremities of the fibers and lengthens them; therefore, it decreases their strength and their spring. Therefore, men are more vigorous in cold climates. The action of the heart and the reaction of the extremities of the fibers are in closer accord, the fluids are in better equilibrium, the blood is pushed harder toward the heart and, reciprocally, the heart has more power. This greater strength should produce many effects: for example, more confidence in oneself, that is, more courage; better knowledge of one's superiority, that is, less desire for vengeance; a higher opinion of one's security, that is, more frankness and fewer suspicions, maneuvers, and tricks. Finally, it should make very different characters.[64]

And again:

> The peoples in hot countries are timid like old men; those in cold countries are courageous like young men.[65]

And finally:

> The heat of the climate can be so excessive that the body there will be absolutely without strength. So, prostration will pass even to the spirit; no curiosity, no noble enterprise, no generous sentiment; inclinations will all be passive there; laziness there will be happiness; most chastisements there will be less difficult to bear than the action of the soul, and servitude will be less intolerable than the strength of spirit necessary to guide one's own conduct.[66]

Although such discourse was counteracted by Winckelmann in his *History of the Art of Antiquity* (1764)[67] where, in the footsteps of Polybius,[68] he partly attributes the progress of the arts in ancient Greece to the more favorable climate of that nation, the opinions expressed by Montesquieu about southern peoples were more deeply rooted. And such reasoning applied not only to the major divide between nations north and south of the Alps; it also pertained to Italian regions north and south of the Tiber. Consequently, it is not surprising that most travelers to Naples 'simply sought confirmation of what they had read about the customs of a lazy and ignorant nobility' and a plebs that Montesquieu labeled 'much more plebeian than any other'.[69]

When it came to describing Neapolitan art and artists, however, there are two notable exceptions.

In 1751, Charles-Nicolas Cochin issued the first edition of *Voyage d'Italie* in manuscript form.[70] Unlike other travel guides, the author – as engraver and art connoisseur whose task had been that of accompanying the future Marquis de Marigny on his grand tour – is bent primarily on imparting artistic concepts that will allow the travelers to *judge* the quality of works of art and not present his readers with a history of painting.[71] Indeed, he surprised his audience by the occasional irreverent treatment or neglect of what were considered venerable icons of Italian art – such as Giotto or Raphael – and focused strictly on painterly and compositional aspects, his leanings being more in favor of *colore* than *disegno*. And while his ultimate artistic taste is defined by his admiration for the art of Guido Reni, he devoted seventy-three pages to the paintings and frescoes he saw in Naples. In his descriptions he demonstrates an unbiased eye and an ability to appreciate both the works of classical artists such as Lanfranco and Domenichino in the *Tesoro* of the Cathedral of Naples, as well as the striking, highly realistic paintings of Jusepe de Ribera in the same chapel and in the Certosa di San Martino.[72] An instance that demonstrates his catholic taste, for example, is his appreciation of Caravaggio's *Flagellation* in the Church of San Domenico, which he found beautifully designed and executed with beautiful colors.[73]

While most guidebooks written by foreigners tended to concentrate on the climate, customs, people, and architecture of the city of Naples, following Cochin's lead, Jérôme Lalande's *Voyage d'un François en Italie* (1765–6) was remarkable for providing more guidance and a relatively objective evaluation of local artists.[74] In fact, the author was so aware of the merit of his approach that in the title of the expanded, second edition of his work he emphasised the novelty of his opus by declaring that it 'included assessments' – 'avec des jugemens' – of the works of art described. Thus, for example, while showing his classical leanings when praising Duquesnoy's and Bolgi's statues of *Saint Andrew* and *Saint Helen*, respectively, in the crossing of Saint Peter's at the expense of Mochi and Bernini's sculptures of *Saint Veronica* and *Saint Longinus*, Lalande also demonstrated a laudable objectivity, like his compatriot Cochin, in praising the works of Jusepe de Ribera. Indeed, in citing a letter from M. de Seine, he informs his readers that 'this artist was worthy to be on a par with the greatest masters' and that his paintings of the twelve prophets in the nave of the Certosa di San Martino are 'masterpieces'.[75] And although at the end of a chapter devoted to the Sciences and the Arts of Naples, in which he included a summary of the most notable painters, sculptors, and architects, he repeated the worn-out cliche that 'the arts have not been as cultivated in Naples as in Rome and Florence', he displays a dispassionate judgment when he praises the Neapolitans' 'natural ingenuity and vitality' which allowed this society to produce distinguished individuals.[76]

Cochin and Lalande's greater openness to Neapolitan art paved the way for the publication of the Abbé de Saint-Non's *Voyage pittoresque, ou description des royaumes de Naples et de Sicile* (1781) whose merit was owed not so much to his deeper assessment of the works of some of the more important Neapolitan painters – who, according to him, never formed a true school to merit inclusion among the great Italian schools of painting – as to his having included a series of engravings of the works he described, thus allowing a wider European audience to *see* with their own eyes some of the masterpieces otherwise inaccessible and unimaginable through the means of literary description (ekphrasis).[77] In fact, this is exactly what in an earlier context Domenicus Lampsonius had stressed: the superiority of prints over ekphrasis 'as the means through which visual paradigms are disseminated'.[78] Despite Saint-Non's achievement, some of his observations raise doubts about the reliability of his comments, as when, for example, in comparing Solimena's *Expulsion of*

Heliodorus from the Temple in the Church of Gesù Nuovo, dated 1725, with Giordano's *Expulsion of the Merchants from the Temple* of 1684 in the Church of the Santi Apostoli, he states he does not know which was executed first, even though both frescoes are signed and dated in bold letters.[79]

By the Age of Enlightenment, then, not everyone's reasoning powers were obfuscated by cliches and prejudice about Naples, its inhabitants, or its artists. Some observers were, in fact, able to go beyond traditional stereotypes.[80] For instance, the Scottish physician and writer John Moore, who was in Naples in 1776, observed:

> The Neapolitans are generally represented as a lazy, licentious, and turbulent set of people; what I have observed gives me a very different idea of their character. Their idleness is evidently the effect of necessity, not of choice; they are always ready to perform any work, however laborious, for a very reasonable gratification. It must proceed from the fault of Government, when such a number of stout, active citizens remain unemployed; and so far are they from being licentious and turbulent, that I cannot help thinking they are much too tame and submissive.[81]

Likewise, in 1787 Goethe acknowledged that, although there were many poorly dressed, tattered people at every step one took, he could not spot any truly lazy individual in Naples and goes so far as to say that, all things considered, the lower class was the more industrious one.[82]

This does not mean that even someone as open-minded as Goethe could be totally removed from his *Zeitgeist*. Like many others, for example, he believed that all Neapolitans 'work not merely to *live* but to *enjoy* themselves: they wish even their work to be a recreation'[83] and this attitude, he explained, is the reason 'why in most kinds of skilled labour, their artisans are technically far behind those of the northern countries' and 'why no painter of the Neapolitan school has ever been profound or become great'.[84] Even for Goethe, in other words, as Passeri stated much earlier, Neapolitan artists, like the rest of their countrymen, were *genetically* predisposed not to take their art as seriously as artists working and living north of their city. But Goethe was also aware that to truly understand and appreciate Parthenopean art and society, one need not rely on hearsay or on centuries of biased opinions that had been propagated in every corner of Europe. In his view, there was only one way for northerners to really appreciate and understand this 'microcosm of the world',[85] as Giulio Cesare Capaccio proudly referred to his hometown, and this required an unprejudiced visit to Naples itself. Insightfully and dispassionately, Goethe observed 'the Neapolitan school of painting can only be properly understood in Naples'.[86]

* * *

Given the foregoing, the question that comes to mind is to what extent was 'Bernini the Neapolitan sculptor', that Ottavio Leoni immortalised in his engraving, really Neapolitan? Certainly, if one were to judge by the (in)famous incident involving his lover Costanza Piccolomini (fig.1.12), wife of his assistant Matteo Bonarelli or Bonucelli, one would have to say that his character is in keeping with the stereotypical, fiery mold referred to by many authors. Having surprised his brother Luigi coming out of Costanza's house and discovering their liaison, Gian Lorenzo went after his brother with an iron rod, breaking two ribs; then still not fully avenged of Costanza's betrayal, he sent a servant to slash her cheek with a blade.[87] Indeed, his explosive temperament reached such extremes that the following day, after having furiously searched for his brother in their family home across from the Basilica of Santa Maria Maggiore and then forcing his way inside the church itself, his mother felt compelled to write to Cardinal Francesco Barberini begging him to intervene to protect the life of her younger

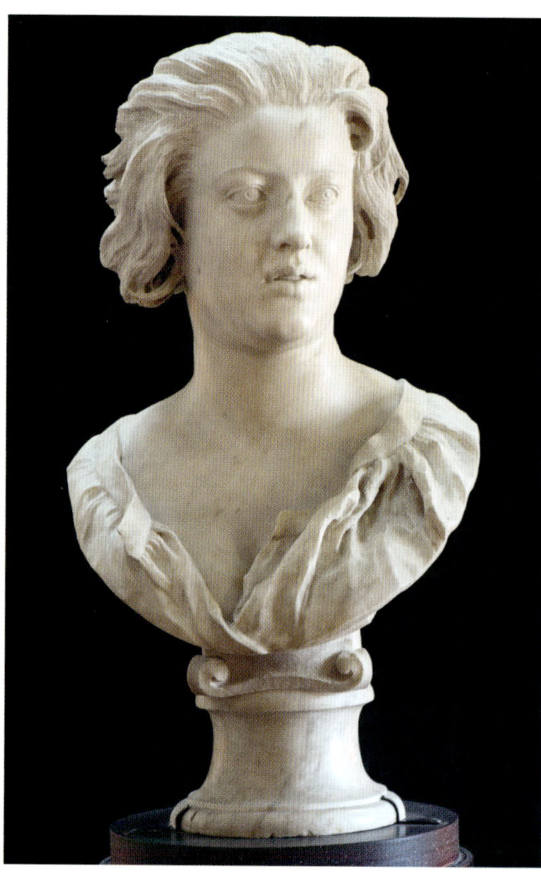

1.12 Gian Lorenzo Bernini, *Costanza Bonarelli*, 1636–8, marble, height 72 cm (28⅜ in), Museo Nazionale del Bargello, Florence

son and restrain Gian Lorenzo, who was behaving so boldly and irrationally, as if he were the Master of the World ('Padron del Mondo').[88]

But apart from this volcanic incident, we have few indications of Bernini's Neapolitan traits. These are found in the four contemporary, or near-contemporary, biographical works that inform us about his life and works: Filippo Baldinucci and Domenico Bernini's biographies, Paul Fréart de Chantelou's *Journal de voyage du Cavalier Bernin en France*, and Pierre Cureau de la Chambre's *Eloge du Cavalier Bernin* (originally published in 1681) along with its *Préface pour servir à l'histoire de la vie et des ouvrages du Cavalier Bernin* (originally read at the Académie française in Paris in 1685).[89]

While Cureau de la Chambre, by prefacing his booklet with Ottaviano Leoni's engraving executed fifty-nine years earlier, reinforced the idea of Bernini's Neapolitan roots and informs his readers that Gian Lorenzo was used to gesticulating when he spoke (something peculiar to the Neapolitans according to him),[90] both Baldinucci and Domenico Bernini only mention a weakness that the artist himself believed was peculiar to anyone who was born in Naples: a passionate love of fruit. However, whereas his son contrasts his father's virtuous restraint at the table – Gian Lorenzo's repasts comprised one course only – with his avid consumption of fruit ('a trait typical of those who are born in Naples'), Baldinucci does more than relate this indulgence to Bernini's sense of humor. When he wrote that 'He [Bernini] used to say, jokingly, that this gluttony for fruit was the original sin of those who are born in Naples', both Baldinucci and the artist must have certainly expected to elicit a smile and a subliminal concern from their audiences.[91] For it had been exactly over a tax on fruit that the aforementioned anti-Spanish, Neapolitan insurrection occurred in 1647. Indeed, the rebellion began when Viceroy Rodrigo Ponce de Léon, Duke of Arcos, reintroduced an unpopular tax on fruit which his predecessor had eliminated. It was at this time that the Neapolitan plebs, headed by the young fishmonger Masaniello, rebelled in Piazza del Mercato.[92] When Anaclerio, the *eletto del popolo*, tried to quell the uprising, rather than threatening the general crowd and the shopkeepers, he thought it more prudent to intimidate only the fruit vendors by saying he would have them beaten and sent to the galleys. Unfortunately for him, his words had the opposite effect. To the chant of '*senza gabella, senza gabella*' ('no tax, no tax'), not only the fruit vendors but all of the crowd began throwing figs, apples, and other fruits at him, before resorting to stones.[93] And it was not coincidental that later in the revolt the head of an unpopular official 'was displayed in the Piazza del Mercato covered with pieces of melon rind and orange peel . . . a reminder that it was the fruit tax for which he had suffered'.[94]

While not all civil unrest was quelled overnight, the immediate uprising lasted only ten days (7–16 July) before it was fiercely suppressed and Masaniello killed. Nonetheless, this alarming, ominous instance of civil disobedience rattled the ruling classes all over Europe, giving rise to a large body of literature in Italy and elsewhere, and remained the most shocking episode in Neapolitan history.[95] Indeed, it has been labeled 'the most spectacular of the "revolutions" of seventeenth-century Europe'.[96] Given the tremendous echo this fruit-generated rebellion had, it is more than likely that the report of Bernini's partaking in the Neapolitans' 'original sin' was meant to be taken as a pun.

A further reference to his countrymen, coming directly from Bernini's mouth, is included in Chantelou's *Diary* but uttered, seemingly, only to distance himself from them. In this occurrence, the author recounts an anecdote that Bernini told Chantelou and the papal nuncio to France, Carlo Roberti de Vittorij (1610–73).[97] The artist related a story of a Neapolitan painter who, having heard of the beauty and magnificence of the Colosseum, decided to travel to Rome to see it for himself. Upon arrival at the site, and seeing the monument in ruins, the Neapolitan exclaimed: '"What, . . . is this the Colosseum which is supposed to be one of the marvels of antiquity, the grandest work surviving from that time!" And he returned back to Naples there and then, without even having entered Rome.'[98] One might suspect that all Bernini was doing by telling this amusing anecdote about one of his countrymen is eliciting a laugh from his French friend and displaying a healthy dose of self-deprecation. However, it is significant that Bernini mentions the anecdote about the Neapolitan painter after having given an answer to a question posed by the papal nuncio as to why some works of art give pleasure immediately whereas others do so after a while.[99] In replying to this question, Bernini relied on the traditional Tuscan-Roman view of the superiority of *disegno* over the charming but insubstantial effects of *colore*, as coloring is an unskilled charm that pleases only the eye and not the mind.[100] But it is noteworthy that Bernini is recorded as having prefaced the above-mentioned anecdote, as stated earlier, by saying: 'in Naples . . . only trifles and gilding are appreciated'.[101] Furthermore, Chantelou reports that Bernini completed his critique of the artistic climate south of Rome by relating another anecdote, which immediately follows upon the one just related, in which he criticised those who at the time controlled the Kingdom of Naples, for 'the Cavaliere added that Spaniards have no taste or knowledge of the arts'.[102] No doubt this sort of denigration could only please the French audience for whom Chantelou's diary was ultimately intended[103] and, perhaps, the statement may even express the artist's resentment for the Spanish Crown's substitution of his bronze statue of the *Crucified Christ* at the Escorial with another executed by Domenico Guidi.[104] Yet, had Bernini still strongly identified with the Neapolitans, one would think that he would have refrained from making such negative statements. The fact is that, as time went on, he not only found it socially more expedient to dissociate himself from Neapolitan artists, but also fully believed and identified with the Tuscan-Roman artistic tradition.

* * *

In Baldinucci's biography of the artist one learns that 'we can with good reason affirm that Cavalier Bernini was most singular in the arts he pursued because he possessed in high measure skill in drawing', giving as proof of this assertion his works in sculpture, painting, architecture, and 'the infinite number of his drawings of the human body which are to be

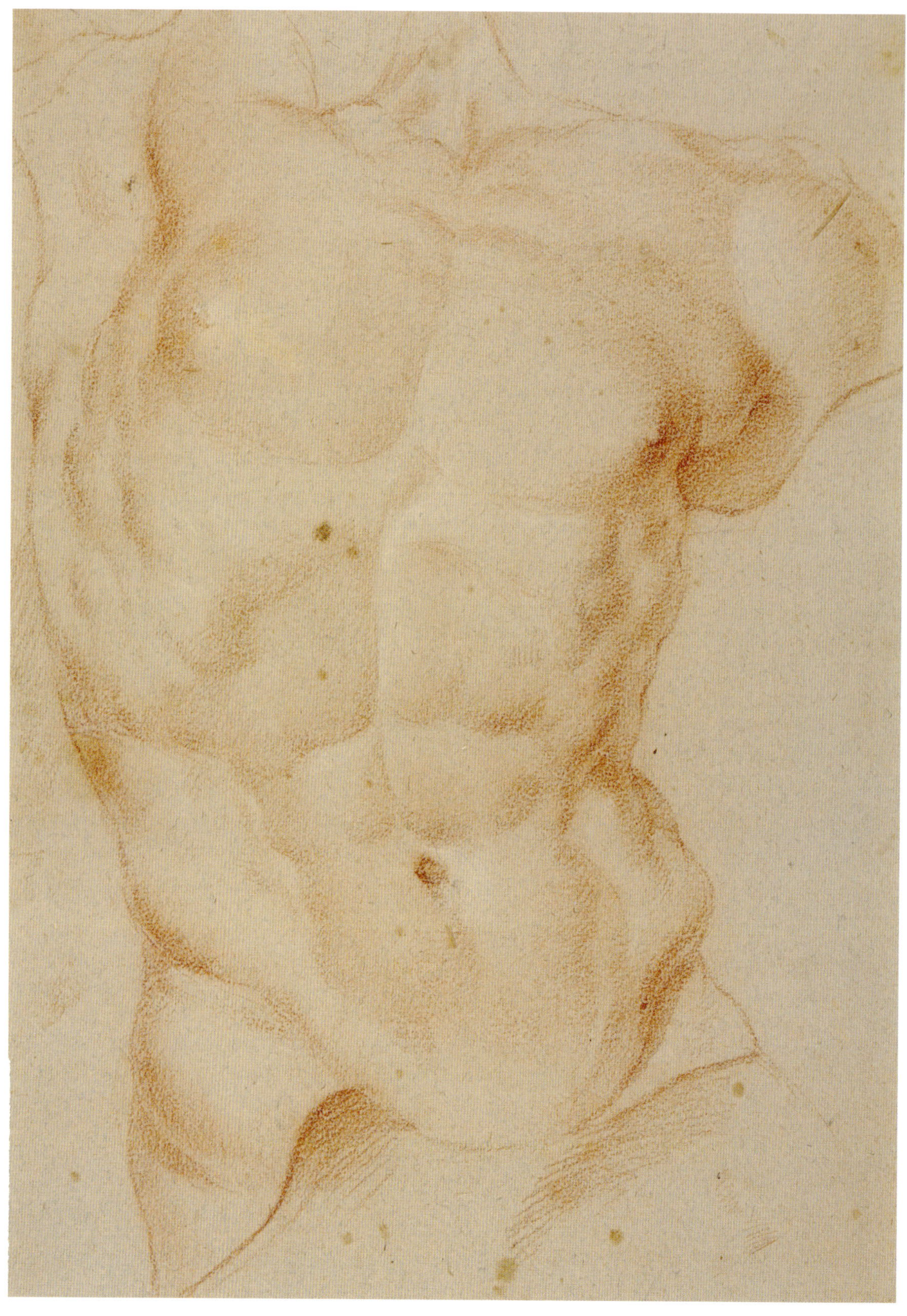

1.13 Gian Lorenzo Bernini, *Drawing after the Laocoön*, drawing, Museum der bildenden Künste, Leipzig, inv. 7903

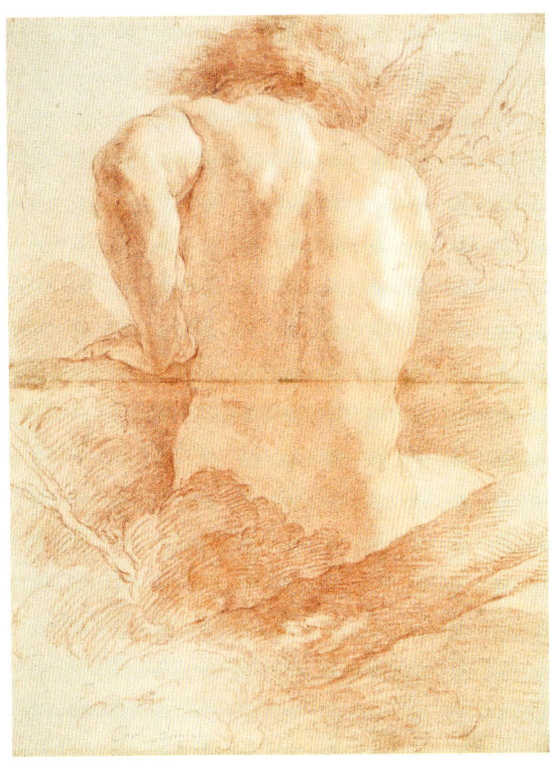

1.14 Gian Lorenzo Bernini, *A Male Nude Seen from Behind*, *c.*1630, red and white chalk on buff paper, 55.6 × 42 cm (21 7/8 × 16 9/16 in), Royal Collection Trust, Windsor Castle

found in almost all the most famous galleries in Italy and elsewhere'.[105] Although there are relatively few extant, fully worked anatomical drawings by Bernini (figs 1.13 and 1.14), coming from a Florentine such as Baldinucci – who lived in the city where the first art academy was founded in 1563 on the premise that *disegno* was the common denominator of the sister arts of painting, sculpture, and architecture – his statement is to be expected and it is certain that for Bernini, the foundations of good art were based on drawing.[106] This conviction, of course, was an offspring of the Renaissance tradition that, ultimately, goes back to Aristotle.[107] Yet, one wonders, as some have done, whether an artist such as Bernini, 'who founded his practice on the optical precepts of *colore* and brilliantly exploited the profound emotional potential of light and color . . . deliberately adapted his views to the classicising ones of his [French] hosts; or alternatively, that such passages owe more to Chantelou than to Bernini'.[108] In fact, this is not the only instance in which Bernini or those who cited his opinions on art seem to be at odds with his artistic production.[109] But as the literary sources and recent studies reveal, *disegno* is doubtlessly what the sculptor emphasised when in 1624 he acted as one of the teachers in the Accademia di San Luca in Rome,[110] as well as in the more private academy led by him under the aegis of Cardinal Francesco Barberini from 1630 until at least 1642, and, of course, in his own studio.[111] But this age-old approach to learning was upheld by Bernini with one caveat. As recorded by Chantelou, in his reply to Colbert's admission that the king would spare no cost to make the arts flourish in France and, for this reason, was willing to subsidise a study period for young artists in Rome, Bernini claimed that it was all well and good but that the training methods had to change. He then explained that,

> it was customary to go to Rome at fifteen and devote the next nine or ten years only to drawing; this meant that artists only began to work at the age of twenty-five; this arrangement should be altered so that they should draw one day and work the next either at sculpture or at painting; by this method they would become much more proficient.[112]

Thus, it makes perfect sense that, when recommending the creation of a French academy to Louis XIV, or just generally when giving advice for the advancement of French artists, he prescribed a sound foundation

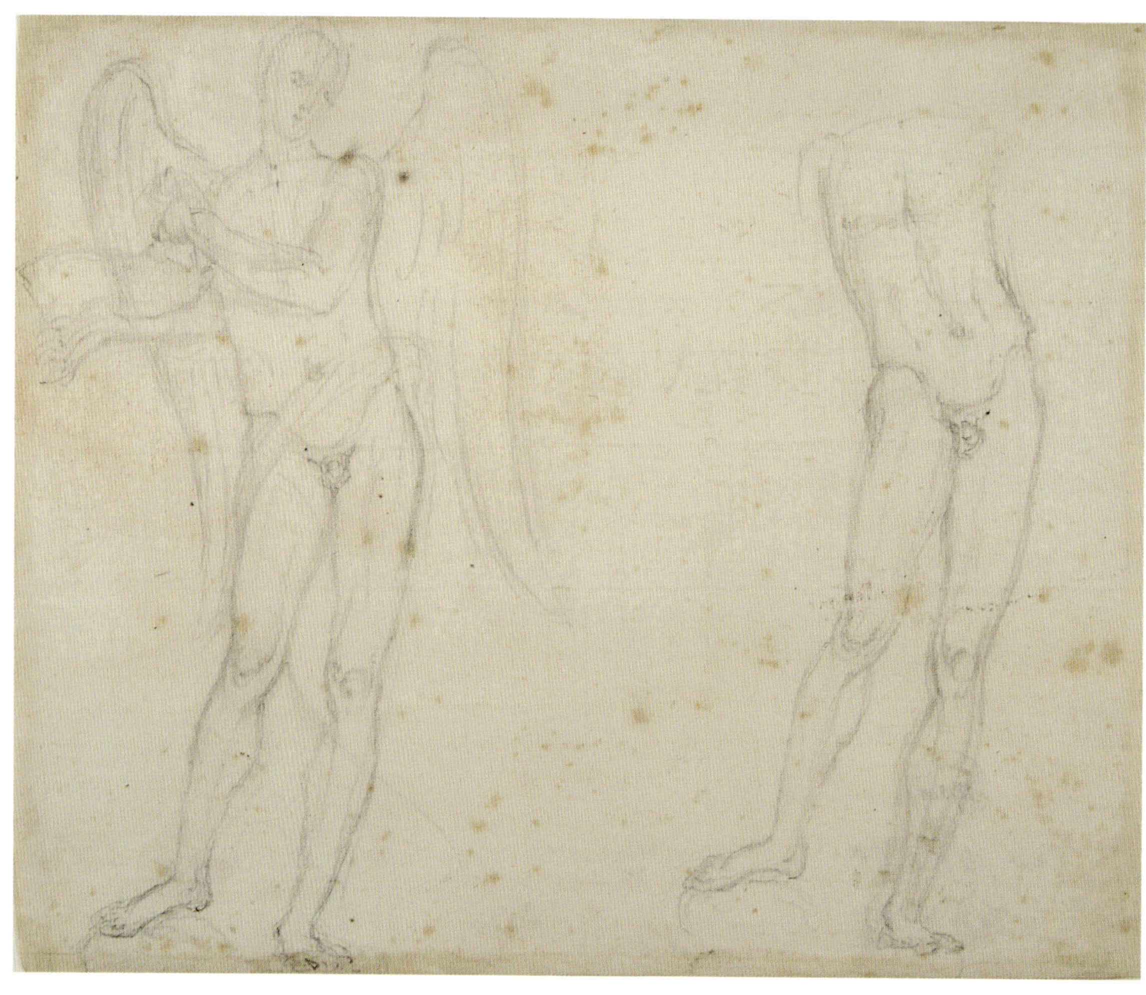

1.15 Gian Lorenzo Bernini, *Two Studies for the Angel with the Superscription*, c.1668, drawing, Istituto Centrale per la Grafica, Rome

in *disegno*, provided they also apply themselves to personal, original creations.

In studying Bernini the draftsman, what stands out is not only his consummate, polished style in the finished drawings but also what one might define as the impetuous, impatient, schematic quality of his sketches and *primi pensieri* (the earliest expressions of his artistic concepts)[113] (fig.1.15). Understandably, it has been suggested that 'he displaced the function that sixteenth-century wax models served – the origination of the invention – onto drawing'.[114] Some recent studies on Bernini's creative or working process have in fact focused on his sketches, drawings, and clay models in an attempt to better understand the 'trope of fire'[115] often associated with his artistic creativity and what has come to be defined as Bernini's 'calculated spontaneity'[116] (figs 1.16 and 1.17), a trope, of course, that was sustained

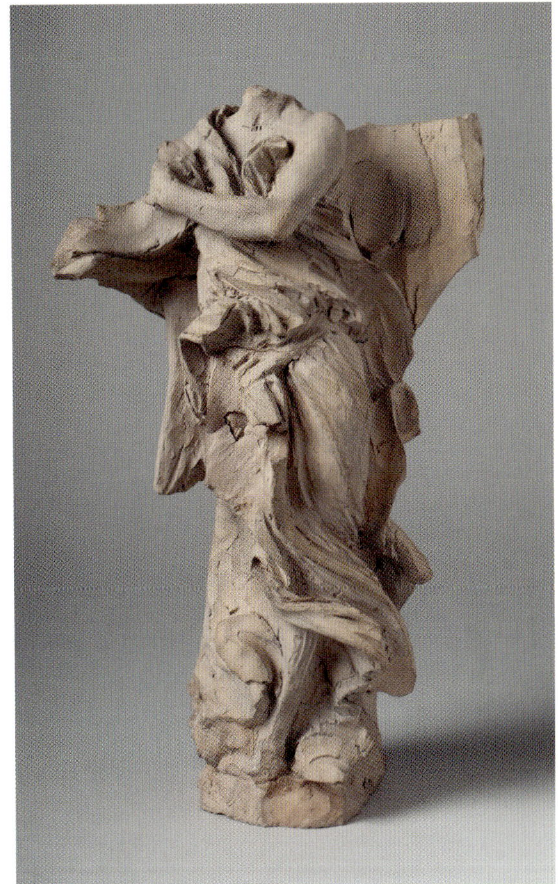

1.16 Gian Lorenzo Bernini, *Angel with the Superscription*, *c.*1667–8, terracotta, 27.8 × 16.5 × 14.2 cm (10 15⁄16 × 6 ½ × 5 9⁄16 in), Harvard Art Museum/Fogg Museum, Alpheus Hyatt Purchasing and Friends of the Fogg Art Museum Funds

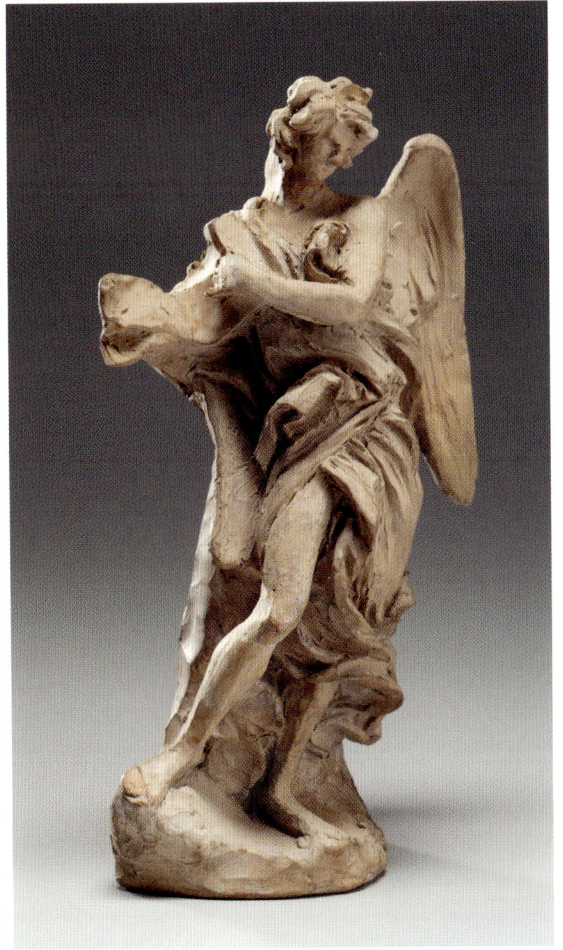

1.17 Gian Lorenzo Bernini, *Angel with the Superscription*, *c.*1667–8, terracotta, 29.2 × 16.2 × 13 cm (11 ½ × 6 3⁄8 × 5 1⁄8 in), Kimbell Art Museum, Fort Worth (AP 1987.02a)

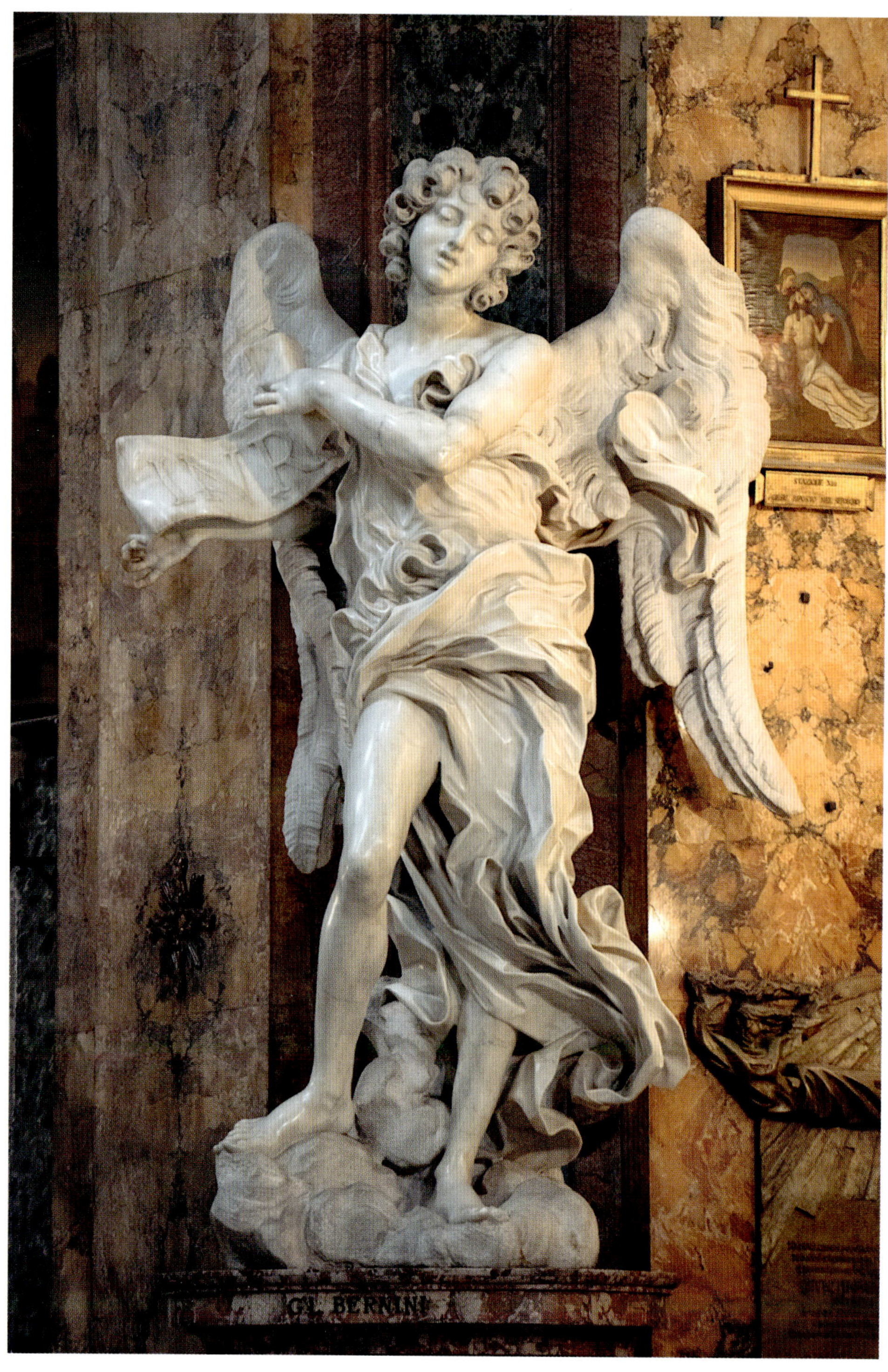

1.18 Gian Lorenzo Bernini, *Angel with the Superscription*, 1668–9, marble, Sant'Andrea delle Fratte, Rome

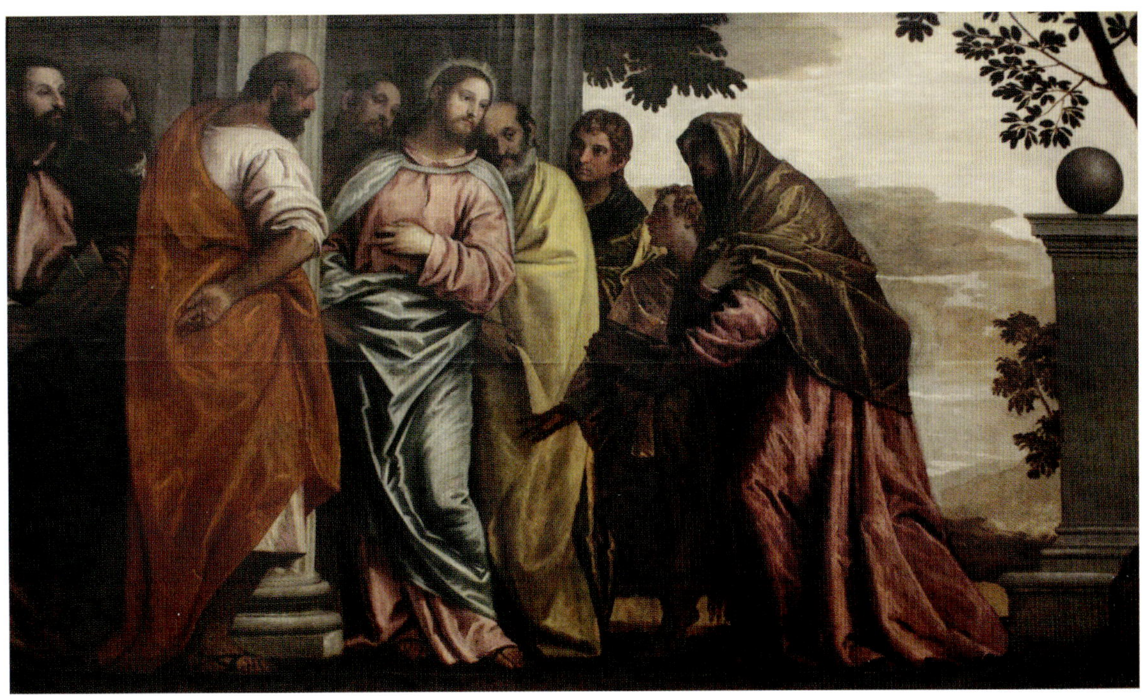

1.19 Paolo Veronese, *The Children of Zebedee Presented to Our Lord by their Mother*, *c.*1565, oil on canvas, 194 × 337 cm (76 ⅜ × 132 ¹¹⁄₁₆ in), Musée de Grenoble

by Baldinucci's description of the artist who was 'inclined to anger and quickly enflamed' and that 'that same fire that seared him more than others also impelled him to work harder than others who were not subject to such passions'.[117]

It is debatable whether the speed of execution of these utilitarian, preparatory artifacts resulted in 'single session pieces', the product of 'unmediated directness',[118] or in a more deliberate, thoughtful process that hid with masterful *sprezzatura* all of the mental and physical labor involved in the creation of a work of art. Indeed, Joachim von Sandrart records that Bernini showed him no less than 22 clay models in preparation for the statue of *Saint Longinus*.[119] But it is likely, for instance, that for every occasion in which one might argue in favor of Bernini's speedy and final execution of a clay model at one sitting, another example of a comparable but more elaborated process could be adduced.[120] What does not change is that the ultimate impression viewers have when confronted not only with sketches, drawings, and clay models but also with the marble works themselves is, indeed, one of an unmatched, volcanic creativity and execution (fig.1.18).

Still, and paradoxically, according to Chantelou, speed of execution is not something Bernini seemingly extolled.[121] For instance, when looking at Veronese's *The Children of Zebedee presented to Our Lord by their Mother* (*c.*1565), possibly the painting now at the Musée de Grenoble (fig.1.19),[122] Chantelou claims that Bernini declared 'that it was a beautiful picture but could not have taken more than eight days at the outside to complete'.[123] And, after looking at this same artist's *Venus and Adonis*, he

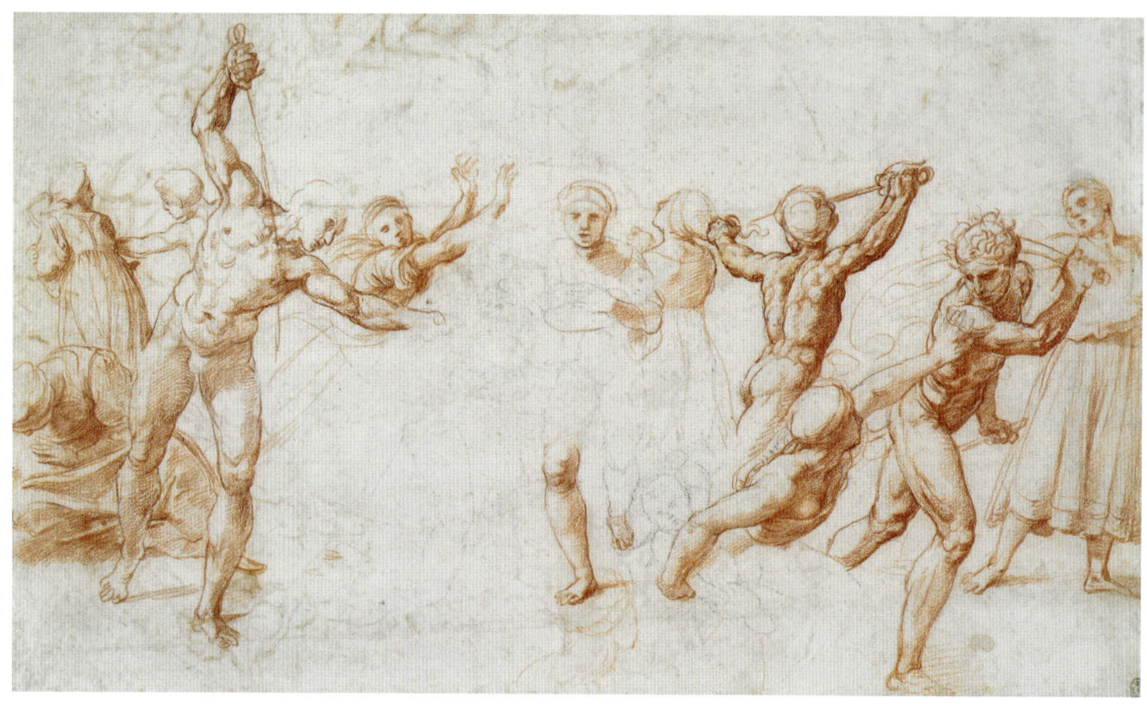

1.20 Raphael, *Study for the Massacre of the Innocents*, *c.*1510–14, red chalk over charcoal pounce-marks, stylus and black chalk underdrawing, 24.6 × 41.3 cm (9 11⁄16 × 16 ¼ in), Royal Collection Trust, Windsor Castle

reiterated the typical central Italian critique of north Italian (primarily Venetian) artists by stating they 'were great painters, but poor draftsmen'.[124] Again, according to Chantelou, Raphael's careful 'attention to detail', which Bernini considered 'extraordinary', was seen in sharp opposition to Tintoretto's and Veronese's 'free and furious style'.[125]

A cursory glance at Bernini's drawings and sculptures at the outset would seem to indicate that he 'said one thing but did another'. With regard to drawings, generally speaking, Raphael's concentration on 'vigorous outline', his gift in registering with clarity the forms before him, or his focusing on compositional groupings[126] (fig.1.20) differ from Bernini's interest in rapid, alternative solutions for his figures' vigorous stances or his composing and drawing by *macchie* (stains or blotches) 'to create a fine contrast of masses'[127] (figs 1.21 and 1.22). Some of Bernini's bold drawings, in fact, are rather distant from Raphael's pondered, sure-handed style. Actually, in some instances Bernini's approach seems closer to Luca Giordano's 'stenographic' *maniera* and one might be tempted to see in his drawings a reflection of Bernini's *napoletanità* (figs 1.23 and 1.24), especially as 'drawing was for Bernini . . . not an end but a means towards an end' – a concept typically associated with Neapolitan artists, as mentioned above.[128]

However, the truth is that his intense, copious, preparatory stages – from his *primi pensieri*, to his sketches, *bozzetti*, and models – *qualitatively* exemplify a break with the Renaissance 'orderly succession of increasingly meticulous studies, culminating in a complete, preferably full-scale

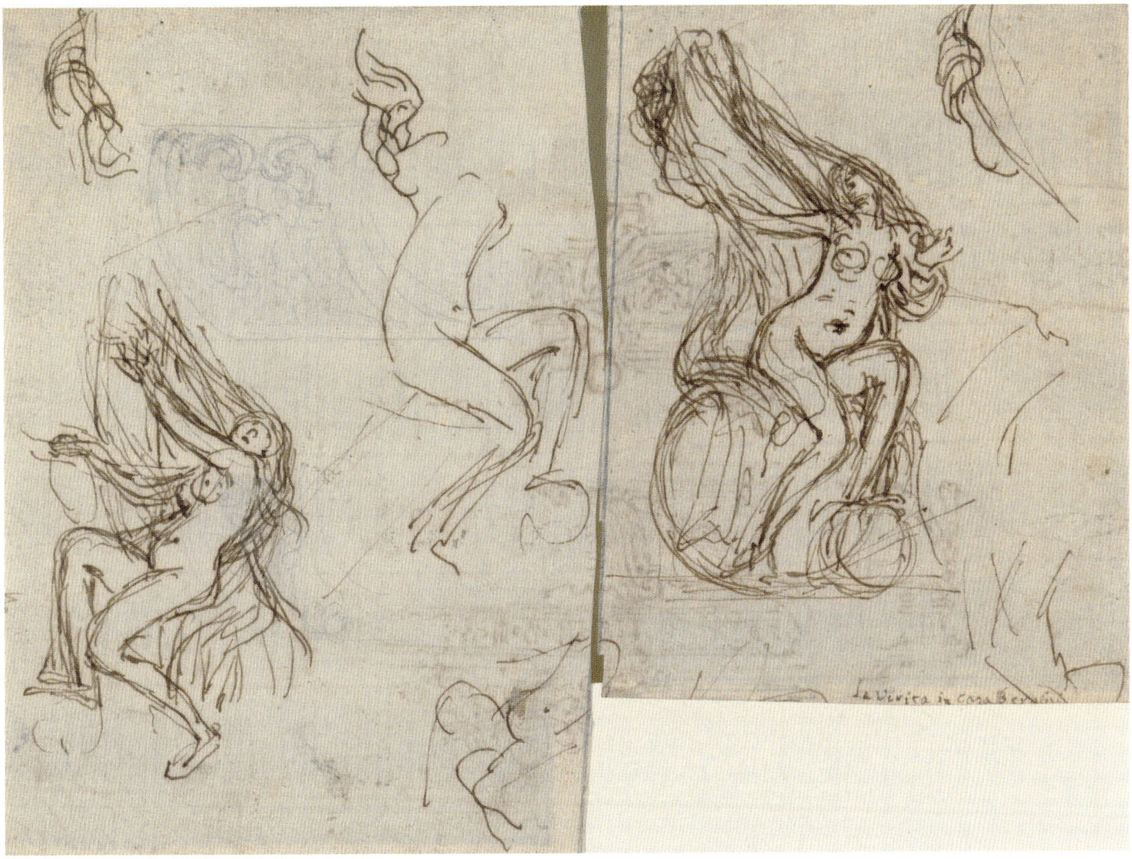

1.21 Gian Lorenzo Bernini, *Sketches for the Statue of Truth*, drawing, Museum der bildenden Künste, Leipzig, inv. 7853

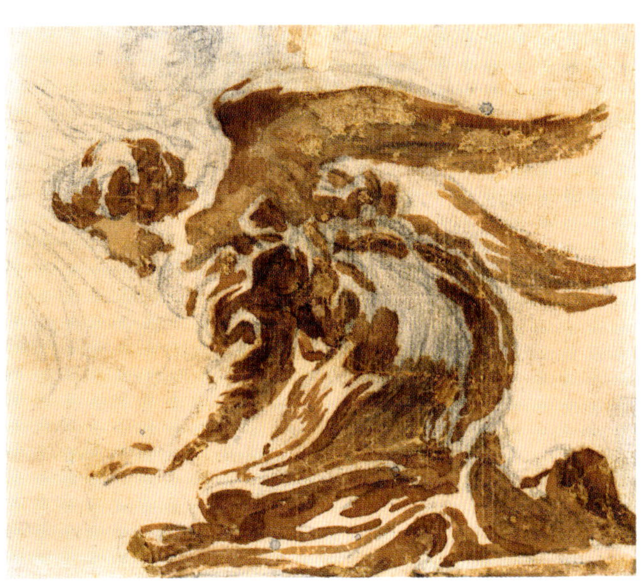

1.22 Gian Lorenzo Bernini, *Study of Angel from the Cappella del SS. Sacramento*, *c.*1673–4, black chalk and brown wash on discolored white paper, 14.4 × 16.8 cm (5 11/16 × 6 5/8 in), The Royal Collection Trust, Windsor Castle

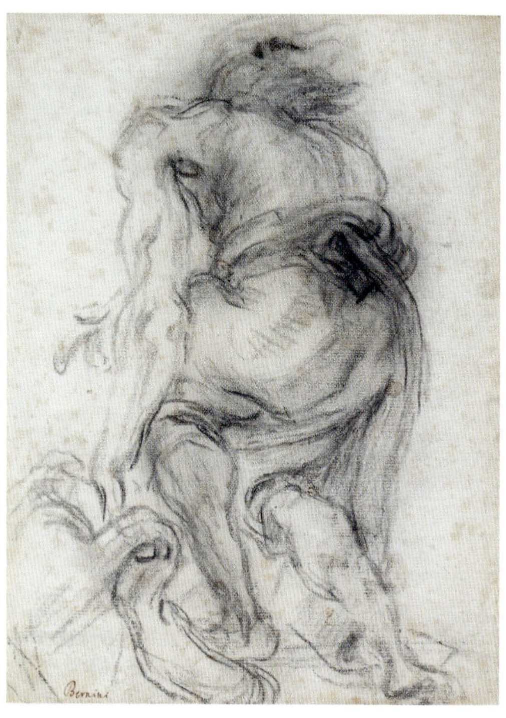

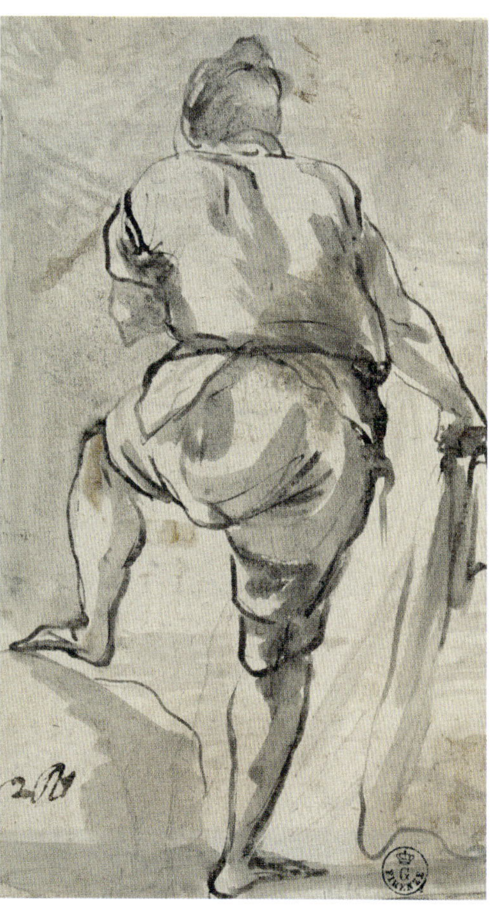

1.23 Gian Lorenzo Bernini, *Study for the Frontispiece of the Third Volume of In Selecta Scripturae Loca Ethicae Commentationes*, 1677, drawing, Istituto Centrale per la Grafica, Rome

1.24 Luca Giordano, *Study of a Man from the Back*, *c.*1684, pen and wash, 15 × 9 cm (5 ⅞ × 3 ⁹⁄₁₆ in), Galleria degli Uffizi, Florence

design from which the final work was copied as accurately as possible'.[129] *Procedurally*, however, they are totally indebted to the Tuscan-Roman tradition of the carefully planned, belabored, preliminary phases that lead up to the final artifact, even if the final work may have differed from the definitive model.[130] And if asked why his style ultimately looked so different from his acclaimed models – classical art and Raphael – Bernini would probably have responded that 'those who do not sometimes go outside the rules never go beyond them'.[131] Thus, an artist should first learn to draw as well as Raphael before going beyond the rules to create one's own, personal style[132] (figs 1.25 and 1.26).

Transferring the above considerations on a parallel, linguistic plane, in Renaissance and Baroque Italy, the Tuscan idiom had become the hegemonic literary and vernacular language. Educated people in different parts of the country, no matter what the local dialect, learned to read and write in Dante's tongue.[133] Although Neapolitan was a language in its own right, people living north of the river Sebeto (Naples' mythic river) considered it an inferior dialect. It is not coincidental that in some of the direct quotations placed in Salvator Rosa's mouth by the Roman Passeri or the Florentine Baldinucci the artist is cited expressing himself in his dialect[134] – a rare, if not unique, occurrence in any of the artists' biographies to have

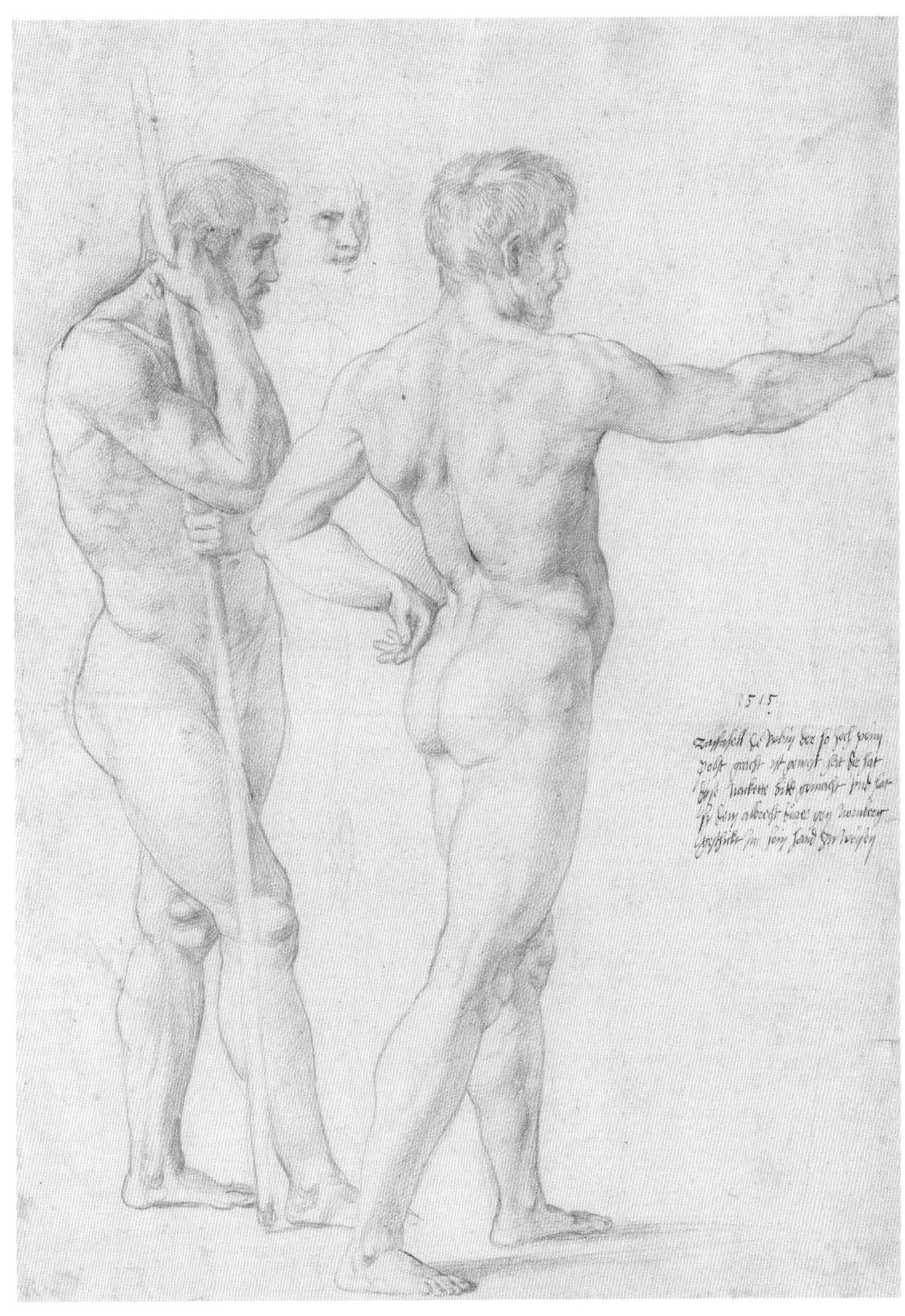

1.25 Raphael, *Study for the Battle of Ostia*, 1515, drawing, 40.3 × 28.3 cm (15 ⅞ × 11 ⅛ in), The Albertina Museum, Vienna

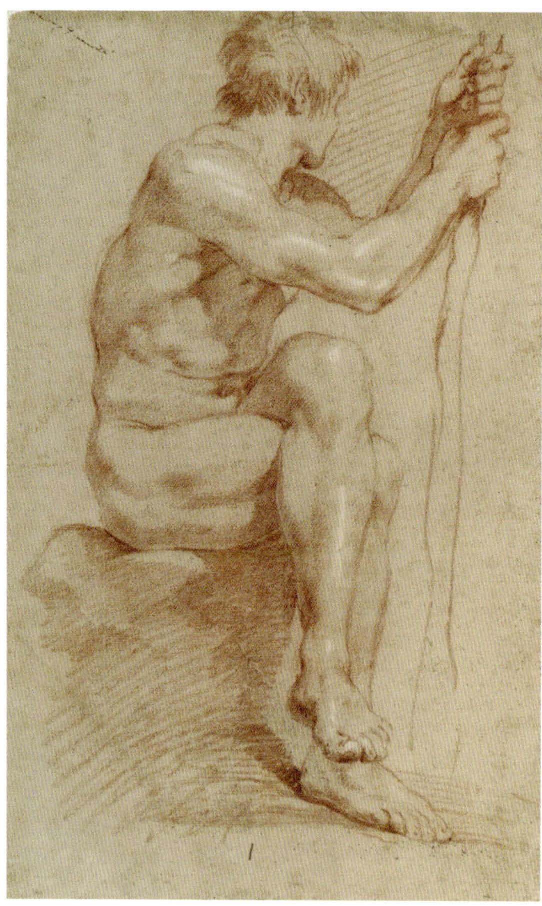

1.26 Gian Lorenzo Bernini, *Seated Male Nude*, *c.*1618–24, red chalk heightened with white chalk on buff laid paper, 42.2 × 27.2 cm (16 5⁄8 × 10 11⁄16 in), Princeton University Art Museum. Museum purchase, Laura P. Hall Memorial Fund and Fowler McCormick, Class of 1921, Fund 2005-128

been published in Italy through the eighteenth century. By so doing the authors did more than just underscore his wit and southern charm; they were plausibly, if indirectly, belittling his nationality for, as Ferdinando Galiani noted as late as 1789, 'it would seem that to speak Neapolitan and buffooning are almost one and the same thing'.[135]

Gian Lorenzo Bernini lived the fundamental, first eight years of his life (1598–1606) in the Neapolitan neighborhood of the *Carità*, near the church of Sant'Anna dei Lombardi. This district had become the artists' quarter and it is logical that his father should establish his home and studio in that part of town.[136] The child was raised hearing his mother and everyone in that section of the city speaking the local idiom.[137] Given his father's Tuscan influence and the early age by which he left his hometown, when speaking as an adult, no doubt, he had lost whatever Neapolitan inflection he might have had in his youth.[138] And even though by 1634–6 Giambattista Basile's *Lo cunto de li cunti* (*The Tale of Tales, or Entertainment for the Little Ones*)[139] – a collection of stories purposely written in the Neapolitan language as a counter-statement to current linguistic trends[140] – had been published and, through it, Parthenope's tongue had made a claim to loftier, more serious considerations by others, in surviving documentation Bernini is never recorded as having reverted to his maternal dialect.[141] This does not mean that in private, or when writing the lines spoken by Coviello – the Neapolitan stock, *commedia dell'arte* character in his plays – he did not do so, but his official *persona* did not indulge in this idiom. In fact, an analysis of his orthographic preferences in the few extant, personal letters show Bernini fluctuating between the Roman-Florentine phonetic and graphic variations typical of the linguistic oscillations of the time.[142] Thus, if language may be considered the equivalent of human behavior,[143] and if it is true that 'we are obliged, through frequent citation, to the legitimacy and advantage of appropriating the language of others to promote our most intimate private sense of self',[144] then this detail in Bernini's biographical accounts may be another indication of his desire to downplay his Neapolitan origin. Despite the occasional reminder that his roots were '*nello*

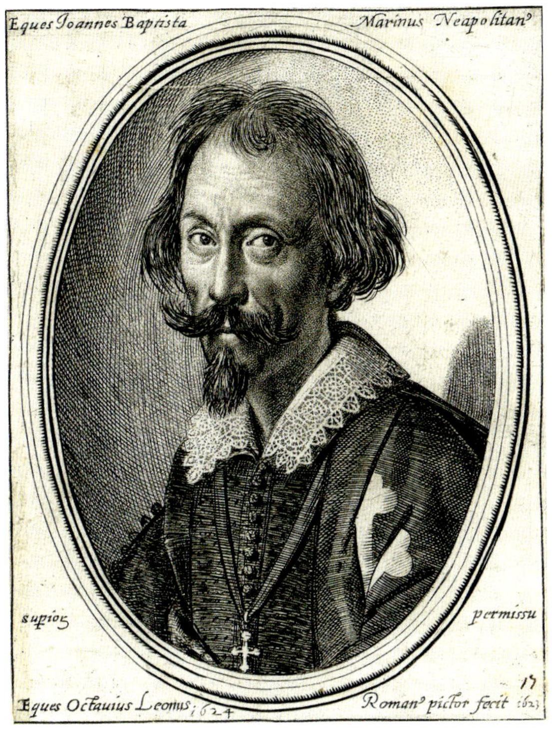

[*sic*] *Sebeto*', as did a compatriot in 1651 in a poem praising his *Four Rivers Fountain* in the Neapolitan language,[145] it is noteworthy that he himself – and, perhaps even more so, those who have informed us of his character and work – preferred that posterity not remember him as a Neapolitan. Indeed, there is no clearer evidence of how little Gian Lorenzo might be considered a '*Neapoletan[us] sculptor*' than the fact that, contrary to another great protagonist of the Baroque, the Neapolitan poet Giambattista Marino (fig.1.27), who after having wandered for years in various northern cities, in the last months of his life felt the need to go back to his hometown, Bernini, once he left, never returned.

1.27 Ottavio Leoni, *Portrait of Giambattista Marino (Eques Joannes Baptista Marinus Neapolitanus)*, 1623, etching and engraving and stipple, 14.2 × 10.7 cm (5 9/16 × 4 3/16 in), The British Museum, London

2

Of Sculptors and Cobblers

Since Ernst Kris and Otto Kurz first published their groundbreaking *Legend, Myth, and Magic in the Image of the Artist: A Historical Experiment*, scholars have been mining artists' biographies not so much for factual information as for a means to understand the way early modern biographers shaped and, not infrequently, manipulated their literary and documentary material.[1] More specifically, Kris and Kurz led the way on how to interpret certain recurring anecdotes employed by biographers and clarify what they reveal about the social and historical context in which such stories were fashioned. In their words: 'Speaking in the most general terms, we can say that we seek to understand *the meaning of fixed biographical themes*. In this sense the anecdote can be viewed as the "primitive cell" of biography. While this is obviously valid of biography in general, it is particularly true and historically proven in the case of the biography of artists.'[2]

Although this line of research has been employed, especially with regard to Giorgio Vasari's *Lives of the Most Eminent Painters, Sculptors and Architects* (1550 and 1568),[3] in recent decades the same approach has also been applied to Filippo Baldinucci's and Domenico Bernini's biographies of Gian Lorenzo Bernini.[4] Starting with Catherine Soussloff's initial studies[5] all the way down to the more recent critical essays published by Maarten Delbeke, Evonne Levy, and Steven F. Ostrow, scholars have become more cognisant of the personal, professional, literary and social agendas that underpin Filippo Baldinucci's and Domenico Bernini's respective works.[6] Paradoxically, however, biographers can reveal equally as much about their agendas by *omitting* to inform their readers about certain details that are known through other sources.[7] A case in point is how both Baldinucci and Domenico Bernini do not devote a single sentence to Gian Lorenzo Bernini's work as a restorer of classical statuary.

In sixteenth- and seventeenth-century Italy modern sculpture was not valued as highly as its classical counterpart, as attested by Bellori's introduction to Alessando Algardi's *vita*.[8] One obvious reason for this state of affairs is that there were only a finite number of ancient statues that could be obtained on the antiquarian market. As Vincenzo Giustiniani poignantly remarked, in his day, excavations had taken place in every corner of the city of Rome and although its soil had copiously surrendered many ancient sculptures, one could not expect them 'to keep growing every year like mushrooms or truffles'.[9] Even when classical statuary was chanced upon through excavations and a patron might consider acquiring it, there was one discriminating consideration that superseded all others. As Donatella Livia Sparti has indicated, 'The value of an ancient sculpture, economic and aesthetic, was proportional to its condition: the more it was damaged and needed to be restored, the less it was esteemed.'[10] Contrary to today's practice – when integration of the missing parts of an ancient statue is generally avoided and the fragment of a classical sculpture does not impede our ability to appreciate its aesthetic qualities – early modern patrons felt compelled to hire a contemporary sculptor to complete the work of art and make it 'whole'.[11] And since 'only complete statues were judged fit for display', the profession of the restorer developed and frequently became the primary source of income for many artists.[12]

Successful sculptors, of course, had enough requests for original work to avoid restoring ancient statuary, unless pressed by powerful patrons.[13] According to Giovan Pietro Bellori, despite the acclaim Alessandro Algardi received for his *Saint Magdalen* (1628–9), soon after he arrived in Rome 'he survived by making models of putti, statuettes, heads, crucifixes, and ornaments for goldsmiths, for sculptures are not in fashion in our age as they were in antiquity due to the magnificence of the Romans; and with everyone seeking ancient statutes, many sculptors live by restoring old fragments and ruins, which are exported from Rome to all parts'.[14]

The young Bernini, like Algardi, had his share in restoring classical statuary. In 1616–17, at the time barely nineteen years of age, he 'must have seen – and perhaps even helped' his father Pietro as he set about to restore the ancient Roman sculpture of a horse discovered about sixty years earlier in the Vale of Tempe at Hadrian's Villa (fig.2.1).[15] Then, a couple of years later, Gian Lorenzo personally restored the *Hermaphrodite* currently at the Louvre (fig.2.2). Discovered in the spring of 1619 in the cloister of the Church of Santa Maria della Vittoria (in the former gardens of Sallust, near the Quirinal Hill), the statue was acquired by Cardinal Scipione Borghese and delivered to Bernini's atelier on 29 September.[16] Gian Lorenzo received a payment of 15 *scudi* for the virtuoso rendition of the mattress on which the statue was placed on 14 October 1619, and then transported to the cardinal's Villa Borghese on 3 January 1620.[17] In essence, instead of setting the antique statue on a base that might recall a classical context, such as a grassy ground, the young sculptor's dexterous treatment of the marble emphasised its erotic potential by showing the half male-half female offspring of Hermes and Aphrodite reclining on a seventeenth-century mattress.[18] The optical and tactile *trompe l'œil* restoration – the 'supple', polished mattress prods viewers to press their fingers into it[19] – mirrored the leather couch that was placed

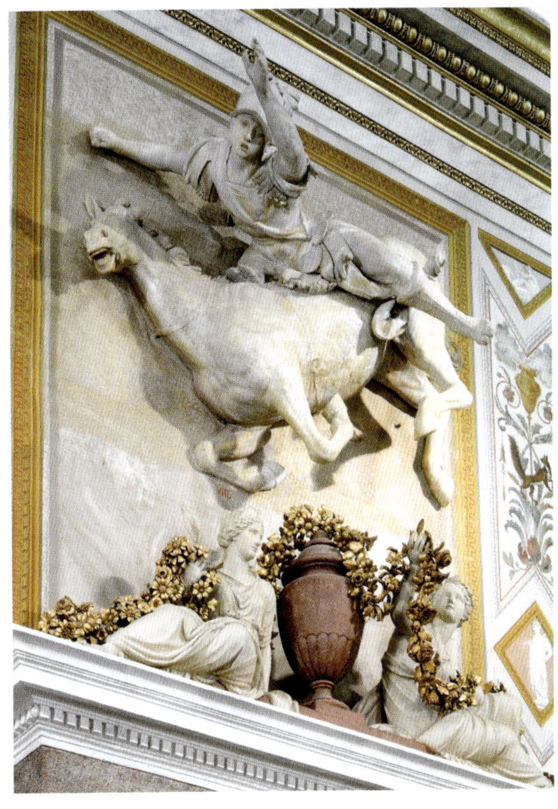

2.1 Pietro Bernini, *Marcus Curtius Throwing Himself into the Chasm*, fragment of a monument with a yoked horse, restored as *Marcus Curtius*, Roman sculpture, second century AD, restoration 1617, marble, height 220 cm (86 ⅝ in), Galleria Borghese, Rome

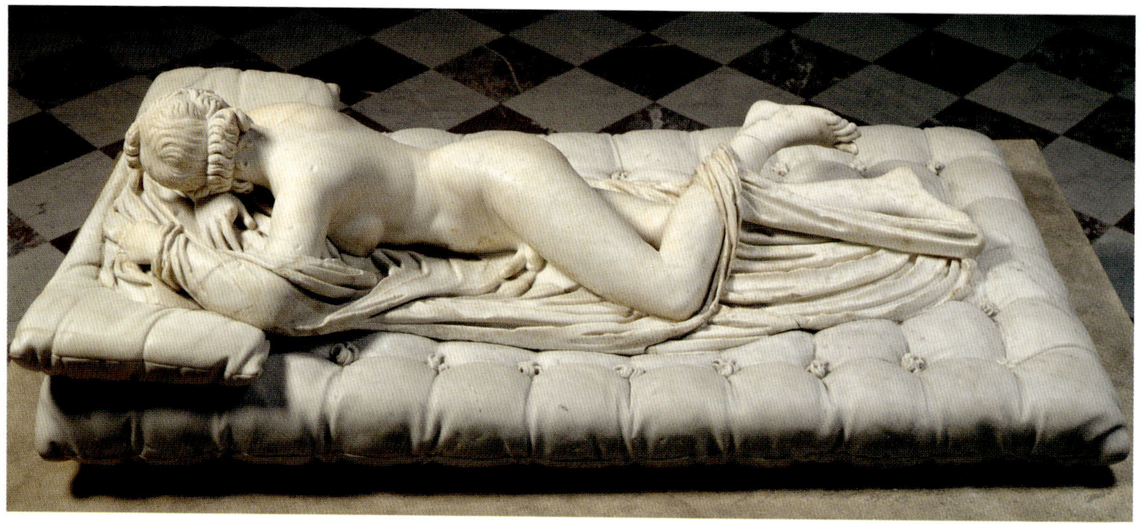

2.2 Gian Lorenzo Bernini, *Hermaphrodite*, second century AD (?), addition of mattress 1619, marble, 46.5 × 173.5 × 90.5 cm (18 5/16 × 68 5/16 × 35 5/8 in), Musée du Louvre, Paris

across from it on the window wall.[20] From such a vantage point the visitor to Cardinal Borghese's villa could pause and admire the realistic treatment of the marble mattress, the beauty of the classical statue, and the male genitalia that complemented the adolescent female breasts visible from both sides of the sculpture.[21] That the sculpture had a prurient effect on viewers is substantiated by the fact that the carpenter, Giovan Battista Soria, was paid 230 *scudi* on 28 June to create an encasement for the sculpture. This wooden box comprised the Borghese eagle and dragon family heraldry, eight small putti, as well as a lid to screen the 'boudoir' sculpture from an indiscreet gaze.[22]

In the summer of 1622, Bernini was asked once again to restore an antique statue. Although by this time he had already embarked on his astonishing trajectory to fame – for Scipione Borghese he had already completed the *Aeneas, Anchises and Ascanius Fleeing Troy* (1618–19) and the *Pluto and Proserpina* (1621–2) (figs 2.3 and 2.4) – he could not decline the request to restore a seated, contemplative statue of *Mars* (fig.2.5) since the patron was Ludovico Ludovisi, Cardinal Nephew of the reigning Pope Gregory XV.[23] Discovered in 1621–2 while excavating a sewer in what is today Piazza Capizucchi, the beautiful, second- or first-century BC Roman copy of a third-century BC Greek marble statue and accompanying Eros was subsequently restored by Bernini by carving anew the lost parts – primarily the nose, hilt of the sword, and right foot of the mythical hero, as well as the head, left arm, and right foot of the Cupid.[24]

From the account books of the Ludovisi collection one learns that 60 *scudi* were disbursed on 20 June 1622 'to Cav[alie]re Bernini, sculptor, for the restoration of an ancient statue of Adonis [*sic*] and all other work done for the *casino* of said vineyard up to the 14th of this month'.[25] Besides the understandable confusion between Mars and Adonis – Adonis, like Mars, was subjugated by Love[26] – Bernini's involvement in the restoration of this

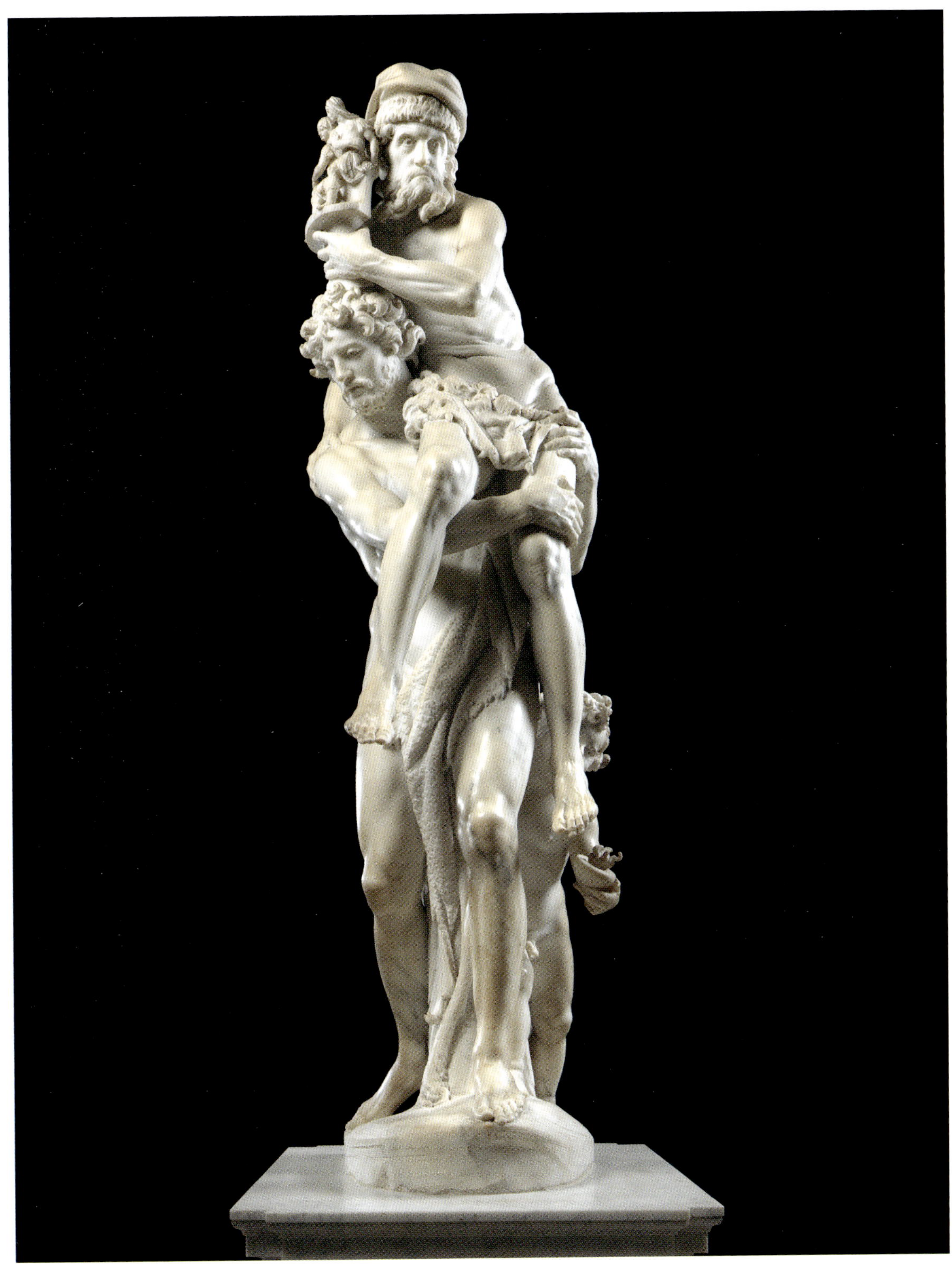

2.3 Gian Lorenzo Bernini, *Aeneas, Anchises and Ascanius Fleeing Troy*, 1618–19, marble, height 220 cm (86 ⅝ in), Galleria Borghese, Rome

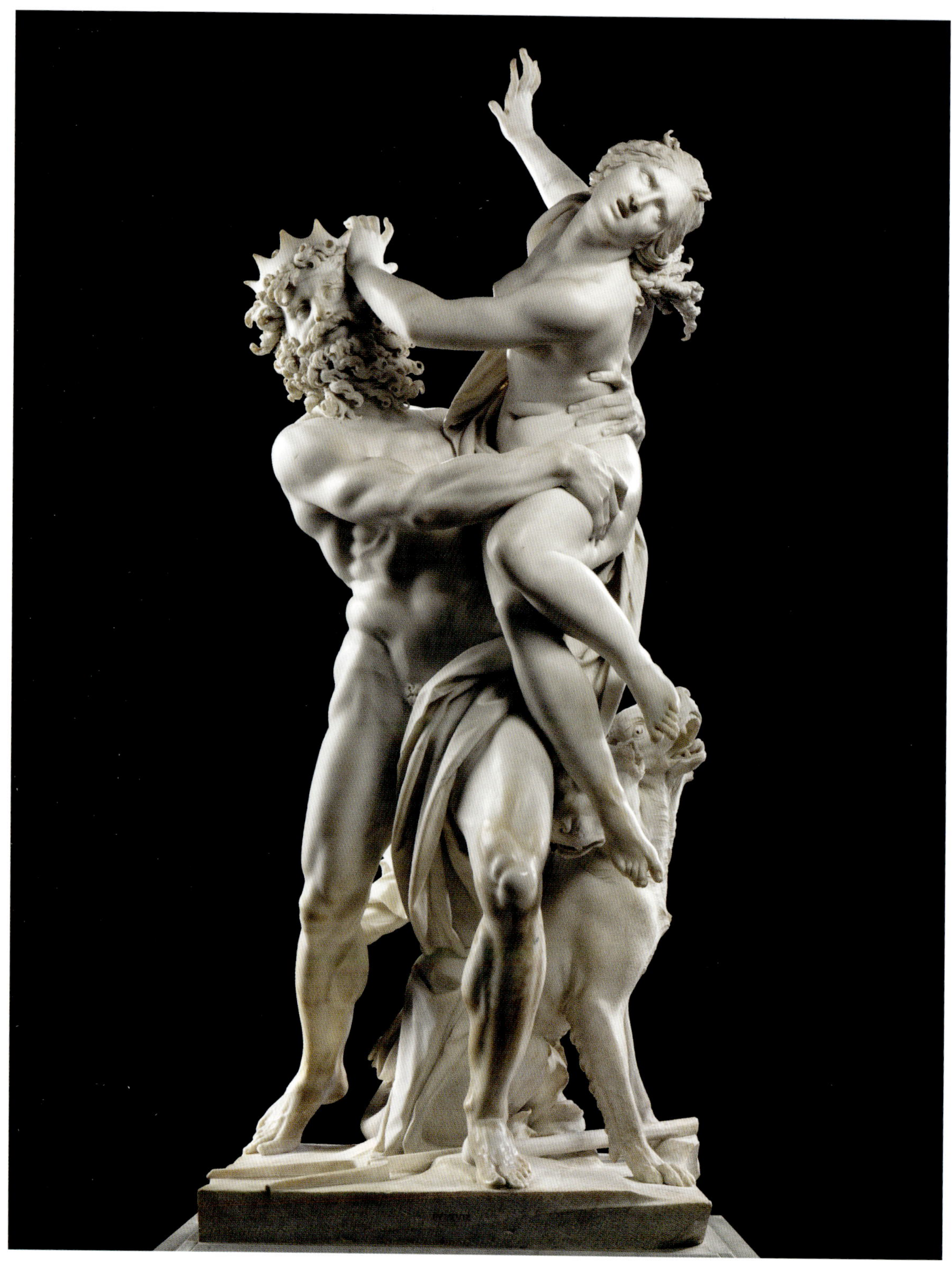

2.4 Gian Lorenzo Bernini, *Pluto and Proserpina*, 1621–2, marble, height 225 cm (88 9/16 in), Galleria Borghese, Rome

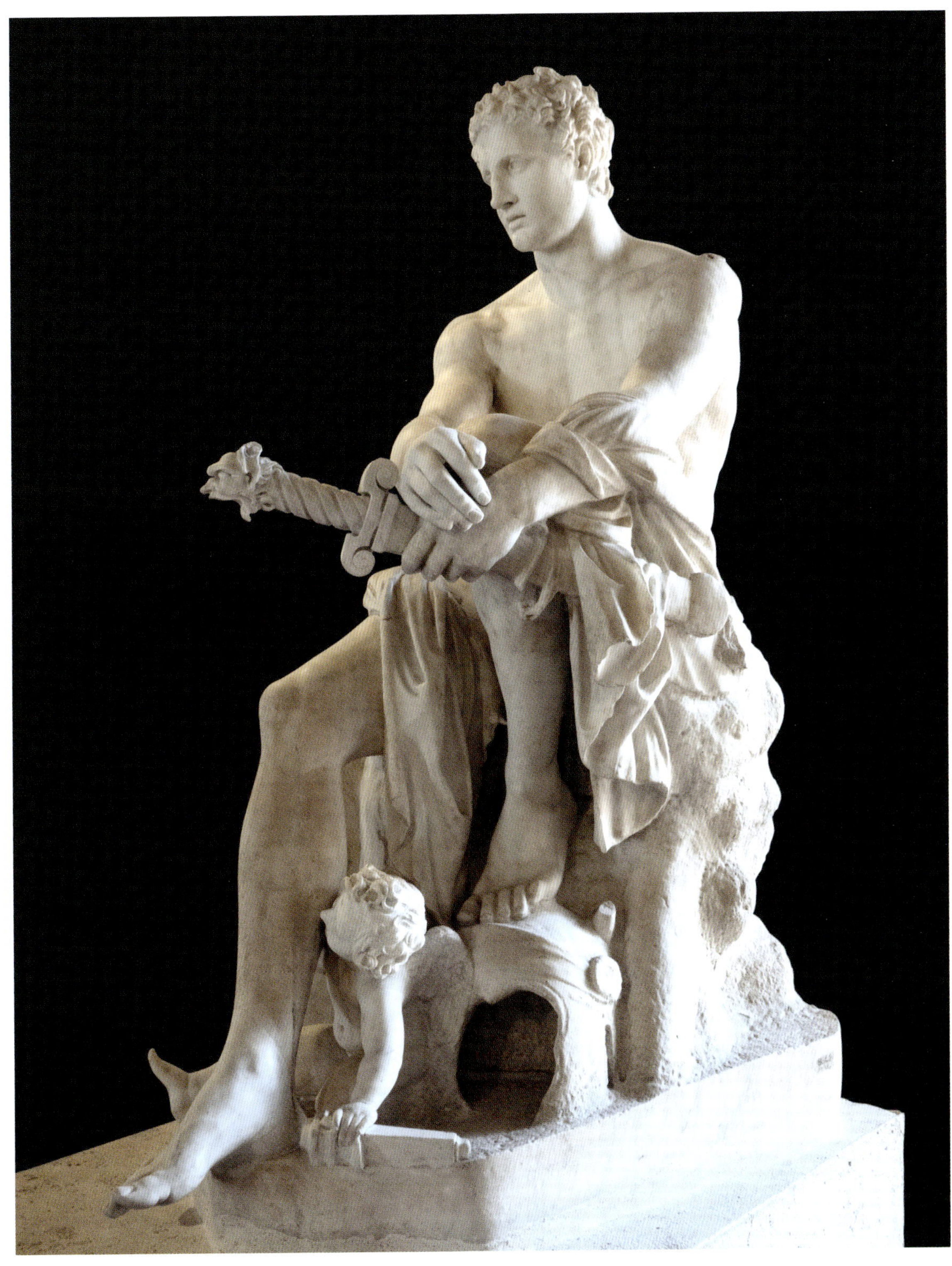

2.5 Gian Lorenzo Bernini, *Ludovisi Mars*, second century AD, restored 1622, marble, height 156 cm (61 7/16 in), Museo Nazionale Romano, Palazzo Altemps, Rome

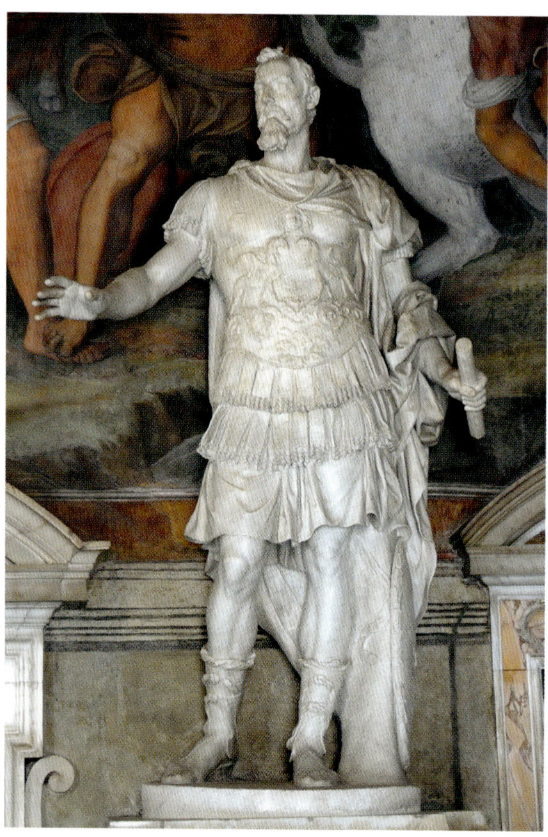

2.6 Gian Lorenzo Bernini, *Head of the Memorial Statue for Carlo Barberini*, 1630, marble, height 230 cm (90 9/16 in), Palazzo dei Conservatori, Rome

sculpture is corroborated by Orfeo Boselli who, in his *Osservazioni della scoltura antica*, praised him for his work on the statue which he thought represented a gladiator.[27]

Bernini was asked to perform one final, *recorded* restoration in 1630, after the Conservatori of Rome held a secret meeting,[28] at which time it was decided to commemorate Carlo Barberini, General of the Holy Church and brother of the reigning Pope Urban VIII, who had died in February of that year (fig.2.6).[29] The patrons' decision, made public on 30 March, involved the reutilisation of a torso fragment of the statue of an emperor.[30] While Alessandro Algardi restored the missing arms and legs, Bernini was asked to carve the head.[31] This division of labor, which resulted in an overall 'clumsy' appearance of the man, was probably dictated by three considerations: the time factor, Carlo Barberini's family ties to the pope, and Bernini's renown as a sculptor of portrait busts.[32] As it turned out, the work was carried out expeditiously since the restored statue was already in place in the Palazzo dei Conservatori by 3 August, with Algardi receiving his final payment on 12 September and Bernini on the 28th of that month.[33]

Bernini lived another fifty years after the Carlo Barberini sculpture was completed. And while it is known that starting in 1663 Cardinal Flavio Chigi from time to time relied on Bernini to estimate the value of restorations executed by others,[34] and that three of his assistants were called upon to do such work – Baldassare Mari from 1669 to 1673, Antonio Raggi from 1673 to 1686, and Giuseppe Mazzuoli from 1677[35] – as far as documented works are concerned, he never again put his hands to hammer and chisel to execute the restoration of an ancient statue.[36] Given that neither of his biographers mentions this aspect of his early works, it has been plausibly assumed that 'in all probability he wanted to prevent that aspect of his youthful period, prior to the pontificate of Urban VIII, from being passed down to posterity'.[37] The question is *why* should the elderly Bernini, who supplied many of the anecdotes and general information about his long career to his sons Pier Filippo and the younger Domenico (and through them to his first biographer Filippo Baldinucci), wish to hide his having participated in such activity. Certainly, next to Bernini's lifelong major accomplishments – from the *Apollo and Daphne* (completed in 1625) (fig.2.7) to the papal tombs for Urban VIII (1647) and Alexander VII (1678), the *Baldacchino* in the crossing of Saint Peter's Basilica (1633), the *Four Rivers Fountain* (1651), and the Cornaro Chapel (1652) – his restoration work pales in significance. But, besides Bernini's recorded

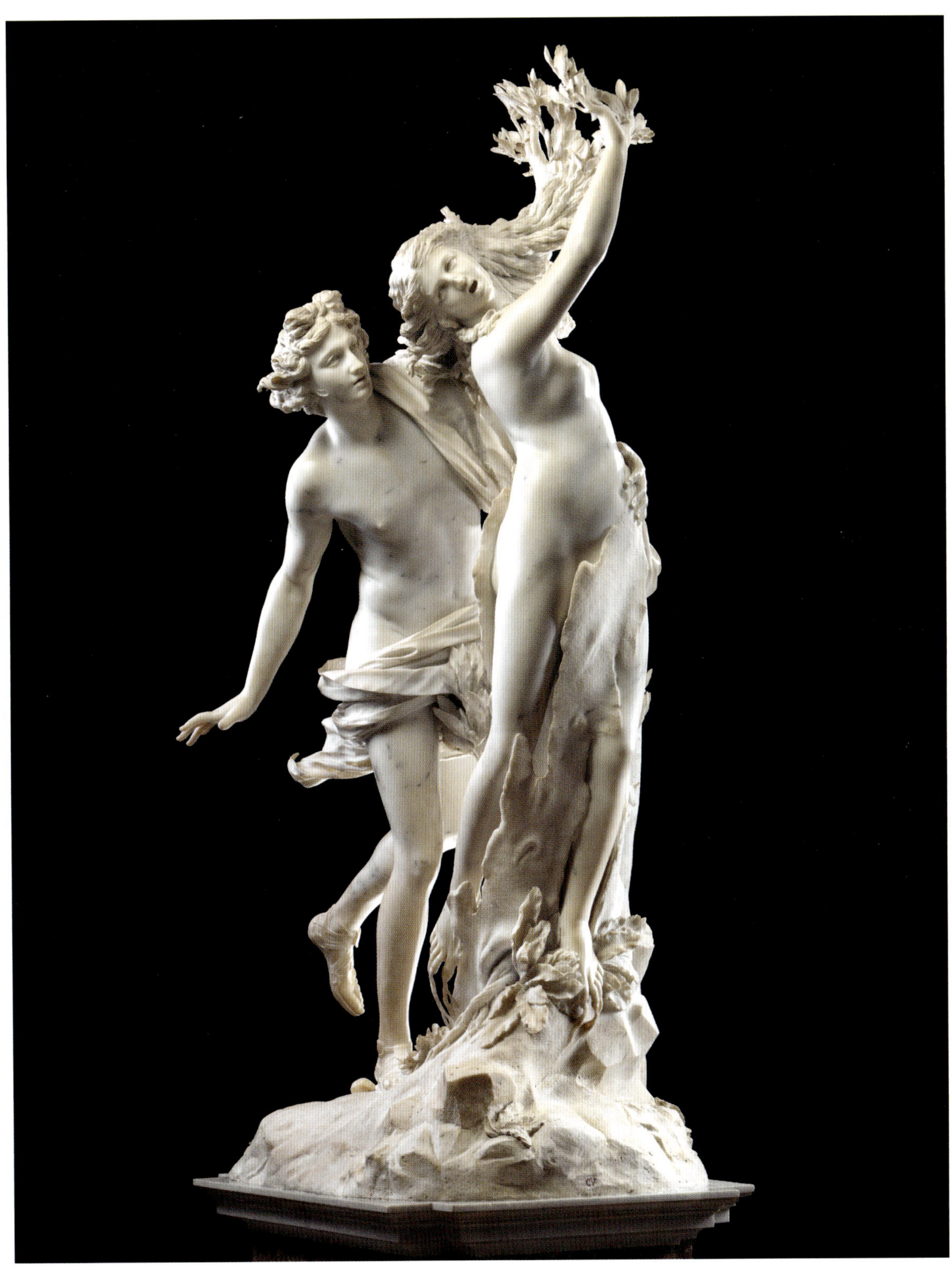

2.7 Gian Lorenzo Bernini, *Apollo and Daphne*, 1625, marble, height 243 cm (95 11⁄16 in), Galleria Borghese, Rome

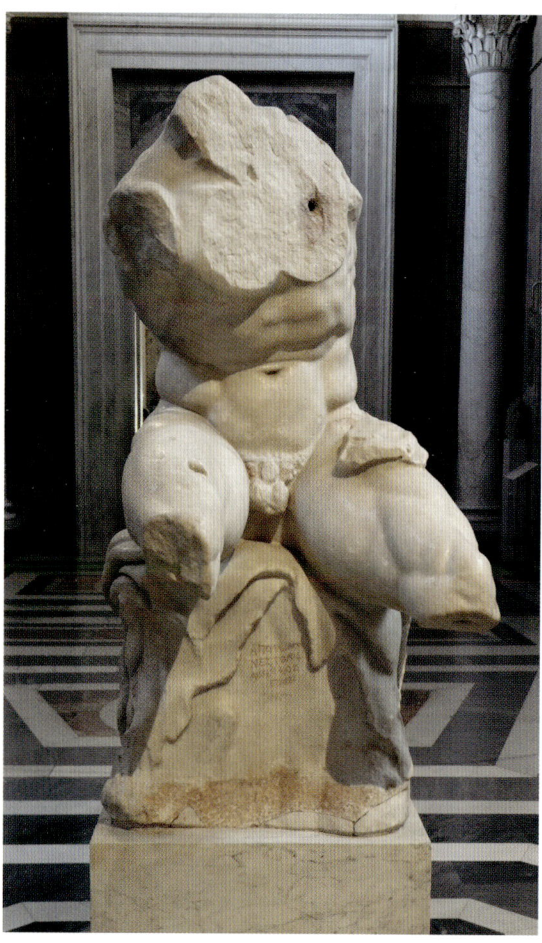

2.8 *Belvedere Torso*, first century BC, marble, 159 × 84 cm (62 5⁄8 × 33 1⁄16 in), Vatican Museums, Rome

admiration for two ancient fragmentary statues that needed no modern restoration to be appreciated – in his view a person could easily recreate in one's mind's eye the missing parts of the *Belvedere Torso* (fig.2.8) and the *Pasquino* (fig.2.9)[38] – there may be professional and social reasons with far-reaching historical roots and implications that justify his and the biographers' reticence on the subject.

No doubt there were people such as Vasari who saw restoration as a worthy enterprise for sculptors. In describing Lorenzetto's 'rehabilitation' of some ancient sculptures, for example, he wrote: 'and, in truth, antiquities restored in this way have more grace than those mutilated trunks, members without heads, or figures in any other way maimed and defective'.[39] He also claimed that, in trying to help Jacopo Sansovino obtain a commission from Julius II, Bramante had him restore some antique sculptures that impressed the pope and others with his ability.[40] Nevertheless, the general sentiment normally contradicted such views. In Benvenuto Cellini's *Autobiography* (1558–62), for instance, the artist informs his readers that one day, when he went to see Cosimo I of Florence, the Duke asked him to open a box he had received from Stefano Colonna in Palestrina. Upon discovering it contained a beautiful fragment of a classical statue the sculptor exclaimed:

> I must say that I have never seen a boy's figure so excellently wrought and in so fine a style among all the antiques I have inspected. If your Excellency permits, I should like to restore it – head and arms and feet. I will add an eagle, in order that we may christen the lad Ganymede. It is certainly not my business to patch up statues, that being the trade of *botchers* [*ciabattini*, i.e., cobblers] who do it in all conscience villainously ill; yet the art displayed by this great master of antiquity cries out to me to help him.[41] (italics mine)

This citation is noteworthy for at least two reasons: first, it demonstrates the ascendancy that classical art had among Renaissance collectors; second, patching antique fragments was considered a 'subordinate occupation' that was beneath the role of a master sculptor.[42] Equally important, however, is to comprehend why Cellini uses the term 'cobblers' to refer to those chiselers who made ends meet by restoring ancient statuary. To understand this, one must go back in time.

* * *

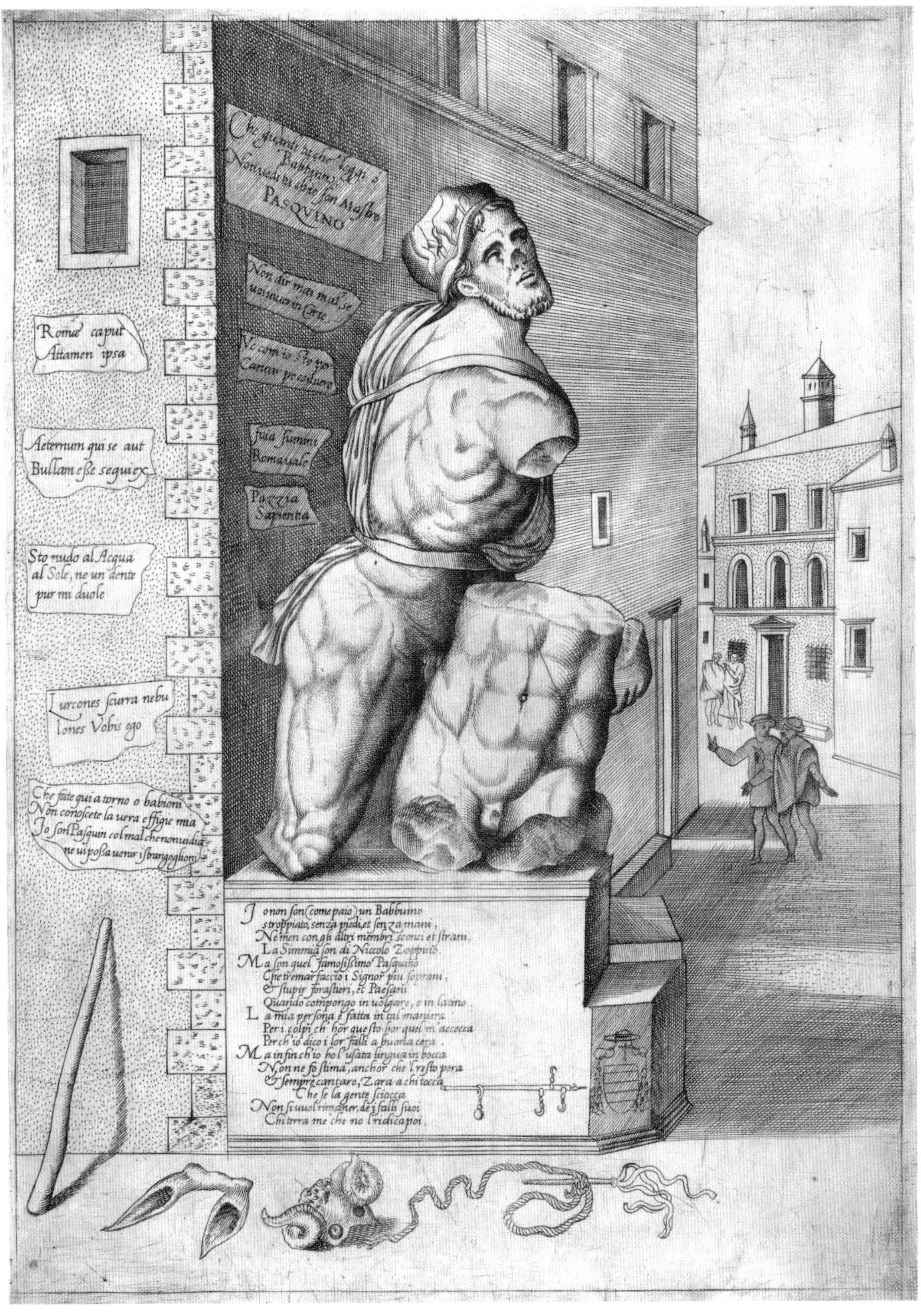

2.9 Nicolas Beatrizet, *Pasquino*, 1550, from Antonio Lafreri, *Speculum Romanae Magnificentiae*, engraving and etching, 47 × 34.5 cm (18½ × 13⁹⁄₁₆ in), Piazza del Pasquino, Rome

There are numerous examples found in classical literary sources to remind readers that in Greek and Roman societies those who busied themselves with the making or repairing of footwear were considered the lowest members of society. This concept was so pervasive that it became a well-known *topos*.[43] Indeed, it is not surprising that, in emphasising the key role that the guardians of the law played in his ideal state, Plato should juxtapose these guardians to cobblers, for his audience would have understood that he was contrasting the most to the least significant members of society.[44] References that corroborate this sentiment, for example, are found in Pliny, Horace, and Juvenal.[45] However, a more factual example that apprises us of the status these artisans held in the ancient world is found in one of Libanius' orations (*Oratio 46: Contra Florentium*). With reference to the *collatio lustralis* or *chrysargyron*, the gold and silver tax that marked a shift in the balance of taxation from the upper to the lower class, Libanius bemoaned: 'While merchants can recoup themselves by speculation, those for whom the work of their hands scarcely furnishes a livelihood are crushed beneath the burden. The lowest cobbler cannot escape from it.'[46]

This ancient elitist view, which placed shoemakers and cobblers on the lowest rung of the social ladder, was inherited by future generations because to earn a living by using one's hands was disreputable, according to classical, medieval, and Renaissance aristocratic worldviews. If those hands, furthermore, were to busy themselves exclusively with the covering of the feet – the lowest part of the body, literally and figuratively – classical prejudices were even more accentuated.[47] Consequently, shoemakers appear copiously as the negative term of comparison or the butt of jokes and snide remarks in Italian literature until modern times and with comparable, though attenuated, force and possibilities in paintings.[48] Thus Dante in the *Convivio* (IV.xvi.6), distinguishing between the concepts of nobility and fame, explains that if the etymological root of the word *noble* had derived from the Latin verb *noscere* (to know), as was erroneously maintained by some, then the famous thirteenth-century soothsayer, the shoemaker Mastro Benvenuto of Parma, known as Asdente, would have been nobler than any other citizen of that city – a nonsensical thought in Dante's opinion.[49]

Comparably, in the prolific world of medieval *novelle*, one finds numerous stories that demonstrate in their wording, anecdotes, or plots how ancient biases were fluidly transmitted from one era to the next. An instance is found in Boccaccio's *Decameron*, which clearly echoes the above-mentioned juxtaposition of cobblers and guardians of the law in Plato's *Republic*. By way of emphasising the strange manner in which Fortune achieves her aims, the author has one of his characters claim, 'What do I care if a shoemaker, rather than a philosopher, manages some affair of mine in his own way, whether openly or furtively, so long as the end result is a good one?'[50]

However, although Leonardo Fioravanti (1518–88) in *Dello specchio di scientia universale* claims that 'there has never been in the world a meaner craft than the shoemaker's',[51] in the highly stratified social context of early modern Italy, making shoes was not really the meanest craft. The lowest of the low were actually the cobblers, or *ciabattini*. While shoemakers were primarily engaged in creating something new and worked in a shop, cobblers merely repaired worn-out shoes and typically 'set up shop' outdoors with nothing to their name but their tools and a bench.[52] The distinction between shoemakers and cobblers at the beginning of the seventeenth century – at the very time Bernini began restoring classical statues – is made clear in Tommaso Garzoni's *La Piazza Universale di tutte le Professioni del Mondo* (1617).[53] In this book, which formed part of Gian Lorenzo's or his brother Luigi's library,[54] the author claims that 'the difference between shoemakers and cobblers with regard to rank is comparable to that between a prince and a servant'.[55] Considering that as late as in the 1878 edition of the *Vocabolario degli Accademici della Crusca* – and, for that matter, in any good Italian dictionary even today – one of the definitions of the word *ciabattino* is 'a term of scorn used to describe anyone who performs his art or craft badly, be it because of carelessness or incompetence',[56] one can understand why Benvenuto Cellini, who deemed restoring antique fragments a task worthy of only second-rate sculptors, chose the term *ciabattini* as their appropriate epithet.

Evidently, the social and professional stigma attached to those who patched sculptures was deep-seated in Italian society. And even though the term *ciabattini* does not seem to have been used in seventeenth-century art treatises or other literature that refers to sculpture, the social disgrace attached to those who 'patched' the object of their craft would no doubt have been present in people's minds.[57] Indeed, closer to Bernini's time, in his *Discorsi morali* (1627) Agostino Mascardi criticised those sculptors who 'patched' fragments of ancient statues ('*rappezzatori di pietre vecchie*') and for being unable, as Bernini had shown in his *Apollo and Daphne* (1622–5), to give life to a sculpture out of a single marble block.[58] And whatever the merits and mastery necessary to bring important restorations to a positive conclusion, in an age when the *paragone* between painting and sculpture was hotly debated, there is no doubt that a restorer ranked lower than a sculptor because restoring did not require as much creativity.[59] Thus, it seems reasonable to assume that the reason why Baldinucci and Domenico Bernini did not include any information in their biographies about Gian Lorenzo Bernini's work as a restorer is that it would not have added luster to his reputation; if anything, it would have detracted from it. Consequently, Bernini himself, as well as Filippo Baldinucci and Domenico Bernini, were probably all too willing to let this aspect of his *curriculum vitae* fall into oblivion.

* * *

In the above-quoted texts by Cellini and Mascardi, restoring ancient sculptures by adding the missing pieces of marble was described indiscriminately by the verb 'to patch' (*rattoppare*, Vasari, and *rappezzare*, Mascardi).[60] In other words, regardless of the technique employed – such as joining a newly carved limb to the ancient statue through the use of pins or rods, or filling a void in the original piece with a marble patch by means of some binding agent[61] – restoring classical statuary was described as patching and all artists involved in this activity were considered 'cobblers'. But patching Greek or Roman sculptural fragments in early modern Italy was one side of the coin. The other side pertains to the patching or addition of pieces of marble to the core of *modern* statuary. This approach to sculpture in the latter part of the sixteenth century introduces a fundamental change in sculptural practice that was responsible, at least in part, for contributing to the development of a new aesthetics in the Baroque period.

In Chapter IX of his 'Introduction' to *The Lives of the Most Excellent Painters, Sculptors and Architects*, in which Giorgio Vasari discusses the technical aspects of architecture, sculpture, and painting, the author addresses the procedure by which sculptors should progress from their clay or wax models to full-sized *modelli* and their transference to the full-scaled marble statue.[62] Wishing to warn about the 'danger of dispensing with the Full-sized Model', Vasari cautions:

> Those artificers who are in a hurry to get on, and who hew into the stone at the first and rashly cut away the marble in front and at the back, have no means afterwards of drawing back in case of need. Many errors in statues spring from this impatience of the artist to see the round figure out of the block at once, so that often an error is revealed that can only be remedied by joining on pieces, as we have seen to be the habit of many modern artists. *This patching [rattoppamento] is after the fashion of cobblers and not of competent men or rare masters, and is ugly and despicable and worthy of the greatest blame.*[63] (italics mine)

Thus, be it the restoration of ancient sculptural fragments or the addition of extra pieces of marble

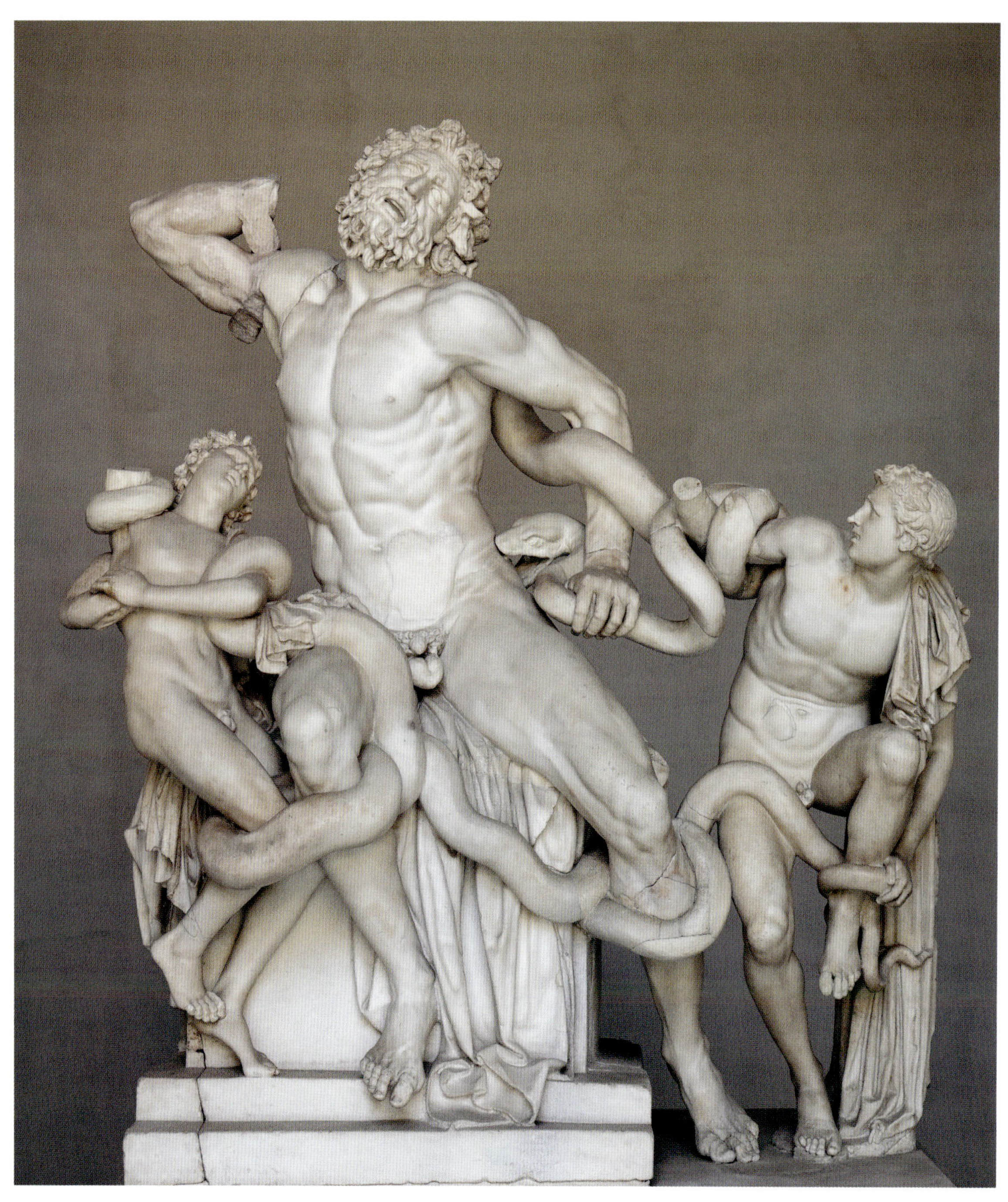

2.10 *Laocoön*, first century AD, marble, 208 × 163 × 112 cm (81 7/8 × 64 3/16 × 17 5/16 in), Vatican Museums, Rome

to modern statues, it is clear that by the middle of the sixteenth century – Cellini's *Autobiography* was written between 1558 and 1562 and Vasari's *Lives* were published in 1550 and in 1568 – a relatively significant segment of the artistic community felt such activities were demeaning for master sculptors, since they were seen as patching or botching the object of their trade as cobblers did theirs.[64]

At the root of such an equation was the classical notion propagated by Pliny the Elder who praised the technical ability of marble sculptors with regard to works of great complexity with the expression *ex uno lapide* ('out of one marble block').[65] As one of the four examples of such a technical *tour de force*, Pliny mentions the *Laocoön* (fig.2.10) that in antiquity was located 'in the palace of General [i.e., Emperor] Titus'.[66] It is difficult to overestimate the impact that this statue had on society at large and on sculptors in particular when it was unearthed on 14 January 1506.[67] Memorably described by Pliny as 'a work superior to any painting and any bronze',[68] the statue's discovery had at least two significant side-effects: on the one hand it reinforced Pliny's authority and historical reliability; on the other, it revealed to sculptors and connoisseurs that it was actually made of not one but four marble blocks (today we know that there are at least seven).[69] Writing to his brother Pomponio from Rome on 1 June 1506, Cesare Trivulzio observed:

> Pliny's testimony is quite important [and] truly great, so much so that the Roman citizen who unearthed it from his orchard, did not wish to sell it to the Cardinal of Saint Peter in Chains [Galeotto Franciotti della Rovere], although a Roman, for six hundred golden *scudi* . . . This statue [the Laocoön], that together with his sons Pliny claims was made of a single piece was challenged by the leading sculptors in Rome, Giovanni Cristofano Romano and Michelangelo the Florentine, who deny it was made of one marble block. They point out that there are about four joins but these are so well connected and stuccoed that they are difficult to discern, except by persons most expert in this art.[70]

In fact, ancient sculptors had not only used struts but also attached, by mortise and tenon or plainly glued, additional pieces to their marble statues 'to transcend the limits of the medium'.[71] Ultimately, the lesson that sixteenth-century sculptors and observers learned when the *Laocoön* was discovered was the *equivalence* between a sculpture that was carved out of a single marble block and one that *seemed* to have been sculpted *ex uno lapide*;[72] that is, the term became accepted as 'an ideal, a criterion of conceptual integrity rather than material fact'.[73] Despite – or rather, because of – such a realisation, the challenge posed by Pliny's praise of a sculpture carved *ex uno lapide* was accepted by artists as a paragon of artistic achievement in their attempt to surpass the reputedly most famous sculpture from antiquity.[74] Most notable among these endeavors were Michelangelo's Florence *Pietà* of the 1550s (fig.2.11), Bandinelli's version of the same theme in SS. Annunziata of 1559, Cellini's

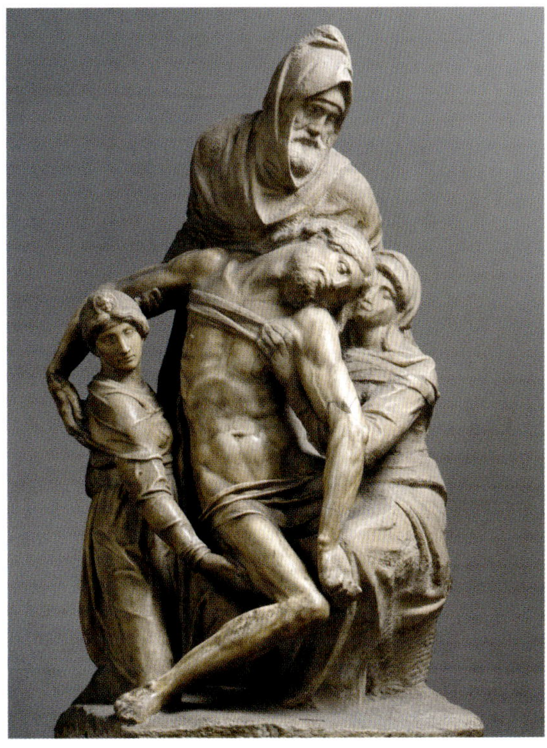

2.11 Michelangelo Buonarroti, *Pietà*, 1547–55, marble, 226 cm (89 in), Museo dell'Opera, Florence

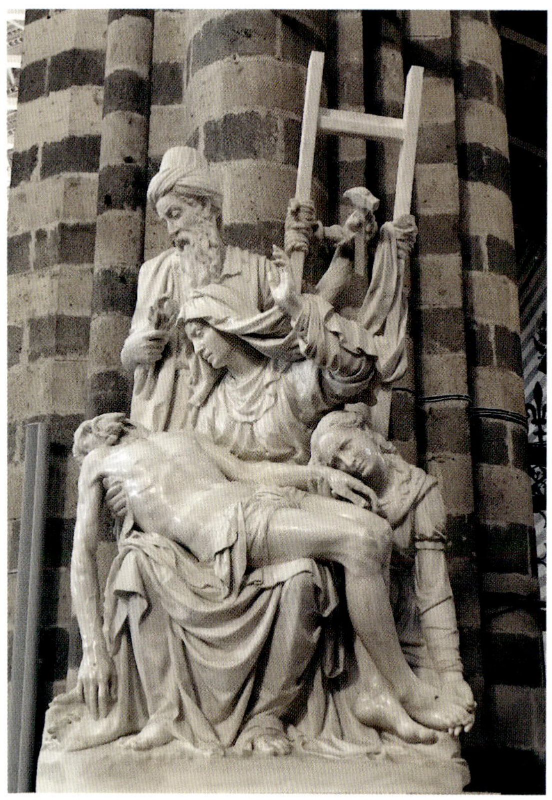

2.12 Ippolito Scalza, *Pietà*, 1579, marble, Orvieto Cathedral

Crucifix (*c.*1562), Ippolito Scalza's *Pietà* (1579) (fig.2.12) and Tommaso della Porta's *Deposition from the Cross* (1586–96).[75]

Nevertheless, thanks to the discovery of the *Laocoön*, Bandinelli himself understood that the classical equation 'one sculpture-one marble block' could be dismissed.[76] Thus, having executed his replica of the statue now in the Uffizi (fig.2.13), he boasted of having achieved as much as the classical sculptors with only three marble blocks.[77] To be sure, opinions on 'patching' sculptures continued to differ. For example, Francesco da Sangallo felt that by patching ('*rapiccare*' or '*rappiccare*') additional pieces to their marble sculptures, sculptors 'vilify themselves and have deprived sculpture ["*l'arte*"] of its nature'.[78] Similarly, Benedetto Varchi criticised Bandinelli in his *Due Lezzioni, Disputa seconda* saying: 'we also see that colossal statues are made of [multiple] pieces, either because of a lack of material, as it has happened a thousand times, or a lack of artistic ability, as one witnessed in the *Hercules* [sculpted by Bandinelli] in Piazza [della Signoria], when a piece [detached and] fell off with great harm upon [him] who was beneath it'[79] (fig.2.14). On the other hand, Bronzino remarked, 'even if a statue were made of infinite pieces, so long as they are well joined, they would not harm the excellence ["*bontà*"] of art'.[80] But the way was paved for marble sculptures to be conceived with a 'centrifugal' rather than a 'centripetal' design, thereby unleashing a freedom 'expressive of a deep spiritual change'.[81] As Detlef Heikamp has sagaciously observed: 'Even patching is in and of itself an extraordinary step that announces the art of sculpture of the following century, the great revolution that finds its crowning [feature] in Bernini. To patch marble means to enjoy a much greater freedom of action in the creation of the shapes and the contours of a statue or a group.'[82]

An early, if aborted, attempt to achieve such freedom is signaled by the statue of *Neptune* that Bartolomeo Ammannati wished to execute for the fountain in Piazza della Signoria (fig.2.15). As discernible from Pier Paolo Galeotti's commemorative medal of 1567 (fig.2.16), Ammannati's intention had been to pose the mythical god with raised arms, a fact that is confirmed by Raffaello Borghini in his *Il Riposo*.[83] However, the project must have been abandoned by 1559, when a different model of the statue was brought by Vasari to Rome to obtain Michelangelo's 'seal of approval'. The great sculptor would no doubt have refused his approbation of Ammannati's original intentions since a figure with raised arms ('braccia alzate') would have necessitated the employment of additional pieces of marble – a concept foreign to Michelangelo, if one excepts his

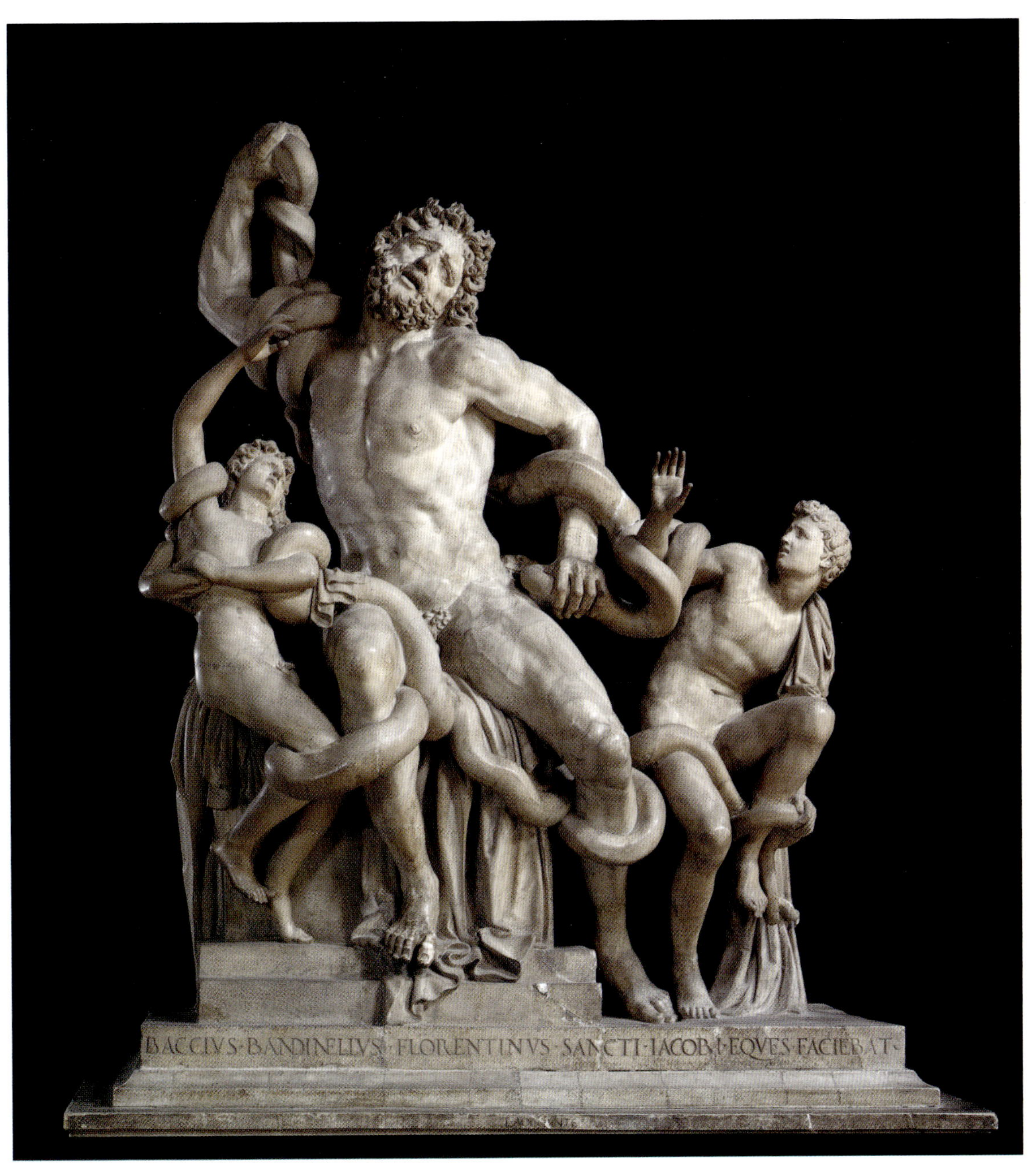

2.13 Baccio Bandinelli, *Laocoön*, 1520–25, marble, height 213 cm (83 7/8 in), Uffizi Gallery, Florence

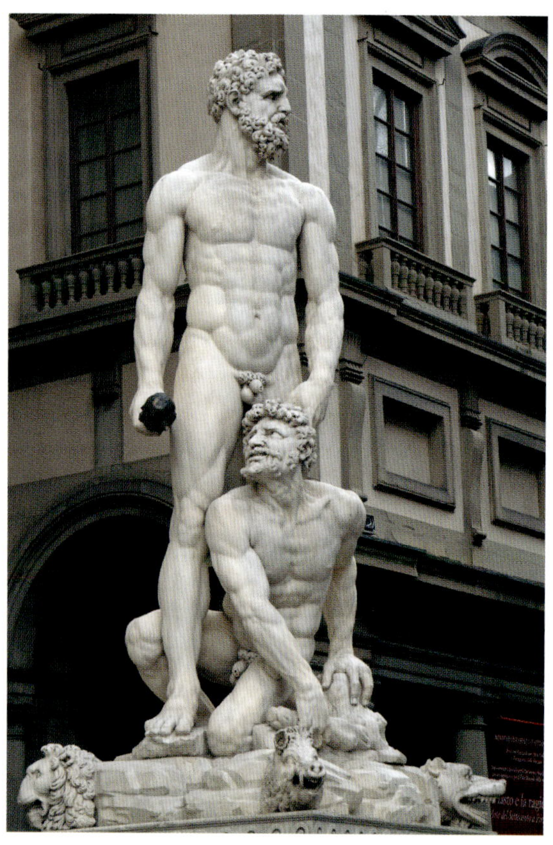

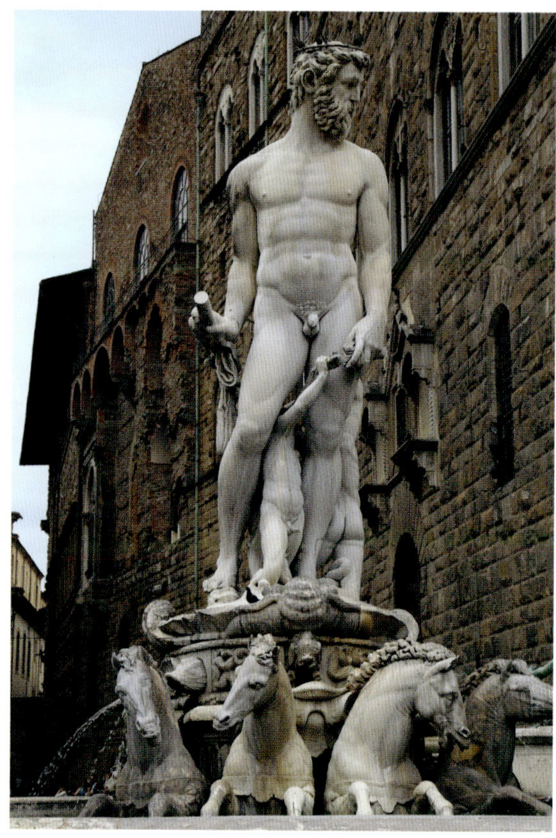

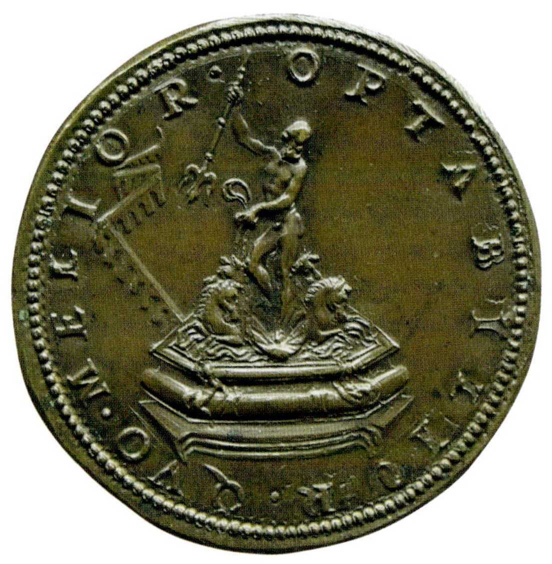

2.14 Baccio Bandinelli, *Hercules and Cacus*, 1524–34, marble, height 505 cm (198 13/16 in), Piazza della Signoria, Florence

2.15 Bartolomeo Ammannati, *Neptune*, 1560–74, marble, Piazza della Signoria, Florence

2.16 Pier Paolo Galeotti, *Medal of Cosimo I*, 1567, obverse with Neptune Fountain and Boboli aqueduct, bronze, Museo Nazionale del Bargello, Florence

2.17 Gian Lorenzo Bernini, *Saint Longinus*, 1635–8, marble, height 450 cm (177 3/16 in), Saint Peter's Basilica, Rome

2.18 Francesco Mochi, *Saint Veronica*, 1635–8, marble, height 500 cm (196 7/8 in), Saint Peter's Basilica, Rome

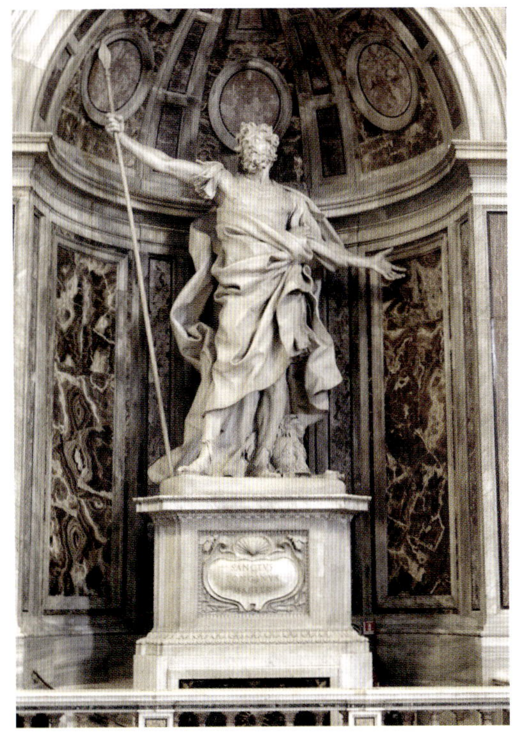

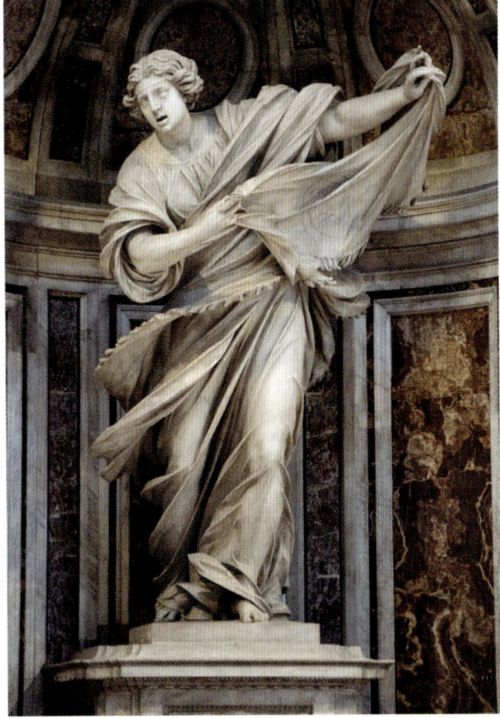

statue of the *Risen Christ*.[84] Ironically, the statue that was ultimately executed, made up of nine different pieces of marble,[85] was not well received and this failure stained Ammannati's reputation for posterity.[86] Nevertheless, seventeenth-century sculptors and their contemporaries were now willing to accept the idea that sculptures, especially those on a large scale, could be executed with more than one marble block. Thus, even though initially the documentation relating to the four colossal statues in the crossing of Saint Peter's Basilica informs us of the desire to have the sculptures executed out of a single marble block,[87] Bernini and his collaborators on this project could *conceive* at the intellectual level of sculpting the over fourteen-foot statues of *Saints Longinus* (fig.2.17), *Veronica* (fig.2.18), *Andrew* (fig.2.19), and *Helen* (fig.2.20), using multiple blocks.[88] That is, leaving aside the technical and economic aspects of a sculpture as large as the *Saint Longinus* – it was less expensive to quarry in Carrara and deliver to Rome multiple smaller blocks of marble rather than a giant one – Bernini had arrived at a conceptual, theoretical dismissal of Renaissance sculptural ideals, including that of clothing figures in such a way that the proper anatomy of the body beneath the drapery be legible from without.[89] Indeed, his 'freedom from thinking in stone'[90] was not limited to colossal statues alone. From his earliest sculptures such as the *Pluto and Proserpina* (1621–2) and the *David* (1623–4), to the late *Angel with the Crown of Thorns* (1668–69) and *Angel with the Superscription* (1668–9), as well as the equestrian statue of *Constantine the Great* (1654–70), Bernini

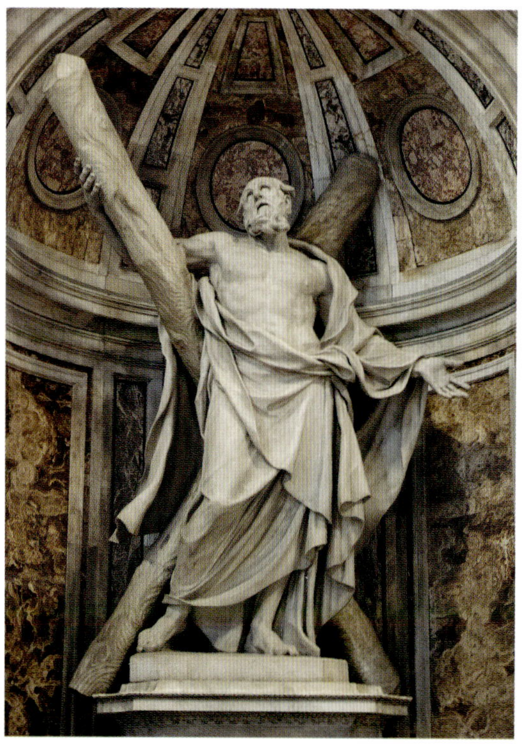

2.19 François Duquesnoy, *Saint Andrew*, 1635–8, marble, height 450 cm (177 3/16 in), Saint Peter's Basilica, Rome

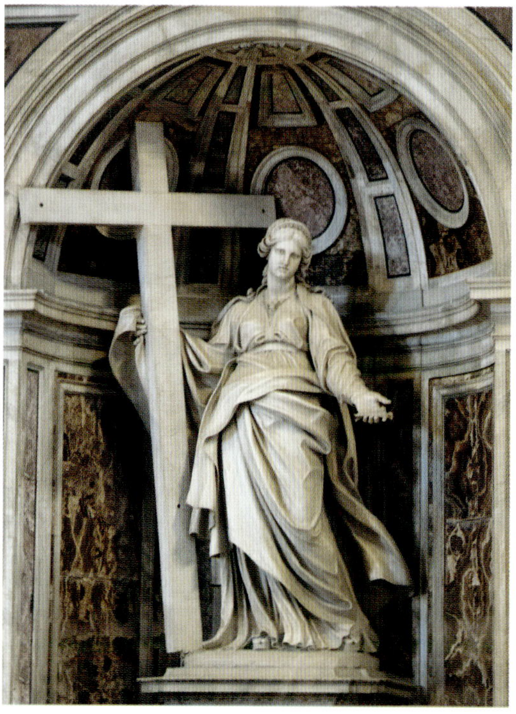

2.20 Andrea Bolgi, *Saint Helen*, 1635–8, marble, height 450 cm (177 3/16), Saint Peter's Basilica, Rome

had no reservations '*alla* Michelangelo' when it came to adding extra marble or plaster 'patches' to his original marble blocks in order to achieve his aesthetic ends.[91] Such practice allowed him to give greater vent to his flights of fancy by combining, as it were, both the traditional marble sculptors' 'subtractive' method (removing the excess marble) and the clay or wax modelers' 'additive' process (adding pieces to the core of a model or sculpture).

Certainly, the use of multiple blocks of marble in colossal statuary could pose other problems, as revealed by a letter dated 6 September 1704, from Filippo Patrizi in Rome to Archbishop Lorenzo Corsini in Florence, in which Patrizi reports that the sculptors involved in the execution of the fourteen-foot (425 cm) statues of the twelve apostles for the nave of the Basilica of Saint John Lateran insisted that they each be supplied with a single marble block (fig.2.21). The demand was made because, as noticeable in the above-mentioned giant statues in the crossing of Saint Peter's executed about seventy years earlier, the blocks had shown signs of shifting.[92] Although no corroborating document on the moving blocks has yet been found in the archives of the Fabbrica di San Pietro, it was by doing away with the classical 'straightjacket' of the *ex uno lapide* dogma and, paradoxically, with the sculptors turning into 'cobblers' that, at least in part, Baroque artists ushered in a new era in Italian sculpture.[93]

* * *

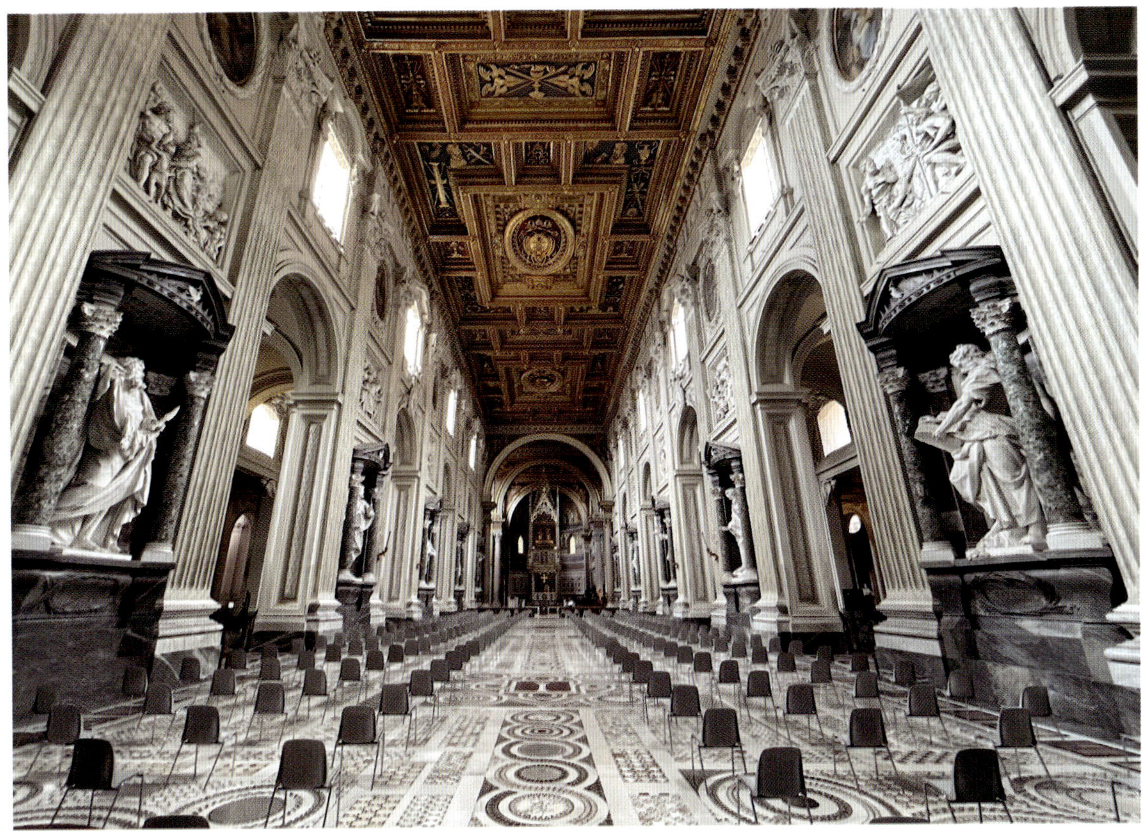

2.21 Saint John Lateran, nave

The importance that the decoration of the crossing of Saint Peter's Basilica has had in the evolution of a new artistic vision representative of seventeenth-century art and sensibility has been commented on most notably by Irving Lavin.[94] Despite the changes that occurred between the initial planning stages and the final decision to place the four giant statues of *Saints Longinus*, *Veronica*, *Andrew*, and *Helen* in the niches they currently occupy – *Saint Veronica* is the only statue that occupies the niche for which it was originally conceived[95] – when standing in front of them, the observant visitor will inevitably feel psychologically involved in a sort of passion play. As the two saintly, female *witnesses* confront the faithful with their respective reminders of Christ's sacrifice – *Veronica* with the sudarium and *Helen* with the cross (figs 2.18 and 2.20) – and the two male saints look upward holding the symbols of their spiritual transformation and martyrdom – *Longinus* with the lance and *Andrew* with the saltire (figs 2.17 and 2.19) – transfixed, as they are, in a celestial vision of their resurrected Lord and his promise of redemption, 'the observer is associated with them and hence, inevitably, becomes a participant'.[96] And, if it is true that the birth of the Baroque began in Casa Borghese (Cardinal Scipione Borghese's villa on the Pincian Hill),[97] then Bernini's orchestration of the refurbishing of the crossing of Saint Peter's represents its affirmation. Under the patronage of Pope Urban VIII, Bernini's ideation of the *Baldacchino* over the tomb of Peter, the decoration of the niches, and the four giant statues in the piers that uphold the dome of Saint Peter's, as well as the balconies over them that house the relics, remains perhaps the most significant project of seventeenth-century Rome. Within the context of this undertaking, Bernini's statue of *Saint Longinus* represents the most tangible expression of the new sculptural phase. In Estelle Lingo's apt definition, this was the place 'where Bernini became Bernini'.[98]

The first statue of the female saints, Andrea Bolgi's *Saint Helen* (1635–8) (fig.2.20), resulted in a weak attempt on the part of the young sculptor to capture what in the eighteenth century became a call to arms by the supporters of a Neoclassical style: 'noble simplicity and quiet grandeur'. While the saint's visage is clearly reminiscent of ancient sculpture, the rendition of the deeply carved garments, more in keeping with modern statuary, strays away from classical standards, thus creating a visual oxymoron.[99] The statue ultimately represents a good example of a stylistic compromise that fails to appeal to proponents of either the contemporary or the classical styles. The comments in the next century by one of the exponents of Neoclassicism, such as Leopoldo Cicognara, are revelatory. In his history of Italian sculpture, Cicognara not only denigrates Bolgi, stating that in the *Saint Helen* the sculptor failed to rise above mediocrity, but further vents his barbs at Bernini by suggesting that it was he who, in order to shine above the other artists, had a role in the choice of Bolgi for this important project.[100] Paraphrasing another nineteenth-century art critic's comment on Duquesnoy's *Saint Susanna*, one might say that Bolgi's *Saint Helen* has more the appearance than the substance of a classical statue.[101] Thus, while meeting with initial approval, the statue subsequently registered with the viewers, as it does today, as the least interesting of the four.

As mentioned, though documentation shows that the initial intention had been that of sculpting the four statues at the crossing of Saint Peter's out of one marble block, it was eventually decided to use multiple pieces seamlessly joined together.[102] Whereas three of the statues are basically made of two marble blocks with smaller pieces added to integrate them – Bernini's *Saint Longinus* consists of four blocks, while Duquesnoy's *Saint Andrew* possibly of six – Francesco Mochi's *Saint Veronica* is made of only three pieces.[103] The sculptor was very proud of this accomplishment and in a letter stressed how the three blocks were 'put together in a most difficult way in which the joins are never seen again', thus showing he was still clinging to the *ex uno lapide* ideal.[104] When Urban VIII went to Saint Peter's to inspect the completed statue on 4 November 1640, he was very pleased with the end result, as recorded in a memo written in the third person by the sculptor himself.[105] Most of all, the pope was apparently pleased with the way Mochi had succeeded in displaying the physical presence of the saint's body without contravening the religious decorum prescribed by the cardinals at the Council of Trent (1545–63). According to Mochi, the pope felt 'The movement of the drapery so beautiful, so skilfully expressing the thighs and the legs, so well draped and artful, that in truth this was the best view of all, saying that he liked all the views, but this one particularly; [and adding] that of this statue one could say, that here was a whole new way of making sculpture.'[106] In fact, with the *Saint Veronica*, the sculptor had reconciled two worlds, the Florentine Renaissance and the Catholic Counter-Reformation. Nevertheless, while in a league of his own, one could hardly claim that this artist had devised a new way of sculpting.[107] Indeed, it is quite likely that the words put in Urban VIII's mouth reflect much more Mochi's personal opinion rather than the pope's.

Mochi's *Saint Veronica* is *compositionally* the most dynamic of the four statues in the crossing of Saint Peter's. Caught in the act of rushing out of her niche towards the approaching viewer, with sharp-edged garments billowing out like bark mushrooms on a tree trunk, *Saint Veronica* seems to encapsulate the very notion of the avant-garde style now labeled Baroque. In fact, the brilliant son of a cobbler, Johann Joachim Winckelmann, mistook it as the work of Bernini.[108] However, despite its forward-leaning posture and seemingly unstable bearing, *structurally* the statue is quite static thanks to Mochi's understanding of the distribution of weight of the marble blocks.[109] Still, the exigency of such an approach limited the possibilities of how limbs or various accoutrements could be liberated into the viewer's space, since the likelihood of breakage increases commensurately to the distance each of these limbs obtains from the statue's center of gravity. To circumvent such difficulties, sculptors working in marble buttressed protruding, more vulnerable features of their statues by subtly linking them to the statue's core. This situation is exemplified by Mochi's solution for the way *Saint Veronica* holds the sudarium.

As observable from a bronze statuette cast from a model for Mochi's initial design, *Saint Veronica* was meant to display the image of Christ's face imprinted on a limb of her own garment – a conception not supported by either the visual or literary traditions and consequently dismissed (fig.2.22).[110] In Mochi's original intentions, *Saint Veronica* holds the image with her outstretched left arm slightly raised above her head. To give greater support to this arm on what would be the eventual full-size marble sculpture, the sculptor designed the model with a large swath of her garment starting below her arm and extending above it in a swirl. The final design for the statue, however, was to resort to a more traditional depiction of the sudarium as a separate cloth held between *Saint Veronica*'s hands (fig.2.18).[111] Thus, with the left arm now placed more horizontally and the marble limb subject to greater tensile stress, Mochi found it expedient to copiously increase the thickness of the mantle that is wrapped around *Saint Veronica*'s left shoulder. He also designed the sudarium in a concave, swelling curve that connects the hands to her torso,

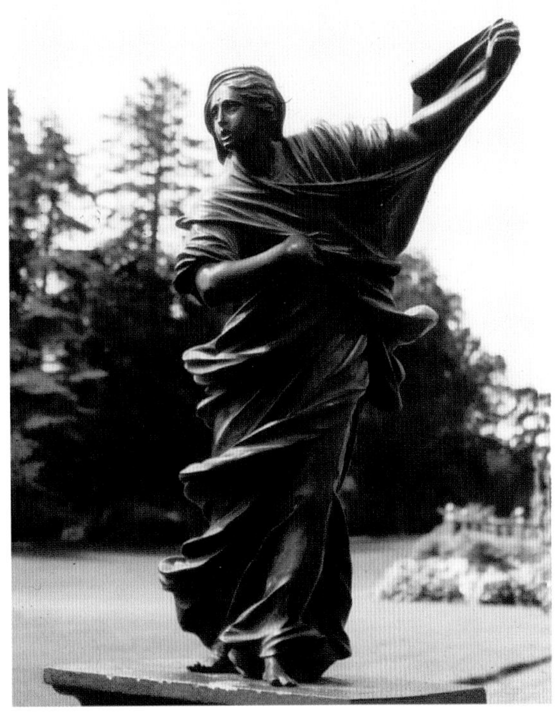

2.22 Statuette cast from Francesco Mochi's model of *Saint Veronica*, *c.*1633, bronze, height 47.8 cm (18 13/16 in), private collection, England

not only to comply with the forward movement implied by her stance but also to act as a 'figural strut', or carved detail, that anchors her arms and hands to the marble block from which they are fashioned (fig.2.23).[112] By so doing, *Saint Veronica*'s limbs were only minimally unshackled from the core of the statue. Even so, having learned in 1642 that there were plans to dust off the four statues on a weekly basis, Mochi wrote to the cardinals of the Fabbrica di San Pietro – the ecclesiastical governing body that oversaw the works executed in Saint Peter's Basilica – asking that his statue be spared such care. Fearing that the cleaners might accidentally cause damage to his statue, Mochi expressed his concern about the breakage of the 'arm, hand, veil, or another part'.[113]

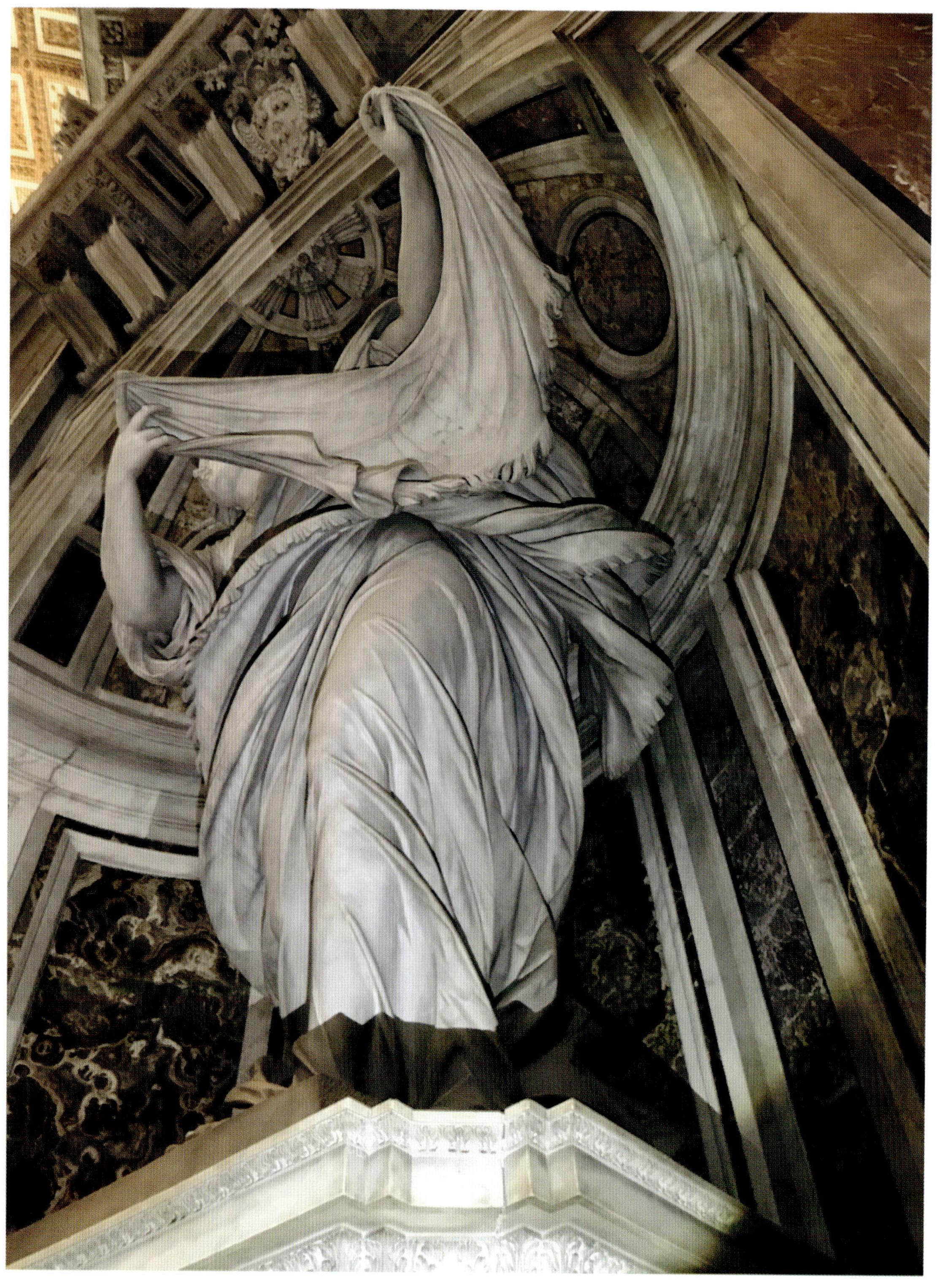

2.23 Francesco Mochi, *Saint Veronica*, detail of fig.2.18, marble, height 500 cm (196 ⅞ in), Saint Peter's Basilica, Rome

Unveiled on 2 March 1640, Duquesnoy's *Saint Andrew* is shown embracing with his right arm the instrument of his martyrdom: a saltire (fig.2.19). In this sculpture the artist's penchant and affinity for classical art is especially evident in the saint's attire, as the folds of his mantle fall in a more rational fashion in compliance with the expected gravitational pull exerted on cloth and its ability to reveal the human form beneath it.[114] Unlike Mochi, however, Duquesnoy was willing to rely on more than the two or three core marble blocks out of which the statues in the crossing of Saint Peter's were carved so as to obtain the desired results, and further availed himself of copper for the execution of parts of the cross that he then covered with stucco to simulate marble.[115] Duquesnoy also adopted the chiastic stance so prevalent in ancient statuary and shows his saint with open arms in a gesture that signals his acceptance of the divine call.[116] What this statue shares with Mochi's, however, is the way the Flemish sculptor anchors the spreading arms to the nucleus of the statue by way of carved or compositional supports. In Duquesnoy's case, *Saint Andrew*'s left arm is sustained by the ample spread of the mantle that reaches out to his wrist (fig.2.24), while his right arm is supported in such an ingenious way that it may be considered a feat worthy of an illusionist (fig.2.25). For the embracing arm, seemingly supporting the cross, is actually supported at the biceps by the upper main block of the statue through the use of a rod – the join is barely visible when standing in front of the statue (fig.2.26) – and, at the level of the hand, by fitting the marble limb into the upper segment of the copper cross, as if it were the piece of a jigsaw puzzle (fig.2.27).[117] This section of the saltire, in turn – the four arms of the cross are independent of each other – is held in place by the insertion of the same crossbeam into the funnel-like casing formed by the marble folds of his mantle that envelop the cross (fig.2.25). The solution to the propping of this extended right arm, which thus forms a sturdy scalene triangle linking shoulder–hand–hip, is further assured, most likely, by the metal bar for which Ascentio Latini and Paolo Rafuti '*compagni ferrari*' (metalwork associates) were paid in 1639 'to support the trunk of the Cross of Saint Andrew'.[118] Plausibly, the said bar was somehow affixed inside or, more likely, on the back of the six visible, conjoined, cylindrical segments that form this beam of the cross so as to provide further reinforcement for the saltire and the saint's protruding arm.

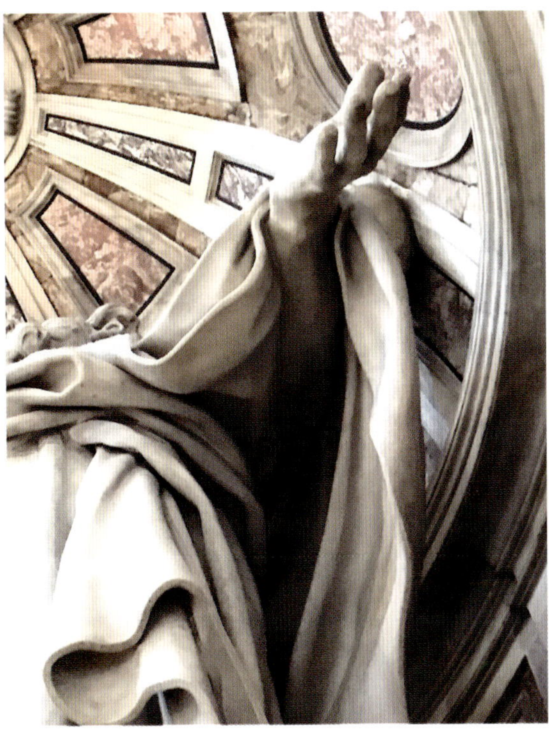

2.24 François Duquesnoy, *Saint Andrew*, detail of fig.2.19, marble, height 450 cm (177 3/16 in), Saint Peter's Basilica, Rome

As underscored by many observers, Bernini's *Saint Longinus* (fig.2.17) departs from Renaissance carving technique not only because he was willing to create his sculpture from multiple marble blocks, but also, and most strikingly, for the way he transmitted

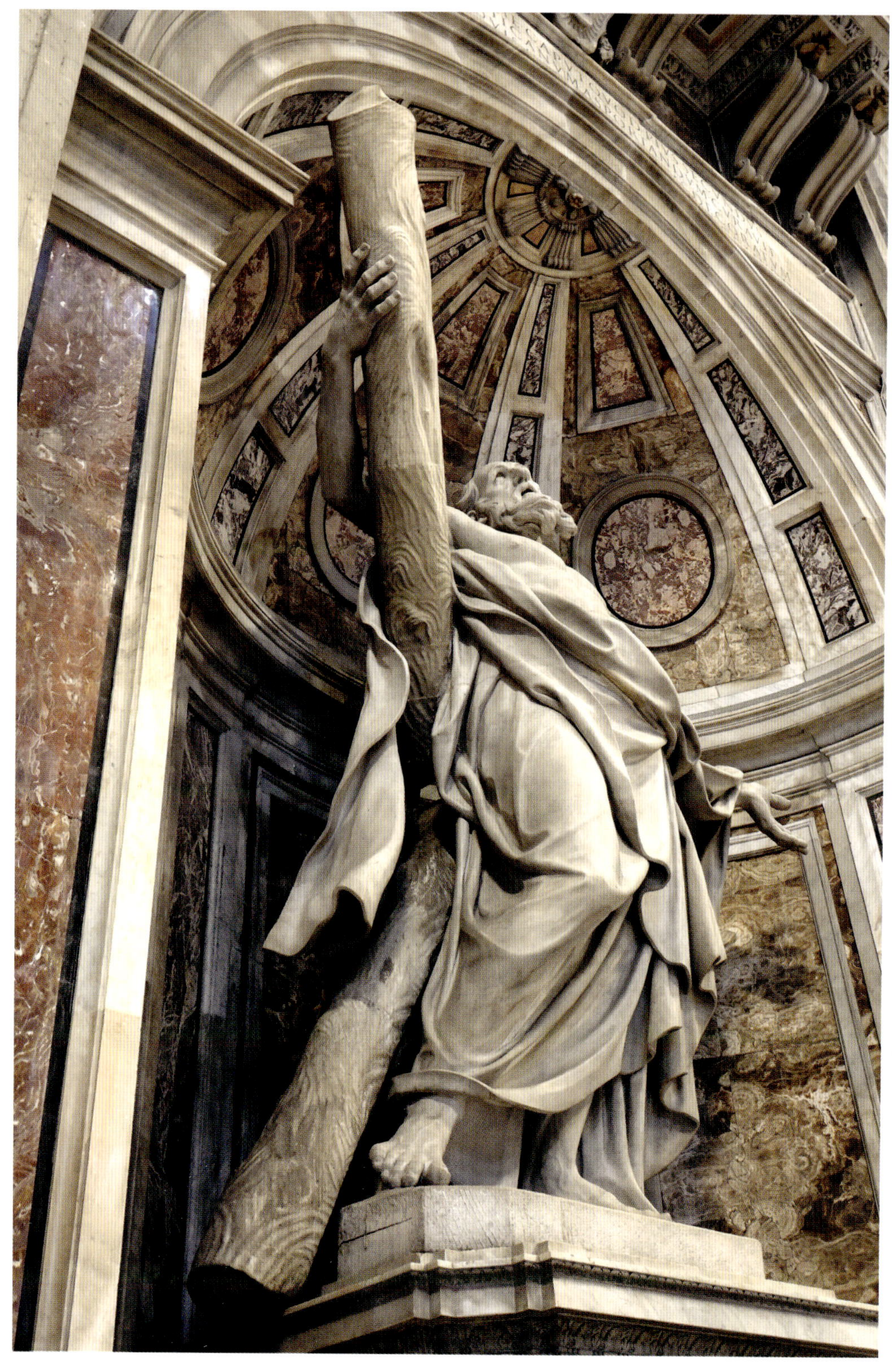

2.25 François Duquesnoy, *Saint Andrew*, detail of fig.2.19, marble, height 450 cm (177 3⁄16 in), Saint Peter's Basilica, Rome

2.26 François Duquesnoy, *Saint Andrew*, detail of fig.2.19, marble, height 450 cm (177 3/16 in), Saint Peter's Basilica, Rome

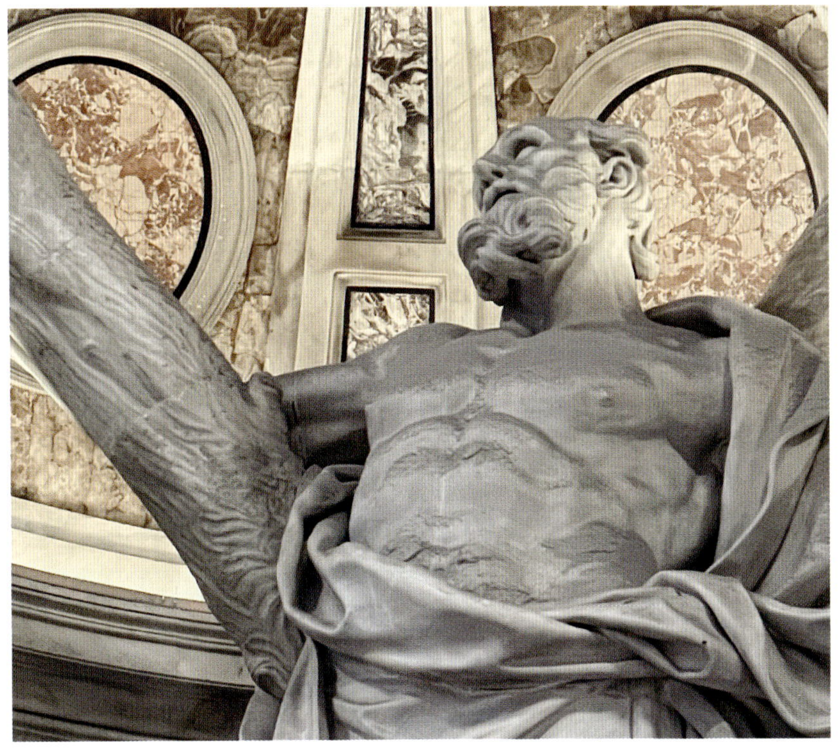

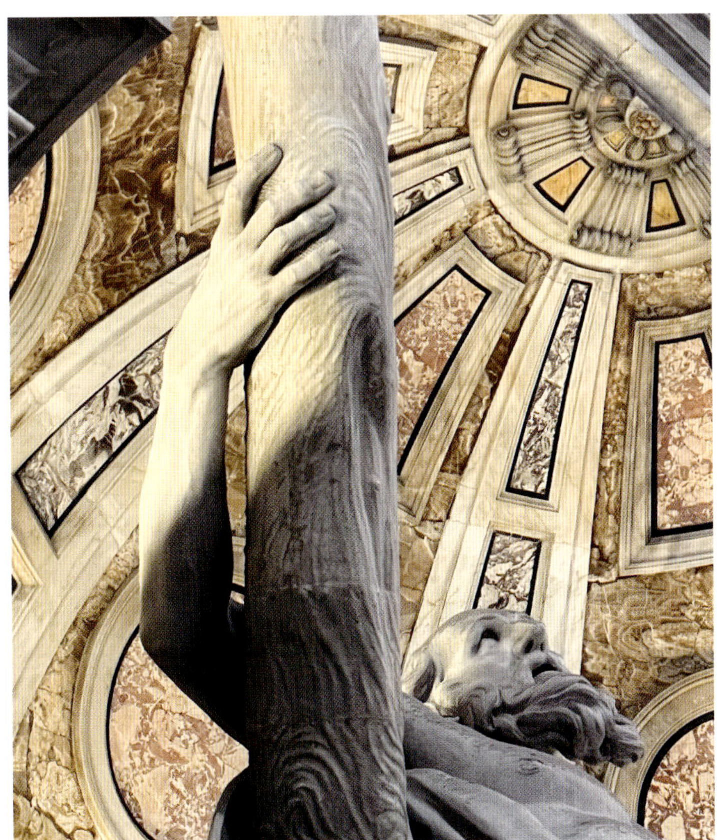

2.27 François Duquesnoy, *Saint Andrew*, detail of fig.2.19, marble, height 450 cm (177 3/16 in), Saint Peter's Basilica, Rome

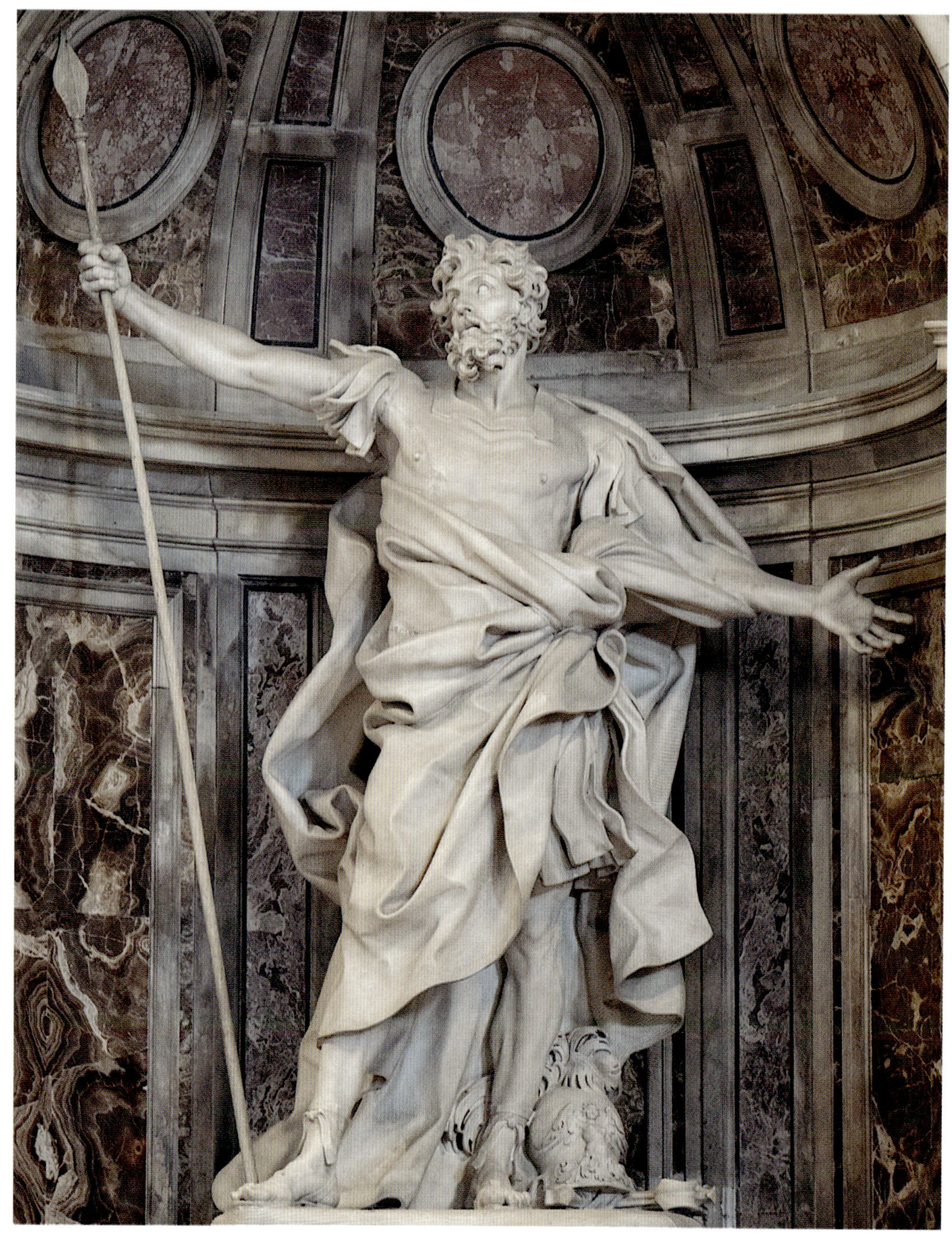

2.28 Gian Lorenzo Bernini, *Saint Longinus*, 1635–8, marble, height 450 cm (177 3/16 in), Saint Peter's Basilica, Rome

to the viewer the saint's intense, intimate, spiritual transformation through the stirring treatment of his attire. In this sculpture, the long-standing reverence for the rational correspondence between outer garments and the bodies they covered was surrendered in favor of the psychological impact that the irrational manipulation of the 'cloth' would have on the viewer.[119] But what is equally, if not more, significant in this statue is the way the saint's arms are freed into space. While *Saint Longinus*' left arm is already given greater visibility than Duquesnoy's corresponding limb in the *Saint Andrew* – as it protrudes farther out from the supporting mantle – his right arm projects out of the statue's core on a 'heroic diagonal' unpropped by any figural attributes (fig.2.28).[120] That is, while in the other three statues the sculptors employed figural features of the statue to sustain the extended arms – Bolgi also buttressed *Saint Helen*'s right hand and the free-standing cross she (seemingly) holds by the swath of marble representing her heavy mantle (fig.2.29) – in Bernini's *Saint Longinus* the right arm is self-supporting and, in fact, it is this very limb that holds in place the symbol of his conversion, instead of being sustained by it.[121] To achieve such liberty of expression, of course, Bernini had to have been willing to carve the arm separately from the statue itself and join it to the torso through the use of an iron rod, as if it had been a missing arm to be applied to the restoration of an unearthed fragment of an ancient sculpture.[122] Of course, Duquesnoy, too, had carved *Saint Andrew*'s right arm separately, but he additionally propped that limb with the support of the cross he supposedly

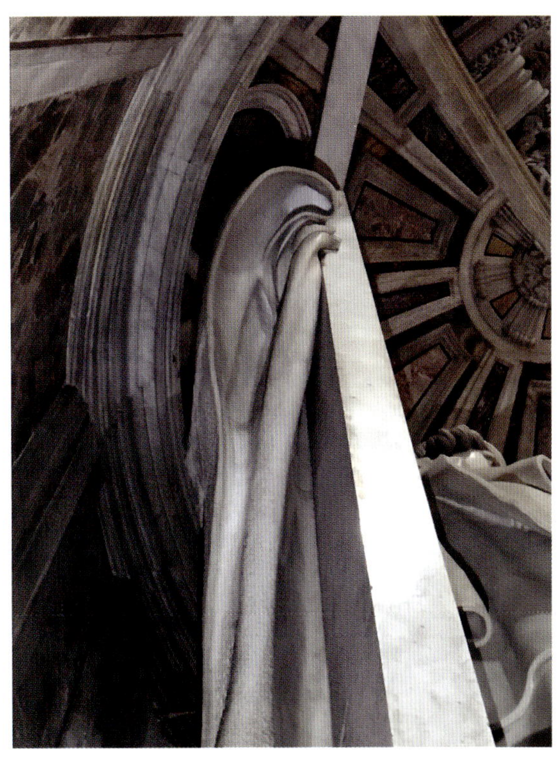

2.29 Andrea Bolgi, *Saint Helen,* detail of fig.2.20, marble, height 450 cm (177 3/16 in), Saint Peter's Basilica, Rome

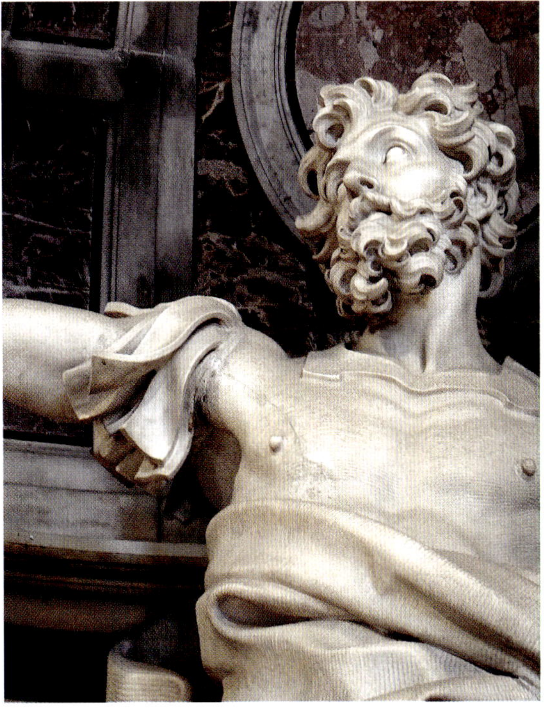

2.30 Gian Lorenzo Bernini, *Saint Longinus*, marble crack, detail of fig.2.17, marble, height 450 cm (177 3/16 in), Saint Peter's Basilica, Rome

holds. Bernini's solution, instead, was so bold and risky that at some point the weight of the arm caused a crack in the marble that stretches from the saint's right shoulder, around his nipple, and down to his chest (fig.2.30). Indeed, the stability of the limb was so compromised that, to safeguard its permanence, it subsequently necessitated the addition of a metal bar affixed to the back of the arm that extends from just above his elbow to the shoulder (fig.2.31). It was, thus, by joining this separately carved arm onto his statue like a cobbler – 'patching it', as Benvenuto Cellini would have criticised – that Bernini achieved the illusion of a material weightlessness typically available to sculptors working in bronze but negated to marble carvers. Ultimately, in this work Bernini turned away from Michelangelo's devotion to the *ex uno lapide* canon and reverted, probably unknowingly, to a stance similar to Ammannati's initial design for his *Neptune* sculpture for the fountain in Piazza della Signoria (fig.2.15). Therefore, through the illusion of the 'bearable lightness of being'[123] of *Saint Longinus*' right arm, one could truly say that the mature, forty-year-old sculptor brought to fulfillment the burgeoning talent he had precociously demonstrated in his youthful sculptures executed for Casa Borghese and provided the most mature embodiment, to date, of the emancipation that Baroque marble sculpture could obtain from its material limitations.

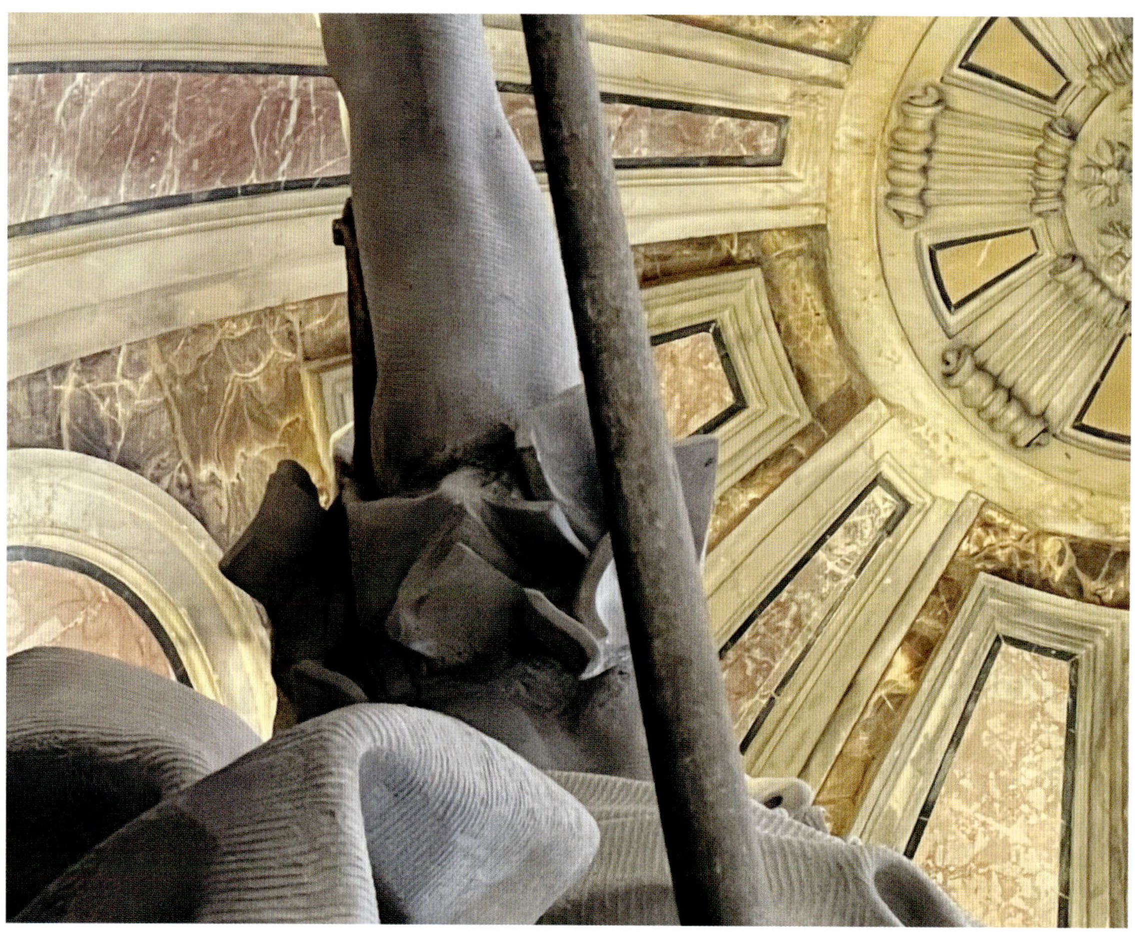

2.31 Gian Lorenzo Bernini, *Saint Longinus*, metal bar supporting right arm, detail of fig.2.17, marble, height 450 cm (177 3⁄16 in), Saint Peter's Basilica, Rome

3

Tall Tales

Filippo Baldinucci's biography of Gian Lorenzo Bernini relates an amusing anecdote about the artist's notable discretion when criticising the work of others – a faculty, apparently, Bernini developed out of his 'moderation in self-esteem'. In Baldinucci's words:

> He was accustomed to praise the good and to remain silent about what was lacking, and if there was nothing to praise, to invent ways of speaking without committing himself. Thus one time being brought by a cardinal to see a dome that the cardinal had had painted by one of his very favorite artists who had made a very bad job of it, when asked by the prelate in the presence of many masters of arts what he thought of it, Bernini observed it closely. He then said to the cardinal who, knowing little of art, expected to hear his painter praised, 'Truly, the work speaks for itself,' and he repeated the words energetically at least three times. Since one takes things in the way one wants to take them, the cardinal took Bernini's words as high praise, while the artists, looking into each others [*sic*] faces, laughed among themselves at the work.[1]

This anecdote, like others in the biography, was obviously included because it not only sustained Baldinucci's intention of extolling Bernini's sagacity and witticism; it also enhanced the appeal of his narrative.[2] For, besides learning about the exceptional personality of the great sculptor, the readers, like the artists present at the scene, are induced to laugh at the expense of the naive cardinal and feel included among 'those who know'.

To complete the picture, however, it is important to realise that Filippo Baldinucci, as other biographers before him, was working within a literary tradition that went back to Plutarch's *Lives of the Noble Greeks and Romans*. Baldinucci, in this instance, was adapting to his purposes an anecdote that Giovanni Paolo Lomazzo had mentioned about Giorgio Vasari's frescoes in the Sala dei Cento Giorni in the Palazzo della Cancelleria. Supposedly, when Michelangelo was shown the frescoes Vasari had painted in that palace in only one hundred days, he exclaimed: 'And it shows.'[3] Lomazzo, in turn, was repeating a tale related by Vasari himself in Michelangelo's *Vita* for 'Being shown the drawing of a boy then beginning to learn to draw, who was recommended to him, some persons excusing him because it was not long since he had applied himself to art, he replied: "That is evident."'('E' si conosce').[4] Unsurprisingly, Vasari was mining Leon Battista Alberti's *De pictura*. In Alberti's version of the story, when Apelles was shown a painting by an artist who had apparently completed it in a day, the famous painter responded: 'I would not be surprised if you had done many such.'[5] Alberti, on his part, was just repeating what Plutarch had mentioned in *De liberis educandis*. In this earliest version of the anecdote Plutarch tells of a 'wretched painter' who, when showing a painting to Apelles, remarked: 'This I have only this moment painted.' Whereupon Apelles replied: 'Even should you not say so, yet I know that it was painted hastily, and I only wonder that you have not painted more of like sort.'[6] Finally, a similar repartee was reiterated in Plutarch's *Life of Pericles*, where Zeuxis, in reply to Agatharchus' 'boasting of the speed and ease with which he made his figures', retorted: 'Mine take, and last, a long time.'[7] Thus, whether the source of some anecdotes included in Bandinucci's and Domenico Bernini's biographies of Gian Lorenzo are to be found in Plutarch's *Lives*, Pliny the Elder's *Natural History*,[8] or one of their Renaissance emulators, strictly speaking, they are not to be considered fictions; rather, they were fabrications. That is, these stories need not be true but true to life, verisimilitude being the primary requirement and morally edifying.[9] It is inconsequential, in other words, whether Bernini actually responded to the artistically unknowing cardinal who showed him the dome painted by one of his protégés by saying 'Truly, the work speaks for itself.' What mattered is that Bernini could have – and, indeed, given that the quality of the fresco was rather poor, should have – replied this way.

This, of course, is only one instance in which the objective truth of comments made about or attributed to Bernini may be questioned. The present chapter will investigate other anecdotes that merit greater scrutiny.

* * *

In his biography Baldinucci informs the readers about a reaction Bernini had to an ancient anecdote involving Zeuxis, the famous Greek painter. Desiring to execute an image of absolute female beauty in the person of Helen of Troy, the painter selected five of the most beautiful Crotonian women as his models.[10] Since nature does not endow any single individual with all perfect features, Zeuxis selected the best qualities from each of the girls, thereby achieving what he considered the ultimate Beauty. This classic example of selective imitation and a transcendent Beauty that must be filtered through the artist's inner eye to achieve perfection seemed absurd to Bernini:

> He held that the story of the Venus [*sic*] that Zeuxis made was a fable: that is to say, the story that Zeuxis had made her from the most beautiful parts of many different girls, taking one part from one and another part from another; [because] he said that the beautiful eyes of one woman do not go well with the beautiful face of another woman, and so it was with a beautiful mouth, and so on.[11]

Thus, we are told that Bernini found the Zeuxis anecdote a tall tale that amounted to nonsense for the discerning reader – a concept, like others attributed to the artist, that perhaps originated with his good friend Cardinal Sforza Pallavicino.[12] Ironically, both the artist and his biographers were not exempt from creating their own mythopoeic fables when it came to Gian Lorenzo himself. One of these anecdotes pertains to the two marble busts of Cardinal Scipione Borghese (1577–1633) on display to this day in the Borghese Gallery (figs 3.1 and 3.2).

In Baldinucci's biography published in 1682, just two years after Bernini's death, the author states the following:

> His Holiness, Pope Paul V, also wished to have his portrait made by Bernini. Afterwards, the artist carved the portrait of Cardinal Scipione Borghese, the Pope's nephew. This handsome work was almost completed when a mishap occurred. A crack [*un pelo*, 'a hair', i.e., a hairline crack] appeared in the marble across the whole of the forehead. Bernini, who was very bold and who already had a marvelous knowledge of the working of marble, in order to free himself, and even more the Cardinal, from the embarrassment resulting from bringing such news to him, *had a sufficiently large piece of marble of known quality secretly brought to him. Without telling a soul, he worked for fifteen nights (which was all the time he had for that tedious task) on another*

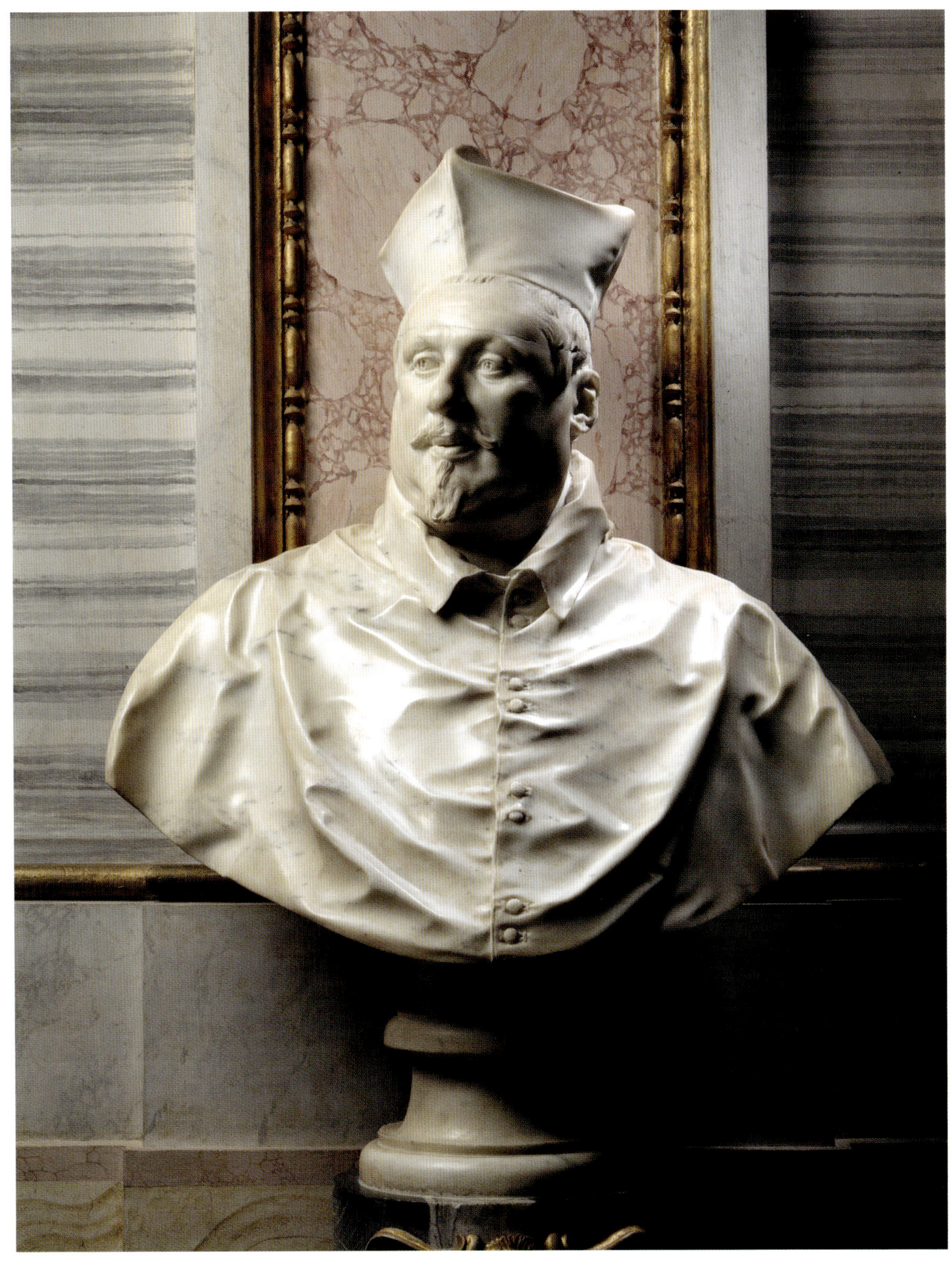

3.1 Gian Lorenzo Bernini, *Scipione Borghese*, first version, 1632, marble, 78 cm (30 11⁄16 in), Galleria Borghese, Rome

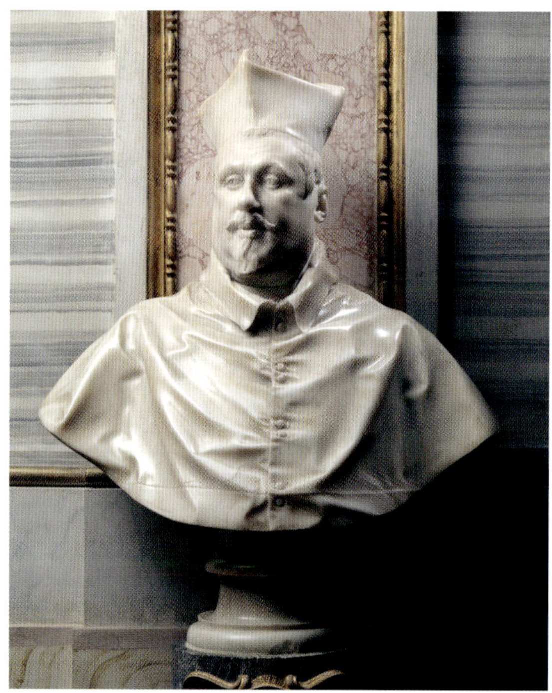

3.2 Gian Lorenzo Bernini, *Scipione Borghese*, second version, 1632, marble, 78 cm (30 11⁄16 in), Galleria Borghese, Rome

bust exactly like the first and not one jot less in beauty. He then had the first bust transported to his studio, well wrapped, so that no one in his household would be able to see it. Then he waited for the Cardinal to come to see the completed work. That gentleman finally arrived and saw the first portrait, whose defect in the polished state appeared even more prominent and disfiguring. At first glance the Cardinal became agitated, but he masked it in order not to distress Bernini. The astute artist, meanwhile, pretended to be unaware of the Cardinal's disappointment, and since relief is more satisfying when the suffering has been most severe, he engaged the Cardinal in conversation before finally uncovering the other beautiful portrait. The gaiety that the prelate displayed upon seeing the second portrait without defect made very evident how much pain he had felt when he beheld the first one. The diligent care that Bernini employed to avoid offending him pleased the Cardinal so much that from that day onward he loved him tenderly. Today both portraits are to be found in the Palace of Villa Borghese. They are such fine and splendid works that Bernini himself, when coming upon them with Cardinal Antonio Barberini forty years later, exclaimed, 'How little progress I have made in the art of sculpture through these long years becomes clear to me when I see that as a boy I handled marble in this manner.'[13] (italics mine) (fig.3.3)

Before addressing the anecdote itself, a few comments are in order; for in the only English translation of Baldinucci's text here quoted, Catherine Enggass does not fully capture the biographer's words and intentions in three instances and it is fruitful, for a better understanding of the anecdote itself, to ponder them at greater length. In the first, by writing '[he] *had a sufficiently large piece of marble of known quality secretly brought to him*' she fails to specify where the block was brought. It was not just vaguely 'brought to him'; rather, it was brought *in camera*, that is 'to his room', the implication being his private room. Indeed, in Italian the word *camera* typically means one's bedroom and this is exactly how Baldinucci himself defines it in his *Vocabolario toscano dell'arte del disegno*: 'a room in which one sleeps'.[14] Actually, this is what Baldinucci states:

> . . . fattosi condurre *in camera* un pezzo di marmo di sufficiente grandezza, e di conosciuta bontà, senza darne notizia a persona, nel corso di quindici notti, che solamente impiegò in quel lungo lavoro, ne condusse un'altro [*sic*] simile, di non punto minor bellezza del primo; poi fattolo portar nel suo studio ben coperto, acciocchè da niuno de' suoi familiari potesse esser veduto, attendeva la venuta del Cardinale a vedere il ritratto finito.[15] (italics mine)

Only by specifying that the replica of the bust was sculpted *in his room* does the subsequent sentence

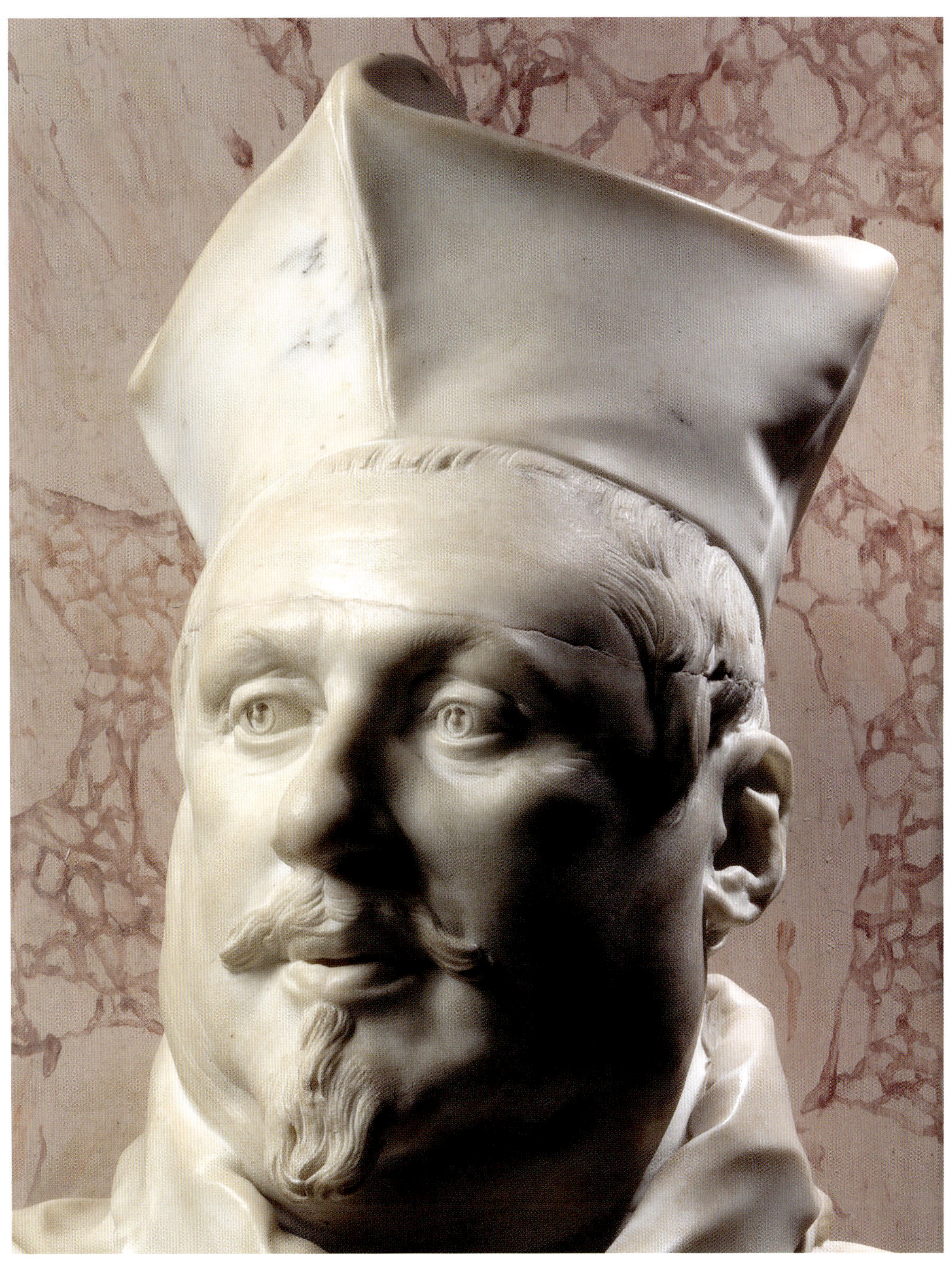

3.3 Gian Lorenzo Bernini, *Scipione Borghese*, first version, 1632, detail of fig.3.1, marble, 78 cm (30 11/16 in), Galleria Borghese, Rome

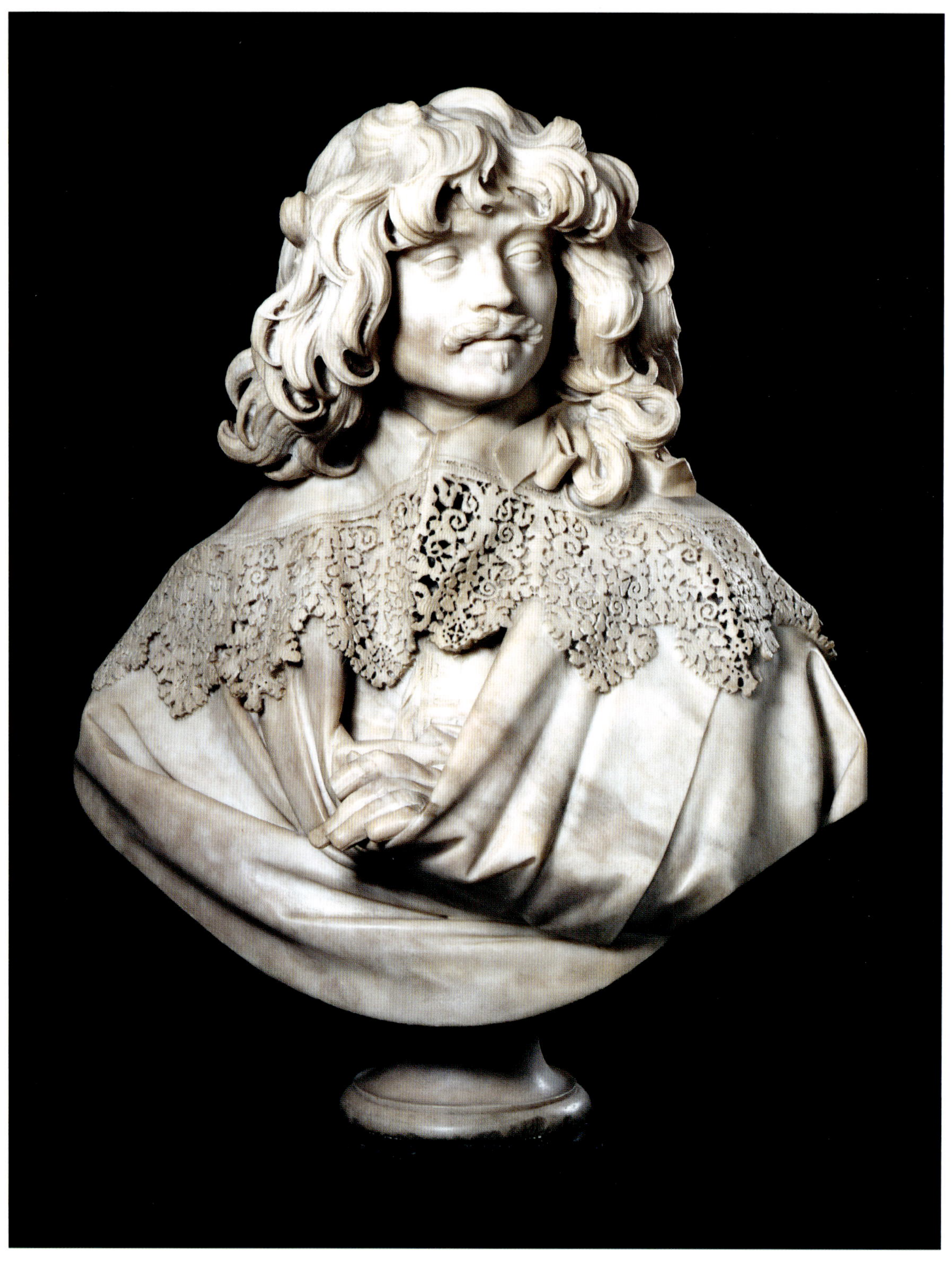

3.4 Gian Lorenzo Bernini, *Thomas Baker*, 1637–8, marble, 82.5 × 70 × 36 cm (32½ × 27⁹⁄₁₆ × 14³⁄₁₆ in), Victoria and Albert Museum, London

make sense. That is to say, in the secrecy of his room, without letting anyone know about it, the young Bernini sculpted the second version of the bust – that he was sculpting *in his room*, with all of the noise that carving entails, suggests that, if the rest of the family was unaware of what he was up to, they must have been afflicted by a severe case of impaired hearing – he then had it taken to his studio 'well wrapped, so that no one in his household would be able to see it'. Moreover, it is incorrect to write 'He then had *the first bust* transported to his studio' (italics mine). The first bust was already in his studio. Rather, it was the second version, which he supposedly executed secretly, that was taken to the studio 'ben coperto'. It was only after Bernini noticed the disappointment on his patron's face ('a prima vista si turbò') that the replica was unveiled; a staged revelation that achieved the artist's end ('L'allegrezza, che mostrò quel Prelato nel vedere il secondo ritratto senz'alcun difetto, fece ben conoscere quanto era stato il dolore, ch'egli avea concepito nel rimirare il primo'). Furthermore, were one to accept this tall tale, then the logical conclusion would be to consider the two busts as 'independent derivations from the same model', with the first version executed directly on the marble with the cardinal in front of the sculptor ('avendo sott'occhio il cardinale'), 'in a most daring and rarely attempted approach', and the second sculpted from recollection ('tutta realizzata a memoria').[16] Without denying Bernini's mnemonic powers, which must have been considerable, the idea that Bernini should tackle a portrait – and one identical to the first version, to boot – without relying on a clay model is to ignore how sculptors worked.[17] For it was clay or wax modeling – not drawing – on which bronze, relief, and marble sculptors relied prior to approaching a three-dimensional work of art, for, as Pasiteles said as far back as the first century BC, 'modeling was the mother' of all sculptural activity.[18] It was only by first having executed a full-scale clay bust that a Bernini, a Finelli, and an Algardi in the seventeenth century or a Camillo Rusconi and a Bouchardon in the eighteenth could hope to achieve such impeccable resemblance to their sitters without spoiling the marble bust.[19] Not that good sculptors are not able to sculpt a portrait or a statue without the aid of a model, but this is, indeed, how Bernini progressed with the portraits of Costanza Bonarelli, Charles I, and Scipione Borghese, as intimated in a letter of 1641 from a Roman correspondent to Cardinal Mazzarino who reports seeing the clay models in Bernini's home.[20] And *a fortiori*, given the importance of the sitter, this is the procedure he followed prior to sculpting Louis XIV's portrait, as testified in a letter written by Paul Fréart de Chantelou to Jean-Baptiste Colbert ('he has worked with great devotion these past two days at the model of his [Louix XIV's] bust'), and in another written by Mattia de' Rossi on 20 June 1665 ('. . . il mercordi principiò il modello di creta, et hora lo sta facendo').[21] In fact, Domenico Bernini himself writes that, having made two portrait drawings of Louis XIV – one in profile and another *en face* – subsequently his father 'created many others in clay and finally began the portrait in marble'.[22] This practice is further corroborated by the diary of Nicholas Stone who, during a visit of 22 October 1638, is told by Bernini that to execute Thomas Baker's portrait 'he began to imbost [emboss] his physyognymy and being finisht and ready to begin in marble, itt fell out that his patrone the Pope came to here of itt who sent Cardinall Barberine to fobid him . . . for the Pope would haue no other picture sent into England from his hand but his Mai[es]ty [Charles I]'[23] (fig.3.4). In fact, this method is exactly what Lelio Guidiccioni describes in the renowned letter he wrote to the sculptor in 1632:

> I will never forget the delight I took in being present at your work all those times, seeing you every morning, always making a thousand opposing movements with extraordinary gracefulness; chatting away, always up to date with the latest events, the hands moving far away from the conversation; crouching down, stretching yourself, placing the fingers on the model with the

> speed and variety of one playing the harp; making charcoal marks on the marble in a hundred places, striking with the mallet in a hundred others; striking, I say, in one place while looking in the opposite direction; pressing the hand onwards, and turning the head looking back; overcoming impediments and with great spirit solving them instantly; the marble splitting in two, due to a hairline crack, when the work was already underway; commence the new work with a new block and complete it with such speed without anyone being aware of it; nor would this be credible if they were not seen side by side.[24]

Thus, as Bernini sculpted the second bust – most likely in his studio and not 'in his room', as Baldinucci would have us believe – he was not relying simply on his memory; he was undoubtedly looking very carefully at the clay model that had already guided him when sculpting the first version of the portrait, which was possibly the very 'ritratto del Cardinale Burghese [*sic*] di creta cotta con suo busto e piedi indorati' described in the 1681 inventory of the objects found in Bernini's household.[25] As a matter of fact, Guidiccioni is quite explicit as to how the sculptor proceeded: first he records how Bernini molded his clay model, then – as artists typically do after taking a number of points as their reference marks on the model – with the aid of calipers or compasses he transferred his measurement by marking his marble block with charcoal 'in a hundred places'.[26] That is, it was by transferring the points indicated on the clay bust to the corresponding spot on the marble block – achieved by the intersection of the radii of a compass measuring the height and the width of the spot under consideration – that the sculptor then proceeded to gradually arrive, via a third measurement to indicate the depth, at the exact point desired by removing the excess marble. It was by repeating this operation numerous times, with all of the points referring back to the clay model, that the marble portrait eventually emerged 'miraculously' from the hard stone.[27] Bernini had unsurpassable talent in envisioning the final sculpture within the marble block but could not afford – as all artists who wished to avoid mistakes, especially in portraiture – to chisel away without making reference to his clay model. As mentioned in Chapter 2, this is exactly what Vasari warned sculptors not to do: 'dispensing with the Full-sized Model'.[28]

Finally, a third misleading interpretation of Baldinucci's Italian text by Enggass pertains to the reason given for the time Bernini spent sculpting the second bust: 'Without telling a soul, he worked for fifteen nights (*which was all the time he had for that tedious task*) on another bust exactly like the first and not one jot less in beauty' (italics mine). What Baldinucci actually said is 'senza darne notizia a persona, nel corso di quindici notti, *che solamente impiegò in quel lungo lavoro*, ne condusse un'altro [*sic*] simile, di non punto minor bellezza del primo' (italics mine). The biographer was not implying that the task was 'tedious'; rather, that it was 'laborious', and obviously wished to emphasise the brief time it took to execute the work. However, more important to Baldinucci, as we shall see, was the time of day when the carving was carried out.

The cardinal's portraits were executed in 1632, Scipione being at the time fifty-five years old and Bernini thirty-four.[29] Thus, the hagiographic claim that Bernini sculpted these busts when he was 'a boy' – in the next section of the biography one learns the artist was supposedly fifteen years old – is an obvious manipulation of the facts by the biographer, possibly suggested by members of Bernini's family. Indeed, when Domenico Bernini published his biography in 1713 – thirty-one years after Baldinucci's – on the one hand, he redoubled the claim by discussing the sculptures immediately after Gian Lorenzo's youthful encounter with Pope Paul V and, on the other, by claiming that at the time he was a 'little artist' ('*picciol'Artefice*').[30] One reason why the biographers predated the execution of the two portraits to Bernini's boyhood is quite obvious. In their attempt to equate Bernini with 'the Michelangelo of his century' they wanted to create a parallel between Bernini's claim of how later in life he felt he had made little progress in the art of sculpture since his youth ('They are such fine and splendid works that Bernini himself, when coming upon them with Cardinal Antonio Barberini forty years later, exclaimed, "How little progress I have made in the art of sculpture through these long years becomes clear to me when I see that as a boy I handled marble in this manner"'), with a similar statement Michelangelo made when later in life he worked primarily as an architect. According to Condivi, upon seeing his youthful work of the *Battle of the Lapiths and the Centaurs* executed around 1492, when he was about seventeen years old, Michelangelo realised how much he had wronged his God-given talent by not continuing to assiduously pursue the art of sculpture.[31] But in Baldinucci's story there is more than meets the eye.

All commentators of this factual sleight of hands – the antedating of the Scipione busts – have indicated reasons why Baldinucci and Domenico Bernini might have been compelled to do so;[32] just as many authors have commented on the amount of time it took the sculptor to execute the second version of the portrait: fifteen nights, according to Baldinucci; three days, in Domenico's version.[33] Certainly, as Rudolf Wittkower noted, 'it must have been a staggering performance whatever the duration'.[34] If, however, one keeps in mind that Bernini's bust of Louis XIV (fig.3.5) took three months to complete (5 July – 5 October 1665), it is understandable why no one felt his intelligence was being more insulted by such fanciful claims than one of the most consummate eighteenth-century art connoisseurs: Pierre-Jean Mariette (1694–1774).[35]

In the *Abecedario*, published from his manuscript notes in the nineteenth century, Mariette opens his commentary on Gian Lorenzo by stating that those who claimed the artist had executed the two busts in his tender youth had garnished their stories with such details that their fantasy ('le merveilleux') could not be sustained by a modicum of probability.[36] In fact, given the inflated nature of the narratives, Mariette

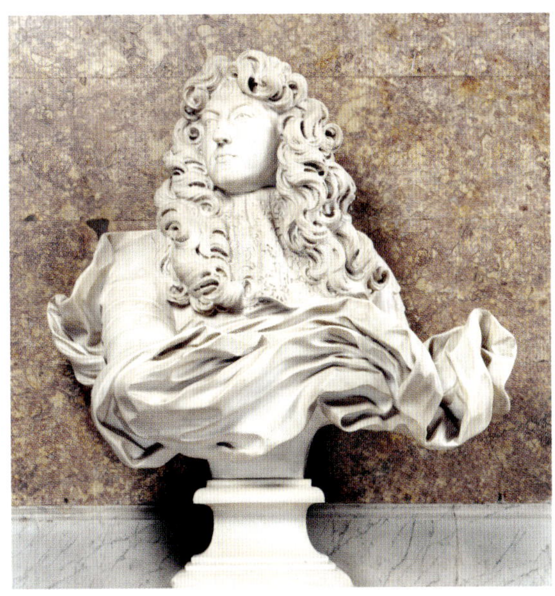

3.5 Gian Lorenzo Bernini, *Louis XIV*, 1655, marble, 105 × 99 × 46 cm (41 5⁄16 × 39 × 18 1⁄8 in), Châteaux de Versailles et de Trianon, Versailles

could not refrain from affirming that 'from that moment on, I was tempted to doubt the truthfulness of the rest of the story'[37] and went on to say, to those people who might respond to his objections by stating that all of Rome had been witness to the prodigious execution of the two portraits, that if those who lived in Bernini's time had wished to be duped, it had been their choice. However, he did not care to be counted among them.[38]

Besides objecting to the artist's reported youthfulness at the time of Scipione's portraits – again, archival documentation would prove Mariette right[39] – it was his knowledge of the sculptors' craft that prevented him from accepting the biographers' tale:

> It may also be that, *after the carving began* and the hair [the crack] in the marble forced Bernini to start another bust, a new bust was secretly prepared and that

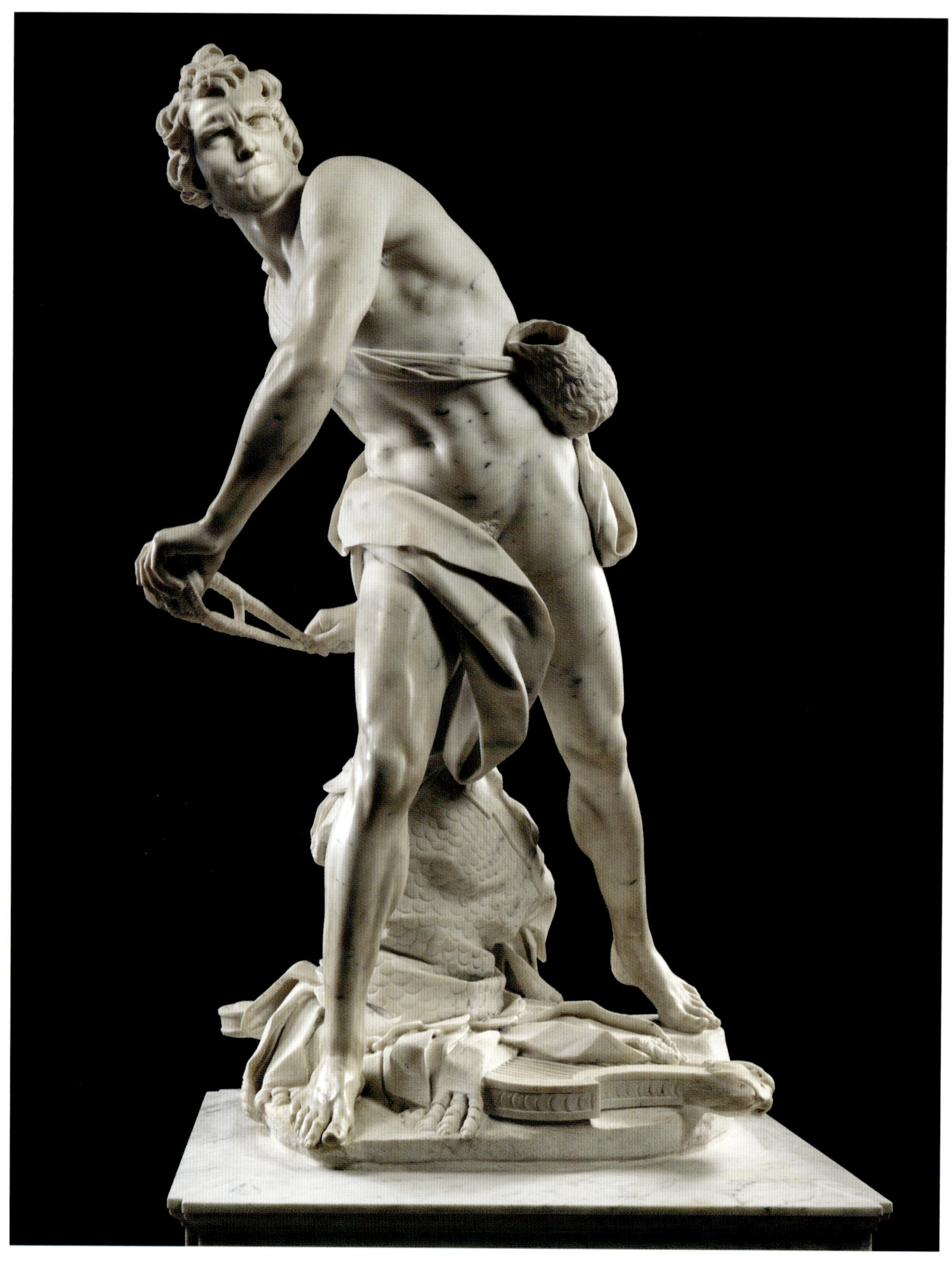

3.6 Gian Lorenzo Bernini, *David*, 1623–4, marble, height 170 cm (66 15/16 in), Galleria Borghese, Rome

it was revealed at the opportune time so as to conclude the staged event [for Scipione Borghese] in its entirety. Because, if one does not allow for such a scam, I doubt anyone who knows the mechanics of working marble could be persuaded otherwise.[40] (italics mine)

The actual timing when the crack appeared is of consequence, as will be seen. But equally objectionable to Mariette was the impression the biographers gave of Bernini working single-handedly on his sculptures, whereas people with any knowledge of the craft understood that carving is typically a collaborative effort that involves various assistants specialising in different phases of the carving process: from the creation of a *bozzetto* (sketch) in wax or clay, to the full-size *modello* to guide the sculptor in the carving of the marble, the *sbozzatura* (roughing out) of the marble block to approximate the overall shape of the sculpture, the actual carving process, the completion of the finer details of the sculpture through the use of a drill, the filing of the surface with rasps, to the final polishing of the statue with various abrasive agents such as pumice-stone.[41]

With regard to the execution of the two Scipione Borghese busts, an example of Bernini's employment of assistants in the preparatory stages of a portrait is provided by the one he made of Louis XIV. Having learned from other sources that the king would like to have one by his hand, even prior to the monarch's personal request (20 June), on 11 June he had asked that some clay be brought to him 'so that he could try out a pose while waiting to start work on the likeness'.[42] The day after, two marble blocks were selected and brought to him.[43] Two weeks later, on 6 July, while he was still working on his clay model, he had his assistants begin roughing out the marble block.[44] As late as 13 July he was still busy working on the model.[45] It is only on the following day, 14 July, that Chantelou records him working on the marble bust.[46] What happened once he began carving the marble is recorded by Domenico Bernini:

As he progressed in the work on this portrait, Bernini began to fear that the marble block that he was carving might one day reveal some unsightly veining or other defect as more stone was cut away from it. He therefore decided to prepare a second one, as he had done in the past, giving orders to his student Giulio Cartari to begin blocking out the outline in another piece of marble, which, should the first prove defective, he could then finish himself. However, fortunate was that first block of stone, which never revealed any stain whatsoever in itself and could fittingly receive the great image of so revered a monarch. The Cavaliere was thus able, with greater ease, to complete the work on the portrait. (In the execution of the king's portrait, let us mention, the aforementioned Giulio Cartari also distinguished himself through the continual assistance he lent to his master).[47]

Thus, it is with knowledge of the sculptor's praxis that Mariette objected to the anecdote related by Bernini's biographers.

Of course, this awareness did not prevent the French connoisseur from accepting the authorship of Bernini's sculptures. From the Renaissance on, hardly anyone would dispute that the artist who ideated the piece, guided his assistants, and personally tackled the most important features of a work of art, was rightfully regarded as the author. However, Mariette went so far as to claim that it was impossible that in the short span of 'two years' (actually six), and at the tender age of twenty, Bernini could sculpt all alone four major sculptures such as the *Aeneas, Anchises and Ascanius Fleeing Troy* (1618–19), the *Pluto and Proserpina* (1621–2), the *Apollo and Daphne* (1622–5) and the *David* (1623–4) (figs 2.3, 2.4, 2.7, 3.6). In his view, as prodigious as Bernini was, he had to have made extensive use of assistants. Indeed, he believed that Bernini only executed a model of the *Apollo and Daphne*, which was then sculpted by a 'Flemish sculptor' employed by his father. Furthermore, he was aware that at the time Bernini availed himself of Giuliano Finelli's incredible technical dexterity – a collaboration also proven by documents.[48] Mariette then concludes his criticism by clarifying his point of view:

> I do not intend, given everything that I have stated, to diminish the glory so rightly deserved by Bernini. But I think that his beautiful works have immortalized him sufficiently not to warrant – in an attempt to make him appear even greater – the inclusion of facts void of any plausibility and, I dare say, the employment of the language of fables.[49]

Ironically, then, Mariette believed that the tall tales spun by Gian Lorenzo's biographers amounted to as much nonsense as the Zeuxis fable had to Bernini.

But Mariette's assertions about Bernini's reliance on assistants in the sculpting of the Scipione Borghese busts deserves further analysis for, as rightly observed by Ursula Schlegel: 'Almost always, the master of a large workshop that received many commissions executed only the very last chisel work for surface effect and finish, and in many cases not even that. As a rule, the style of a sculptor is much more clearly reflected in his handmade *bozzetto* than in the finished work.'[50] At the time the two Scipione portraits were executed (1632), Bernini was very much occupied with the giant statue of *Saint Longinus*, the overseeing of the decoration of the four niches in the enormous piers that uphold the dome of Saint Peter's, the final phases of the *Baldacchino* in this same basilica, as well as two marble and two bronze portraits of Pope Urban VIII.[51] Scipione Borghese had been Bernini's first major patron and had entrusted him with the execution of the early masterpieces that revealed the artist's exceptional genius. Whether the request to carve his portrait was issued by Scipione himself, as mentioned by Domenico Bernini, or Pope Urban VIII, is unclear. In fact, even a document published by Stanislao Fraschetti does not fully clarify the matter.[52] Certainly, Bernini must have welcomed the opportunity to immortalise his cardinal friend. Nonetheless, after the *pelo* appeared across the bust's forehead, sculpting a second version was probably a task that for the most part he relegated to assistants, applying only finishing touches here and there. And this, contrary to what John Pope-Hennessy believed, was not 'a critique of the first [bust]';[53] rather, a necessary and genial expedient to save face and please his patron. The question is, when did the hairline crack occur and how soon did Bernini initiate the second version?

It is instructive to compare how the two biographers prance around the timing and the technical problem posed by the crack on the first Scipione Borghese portrait.[54] In Baldinucci's narrative, the *pelo* appeared when the 'work was almost completed' and having 'a marvelous knowledge of the working of marble . . . had a sufficiently large piece of marble of known quality secretly brought to his room (*camera*)'. In other words, the *pelo* did not appear until the very last phase of the process and, to make up for the faulty stone, Bernini made sure that the next marble block be of excellent quality.[55] Baldinucci clearly blamed the material for the mishap, rather than the hands behind the hammer and chisel that struck the marble.

Domenico Bernini, also, goes out of his way to imply that the problem was 'connatural' to the marble block and, if there was any human to blame for having caused the crack to come to the surface, it was his father's assistants: 'In finishing the face of the portrait with their pumice-stone, the polishers uncovered a vein in the marble, or, as we say, a "hair," that crossed the entire forehead and noticeably altered the likeness of the sitter.' This unexpected flaw in the marble block, according to Domenico Bernini, 'greatly troubled the heart of Gian Lorenzo's father, so anxious for his son's success', even though, it should be noted, Pietro Bernini had actually died three years before the execution of the bust.[56] Domenico further specifies that: 'The studio assistants, well aware that the pope was anxiously awaiting the portrait, strove in vain to eliminate the blemish, which, in fact, was a natural feature of the marble itself.'[57] In other words, when the sculptor had finished his work the bust was still intact. The crack appeared only when the assistants, in polishing the bust, intervened. If any agent was to be blamed for mishandling the sculpture, that person could not have been Gian Lorenzo.[58]

Again, it is just this sort of manipulation of the events that Mariette found difficult to accept. Although the above-mentioned 'eyewitness report', in the form of a letter written by Lelio Guidiccioni recalling his visits to the sculptor's studio, states that 'the marble splitting in two, due to a hairline crack, when the work was already underway' ('*spezzarsigli il marmo per un pelo in due pezzi quando era già il lavoro condotto*'),[59] in Mariette's view, evidence of the crack probably occurred not at the end of the sculpting process but 'after the carving began' (*dès les commencemens dans le marbre*), that is, sooner than most people were willing to admit. And, rather than being defeated by the appearance of the *pelo*, the artist made virtue out of necessity and proceeded to work almost simultaneously on the second version with the aid of assistants. In fact, that this is just what might have happened is supported by Baldinucci:

> Bernini had splendid precepts concerning architecture: first of all he said the highest merit lay not in making beautiful and commodious buildings, but in being able to make do with little, to make beautiful things out of the inadequate and ill-adapted, to make use of a defect in such a way that if it had not existed one would have to invent it.[60]

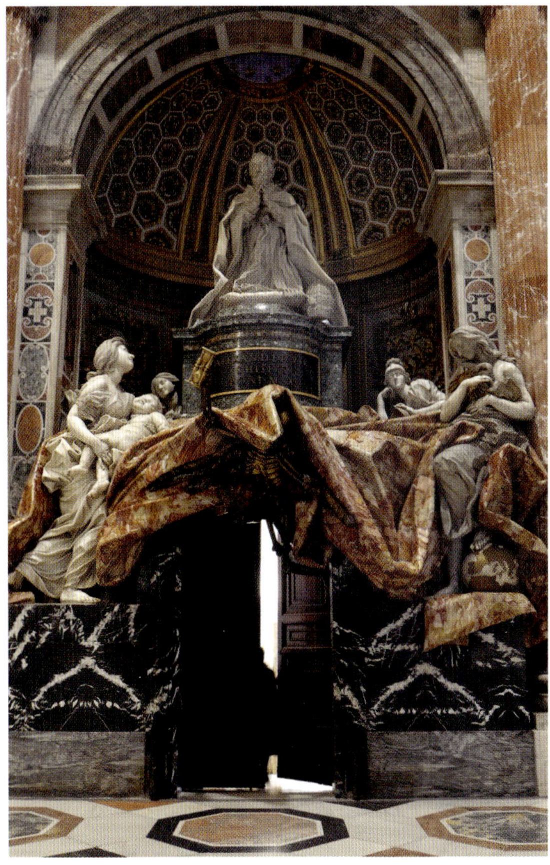

3.7 Gian Lorenzo Bernini, *Tomb of Alexander VII*, 1671–8, marble, Saint Peter's Basilica, Rome

A clear example that illustrates this concept in Baldinucci's biography was the way Bernini made virtue out of necessity in the *Tomb of Alexander VII* (1671–8) (fig.3.7) where the presence of a door beneath the location selected for the monument was turned to advantage and incorporated in the overall design by transforming it into a symbol of the threshold that separates this life from the next: 'He set the tomb in a great niche containing a door through which there is a continual coming and going. But he made such good use of the door; which to others would have seemed a great impediment, that it served him as an aid, or rather, a necessary component for working out his splendid concept.'[61] Indeed, even though Bernini's comment 'If you want to see what a man knows, put him in a difficult position' ('Chi vuol' vedere quel che un uomo sa, bisogna metterlo in necessità') refers to an architectural project – the Louvre – there is no doubt that he brought this mindset to bear on all of his artistic creations.[62]

There is truth in Mariette's observations. Despite the objective, excellent quality of both versions of Scipione's portrait – indeed, Domenico Bernini actually claimed the second portrait had a more

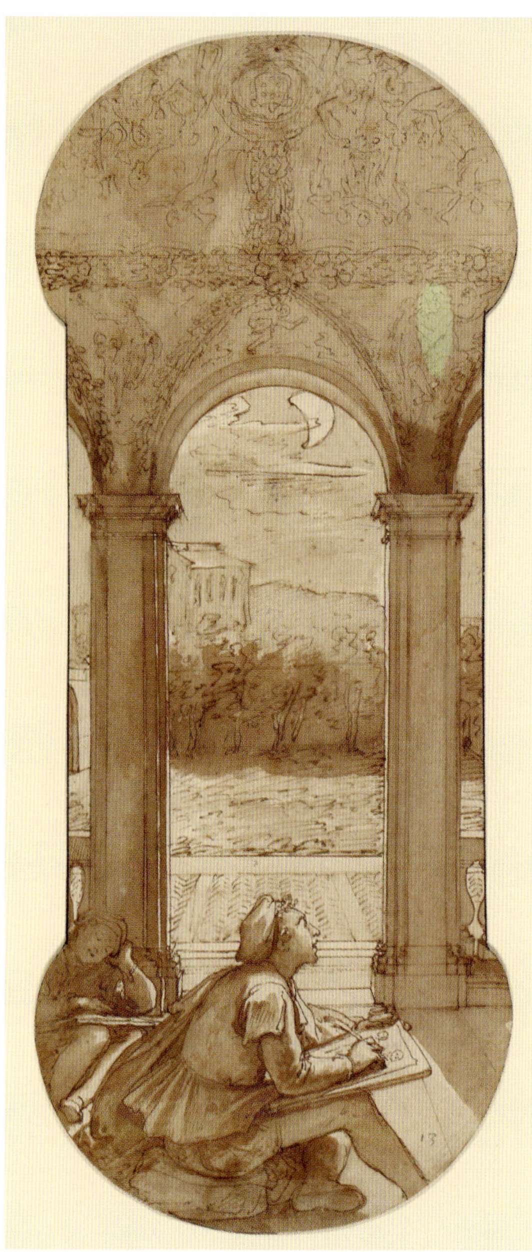

3.8 Federico Zuccari, *Taddeo Zuccari Copying Raphael's Frescoes in the Loggia of the Villa Farnesina*, pen and brown ink, brush with brown wash, over black chalk and touches of red chalk, 42.4 × 17.5 cm (16 11⁄16 × 6 7⁄8 in), J. Paul Getty Museum, Los Angeles

lively expression[63] – it is undeniable that the first bust is the better of the two and it shows Bernini's greater, direct involvement.[64] The second version lacks the superior psychological penetration of the first – in part obtained by the deeper drilling of the irises – and the crisp, tense treatment of the mozzetta folds. And even though Baldinucci alleges that the artist himself, when seeing these works years later, was in awe of his own sculptural ability as a 'boy', and Domenico informs us that 'the amount of praise accorded Gian Lorenzo after the subsequent comparison of the two portraits was simply beyond belief', a more nuanced understanding of the actual reception the sculptures received may be inferred by the fact that the first version was placed, probably from the beginning, on the ground floor of the Villa Borghese, in the Salone degli Imperatori, while the second, implicitly less appreciated by the patron, was exhibited in the small Room XI, the so-called Sala dei Ritratti, on the second floor.[65]

A further point needs to be made with regard to Baldinucci's word selection when referring to the amount of time it took Bernini to complete the second portrait. The attentive reader will have realised that Domenico Bernini, while making a hyperbolic claim, states that his father worked relentlessly for 'three days' to execute the bust; that is, he computes the time in terms of 'days', which is the way most people would refer to the period needed to carry out a work of art. Not so Baldinucci: he upends the readers' expectations by adopting a nocturnal clock, so to speak, stating that it took the young artist 'fifteen nights' as opposed to fifteen days. The reason for this word choice has classical and Renaissance roots and reflects seventeenth-century artists' social and intellectual aspirations to a professional nobility. As expounded in Cesare Ripa's *Iconologia* under the heading *Studio*, youths who wished to achieve fame and nobility of mind had to burn the candle at both ends.[66] That is, they had to study important classical and Renaissance works of art during the day and, at night, rather than imbibing wine by partying with

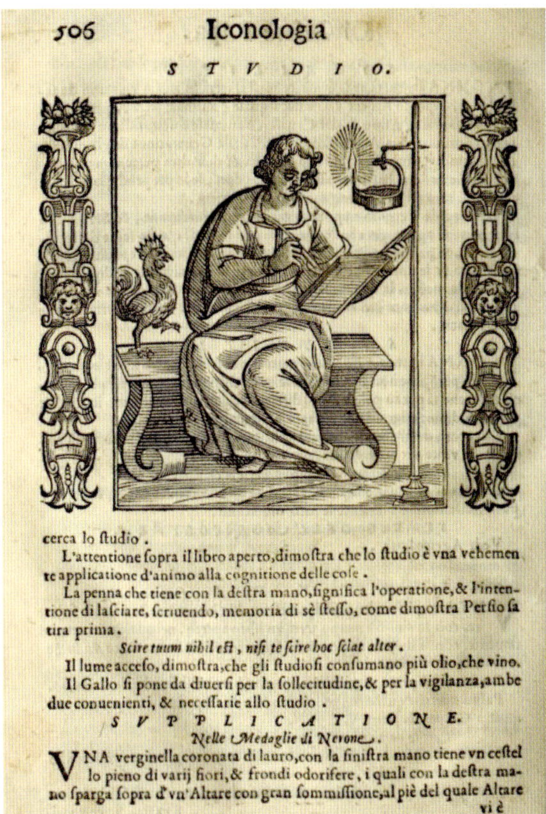

506 Iconologia

S T V D I O.

cerca lo ſtudio.

L'attentione ſopra il libro aperto, dimoſtra che lo ſtudio è vna vehemente applicatione d'animo alla cognitione delle coſe.

La penna che tiene con la deſtra mano, ſignifica l'operatione, & l'intentione di laſciare, ſcriuendo, memoria di sè ſteſſo, come dimoſtra Perſio ſatira prima.

Scire tuum nihil eſt, niſi te ſcire hoc ſciat alter.

Il lume acceſo, dimoſtra, che gli ſtudioſi conſumano più olio, che vino.

Il Gallo ſi pone da diuerſi per la ſollecitudine, & per la vigilanza, ambedue conuenienti, & neceſſarie allo ſtudio.

S V P P L I C A T I O N E.

Nelle Medaglie di Nerone.

VNA verginella coronata di lauro, con la ſiniſtra mano tiene vn ceſtello pieno di varij fiori, & frondi odorifere, i quali con la deſtra mano ſparga ſopra d'vn'Altare con gran ſommiſſione, al piè del quale Altare

vi è

3.9 Cesare Ripa, *Studio*, from *Iconologia, overo Descrittione D'Imagini Delle Virtù, Vitij, Affetti, Passioni humane, Corpi celesti, Mondo e sue parti*, Padua, 1611, p.506, Internet Archive

friends, should consume the oil in the lamps that allowed them to work in the absence of sunlight; to be exact, they should continue studying after hours by applying themselves to their art, as exemplified by Federico Zuccari's drawings of events from the life of his brother Taddeo, or Cesare Ripa's illustration of *Studio* in his *Iconologia* (figs 3.8 and 3.9). As Kris and Kurz pointed out long ago, 'zeal and industry are common to all who are involved in creative efforts'.[67] Bernini, of course, was actually knighted by Gregory XV in 1621 when he was twenty-three years old, as discussed in Chapter 1. But, in keeping with Baldinucci's tale, at the time of Scipione Borghese's portraits he was still 'a boy'. Thus, Bernini not only 'spent three continuous years from dawn until the sounding of the Ave Maria in the rooms of the Vatican drawing the objects of greatest rarity, those with qualities of excellence and exoticism as well as examples from antiquity'[68] but also, after sunset, he wasted no time. In merely 'fifteen nights' he achieved the miracle of sculpting a nearly identical replica of Scipione's bust by 'burning the midnight oil'.[69] In the author's mind, there was no better example to foreshadow the glory that the young Bernini would achieve as he grew older. Indeed, Baldinucci's anecdotes pertaining to Bernini's youth were true 'Intimations of Immortality from Recollections of Early Childhood'.[70]

* * *

Even before Mariette brought his artistic expertise and critical eye to bear on Bernini's biographies, another Frenchman, the Abbé Pierre Cureau de la Chambre, followed a similar course. In his *Preface pour servir à l'histoire de la vie et des ouvrages du Cavalier Bernin* (*Preface at the service of a history of the life and works of Cavalier Bernini*) written in 1685, three years after Baldinucci's *Life* was published, the Abbé sketched the main lines of a biography that would never see the light of day.[71] In contrast to biographers who preceded him – authors, in his view, primarily engaged in writing panegyrics and flattery rather than history – Cureau de la Chambre was intent on applying his rationalistic, Cartesian outlook to Bernini's life and works.[72] 'How', he asked, 'could one recognize therein [in previous biographies] the ordinary course of man's life, such as he really is, feeble, flawed, subject to a thousand injustices, and so often more worthy of pity than admiration and envy?'[73] Equally at fault as those painters who, not having been exposed to ancient art, simply copied nature without idealising it, the

Abbé felt that previous biographers had gone to the opposite extreme by embellishing the characters of the individuals whose lives they narrated to such an extent that one could not discern in them any relationship to reality.[74] 'The [literary] portraits they painted of their subjects were extremely accomplished but shaped by pure caprice and fantasy, colorful portraits designed to please: nothing natural or recognizable, nothing manifest because everything is studied, everything suited for the theater, spectacle and pomp.'[75] Cureau de la Chambre wondered whether such writers qualified as historians at all. Indeed, he claims that they should be more accurately considered novelists, authors who busied themselves in writing fiction. As for himself, Cureau de la Chambre wished to avoid such pitfalls: 'I will boldly recount the strengths and the weaknesses, the good and the bad [features] of Cavalier Bernini.'[76] He did not wish to portray him as a man without faults, for posterity would not esteem Bernini any less even if aware of his shortcomings, 'since the master did not always equally succeed in all of his enterprises'.[77] His critique of Baldinucci could not have been more explicit. But what are some other tales, besides the Scipione Borghese anecdote, that are objectionable in the Florentine biographer's 'novel'?

The first questionable event presented by Baldinucci relates to Bernini's well-known encounter with Pope Paul V.[78] Having heard of the acclaim the child was receiving, he asked that the ten-year-old Gian Lorenzo be brought before him.[79] When he requested 'in jest' ('*come per ischerzo*') the sketch of a head – the implication being the pope did not think the child was capable of doing so – the boy inquired which head he wished. The pope, taken aback by the reply, realised that the child must have known how to draw any head ('*Se cosí è le sa far tutte*'). Paul V thus asked Bernini to draw the head of his namesake, Saint Paul, and within half an hour Bernini did so to perfection. The conclusion to the story is that the pope solicited Cardinal Maffeo Barberini, the future Pope Urban VIII and most important patron of the artist, to become the child's mentor. Thus, just as Bernini embarked on his way to stardom, Paul V supposedly exclaimed: 'We hope that this youth will become the Michelangelo of his century.'[80]

As with a number of other events narrated by the biographer, the story may have actually occurred. On the other hand, it is legitimate to question its factuality since it has clear roots in Vasari's anecdote of Giotto's 'O', which ultimately was inspired by Pliny's anecdote about Apelles' line.[81] But whereas in Pliny's tale the contest is between two artists, Protogenes and Apelles, as to who could paint freehand the thinnest straight line – that is, a strictly technical competition[82] – in Vasari's tale the anecdote is enriched as it refers not only to Giotto's skill, but also to his wit, and the artist's introduction to the highest religious figure in Christendom: Pope Benedict XI.[83] As is well known, the pope had sent one of his emissaries to Tuscany to find a master from whom to commission some paintings in Saint Peter's. After having obtained some drawings from other painters as proof of their skill, the envoy asked Giotto for one of his. The artistically uninformed messenger felt duped by Giotto when the artist, with a brush dipped in red paint, proceeded to paint freehand a perfect circle and nothing more. Although the unknowing envoy failed to appreciate the technical skill involved, he was told to take it to the pope and 'see whether it is understood or not'. When the pope and a number of knowledgeable courtiers were told that Giotto had painted the circle 'without moving his arm and without the help of a compass' it proved to them 'how much Giotto surpassed all other painters of that time'.[84]

As mentioned in Chapter 2, in Ernst Kris and Otto Kurz's *Legend, Myth, and Magic in the Image of the Artist*, the authors focused on a number of recurring themes in the *Lives* of artists. As one of the derivative anecdotes from the Apelles and Protogenes contest, they singled out the one on Giotto's 'O' as a most obvious variation on the theme and explained that it was included by the sources of the biographical sketches to indicate 'the mark of artistic attainment'. Kris and Kurz elaborate the significance of the event by stating that the artist's virtuosity represented 'a value in its own rights: technique becomes an end in itself'.[85] This is exactly what Baldinucci wished to accomplish when he included Bernini's youthful, 'off the cuff' drawing of the head of Saint Paul for the pope. He also wished to draw an analogy between the biographies of the two artists by having Bernini meet a pope, Paul V, just as Giotto had met Benedict XI.

But while Baldinucci places this anecdote in the opening passages of the *Vita*, in Vasari's biography of Giotto it occurs much later, when he had already become an accomplished artist. Nevertheless, Baldinucci's adaptation of Vasari's trope of the epiphanic moment is only seemingly asynchronous. For Vasari's introduction of Giotto's artistic virtuosity exemplified by a drawing occurs even earlier than the execution of his famous 'O'. It happens at the outset of his *Life* of the painter, when Giotto, aged ten like Bernini, is discovered by Cimabue drawing a sheep on a rock with the help of a sharp stone while tending to a flock.

Thus, just as Vasari had relied on Pliny to introduce the sign of artistic dexterity by adopting the Apelles anecdote, so too did Baldinucci depend on Vasari when including the earliest revelation of Bernini's graphic skill. By conflating the artist's encounter with the pope with the youthful, revelatory drawing to his tenth year, Baldinucci was implicitly claiming for the young Bernini a comparable revolutionary role in seventeenth-century art as Giotto had played in the thirteenth.

* * *

Among the various fabrications relating to Bernini, there is one that Cureau de la Chambre did not have to comment on since it was omitted by Baldinucci – whom he read – but introduced by Domenico Bernini in the *Life* of 1713, when the Abbé had been dead for twenty years. It pertains to Bernini's statue of *Saint Lawrence* executed in 1617 (fig.3.10). Included in the narrative immediately after the Scipione Borghese portraits, Baldinucci simply states: 'Meanwhile, still in his fifteenth year [actually his nineteenth], he carved the figure of Saint Lawrence (his namesake) on the gridiron for Leone Strozzi, which was placed in the Strozzi villa.'[86] Domenico, instead elaborates the tale in ways that have been rightly interpreted as 'a metaphor of auto-creation' by which 'Bernini reformed and perfected himself . . . having only his *ingegno* as his teacher'.[87] Domenico's version claims as follows:

> Out of devotion toward the saint, whose name he bore, Gian Lorenzo wished to depict in marble Saint Lawrence in the act of being burned naked on the grill. In order to adequately reflect in the saint's face the pain of his martyrdom and the effect that the fire must have had on his flesh, he placed his own leg and bare thigh near burning coals. Thus coming to feel in himself the saint's suffering, he then drew with his pencil, before a mirror, the painful contortions of his face and observed the various effects that the heat of the flame had on his own flesh. Even more meritoriously than the ancient Scaevola, who placed his hand in fire in order to punish himself for having erred, our Gian Lorenzo caused his own flesh to be burned out of a desire not to fall into error.[88]

Clearly a hyperbolic assertion adding both hagiographic[89] and Roman historical overtones to the artist's profile, had this event really taken place, no doubt the two biographers would have taken an opportunity at some point later in the artist's *Life* to refer to the singed epidermis that the burning coal had left on his leg, if for no other reason, as a reminder of Bernini's saintly nature; a fact underscored at this point in Domenico's biography who claims that his father saw 'il figliuolo in quell'atto di martirio' ('his son [carrying out] that sacrificial act').[90] Moreover, placing his leg in the fire

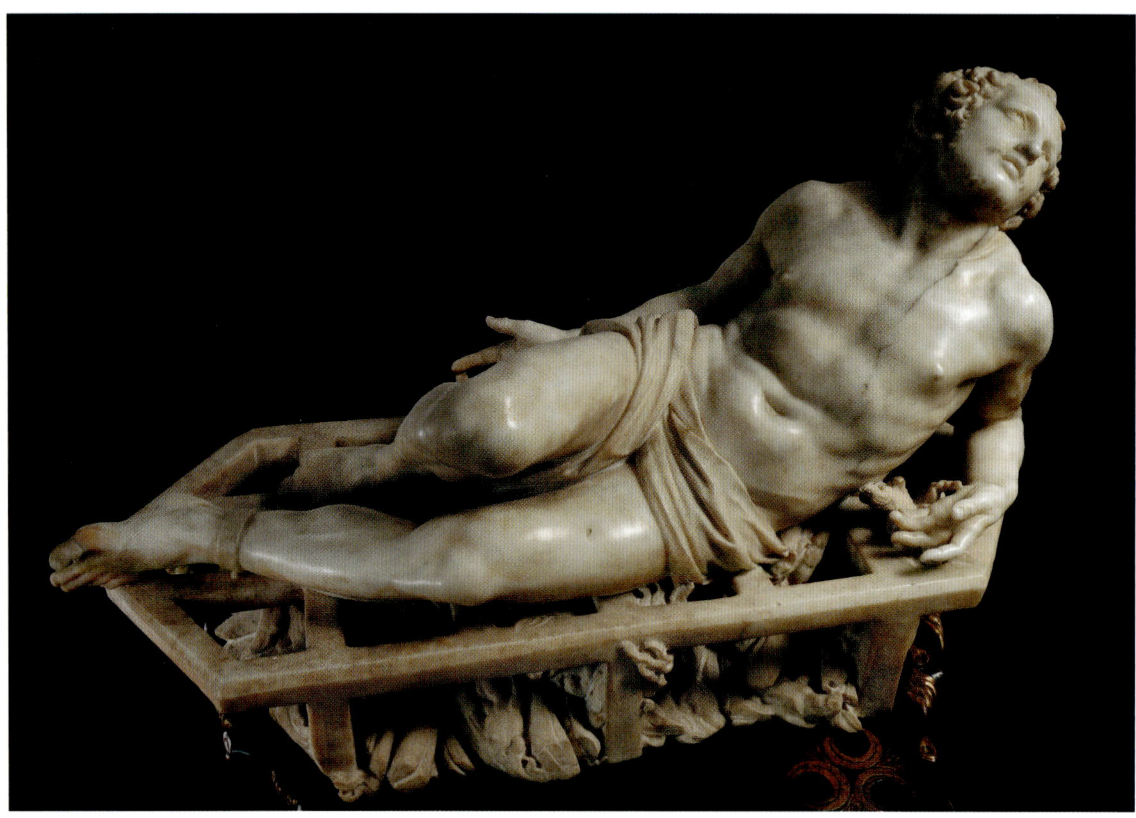

3.10 Gian Lorenzo Bernini, *Martyrdom of Saint Lawrence*, 1617, marble, 66 × 108 cm (26 × 42½ in), Galleria degli Uffizi (from the Contini Bonacossi Collection)

to observe 'the various effects that the heat of the flame had on his own flesh' would have been a futile exercise, for the saint's expression in the sculpture does not reflect the pain Bernini would have felt. Rather, *Saint Lawrence* is shown in a transcendent, spiritual dialogue with his Maker. Regardless, and as others have abundantly pointed out, this tale is based on a classical *topos* that has roots in Aristotle, Horace, and Quintilian.[91] In his *Poetics*, Aristotle observed that the poet (actually a playwright) 'should even act his story with the very gestures of his personages. Given the same natural qualifications, he who feels the emotions to be described will be the most convincing; distress and anger, for instance, are portrayed most truthfully by one who is feeling them at the moment.'[92] Similarly, Horace states: 'Not enough is it for poems to have beauty; they must have charm, and lead the hearer's soul where they will. As men's faces smile on those who smile, so they respond to those who weep. If you would have me weep, you must first feel grief yourself.'[93] Quintilian, likewise, in advising young orators, wrote: 'The prime essential for stirring the emotions of others is, in my opinion, first to feel those emotions oneself.'[94] And echoes of this concept may be heard in Dante's *Convivio* where he wrote: 'No painter could depict any form if he did not first conceive in his imagination how he wishes it to be.'[95] In fact, closer in time to Bernini's *Saint Lawrence*, in 1594 the Jesuit Antonio Possevino had stated as much in his treatise on poetry and painting, as would also Federico Borromeo in his *Sacred Painting* in 1624.[96] But while these examples refer primarily to theatrical and poetic *mimesis* (imitation), there is a more specific artistic reference that was doubtlessly known to Domenico, who was an accomplished historian.[97]

In Seneca the Elder's *Declamations*, in which he presents *Controversiae* intended for students training for the law court, the author typically gives first a recap of the law, then the theme of the subject at hand, and, subsequently, two sides of the argument in the form of epigrams placed in the mouths of various characters.[98] In one of these, Seneca concisely wrote:

> The Athenian painter Parrhasius purchased an old man from among the captives from Olynthus put up for sale by Philip [II of Macedon], and took him to Athens. He tortured him, and using him as a model painted a Prometheus. The Olynthian died under the torture. Parrhasius put the picture in the temple of Minerva; he is accused of harming the state.[99]

Thus, in wishing to render Prometheus' grimacing face as realistically as possible, this artist was credited with having tortured a slave. Arguments *pro* and *con* are given to assess whether the end justifies the means,[100] even though the debate is ultimately given no resolution.

This classical source had already been culled by Carlo Dati in his *Vite de pittori antichi* of 1667 where he relates the questionable, spurious story involving Parrhasius to another equally specious tale that claimed Michelangelo had actually crucified and killed his model for the sake of greater realism in depicting the face of Christ on the cross – something Dati denounces as absolutely false and Carlo Cesare Malvasia as one of the usual, unfounded '*voci popolari*' that spread like wildfire.[101] Therefore, quite plausibly, this had been Domenico's most compelling reason for including the *Saint Lawrence* anecdote in his work since, besides giving Gian Lorenzo the aura of a modern-day Christian martyr – it is not accidental that Baldinucci refers to the 'persecutions' the artist had to endure when his bell tower on the facade of Saint Peter's was demolished[102] – and being an example of his interest in naturalism in his early years, it provided further evidence of Bernini's Michelangelesque pedigree, as repeatedly underscored by both biographers. With a major difference: while Michelangelo's purported interest in realism in his art was achieved at the expense of another human being, Bernini's pursuit of greater adherence to reality was a self-effacing – indeed, a superhuman – 'martyrdom' in emulation of his eponymous saint.[103] As Domenico put it: 'the boy had re-created in himself the torment of a real Saint Lawrence in order to sculpt an artificial one'.[104]

* * *

Gian Lorenzo Bernini's interest in sculpting portraits that not only faithfully reproduced the outer physiognomy of his sitters but, more importantly, revealed the inner workings of their minds is certainly not the product of the fecund imagination of his biographers. Nor does one have to rely on the scholarly articles that in recent years have probed every aspect of Bernini's approach and innovations in portraiture to realise that, when looking at one of his busts, we are in the presence of sublime artistry. Even if someone were to close one's eyes and merely investigate through the sense of touch a Bernini bust, that person would feel the superlative portrayal of 'the transitoriness of the psychological moment'.[105] Indeed, his busts display an ability to capture the quintessence of a person that, as Bernini noted about sculpture in general, 'even a blind person is able to judge';[106] a concept beautifully rendered in a drawing by

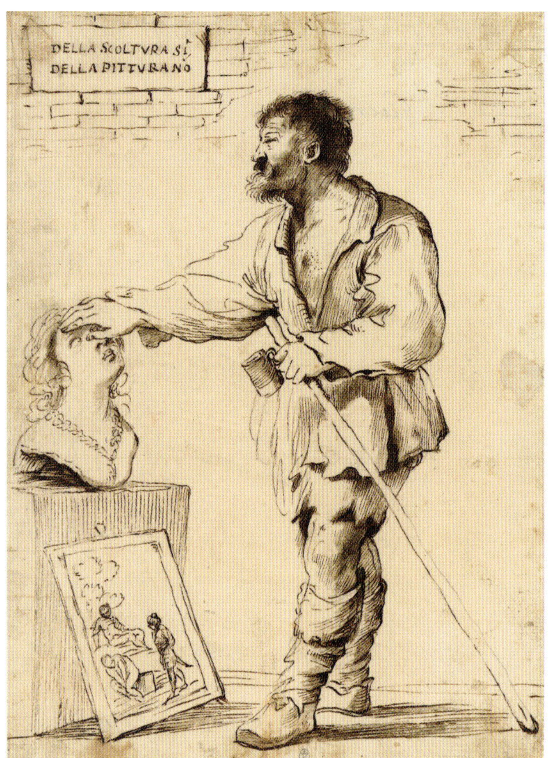

3.11 Giovanni Francesco Barbieri (Guercino), attributed, *Allegory of the Superiority of Sculpture over Painting*, brown ink, brown wash, black chalk quill, 26.9 × 20.1 cm (10 9⁄16 × 7 15⁄16 in), Musée du Louvre, Paris

Guercino that underscores, at least with regard to the haptic 'truthfulness' of a work of art, the superiority of sculpture over painting by declaring 'DELLA SCOLTURA SÌ, DELLA PITTURA NO' (fig.3.11).[107] Certainly, his portraits of Scipione Borghese (figs 3.1 and 3.2) took the genre to an unprecedented level and this he partly achieved by studying his subject, not by having the person pose perfectly still, as other artists were wont to do, but as they spoke and moved about (fig.3.12).[108] As we learn from a procedure explained by Chantelou, as well as Domenico Bernini with regard to Louis XIV's portrait,[109] he did so by executing multiple drawings,[110] thereby absorbing and imbibing ('*inzupparsi et imbeversi*') every aspect of his subject.[111] Thus, when he subsequently molded the clay model or sculpted the marble bust, he would be recollecting the overall image of the sitter captured in the drawings and creating an original work of art instead of a copy of what he had previously done.[112]

Although the truthfulness of Domenico Bernini's anecdote about Gian Lorenzo studying his own visage when planning his sculpture of *Saint Lawrence* is undermined by the sculpture itself,[113] his biographers' descriptions of the artist's working method are reliable. For, as he mentioned to Paul Fréart de Chantelou, when trying to capture the expression of a figure he wished to represent, he reverted to a technique he had devised himself; that is, he would place himself in the position and in the act he wished to give that figure and have an assistant draw him. A blatant example of unjustified pride – as mentioned, Aristotle, Horace, and Quintilian had prescribed this approach centuries earlier – Bernini's claim does reflect the importance he placed on achieving a most faithful depiction of his sitter's expression which, after all, he considered the 'soul of painting'.[114] Nevertheless, this reliance on his own person as a model leads to the consideration of another anecdote recounted in the *Lives*: the one regarding the *David*.

In Baldinucci's version of the anecdote one learns the following:

> In this work Bernini overwhelmingly surpassed himself. He completed it within a period of no more than seven months, thanks to the fact that from youth, as he was wont to say, he devoured marble and never struck a false blow, an accomplishment of those who have made themselves superior to art itself rather than of those who are merely expert in art. He modeled the beautiful face of this figure after his own countenance. The powerful knitted brows, the terrible fixity of the eyes, and the upper jaw clamped tightly over the lower lip wonderfully express the rightful wrath of the young

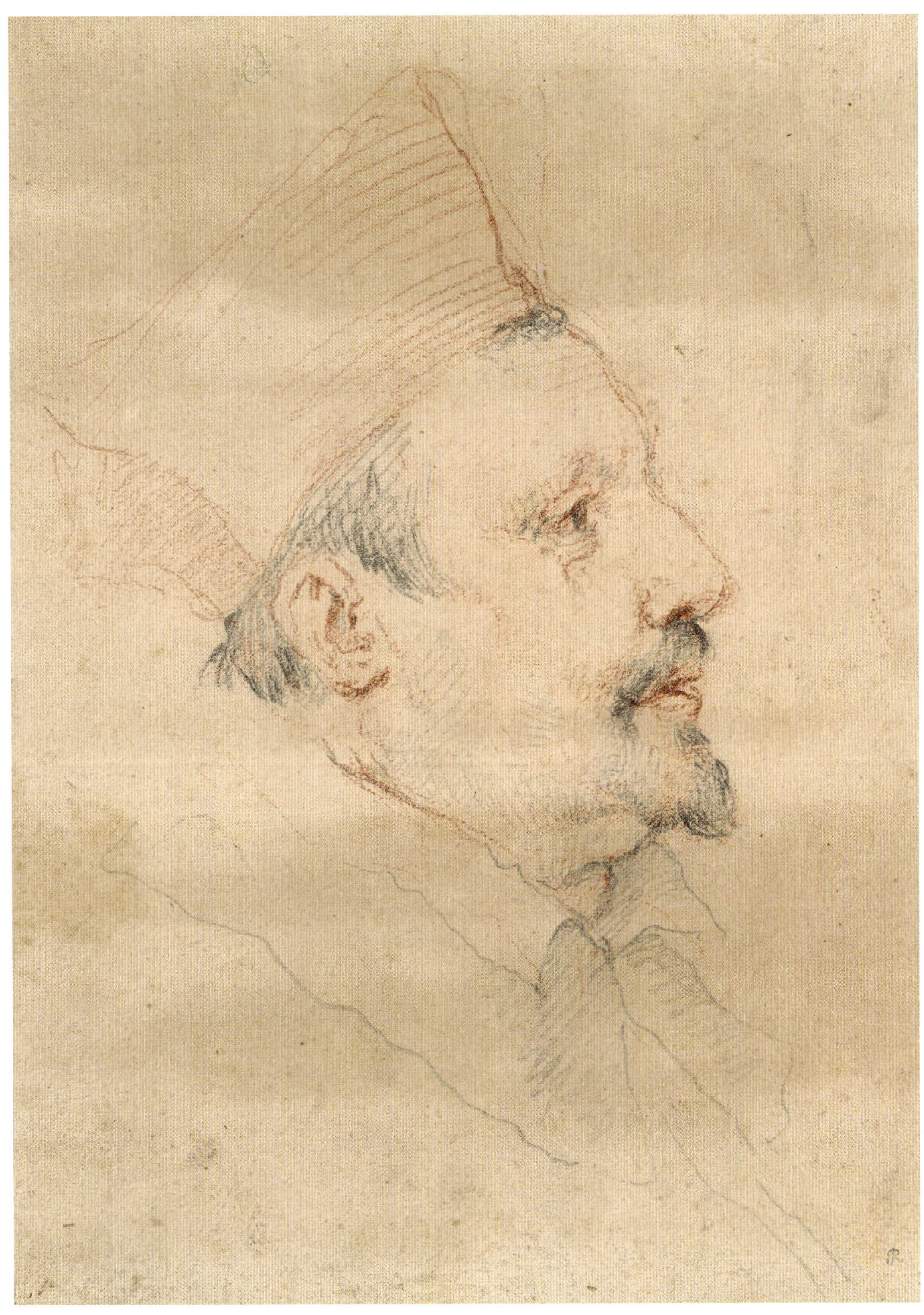

3.12 Gian Lorenzo Bernini, *Portrait of Cardinal Scipione Borghese*, 1632, red chalk over graphite on laid paper, 25.3 × 18.4 cm (9 15⁄16 × 7 1⁄4 in), The Morgan Library and Museum, New York. Purchased by Pierpont Morgan (1837–1913) in 1909

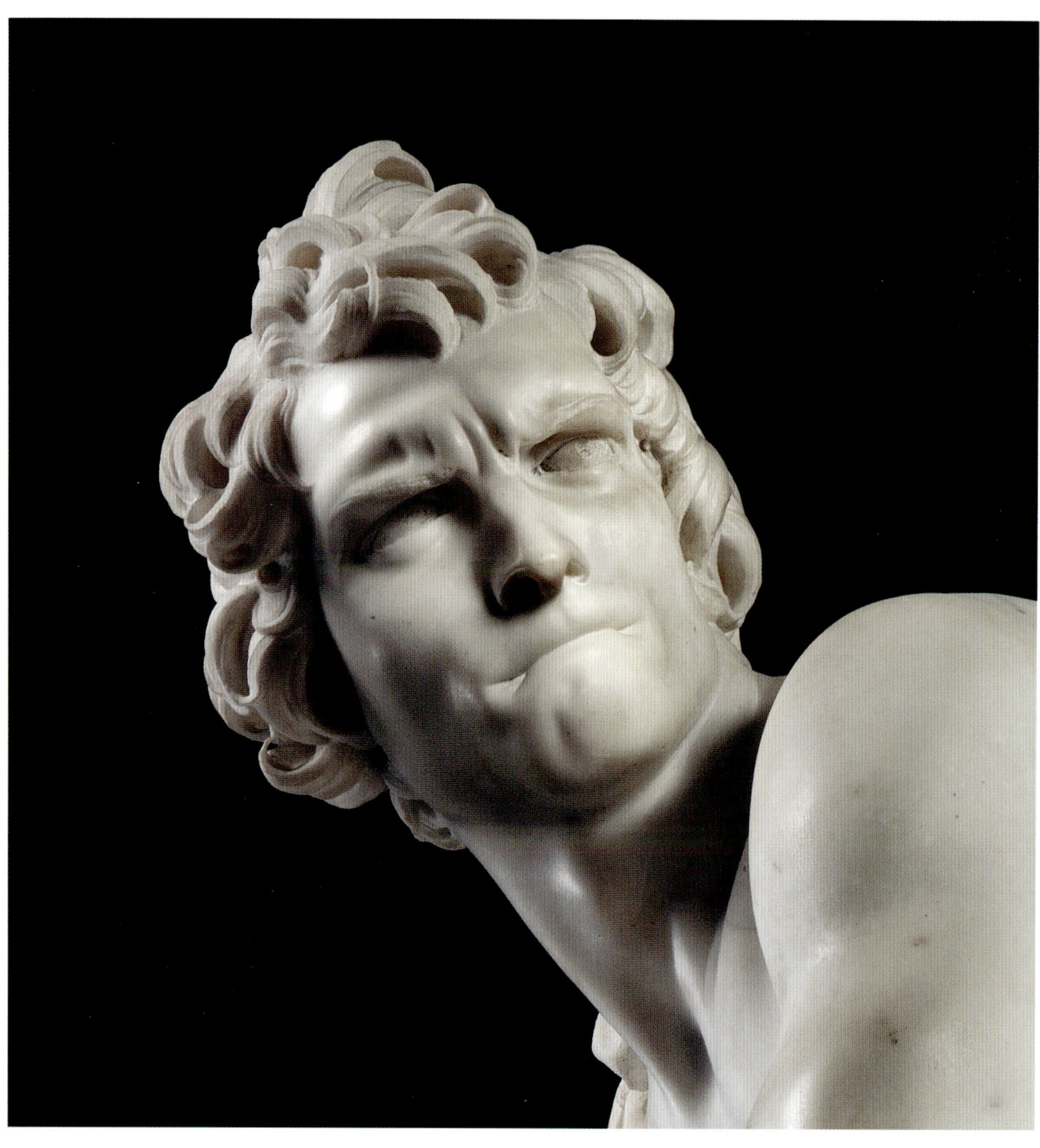

3.13 Gian Lorenzo Bernini, *David*, detail of fig.3.6, 1623–4, height 170 cm (66 15⁄16 in), Galleria Borghese, Rome

> Israelite in the act of aiming his sling at the forehead of the giant Philistine. The same spirit of resoluteness and vigor is seen in all parts of the body, which lacks only movement to be alive. It is worth recording that while Bernini was working on the figure in his own likeness, Cardinal Maffeo Barberini came often to his studio and held the mirror for him with his own hand.[115]

Domenico Bernini, similarly, claims that 'as far as the statue of David is concerned, in carving its face, Bernini with the help of a mirror, depicted his own features, doing so with an expressivity completely and truly marvelous. And it was Cardinal Maffeo Barberini himself, a frequent visitor to the artist's studio, who many times held the mirror with his own hands' (fig.3.13).[116] Both authors based their biographies on the earliest biographical sketch of Bernini's *Life* penned by Pier Filippo Bernini, the artist's eldest son, in 1674 when Gian Lorenzo was still alive.[117] Unlike the former two, however, all Pier Filippo wrote about the *David* statue is that 'he sculpted [it] giving the face and body his own likeness'.[118] It is totally credible and in keeping with the artist's method that he used his own person in trying to capture David's expression with furrowed brows and sealed lips, as the biblical hero is about to fling the stone that would fell Goliath, even though one is hard put to find a true physiognomic resemblance between the young hero and the known self-portraits of the artist.[119] But even though the most influential Bernini scholar of the twentieth century, Rudolf Wittkower, stated that there was no reason to doubt the truthfulness of the biographers' claim about Maffeo Barberini (1568–1644) holding the mirror for the young sculptor,[120] it is extremely unlikely that in a highly stratified, hierarchical society, such as seventeenth-century papal Rome, the fifty-four-year-old cardinal would lower himself to play such a subservient role to a twenty-two-year-old sculptor. For the man who about a month after the sculptor began the *David* was elected pope[121] and who was so keenly aware of the impact ceremonials and outward appearances had on contemporaries, the propagation of this anecdote would have sounded at the very least inappropriate.[122] One must remember that the context in which this tale was spun was the same in which social etiquette prescribed where in his palace a cardinal should meet a visiting dignitary, where each of the retinue should be seated according to rank, how many candles should accompany the visitor in the evening hours as he was escorted from one room to another, and how far the cardinal was to accompany his guest on the way out. Depending on the guest's rank, a cardinal would decide in which room to bid his guest adieu, how close to the exit door, to the top of the stairs, and even, in the case of 'first-class ambassadors', to 'pretend to wish to go downstairs';[123] it was an etiquette that applied to the secular world as well and that Bernini himself followed – or, to be precise, failed to follow more than once while in Paris.[124] In fact, all one needs to do is read Francesco Sestini's *Il maestro di camera* (1646) to see the implausibility of Baldinucci's and Domenico Bernini's story, especially with reference to a cardinal. If, for example, there was any doubt about the thorny issue of 'precedence' when two carriages crossed paths, such a conundrum, Sestini states, could not arise when these belonged to two cardinals since 'each knows his rank'.[125] Given such guidelines for a cardinal's behavior, it takes a stretch of the imagination to believe that Maffeo Barberini would perform the task of a studio assistant by holding the mirror to the young artist's face.

Instead, this tale should be understood as a fable comparable to Vasari's claim that, to soothe the pain of the dying Leonardo, 'the king [Francis I] held his head' and 'conscious of the great honour being done to him, the inspired Leonardo breathed his last in the arms of the king',[126] or, to stay within the context of Bernini's *Lives*, the analogous incident which occurred when Queen Christina of Sweden visited the sculptor in his studio:

Bernini received her in the heavy rough (*'grosso, e rozzo'*) garment he was accustomed to wear when working in marble. Since it was what he wore for his art, he considered it to be the most worthy possible garment in which to receive that great lady. This beautiful subtlety was quickly perceived by the Queen's sublime genius. His action not only increased her concept of his spirit, but even led her, as a sign of her esteem for his art, to wish to touch the garment with her own hand.[127]

Domenico also refers to the incident and makes much of Gian Lorenzo's coarse attire, describing it as the garment of his profession, as will be discussed in the next chapter.[128] What is clear is that here the biographers dipped their quills deep in the inkwell of hagiography where contact relics (*brandea*) were a confirmation of the 'wonderworking *virtus*' of a saint's body itself.[129] But while for Rudolf and Margot Wittkower the story might be true, they also point out how the anecdote sounds like the familiar *topos* fabricated 'in praise of the dignity of the artistic profession, best illustrated by the famous story according to which Charles V picked up Titian's brush'.[130] And one might add, to mention one further example, the rehashing of the *topos* describing how, when Queen Christina honored the painter Guercino with a visit to his studio in Bologna, in recognition of a painter who had worked wonders, 'she touched his hand'[131] – an anecdote reminiscent of the 'appropriation of religious forms for secular purposes' such as the kissing of the hand of a nobleman.[132]

Ultimately, however, while one might doubt the extent to which the anecdotes that Bernini's biographers inserted in their narrative are based on events that really took place, one thing is certain: the *Imitatio Buonarroti* that Baldinucci and Domenico Bernini stressed throughout their biographies was something the artist himself fully embraced.[133] Although it is unlikely, as stated, that a cardinal would play a subservient role to the young artist by literally holding the mirror so he could study his face when sculpting the *David* (1623–4), it was not unusual for an artist to act as his own model when executing a work of art.[134] In Bernini's case, there was an even more significant reason why he worked on the figure 'in his own likeness', for Michelangelo's consecration as the most talented sculptor of the Renaissance came with the completion of the giant marble statue of the same biblical hero.[135]

As is known, beside the sketch for the bronze *David* (*c.*1501–2) executed for Pierre de Rohan, Maréchal Gié (fig.3.14), Michelangelo also drew – upside down in relation to this sketch – the right arm of the marble *David* (1501–4). Next to this arm, the twenty-seven-year-old sculptor declared his personal identification with the biblical hero by writing 'Davicte cholla Fromba/e io collarcho/ Michelagniolo' ('David with his sling and I with the bow. Michelangelo'), and below: 'Rocte lalta cholonna elverd'. ('Broken is the tall column and the green').[136] While it is nowadays generally accepted that by the word 'collarcho' ('with the bow') Michelangelo meant the sculptor's drill – references have also been made to David's harp and a weapon[137] – it is much more likely, as Irving Lavin has ingeniously suggested, that *arco* combines multiple connotations referring to the *arco dell'intelletto* (the mental effort required to execute a sculpture), the *arco della schiena* (the 'bowed' or arched back of a person performing a strenuous physical task), as well as the *seste ad arco* (the bowed calipers or compass a sculptor uses to transfer the measurements from a model to the marble block).[138] Ultimately, however, the meaning of Michelangelo's inscription is very clear: just as David defeated the giant Goliath with the implement available to the youthful shepherd (the sling), so, too, has the young Florentine artist succeeded in conquering the giant marble column (*gigante*) with the instruments available to him: the sculptors' tools and his genius.

Bernini most likely never saw Michelangelo's drawing, although he conceivably heard about

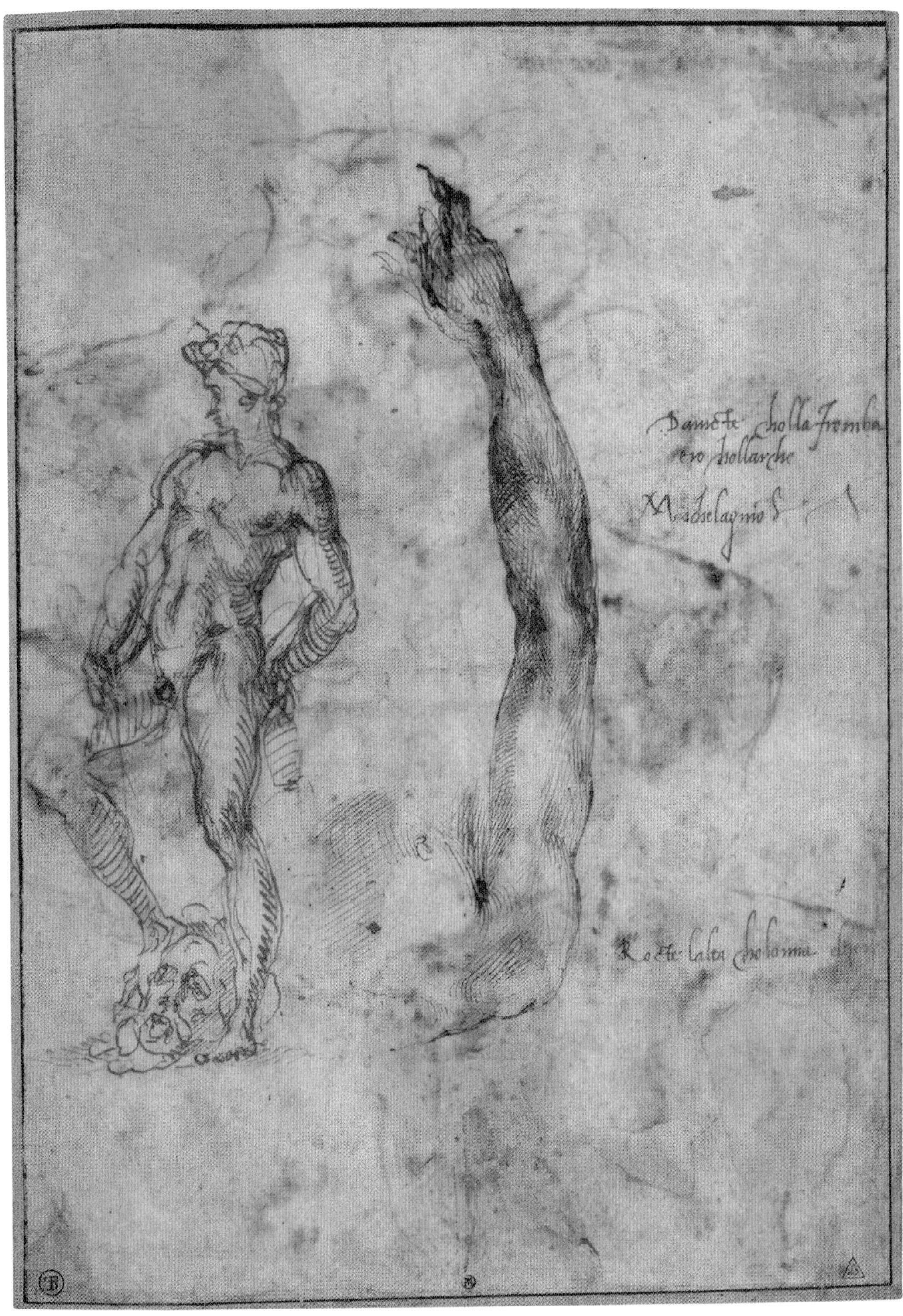

3.14 Michelangelo Buonarroti, *Studies for the Figure of David*, pen and brown ink, 26.3 × 18.8 cm (10⅜ × 7⅜ in), Musée du Louvre, Paris

it through Cardinal Maffeo Barberini, who was a close friend of Michelangelo's great-nephew, Michelangelo the Younger. In fact, the two had known each other from early childhood in the neighborhood of Santa Croce in Florence, had become close friends when studying in Pisa between 1586 and 1588 while lodging together in the house of Giovanni Uguccioni,[139] and remained in epistolary contact through 1623, when Maffeo was raised to Saint Peter's throne as Urban VIII.[140] Indeed, when publishing the first printed edition of his great-uncle's poems in 1623, Michelangelo the Younger dedicated the volume to the then Cardinal Barberini;[141] and the latter, on his part, did not forget his dear friend by admitting him into the pontifical court from the spring of 1629 through the spring of the following year.[142] Regardless of whether Bernini had been made privy to the association that Michelangelo had drawn between himself and the *David*, as he temporarily ceased working on the *Apollo and Daphne* he was executing for Scipione Borghese so as to tackle the *David* for Cardinal Alessandro Peretti Montalto,[143] he must have welcomed the opportunity to prove, as his Renaissance precursor had done with the Florence *David*, that he was, in fact, the best sculptor of his age. With the inclusion of the anecdote of the mirror held by Cardinal Barberini, his biographers implicitly emphasised, once again, not only the identification of Gian Lorenzo with the Old Testament hero but also with the artistic 'giant' who had preceded him in the previous century. Actually, one might argue that Gian Lorenzo had even surpassed his precursor for, while Michelangelo had created a sculpture that gave only a premonition of the ensuing confrontation between the biblical hero and the Philistine giant, Bernini transcended the temporal, descriptive limitations of sculpture by *narrating*[144] a story *in medias res*, as Horace had suggested, drawing the viewer 'in the story's midst'[145] and recreating the confrontation as if it were occurring in front of the viewer. Whether inspired by him or not, Bernini achieved in sculpture what Leon Battista Alberti had claimed was the main purview of painting: the ability to represent an *istoria*. This capability was traditionally achievable by sculptors when using their chisel as if it were a brush, that is, when sculpting reliefs, but not when carving statues in the round.[146] Instead, as Leon Battista Alberti had advised, by depicting David not after the event (as Donatello had done), nor before (like Michelangelo did), but at the very apex of the action – just as he is about to fling the stone that will defeat Goliath – Bernini succeeded in revealing to the viewers the 'movements of the soul' through the 'movements of the body'.[147] Thus, in contrast to Michelangelo, who had assumed his own biblical persona 'short of physical self-portraiture' by traversing the gap that separated the man from the statue via the medium of the written word ('David with his sling/and I with the bow/Michelangelo'),[148] Bernini's biographers were eager to emphasise that Gian Lorenzo, by not relying on the written message and remaining strictly within the bounds of his art, had achieved as much as Michelangelo, if not more. For by working the figure of *David* 'in his own likeness' with the aid of a mirror, he had infused the sculpture with the movements of his body (literally) and those of his soul (metaphorically).

4

Biographies, Garments, and Bernini's '*Abito . . . grosso, e rozzo*' in Perspective

In the oft-quoted, opening passages of the *Life of Pericles*, Plutarch (46– after 119 AD) succinctly explains his reason for writing biographies while, concomitantly, revealing a basic fact about Greek and Roman societies. Human vision, he states, apprehends all objects that present themselves to the eyes, be these useful or useless. It is up to man's mind to 'pursue what is best, to the end that he may not merely regard it, but also be edified by regarding it'.[1] This same approach, he further elucidates, is to be followed when it comes to deeds, as these instill in 'those who search them out a great and zealous eagerness which leads to imitation'.[2] In fact, elsewhere he specifies that, while he had begun his biographies for the benefit of others, he found himself 'continuing the work and delighting in it now for my own sake also, using history as a mirror and endeavoring in a manner to fashion and adorn my life in conformity with the virtues therein depicted'.[3] In some cases, however, admiration of the deed does not lead to imitation or emulation. Rather, Plutarch argues, there are instances when, 'while we delight in the work, we despise the workman'. To make the point all the more poignant, he focuses the reader's attention on the artistic creations of renowned artists and poets:

> Labour with one's hands on lowly tasks gives witness, in the toil thus expended on useless things, to one's own indifference to higher things. No generous youth, from seeing the Zeus at Pisa, or the Hera at Argos, longs to be Phidias or Polycleitus; nor to be Anacreon or Philetas or Archilochus out of pleasure in their poems. For it does not of necessity follow that, if the work delights you with its grace, the one who wrought it is worthy of your esteem.[4]

Thus, while, on the one hand, Plutarch finds a biography's reason for being in its affinity with moral philosophy – it should incite the reader to ethical, edifying behavior – on the other, he reveals a social bias by making a clear distinction among artists, their work, and the educated readers. For, reflecting the aristocratic mindset of classical cultures that were sustained by a slave economy, the quotation clearly indicates that, for him, to earn one's living or acquire fame through the sweat of one's brow is deemed beneath the status of a free man. Consequently, as much as one might admire the work of renowned artists such as Phidias or Polycleitus, Plutarch reminds his patrician audience they would not want to be one of them.[5] Echoing this very concept Lucian (*c.*120–190 AD) wrote:

> Even if you should become a Phidias or a Polycleitus and should create many marvelous works, everyone would praise your craftsmanship, to be sure, but none of those who saw you, if he were sensible, would pray to be like you; for no matter what you might be, you

would be considered a mechanic, a man who has naught but his hands, a man who lives by his hands.[6]

Actually, although in classical Greece artists were typically thetes – the lowest rung of free men who did not own property – they were seen on a par with slaves as they often worked in a foreign land and earned their bread by performing manual labor.[7] This mindset clearly reflected the hegemonic, land-owning, aristocratic mentality that prized the *otium* of economic inactivity, as opposed to that of the poor who begged in order to survive. As Aristotle phrased it: 'it is noble not to practice any sordid craft, since it is the mark of a free man not to live at another's beck and call'.[8]

This prejudice against banausic, manual activity was also shared by the Romans, as artists in their society were frequently foreigners, freedmen, or slaves.[9] As exemplified by Valerius Maximus at the beginning of the first century AD in a paragraph on how to achieve glory, he not only criticises the aristocratic painter, Fabius Pictor, for engaging in a *sordidum studium* ('a base pursuit') – a scandalous activity for a man of his rank – but also reproached him for having signed his frescoes in the temple of Salus (304–303 BC).[10] Pliny, on his part, in writing of the poet and painter Pacuvius (220–130 BC), nephew of the poet Ennius, stated that the manual work required by the art of painting was not esteemed reputable for persons of station ('non est spectata honestis manibus').[11]

This worldview did not come to an end with the advent of Christianity, as the same economic system was supported by the ecclesiastical aristocracy.[12] Indeed, the very stigma that accompanied manual work in the eyes of the upper classes in the classical world was maintained in medieval, Renaissance, and early modern European societies. Thus, when in fifteenth- and sixteenth-century Italy the *paragone* – the dispute over the superiority of painting or sculpture – was a hotly debated issue, physical or manual exertion was a factor in the equation that painters emphasised at the expense of sculptors. A famous rumination on the subject by Leonardo da Vinci is indicative of this sentiment:

> I find no difference between painting and sculpture other than [to say] the sculptor executes his works with greater physical exertion than the painter, and the painter executes his works with greater mental exertion. Proof of this is that the sculptor accomplishes his work by percussion through the toil of his arms, removing the marble or stone in excess of the figure contained within the block. This labor is very mechanical, often accompanied by much sweat mixed with dust that turns to sludge. [The sculptor's] face is covered with this paste and his body enveloped by marble dust makes him look like a baker. He is covered by minute marble chips, as if shrouded by snowflakes. His abode is soiled, full of specks and marble dust. This is the exact opposite of what happens to a painter, [and I am] talking about master painters and sculptors. This is because the painter comfortably sits in front of his canvas, well dressed, [effortlessly] handling a light brush with beautiful colors, clothed in whatever apparel he pleases. And his home is full of pleasant paintings, clean, often resonating with music or recitations of various, beautiful works which, without the deafening sound of hammers or other noise, are heard with the greatest delight.[13]

In contrast to the sculptor's strenuous, dusty, noisy activity, Leonardo praises the painter's clean, quiet environment and craft. In support of such differences he twice mentions the possibility the painter has of sporting a more decorous apparel: unlike a sculptor, the painter can be 'well dressed' ('ben vestito') and 'clothed in whatever apparel he pleases' ('ornato di vestimenti come a lui piace').

Although Leonardo's comments about a sculptor's dusty studio and garments were observations that anyone paying a visit to a sculptor could make, it is probable that Lapo da Castiglionchio's 1434 translation of Lucian's *The Dream, or Lucian's Career* had its impact on the cultural-artistic climate of Renaissance Italy and influenced, if indirectly, Leonardo's formulation of the above-quoted *paragone* between painters and sculptors.[14] For, in his autobiographical work, Lucian tells of how his programmed career as a sculptor – his grandfather and two uncles were sculptors themselves – was averted in favor of intellectual pursuit by a dream he had. Narrated in the form of an allegory in which two women, personifying Sculpture and Education, vie for his attention, the latter ultimately prevails. However, more pertinent to the topic at hand, in describing their appearance Lucian writes, 'One was like a workman, masculine, with unkempt hair, hands full of callous places, clothing tucked up, and a heavy layer of marble-dust upon her, just as my uncle looked when he cut stone. The other, however, was very fair of face, dignified in her appearance, and nice in her dress.'[15] Nevertheless, Sculpture reminds Lucian that although he might be disgusted by her humble figure and soiled clothing, Greek sculptors had achieved great fame and received homage 'second only to the gods'.[16]

Lady Education, by contrast, points to her own clothing, as 'she was very splendidly dressed',[17] and warns Lucian that 'if you turn your back upon these men [philosophers and orators] . . . you will put on a filthy tunic, assume a servile appearance, and hold bars and gravers and sledges and chisels in your hands, with your back bent over your work; you will be a groundling, with groundling ambitions, altogether humble; you will never lift your head, or conceive a single manly or liberal thought.'[18] And while concerned about the aspect of his statuary, should he opt to follow the illiberal profession of a sculptor, Education warns him that he would be making himself 'a thing of less value than a block of stone'.[19]

It is evident, then, that in antiquity, Renaissance Italy, and, as will be seen, even more so in 'Bernini's World', much emphasis was placed on the artists' sartorial attributes as these contributed to the characteristics that signaled their relative success and liberal pursuits. An indication of the significance these descriptions had in the seventeenth century is provided by Baldinucci's anecdote of how Gian Lorenzo Bernini welcomed Queen Christina in his studio:

> There are many indications of that great esteem which he always engendered. As proof it will suffice to tell of the first time that Her Majesty the Queen of Sweden did him the honor of going to see him at work in his own house. Bernini received her in the heavy rough garment ['Abito . . . grosso, e rozzo'] he was accustomed to wear when working in marble. Since it was what he wore for his art, he considered it to be the worthiest possible garment in which to receive that great lady. This beautiful subtlety was quickly perceived by the Queen's sublime genius. His action not only increased her concept of his spirit, but even led her, as a sign of her esteem for his art, to wish to touch the garment with her own hand.[20]

Besides remarking the unlikelihood of such an epilogue to the visit, as discussed in the previous chapter, to fully appreciate the anecdote one might consider what could have been a more probable behavior on the part of an artist. Such an instance is provided by Admiral George Byng's visit to the studio of the Neapolitan painter Paolo de Matteis (1662–1728). The biographer, Bernardo De Dominici, briefly describes the event as follows: 'And to receive that Lord, he had a housecoat made of golden cloth, with a comparably long cap and golden ribbon. When that [Lord] visited him, he feigned not having been informed of his arrival. And this he did because of his affectation [wishing] to welcome him in such a fashion.'[21] The garment that de Matteis donned on this occasion is probably the very attire he depicted himself wearing in the fragment of a large painting of the *Allegory of the Peace of Rastatt and Utrecht* (*c.*1714) (fig.4.1). Finding the *robe de chambre* and slippers discordant with the elevated subject of a history painting, De Dominici further criticises the

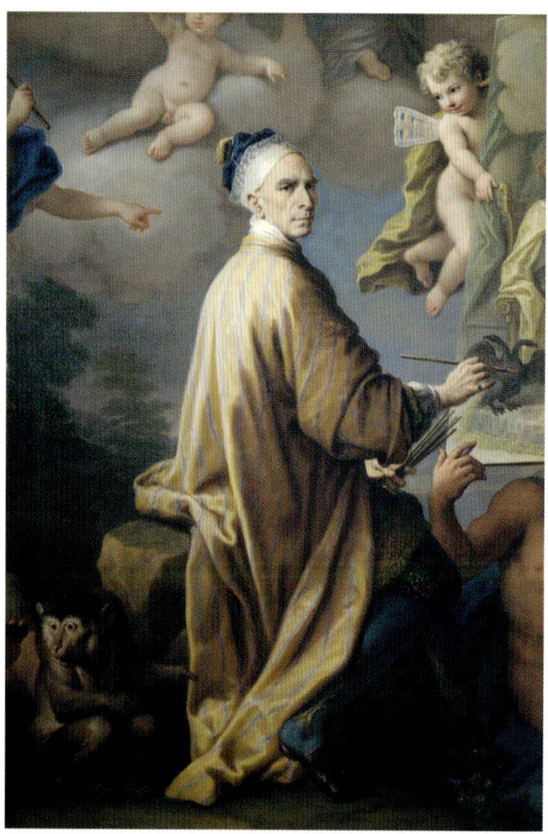

4.1 Paolo de Matteis, fragment with self-portrait, detail of *Allegory of the Peace of Rastatt and Utrecht*, *c.*1714, oil on canvas, 118 × 170 cm (46 7⁄16 × 66 15⁄16 in), Museo di Capodimonte, Naples

painter for this 'base concept'.[22] What the biographer failed to appreciate, however, was de Matteis' avant-garde quotation of the up-to-date sartorial fashion in which French artists, men of letters, scientists, and their ilk dressed in the most sophisticated capital of Europe.[23] Indeed, Paolo's Parisian sojourn from 1702 to 1705 had given him the opportunity to see the portraits of artists such as Charles Le Brun and Pierre Mignard who are depicted flaunting their *à la mode* housecoats (or banyans) and slippers in the intimacy of their studio or home.[24] Regardless of the criticism voiced by people such as De Dominici, and although not all artists were as conceited as de Matteis, given the significance a social call of an important dignitary should have had for Bernini – one is reminded of Alexander the Great's visits to Apelles' studio[25] – the expectation is that the sculptor would have worn more distinguished clothes. Instead, according to his biographer, he surprisingly chose to downplay his appearance by electing to wear mean attire. This chapter investigates how descriptions of artists' vestments were employed in biographies from antiquity to early eighteenth-century Italy and what they tell us about both the artists themselves and the biographers' intentions, since, by being cognisant of this biographical tradition, one may more fully appreciate and grasp what motivated Baldinucci as well as Domenico Bernini to include this anecdote in their biographies of Gian Lorenzo Bernini.

* * *

One of the earliest examples of refined apparel as an indication of the artist's success and, at least in the artist's mind, of a claimed superiority vis-à-vis mere craftsmen is provided by Pliny the Elder's description of Famulus.[26] Commemorated for having primarily decorated Nero's Golden House – so much so that the imperial palace was considered his 'prison' – Pliny underscores two aspects of his activity: the time he spent applying his hand to the brush and the garment he wore while doing so: 'Famulus used to spend only a few hours a day in painting, and also took his work very seriously, as he always wore a toga, even when in the midst of his easels.'[27] Presented as an example of a painter's exceptional pride and earnestness, it would seem that Famulus not only felt too important to devote more than a few hours a day to his art but, more significantly, wore a toga while doing so. Lest one miss the point, it must be remembered that the toga was an impeccably white, woolen garment, the 'formal and official civilian dress of the Roman citizen', that could easily soil if one were to undertake any manual, physical labor.[28] Simply stated, by painting only a few hours a day and flaunting his toga, Famulus stressed his status as a Roman citizen and a free man who claimed a higher consideration than your run-of-the-mill painter or craftsman.[29]

Famulus was not the only artist in antiquity who displayed the high opinion he had of himself 'on his sleeve', so to speak. According to Aelian (*c.*175–235 AD), the Greek painter Parrhasius, besides wearing 'a purple cloak and a golden crown . . . had a stick decorated with gold bands around it and he fastened the straps of his sandals with gold laces'.[30] From Pliny, one further learns that another painter, Zeuxis of Heraclea, became so rich that he exhibited his name 'embroidered in gold lettering on the checked pattern of his robes'.[31] In fact, he became so full of himself that eventually 'he set about giving away his works as presents, saying that it was impossible for them to be sold at any price adequate to their value'.[32]

Since the sources just cited refer to artists who lived many centuries earlier, care must be taken not to assume that the views there expressed applied equally from the fifth century BC to the third century AD.[33] Still, the emphasis that classical authors placed on the apparel of successful painters – but not sculptors, who were truly seen as manual, mechanical craftsmen – was a recurrent leitmotif.[34] When turning to the Middle Ages, however, documents are much more reticent. To my knowledge, no known record from this later period informs us as to whether artists were criticised for being either extravagantly or indecorously dressed according to current societal norms.[35] Although studies pertaining to apparel from the sixth through the twelfth centuries indicate that garments had both cultural and moral overtones, all one may assume about the artists' attire for this epoch is derived from visual records. Accordingly, for the period that spans from the twelfth through the fifteenth centuries, short, practical vestments – such as a tunic often covered by an apron – that allowed freedom of movement, along with a head-covering, were typically worn by craftsmen who practiced a 'mechanical' task.[36] Longer, more sumptuous garments instead, starting from the end of the twelfth century, designate the artist – especially a painter – as a 'scholar' or the *auctor* of the work being executed.[37] Thus, even though the traditional anonymity associated with artists from this period has by now been proven mere 'fiction', and knowing that even in geographic areas where artists were traditionally considered self-effacing there were strong artistic personalities who, along with their signature, included their self-portrait in a work of art, when searching for artists' sartorial features one has to turn to early modern sources.[38] For, just as artists of the fifteenth, sixteenth, and seventeenth centuries found inspiration in classical art, so too did writers and biographers of that same era follow in the footsteps of their Greek and Roman precursors.

* * *

A known feature of Vasari's *Lives* and, consequently, of the writings of later biographers is their reliance on epideictic rhetoric – a form of oratorical argumentation that depends on praise and blame.[39] Through the juxtaposition of the good qualities of one artist with the negative ones of another, these authors informed their readers – and, even more so, artists – as to what constituted proper, edifying behavior. Embedded in this discourse were also hagiographical overtones that exalted the pious conduct of good Christian artists and significantly, but in an ancillary role, the moral and social importance authors ascribed to their vestments. It is with these modern *Lives* that apparel became a fixed feature in the description of artists.

A *locus classicus* of Vasari's 'morality plays', for example, is his description of Giovanni Antonio Bazzi, known as Sodoma. In the biographer's account, besides always surrounding himself with 'boys and beardless youths, whom he loved more than was decent' – thus his sobriquet – Sodoma cared 'for nothing so earnestly as for dressing in pompous fashion, wearing doublets of brocade, cloaks all adorned with cloth of gold, the richest caps, necklaces, and other suchlike fripperies only fit for clowns and charlatans'.[40] Clearly, in Vasari's intentions, Sodoma's expensive, ornate apparel was not just a sign of professional status and economic success. More importantly, his display of extravagant garments was evidence of an effeminate, deviant nature.[41] Vasari's description of Luca Signorelli's fine garments, on the other hand, has totally different implications. According to the biographer, 'he lived splendidly, and took delight in clothing himself well'. Nonetheless, because he 'was a man of the most excellent character, true and loving with his friends, sweet and amiable in his dealings with every man', Signorelli was held 'in the highest veneration'.[42] Therefore, in Vasari's *Lives* the 'handsome vestments' artists wore were not in themselves necessarily good or bad. They simply reflected the perceived or known human qualities of the artist who wore them.[43]

At the other end of the spectrum, Vasari also includes comments about artists who were poorly dressed or unconcerned with their appearance, such as Buonamico di Cristofano – called Buffalmacco – and Vasari's own protégé, Cristofano Gherardi.[44] The former, mentioned by Boccaccio and Franco Sacchetti in their *novelle*,[45] is the protagonist of an anecdote involving the Convent of the Nuns of Faenza whose members judged Buffalmacco's frescoes not by the quality of his work, but by his garments. Seeing him wearing a doublet instead of the mantle and cap fashionable at the time, for he 'was very eccentric and careless both in dress and in manner of life', the nuns complained to the abbess that the artist executing the painting was not the master, but an assistant. Upon learning this, Buffalmacco decided to play a prank on them. By devising a contraption comprising two stools – one upon the other – surmounted by a water-jar with a brush projecting from its spout, and by covering it with a mantle and cap, he fooled the nuns into thinking, as they looked through a screen, that it was the silhouette of the 'master' at work. After they realised they had been duped, Buffalmacco reprimanded the nuns by saying 'it is not always by their clothes that the works of men should be judged'.[46]

A comparable disregard for external looks is found in Vasari's *Life of Cristofano Gherardi*. Described as being totally engrossed in his work, but careless in his person – so much so as to walk out of the house wearing mismatching shoes – in reply to Cosimo I's observation as to why he wore his mantle inside out Cristofano said, 'let your Excellency look at what I paint, and not at my manner of dressing'.[47] Indeed, despising new clothes because he felt constricted by them, Vasari at times reverted to having new garments made for him in secret and removing the old ones from his room, so Cristofano was forced to wear what he found. In response to the ruse Gherardi would complain that 'such fashions . . . kept men bound in chains like slaves'.[48]

As sagaciously indicated by Paul Barolsky, Vasari's anecdotes on the disregard that some artists had for their apparel, besides making for some amusing reading, find their classical source in Diogenes Laertius' and Aristophanes' description of Socrates, whose reputed disregard of outward appearance was an analogue for his physical shortcomings in opposition to his inner virtue.[49] Thus, while in classical sources one primarily hears of painters who display sumptuous garments as a reflection of their success or their self-proclaimed higher social status, by the thirteenth century, Italian authors with a humanist background began also describing artists as individuals who downplayed exterior ostentation in favor of inner uprightness. This extended scope of sartorial possibilities marked a shift that by the sixteenth century led to 'a broader Socratic typology of the artists' in Vasari's *Lives*.[50] The ultimate example of this carelessness for vestments, of course, is Michelangelo who 'in his youth . . . slept in his clothes, [for] being weary with labour and not caring to take them off only to have to put them on again later'.[51] Indeed, Michelangelo was so unconcerned about clothing that, 'In his latter years he wore buskins of dogskin on the legs, next to the skin, constantly for whole months together, so that afterwards, when he sought to take them off, on drawing them off the skin often came away with them.'[52]

Generally speaking, however, Vasari's comments on artists' garments either record how they depicted themselves in their own works or tend to document the way their vestments fall somewhere between the two poles just described. Thus, Agnolo Gaddi is reported as having painted his self-portrait in the Alberti Chapel in Santa Croce 'with a rose-coloured cap on his head according to the use of those times',[53] while Gherardo Starnina's self-portrait shows him 'with a cap wound round the head and wearing a buckled mantle'.[54] Andrea Castagno, we are told, 'lived in honourable style, and since he spent his money freely, particularly on dress and on maintaining a fine household, he left little property when he passed to the other life at the age of seventy-one'.[55] And whereas Giulio Romano was 'very loving, regular in all his actions, and frugal in eating, but fond of dressing and living in honourable fashion',[56] Benvenuto Garofalo, having lost the sight of his right eye and fearful of losing the other, 'having recommended himself to God and made a vow that he would always dress in grey, as he afterwards did, by the grace of God he preserved the sight of the other eye'.[57]

It is in keeping with Vasari's approach that some seventeenth- and early eighteenth-century biographers included sartorial details to round off their account of many artists' lives, as if they were the crowning feature of a person's 'portrait' and character. While this biographical approach is basically absent from Giovanni Baglione's *Le vite de' pittori scultori et architetti* (1642) and seldom relied upon in Carlo Cesare Malvasia's *Felsina pittrice* (1678), one finds abundant examples of it in the *Lives* written by Giovanni Battista Passeri (published in 1772 but begun around 1653–63 and still incomplete when he died in 1679), Giovan Pietro Bellori (1672), and Lione Pascoli (1730–36).[58]

Thus, for example, in Passeri's description of Agostino Tassi one perceives sartorial echoes of Vasari's Sodoma. For, being a braggart who loved to ride about town on horse with sword by his side, he ostentatiously wore pompous, noble garments and a gold chain that were an indication, according to this biographer, of a 'weak mind' ('*debolezza di cervello*').[59] Alessandro Algardi and Francesco Albani, on the other hand, are described as dressing decorously. The former 'always dressed civilly, unpretentiously and discretely', just as the latter did so 'nobly, but with moderation', and, by doing so, both were appreciated by their contemporaries and worthy of respect.[60]

More significant for the impact he had on seventeenth- and early eighteenth-century art was the literary progeny of Giovan Pietro Bellori (fig.4.2). According to him, while Rubens' attractive garments were evidence of his dignified, kind nature ('noble in manners and dress', he wore a gold chain about his neck, and rode about 'like other knights and titled persons'), Guido Reni's modesty, humility, and desire not to appear above his station was revealed by simply dressing in an honorable manner, 'like the gentlemen of his time'.[61] In opposition to these signs of proper clothing, Bellori saw the analogue for Caravaggio's tenebrous, painterly style in his physiognomy ('he was dark, and he had dark eyes and black eyebrows and hair') and his human qualities in his apparel: 'We shall not fail to note the same ways in his attire and way of dressing, for he decked himself in fine cloths and velvets, but then once he had put on a suit of clothes, he never would change it until it was falling off him in rags' (fig.4.3).[62] But while Caravaggio – that is, Michelangelo Merisi – was as careless about his garments as his Renaissance namesake had been, the description of his unkempt apparel was also a signifier of Bellori's ultimate disapproval of the painter's style and indecorous behavior ('He was extremely negligent about washing; and for many years he had his meals on the canvas of a portrait, using it as a tablecloth morning and

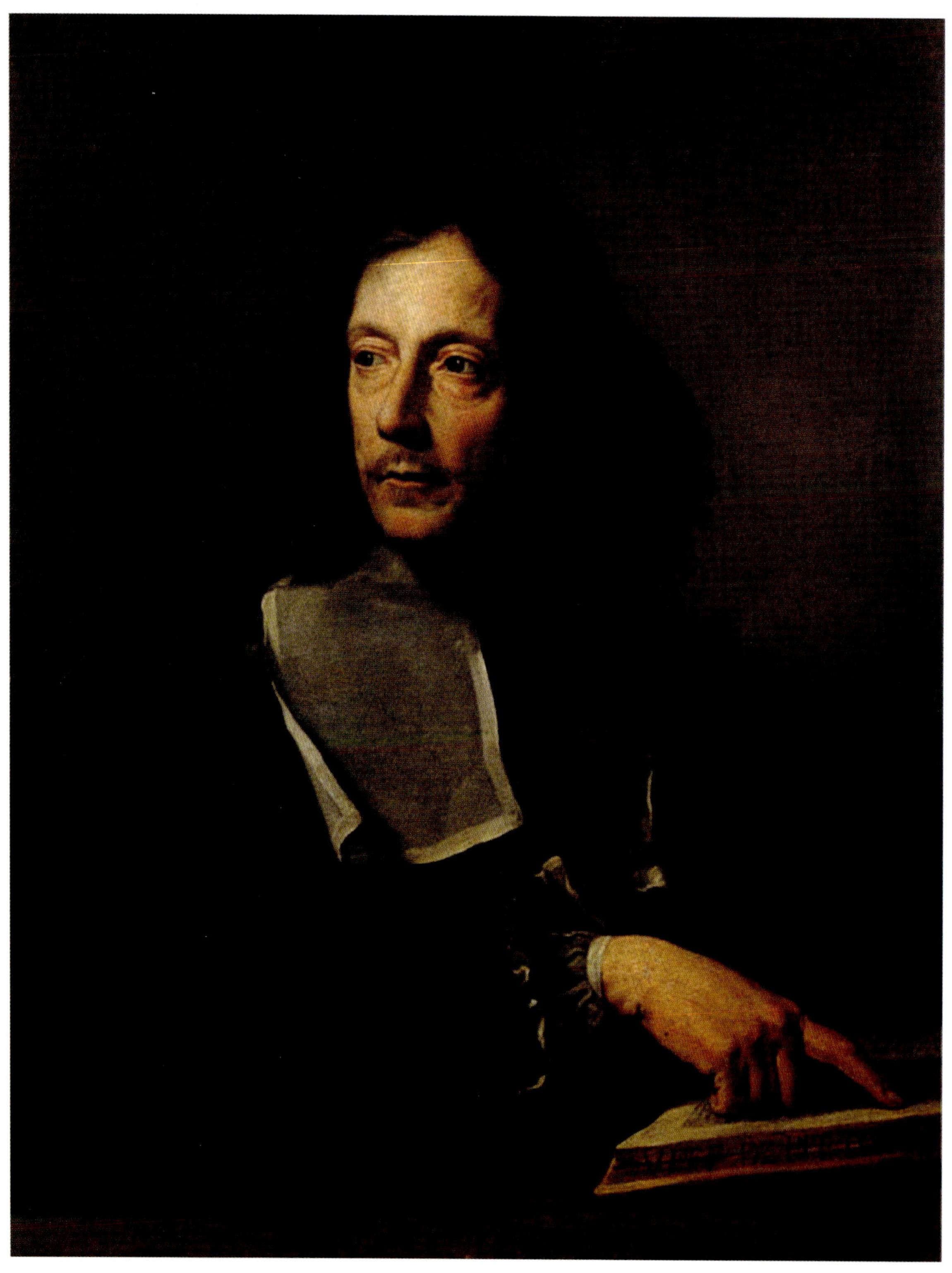

4.2 Carlo Maratta, *Portrait of Pietro Giovanni Bellori*, 1650, oil on canvas, 97 × 72.5 cm (38 3⁄16 × 28 9⁄16 in), private collection

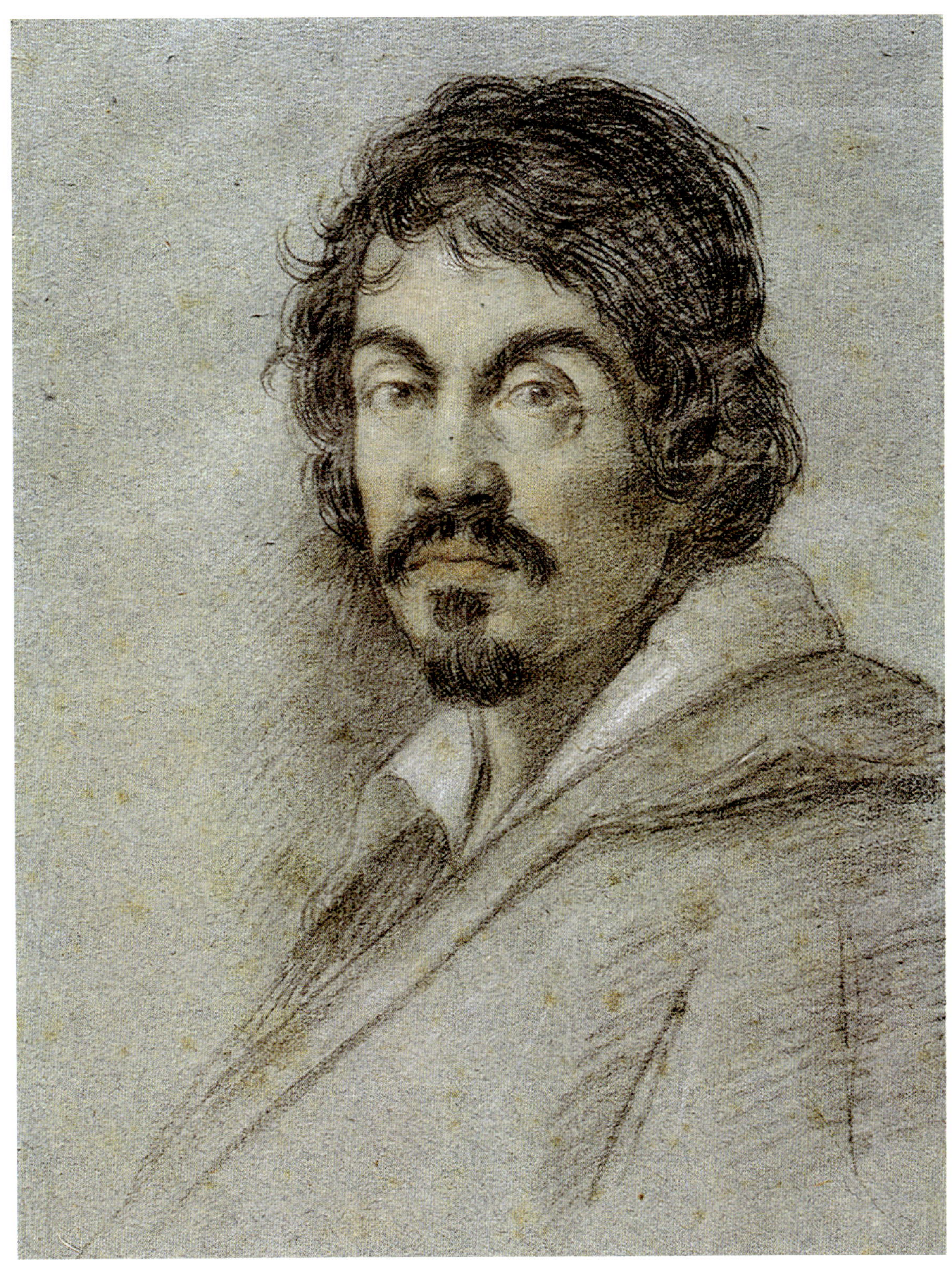

4.3 Ottavio Leoni, *Portrait of Caravaggio*, 1621–5, chalk, 23.4 × 16.3 cm (9 3/16 × 6 7/16 in), Biblioteca Marucelliana, Florence

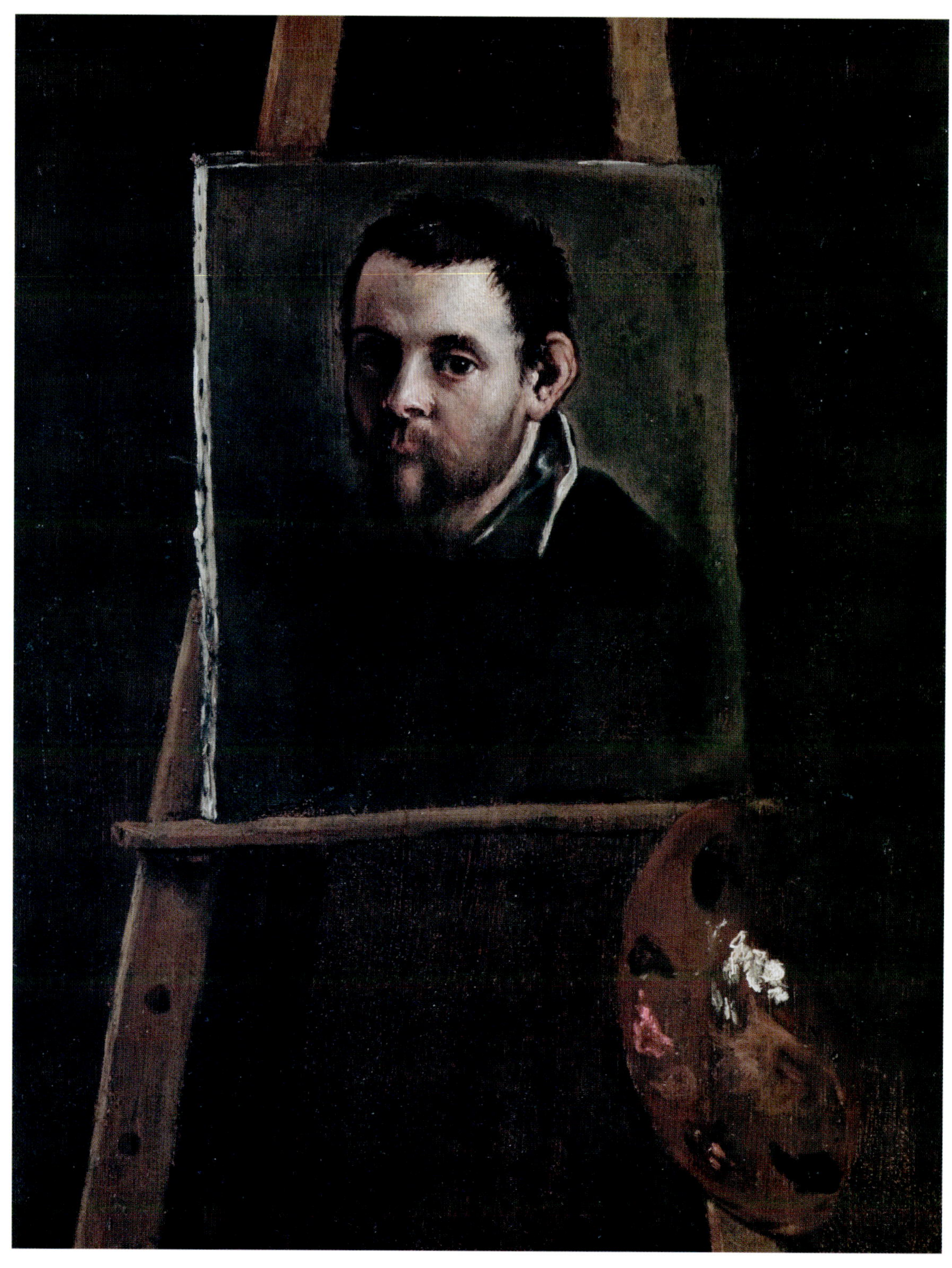

4.4 Annibale Carracci, *Self-portrait with Easel*, detail, 1605, oil on canvas, 42 × 30 cm (16 ⁹⁄₁₆ × 11 ¹³⁄₁₆ in), Vasari Corridor, Uffizi Gallery, Florence

evening').[63] Annibale Carracci's unpretentious apparel, on the other hand, is presented by Bellori as a reflection of 'a certain temperament which is truly that of a philosopher' (fig.4.4).[64] As a matter of fact, his description of the way two members of the same family dressed – Annibale and his older brother Agostino – provides one of the most poignant examples of how sartorial anecdotes in artists' biographies are reliable conduits of an engaging narrative and revealing indicators of the biographers' underlying socio-artistic agendas. In Bellori's case, of course, the fundamental 'program' was that of upholding the supremacy of classical, idealised art. And although well known, it will be fruitful to revisit his account of the Carracci brothers' internecine quarrel since, while both painters were the promoters of a style that reflected Bellori's artistic preferences, the way he describes their differing sartorial inclinations reveals the biographer's view of the artists' social status.

Annibale despised money and ostentation, sought the company of men who were simple and without ambition, stayed away from courtiers and courtly life, and had no appreciation for a social context that judged by appearances and did not esteem him.[65] Rather than wasting his time on superficial social contacts, he passed his days painting and teaching his assistants.[66] Consequently, it is no surprise that he had little patience for his brother Agostino who, instead, was attracted to and frequented courtiers. Annibale, by contrast, was only concerned with his art and 'paid only so much attention to his beard and collar'.[67] And if he encountered Agostino 'among gentlemen in grand attire', he would be embarrassed by his brother's affectation to the point that Bellori records him telling his brother: 'Remember, Agostino, that you are the son of a tailor.'[68] And, to drive the point home, Annibale sent him a visual reminder. According to the biographer, the drawing showed 'their father with his spectacles, threading a needle, with his given name Antonio written above, and

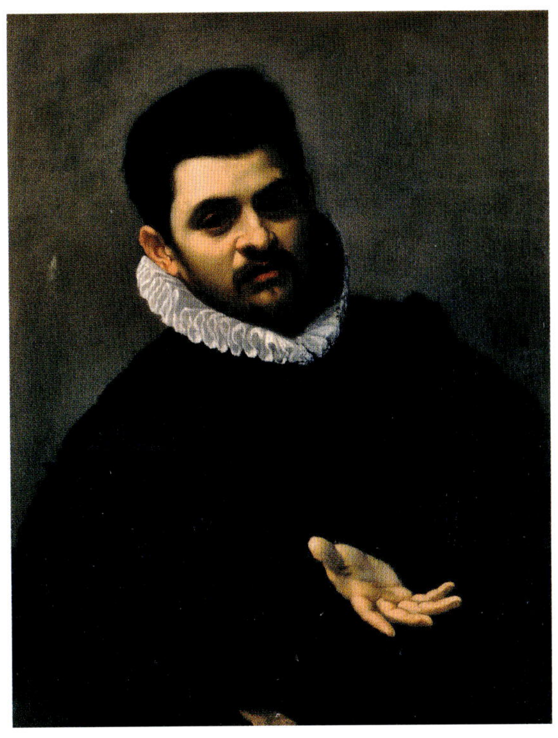

4.5 Agostino Carracci, *Self-portrait*, 1580–90, oil on canvas, 70.8 × 56.2 cm (27⅞ × 22⅛ in), Vasari Corridor, Uffizi Gallery, Florence

beside him their old mother with scissors in her hand'.[69] Apparently, this artistic memento stung Agostino to the core, for he abandoned his brother and the city of Rome.

Juxtaposed to Annibale's slovenly apparel, one also learns from Bellori's biography of Agostino that the latter 'dressed with decorum and his manners were sincere, affable, and kindly with everyone; nevertheless he had a fondness for frequenting the great and the court, and he assumed the ways of the courtiers, in which he differed from his brother' (fig.4.5).[70] To complete the picture, though, one must remember that in Annibale's biography Bellori stated that it was not commendable for artists to frequent the courts and, 'being artistically inadequate

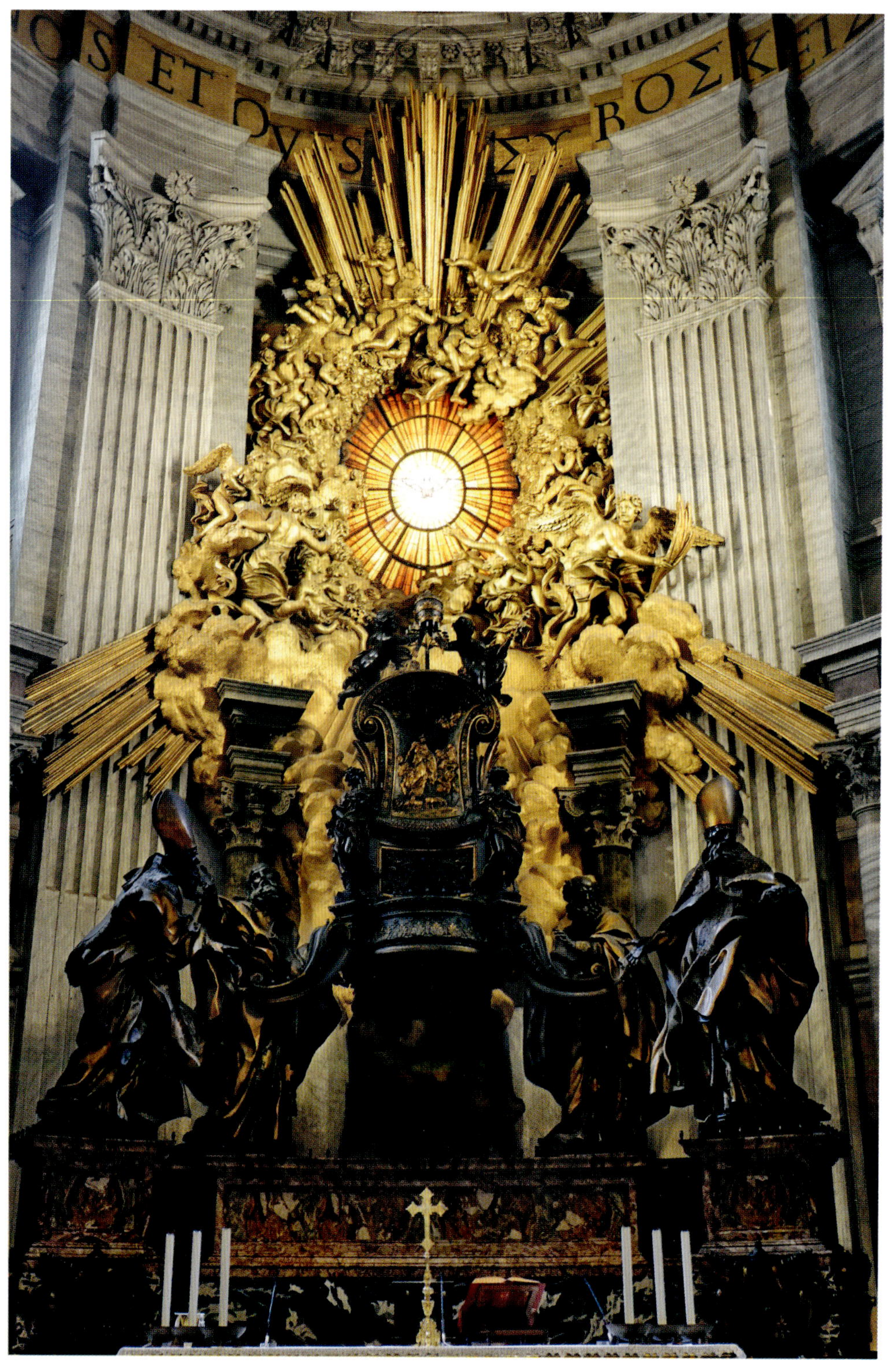

4.6 Gian Lorenzo Bernini, *Cathedra Petri*, 1660–66, gilt bronze, Saint Peter's Basilica, Rome

in art, take advantage of the grace of princes and the acclaim of the crowd, which in the end fades to naught'.[71] Thus, while still holding Agostino in great esteem for his knowledge of the sciences and the arts, and especially for having painted one of the most lauded paintings of the era, *The Last Communion of Saint Jerome*, Bellori indirectly rebukes him for having attempted to rise above his station in life. For this is Bellori's sartorial 'lesson': artists should dress decorously between the two extremes of arrogant ostentation and unpretentious modesty, which, of course, reinforced their acquiescence to societal roles and expectations. As Joseph Connors observed long ago, 'it is status, not style, that is the golden thread running through the *vite*'.[72]

Given these premises, it is understandable why 'the last continuator of Vasari', Lione Pascoli, in conjunction with the description of artists' vestments, most often employed the adverbs *nobilmente* and *civilmente* as these signaled their conformity with the decorous, proper, and, ultimately, conservative attire of the gentlemen they had long aspired to be.[73] Thus, Luigi Scaramuccia 'loved cleanliness to no end and dressed nobly',[74] Francesco Cozza 'dressed civilly, almost always in black, and cared for his linen more than anything else',[75] Giammaria Morandi 'dressed very civilly, and treated himself just as civilly',[76] Filippo Lauri 'dressed very civilly, for the most part in black, and [had] a particular penchant for dealing with the nobility',[77] Giovanni Battista Benaschi 'dressed very civilly, and very civilly treated himself at the table',[78] as did Ludovico Gimignani, Giovanni Odazzi, and Giuseppe Mazzuoli – the latter of whom 'dressed civilly' and, avoiding tight-fitting clothes, would remind others that from the way a person dressed one could 'perceive his inner soul'.[79] Francesco Mochi, finally, stood out not only for his garments, but also for the 'air' about him, for he 'dressed nobly, and complementing the nobility of his attire with that of his looks, would have been taken, by anyone who might not have known him, for an illustrious personage'.[80]

Sartorial details in the *Lives* of artists could also imply a sign of disrespect. Thus, from a late anecdote narrated by Lione Pascoli we learn that, although Bernini and Andrea Sacchi had some disagreement – according to this biographer, Sacchi frequently criticised the work of others – the former invited him to see the *Cathedra Petri* in the apse of Saint Peter's before it was unveiled, so as to solicit his opinion (fig.4.6).[81] When Bernini arrived at Sacchi's house to drive him in his carriage to Saint Peter's, Sacchi supposedly appeared wearing a doublet, cap, and slippers ('in farsetto, in berretta, ed in pianelle'). Despite the probable spurious nature of this anecdote, the meaning of Sacchi's attire on this occasion is evident. Still, Pascoli elaborates his comments, lest the reader miss the point: 'nor had he [Sacchi] any intension of dressing differently, even though he had been alerted [of Bernini's arrival]. This, however, was no coincidence, since he was very forthright, shrewd, and never did anything unintentionally. Nonetheless, even though it was generally interpreted as [a gesture of] contempt, one could never really know what his intension had been since he always refused to say.'[82]

Finally, sartorial details could also be important indicators of the historical, cultural climate of early modern Europe. For even a person's allegiance to either one of the two hegemonic powers, France and Spain, could be deduced from the way one dressed.[83] Hence, while Passeri informs us that Francesco Borromini attracted attention because, not wishing to follow current trends, he always wore old fashioned clothes ('he wore a Spanish-styled ruff'), and Pascoli writes that Borromini 'always dressed in black, almost in the Spanish fashion, but with a peruke and sideburns',[84] the former also alerts us that such a display of national partisanship via clothes could be a dangerous affair. Accordingly, Passeri points out that even after his arrival in Rome, Nicolas Poussin continued to dress *alla francese*. However, following a brush with the papal guards at a time of political friction between the papacy and the French crown, he 'converted' to dressing in the more measured

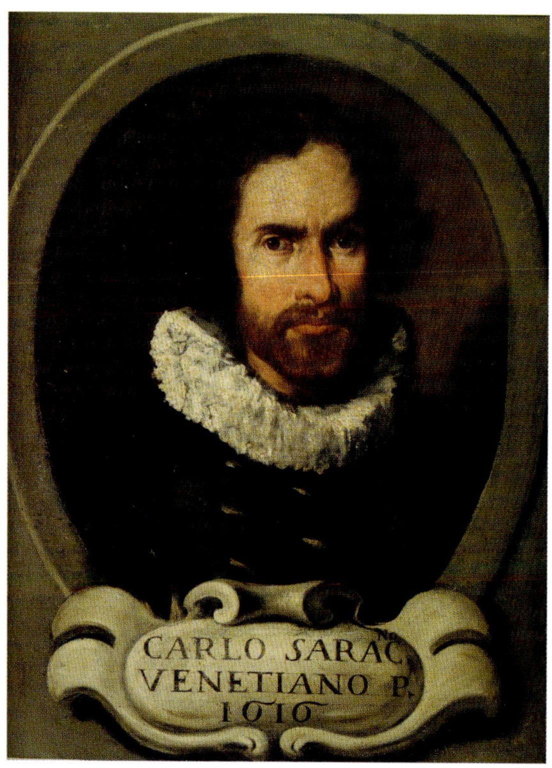

4.7 Carlo Saraceni, *Self-portrait,* 1616, oil on canvas, 63 × 47 cm (24 13⁄16 × 18 ½ in), Accademia di San Luca, Rome

Italian fashion.[85] Thus, in Baroque Rome, artists are occasionally recorded as dressing *alla spagnola* or in the style in vogue north of the Alps, as did the painter Carlo Saraceni who, Baglione claims, 'always dressed in the French fashion, although he had never been to France, nor could utter a word in that language' (fig.4.7). Saraceni, of course, is ridiculed for believing 'that virtue resides in outward appearances',[86] for French attire was seen as flashy, over the top, and associated with narcissism for the way the body related to public space.[87]

Politically divided in their support of either of the two leading European powers, and having succumbed to them even on sartorial matters, some individuals, such as Giovanni Sonta Pagnalmino – a pseudonym for the Benedictine abbot Agostino Lampugnani – tried to uphold a modicum of national pride in fashion or, as it had come to be known by that time, '*Moda*'.[88] He criticised youths for their 'eccentricity' and 'madness' as they were easily overwhelmed by the latest foreign trends. So much so, Pagnalmino believed, that their allegiance to Spain or France had become 'connatural'. Therefore, he scolds them for forgetting they were Italian.[89] In truth, as Rosita Levi Pisetzky points out in her thorough study of Italian fashion through the ages, although Italian style had been influential in the late fifteenth and early sixteenth century, after the first two decades of the Cinquecento, when the peninsula went from being subjugated by the French to the Spanish, foreign influence became felt also in the sphere of vestments.[90] But actually, there are premonitions of Pagnalmino's lamentation already in Baldassare Castiglione's *The Courtier* (1528). Through the persona of Federico Fregoso, Castiglione bemoaned:

> I do not know by what fate it happens that Italy has not, as it was wont to have, a costume that should be recognized as Italian: for although the putting of these new fashions into use may have made the former ones seem very rude, yet the old ones were perhaps a badge of freedom, as the new ones have proved an augury of servitude, which I think it is now very clearly fulfilled . . . So our having changed our Italian garb for that of strangers seems to signify that all those for whose garb we have exchanged our own must come to conquer us: which has been but too true, for there is now left no nation that has not made us its prey: so that little more is left to prey upon, and yet they do not cease preying upon us.[91]

As for Castiglione's sartorial advice to courtiers, he recommended they wear something common and appropriate to their profession, suggested their garments 'tend a little towards the grave and sober rather than the gay', thought 'black is more suitable for garments than any other colour', and, if not black, 'let it at least be somewhat dark'.[92] Already by the sixteenth century, then, Italian fashion had basically given way to a compromise between the two prominent dressing trends of Spain and France – with a definite preference for the sobriety associated with the former – and black had become the advisable color of a gentleman's attire.[93]

* * *

An overview of Roman Baroque portraits reveals that in the seventeenth century the apparel frequently sported by artists, members of the intelligentsia, and the upper class was a black garment with white collar and, when more of the body was depicted, white wrist cuffs.[94] While in the medieval religious context, the contrast between the spotless, inner white garment and the outer black habit of the Dominicans referenced 'the soul to be redeemed from black sin', prevalence of black vestments in lay society evolved in the fifteenth-century in the Burgundian court of Philip the Good where his black garments, and, subsequently, those of his emulating ministers, acquired the meaning of greater 'moral height' or 'moral fortification'.[95] But it was the adoption of this grave color by Philip II in sixteenth-century Spain that was responsible for the propagation of black garments all over Europe, since it implied a 'dignified solemnity'.[96] As John Harvey points out, 'Black became the uniform of officials and men of power throughout Philip's possession – in New Spain as well as Spain, and Naples as well as the Netherlands.'[97]

Portraits of Italian intellectuals and artists, such as those of Giovan Pietro Bellori and Pietro da Cortona (figs 4.2 and 4.8), are indicative of the sartorial trend just described, as are generally those of seventeenth-century gentlemen, like the one drawn by Bernini in 1638 of his young friend, Sisinio Poli (1620–96), or that painted by Giuseppe Passeri of the same man fifty years later[98] (figs 4.9 and 4.10). This, in fact, is also how Bernini depicted himself or was portrayed by others in most paintings and drawings, as in his first self-portrait of about 1623 in the Borghese Gallery (fig.4.11), the Montpellier portrait by one of his followers of about 1630 (fig.4.12), the so-called 'melancholic' self-portrait of about the same date (fig.4.13), the self-portrait as a man in his late thirties in the Uffizi Gallery (fig.4.14), and the impressive, penetrating self-portrait as a man in his early forties, also in the Borghese Gallery (fig.4.15). In all of these works, Gian Lorenzo is shown wearing a small, flat white collar – what the French called *collet plat à l'italienne* – over a black garment.[99] But even in the splendid, late self-portrait drawing of about 1678 at Windsor Castle (fig.4.16), the very presence of the rabat

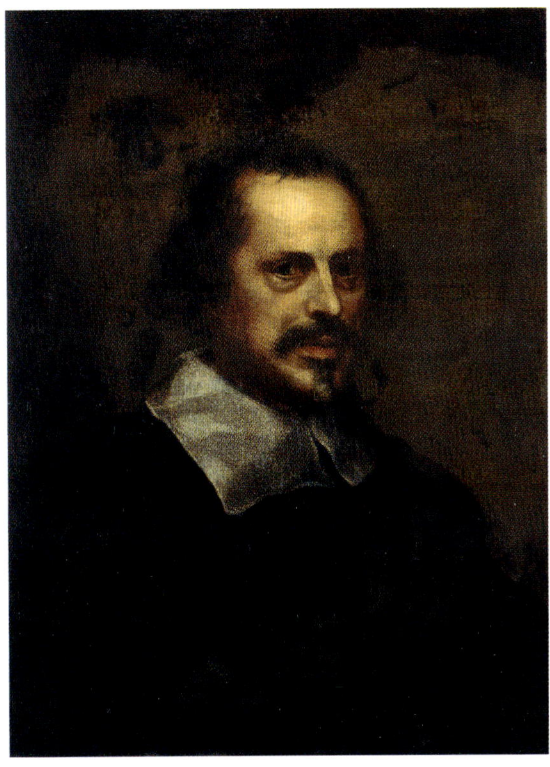

4.8 Pietro da Cortona, *Self-portrait*, oil on canvas, 72 × 58 cm (28 3/8 × 22 13/16 in), Vasari Corridor, Uffizi Gallery, Florence

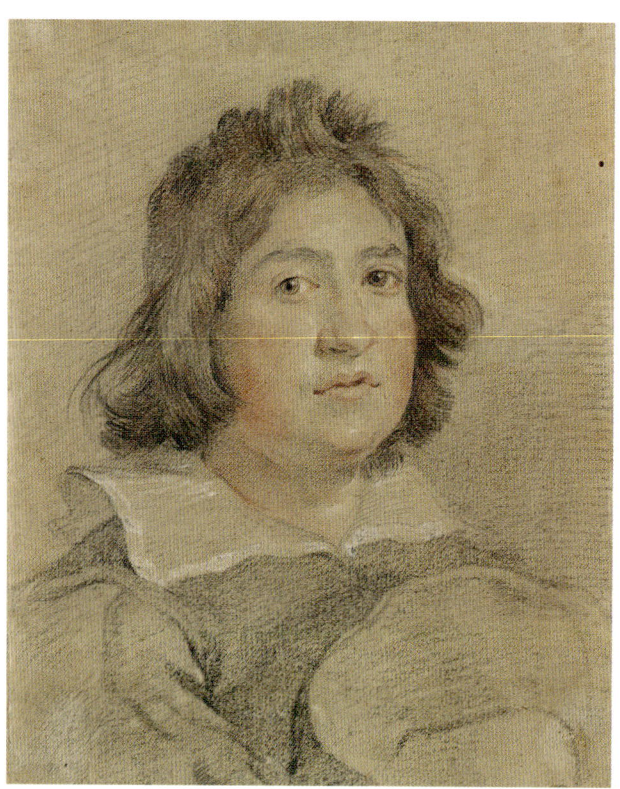

4.9 Gian Lorenzo Bernini, *Portrait of Sisinio Poli*, 1638, black, red and white chalk on light brown laid paper, 27 × 20.7 cm (10⅝ × 8⅛ in), The Morgan Library & Museum, New York. Purchased by Pierpont Morgan (1837–1913) in 1909

4.10 Giuseppe Passeri, *Portrait of Sisinio Poli*, 1688, oil on canvas, 72.8 × 61.5 cm (28 11⁄16 × 24 3⁄16 in), Kunsthalle, Bremen

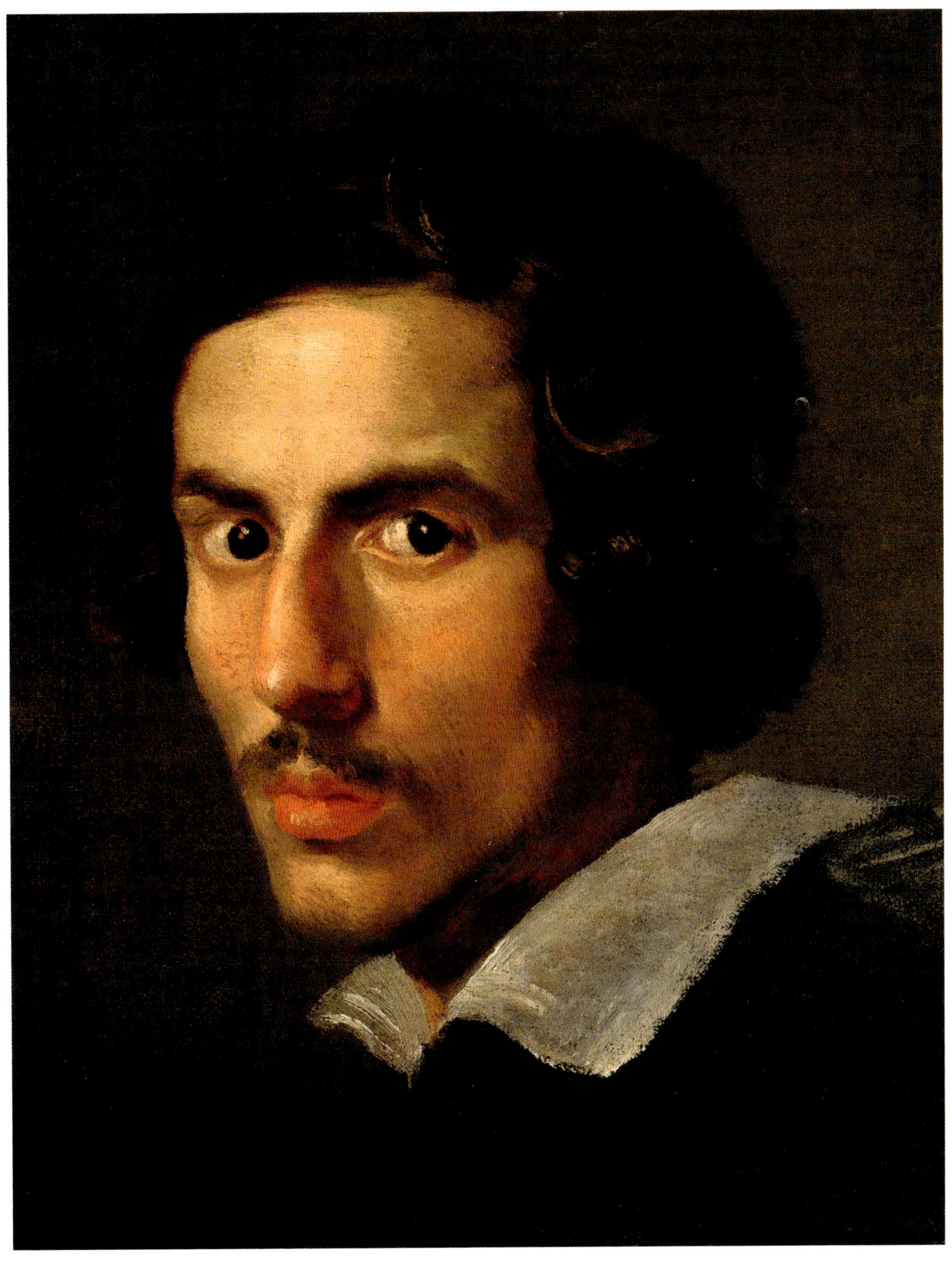

4.11 Gian Lorenzo Bernini, *Self-portrait*, *c.*1623, oil on canvas, 38 × 30 cm (14 15⁄16 × 11 13⁄16 in), Galleria Borghese, Rome

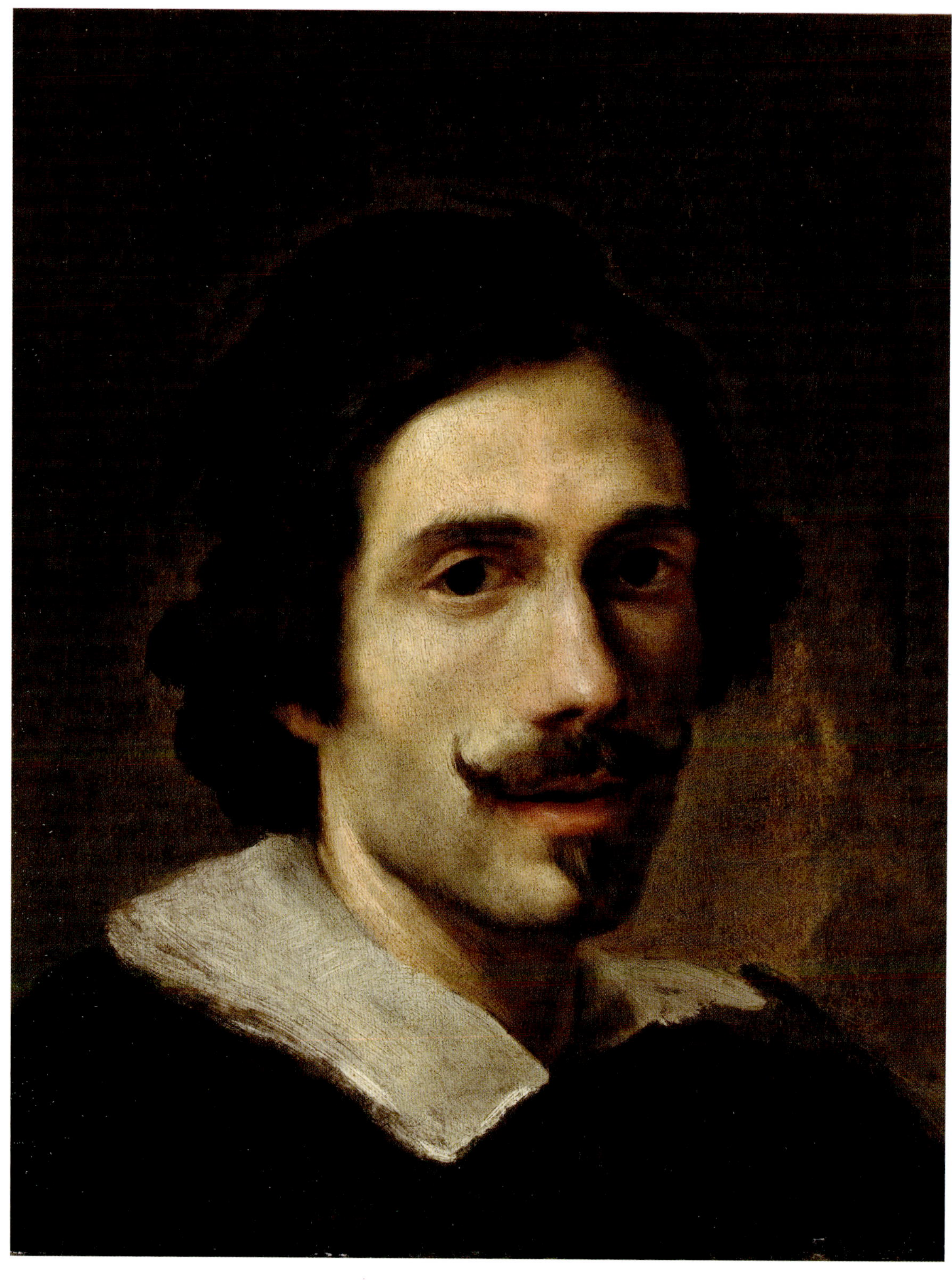

4.12 Gian Lorenzo Bernini, follower of, from a *Self-portrait*, *c.*1630, oil on canvas, 43.5 × 35.2 cm (17⅛ × 13⅞ in), Musée Fabre de Montpellier Méditerranée Métropole, Montpellier

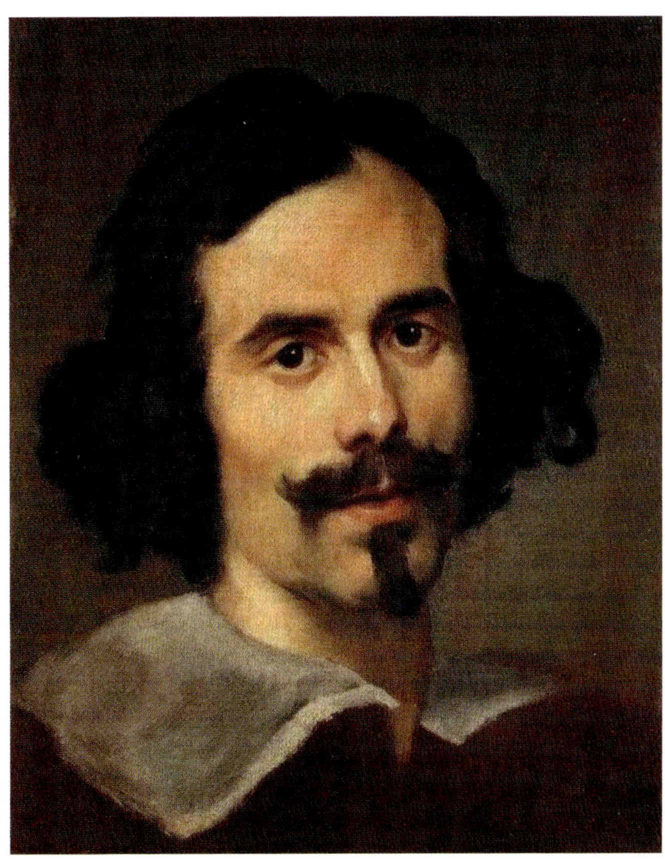

4.13 Gian Lorenzo Bernini, *Self-portrait* ('Melancholic portrait'), *c.*1630, oil on canvas, 43 × 34.2 cm (16 15⁄16 × 13 7⁄16 in), private collection

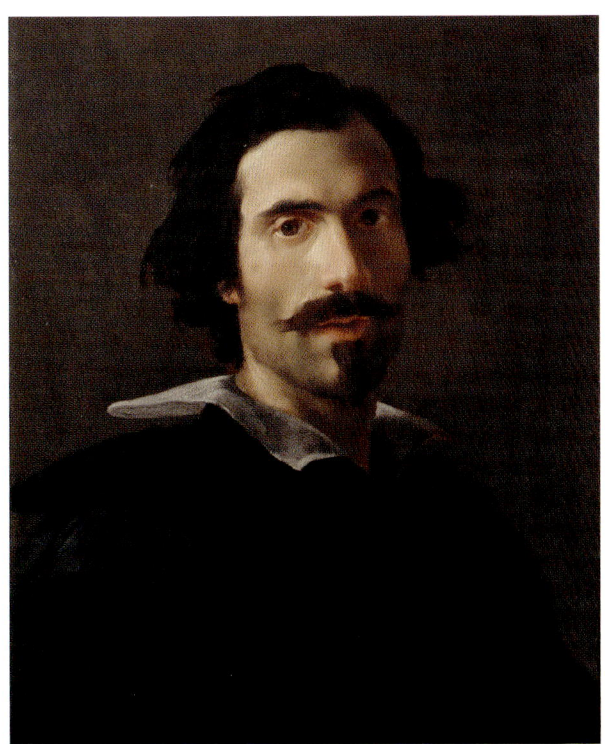

4.14 Gian Lorenzo Bernini, *Self-portrait*, *c.*1636, oil on canvas, 62 × 46 cm (24 7⁄16 × 18 1⁄8 in), Vasari Corridor, Uffizi Gallery, Florence

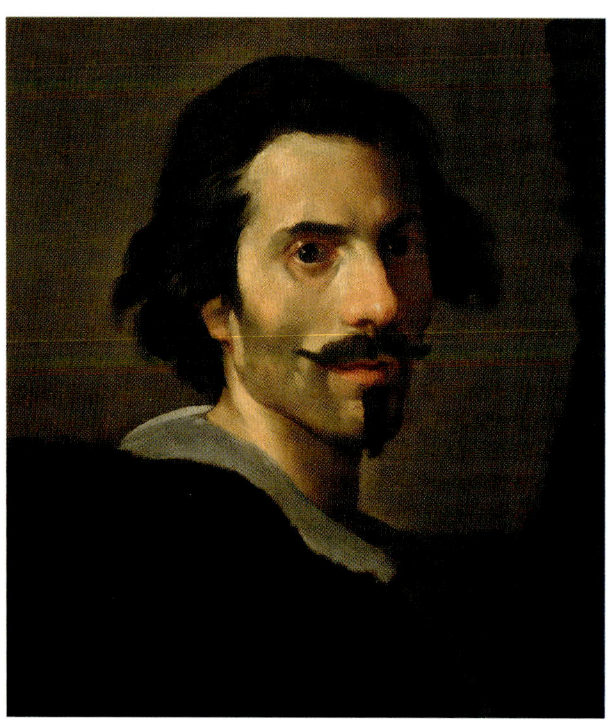

4.15 Gian Lorenzo Bernini, *Self-portrait*, *c.*1638–40, oil on canvas, 53 × 43 cm (20 ⅞ × 16 15⁄16 in), Galleria Borghese, Rome

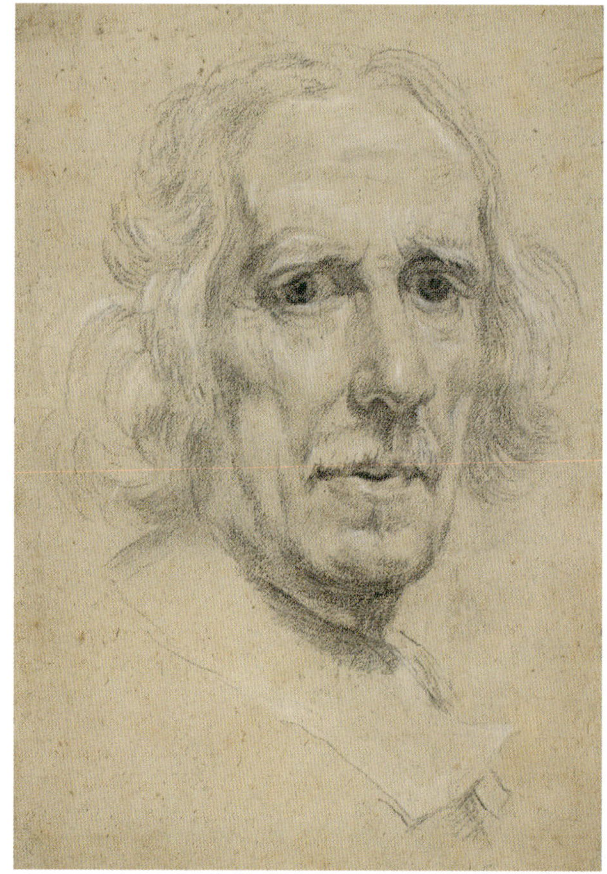

4.16 Gian Lorenzo Bernini, *Self-portrait*, *c.*1678, black and white chalk on buff paper, 41.3 × 27.1 cm (16 ¼ × 10 11⁄16 in), The Royal Collection, Windsor Castle

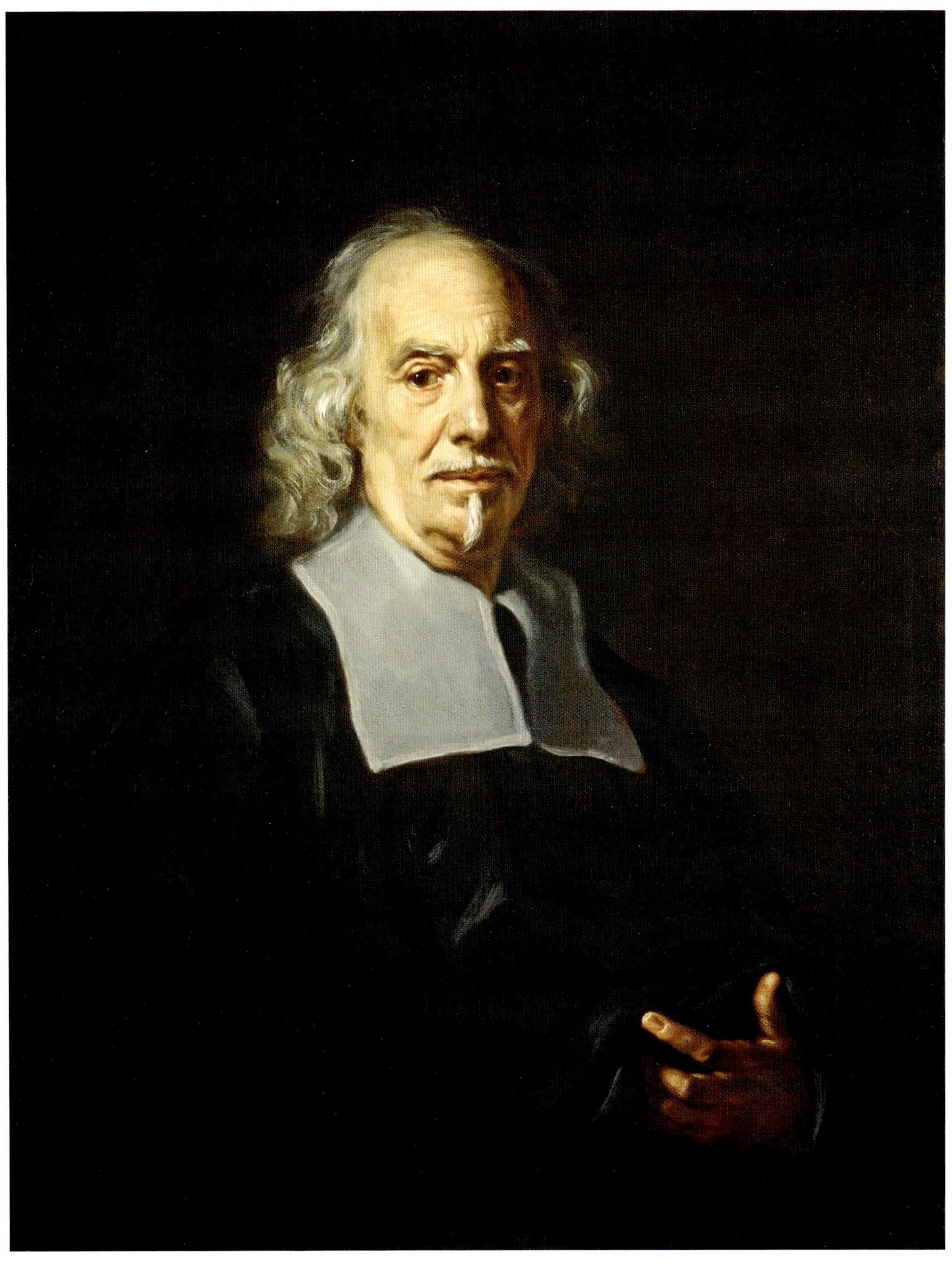

4.17 Giovan Battista Gaulli, *Portrait of Gian Lorenzo Bernini*, *c.*1675, oil on canvas, 99 × 74.5 cm (39 × 29 5/16 in), National Galleries of Scotland. Purchased with the aid of the Art Fund 1998

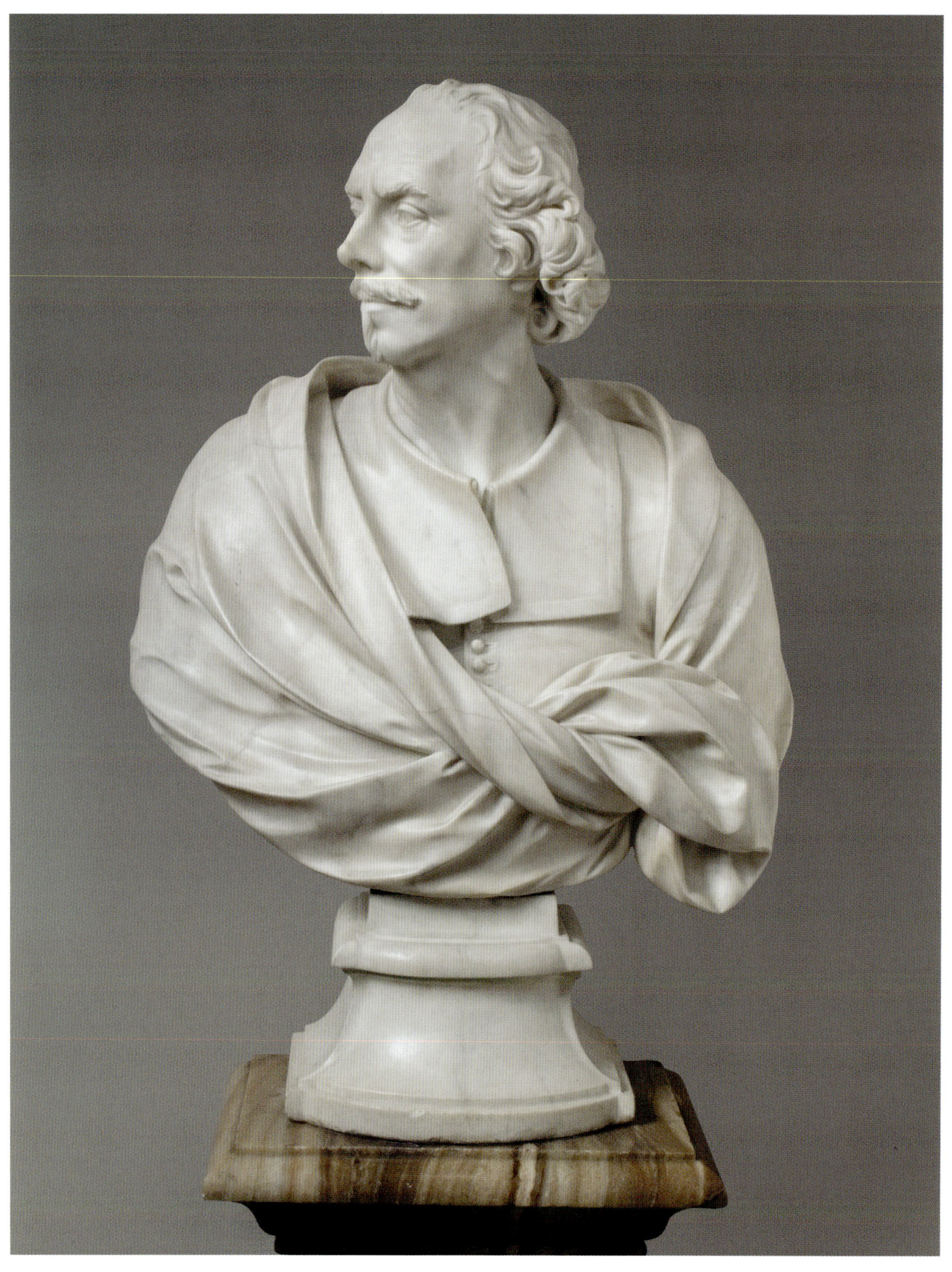

4.18 Bernardo Fioriti, *Bust of Gian Lorenzo Bernini*, *c.*1660, marble, 88.9 × 63.5 × 40.6 cm (35 × 25 × 16 in), Philadelphia Museum of Art. Gift of R. Sturgis and Marion B.F. Ingersoll, 1956

collar signals that in the lower part of the portrait he would have donned the usual black apparel, as he does in Gaulli's portrait now in Edinburgh (fig.4.17), and, paradoxically in this context given the 'color' of the material out of which it is made, beneath the rabat collar in the bust sculpted by Bernardo Fioriti in the Philadelphia Museum of Art (fig.4.18).[100] Furthermore, and quite expectedly, given the ceremonial context of the event represented, in the only full-length representation of the artist – depicted in the act of presenting his project for the reliquary niches in the crossing of Saint Peter's Basilica to Urban VIII – he is shown wearing a formal, elegant black mantle over a white collar that distinguished people of rank from the common folk (fig.4.19).[101] And, finally, in both the commemorative medal of Bernini aged seventy-six executed by François Chéron (1625–98) (fig.4.20) as well as in the engraving by Sébastien Leclerc portraying the personification of Sculpture carving Bernini's own bust (fig.4.21) – an actual marble portrait of Bernini that Cureau de la Chambre claims to have recently received and that either no longer exists or, perhaps more likely, is to be identified with the one by Fioriti – Bernini is shown donning a cloak worthy of a *cavaliere* over the ubiquitous rabat collar.[102] But while some artists, such as Michael Sweerts, could consider representing themselves either in working

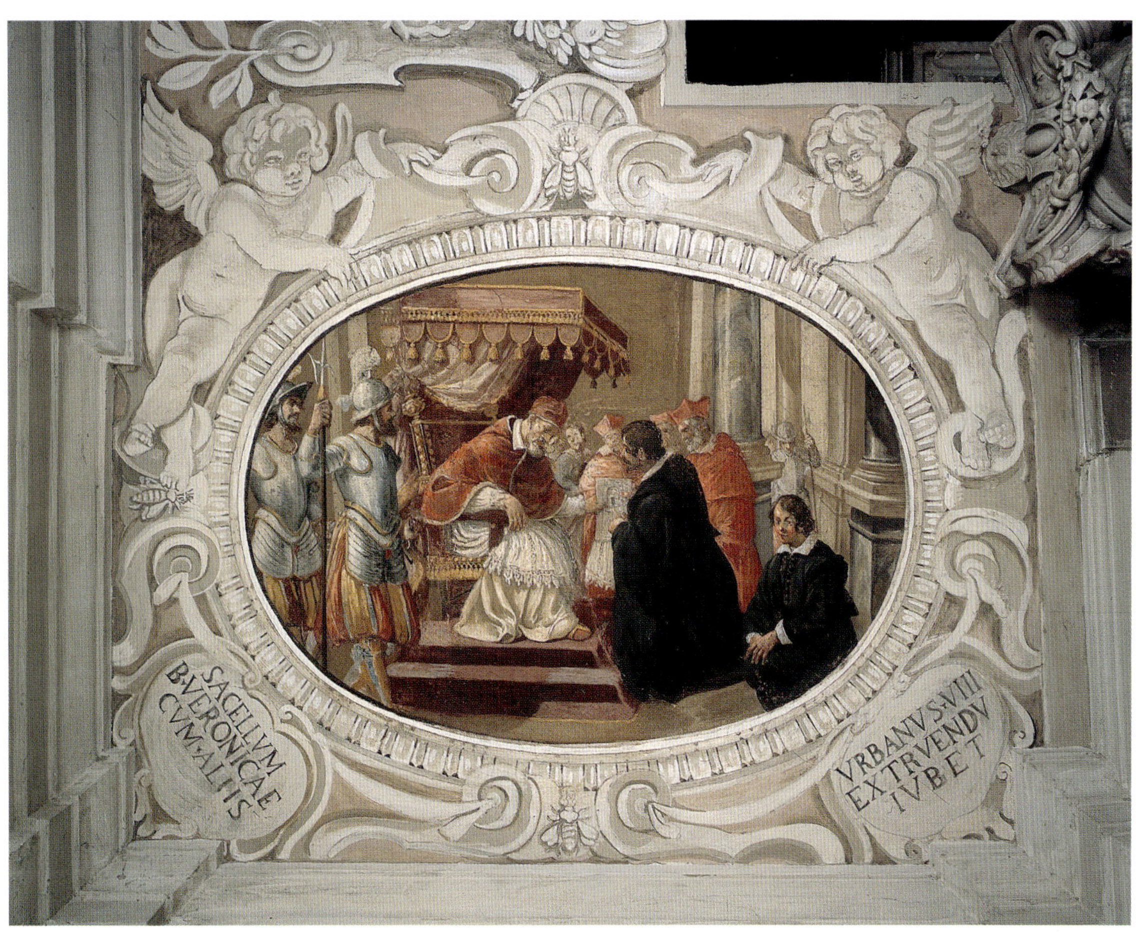

4.19 Guido Ubaldo Abbatini, *Bernini Presenting his Project for the Reliquary Niches in the Crossing of Saint Peter's to Urban VIII*, 1633, fresco, Grotto Chapel of Saint Veronica, Saint Peter's Basilica, Rome

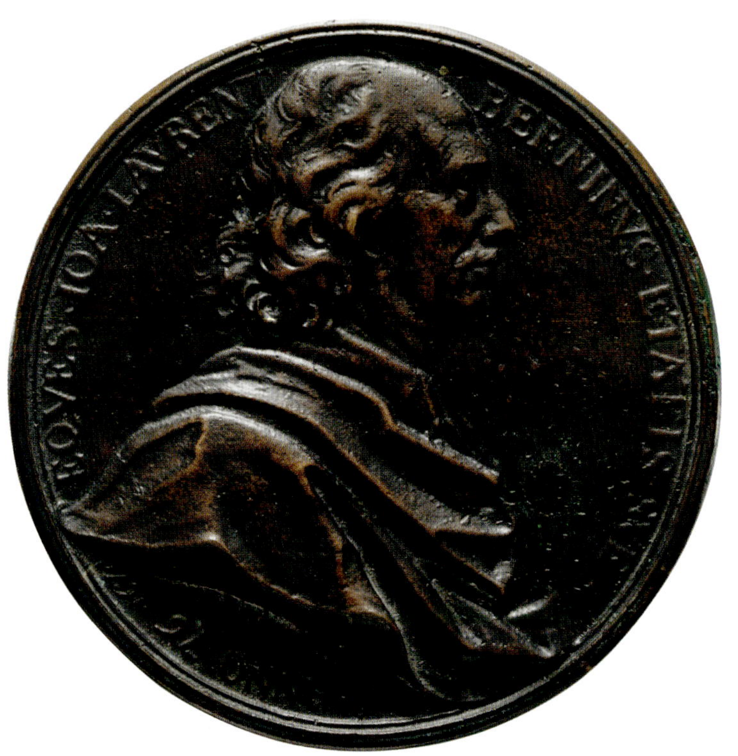

4.20 François Chéron, Gian Lorenzo Bernini's commemorative medal, obverse, 1674, bronze, diameter: 7.3 cm (2 ⅞ in), Metropolitan Museum, New York. Purchased, Gift of Ogden Mills, by exchange, 1987

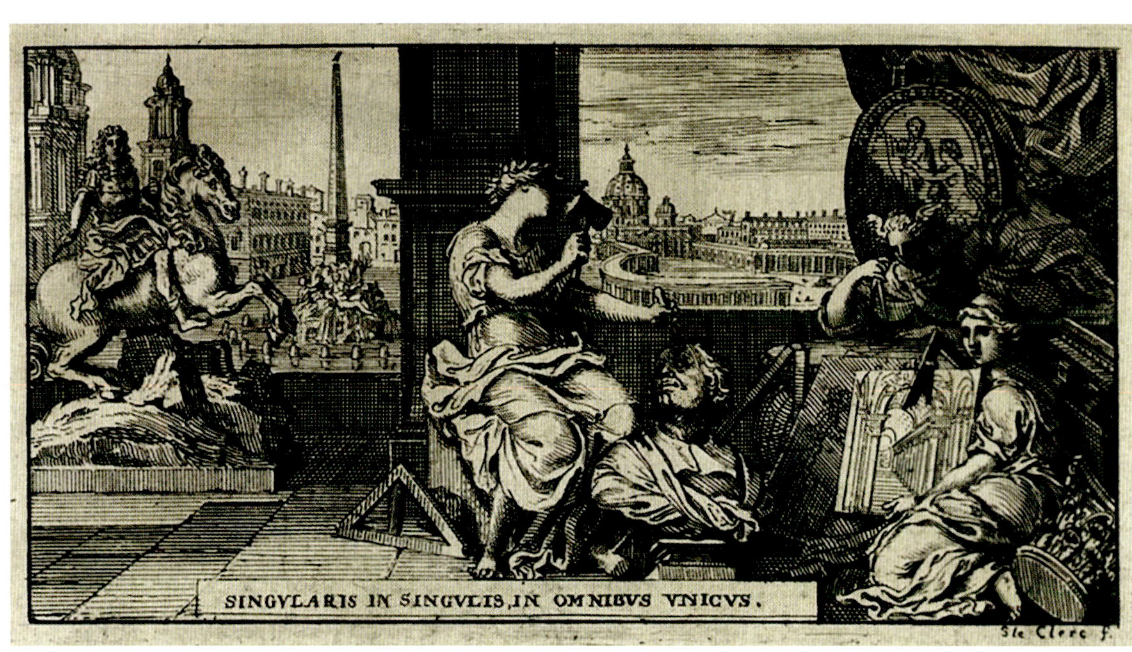

4.21 Cureau de la Chambre, *Eloge du Cavalier Bernin*, 1681, Bibliotheca Hertziana, rare book collection, Rome

4.22 Michael Sweerts, *Self-portrait*, oil on canvas, 35.5 × 30.2 cm (14 × 11 7/8 in), private collection

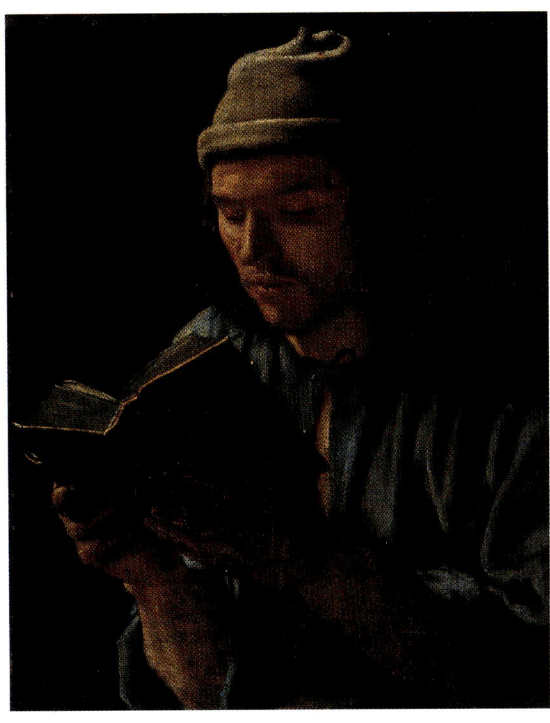

4.23 Michael Sweerts, *Self-portrait*, *c.*1656, oil on canvas, 94.5 × 73.4 cm (37 3/16 × 28 7/8 in), Allen Memorial Art Museum, Oberlin College, Ohio. R.T. Miller Jr. Fund

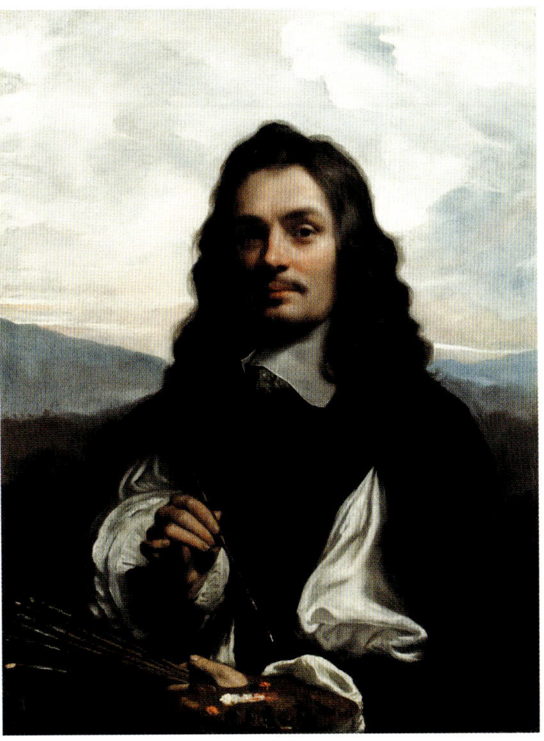

clothes or as a 'man in black' (figs 4.22 and 4.23),[103] Bernini never dropped his guard by portraying himself in the sculptor's garment that, at least until 1630, had defined his artistic identity.[104] To be sure, he was so attentive to garments that he even saw the architectural relationship between the marble pedestals and the bronze Solomonic columns of his *Baldacchino* in such terms, claiming that these corresponded 'to the relationship that obtains between the coarse materials of a man's shoe and the fine silk of his stocking'.[105]

Given the frequency with which early modern biographers refer to sartorial details and the consistency with which images of Bernini depict him in conventional attire, it is surprising that Filippo Baldinucci should not mention Gian Lorenzo being dressed, like other artists, *civilmente* or *nobilmente*. Instead, the only instance in which he describes Bernini's clothing is when Queen Christina visited the artist in his studio. The event is so essential to the mythopoeic nature of his biography that even Domenico Bernini, who also makes no other reference to his father's garments, gives a more elaborate version of the anecdote, as he wished to emphasise the deliberate choice Gian Lorenzo supposedly made on this occasion, even against the advice of others:

> The queen . . . one day, while the Cavaliere was least expecting such an honor, she herself, along with a multitudinous retinue, came to pay him a visit in his

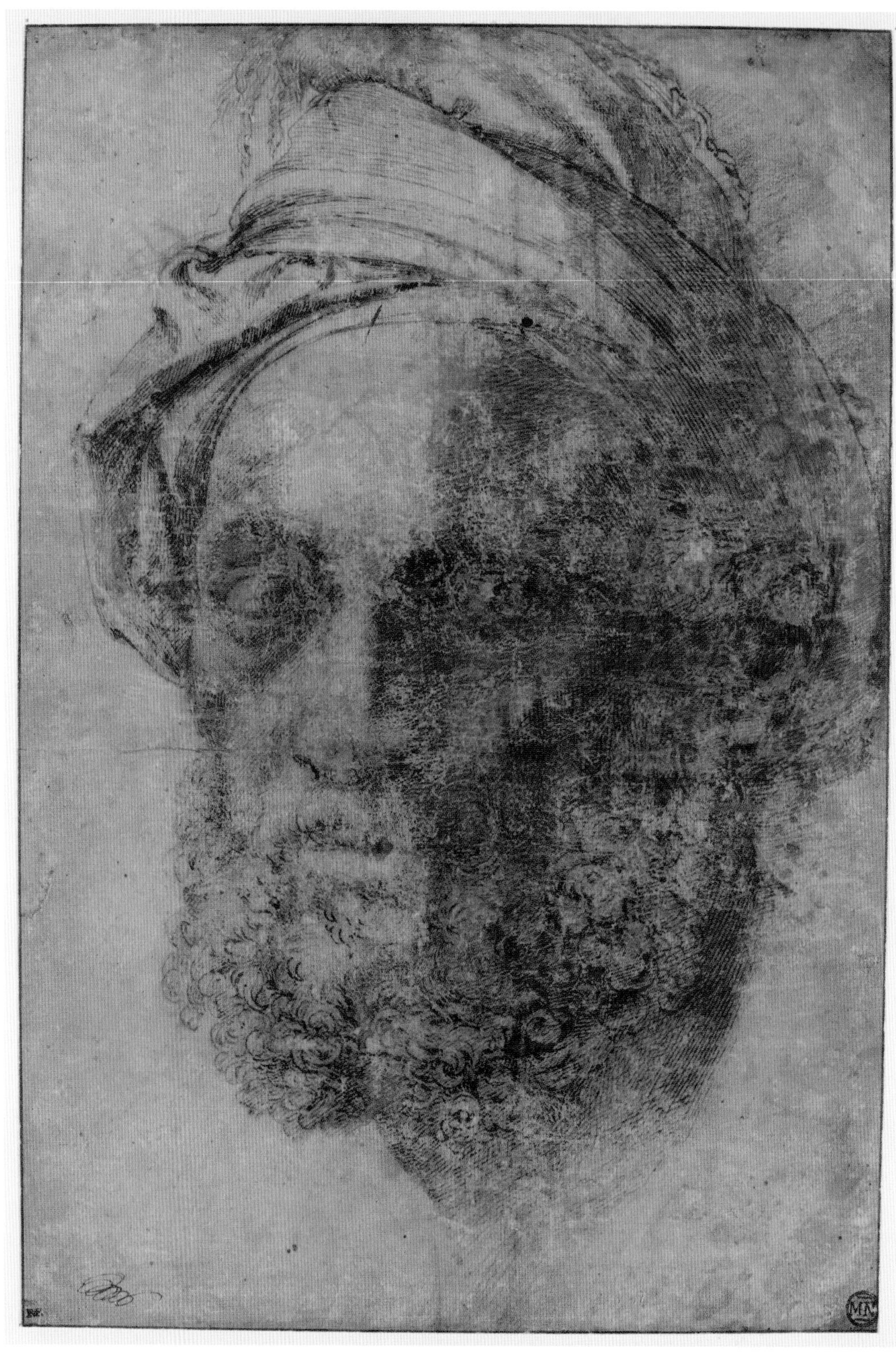

4.24 Anonymous, *Portrait of Michelangelo with Head Covering*, drawing, 36.4 × 24.8 cm (14 5⁄16 × 9 3⁄4 in), Musée de Louvre, Paris

home. Bernini, who was at that moment absorbed in his work, received her, dressed just as he was, wearing the clothes of his profession, even though he had had the time to change into something different. *To those who had advised him to change his clothing*, the artist replied that 'he had no attire more appropriate with which to receive a queen wishing to visit an artist than this coarse, rough garb ['abito . . . grossolano, e rozzo'], which was indeed proper to that talent that had elevated him to the status of artist in the estimation of the world.' The sublime mind of that great lady was able to penetrate the significance of this gesture on Bernini's part and not only did her opinion of him consequently rise all the more, she, as further demonstration of her esteem, actually touched the garment with her own hands.[106] (italics mine)

As discussed in the previous chapter, the anecdotal precedents to this tale lead one to suspect that the epilogue was a mere fabrication to augment the readers' belief in the artist's superhuman talent. Nevertheless, it is not impossible that Bernini chose to upend expectations by wearing a sculptor's smock during an important regal visit. In truth, in at least one instance he did wear his working clothes in front of visitors, but this occurred because the social call was unannounced. In Chantelou's eyewitness report dated 6 September, Bernini called upon his valet 'to bring his working jacket ['*sa casaque*'] and began to give a touch or two to the drapery of Signor Paolo's figure of the *Christ Child*. Then Mme. de La Baume arrived, accompanied by M. D'Albon, which annoyed the Cavaliere very much, but went on working.'[107] It is known that Bernini did not object to having visitors come to his atelier, as recorded in an *avviso* of 19 November 1668, provided he be notified in advance.[108] Plausibly, therefore, the unexpected arrival of these visitors caused Bernini's irritation not because they saw him sculpting, but rather because he was seen in his menial working clothes.[109] But if this is true, then one wonders why during Queen Christina's visit Bernini purportedly made it a point to be seen wearing his 'abito . . . grosso, e rozzo', for this decision referenced 'the harsh work of the chisels', as Father Oliva, Superior General of the Jesuits, would say, rather than the intellectual elucubrations that went into the creation of a work of art.[110] In fact, and quite expectedly, Bernini was so attuned to the social implications of vestiary differences that in his only extant play, *The Impresario*, he has the protagonist's rival producer, Alidoro, be willing to submit to such a sartorial downgrading when, in his attempt to steal Gratiano's stage secrets, he affirms 'Don't judge me by these [fine] clothes . . . I so ardently long to learn something of his art that if necessary I'd don a smock, I'd mix glue, I'd spread plaster, anything whatever!'[111] Thus, one might ask, what ulterior motive lay behind Baldinucci's and Domenico Bernini's decision to include the Queen Christina anecdote in their narratives which, unlike other seventeenth-century biographies, are otherwise void of references to his garments?

Although Leonardo and others before him denigrated the physical exertion expended by sculptors on their creations, it is important to note that by the sixteenth century the personification of *Labor* combined the 'artes meccanicae' and the 'artes liberales'.[112] The one individual who exemplified both of these concepts at the highest level in Cinquecento Italy was, of course, Michelangelo. Unsurprisingly, in a portrait drawing (fig.4.24) and in a painting of the artist aged forty-seven by Giuliano Bugiardini at the Louvre, as well as in another version of the painting in Casa Buonarroti (fig.4.25), he is depicted with a head-covering – a towel wrapped around his head like a turban – that was also a symbol of physical exertion; for towels were used by sculptors to prevent marble dust and chips from settling on their head as the chisel struck the marble block.[113] These depictions of Michelangelo, which are evidence of physical work, are complemented in a number of prints and paintings of the time by other signs of toil.[114] Two

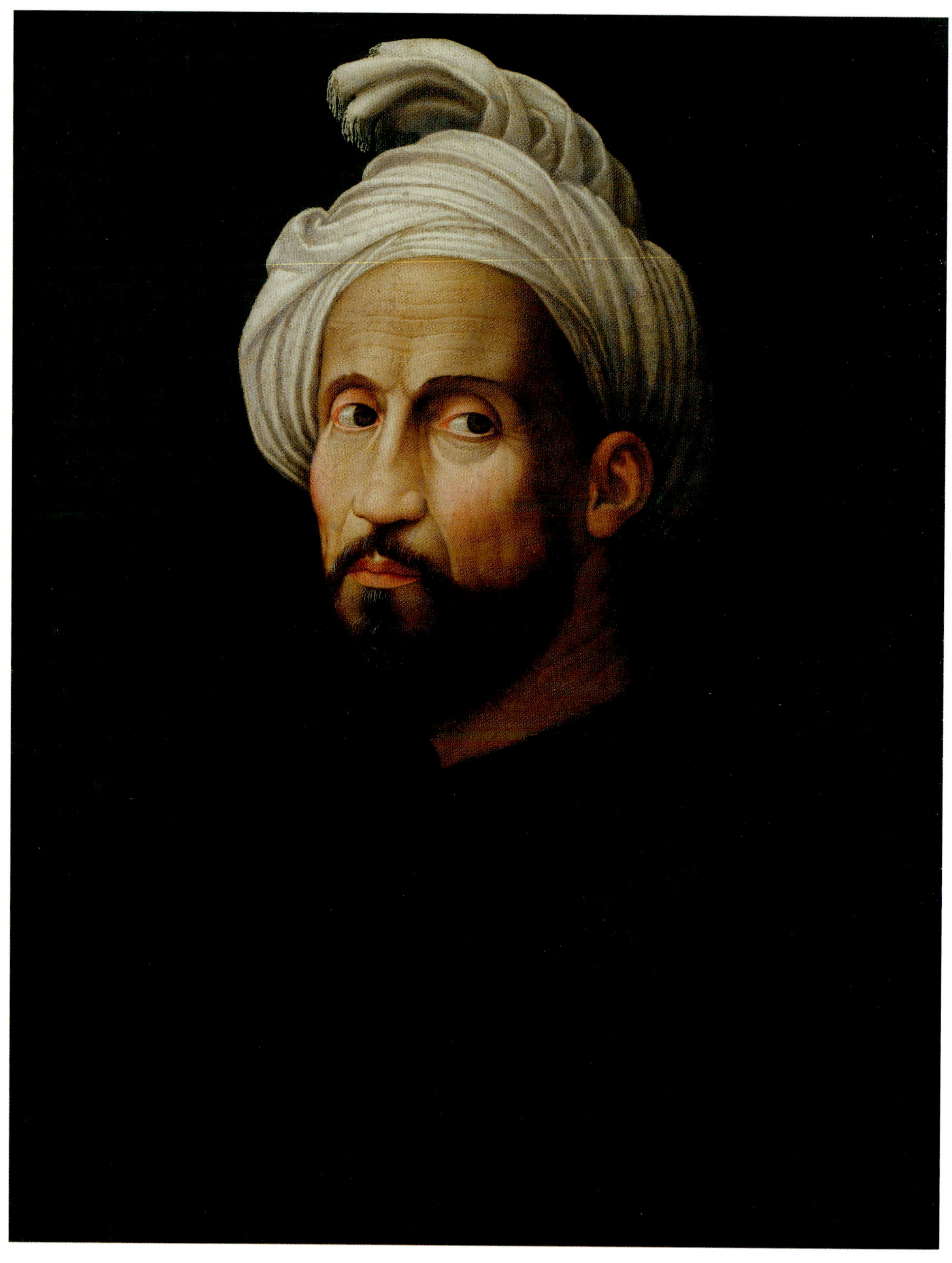

4.25 Giuliano Bugiardini, *Portrait of Michelangelo*, 1522, oil on canvas, 55.3 × 43.5 cm (21¾ × 17⅛ in), Casa Buonarroti, Florence

4.26 Philips Galle, 'Labor', from *Prosopographia, sive virtutum animi, corporis, bonorum et externorum, vitiorum, et affectuum variorum*, *c*.1585–90, engraving, 15.1 × 9.2 cm (5 15⁄16 × 3 5⁄8 in), purchased with the support of the F.G. Waller-Fonds

4.27 Cornelis Cort, engraving after Federico Zuccari's drawing of *The Lament of Painting*, 1579, detail, engraving; two plates on two sheets, 37.3 × 53.7 cm (14 11⁄16 × 21 1⁄8 in), Metropolitan Museum, New York. Charles Z. Offin Fund, 1988

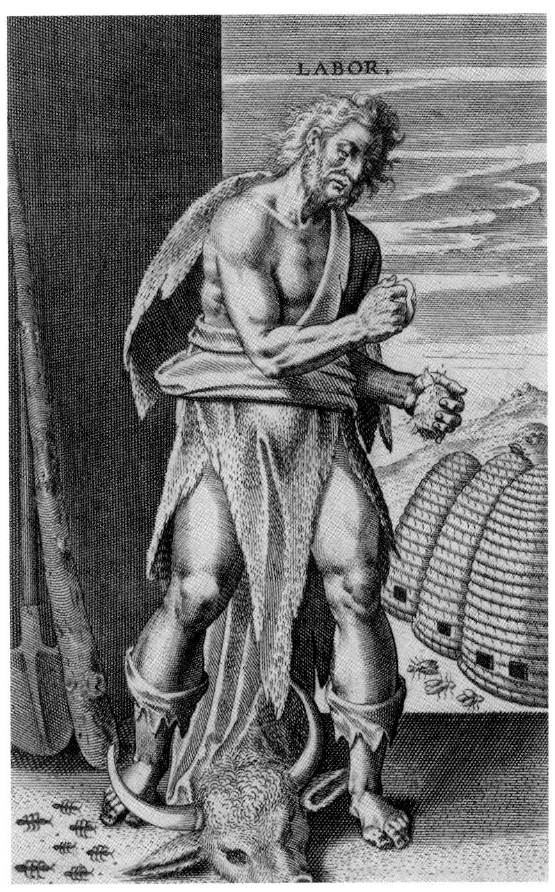

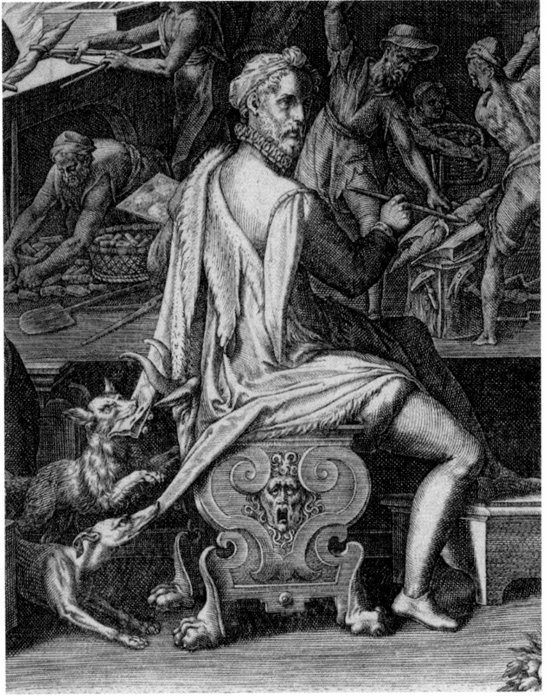

examples of such iconographic details are discernible in Philips Galle's engraving of 'Labor' showing a man with symbols of industry – club, spade, flint, ox-hide, as well as bees and ants[115] (fig.4.26) – and Cornelis Cort's engraving after Federico Zuccari's drawing of *The Lament of Painting* (1579), in which Zuccari dons the ox-hide over his more stately garment (fig.4.27). Even as the theme of *Labor* was less popular in the Baroque period than it had been in the Renaissance, the coarse ox-hide was deemed as the appropriate signifier for sculpture because of the strenuous nature of the ox's activity, as seen in the background of Jan Müller's engraving after Spranger's *Minerva Crowning the Young Artist* (1592), where the personification of sculpture in the background wears the ox-hide, as does the young artist kneeling in front of Minerva (fig.4.28).[116] There is no doubt that the Florentine Baldinucci was aware of Bugiardini's portrait of Michelangelo as he would have seen it hanging in Casa Buonarroti in Florence.[117] Clearly, Bernini's 'abito . . . grosso, e rozzo' is not quite the same as the ox-hide of Renaissance and Baroque allegorical images but symbolically it is its analogue, as it is of Michelangelo's headgear. By including this sartorial detail in his biography, Baldinucci first, and Domenico Bernini later, were surely interested in emphasising Gian Lorenzo's inner virtue while eschewing outward appearances.[118]

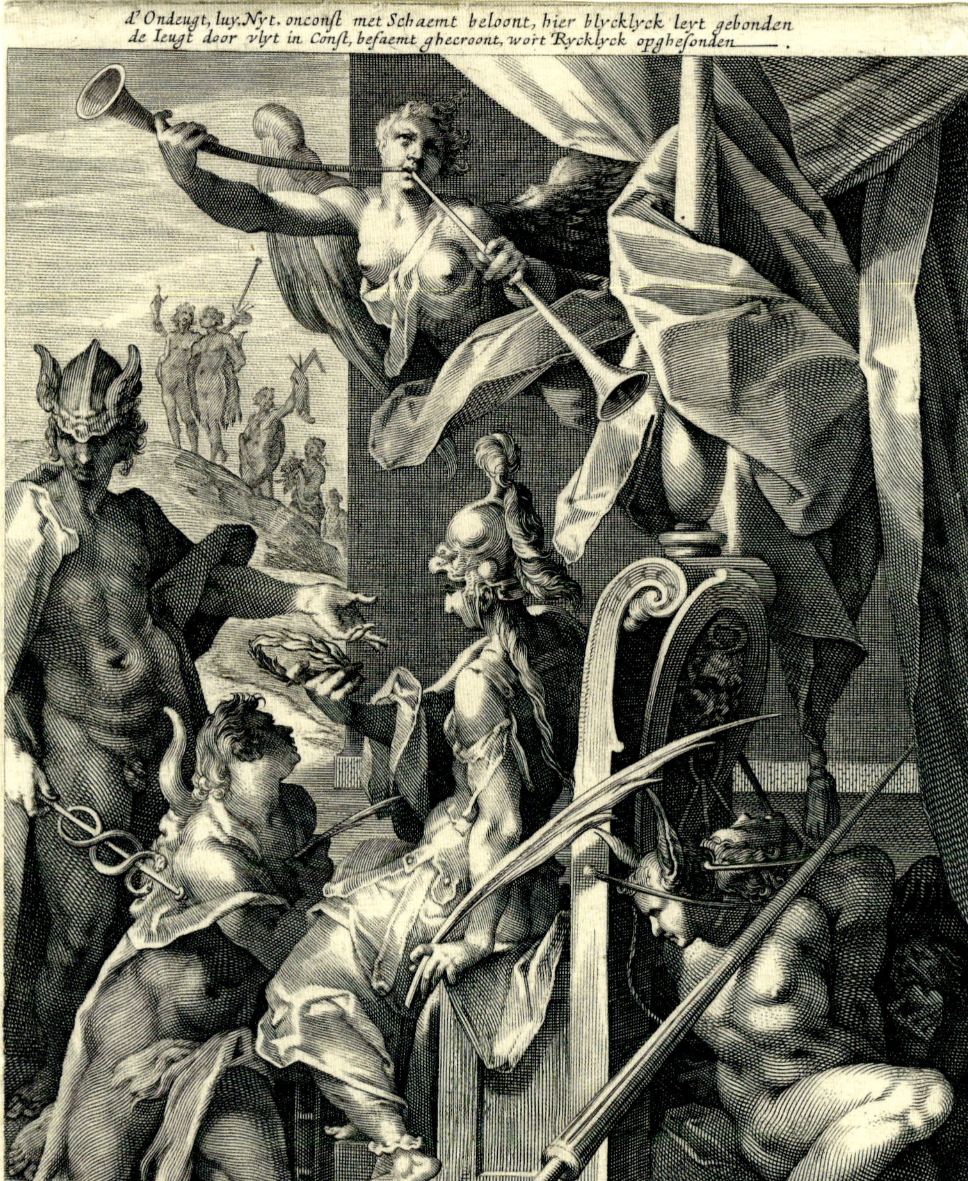

4.28 Jan Müller, from Bartholomeus Spranger, *Minerva Crowning the Young Artist*, 1628, engraving, 25.3 × 17.2 cm (9 15⁄16 × 6 3⁄4 in), The British Museum, London

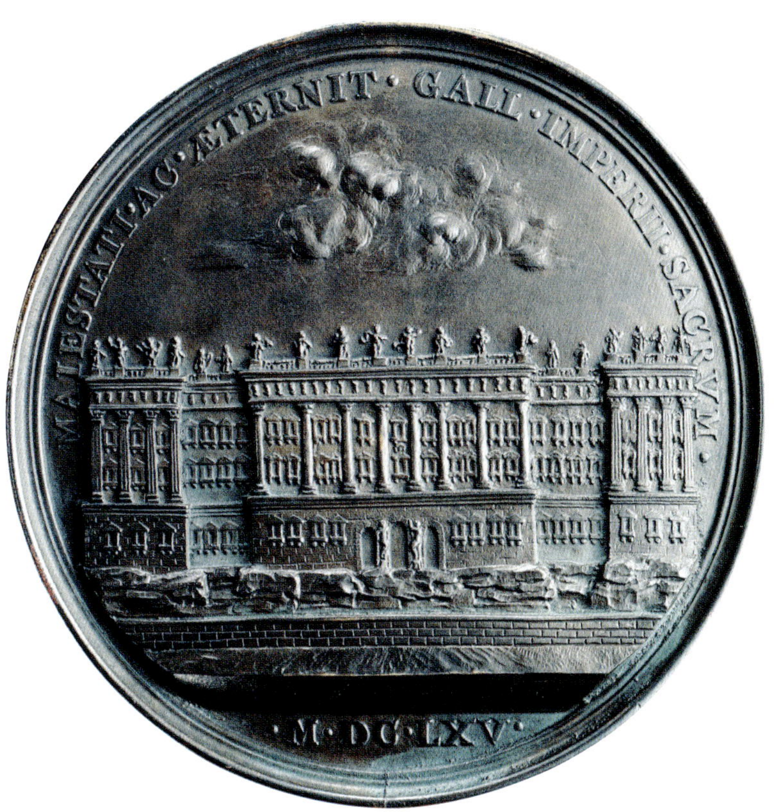

4.29 Jean Warin, the facade of the Louvre as conceived by Bernini, medal of Louis XIV of France, detail of fig.5.1, reverse, 1665, gunmetal, diameter 10.8 cm (4¼ in), The British Museum, London

In an unpublished treatise on the arts that Pirro Ligorio (1514–83) had been planning for a number of years, the Neapolitan artist bemoaned how good artists were being ignored while the stupid and the wily progressed:

> So as to appear as excellent as was Michelangelo Buonarroti they put on a hat and short boots with shoes over them and have bushy eyebrows under the shaggy hat to imitate his knowledge, and if that were in the hat or boots, and as associating with a doctor one learns to go dressed as one without having the knowledge or method to be able to study as they do in order to go about so dressed, they wish to appear doctors or Michelangelos.[119]

Obviously, Ligorio was underscoring the truth that underpins the popular proverb 'the habit does not make the monk'. However, the dictum uttered by Polonius in *Hamlet* – 'the apparel oft proclaims the man' – also conveys a converse reality.[120] Ultimately, this is exactly what Bernini's biographers achieved when they included the 'abito . . . grosso, e rozzo' anecdote in their narrative. For a fundamental feature of Bernini's *Lives* is the consolidation of the claim that Bernini was the new Michelangelo. Repeatedly, the authors underscore this analogy explicitly, as Paul V supposedly stated when he first met Bernini, or implicitly, as various details of his life and work indicate.[121] It is impossible to know if, when Queen Christina called on Bernini in his studio, the sculptor really opted not to change his working clothes. Certainly, he was cognisant of the significance that contemporaries ascribed to the Herculean theme of virtue and labor as the necessary path to overcoming obstacles that lead to greatness, since

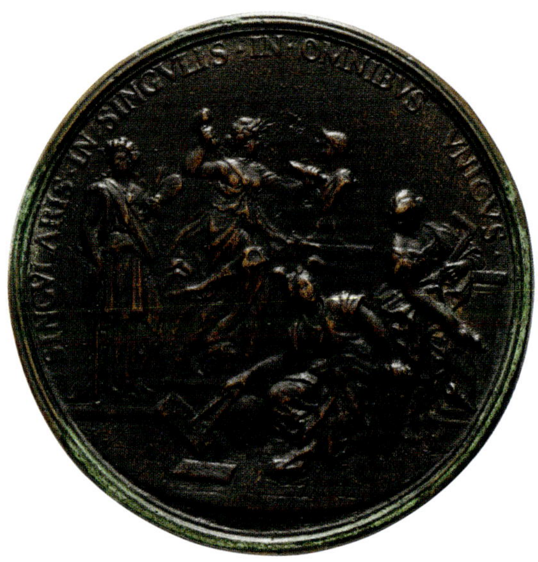

4.30 François Chéron, Gian Lorenzo Bernini's commemorative medal, 1674, reverse of fig.4.20, bronze, 7.3 cm (2 ⅞ in), Metropolitan Museum, New York. Purchased, Gift of Ogden Mills, by exchange, 1987

he himself is reported having commented as much about the two giant statues of Hercules he wished to sculpt on either side of the main entrance to the Louvre (fig.4.29).[122] Indeed, when the Abbé Jacques Carpentier de Marigny went to visit Bernini in Paris while he was working on Louis XIV's bust, the sculptor emphasised the strenuous nature of sculpting. In response to the Abbé's compliments and praise for the ease with which he carved marble, Bernini retorted by quoting Michelangelo who reportedly said: '*Nelle mie opere caco sangue*' ('I shit blood while I work').[123] Clearly, assiduous diligence and labor were considered fundamental to achieve glory and, although not a nobleman by birth, an artist could attain such a social rank not through one's blood, but rather through the sweat of his brow. Therefore, if according to Vasari the elderly Michelangelo claimed that 'the exercise of the hammer kept him healthy in body',[124] Baldinucci informs us that, when not engaged in architectural projects, Bernini 'spent up to seven straight hours without resting when working in marble',[125] and, while not expressing himself as scatologically as Michelangelo had done, Baldinucci asserts that at the end of a working session Bernini, too, would show signs of physical exertion as he 'would be bathed in perspiration and, in his last years, very lowered in spirits. But because of his excellent constitution a little rest would restore him.'[126] Thus, wearing the rough garment that sculptors donned while working was a metaphor of the very theme of *Labor*. But regardless of whether one accepts the truthfulness of the epilogue to this story, what should be obvious to the readers of Filippo Baldinucci's and Domenico Bernini's literary offspring is that the authors included the only sartorial detail in their respective biography of the sculptor to draw an ulterior equivalence between Michelangelo and his Baroque 'reincarnation'.

Biographical accounts of the way artists dressed through the centuries indicate how they had a twofold approach to garments: one which emphasised their outward appearance as a sign of success, and, at the opposite end of the sartorial spectrum, another that, by downplaying exterior looks, focused on interior virtue. Either tactic, consciously or not, was a way of communicating the image the artists had of themselves and to emphasise their individuality and peculiarity. But while Bernini's images of himself and those that other artists have left us of Gian Lorenzo typically record his sartorial, gentlemanly conformism to the 'men in black', by including a single reference to his mean garments, quite conversely, his biographers cared to point out that, even during the noteworthy instance of a royal visit, in his selection of clothes Bernini was unique. For Baldinucci and Domenico Bernini, the sculptor was exactly as the obverse of the above-mentioned Bernini commemorative medal executed by Chéron and the engraving by Sébastien Leclerc claimed: 'Singularis in singulis, in omnibus unicus' ('Alone of his kind in individual things, but unique in everything') (figs 4.30 and 4.21).[127]

5

Pride and Prejudice: Paris–Rome

Rather late in life, on Saturday 25 April 1665, Bernini left Rome on a trip that would get him across the Alps and into Paris by 2 June.[1] Accompanied by his second-born son Paolo, then eighteen years old, his favorite architectural aide, Mattia de' Rossi, and Giulio Cartari (Cartarè), 'his young [assistant] sculptor',[2] and having received an advance payment of 10,000 *scudi* to cover travel expenses,[3] the great artist went to France because he had been invited to contribute to the Sun King's political and cultural solar system by redesigning what was to be 'the most magnificent palace in the world': the Louvre (fig.5.1).[4] Besides the artistic and cultural motivations as to why Louis XIV invited Gian Lorenzo, there was also a significant political factor that contributed to Bernini's decision to make the journey. In the wake of the diplomatic tensions resulting from the 1662 skirmish between the French guards of Ambassador Duke de Créqui and Alexander VII's Corsican militia around Palazzo Farnese over the French claim to

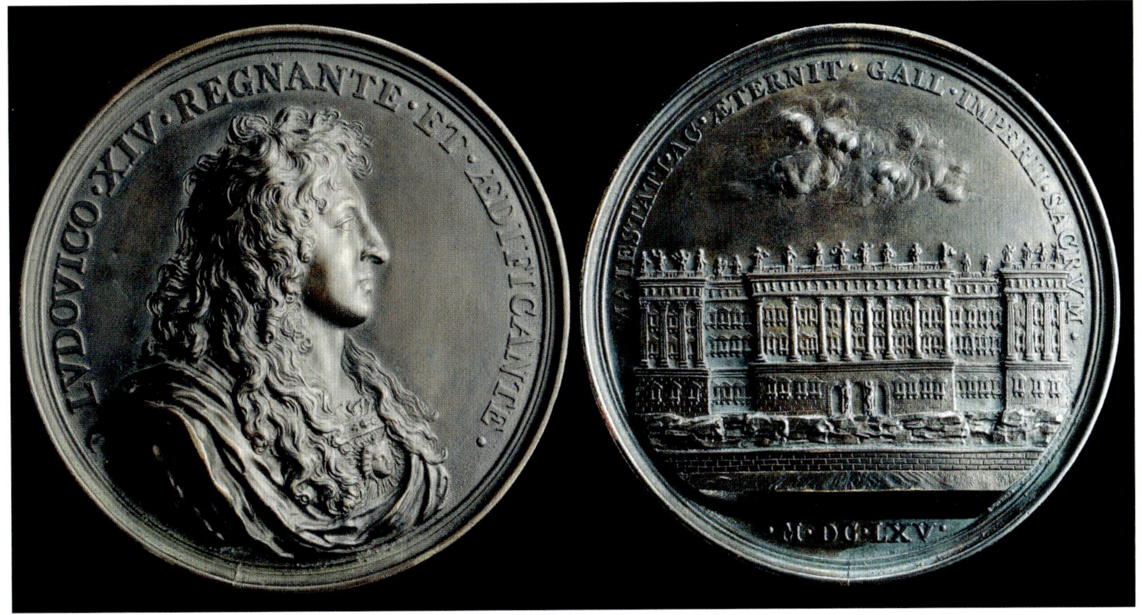

5.1 Jean Warin, cast medal of Louis XIV of France, 1665, gunmetal, diameter 10.8 cm (4.3 ins), The British Museum, London

the 'droit de quartier',[5] as well as the subsequent Peace of Pisa (1664) that limited the power of the Church, the rapport between the pope and the king remained strained.[6] Thus, Alexander VII's approval to lend his architect for three months to Louis XIV was part of a diplomatic effort to assuage the French monarch's anger.[7] Despite Bernini's apprehensions in undertaking such an arduous trip[8] – at the time he was sixty-seven years old and busy overseeing the execution of the *Cathedra Petri* in Saint Peter's Basilica and the colonnade in Saint Peter's Square – he was ultimately persuaded, at least in part, by his good friend Father Gian Paolo Oliva, the General of the Society of Jesus, who told him that 'to submit to such a summons, even at the cost of life itself, was an admirable action'.[9]

Bernini's four-and-a-half-month sojourn in the French capital (2 June – 20 October), despite official proclamations, did not produce the desired results for either the artist or the patron.[10] In retrospect, Bernini being Bernini – the proud artist who was acclaimed 'not only the best sculptor and architect of his century but, to put it simply, the greatest man as well', and who believed as much himself[11] – and the French being French – the proud protagonists of the *grand siècle* who, in the planning phase of the Louvre, asked for Bernini's advice but consistently refrained from taking it[12] – the outcome could have been foreseen.[13] In fact, in a letter dated 25 November 1664 from the Duke de Créqui to the Superintendent of the King's Buildings in Paris, Jean-Baptiste Colbert, the former states: 'However, having seen all of the beautiful buildings that are here [in Rome], I tell you that there are certain features of Italian architecture that could never be adapted to ours.'[14] Certainly, Bernini's inability or unwillingness to refrain from comparing (negatively) Parisian to Roman art and architecture did not help,[15] as did not, according to Bernini, the objections he received about his first project for the Louvre – in another letter from the Duke de Créqui to Colbert, Bernini supposedly complained that they had 'found more faults than it would take stones to build it', and that 'the French architects would not fail to criticize whatever he did, having no interest in executing the project of an Italian'.[16] And, no doubt, the condescending opinions that Bernini supposedly expressed about the king's apartment, as well as other faux pas he made, were not likely to elicit goodwill.[17] But the obstacles to a more positive outcome were primarily the result of two different conceptual approaches to the project. Bernini's concern with creating an architectural analogue for *la grandeur* of Louis XIV – a tectonic 'portrait of the prince's soul'[18] – was bound to clash with Colbert's legitimate concern with functionality as well as with his national pride.[19] In fact, Colbert's extensive, punctilious annotations to Bernini's designs reveal what each of the two protagonists of this saga was up against.[20] Yet, as suggested by the Abbé Elpidio Benedetti, a solution to the impasse could have been that of combining the best of the French and Italian architectural traditions to obtain 'un buon misto'; a compromise typical of a well-established tradition in architectural contests, at least in Italy.[21] But, ultimately, it became 'a tussle between display and amenity', as it has been aptly defined.[22] For, besides what might have been Colbert's genuine worries about practical issues such as 'water closets and conduits',[23] the Superintendent of Buildings would have been better served by an obedient, manual executant of his ideas, rather than by the artistic genius of a man whose flights of fancy addressed architectural challenges with the same allegorical approach as when sculpting the portrait of a monarch, by focusing on ideals such as monarchy, grandeur, and virtue.[24] And although it may not have been his initial intention, Colbert was ultimately more concerned with consecrating *his* glory rather than that of the Italian artist.[25] Of course the barricades obstructing the implementation of Bernini's designs were also the outcome of a pernicious, belittling campaign set in motion by the king's inner circle, among whom were the architects Louis Le Vau (who preceded Bernini in the initial planning of the new Louvre), François

Dorbay, Claude Perrault, as well as the court painter Charles Le Brun, maréchal de Grammont, and, last but not least, Colbert's right-hand man and Claude's brother, Charles Perrault. All of these individuals were in fact, as Bernini had predicted, 'resolved to oppose the foreigner'.[26] Thus, despite the laying of the first stone on 17 October – three days prior to Bernini's return to Rome – his plans for the Louvre were eventually aborted.[27] Consequently, the planning and execution of the new project were assigned to a team of individuals over whom Colbert had complete control.[28] By so doing, no doubt he also trusted he would be asserting the triumph of a national architecture that, in contrast to the Roman Baroque penchant for stunning, striking solutions, allowed the eye to be 'never surprised and always enchanted'.[29]

The changing relationship between the artist and Colbert is well chronicled in Paul Fréart de Chantelou's *Diary of the Cavaliere Bernini's Visit to France*. Begun on 1 June 1665, by 15 July this document already records how the artist's rapport with his French hosts was turning sour. Being used to practically unlimited trust and reverence in papal Rome, the observations and critiques that Bernini received for his designs of the Louvre resonated in the artist's bosom as lèse-majesté. By 18 October, the pot had reached boiling point. After hearing Colbert's additional concerns about his layout for the new Louvre, in a rage Bernini told Chantelou 'that he now wished to leave, that they were making fun of him, that M. Colbert treated him like a small boy; he took up whole meetings with long and useless discussion on privies and water pipes; he wished to show off his knowledge and he understood nothing at all; he was a real *couillon*'.[30] From the available documentation it is clear that both parties were at fault and victims of their respective pride and prejudice. As Carlo Vigarani – chargé d'affaires to Duke Francesco II d'Este and responsible for festivities at the French court[31] – reported on 19 June, two weeks after Bernini's arrival, the great artist had not been well advised:

> I greatly fear that the many honors received when he first arrived did not prevent him from making brash statements on the imposing structure of the Louvre that were disadvantageous to him. By so doing he paved the way for malicious [enemies] to negatively influence the King since from the day of his arrival he stated that it was necessary to knock down all of the [old] Louvre if they wished to create anything good. This, added to many other critical comments which reached His Majesty's ear, did not serve him well. And if he later changed his way of talking, it is believed that it was due to M. Colbert's advice. But this did not prevent him from spoiling matters for himself. He needed good counsel upon arrival, which he did not receive. And all that I state is true, because I know what His Majesty said in Versailles in front of fifty great Lords after having honored me by asking if I had seen him. The discussion ended by my being told that he did not want Bernini present at the festivities [being organised] at Versailles since, in the half an hour he had met and spoken with him, he could tell that he was a prejudiced man bent on not finding anything that was well executed in France.[32]

Although Bernini's undiplomatic personality contributed to the final decision to not carry out his design for the Louvre, the outcome of his ultimate failure in Paris showed that the French could do without the aid of the Italians in their rise to artistic supremacy in Europe, even in a field in which Italy had been the uncontested leader.[33] The shift in the artistic 'balance of power' since the time of Francis I could not be starker, and the contribution that Italian artists such as Rosso, Primaticcio, and Nicolò dell'Abate had made to the transformation of French art from 'hybrid and provincial' to experimental in the latest Mannerist principles was certainly something of the past.[34]

Bernini's negative incident in France is not an isolated case. At least three other Italian artists had similar experiences: the Neapolitan Paolo de Matteis (1702–5), the Venetian Giovanni Antonio Pellegrini

(1721), and the Roman Gregorio Guglielmi (1770).[35] All these artists felt the resistance, if not the hostility, of French artists who, buttressed by a heavy dose of chauvinism, believed they were being unjustly penalised by those patrons who commissioned works from foreign artists, since they were convinced these could be executed equally well by local artists.[36] But what these examples underscore are two interwoven leitmotifs also present in the competitive artistic context of early modern Rome: the tensions that arose when important commissions were assigned to non-Italian artists, and Paris' usurpation of Rome's role as the leading cultural and artistic center. This chapter will consider whether, contrary to what occurred in Paris, foreign artists fared any better in Rome and investigate what might have been the artistic and social conditions that made the interaction between local and non-local artists not as thorny an issue as it might have been in other cities. To achieve this aim, the following pages will also take a closer look at three 'case studies' which may be considered indicative of the pride and prejudice that Italian artists exhibited, especially when French sculptors gained ascendancy in late seventeenth- and early eighteenth-century Rome.

* * *

As was the case with Naples in Chapter 1, one might start by considering how a few influential, foreign observers perceived the Eternal City. Unsurprisingly, what stands out most is the impact that classical vestiges, historical and artistic, had on visitors. Johann Goethe (1749–1832), for example, in 1786 expressed the overwhelming awe he witnessed when confronted by the classical heritage in the city by claiming that 'Nothing, above all, is comparable to the new life that a reflective person experiences when he observes a new country. Though I am still always myself, I believe I have been changed to the very marrow of my bones.'[37] He also provided his readers with an intimation as to how said change occurred: 'The most important monuments I take very slowly; I do nothing except look, go away, and come back and look again. Only in Rome can one educate oneself for Rome.'[38]

A hundred and forty years earlier, John Evelyn (1620–1706) also expressed the overpowering impact that the art and architecture of ancient Rome had on individuals who had been reared on the classical paideia. As he paused and looked back at the city from a high ground at the end of his sojourn, in a wistful mood he mused 'More glorious than be other *Citties* far:/With speaking stones, & breathing *Statues* set,/Justly art term'd the *Worlds sole Cabinet*:/ Of all the *Vniverse* none dares Contend/With thee ô *ROME*, nor will thy Praises End.'[39] An even earlier, perspicacious visitor, Michel de Montaigne (1533–92), indicated a further reason why this city had a strong appeal for people from all corners of Europe. While not ignoring the lure and significance of the classical tradition, in his *Journal de voyage en Italie* (1580–81) he wrote:

> I find it, of all towns in the world, the one most filled with the corporate idea, in which difference of nationality counts least; for, by its very nature, it is a patchwork of strangers, each one being as much at home as in his own country. The authority of its ruler lies over the whole of Christianity.[40]

For Montaigne, in addition to its historical lure, it was Rome's ecumenical nature, its leading role in 'shaping and defining a common Christian identity for the disparate peoples of Europe'[41] that made the city a major pole of attraction.[42] As he reiterated in his *Essays*, Rome was 'the only city common to all men and universal. The sovereign magistrate who rules there is similarly acknowledged everywhere; it is the mother city of all Christian peoples: both Frenchman and Spaniard are at home there.'[43] To be sure, had his readers doubted his claim, all they needed to do was to consider the numerous national churches present in Rome.[44] In fact, Roman churches with a foreign affiliation typically developed during the Middle Ages, when pilgrims from all over Europe flocked to the Holy City, especially during Jubilee Years. Connected with these houses of prayer were hospices and fraternities where foreigners found religious, social, medical, and monetary support from their fellow countrymen who resided in the city.[45] Consequently, it is not surprising to learn that in the sixteenth and seventeenth centuries those national churches amounted to about fifty, of which one third belonged to Italian nationals and two thirds to European citizens,[46] such as San Giuliano dei Fiamminghi (Flemish), San Girolamo degli Schiavoni (Slavs), San Luigi dei Francesi (French), Sant'Ivo dei Bretoni (Breton), Santa Maria dell'Anima (German), San Tommaso di Canterbury (English), Sant'Antonio dei Portoghesi (Portuguese), San Giacomo degli Spagnoli (Spanish), Santa Brigida (Swedish), and Santo Stefano Rotondo (Hungarian).

Moreover, besides the cosmopolitan nature of the papal court, with hundreds of foreign subjects in the retinue of cardinals and bishops,[47] it is quite indicative of the international character of the city that, for example, among the 1268 notaries working in the Holy City between 1507 and 1519, 319 were French, 160 Spanish, 135 German, and 39 Flemish.[48] Their presence in Rome can only be understood in relation to there being a consistent component of compatriots in town who needed their bilingual assistance and expertise.[49] Furthermore, recent studies have also stressed the transnational character of Rome – 'a mosaic of nations', as it has been described[50] – by investigating other factors, such as the creation of educational institutions that attracted young men especially from northern Europe – namely the Collegio Germanico (1522) and the Collegio Urbano di Propaganda Fide (1627)[51] – or the 'colonization and conquest' of the Eternal City sustained by the Spanish monarchs' desire to reinforce a nation-building process at the local level that filled the city with a preponderant presence of members of the 'Spanish nation'.[52]

Such diversity in the social fabric of early modern Rome was comparably reflected in the multinational character of the artists who chose to visit and, occasionally, become permanent residents of this city.[53] Indeed, this international feature was sustained, not in the least, from the Renaissance well into the eighteenth century, by familial and professional networks of the artistic community that helped to blur the national divide.[54] These individuals, especially Netherlandish 'artists on the move',[55] most often crossed the Alps into Italy, 'the universal school of painting', as Karel van Mander labeled it,[56] and went on to Rome hoping to find primarily employment opportunities.[57] Indeed, the Holy City had developed into a lucrative artistic milieu. As a Milanese patron learned in 1625, artists knew that Rome was the city 'where you go to get rich'.[58]

And while many of these artists on their way south might choose to work or settle in other parts of Italy, 'in the final analysis, Rome was what it was all about'.[59] Indeed, according to Giulio Mancini, Urban VIII's personal doctor, around 1620 there were so 'many French and Flemish [artists] who come and go that one cannot contain them'.[60] Certainly, as Jacques Thuillier perceptively pointed out, during the period of the European wars of religion that culminated in the Thirty Years' War (1618–48), when the exigencies of reconstruction discouraged any form of luxury, thus impacting negatively moribund artistic ateliers, a trip to Italy was for many young artists not only a noble solution, but also a practical one.[61] In fact, starting in 1568 – the beginning of the Eighty Years' War – until the end of the century, there was an 'exodus' of artists from the Low Countries and, among these, twenty-three sculptors settled in Rome.[62] Nevertheless, the main reason these artists went south was a desire to improve their talent by imbibing directly at the spring of classical art, as well as benefiting from studying the works of those Renaissance artists who were recognised (by northerners) and celebrated (by the Italians) as having made the greatest advances in modern art.[63] Ultimately, a sojourn in the Eternal City became a deliberate investment in their career.[64] Yet, despite the efforts of authors such as Karel van Mander, whose biographies were written with the clear intention of rebutting Vasari's claims about the superiority of Italian art over that produced in northern countries, from the Renaissance through the Baroque period there was an obvious inferiority complex on the part of northern artists vis-à-vis their Italian counterparts and Italian art in general.[65] A clear example of this mindset is provided by van Mander's opening statements in his *Lives of the Illustrious Flemish, Dutch and German Painters* (1604), where he concedes that 'art-loving Italy' ('*het Const-liebende Italien*')[66] was the leading country in painting, for its artists were the first to have followed the 'best method' of learning: studying classical art.[67] And indicative of the cultural, if not technical, divide between northern and southern European artists is Lampsonius' comment that 'the Netherlanders are usually praised for their paintings of landscapes, and the Italians for their representation of the humans and divinities. This should not elicit any wonder and should rather be taken as the truth, because the Italians have their brain in their head. It is not unjust to assert, however, that the Netherlanders have their intelligence in their hands.'[68]

Even so, while this palpable admission of artistic subordination to the Italians on the part of northerners found its counterpoint in van Mander's equally proud praise of northern artists for their superior skill in landscape paintings and engravings,[69] the author's piqued attitude towards the Italians' arrogance is equally manifest. Thus, while in his didactic poem addressed to young Flemish artists he exhorts them to go beyond their renown as landscape painters and tackle the difficult fresco medium in which Italians excelled, in his *Life of Hans Holbein*, he complains that Italians are typically quite prodigal in singing the praises of their countrymen, but rather reluctant in extolling foreigners.[70] Indeed, in his biography of Aert Mijtens, van Mander goes so far as to state that this painter's excellence compelled the Italians to claim less frequently that the Netherlanders were incapable of depicting the human figure, forcing them 'to keep their mouths shut and treat us with greater respect'.[71]

In Italy, on the other hand, an indication of the local artists' 'superiority complex' may be summarised by a few statements that Francisco de Hollanda ascribes to Michelangelo in his *Diálogos em Roma* (1538). In response to a question posed by Vittoria Colonna about Flemish painting – for it seemed to her that it was more devout than 'the Italian manner' – Michelangelo supposedly responded by saying that 'it will appeal to women, especially to the very old and the very young, and also to monks and nuns and to certain noblemen who have no sense of true harmony'.[72] Elaborating on this belief, the artist added that 'though it pleases some persons, [it] is done without reason or art, without symmetry or proportion, without skillful choice or boldness and, finally, without substance or vigour. Nevertheless, there are countries where they paint worse than in Flanders.'[73] Finally, in a lapidary tone, Michelangelo reportedly sentenced: 'It is practically only the work done in Italy that we can call true painting, and that is why we call good painting Italian; were it produced elsewhere, we should give it the name of that country or region.'[74]

It is inconsequential whether these statements ascribed to Michelangelo are spurious.[75] The fact that such opinions were recorded at all is sufficient proof that, in early modern Europe, Italian artists were certainly emboldened in their self-esteem because of the achievements attained by their predecessors, from Cimabue and Giotto down to their contemporaries. Indeed, reflecting this state of affairs by the end of the Baroque period is a cutting statement written from Rome by the German-born painter John Closterman in a 1699 missive to Anthony Ashley Cooper, Third Earl of Shaftesbury: 'I durst not pretend to instruct an Italian, they think of themselves above all the world.'[76] However, while the Eternal City had been the epicenter of artistic and theoretical developments during the sixteenth and seventeenth centuries, starting in the second half of the 1600s, Rome began to share and eventually cede centerstage to Paris.[77] This transfer of power was gradual, occurring over decades and well into the first quarter of the eighteenth century,[78] with an evident signal of the changing climate in France's cultural politics as it mutated from 'the age of copies and translations' to that of 'an imperialistic appropriation and extraction of [the] historical identity'; that is, through acquisition not only of plaster casts of classical sculpture but also of the original sculptures from Roman collections.[79] Nonetheless, as it has been pointedly stated, 'If Rome was indeed on the decline as artistic capital at this time, the Romans had apparently not been informed.'[80] So much so that in 1696, for the celebration of the one hundred years since the founding of the Accademia di San Luca, its secretary, the painter Giuseppe Ghezzi, published an oration in *Il Centesimo dell'Anno M.DC.XCV.* (fig.5.2) that to some extent was the Roman reply to Charles Perrault's poem *Le Siècle de Louis le Grand* – a poem that, along with his *Paralelle des Anciens et des Modernes*, was to ignite the so-called *Querelle des Anciens et des Modernes*.[81] Reacting to Perrault's claim that the seventeenth century was the century of Louis XIV, with his booklet Ghezzi cared to assert that in artistic matters the '*Grand siècle*' was still a Roman matter and that Bernini was its guiding star.[82] For these reasons, it is of some interest to observe how French artists were received in Rome at this crucial juncture.

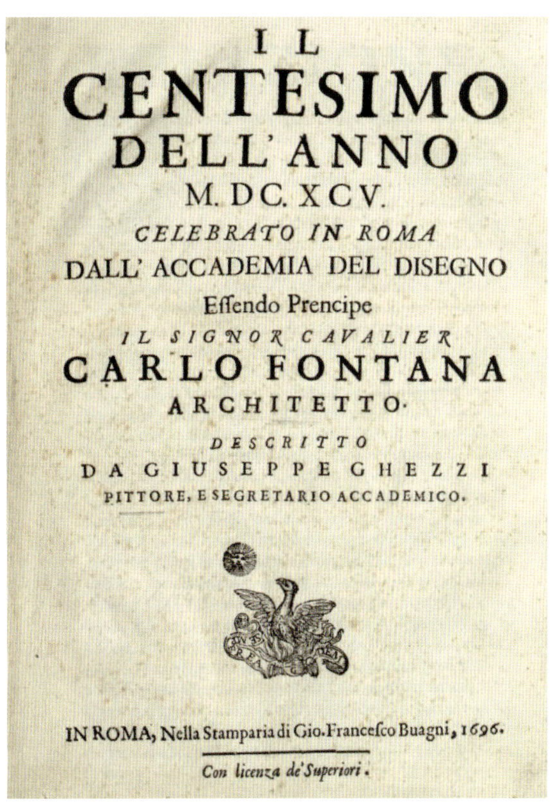
IL CENTESIMO DELL' ANNO M. DC. XCV. CELEBRATO IN ROMA DALL' ACCADEMIA DEL DISEGNO Essendo Prencipe IL SIGNOR CAVALIER CARLO FONTANA ARCHITETTO. DESCRITTO DA GIUSEPPE GHEZZI PITTORE, E SEGRETARIO ACCADEMICO.

IN ROMA, Nella Stamparia di Gio. Francesco Buagni, 1696.

Con licenza de' Superiori.

5.2 Giuseppe Ghezzi, *Il Centesimo dell'Anno M.DC.XCV*, 1696, Rome

* * *

In a 1664 undelivered letter written on behalf of Jean-Baptiste Colbert (1619–83) (fig.5.3) to the painter Nicolas Poussin, then in Rome, Charles Perrault reveals the main justification for Louis XIV's politically wise and culturally commendable support of the fine arts: 'It is certain that he intends to elevate these arts to the highest degree of perfection ever attained, and that he wishes for his reign to be celebrated not only for the great deeds of his own life, but also for the infinite number of famous men in every profession, who have equaled and even surpassed those of antiquity.'[83] Like few before him, this worthy epigone of Emperor Augustus – one of the most shrewd rulers to skillfully enlist the arts at the service of the state[84] – the Sun King realised that not only his contemporaries but also future generations would judge his reign by the cultural and artistic accomplishments he promoted as much as by his political and military achievements.[85] 'To this

5.3 Robert Nanteuil, *Portrait of Jean-Baptiste Colbert*, *c.*1667, engraving, 31.8 × 24.9 cm (12½ × 9 13⁄16 in), National Galleries of Scotland

purpose', the letter continues, 'His Majesty forgets nothing which may naturally encourage virtue in the hearts of those who have some inclination toward great things, and for his own part he offers them every means of improving themselves. To ignite interest in science, he has given monetary awards to all the men of letters who have outstanding reputations, and wherever merit shines forth, not only in France but in all of Europe, there have been tokens of his royal generosity. With respect to painting and sculpture, particularly to glorify him and to transmit his name to posterity, he omits nothing which may bring them to the last degree of perfection.'[86] Consequently, in 1648 the monarch established the Royal Academy of Painting and Sculpture in Paris – the Académie Royale de Peinture et de Sculpture – thereby providing, among other things, instruction, guidance, and prizes for promising artists. Moreover, Perrault continues:

> because it still seems necessary for young people of your profession [painting] to spend some time in Rome, to acquire the taste and manner of the originals and models of the greatest masters both of antiquity and of recent times, and since it happens often that those students who have the greatest talent and aptitude either fail to do this or cannot make the journey because of its cost, His Majesty has resolved to send a certain number of students there every year, who will be chosen from the Academy and who will be supported in Rome during their stay there . . . To this end, His Majesty has decided to have always in Rome some illustrious master, who would have the care and direction of the students whom His Majesty will send there, and he has chosen you, Monsieur [Poussin], and named you as the one whom he now entrusts with this charge.[87]

Clearly, as the French author of a guide to Rome dated between 1677 and 1681 commented, the ultimate objective was to do away with the Crown's dependence on foreign artists for the improvement of national art.[88] The Académie de France in Rome eventually opened in 1666, a year after Poussin's death, with Charles Errard acting as its first director (fig.5.4).

Colbert was well aware that 'genius and good taste come from God', but he was equally convinced that a period of intensive study in the Eternal City could only help raise the quality of national art.[89] And it was certainly thanks to the economic and artistic support of this institution that a constant flow of talented French artists began going to Rome in the mid-seventeenth century, helping them rise to the summit of their profession and compete for the most prestigious local commissions. It is also thanks to the extensive correspondence exchanged between the various directors of the Académie in

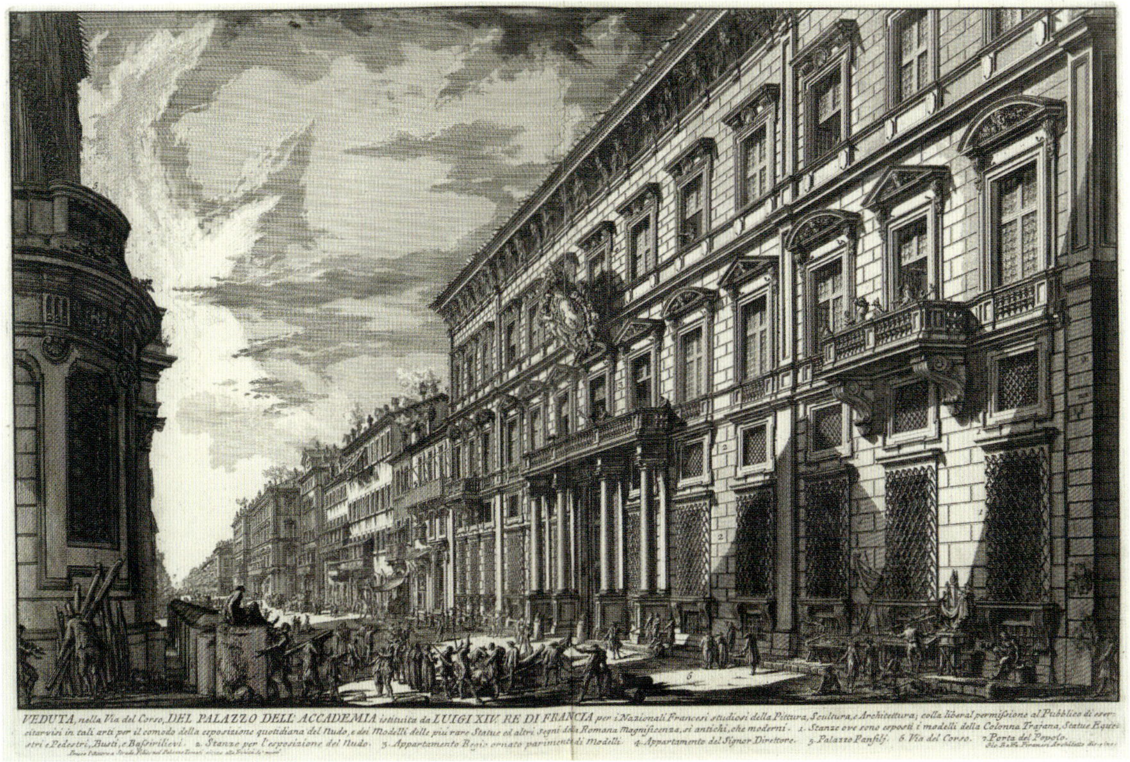

5.4 Giovanni Battista Piranesi, *Palazzo Mancini, Seat of the Académie de France in Rome from 1750 to 1778*, etching, 52 × 74.5 cm (20½ × 29⁵⁄₁₆ in), Metropolitan Museum, New York. Rogers Fund, transferred from the Library

Rome and the supervisors of this institution in Paris that a privileged, if filtered and predictably partial, perspective is obtained on the way Italians were perceived by the French, the way the latter perceived themselves, and on how local artists reacted to foreign competition.

* * *

The publication of the *Correspondance des Directeurs de l'Académie de France à Rome avec les Surintendants des Bâtiments*, begun in 1887 by Anatole de Courde de Montaiglon (1824–95) and completed in 1908 with the issue of the seventeenth volume, is a Herculean feat comprising 9,996 documents that cover the institution's history from its inception in 1666 until 1804.[90] Allowance being made for the common denominator that characterises all group identities – endogenous rather than exogenous empathy – the views expressed in the *Correspondance* reflect a duality inherent in the historical context in which they were formulated. On the one hand, when considering the artistic past of the Italian peninsula, the directors' views were generally positive; on the other, when judging the social, political, and anthropological nature of their host nation or the quality of contemporary art, their tone became more critical, as it reflected the mounting awareness of France's hegemonic status in Europe – a perception, as mentioned, that progressively increased from the second half of the seventeenth into the eighteenth century. Thus, besides the recurrent praise of Michelangelo and, to an even greater extent, Raphael, as well as the acclamation of those artists who were considered the latter's worthy successors – such as Annibale Carracci, Domenichino, and Guido Reni – contemporary Italian artists were seen as coming short of expectations and harmful models to the artistic development of young *pensionnaires* who frequented the Académie. Hence, for example, writing on 9 December 1692, to the Superintendent Marquis de Villacerf in Paris, Director La Teulière condemns Pietro da Cortona and his followers for their 'capricious imagination', for having strayed far from the 'wisdom and soundness' of Raphael's and antiquity's exemplary works, and accused him, along with Bernini and Borromini, for 'having totally ruined the Beaux-Arts'.[91]

When assessing the overall Italian character, instead, one senses all of La Teulière's ethnic distance, claiming not only that 'Italians are much more mistrustful than [people from] the rest of the world'[92] and more 'intractable' than any other nationality when they feel one could do without them,[93] but also that Italians disliked the French more than anyone else.[94] La Teulière further considered local painters and sculptors 'naturally very lazy'[95] – a commonplace about southerners in general, as already discussed in Chapter 1 – while Charles Poerson, in a missive written two decades later to his superintendent, Duke D'Antin, feared the contagiousness of such indolence on the young French artists[96] and described the Italian population at large as being 'poor and lazy'.[97]

With regard to envy – a sentiment La Teulière attributed generally to other nations vis-à-vis the French[98] – Poerson informs us, just as Joachim von Sandrart did about François Duquesnoy's experience when he first arrived in Italy, that Romans were typically reluctant to praise foreigners.[99] Indeed, with regard to *professional* jealousy on the part of Italian artists, the *Correspondance* records two instances between the end of the seventeenth and the first quarter of the eighteenth century when such sentiments could have been engendered. A closer look at these events, along with the international fabric of the Accademia di San Luca and the major Jesuit commission of the period – the Chapel of Saint Ignatius in the Gesù – is revealing of the peculiarity of the Roman artistic milieu.

The first occasion involved the Baptismal Chapel in Saint Peter's and the papal allocation in March 1692 of a Bernini 'trophy' located a stone's throw from the apse of the basilica: the large studio by the foundry known as the 'Fonderia della Fabrica', near the church of Santa Marta (fig.5.5).[100] This was, in fact, where Gian Lorenzo sculpted the equestrian marble statue of Louis XIV.[101] Initially awarded to Lorenzo Ottoni, according to La Teulière's account of the events, the studio was subsequently assigned to his friend, Jean-Baptiste Théodon, thanks to Théodon's deceit and behind-the-scene maneuvers by Cardinal d'Estrée.[102] Ottoni's reaction is not recorded, but given that by September of the same year the two sculptors, along with another Frenchman, Michel Maille, and Girolamo Lucenti, were commissioned to sculpt a *Virtue* each for the chapel – with the more famous Domenico Guidi being assigned the main sculpture of *Christ and Saint John the Baptist* – this subdivision of labor indicates that equal opportunities in the most hallowed place of Christendom were being given to Italian and foreign sculptors alike. This fact, in itself, must have fostered collaboration as much as competition, especially since, as La Teulière records, all of these sculptors were to be granted their own workplace near Saint Peter's.[103] It is true that two years later, on 6 March 1694, with reference to the projected execution of 'four large statues' for the Baptismal Chapel, an *avviso* reported the discontent of the Italian sculptors when they discovered that the sculptures had been assigned to 'four northern artists' ('4 Operarij oltramontani') – an inaccurate statement since Ottoni and Lucenti were born in Rome.[104] Still,

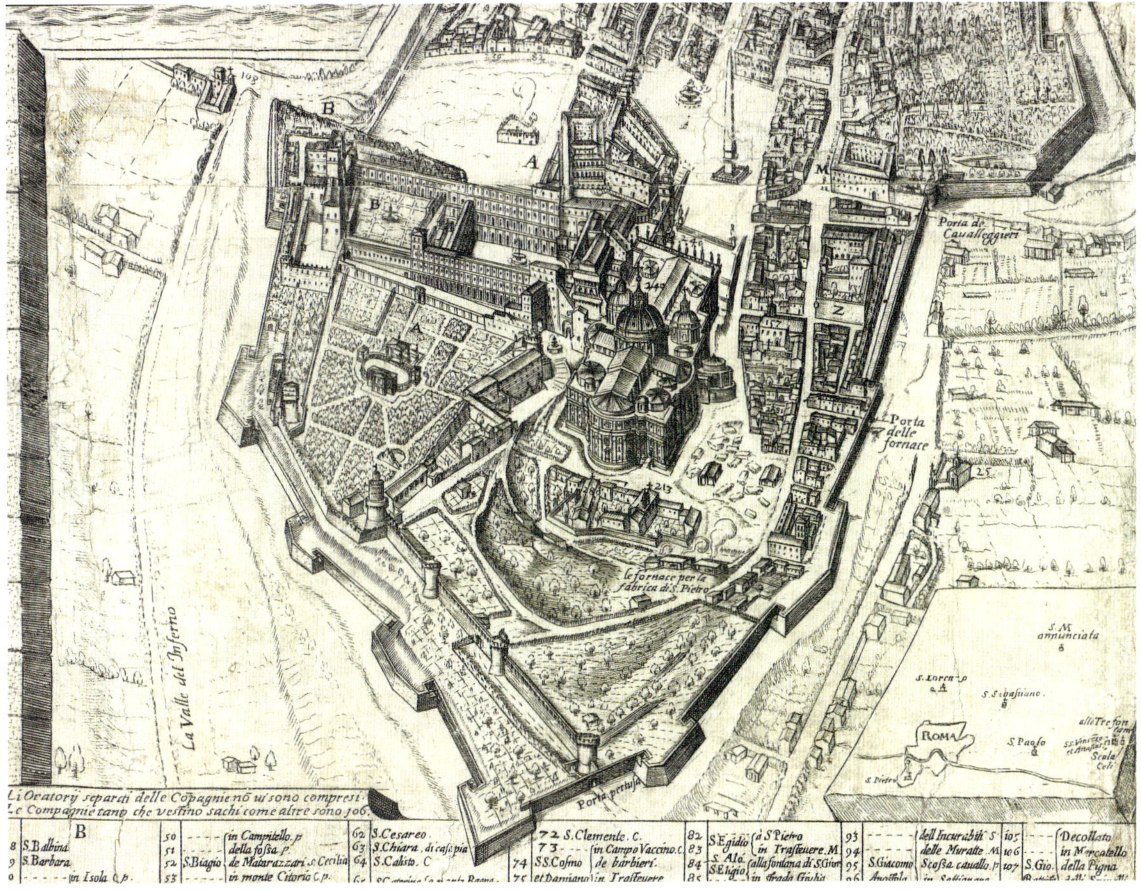

5.5 Matthäus Greuter, map of Rome, detail of the area around Saint Peter's, 1618, paper, 130 × 214.7 cm (51 3/16 × 84 1/2 in), Biblioteca Nazionale Centrale 'Vittorio Emanuele II'

there is corroborating information indicating that the Roman context was not so ill-disposed towards foreign artists, as a statement from the *Diario del Valesio* leads one to understand. Dated 28 November 1700, it declared that 'His Holiness has ordered that Monsieur Théodon, one of the best sculptors that we have nowadays, be retained in Rome. He was already prepared to leave for France and flee Rome, whereby one suspects that Our Lord [the Pope] wants to employ him in some project . . .'[105] If Valesio claimed that Théodon was one of the best sculptors of his time and the newly elected Pope Clement XI – who rose to the throne of Peter just five days prior to Valesio's entry in his diary – prevented the artist from leaving town because he had intentions of assigning a papal project to him, then it would seem that foreign artists must not have been terribly penalised in the Holy City because of their nationality.

The second event that has traditionally been taken as a cabal by Italian artists against the sculptor Lambert-Sigisbert Adam has to do with the competition for the Trevi Fountain project. Writing to Superintendent D'Antin in November 1730, the artist proudly informed him that he had made a model for the fountain: 'If I'll have the pleasure of winning the contest in which I will participate along with my colleagues, and if Your Highness will allow me to execute this grand project, I will endeavor to bring honor upon myself.'[106] In a note by the editor of the *Correspondance*, readers are directed to consult the pages relating to this project that Dom Calmet, Abbé de Senones, wrote in his *Bibliothèque lorraine* of 1751.[107] Besides being the only source describing Adam's project for the fountain – thus giving the impression of his being well-informed on matters pertaining to this artist – the Abbé specifies that, out of the sixteen models of the Trevi Fountain presented by various artists to the pope, Adam's was initially the one selected to be executed.[108] However, since the project was ultimately assigned to the Italian architect Nicola Salvi, according to Calmet, the change of plans was due to national envy: 'the Romans, seeing that this commission was given to a foreigner, suggested to the Pope that he build the facade of Saint John Lateran in place of the Fountain; which is what happened'.[109] As Anne-Lise Desmas has argued, Calmet's biography of the artist is not only the sole document claiming that Adam was the victim of a plot ordained by the Italians, but also the chronology there set forth is inaccurate.[110] Desmas further notes that one should be wary of using Calmet's *Bibliothèque lorraine* as a source, since his statements about Adam and the Trevi Fountain project are a blatant effort to glorify his compatriot – Lambert-Sigisbert was born in Nancy, former capital of the province of Lorraine – at the expense of historical accuracy.[111] Had the Romans really plotted against the French sculptor, the director of the Académie at the time, Nicolas Vleughels, would certainly have communicated the cabal to D'Antin. In other words, this incident of national 'pride and prejudice', if anything, is to be ascribed to Calmet rather than to the Romans. Desmas rightly observes that a French sculptor's design for the Trevi Fountain – Edmé Bouchardon had also submitted a model – had hardly any chance of being selected, not because of Adam's nationality, but rather because of his profession.[112] Vleughels had understood this as early as 4 January 1731, when he wrote that in this project, 'the architects want to be in charge of everything'.[113] Indeed, besides exceptional cases when a sculptor was a recognised master and designer, as were Bernini and Algardi,[114] sculptors working on undertakings that required designing ability normally operated under the supervision of architects – as in the Baptismal Chapel in Saint Peter's, discussed above, overseen by Carlo Fontana[115] – or painters – as with the over-life-sized sculptures of the apostles to be placed in the nave of Saint John Lateran, for which Carlo Maratta was asked to provide drawings to be followed by the sculptors (fig.2.21).[116] And although care must be taken not to generalise, this state of affairs was especially prevalent because designing and inventing was not a talent usually accorded to sculptors.[117] Therefore, as at least these two recorded instances suggest, holding a foreign passport was not a discriminating factor for artists in papal Rome.

An additional glimpse into the rapport between Italian and foreign artists may be gleaned by turning one's attention to the older, Roman artists' enclave: the Accademia di San Luca. Founded in 1577, but reorganised in 1593 – thirty years after the creation of the first artists' academy, the Florentine Accademia del Disegno – in 1677 the Accademia di San Luca sealed a 'twinning' or aggregation agreement with the aforementioned Parisian Académie Royale de Peinture et de Sculpture.[118] Even before the two academies nominally united, in 1672 the French Charles Errard, first director of the Académie de France in Rome, was named *principe* of the Accademia di San Luca, followed in 1676 by Charles Le Brun who, however, presided *in absentia* through Charles Errard.[119] The bestowing of such an honor on a foreign national by the Roman academy at this historical juncture, naturally, reflects a growing recognition on the European scene of *la grandeur française*.[120] Nevertheless, if one considers that from the seventeenth through the eighteenth centuries nine foreign *principi* were selected for the highest post in the Accademia di San Luca, it was probably also due to a less pronounced chauvinism on the part of Italians and a greater acceptance of others. This is especially remarkable if one takes into account that, although five out of those nine *principi* during that period were French, 'the honor was never reciprocal: no Italian was named director of the Académie de France à Rome'.[121] While it is true that the French nominated Domenico Guidi as one of the four rectors of their *Roman* Académie, this lack of reciprocity is all the more striking if one considers that until 1731, when Giovanni Niccolò Servandoni (1695–1766) was admitted to the Parisian Académie Royale, the only other Italian 'member' of this exclusive French consortium had been a model for life-drawing classes.[122] Indeed, it is noteworthy that well in advance of the establishment of the Académie de France in Rome, first a Fleming (Paul Brill, 1620–21) and then a Frenchman (Simon Vouet, 1624–7) were placed at the helm of the Accademia di San Luca; that is, before the French nation acquired the political and cultural clout that it gained under Louis XIV.[123] Furthermore, it is of some significance that, out of the seventy-six students enrolled in the Accademia in 1664 and one hundred and twenty in 1665, a third were foreigners.[124]

While according to Giovanni Battista Passeri the relationship between Italian and foreign artists was always a bit precarious,[125] perhaps the best indication of the dynamics between these artists in Rome may be understood by considering that some of the most prized commissions in late seventeenth- and early eighteenth-century Rome were awarded to foreigners. Although Director La Teulière in 1692 maintained that Italy was 'a country where artifice and ploy hold sway over merit and judgment',[126] and forty years later his successor Nicolas Vleughels, in criticising the selection of Alessandro Galilei's project for the Corsini Chapel in Saint John Lateran, complained that 'according to the custom of this country, the architect was selected even before he entered the contest',[127] one need only reflect about the major sculptural project in late-Baroque Rome to be reminded of the city's particular context and of how a foreigner's merit was readily recognised.

The Chapel of Saint Ignatius Loyola (1695–9) (fig.5.6), designed by Andrea Pozzo for the Jesuits' mother church, the Gesù, was not only the most important commission at the end of the century but also one that involved an army of collaborators: over one hundred, taking into account artists, artisans, and builders.[128] Even as every single aspect of the ensemble contributes to the overwhelming impact that the chapel has on viewers, it is undeniable that the most striking and important sculptural features of the project are the two group sculptures that flank the altar. The artists chosen by the Jesuits to execute *Faith Trampling Heresy with the King of the Congo Rising Converted*, on the left of the altar (fig.5.7), and *Religion Triumphing Over Heresy*, on the right (fig.5.8), were Jean-Baptiste Théodon and Pierre Legros, respectively. It is possible, as suggested by Robert Enggass, that

> the Church was never allowed to forget the power of the French king and the desirability of working out some kind of accommodation with him. It was this the Jesuits had in mind when they urged an elderly and reluctant Bernini to go to France to work for Louis XIV and it is this that must have been in the back of their mind too when they distributed the commissions for the altar of Saint Ignatius.[129]

But while, as mentioned above, local observers were willing to admit that Théodon was one of the best sculptors working in Rome, it does not mean that the choice of two French sculptors for such an important commission did not create waves in the local artistic community.[130]

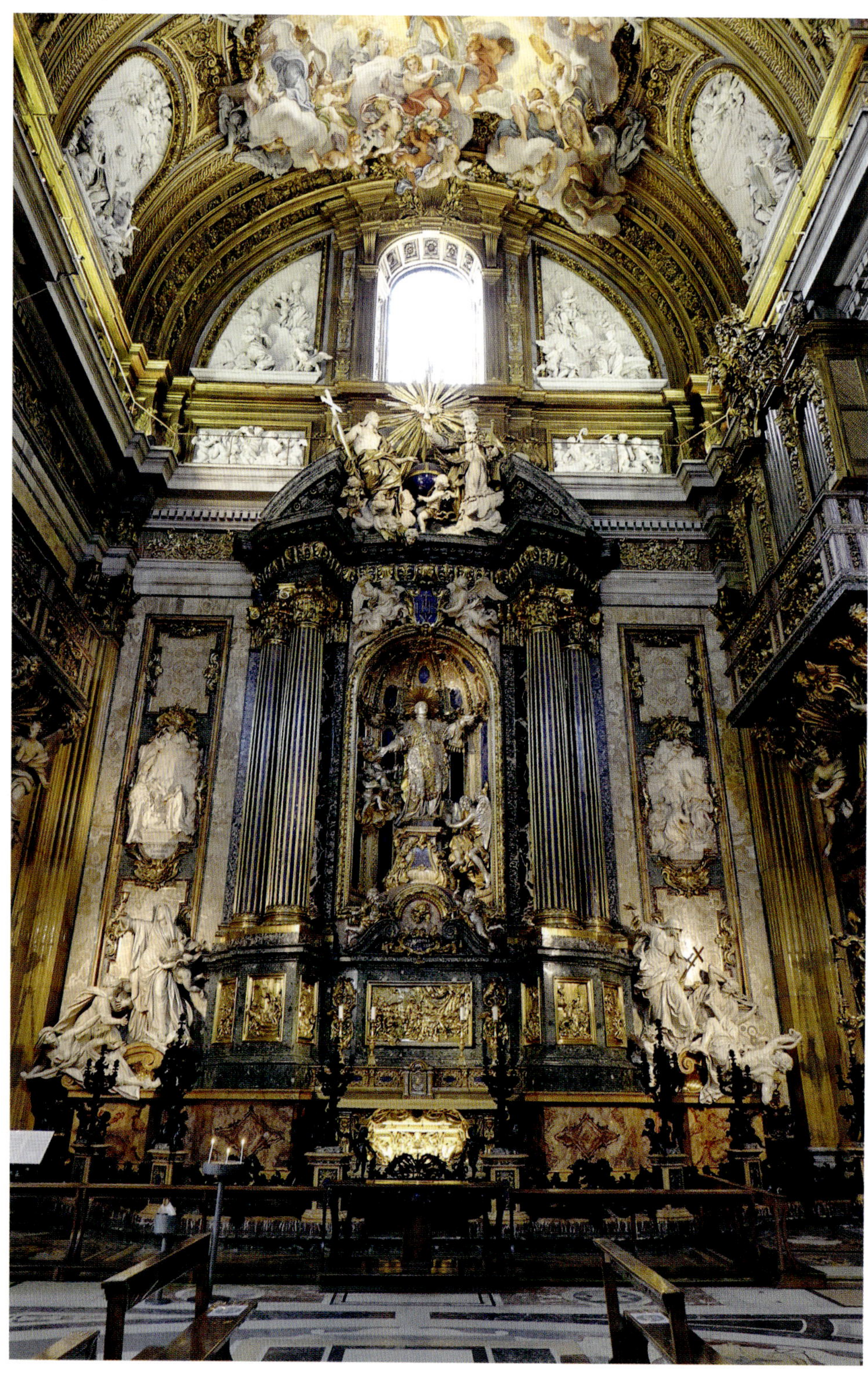

5.6 Andrea Pozzo, Chapel of Saint Ignatius Loyola, 1695–9, marble, bronze, lapis lazuli, silver, Il Gesù, Rome

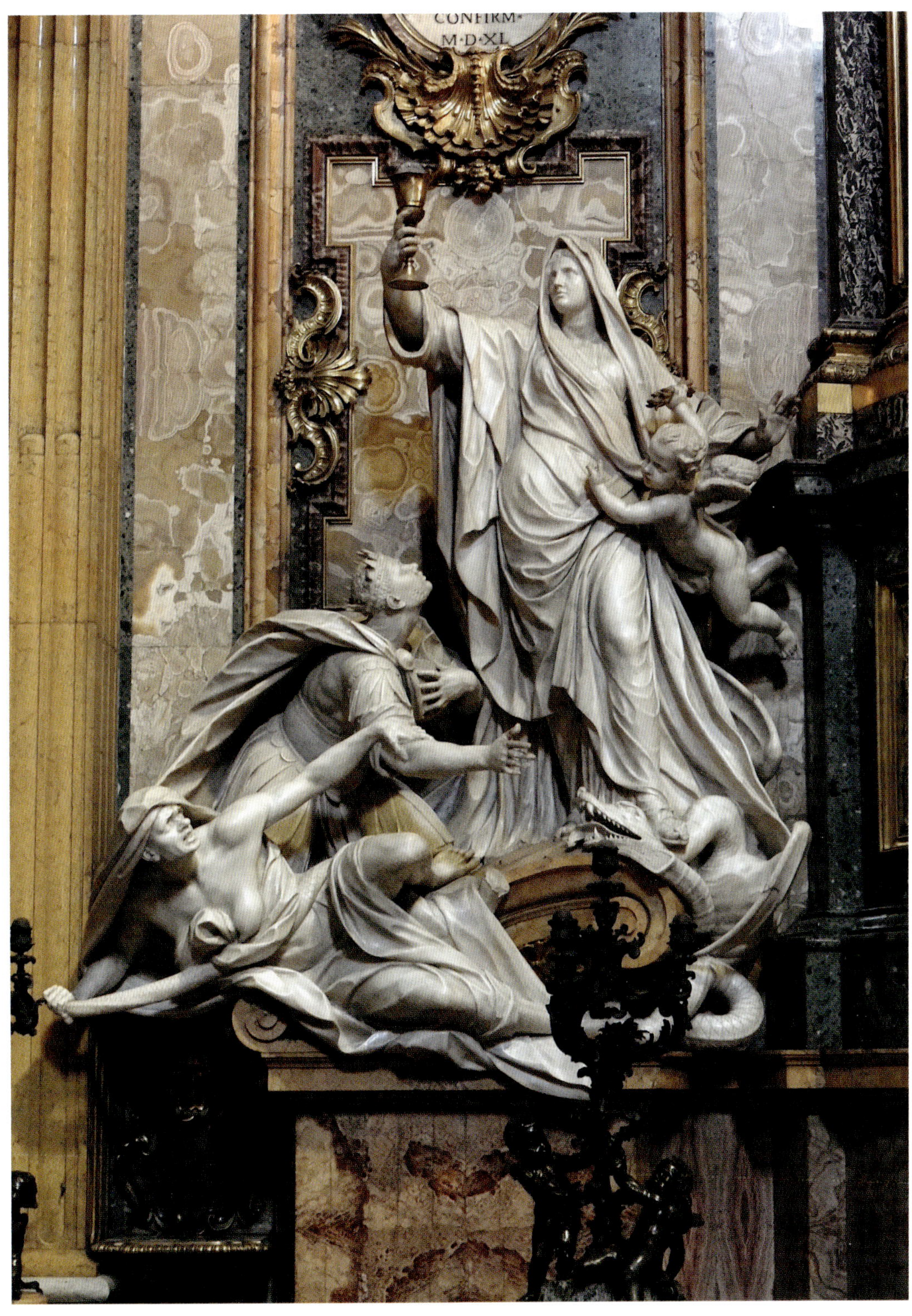

5.7 Jean-Baptiste Théodon, *Faith Trampling Heresy with the King of the Congo Rising Converted*, 1695–9, marble, Il Gesù, Rome

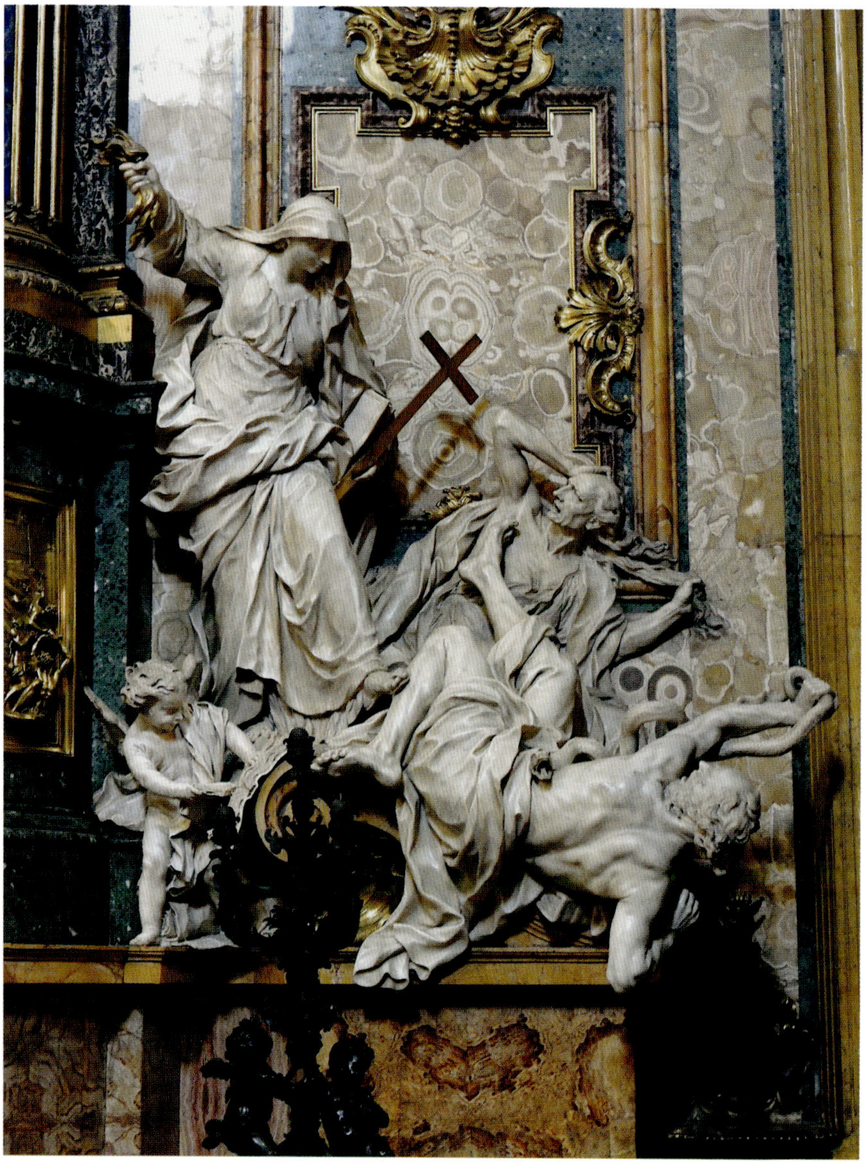

5.8 Pierre Legros, *Religion Triumphing Over Heresy*, 1695–9, marble, Il Gesù, Rome

5.9 Camillo Rusconi, *Angels*, 1696–9, marble, Chapel of Saint Ignatius Loyola, Il Gesù, Rome

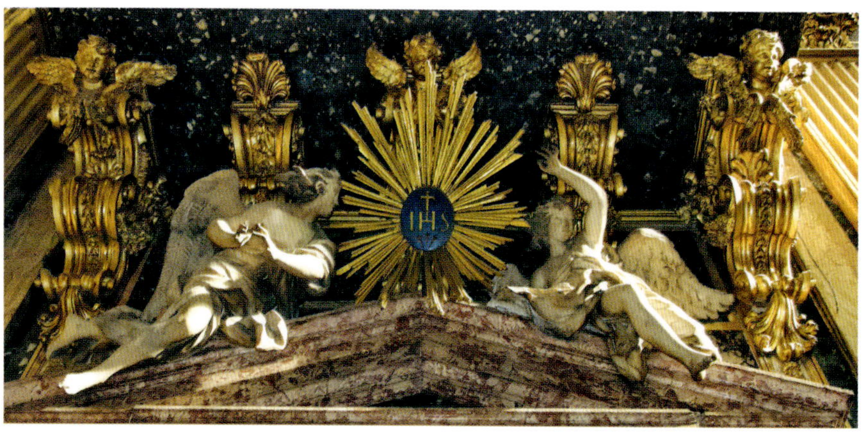

In a letter written in 1732 by Filippo della Valle to Monsignor Giovanni Bottari, who had asked for biographical information about his fellow sculptor Camillo Rusconi (1658–1728), the artist asserts that initially it was Rusconi who had been commissioned to sculpt one of the two multi-figural sculptures for the Chapel of Saint Ignatius. 'However', della Valle elaborates, 'because of the intense pressure [placed on the Jesuits], they were assigned to two Frenchmen and turned out the way everyone can see.'[131] Whereas della Valle does not declare who strongly recommended Théodon and Legros to the point that the Jesuits were dissuaded from allowing Rusconi to sculpt one of the two statues, one does sense a nationalist resentment on his part as he does not even mention the two French sculptors by name. But the apparent criticism of these two foreigners is made more evident as della Valle concludes his comments about the chapel by saying that

> and to him [Rusconi] they just assigned the execution of two angels above the passageway on the [right] side of the chapel where the Epistles are read, which were so excellently executed that they were judged not only the most elegant sculptures of the chapel but [it was] also [deemed] that there were no comparable angels in Rome that could surpass them in beauty (fig.5.9).[132]

Reiterating the idea that Camillo was deprived of the opportunity to prove his mettle because of the pressure exerted on the Jesuits, in 1735 Francesco Saverio Baldinucci – son of Bernini's biographer Filippo Baldinucci – also claimed that Pozzo himself would have preferred to have Rusconi work on one of the two multi-figural sculptures. He further provided the names of the two French artists, Théodon and Legros, and asserted that Rusconi's two angels were not only much better than the two sculptural groups but also that they were considered 'in jest' by some as more beautiful than all other angels in Rome.[133] However, if one may trust a letter written by the director of the Académie de France at the time, Matthieu de La Teulière (1684–99), to the Superintendent Villacerf, the alleged pressure on the Jesuits certainly did not emanate from him – for he was unaware of Legros' surreptitious participation in the contest[134] – or anyone close to the French crown.[135] Rather, according to La Teulière, it was the French engraver Nicolas Dorigny who simply suggested Legros' name to the Jesuits and that the prelate in charge of the project, Father Bonacina, expressly asked the sculptor not to mention it to anyone.[136] More important in the context of the present chapter is that, still according to La Teulière, Legros' model had been 'the one most generally approved of, everyone being unaware of its author, as most people believed the sculptor to be a Genoese'.[137] Thus, at least with regard to this Roman Jesuit commission, anonymity was a remarkable aspect in the process of adjudication.

It is of some consequence that Lione Pascoli's biography of Camillo Rusconi makes no reference to the pressure exerted by members of the French community or their advocates.[138] One would assume that, since Pascoli was aware of the universal praise that Rusconi's angels received, he would have been equally informed – had it actually taken place – about the cabal that prevented the Italian sculptor from obtaining the more prized commission, especially as Pascoli personally knew and was friends with many contemporary artists living and working in Rome, such as Luti, Odazzi, and Rusconi himself.[139] 'Thus', as Alessandro Marabottini points out, 'we can be quite certain that in all these cases he [Pascoli] had direct and certain information, to the extent that one cannot always trust the precise memory of the artists [themselves].'[140] In this instance, had Rusconi been deprived of the important commission, no doubt Pascoli would have heard about it and recorded it in the biography of his friend. Therefore, it seems reasonable to assume that Filippo della Valle's recording of events simply reflects gossip that circulated among some local

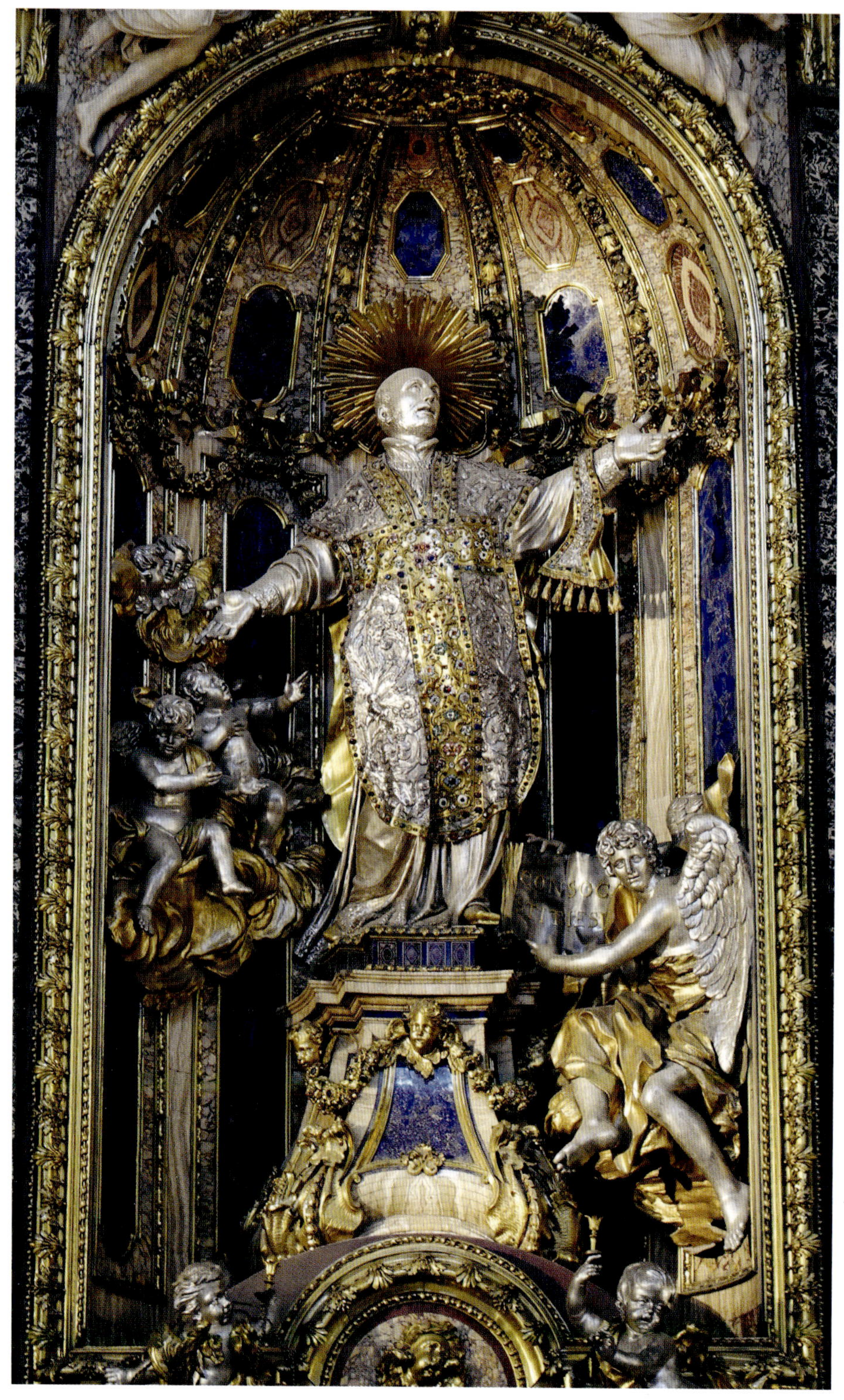

5.10 Pierre Legros, *Saint Ignatius*, 1697–9, silver statue, remodeled by Luigi Acquisti, 1803–4, Chapel of Saint Ignatius Loyola, Il Gesù, Rome

artists and, unsurprisingly, it would indicate that chauvinism and professional jealousy was also an issue for some Italians in Rome as it was for French artists in Paris.

Certainly, human reactions in situations that pitched artists of different nationalities against one another could never be interpreted in a clear-cut fashion. However, in contrast to the Rusconi affair, the impression one gets from a document preserved in the Jesuits' archives is that both the patrons and other artists had a more positive, collegial reaction to the selection of a foreigner for another contest still related to the Chapel of Saint Ignatius. Thus one reads that, after Pope Innocent XII visited the Gesù on 3 August 1697 to inspect the twelve models for the proposed silver statue of Saint Ignatius that was to be the centerpiece of the altar in the chapel dedicated to him, Pierre Legros' model was chosen by the twelve contestants themselves (fig.5.10).[141] Subsequently, the decision was celebrated not only by the French.[142] Recollecting the event in a manuscript dated 15 February 1706, Father Bonacina wrote:

> Once it became known that the first prize had been awarded to Monsù [Monsieur] Le Gros, the large crew of young Frenchmen that was waiting for him, loudly shouted *Long Live Long Live Monsù Le Gros*. As he went down the stairs with a pouch containing one hundred *scudi* in as many coins, he shook it so their jingle could be heard. When he reached the gate to said stairs that lead to the [upper] storey, the French youth surrounded him and, lifting him off the ground, carried him triumphantly, repeating from time to time *Long Live*. The exceptional clamor they made as they went through the streets drew attention from people, who asked what was going on. After having received the honor owed to his talent, Monsù Le Gros decided to honor his personal generosity by treating to a solemn, magnificent banquet *not only his compatriots but also many friends, all [of whom were] excellent Masters*. But I would greatly digress from my intentions were I to recount the loud expressions of joy, good-natured pranks, amusing stunts to which those ingenious, lively youths gave life so as to increase the approbation and glory of their Master.[143] (italics mine)

From Bonacina's description of the events that occurred nine years earlier, one senses his sympathetic attitude towards Rome-based French artists. From this same text it is also reasonable to assume that among the many *Virtuosi* friends who celebrated Legros' success as he stepped outside the Jesuits' Casa Professa were some Italian artists (fig.5.11). Written by Bonacina – a Milanese Jesuit who had felt the effects of Roman *campanilismo* himself from both the religious and lay communities[144] – the documents indicate that first of all, to prevent biased judgments, anonymity was again strictly observed in these contests, and that, second, the artistic commission was awarded by a sort of 'peer review'. Indeed, as Evonne Levy has pointed out with reference to 'the Jesuitness of Jesuit architecture', what distinguishes the 'Jesuit Style' is that their projects were open to public participation. In other words, it was not a matter of 'form', rather of '*process* – organised and controlled by the Society – through which forms emerged'.[145] In the selection of the winning model for the silver statue of Saint Ignatius, as it had been with the selection of the architectural plan for this very chapel designed by the Jesuit Andrea Pozzo, the project became public and the final choice was collegial, even if the patrons retained control of it.[146] Thus, while Filippo della Valle's claim that Rusconi had been deprived of a major commission because 'of the intense pressure [placed on the Jesuits]' is a good example to underscore that national pride and prejudice among artists was certainly present at all latitudes, the sculptural commissions related to the Chapel of Saint Ignatius Loyola are proof that the Roman artistic scene was overall not affected by a chronic form of chauvinism.[147] In fact, if one is to believe

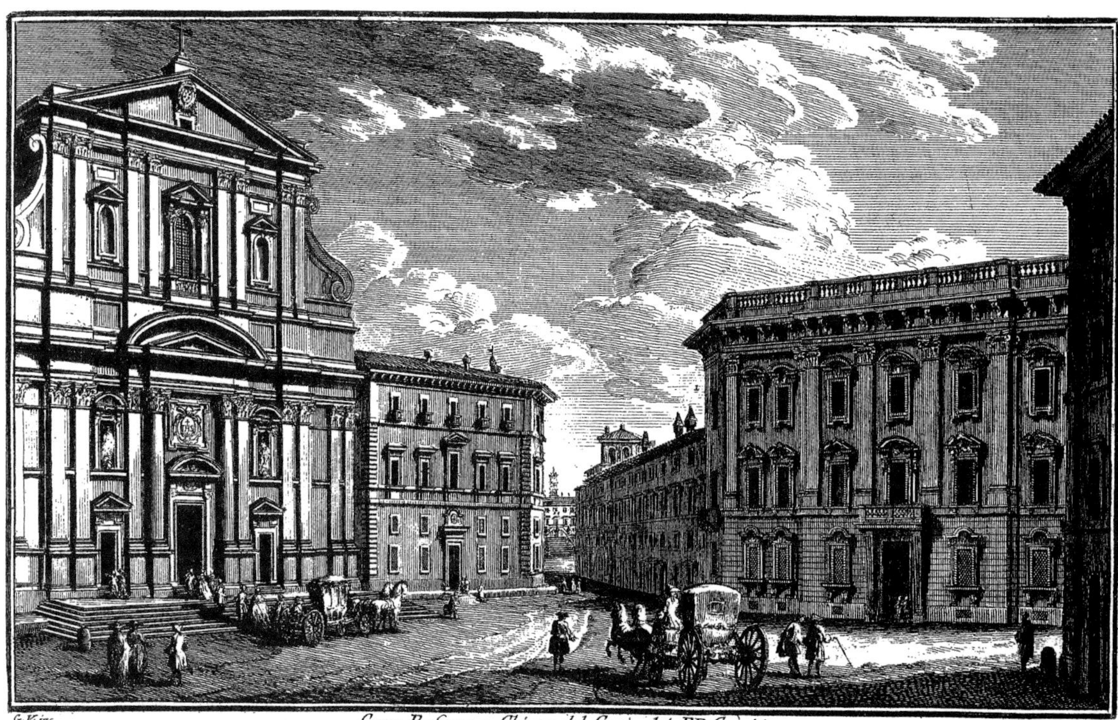

5.11 Giuseppe Vasi, *Il Gesù and the Casa Professa*, 1756, engraving, 33.1 × 21.7 cm (13 1⁄16 × 8 9⁄16 in), *Delle magnificenze di Roma antica e moderna*, vol.7, 1756, public domain

the comments made by Directors Charles Poerson and Nicolas Vleughels, local artists were objective enough to acknowledge foreign talent when they saw it. In a letter of 1711, in which he informs D'Antin of Clement XI's decision to fill the aedicules created by Borromini in the nave of Saint John Lateran with twelve giant statues of the apostles (fig.2.21), Poerson maintained that 'according to the Italians, [Legros] is the most skilled sculptor in Italy'.[148] Vleughels, on his part, in a missive of 1731 to D'Antin referring to Bouchardon's completed portrait of Clement XII, vaunts his national pride by stating that 'it must be truly good, since the Italians praise it'.[149]

In the exhibition catalog *Art in Rome in the Eighteenth Century*, Christopher Johns contrasted the reception that foreign artists received in Rome with that of major centers north of the Alps:

> Surprisingly, their competition with established local artists caused much less friction than might be imagined, evidence of a broad consensus of the cosmopolitan nature of the art world in Settecento Rome. Such an attitude stands in sharp contrast to the nationalistic howls of protest from most British and French artists when a choice commission was awarded to a foreigner.[150]

In this same publication, Dean Walker also questioned the openness of Italian artists to the forays made by foreign sculptors on the Roman art scene, as he pondered the above-mentioned cases involving Lambert-Sigisbert Adam and Bouchardon.[151] Given the foregoing, and keeping in mind that in early modern Italy a Florentine or a Lombard artist was as much of a foreigner in Rome as a Fleming or a Spaniard,[152] one has to conclude that the city's pluralistic, transnational character was the most significant factor that resulted in the filing of those 'rough edges' which caused greater attrition among artists in other European cities. Indeed, it was Rome's catholic nature, its all-embracing 'extreme openness',[153] that made it an exceptional artistic center for Italians and foreigners alike.

* * *

Among the documents from 1776 included in the *Correspondance des Directeurs de l'Académie de France à Rome* under the directorship of Joseph-Marie Vien (1775–81) is an abstract from the Abbé de Fontenai's *Dictionnaire des artistes* (1776).[154] While incorrectly crediting Charles Le Brun for having conceived the idea of creating an artists' academy in Rome, under the heading 'Académie', the author writes:

> Just as the ancient Romans went to Athens, which was the center of eloquence and philosophy, similarly Le Brun thought that, in our days, the French must go to Rome to study the beaux-arts. It is in this city, in fact, that the works of the ancient Greeks, the Michelangelos, the Raphaels, the Domenichinos, convey silent lessons far superior to all of those that the greatest modern masters could impart with their living voice.[155]

While quoting verbatim, without citing his source, the French translation of Francesco Algarotti's *Saggio sopra l'Accademia di Francia che è in Roma*,[156] the Abbé still expressed the mindset that much of Europe had developed through the centuries: a marked obeisance towards Rome as the wellspring from which all good art derives.

As Europe entered the period we have come to know as Neoclassicism, when artists, critics, and art theorists sought to bring back a 'true style' based on 'the reassertion of timeless artistic truths',[157] three notable aspects of the Abbé de Fontenai's claim should be highlighted: first of all, he states that young French artists, by being in Rome, could benefit by studying the works of the ancient *Greeks* rather than those of the Romans;[158] second, the lure of Michelangelo – despite the anti-classical trends of his late works – still held sway, at least for some, well into the end of the eighteenth century; third, Raphael, as well as the Domenichinos – that is, all of the Baroque artists who followed his classical artistic vein – remained the constant guiding light for artists until the nineteenth century. What the Abbé or Vien would not have dreamt of asserting is that Rome, as a cultural center, was superior to Paris. Indeed, as Gilles Montègre has pointed out, if in 1705 someone such as Saint-Évremond could claim 'a gentleman must live and die in a capital and, from my point of view, there are only three capitals: Rome, London and Paris',[159] by 1765 Louis de Jaucourt would express a rather different point of view in the *Encyclopédie*. Besides criticising Rome's poorly maintained palaces, deplorable homes, poorly paved roads, unsightly, dirty, narrow streets cleaned only by the pouring rain, he states: 'This city, that abounds with churches and convents, is practically uninhabited on its east and south sides . . . Thus, those who say that the seven hills, which previously symbolised its ornament, [now] function only as its grave, are right.'[160] In fact, what took final shape during the second half of the eighteenth century is a cultural tug-of-war between France and Italy that had begun in the sixteenth century, as the French intelligentsia became more convinced that their society had superseded the Italian and that they could well do without much of what the latter had to offer.[161] As Voltaire stated in a polite but proud response to Deodati de' Tovazzi's claim on the superiority of the Italian language, 'Having long since left our infancy behind, we have abandoned the lap of a decaying wet-nurse whose milk is spent . . . Equality gratifies the wise, so let us end the contest. It's not so bad to be equal to the French.'[162] Indeed, Italian culture at large was by then seen in France as 'somnolent and archaic', unable to produce significant works capable of attracting the attention of the literati north of the Alps.[163] *De facto*, by the eighteenth century Paris had become the new Athens[164] and everyone in Europe, but especially in Italy, looked up to France as the *dotta nazione*, 'the learned nation'.[165]

It is within the larger context of the cultural war between France and Italy that Algarotti wrote the above-mentioned *Saggio sopra l'Accademia di Francia che è in Roma*. It was a response to the criticism expressed by the Marquis d'Argens in his *Réflexions critiques sur les differentes écoles de peinture* (1752), where Argens clearly asserted that, by his time, it was useless for young French artists to go to Rome to complete their studies.[166] 'Foreigners', he proudly professed, 'and the Italians most of all, presume that, since we send some of our youth to study in Rome, they are justified in maintaining that one cannot become a great painter other than by going there, since we, who claim to be their rivals, go to their country to learn our trade. This type of reasoning might have been valid seventy years ago but it has no basis today.'[167] Supporting his argument by claiming that artists had all they needed in Paris – the royal collection of paintings with masterpieces from all European schools and casts from ancient monuments – he further stated that it was evident to him 'that one may become a very great painter without owing anything to the Italians'.[168]

As if indirectly rejoining a century later Benvenuto Cellini's claim that 'the French are people of no culture', around the year 1670 an anonymous Frenchman wrote 'L'Italie c'est rien'.[169] Scornful and reductive as chauvinistic views can be, the phrases tell us much more about the persons who voiced them than the nations they branded. As it has been perspicaciously observed, such opinions were the fruit of a long process of denigration of 'the other' in the struggle for the cultural hegemony of Europe.[170] Channeled by guidebooks that reproduced stereotypes – as discussed in Chapter 1 – the sentiments expressed by northerners, especially the French, about Italy and Rome in the eighteenth century represent 'the consolidation of a national characterization, typical of the philosophical discourse of the eighteenth century',[171] especially in the wake of Montesquieu's *De l'esprit des loix* (1748–9). However, the reflective observer would have understood that, especially in the field of the arts, far from having descended into a phase of decline, Rome remained, as it had been in Bernini's time, a viable, powerful magnet for European artists and connoisseurs alike.[172] So much so that in the spring of 1802, writing to Talleyrand from Rome, François Cacault asked: 'why does the most famous European painter of the last century happen to be a German, Monsieur *Mengs*? Why is the most famous living sculptor a Venetian, Monsieur *Canova*? . . . I know that in Paris people maintain that during the last century we have had comparable good painters to *Mengs*; but the rest of Europe doesn't think so. The same goes for *Canova*.'[173] In fact, it is unlikely that both foreigners, the German painter or the Venetian sculptor, would have metamorphosed into the extraordinary artists the world has known had they not lived and worked in Rome. For the openness to foreign talent and artistic virtue made the city, as Bellori stated, 'that common fatherland of humanity where the loftiest spirits are wont to congregate'.[174] Significantly, Bernini was well aware of this when he initially refused Louis XIV's invitation to go to Paris, asserting: 'Although Rome's vision at times is impeded, it never loses its sight; by which he implied that Rome was a city in which at times envy undermines merit, but never suppresses it.'[175]

6

Bernini's Shadow

In a letter dated 8 December 1665, Bernini informs Paul Fréart de Chantelou that he has arrived back in Rome and, laconically, also reports at the end of the letter that he has learned that Poussin had died.[1] The artist's contact with the French court continued even after Colbert officially notified him, on 15 July 1667, that his project for the Louvre could not be carried out because of the expenses the nation had to sustain in the so-called War of Devolution (1667–8).[2] As a consequence, false rumors spread in Paris claiming that, in despair, Bernini contemplated suicide.[3] Actually, Gian Lorenzo was not only asked to oversee the young sculptors who were to frequent the burgeoning Académie de France in Rome but also to execute an equestrian statue of Louis XIV (fig.6.1).[4] The statue was to be carried out with the aid of the young *pensionnaires*, while Bernini reserved for himself the execution of the facial features of the king.[5] The monument, according to Colbert's initial plans, was to be located either on the projected stone bridge meant to replace the Pont-Rouge, which connected the left bank to the Louvre, or in the Tuileries gardens.[6] Begun by May 1671, and still in Rome at the time of Colbert's death in 1683, it was embarked in 1684, arriving in Paris in March 1685. As it failed to please the king and other French viewers – evidence that 'the same camarilla in Paris which had prevented the execution of Bernini's Louvre designs had won a new victory'[7] – it was soon transferred to Versailles, where it is to be found to this day.[8]

After his return to Rome, Bernini lived another fifteen years. And while his protégé, 'Le petit Giulio' who had accompanied him to Paris, had become an able sculptor in his own right and was completing the busts of Cardinal Fausto Poli and his nephew, Monsignor Gaudenzio, in their chapel in San Crisogono (1679–81)[9] (figs 6.2 and 6.3) – Bernini's last architectural project commissioned by his friend Sisinio Poli whose portrait he had drawn years earlier (fig.4.9) – the master lay dying in his palace on Via della Mercede.[10] During his final hours Bernini was surrounded by family and intimate friends who witnessed 'a continued coming and going of the most illustrious personages of Rome'.[11] Among his close friends was Bernini's faithful assistant. Filippo Baldinucci's comment that Giulio 'served and aided him [Bernini] until his death',[12] is corroborated by Domenico Bernini who records that in his father's final hours, after the artist fell sick with a fever and subsequently suffered a fit of apoplexy, his assistant was 'constantly at his bedside'.[13]

Despite the sad circumstances and true to his character as described by Baldinucci and his son Domenico, Gian Lorenzo did not lose his sense of humor in his final hours. As he lay in bed with the right side of his body paralyzed, he purportedly uttered: 'it is good that this arm which has so

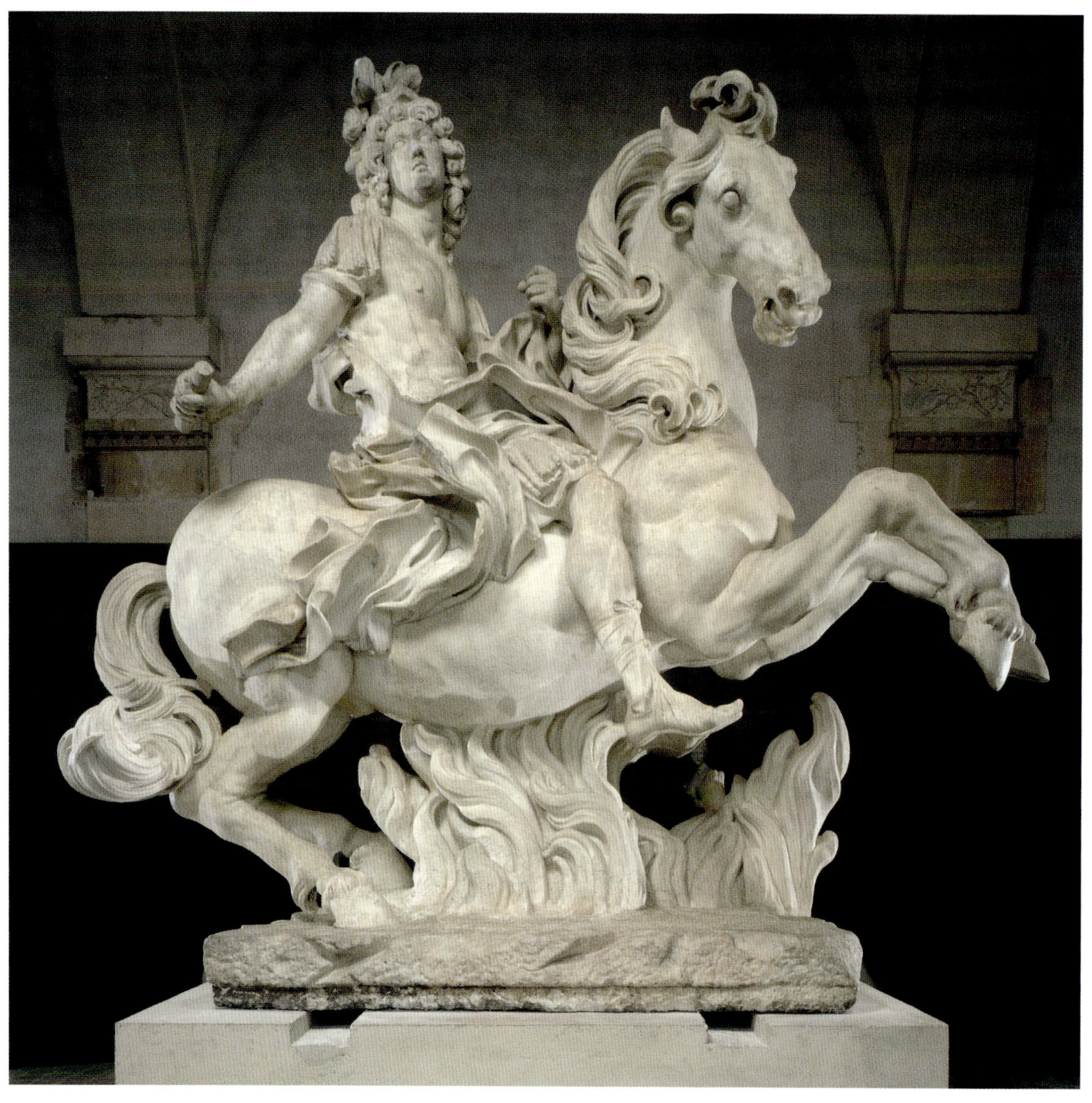

6.1 Gian Lorenzo Bernini, *Equestrian Statue of Louis XIV* (later re-carved as *Marcus Curtius* by François Girardon), *c.*1671–8, marble, 376 × 399 cm (148 1⁄16 × 157 1⁄16 in), Châteaux de Versailles et de Trianon, Versailles

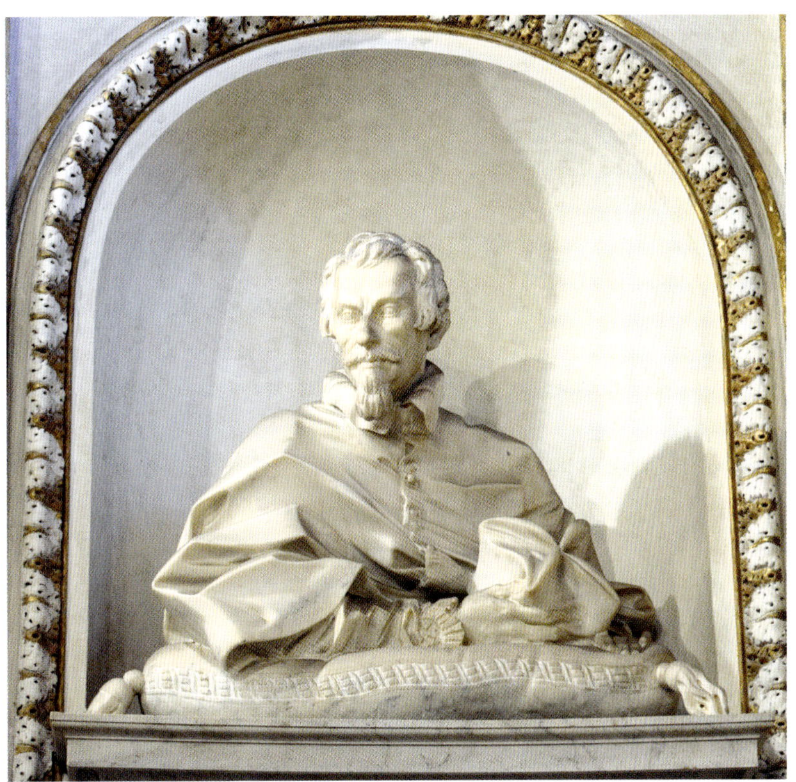

6.2 Giulio Cartari (Cartarè), *Portrait of Fausto Poli*, 1679–81, marble, Poli Chapel, San Crisogono, Rome

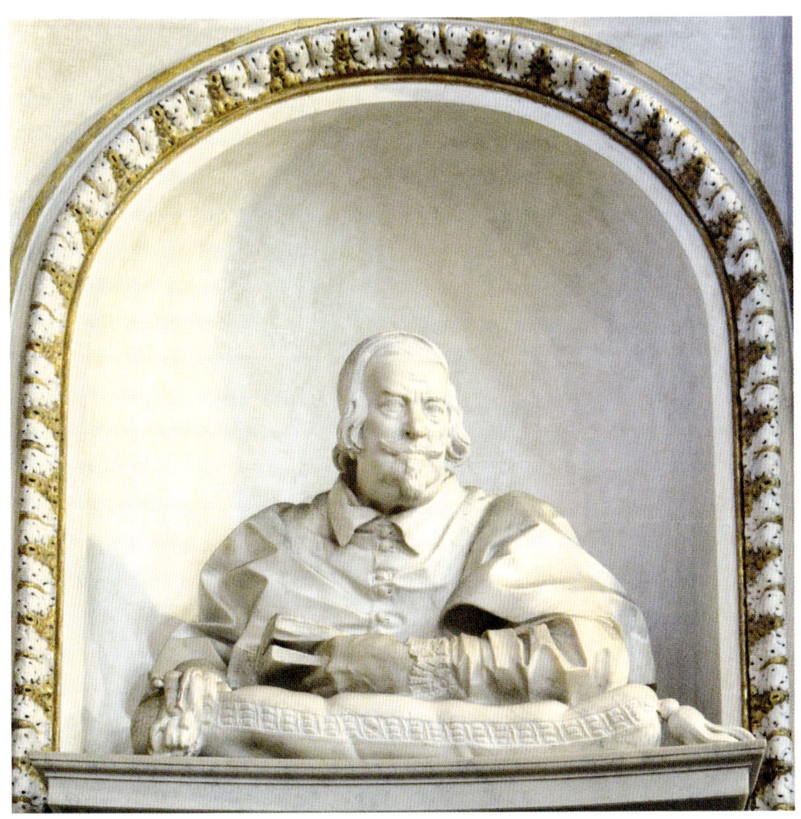

6.3 Giulio Cartari (Cartarè), *Portrait of Gaudenzio Poli*, 1679–81, marble, Poli Chapel, San Crisogono, Rome

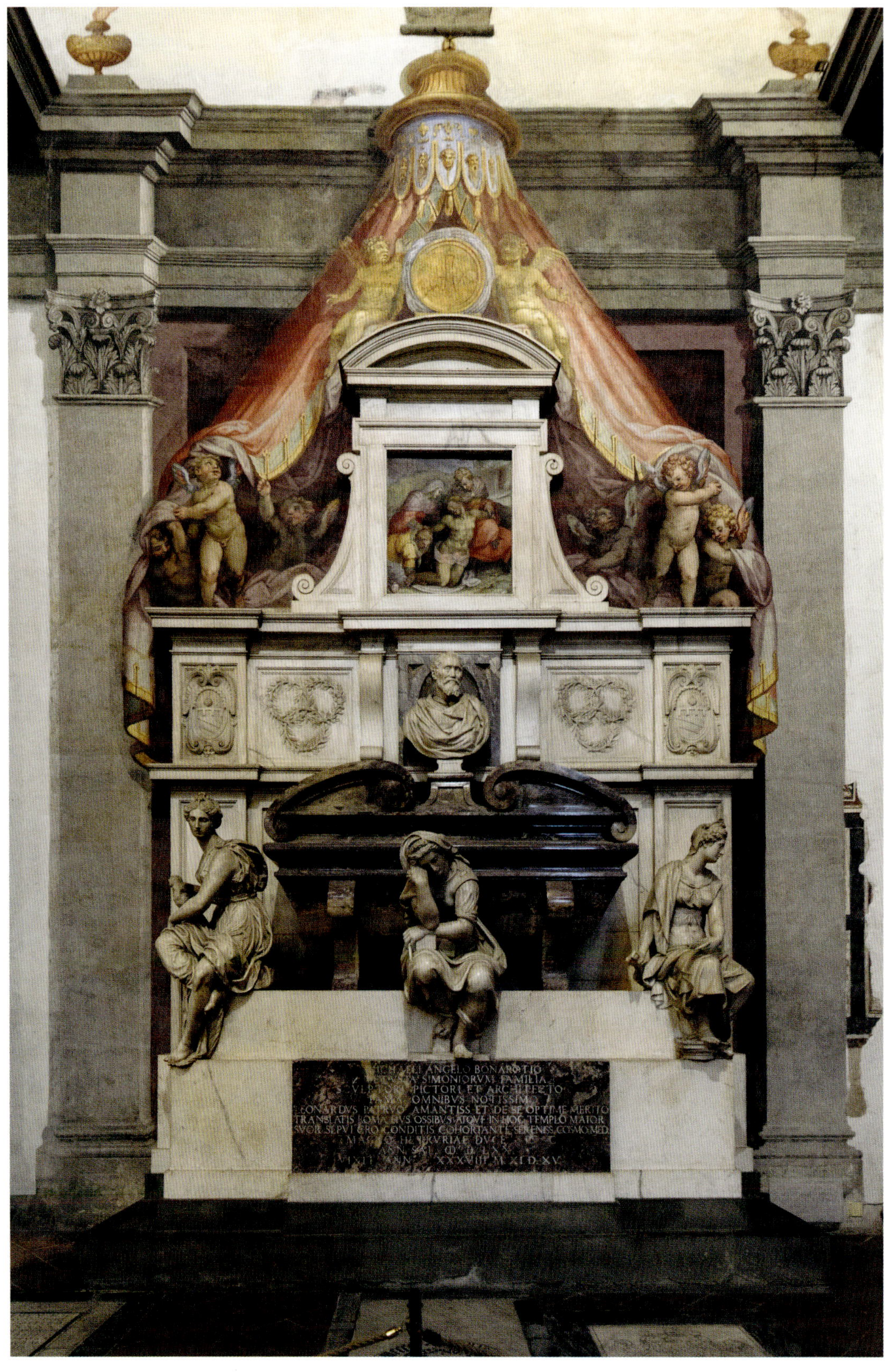
ANGELO BONAROTIO
SIMONIORVM FAMILIA
PICTORI ET ARCHITETTO
OMNIBVS NOTISSIMO
AMANTISS ET DE SE OPTIME MERITO
TRANSLATIS OSSIBVS ATQVE IN HOC TEMPLO MAIOR
CONDITIS COHORTANTE SERENISS COSMO MED
DVCE
VIXIT ANN XXXVIII M XI D XV

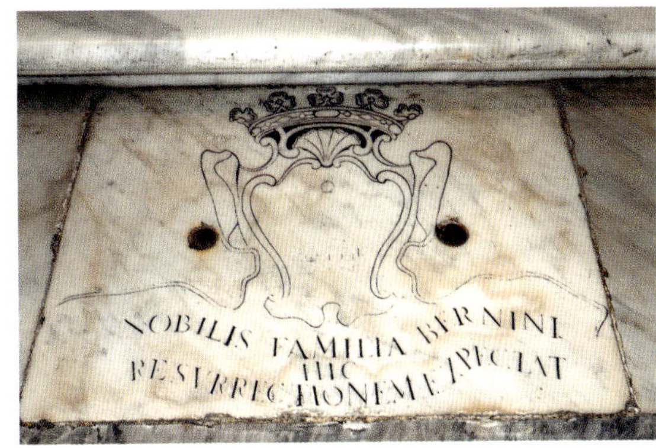

6.4 Giorgio Vasari, *Tomb of Michelangelo Buonarroti*, 1564–78, white Carrara marble, polychrome marble, wall painting, 500 × 600 cm (196 ⅞ × 236 ¼ in), Santa Croce, Florence

6.5 Bernini's family tomb, marble, Santa Maria Maggiore, Rome

wearied itself in life should rest a bit before death'.[14] Subsequently Bernini lost his speech and, having imparted his blessings to his nine children, received the pope's benediction via one of the papal valets.[15] 'Then, at the commencement of the twenty-eighth day of November of the year 1680 and in the eighty-second year of his life Bernini breathed his last.'[16]

Even though the artist's parish church of Sant'Andrea delle Fratte was just across from the palace in which he died, his corpse, 'accompanied by four torches',[17] was taken to his family's parish church: the Basilica of Santa Maria Maggiore. The following morning his remains were exhibited to the public in the middle of the nave with sixty torches surrounding it, the church 'nobly decorated', a mass sung, and candles and bread distributed to the poor.[18] While the records do not reveal the names of the dignitaries who attended the obsequies or the clergyman who delivered the eulogy,[19] Baldinucci claims that so many people came to pay homage to the artist that it was decided to postpone the interment of the body.[20] As to his funeral rite, in his testament Bernini had expressed a wish that it be a simple affair: 'I leave up to my aforementioned heirs the [planning of my] funeral, and I remind them that, for the unfortunate deceased, suffrages in the form of Masses and prayers are more necessary than the pomp of funeral services.'[21] Both biographers refer to the fact that his body was placed in a lead coffin,[22] with his son also specifying that an inscription recording the name and date of his death was attached to it.[23]

To anyone conversant with Bernini's designs for funerary monuments, seeing this artist's tomb in Santa Maria Maggiore comes as a surprise. In contrast to his great predecessor, Michelangelo, whose imposing tomb in the church of Santa Croce (fig.6.4) declared to future generations the esteem in which he was held by his contemporaries, the only indication of Bernini's remains is a simple marble slab with a coat of arms and an inscription that dates to after 1746, when Benedict XIV ennobled the family.[24] On the right aisle pavement, near the main altar, all one reads is 'Nobilis familia Bernini hic resurrectionem expectat.' ('The Noble Bernini Family here awaits resurrection') (fig.6.5).[25] In Gian Lorenzo's case, resurrection must have occurred before 1 July 1931 since, to the disappointment of those who descended into the crypt at that time, there was no trace of his mortal remains;[26] all they found that most likely belonged to him was the hilt of the sword with which he was knighted by Gregory XV (fig.6.6).[27] Nonetheless, from a drawing attributed to Ludovico Gimignani at the Istituto Centrale per la Grafica, one gathers that at some point a full-fledged funerary monument for Bernini was being planned, perhaps under Bernini's own directive, to be placed most likely in the Basilica of Santa Maria Maggiore

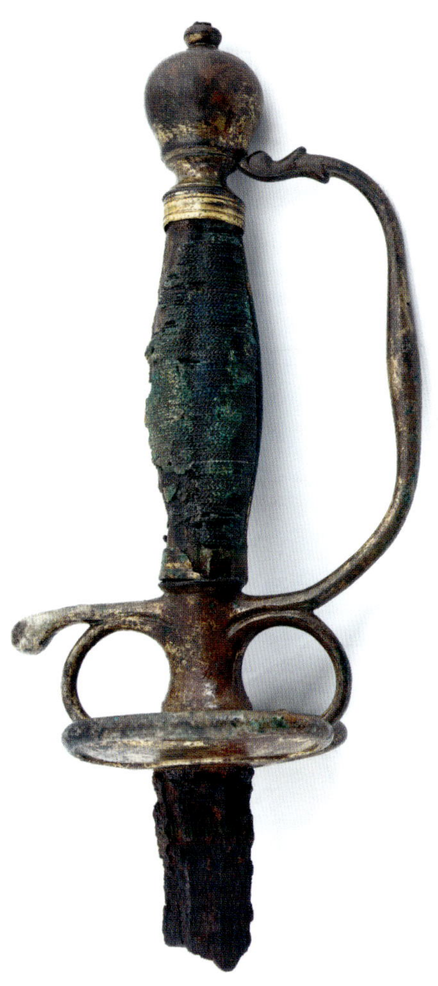

6.6 Dress sword, from the Bernini family tomb, Museo Storico, Santa Maria Maggiore, Rome

(figs 6.7 and 6.8).[28] Set against a niche, the portrait bust of the sculptor looking down to his right rises from an amorphous rocky formation (the 'Mountain of Virtue') as a winged figure (Fame, Virtue, or possibly an angel)[29] crowns it with a wreath. Beneath this rock, a cartouche with Bernini's name separates the bust from two putti and, possibly, the outline of a reclined woman – whose face resembles that of Bernini's drawing for his Saint Teresa (fig.6.9) – looking up towards the bust.[30]

That such a monument was being considered at some point is plausibly corroborated by the presence of a larger-than-life statue of *Fame* recorded as being in the sculptor's courtyard at the time of his death.[31] As to why such a sepulcher was never executed remains unknown, although it has been suggested that, with Clement IX's death and Clement X's replacement of Bernini with Carlo Rainaldi as architect of the planned new apse of Santa Maria Maggiore, the project was dismissed.[32] According to this view, had Clement IX's funerary monument been erected in the new apse of the basilica, Bernini might have succeeded in having a more monumental sepulcher for himself in the same church.[33] Chances are, however, that Bernini never received an approval for a papal tomb in the newly contemplated apse because the papal focus had shifted to a modern reconstruction of the rear of the basilica which would have had a great symbolic and figurative impact on the urban context of the Esquiline Hill, comparable to that achieved by Clement IX's predecessor, Alexander VII, with the colonnade of Saint Peter's.[34]

As to Bernini's own sepulcher, perhaps his preference for 'Masses and prayers', as stipulated in his will, may have been the decisive factor in the final choice of the family's humble tomb. Or, possibly, his choice was determined by a desire to imitate the example set by one of his closest friends, Cardinal Sforza Pallavicino, who, believing that inscriptions were a more appropriate and longer-lasting way to commemorate an individual, stipulated that he be buried 'in the most private and simple manner possible' with a tombstone having only a brief inscription and the design approved by Bernini.[35] Certainly, Gian Lorenzo was no Cato the Elder, who would rather have people ask why he had no statue made of himself rather than why he had one.[36] Such self-abnegation does not reflect what we know about the artist's personality. Still, this mindset was not totally alien to anyone interested in

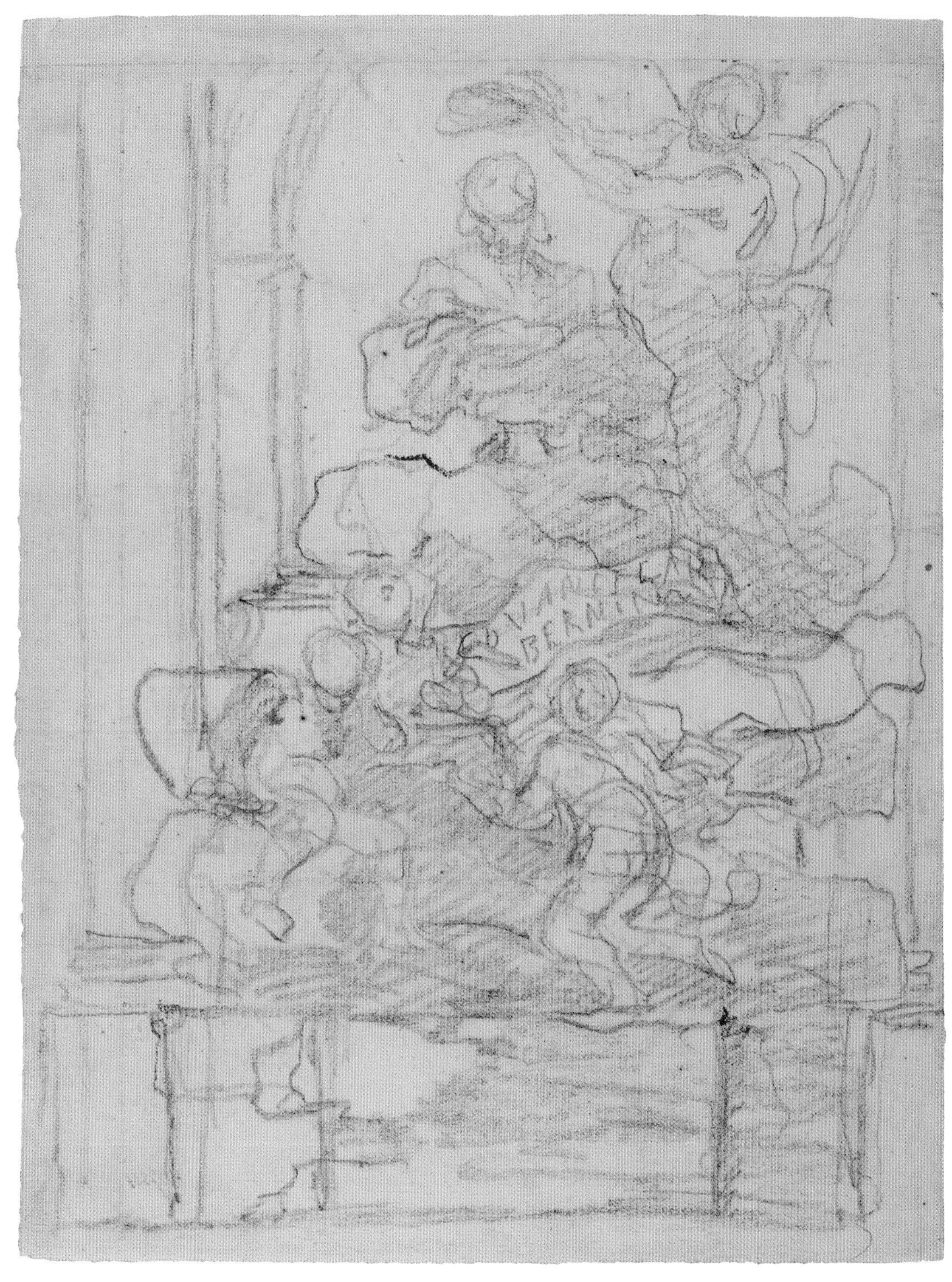

6.7 Ludovico Gimignani, *Projected Tomb for Gian Lorenzo Bernini*, drawing, 22.5 × 17.2 cm (8 ⅞ × 6 ¾ in), Istituto Centrale per la Grafica, Rome

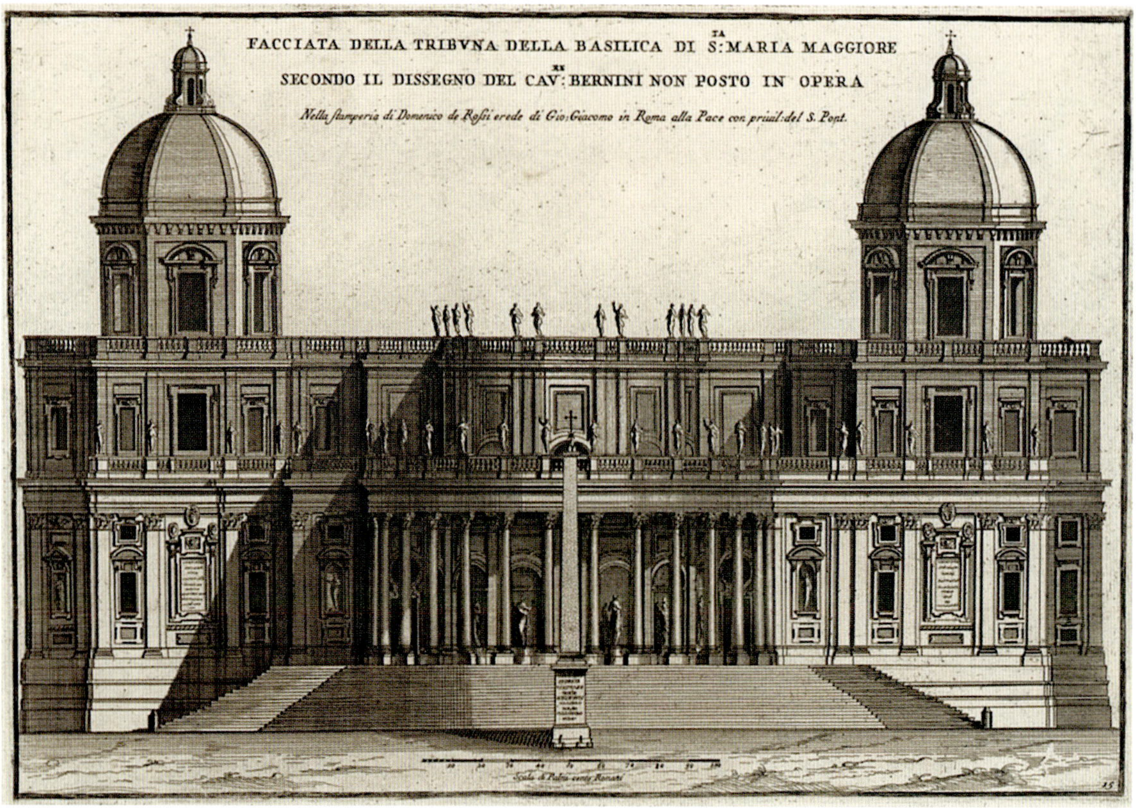

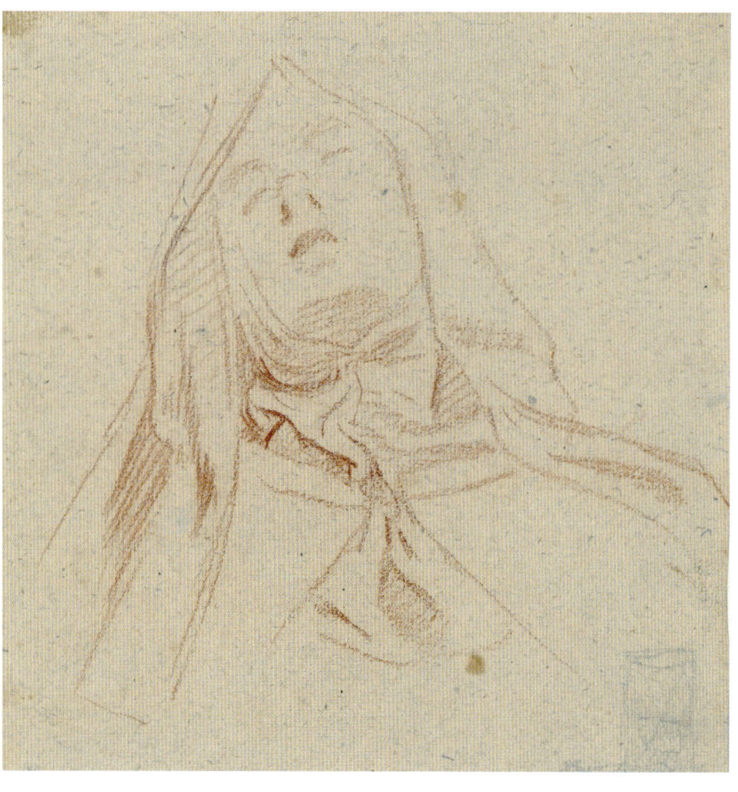

6.8 Domenico de Rossi, *Santa Maria Maggiore*, unexecuted rear facade designed by Bernini, 1720–21, engraving, 47.8 × 34 cm (18 13⁄16 × 13 3⁄8 in), Domenico de Rossi, Studio d'architettura Civile, parte terza, 1720–21

6.9 Gian Lorenzo Bernini, *Study for the Head of Saint Teresa*, red and black chalk, Leipzig, Museum der bildenden Künste

sculpture. A seventeenth-century book specifically dedicated to statuary, Giovanni Antonio Borboni's *Delle Statue* (1661), makes such a claim. After an extensive exposition of individuals meritorious of a public statue from antiquity to the modern era, the author concludes his final chapter with the following statement:

> Now, if one may not only commend those who erect statues with the aims praised [earlier in the book] but also extol their infinite merit, what acclaim and merit shall be bestowed upon him who with an excess of humility refuses [to have one built for himself]? As Paul wrote to the Corinthians, *Qui matrimonio iungit Virginem suam, benè facit, & qui non iungit, melius facit.* Thus I will say [with regard] to my subject: he who has wedded the immortality of his name to a statue, has done well; but he who has remained celibate, has done better.[37]

Ultimately, the family decided to erect an equally grand monument to Gian Lorenzo Bernini: a literary one, in the form of a biography.[38] This project was meant to not only commemorate the sculptor's works but also act as an apology against a series of attacks on the artist that had begun appearing from the mid-1670s. These had taken the form of *avvisi* (news dispatches), handwritten booklets, and influential books, such as Passeri's *Lives of the Artists* (circulated in manuscript form) or Bellori's biographies, which basically ignored Bernini's existence.[39] In the end, no doubt, the family must have felt that the literary medium was an even better choice, for it would have a greater impact on public opinion far and wide, beyond the city's boundaries, while a sumptuous funerary monument could only affect those who were able to see it in person.

Whatever the reason, had the monument been built, it is possible that the psychologically penetrating terracotta portrait of the artist at the Hermitage Museum would have been part of the memorial (fig.6.10).[40] The authorship of this captivating portrait has been attributed in turn to Bernini's workshop,[41] Gian Lorenzo himself,[42] and, more recently, to Giulio Cartari (Cartarè).[43] Although stylistically and qualitatively the superlative clay bust would seem to have been generated by a sculptor more talented than Giulio, one could envision no better tribute for any of his assistants to pay the master, for he had transformed, with their assistance, the Eternal City into Bernini's Rome.[44]

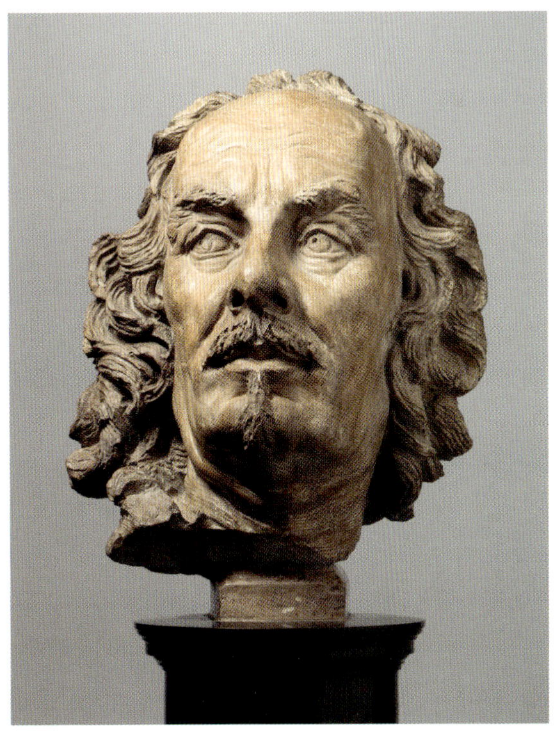

6.10 Gian Lorenzo Bernini, workshop of, *Gianlorenzo Bernini*, *c.*1670, terracotta, height 46 cm (18⅛ in), The State Hermitage Museum, Saint Petersburg

* * *

Contrary to a number of predecessors who wrote biographical accounts of modern or ancient artists, Giovan Pietro Bellori broke a well-established tradition when he penned *The Lives of the Modern Painters, Sculptors and Architects* (1672).[45] Instead of including the biographies of as many artists as possible, he decided to be highly selective: 'But because we propose at present to write of artists of *disegno*, we shall address painting, sculpture, and architecture: since these, like poetry, for their excellence do not allow mediocrity of imitation, they reject mediocre artists and grant the laurels of immortality only to those who are excellent.'[46] Among the twelve artists whose biographies he had completed by publication date, Bellori included eight Italians (six painters, one sculptor, and one architect) and four foreigners (three painters and one sculptor).[47] But, as is known and quite surprisingly for modern readers, Bernini is excluded from such company, as is Borromini. While the omission of the latter from Bellori's *Lives* was uniquely connected to the biographer's classical leanings – a gloss to Borromini's San Carlo alle Quattro Fontane in his copy of Giovanni Baglione's *Lives* censures it as 'ugly and deformed, barbarous, most ignorant and a corruptor of architecture, infamy of our age'[48] – Bernini's exclusion was dictated by both Bellori's aesthetic preferences and the fact that in 1672 the artist was still alive. Nevertheless, one imagines that no greater insult could be flung at the artist who was ultimately employed by seven popes, acclaimed by numerous cardinals, revered by Queen Christina and invited to France by the Most Christian King, than to not have been considered among those who were worthy of 'the laurels of immortality'.[49] Indeed, although the general sentiment of Bernini's Roman admirers is encapsulated in a letter that Cardinal Decio Azzolino wrote to him while the sculptor was in France – 'the great works we have of yours in Rome, which are responsible for having taken you to France, seem to make it pointless to judge your worth by what you will do over there'[50] – Bellori's omission was one of the reasons why Bernini's family ultimately conceived and prompted Filippo Baldinucci to write a biography of the artist.[51]

Until fairly recently, some scholars saw in Bellori's biographies and his endorsement of those artists representative of the classical vein in seventeenth-century Roman art – such as Annibale Carracci, Domenichino, and Poussin – indications of a reversal in Bernini's reputation.[52] There are also historians who believe that the giant statues of the twelve apostles executed for the nave of the Basilica of Saint John Lateran reveal the extent of Bernini's unpopularity and a reaction to his effusive style (fig.2.21).[53] While there is no doubt that the classical ideals championed by Bellori and encapsulated in the sculptures of Duquesnoy and Algardi would ultimately prevail in the eighteenth century, the idea that Bernini's appeal had subsided as early as 1700 is contradicted by documentary and artistic evidence.[54] The truth is that Bernini's influence clearly continued to cast a long shadow for years to come.

It is of some interest, for example, that up to the end of the eighteenth century, when Antonio Canova created his first public masterpiece that inaugurates the new season of Neoclassicism with his tomb for Clement XIV of 1787 in the basilica of Santi Apostoli (fig.6.11), the directors of the Académie de France continued to show interest in one of the least classical sculptures Bernini executed in his early career: the statue of *Saint Bibiana* (1624) (fig.6.12).[55] The representation of this Early Christian saint, caught in the middle of a spiritual experience as she ecstatically looks up towards her Creator with raised right hand and leg as well as deeply carved garments, is the complete antithesis of the calm, noble dignity associated with late eighteenth-century style. True, her human form does not totally disappear under swaths of drapery as do his late sculptures, such as the angels intended for the Castel Sant'Angelo bridge of 1667–9 (figs 6.13 and 1.18), but the heavy vestment that covers her abdomen with a hyperbolic, surging fold is at odds with late eighteenth-century taste.[56] In fact, while by the end of the sixteenth century some sculptors, such as Bartolomeo Ammannati, in compliance with the Post-Tridentine artistic dictates,

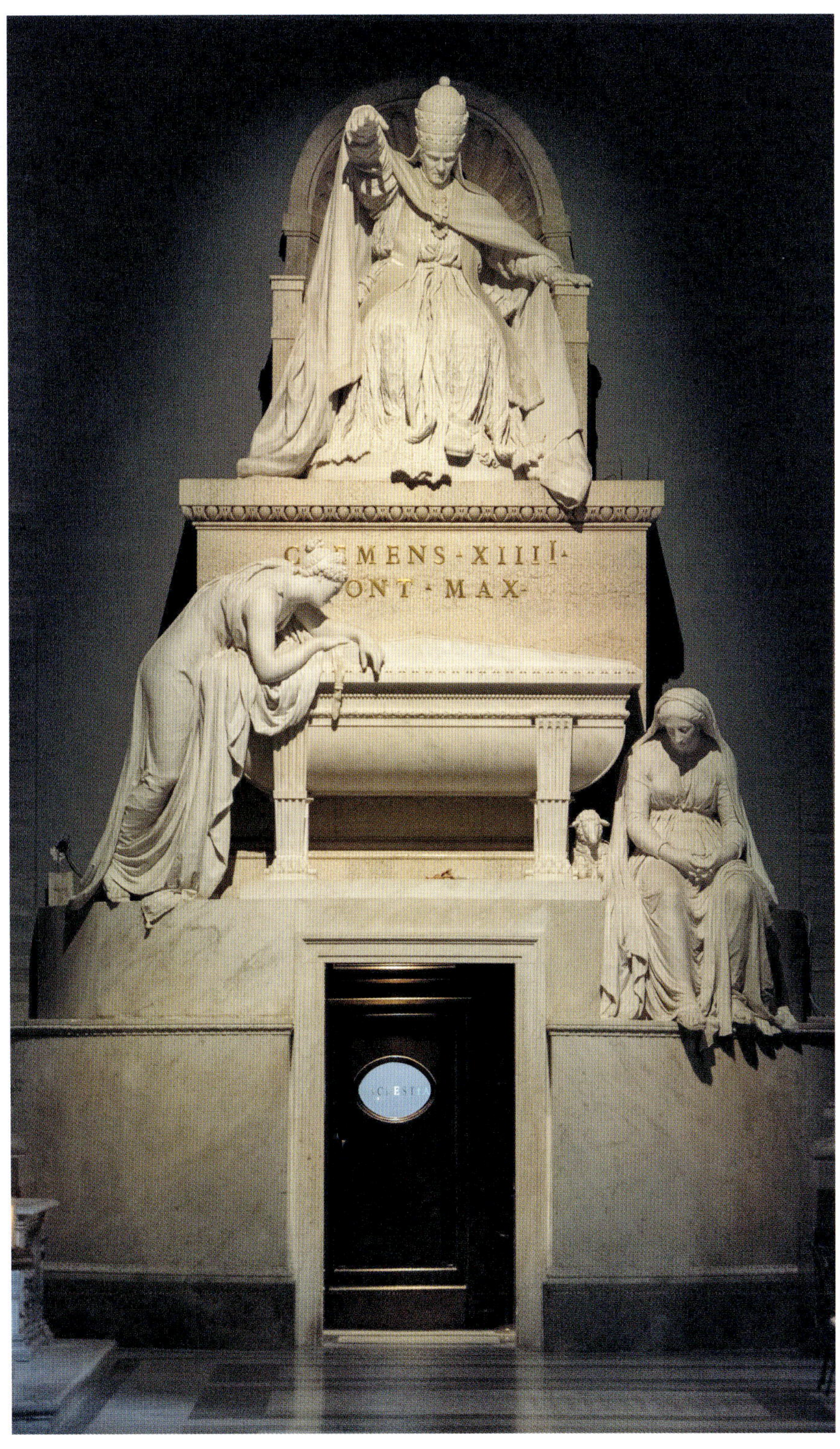

6.11 Antonio Canova, *Funerary Monument for Clement XIV*, 1787, marble, height 740 cm (291 5/16 in), Santi Apostoli, Rome

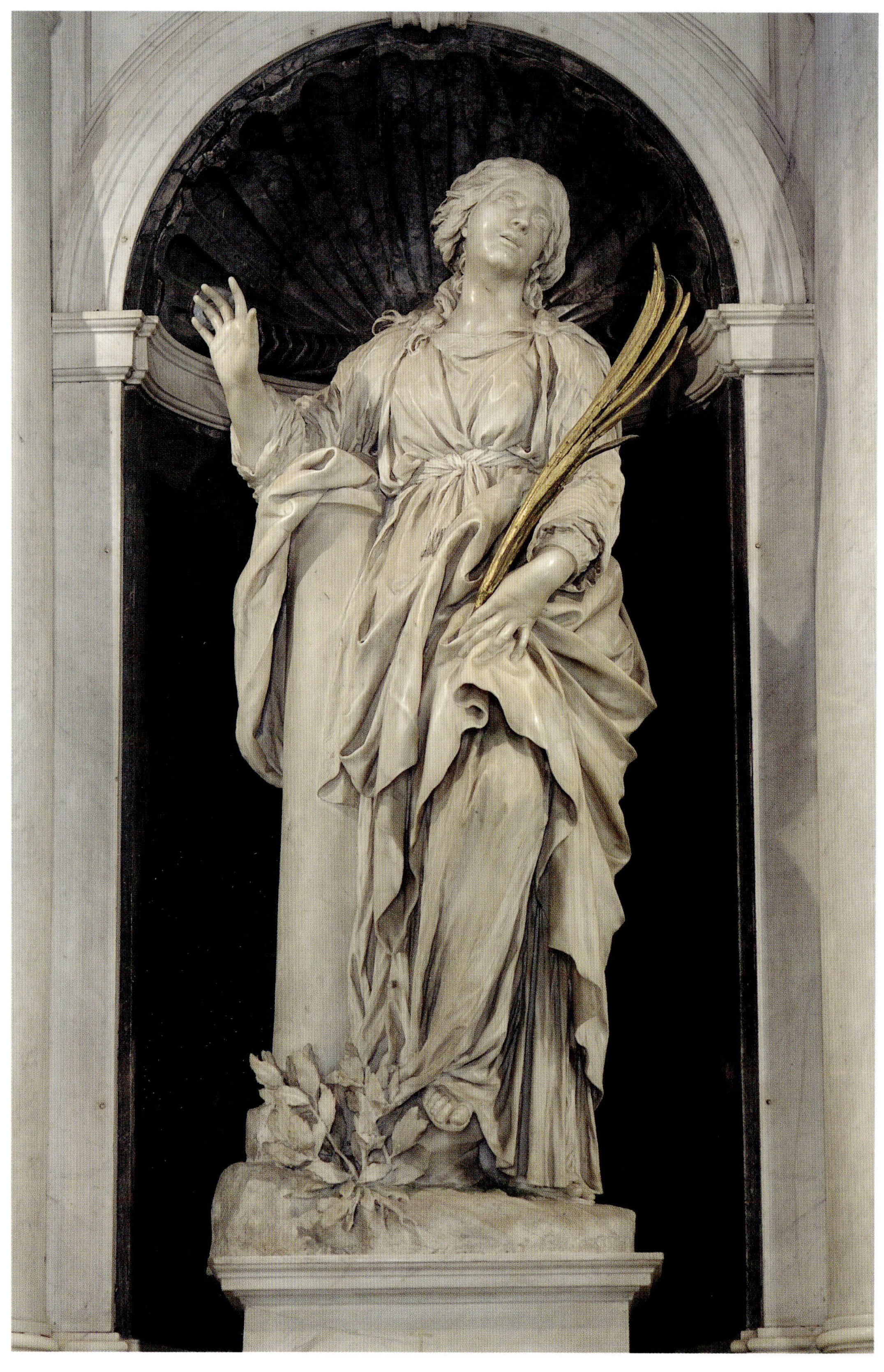

6.12 Gian Lorenzo Bernini, *Saint Bibiana*, 1624, marble, Santa Bibiana, Rome

6.13 Gian Lorenzo Bernini, *Angel with the Crown of Thorns*, 1669–71, marble, Sant'Andrea delle Fratte, Rome

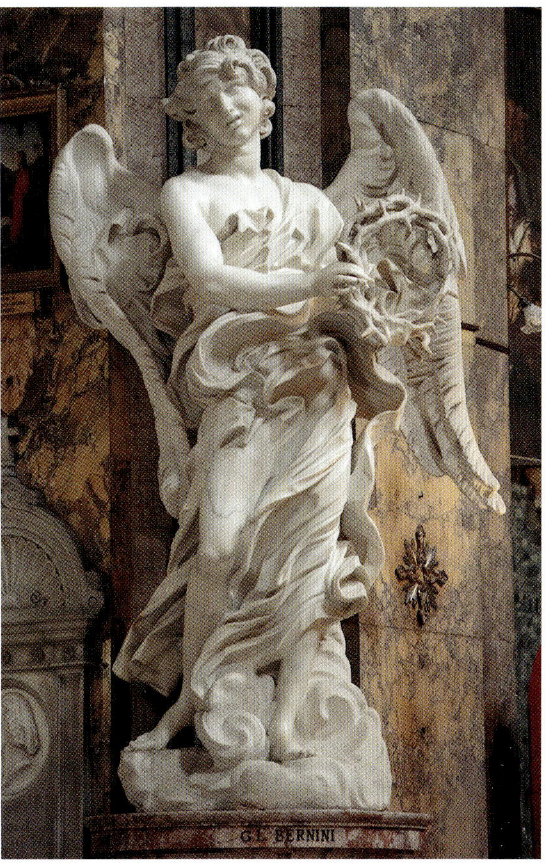

avoided clothing religious figures with clinging drapery so as to conform to religious decorum,[57] Bernini covered *Saint Bibiana*'s anatomy with heavy garments, not out of concern for pious propriety, but rather to accentuate and graphically sustain the emotional rapture of the figure represented and demonstrate his renowned dexterity as a sculptor who treated marble as if it were dough or wax.[58] And although he was criticised by some who saw 'the drapery of his figures as too complex and sharp, on the contrary, he felt this to be a special indication of his skill'.[59] When viewing the statue with the sculptor Lambert-Sigisbert Adam in 1729, Montesquieu observed as much:

> He [Bernini] has endowed all of the draperies with a very large number of folds and, by his art, not allowed the nude figure beneath to appear, such that with much he makes much, unlike the Fleming [Duquesnoy] and Algardi, who use few folds and allow the form of the body to show through. Bernini's art comes from his skill in carving marble.[60]

One would expect that by the eighteenth century in the two institutions for which classical art was the primary source of inspiration – the Académie de France and the Accademia di San Luca – Bernini might have lost his attractiveness. Yet, this was not the case. As regards the Académie, for example, one first hears of the directors' attraction to Bernini's *Saint Bibiana* in a letter dated 13 January 1741, when Jean Baptiste De Troy asks the *Surintendant* Philibert Orry permission to have a plaster cast made of it for the benefit of the young French sculptors who attended the institution.[61] Then, in June of the same year, we learn from De Troy that the young *pensionnaire*, Jacques Saly, asked for permission to make a copy in marble of this statue, which De Troy considers 'une figure admirable'.[62] Although nothing came of it at the time, twelve years later, on 17 January 1753, Director Charles Natoire, in corresponding with Superintendent Abel-François Poisson de Vandières – better known as the Marquis de Marigny – informs him that, with his approval, he could have a plaster cast executed of Bernini's *Saint Bibiana*, 'one of his most beautiful pieces'.[63] When one considers that these views were being expressed

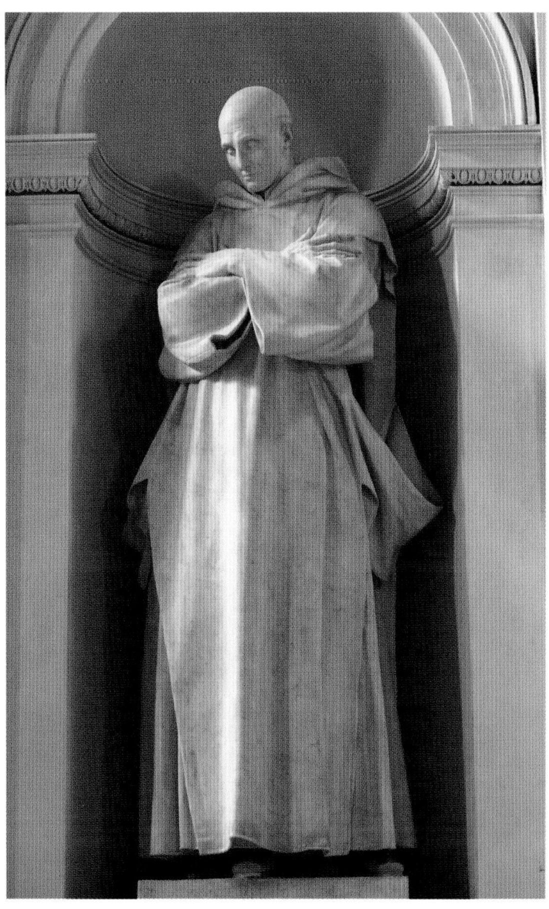

6.14 Jean-Antoine Houdon, *Saint Bruno*, 1766, marble, height 315 cm (124 in), Santa Maria degli Angeli, Rome

at about the time when the Académie's own Jean Antoine Houdon sculpted the acclaimed *Saint Bruno* (fig.6.14) in Santa Maria degli Angeli (1766), a work positioned aesthetically at the opposite end of the spectrum from the *Saint Bibiana*, such statements are quite striking.[64] In fact, mention of Bernini's prized plaster cast recurs on 30 December 1778, when Director Joseph-Marie Vien, corresponding with the Comte d'Angiviller, verifies that it was still part of the Academy's collection.[65] And well into the last quarter of the eighteenth century, on 15 May 1782, the new director Louis-Jean-François Lagrenée informs d'Angiviller that a molder ('mouleur'), in exchange for obtaining permission from the Vatican to make a mold of the *Discobolus*, would give the Académie two free plaster casts of this statue, provided Lagrenée allow him to keep the mold and permit him to make an added mold of Bernini's *Saint Bibiana*.[66] On 28 June, d'Angiviller gave his approval but demanded the molder agree, in writing, that should the academy's plaster cast be damaged in the process, he would supply a new mold taken from Bernini's marble statue, for 'given Bernini's renown, the Saint Bibiana must be a precious work'.[67] Given the interest in this statue by members of the Académie, it is unsurprising that even as late as 1833 there were writers traveling through Italy, such as Antoine Claude Pasquin Valery, who could find some redeeming value in the *Saint Bibiana* (the 'most graceful, and best work of Bernini in sculpture') before, according to him, Bernini had taken 'such pains to corrupt his style'.[68]

The French were not alone in their appreciation of Bernini's sculptures at this late date. His lasting allure through most of the eighteenth century is corroborated by the records of the Accademia di San Luca, which preserve not only the minutes of the academic gatherings but also the drawings made by its students from 1663 to 1870.[69] With a fairly regular frequency from the middle of the seventeenth to the middle of the eighteenth centuries, the topics chosen for the contests – the *concorsi* – of young artists provide an indication of what the academicians believed worthy of emulation. Besides those instances in which students were asked to draw after classical statuary, the first time that a contest involved drawing the work of a modern sculptor occurred in 1692 when the aspiring academicians were required to draw Algardi's spectacular relief representing the *Encounter of Leo I and Attila* in Saint Peter's (fig.6.15).[70] However, it was Bernini's statues that, on a par with classical sculptures, were most often taken as *exempla* for the artistic competitions.

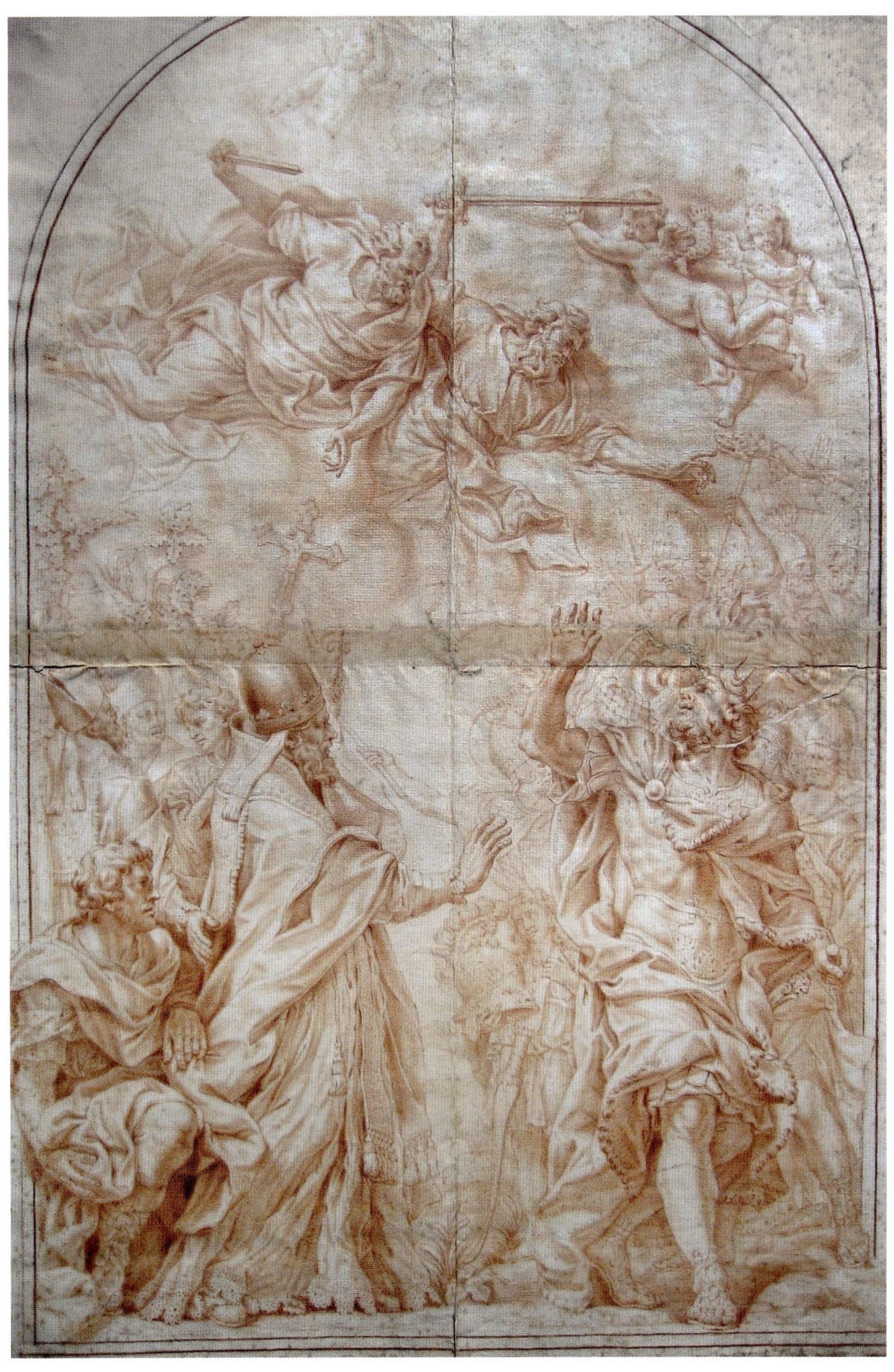

6.15 Anonymous, *Encounter of Leo I and Attila*, 1692, drawing, sanguine, 90 × 58 cm (35 7/16 × 22 13/16 in), Accademia di San Luca, Rome

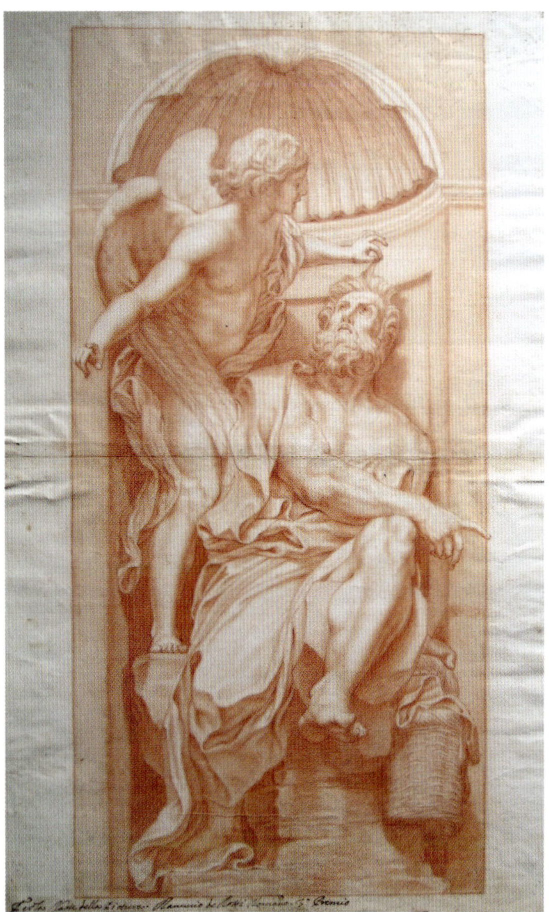

6.16 Ranuccio De Rossi, *Habakkuk*, drawing, sanguine, 62 × 30.5 cm (24 7⁄16 × 12 in), Accademia di San Luca, Rome

While between the end of the seventeenth and the end of the eighteenth centuries the works of Michelangelo, Guglielmo della Porta, Reni, Cordier, Raggi, Menghini, Duquesnoy, Guidi, and Rusconi were drawn only once, and those of Algardi and Raphael twice, sculptures by Gian Lorenzo were chosen nine times. The first instance was in 1694 (*Habakkuk*) (fig.6.16)[71] with a second in 1696 (*Saint Teresa* and *Daniel in the Lion's Den*) (fig.6.17).[72] More importantly, during Carlo Maratta's second presidency of the Accademia (1699–1713) Bernini's sculptures were selected as appropriate *exempla* for the student contests; that is, at a time when the Accademia was under the leadership of the very painter who embodied Bellori's ideal artist and whose preparatory drawings for the Lateran apostles and ensuing sculptures were taken until not too long ago as evidence of Bernini's unpopularity in early eighteenth-century Rome.[73] Subsequently, in 1706 the aspiring academicians drew the *Tomb of Urban VIII*,[74] in 1709 the statues of *Charity* and *Truth* that flank the *Tomb of Alexander VII*,[75] in 1732 the young sculptors executed in clay the statue of *Habakkuk*,[76] and in 1738 the students drew after the statue of *Neptune and Triton*, at the time in the Villa Montalto (fig.6.18).[77] Finally, in 1775, the sculpture after which students were asked to execute a *modello* was the *Saint Bibiana* (fig.6.12) at the same time that the third painting class drew no less an icon of Neoclassical ideals than the *Apollo Belvedere* (fig.6.19), of which Winckelmann had famously written, only eleven years earlier, that 'in gazing upon this masterpiece of art, I forget all else, and I myself adopt an elevated stance, in order to be worthy of gazing upon it', and which others in his wake, such as the Scottish author Tobias Smollett, considered 'the most beautiful statue that ever was formed'.[78]

Thus, if in both the French academy and the Accademia di San Luca Bernini's sculptures were being proposed so persistently to their students as *exempla* through much of the eighteenth century, it is evident that his appeal persisted for decades after his death. Indeed, in 1740 Charles de Brosses described Bernini's *Baldacchino* (fig.6.20) in superlative terms as the most beautiful bronze work in the world, comparable to that other prodigious work, Bernini's *Cathedra Petri*.[79] And, as late as 1780, the twenty-three-year-old Antonio Canova was so struck by Bernini's *Apollo and Daphne* as to record in his diary that it was 'sculpted with such delicacy that it seems impossible [to achieve], there are laurel leaves [executed] with wonderful workmanship,

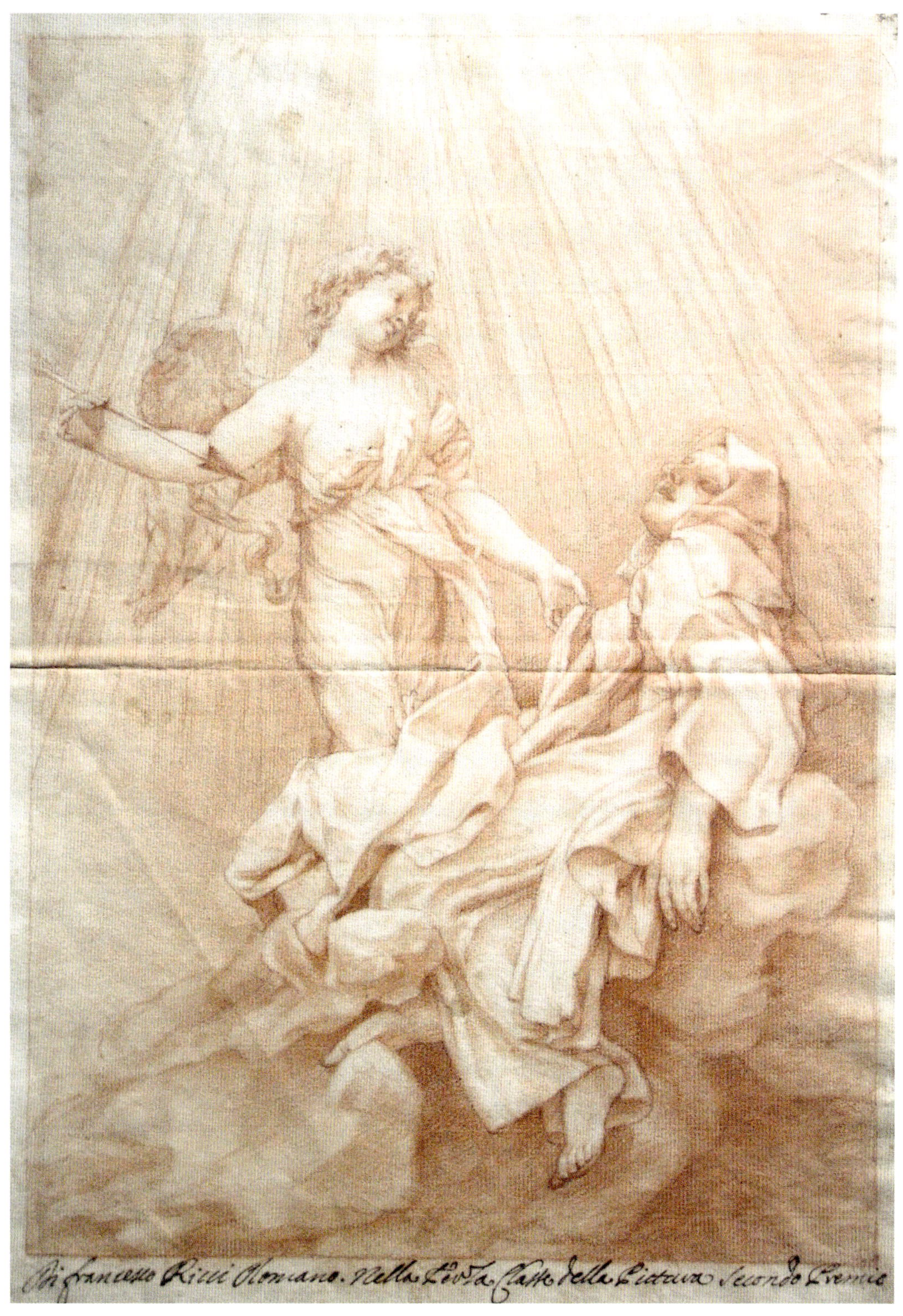

6.17 Francesco Ricci, *Saint Teresa*, drawing, sanguine, 42 × 30 cm (16 9⁄16 × 11 13⁄16 in), Accademia di San Luca, Rome

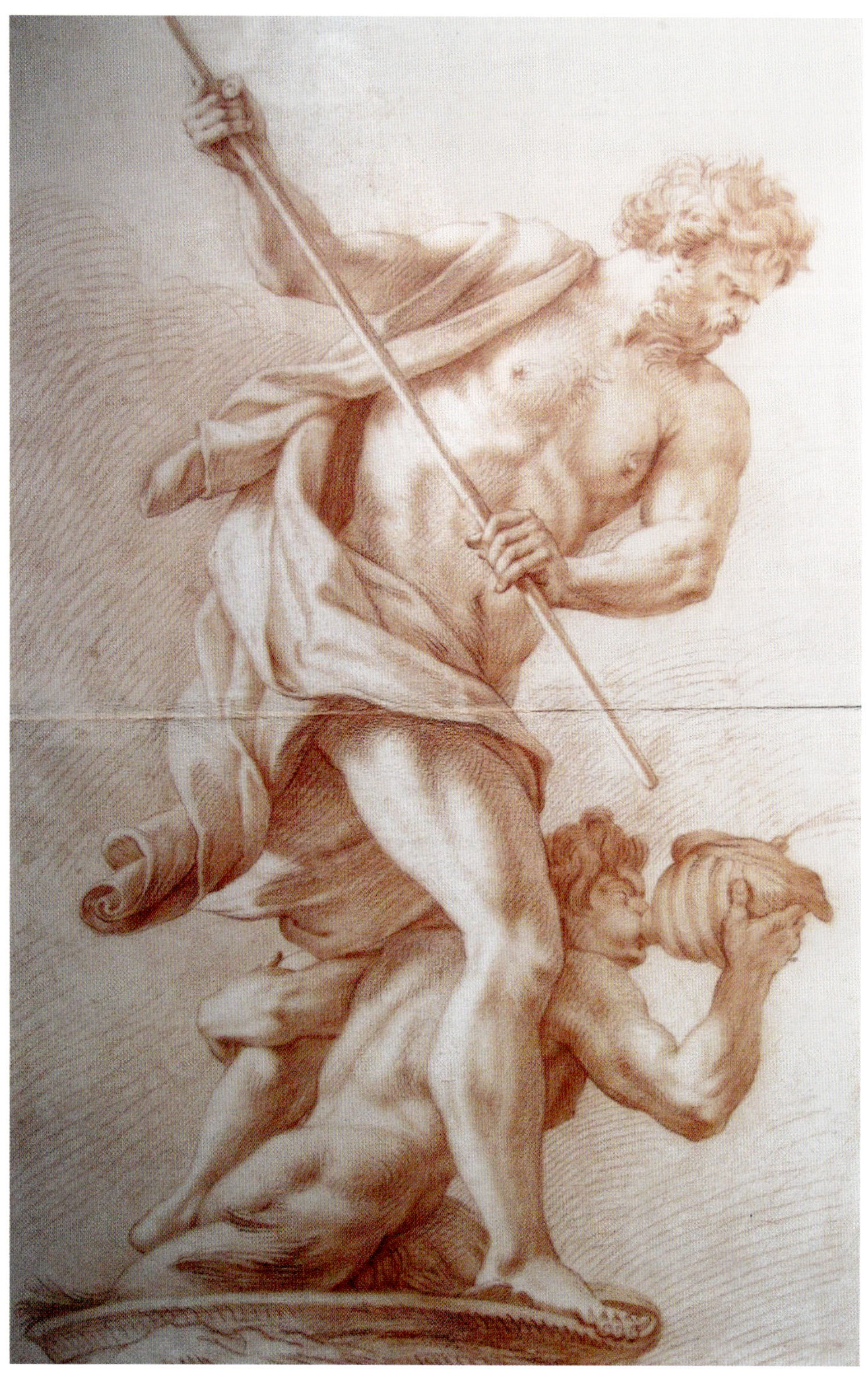

6.18 Girolamo Paladino, *Neptune and Triton*, drawing, sanguine, 66 × 42.5 cm (26 × 16¾ in), Accademia di San Luca, Rome

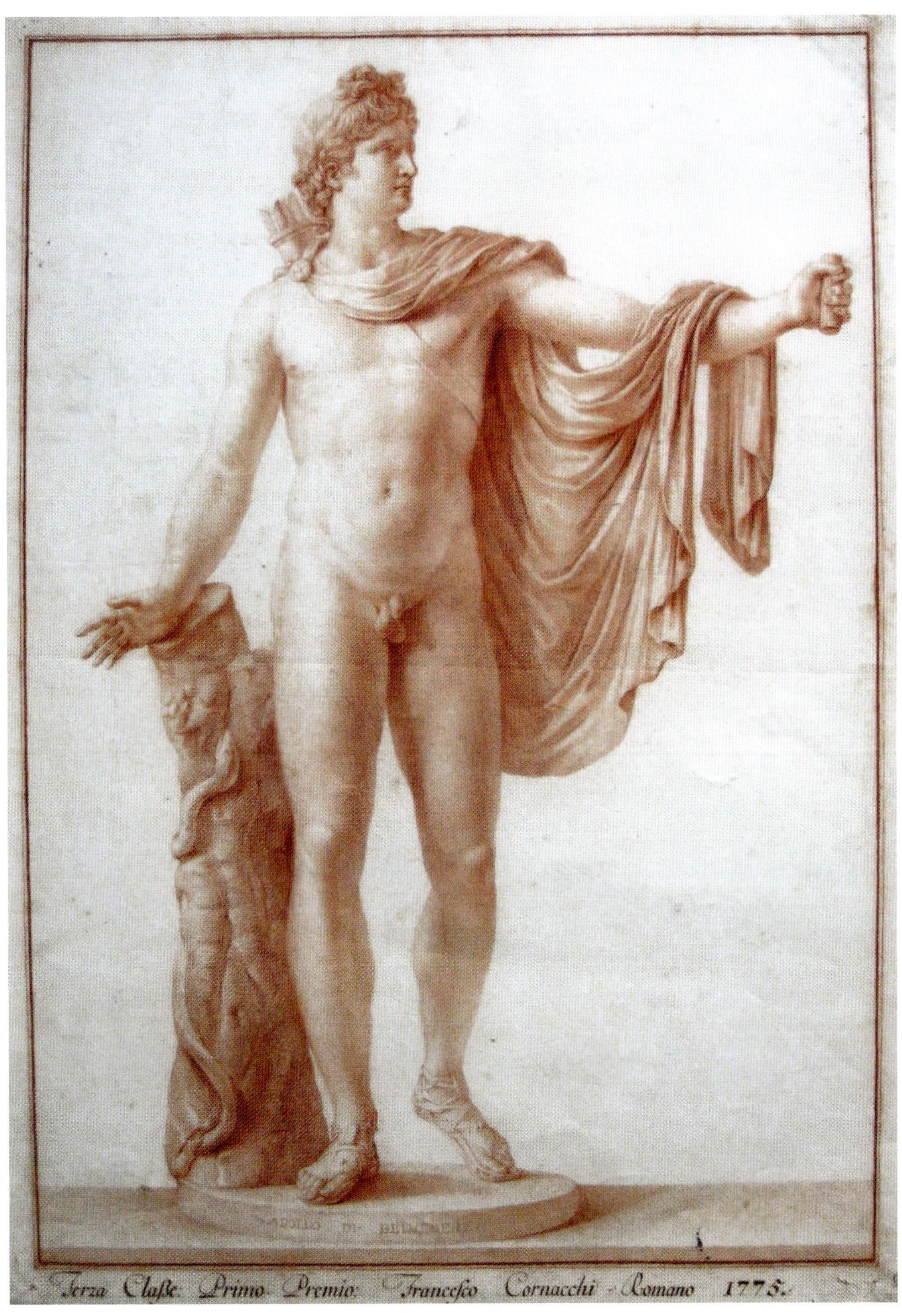

6.19 Francesco Cornacchi, *Apollo Belvedere*, drawing, sanguine, 52 × 36.5 cm (20½ × 14⅜ in), Accademia di San Luca, Rome

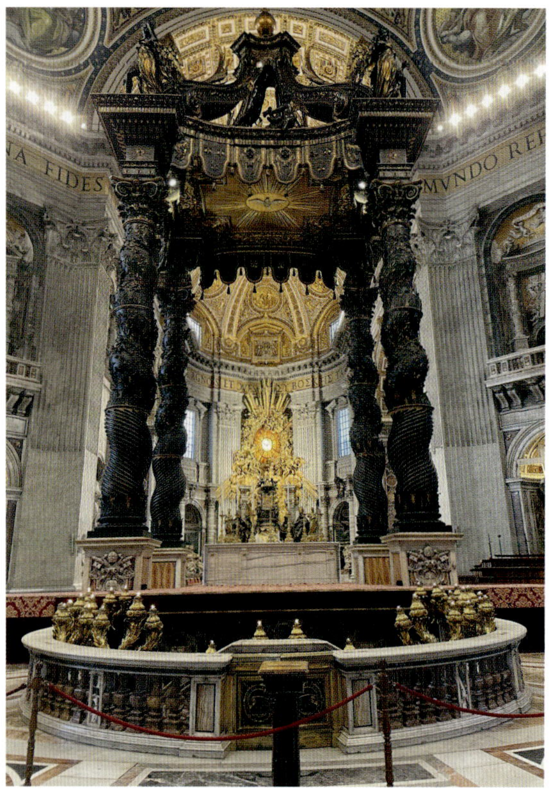

[and] the [rendition] of the beautiful nude is beyond expectation'.[80] In fact, Bernini's popularity and impact on eighteenth-century Romans and foreigners alike is easily apprehended when looking at one of the most sophisticated and yet popular 'postcards' of the age: Giovanni Paolo Panini's *vedute* of the Eternal City.

Two years after his arrival in Rome in 1754, the new French ambassador to Rome, Étienne François duc de Choiseul, commissioned from Panini (1691–1765) the stunning pendants of two imaginary picture galleries displaying 'paintings within the painting' of ancient monuments in one, and modern ones in the other. In the *Interior of an Imaginary Picture Gallery with Views of Modern Rome* (1757) (fig.6.21) Panini assembled a collection of paintings and statues gathered under one roof, which he considered the most memorable views and sculptures of the modern city. Possibly inspired by the vast collection of Cardinal Silvio Valenti Gonzaga (1690–1756) – he owned 892 paintings[81] – and imitating the wall-to-wall 'pictures within a picture' theme already represented in *The Picture Gallery of Cardinal Silvio Valenti Gonzaga* (1749) (fig.6.22) executed for this prelate, Panini's modern Rome gives a clear indication of how much seventeenth- and eighteenth-century Rome was identified with Bernini. Truly, Panini's painting could be taken as the visual 'companion guide' to Baldinucci and Domenico Bernini's biographies or a precursor to the Baedeker's guide to Rome as, among other works, it depicts the following creations that Bernini ideated totally or in part: *Triton Fountain, Elephant and Obelisk, Sant'Agnese, Four Rivers Fountain, Saint Peter's Square, Barcaccia Fountain, Baldacchino, Apollo and Daphne, David*, the 'twin' churches in Piazza del Popolo, the *Angels* on the Castel Sant'Angelo bridge, *Fontana del Moro, Constantine the Great, Neptune and Triton, Sant'Andrea al Quirinale*, the *Villa Borghese Herms*, and Palazzo Ludovisi (Montecitorio) (fig.6.23).[82] Still, the best way for anyone today to personally assess the extent to which Bernini left his imprint on the

6.20 Gian Lorenzo Bernini, *Baldacchino*, 1624–33, bronze, Saint Peter's Basilica, Rome

6.21 Giovanni Paolo Panini, *Picture Gallery with Views of Modern Rome*, 1757, oil on canvas, 170.2 × 244.5 cm (67⅛ × 96¼ in), Museum of Fine Arts, Boston, Charles Potter Kling Fund, 1975.805

6.22 Giovanni Paolo Panini, *The Picture Gallery of Cardinal Silvio Valenti Gonzaga*, 1749, oil on canvas, 198.2 × 268 cm (78 1/16 × 105½ in), Wadsworth Atheneum Museum of Art, Hartford, CT, The Ella Gallup Sumner and Mary Catlin Sumner Collection Fund, 1948.478

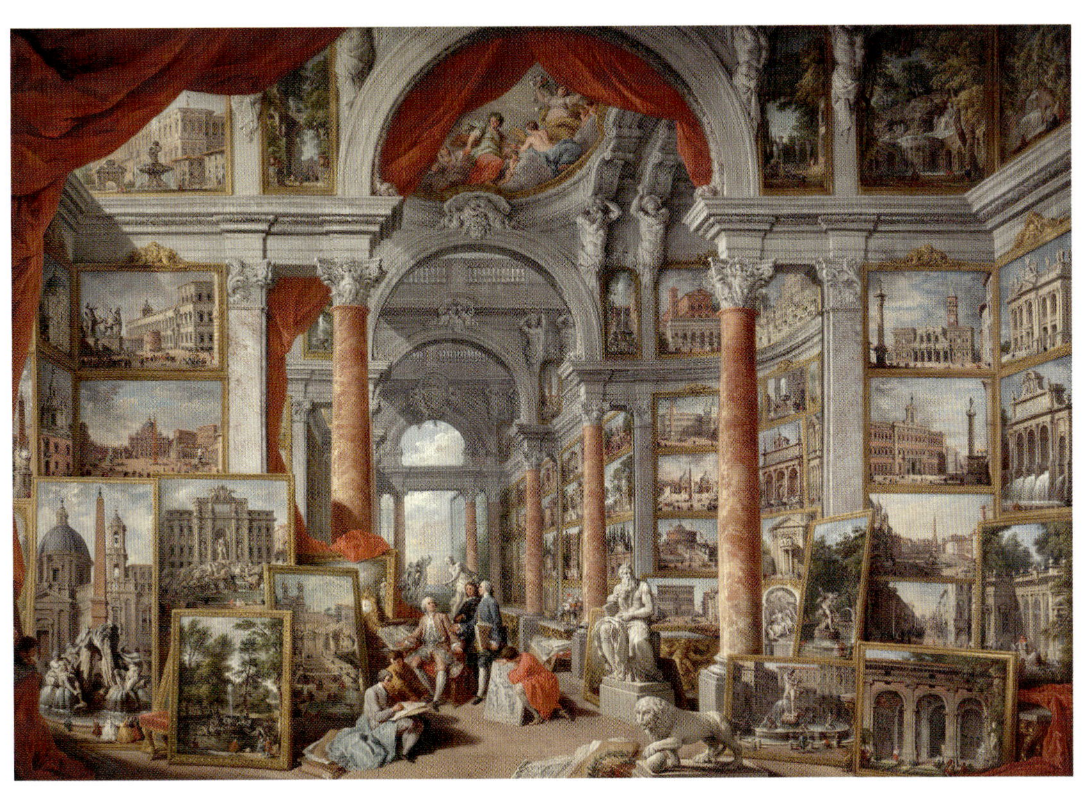

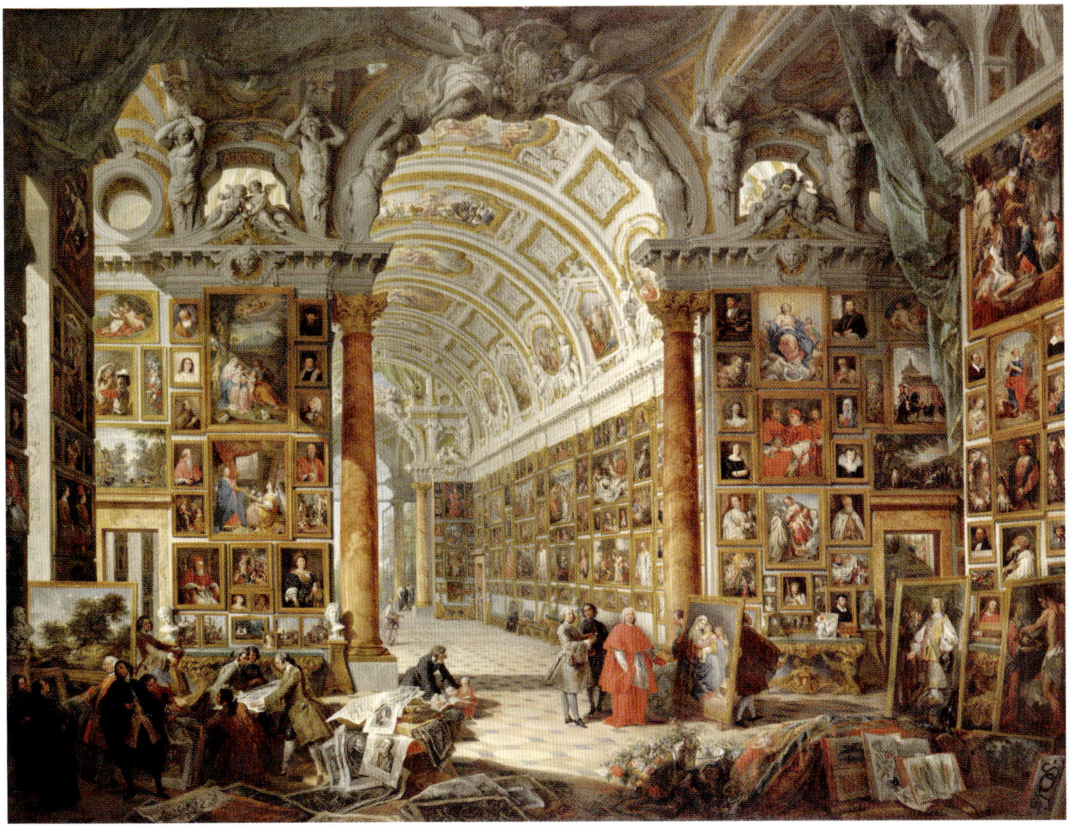

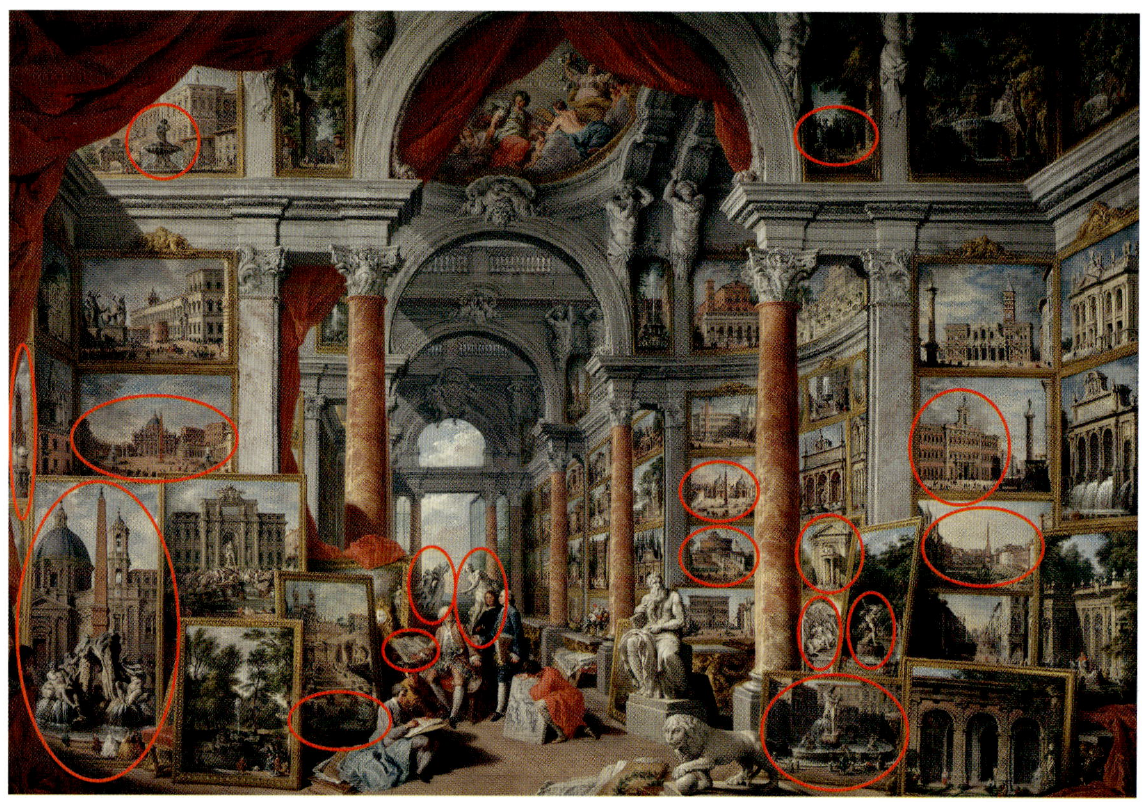

6.23 Giovanni Paolo Panini, as fig. 6.21 highlighting Bernini's works, oil on canvas, 170.2 × 244.5 cm (67 × 96 ¼ in), Museum of Fine Arts, Boston, Charles Potter Kling Fund, 1975.805

art and artists of eighteenth-century Rome is to visit some of its churches, for there his presence will be tangibly felt typologically and stylistically.[83]

* * *

Leo Bruhns' pioneering study, 'The Motif of Eternal Adoration in Roman Funerary Sculpture of the Sixteenth and Seventeenth Centuries', provides a useful guide to a ubiquitous theme found in many Roman churches and, in the process, investigates various types of commemorative monuments.[84] Among these, there is one funerary memorial that involved the conflation of two separate ancient monuments: the pyramid and the obelisk.[85] In the sixteenth and seventeenth centuries both of these structures were taken to symbolise immortality and consequently readily adapted to contemporary tombs.[86] Ironically, even though the inclusion of such a symbol in a modern monument was first conceived by Raphael in 1513 for Agostino Chigi in his chapel in Santa Maria del Popolo,[87] its creation was soon ascribed to Bernini because of the re-modeling of the space the artist undertook in 1652 for Cardinal Fabio Chigi and, more extensively, in 1655 when he became Pope Alexander VII (figs 6.24 and 6.25).[88] As recorded in a *modello* by Francesco Salviati for a 'Seasons' tapestries series (fig.6.26), in designing the famous

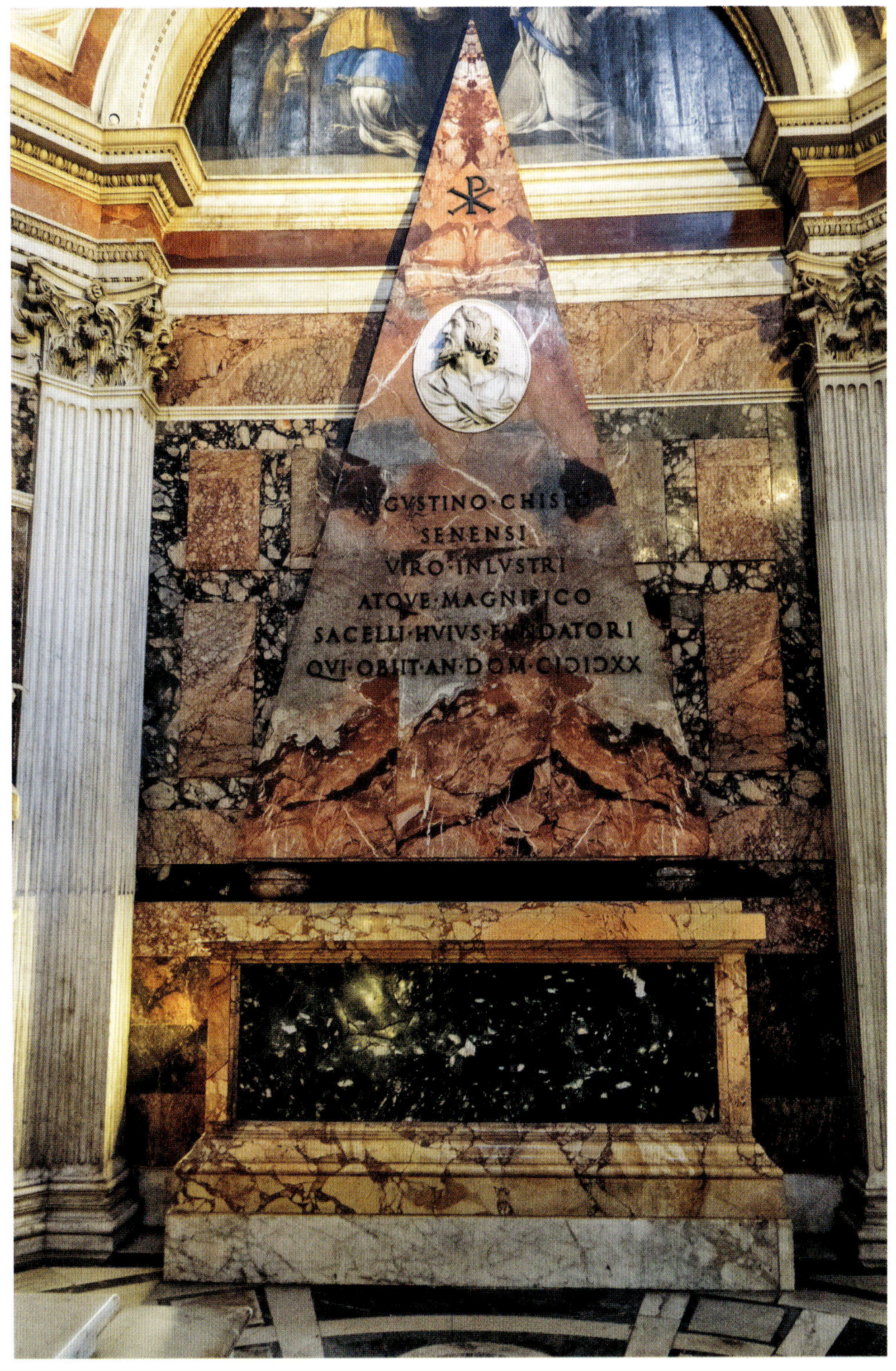

6.24 Gian Lorenzo Bernini, *Tomb of Agostino Chigi*, 1655, polychrome marble, Chigi Chapel, Santa Maria del Popolo, Rome

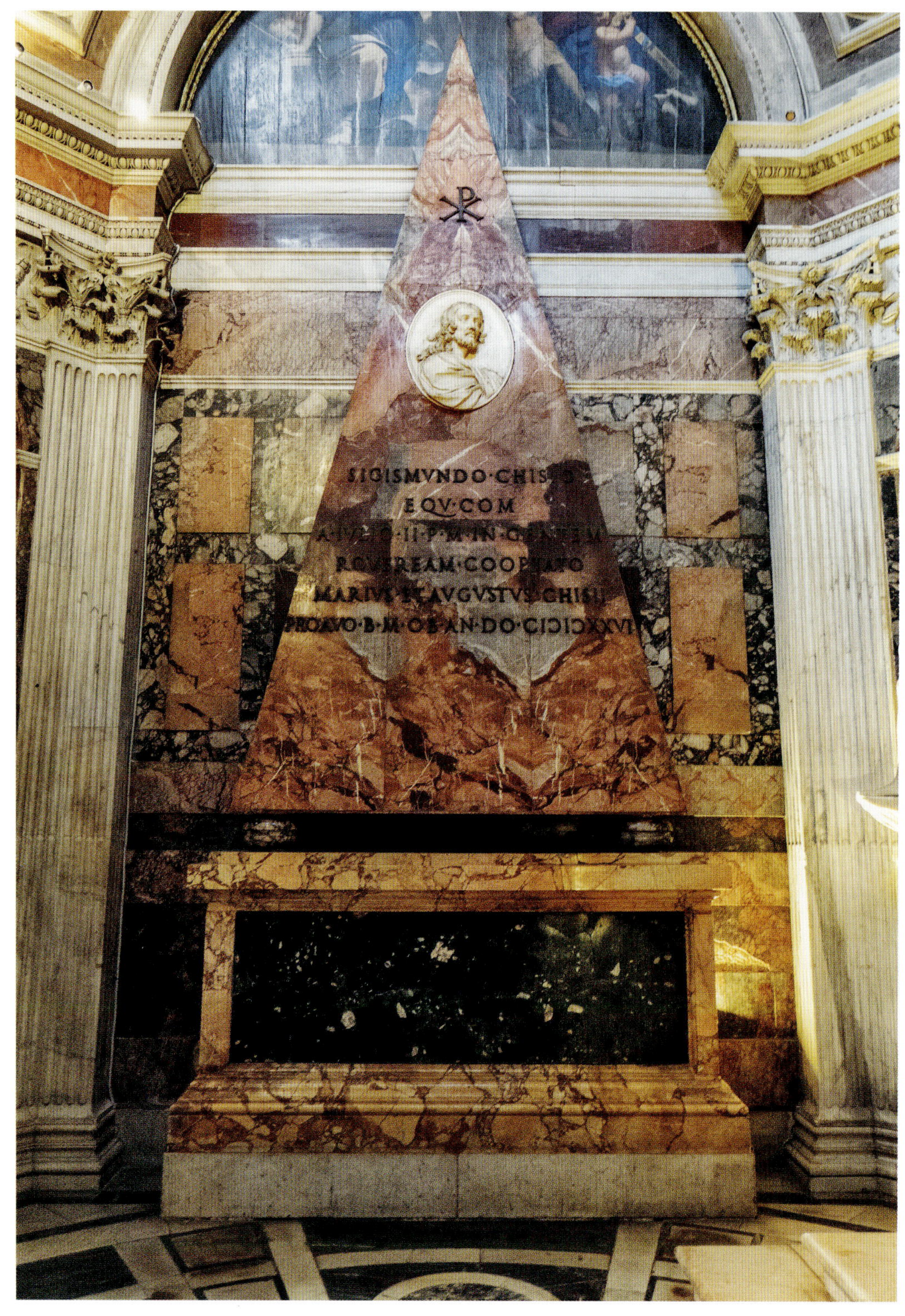

6.25 Gian Lorenzo Bernini, *Tomb of Sigismondo Chigi*, 1655, polychrome marble, Chigi Chapel, Santa Maria del Popolo, Rome

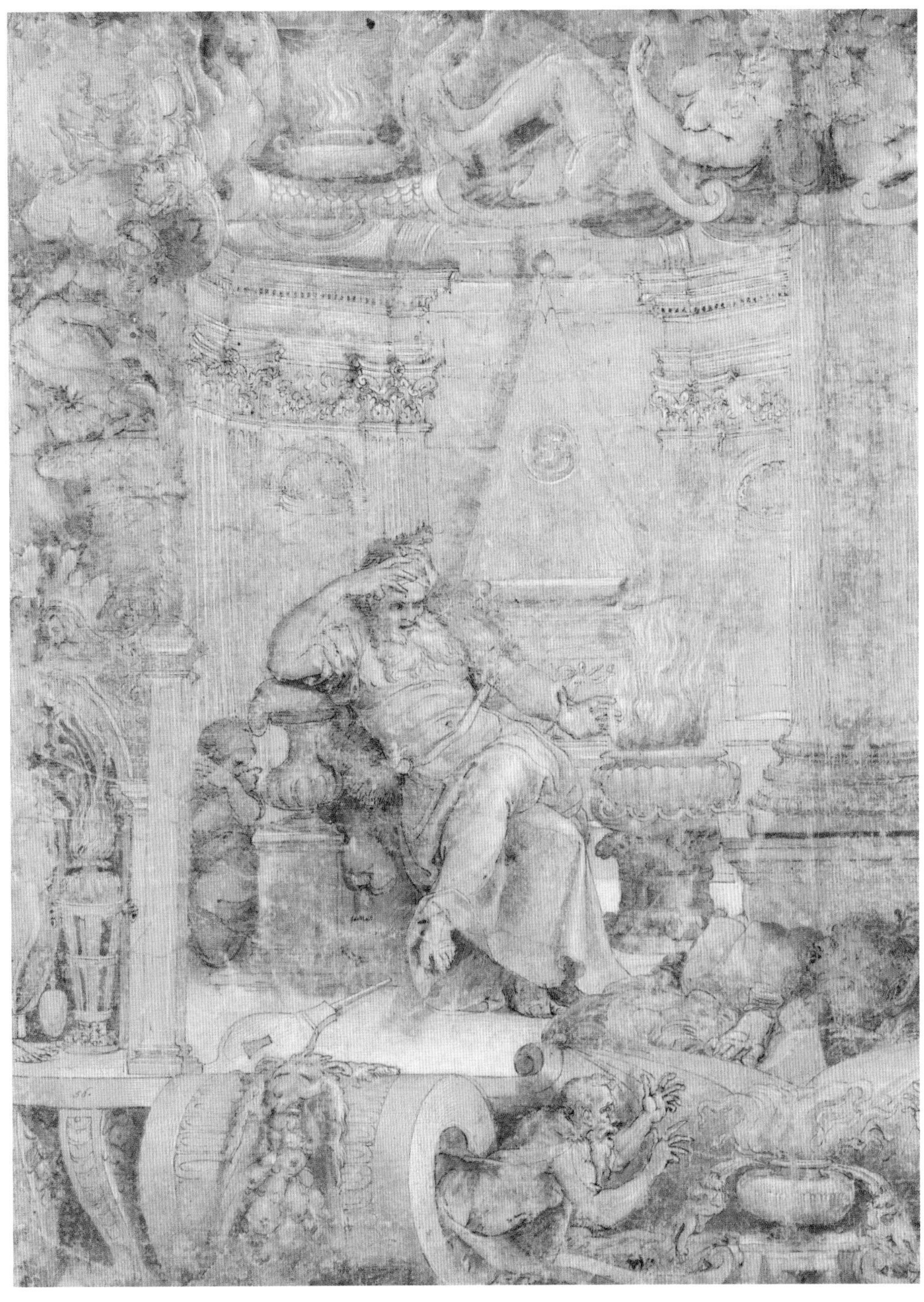

6.26 Francesco Salviati, *Winter*, from *modello* for 'Seasons' tapestry series, detail, pen, wash and white lead on beige paper, Uffizi Gallery, Florence

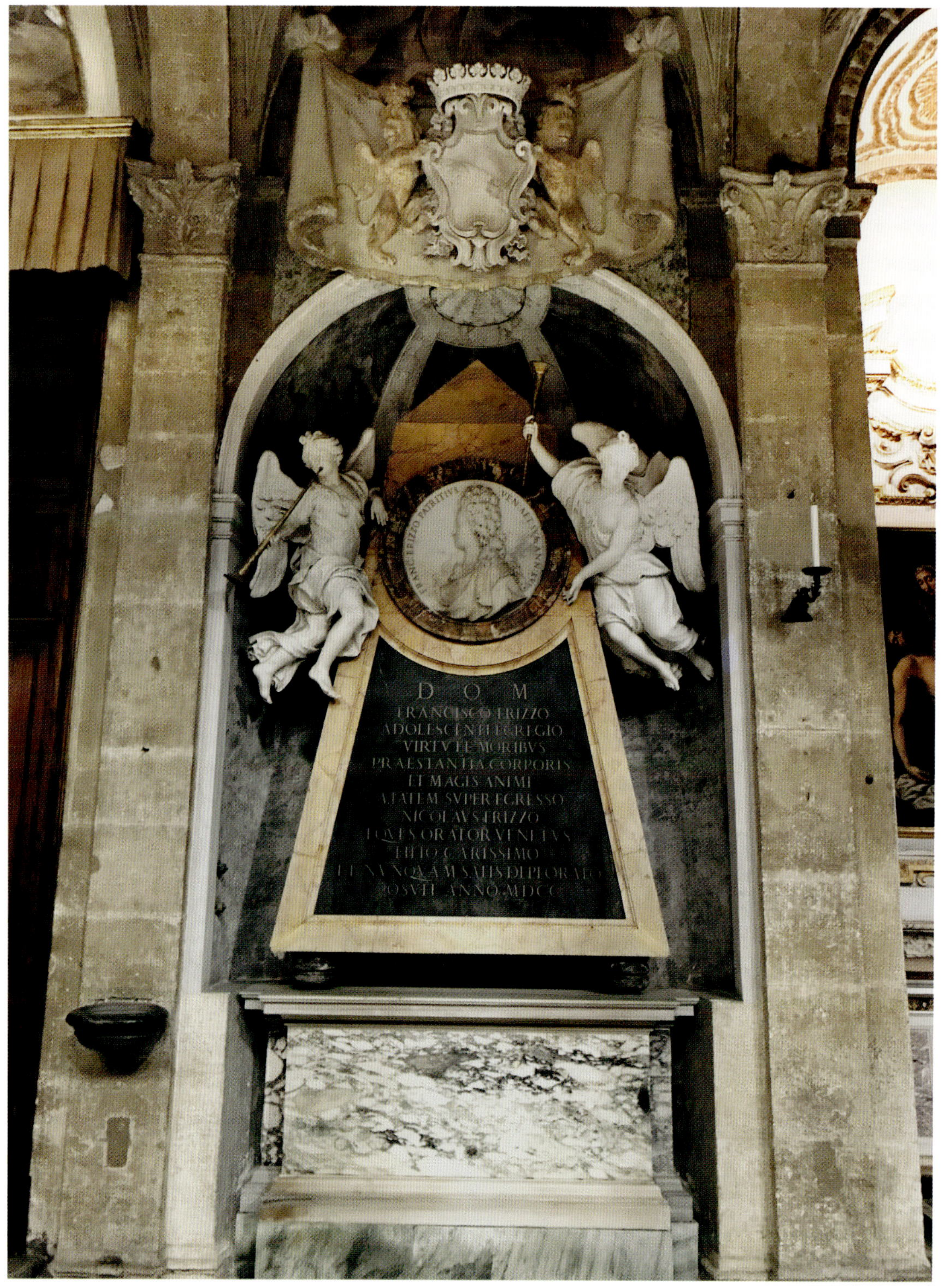

6.27 Francesco Maratti, *Funerary Monument of Francesco Erizzo*, 1700, marble, San Marco, Rome

Sienese banker's monument Raphael had devised a pyramidal structure with a sphere at its summit,[89] a bronze portrait medallion roughly in the middle of the triangular memorial,[90] and bronze reliefs for the three sides of the protruding sarcophagus.[91] When, in anticipation of Queen Christina of Sweden's arrival in Rome, Bernini was asked by the pope to renovate both the church of Santa Maria del Popolo and the pope's ancestral chapel within it, the artist basically simplified the design of Agostino Chigi's tombs. He did so by eliminating the bronze sphere at the top, sculpting the portrait medallions in white marble, substituting green marble slabs for the reliefs on the three surfaces of the sarcophagus, and doing away with the cartouches intended for the dedication while allowing 'the inscription to spread unbounded over the pyramid'.[92] Raphael's pyramidal solution for Agostino Chigi's tomb was not finalised by the time he died in 1520, but Bernini's refurbishing of the sumptuous chapel was significant enough to impress contemporaries and obfuscate traces of Raphael's involvement in that part of the chapel. Consequently, already by 1674 – while Bernini was still alive – in Titi's first edition of his guide to Roman churches, the author asserted: 'In the corners [of the Chigi Chapel] there are four marble statues; the Elijah and Jonah are sculptures [executed] by Lorenzetto on a design by Raphael; the two modern ones, along with the sepulchers and other ornaments, were made by the Cavalier Bernini'[93] – a 'fact' reaffirmed in the 1686 and 1763 editions, and reiterated *verbatim* by Francesco Posterla in *Roma sacra, e moderna* in 1725.[94] Thus, many artists through the eighteenth century looked to Bernini's Chigi memorials when designing their own variations on the theme.[95] This, for example, is what Francesco Maratti did in his monument for Francesco Erizzo in the church of San Marco in 1700 (fig.6.27), the anonymous sculptor who designed Petronilla Paolina Massimi's sepulcher in the church of Sant'Egidio (1726) (fig.6.28), Pietro Bracci in Fabrizio Paolucci's sepulcher in San Marcello al Corso (1726), Filippo della Valle for the Girolamo

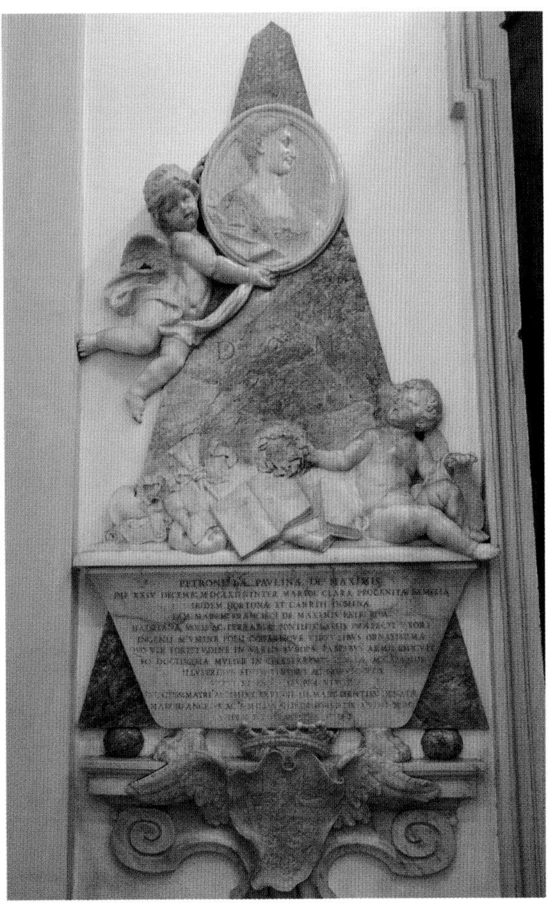

6.28 Anonymous, *Funerary Monument of Petronilla Paolina Massimi*, 1726, marble, Sant'Egidio, Rome

Samminiati memorial in San Giovanni dei Fiorentini (1733) (fig.6.29), Bernardino Ludovisi for Cardinal Giorgio Spinola's tomb in San Salvatore alle Coppelle (1744) (fig.6.30), René-Michel Slodtz for Alessandro Capponi's resting place in San Giovanni dei Fiorentini (1746) (fig.6.31), and Pietro Bracci in the monument for Cardinal Carlo Leopoldo Calcagnini in Sant'Andrea delle Fratte (1748) (fig.6.32). Actually, as late as 1793, the anonymous sculptor who designed the monument for the commander of the papal troops under Pius VI, Enea Caprara, in San Lorenzo

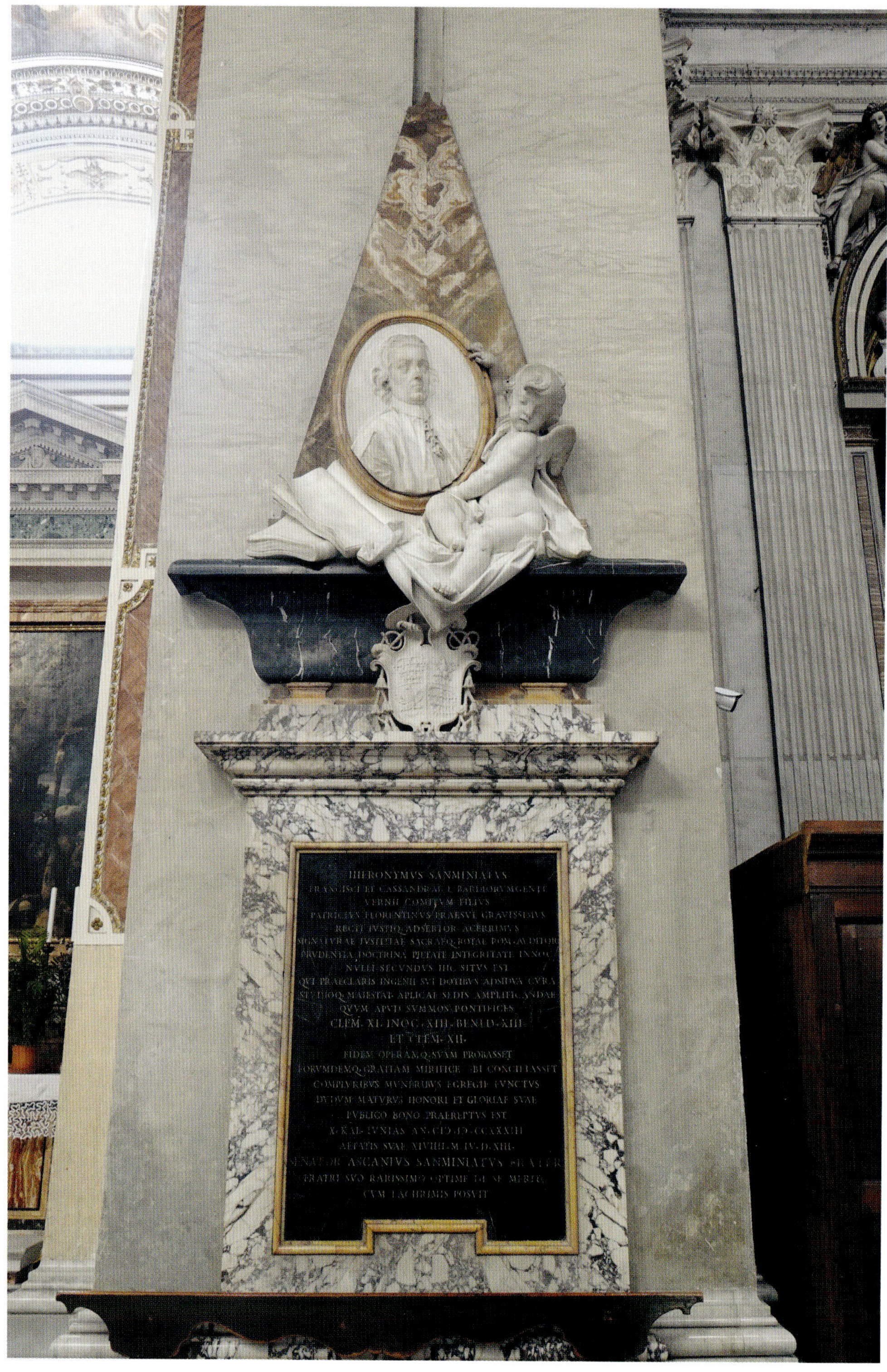

6.29 Filippo della Valle, *Funerary Monument of Girolamo Samminiati*, 1733, marble, San Giovanni dei Fiorentini, Rome

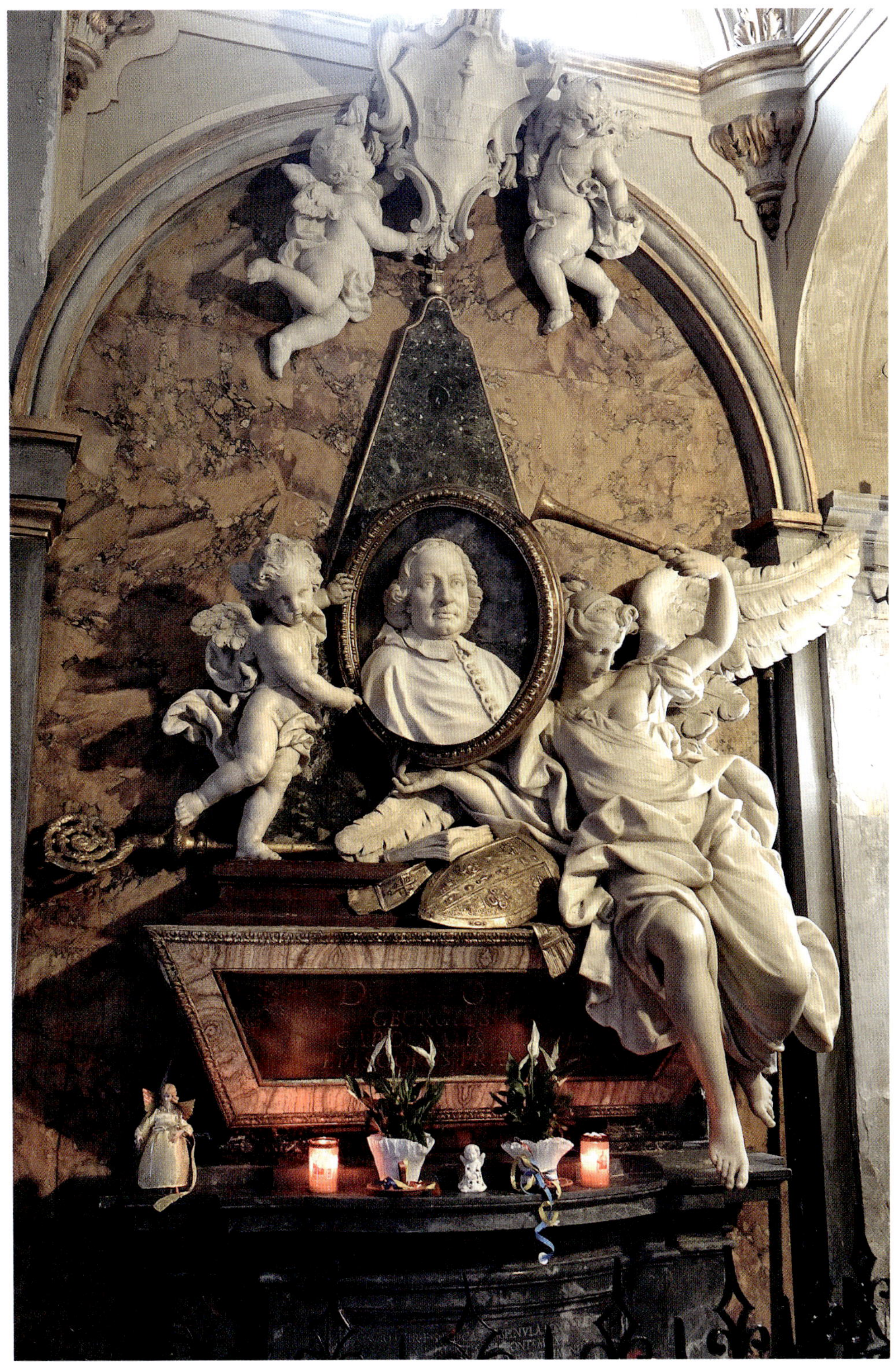

6.30 Bernardino Ludovisi, *Funerary Monument of Cardinal Giorgio Spinola*, 1744, marble, San Salvatore alle Coppelle, Rome

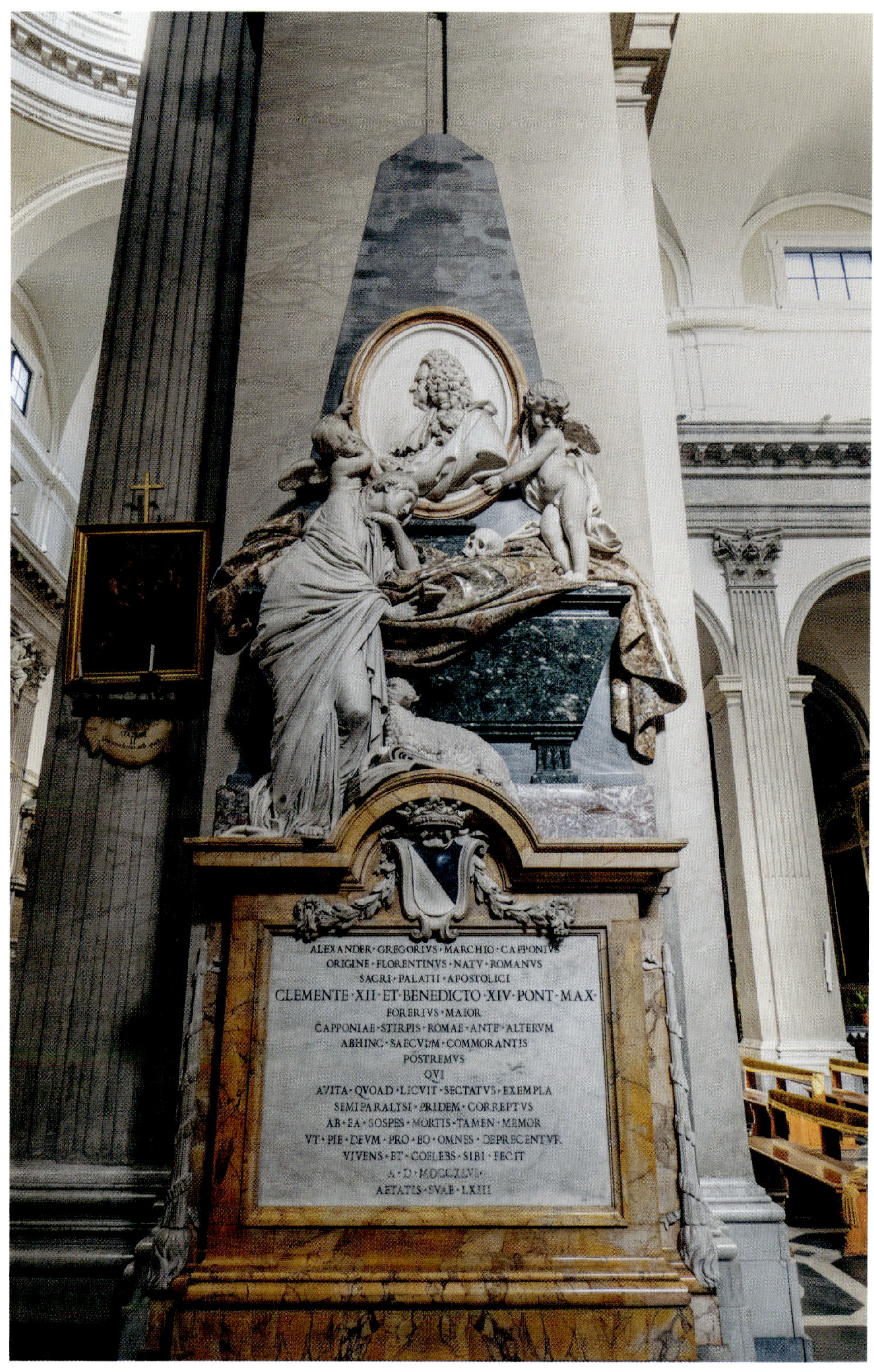

6.31 René-Michel Slodtz, *Funerary Monument of Alessandro Capponi*, 1746, marble, San Giovanni dei Fiorentini, Rome

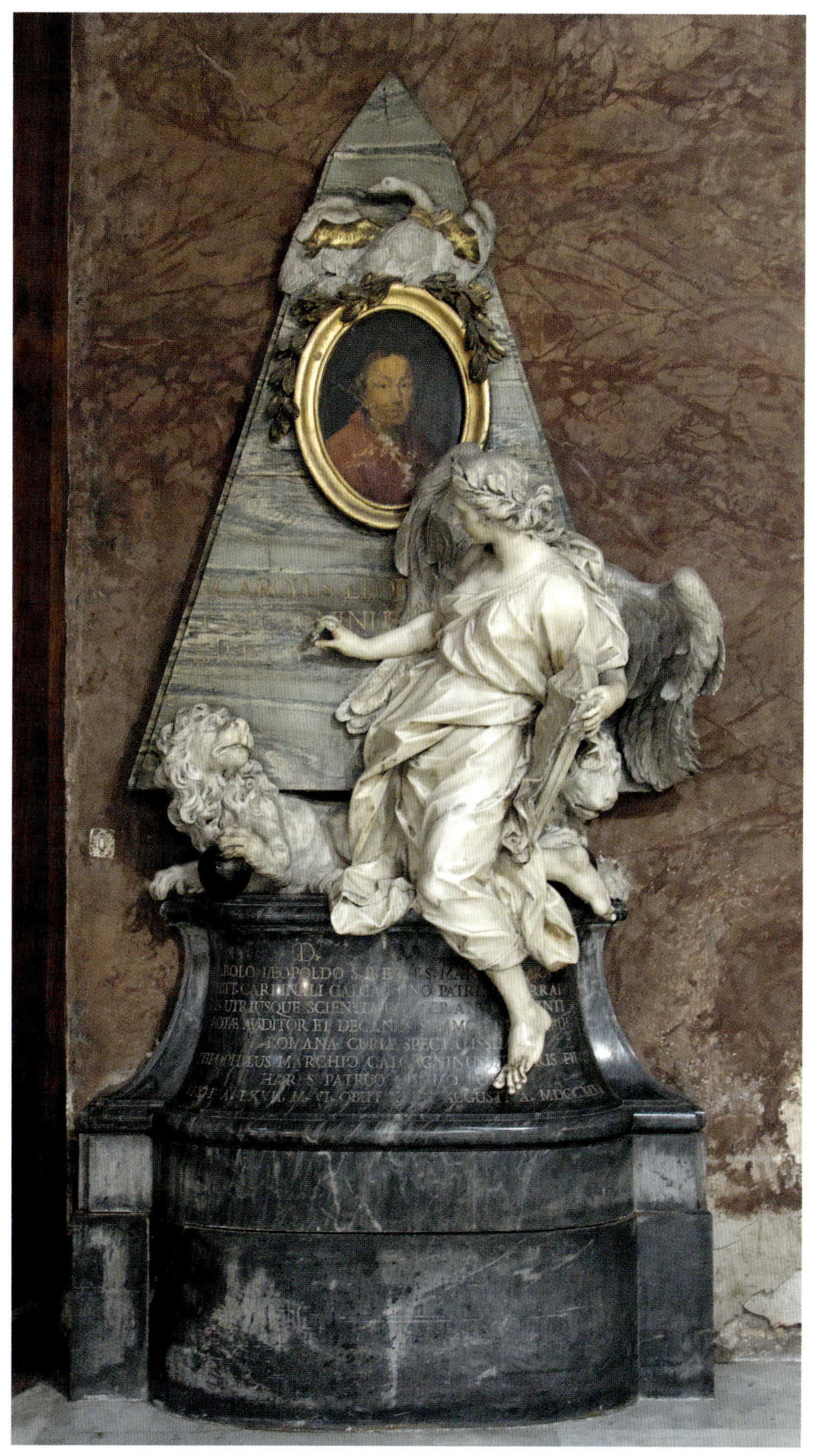

6.32 Pietro Bracci, *Funerary Monument of Cardinal Carlo Leopoldo Calcagnini*, 1748, marble, Sant'Andrea delle Fratte, Rome

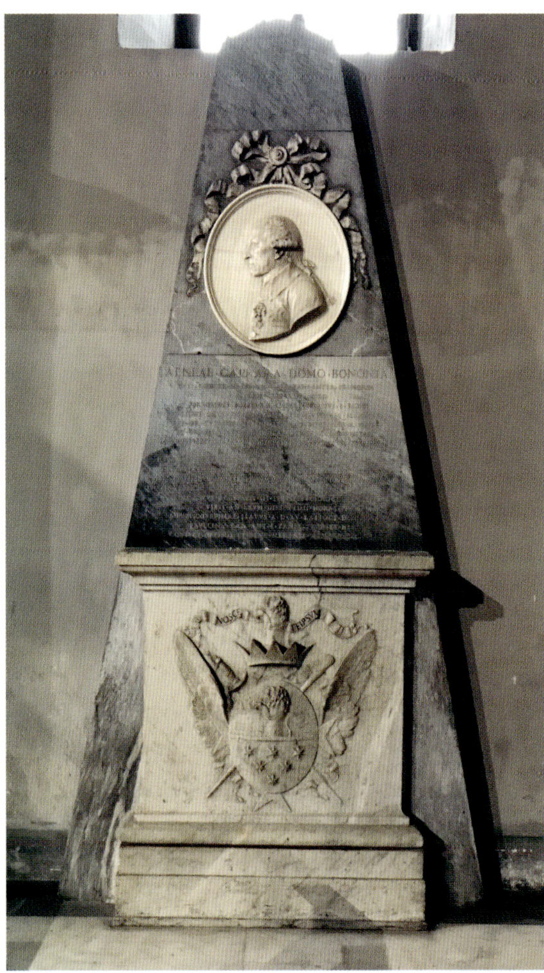

6.33 Anonymous, *Funerary Monument of Enea Caprara*, 1793, marble, San Lorenzo in Damaso, Rome

in Damaso still looked to Bernini's solution for the Chigi tombs for inspiration (fig.6.33).[96]

Even more obvious was Bernini's influence on his successors for a far more engaging, theatrical design for a chapel represented by his two most successful funerary creations: the Raimondi Chapel (1640–47) and, more effectively, the Cornaro Chapel (1647–52) (figs 6.34 and 6.35). Once again, he was certainly not the first sculptor to have included in his compositions sculptures of patrons who, through gestures and facial expressions, underscore their devotion to the image on the altar so as to convey their perpetual worship and hope for salvation.[97] The most successful precedent from the Renaissance, for example, was achieved by Tommaso Malvito (1497–1506) in the Chapel of Saint Gennaro in the Cathedral of Naples where, as Leo Bruhns observed, 'the idea of eternal devotion has been embodied truly splendidly: the petrified [Carafa] archbishop has been calling on the faithful to bend his knees and to worship the patron saint of the city for centuries'.[98] In the Holy City, instead, an influential example had been the Cappella Mellini in Santa Maria del Popolo where Alessandro Algardi's portrait of Cardinal Giovanni Garcia Mellini (1637) – a half-length portrait with book in one hand and the other clutching his breast – became a compositional solution that would be imitated by artists working in Rome through the eighteenth century.[99] However, Bernini's incomparable ability to orchestrate the painterly, sculptural, and architectural aspects of his design in a splendid, choral way – what Filippo Baldinucci described as a *bel composto* (a 'beautiful ensemble')[100] – became the benchmark to which other artists aspired in their conception of funerary chapels. In these spaces the ultimate goal was that of approximating a theatrical setting where, through a heightened visual, spatial, and psychological experience, the visitor would feel an emotional stimulus to piety, in keeping with the Counter-Reformation artistic dictates.[101]

In discussing Bernini's Raimondi Chapel, Leo Bruhns felt that the artist successfully achieved a theatrical 'dramatic tension' by designing a sculptural 'altar stage' at the end of a deep space, lit from the side windows where the architectural setting 'creates the tensions from which a drama can develop'.[102] Although in the Cornaro Chapel the shallowness of the space allowed for a less perfect solution in the way the family members' portraits dialogue with the altar sculpture – the Cornaro cardinal closest to the altar in the right balcony is conspicuously looking at the wall

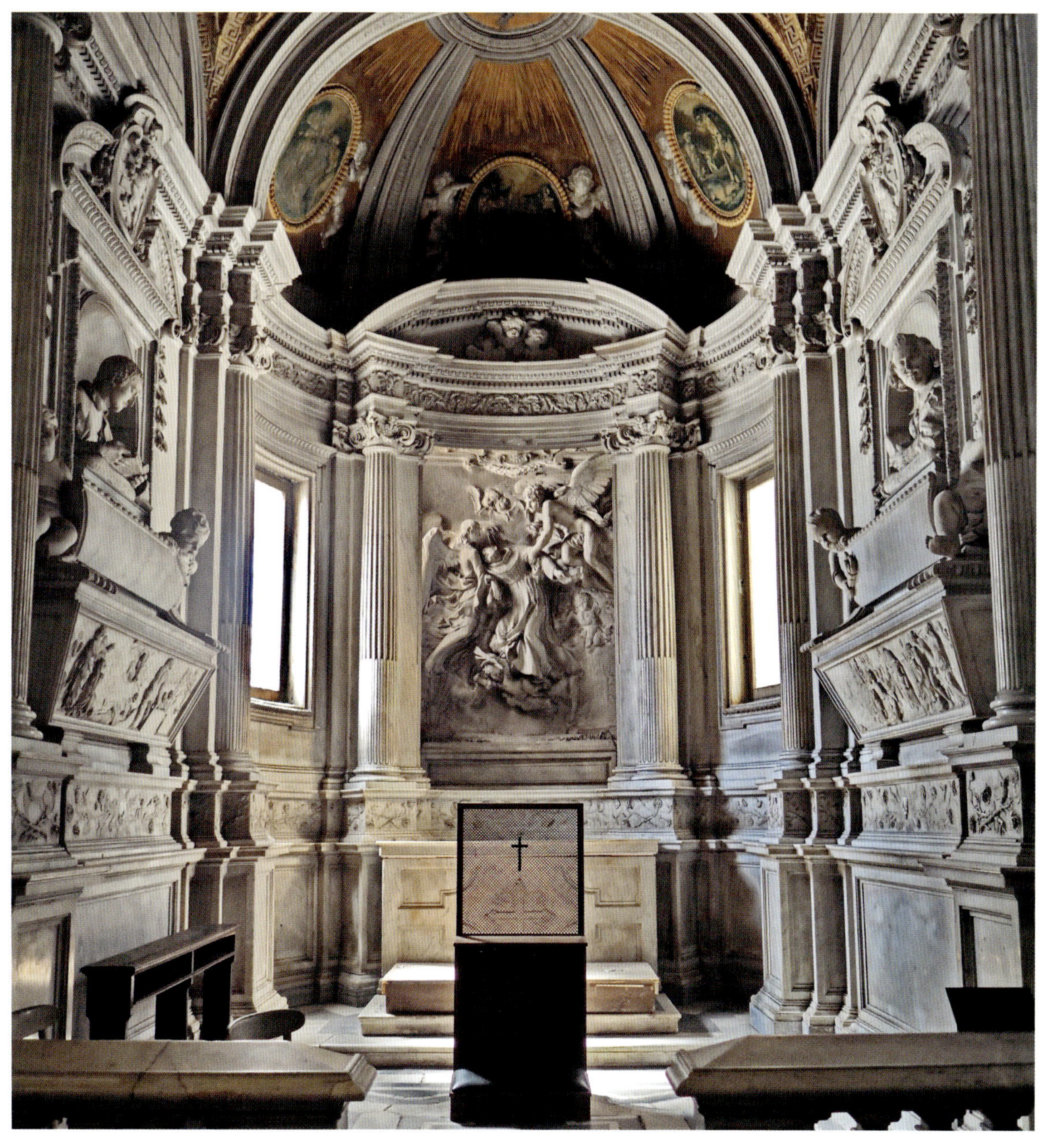

6.34 Gian Lorenzo Bernini, Raimondi Chapel, 1640–47, San Pietro in Montorio, Rome

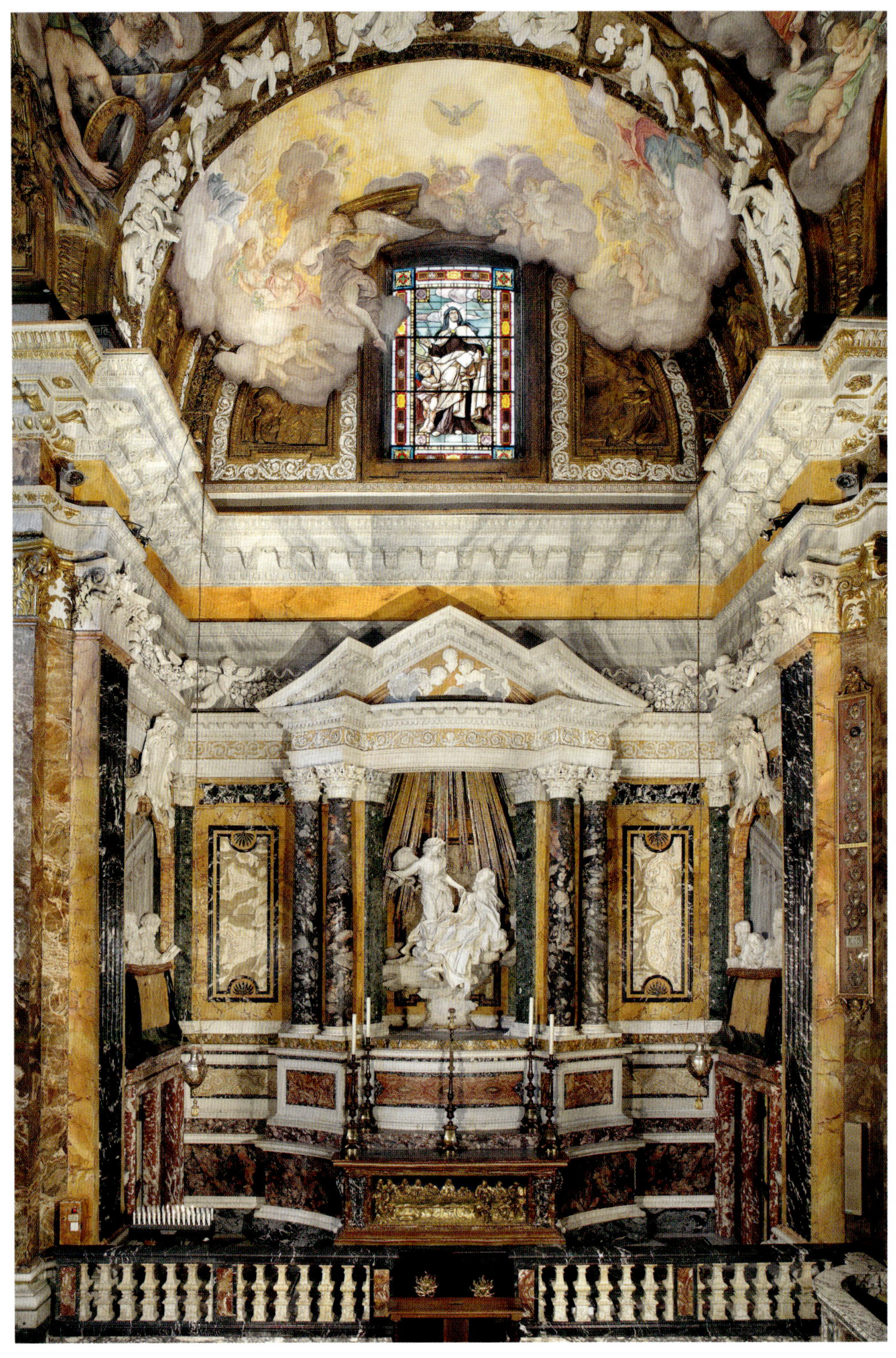

6.35 Gian Lorenzo Bernini, View of the Cornaro Chapel with the *Ecstasy of Saint Teresa*, 1647–52, Santa Maria della Vittoria, Rome

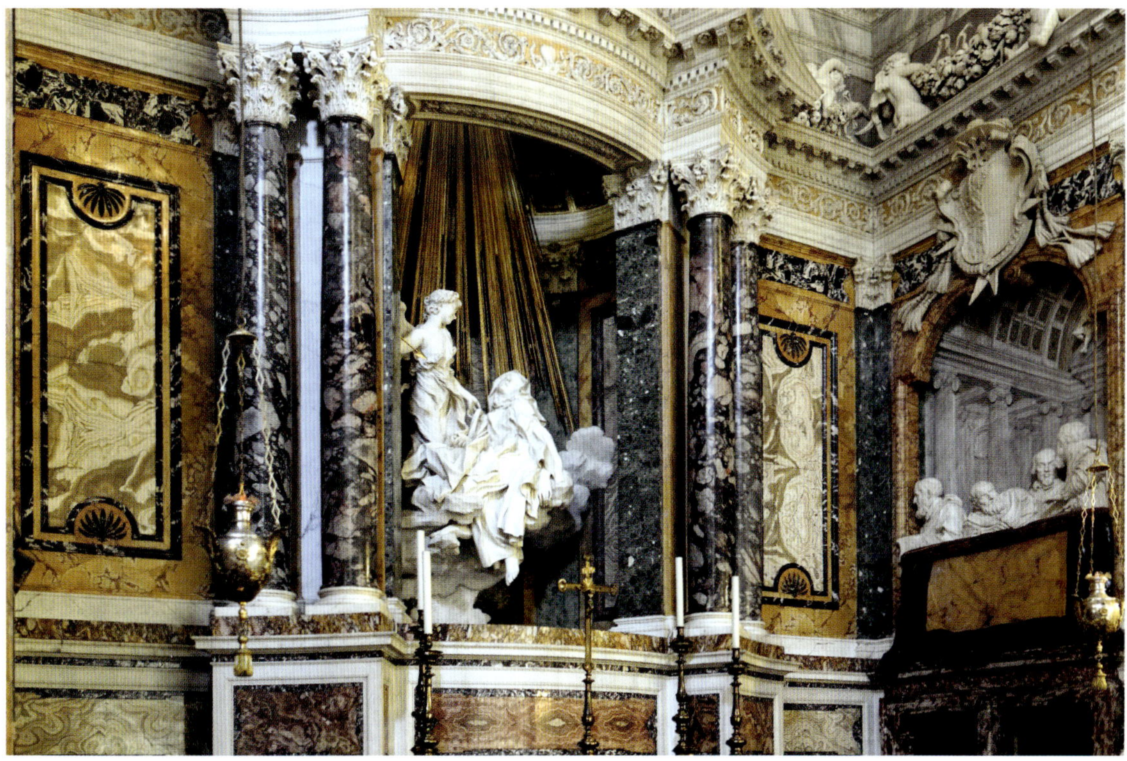

6.36 Gian Lorenzo Bernini, Cornaro Chapel, detail, Santa Maria della Vittoria, Rome

rather than towards Saint Teresa (fig.6.36) – it cannot be denied that it was in this chapel's theatricality that Baroque funerary memorials reached their apogee. Bernini's 'sensualization of the supersensible', as Bruhns described it, attained by the combination of architecture, painting, and, most of all, sculpture in the incomparable representation of spiritual bliss captured in the statue of *Ecstasy of Saint Teresa* (fig.6.37), make this artistic ensemble one of the highest achievements of western art.[103]

A sign of the success, and the earliest adaptation of Bernini's theatrical idea to the context of a whole church, rather than just a chapel, was carried out for the Bolognetti family in the church of Gesù e Maria (figs 6.38, 6.39, 6.40). Perched over the two confessionals that divide the three chapels on either side of the nave, Giorgio Bolognetti, bishop of Rieti (fig.6.41), commissioned Francesco Cavallini to turn the whole space into the tombs of six family members who partake in the 'eternal adoration' on a larger scale. Aided by sculptors Francesco Aprile, Michele Maglia (i.e., Michel Maille), and Giuseppe Mazzuoli, by 1687 Cavallini succeeded in turning the whole church into a grand reenactment of the Raimondi and Cornaro Chapels combined.[104] But obvious imitations of this Berninesque approach to a liturgical-commemorative space extend well into the eighteenth century, as discernible in the Albertoni Altieri Chapel in Santa Maria in Campitelli (1710) (figs 6.42 and 6.43), the Muti-Bussi Chapel in San Marcello al Corso (1725) (figs 6.44 and 6.45), and the tomb of Antonio and Girolama Publicola in Santa

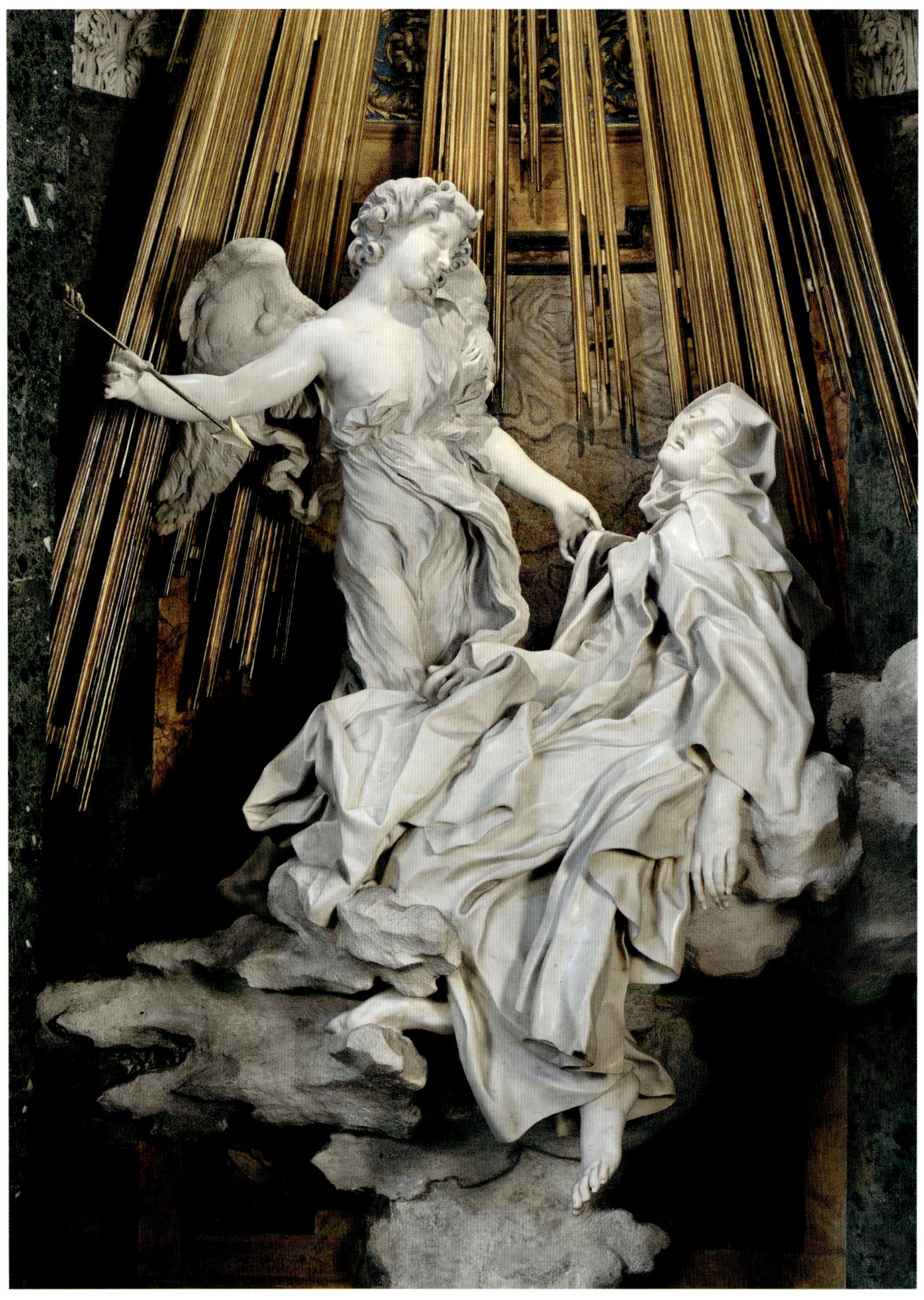

6.37 Gian Lorenzo Bernini, *Ecstasy of Saint Teresa*, Cornaro Chapel, 1647–52, marble, Santa Maria della Vittoria, Rome

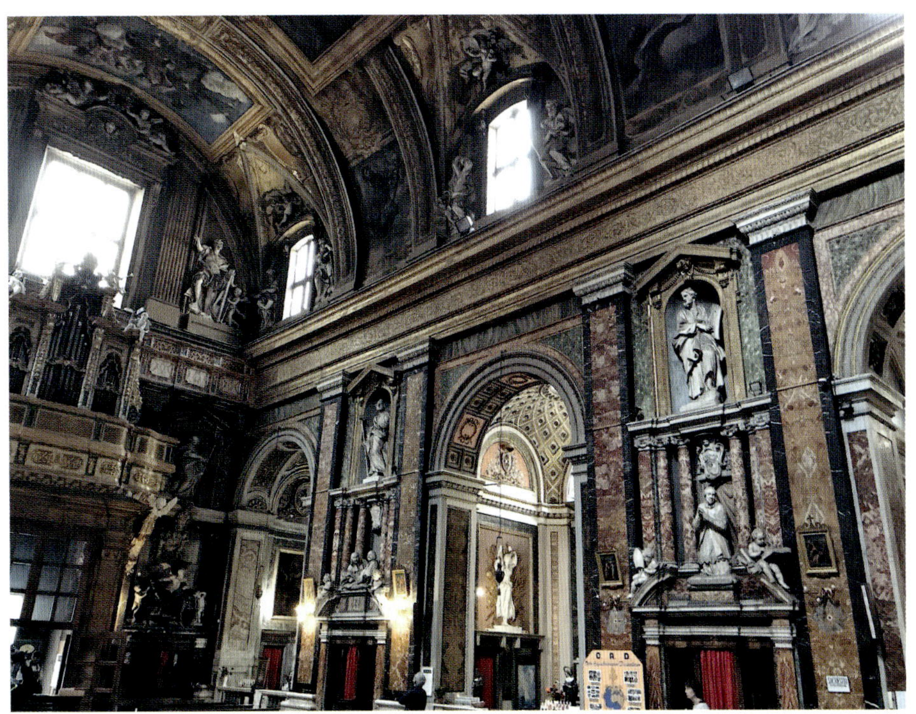

6.38 Francesco Cavallini, *Funerary Monuments of the Bolognetti Family*, 1687, marble, Gesù e Maria, Rome

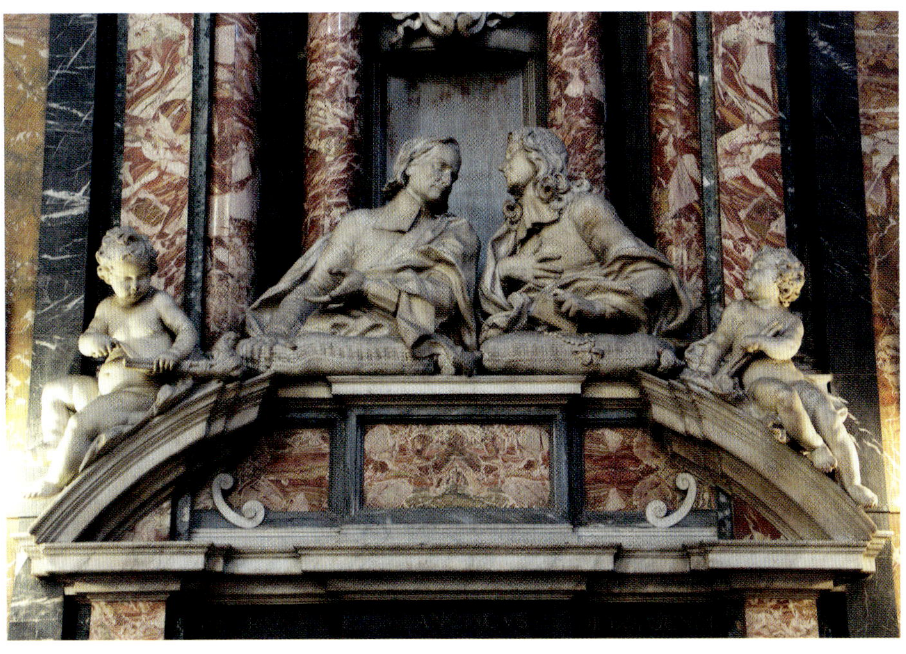

6.39 Francesco Aprile, *Funerary Monument of Pietro and Francesco Bolognetti*, marble, Gesù e Maria, Rome

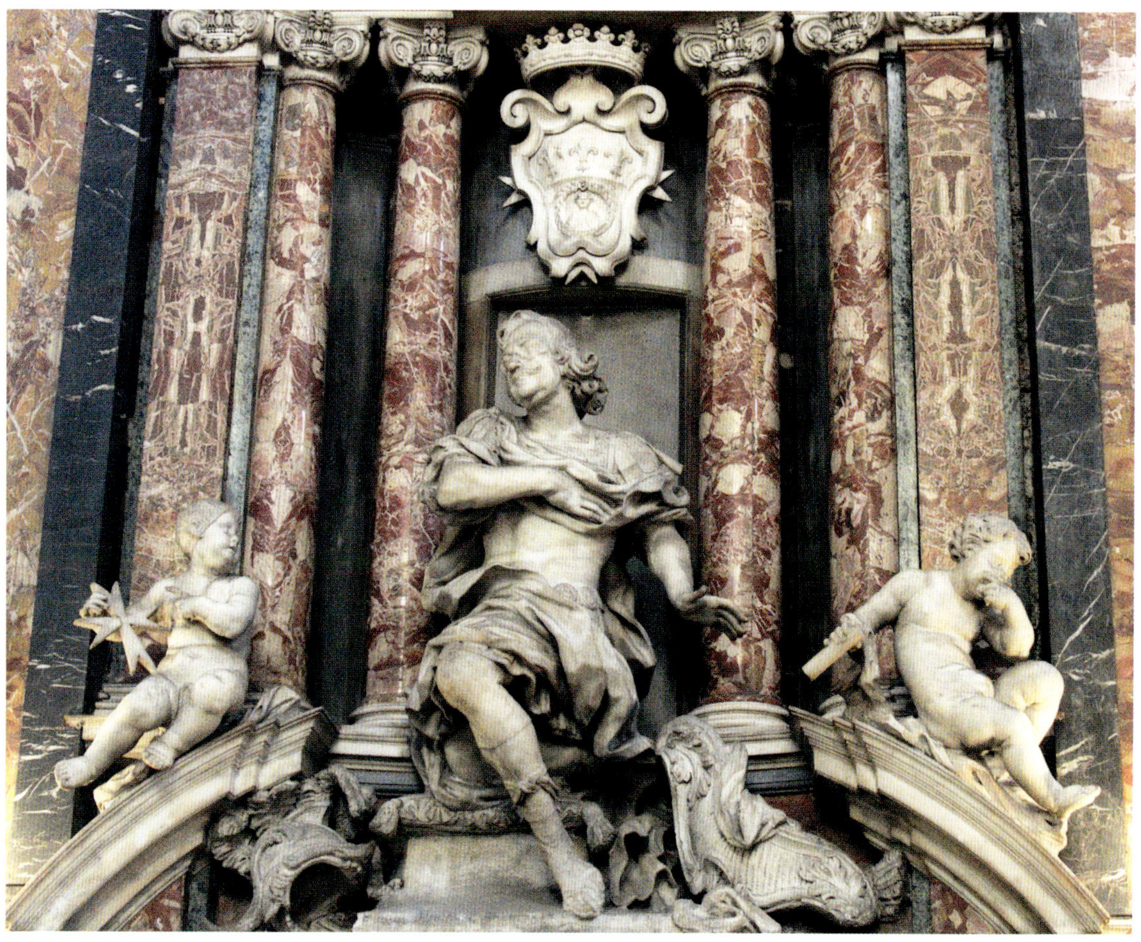

6.40 Francesco Cavallini, *Funerary Monument of Mario Bolognetti*, 1687, marble, Gesù e Maria, Rome

Maria in Publicolis, executed in 1727 by Lorenzo Ottoni (fig.6.46).[105]

Furthermore, and as previously mentioned, Bernini's approach to his figures' garments, though criticised by some as excessive, was frequently emulated.[106] What Bernini had initiated with the stylised, 'agitated' drapery of his *Saint Bibiana* (fig.6.12) in 1624, by 1669 had become an extreme stylistic choice which strained the viewer's belief that underneath the garments there was an actual body, as seen, for instance, in the *Angel with the Superscription* and the *Angel with the Crown of Thorns* in Sant'Andrea delle Fratte (figs 1.18 and 6.13).[107] Despite the reservations expressed by critics, such as the more classically minded sculptor Orfeo Boselli – who in his treatise on sculpture, without mentioning Bernini's name, found his approach totally contrary to that observed by classical artists ('They [ancient sculptors], therefore, had no other aim, goal, or intention than to drape the nude [body] in such a way as to expose it; to drape it so as to reveal it.')[108] – Bernini's angels were studied by and influenced subsequent generations of sculptors at

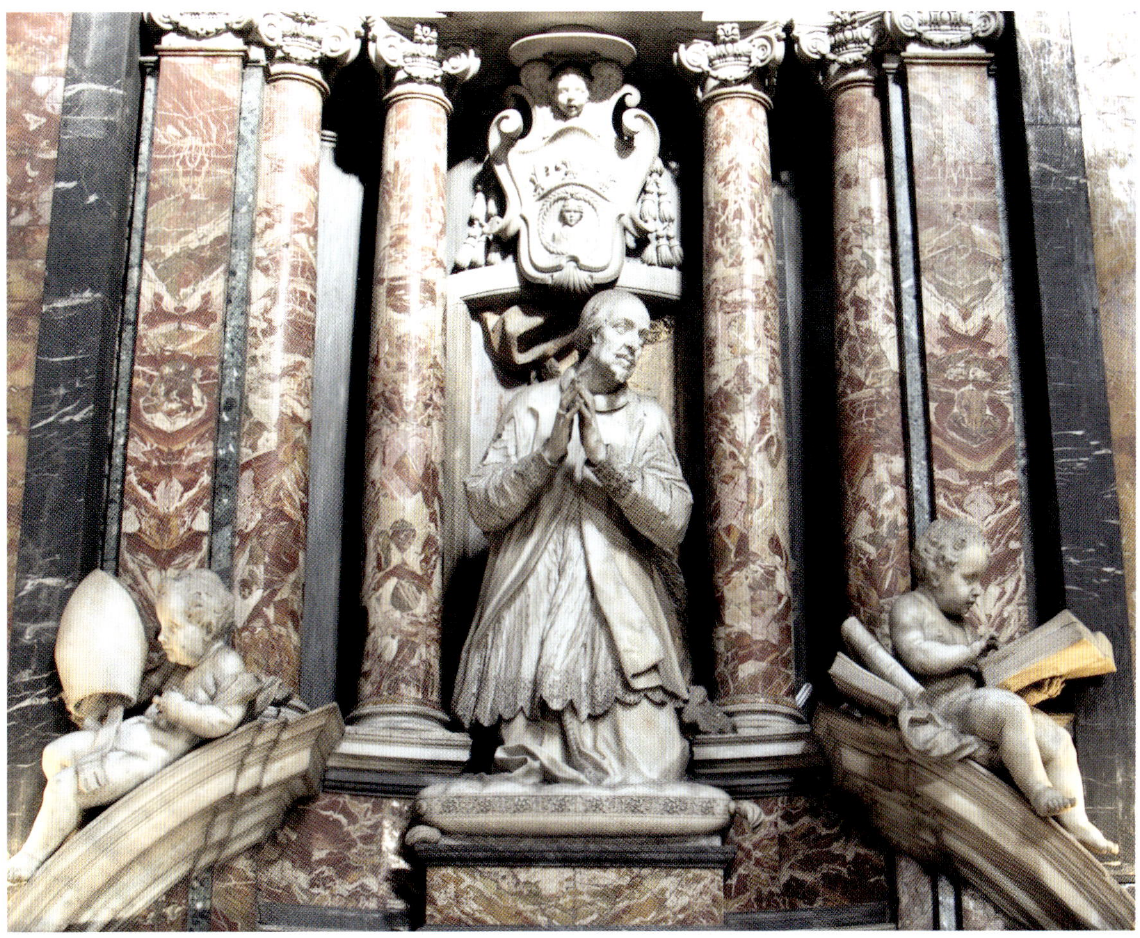

6.41 Francesco Cavallini, *Funerary Monument of Giorgio Bolognetti*, 1687, marble, Gesù e Maria, Rome

least through the middle of the eighteenth century.[109] Note, for example, how not just his most talented assistant, Antonio Raggi, followed Bernini's dynamic approach to his angels' garments on the facade of the church of San Marcello al Corso (1686) (fig.6.47), but some eighteenth-century sculptors also followed suit. Among the latter, there were artists such as Pietro Bracci in his *Angel with Palm Branch* of 1749 in the loggia of Santa Maria Maggiore (fig.6.48), as well as Pietro Pacilli, Giuseppe Vans, and Jean Le Doux, who executed the lovely angelic creatures who uphold the oval paintings in the five aisle 'chapels' – altars, really, but so labeled in the autograph plan – for Ferdinando Fuga's revamping of the basilica between 1746 and 1747 (fig.6.49).[110] Nonetheless, the tide eventually did turn and Bernini's art no longer pleased or succeeded in engaging viewers. In the emerging, Neoclassical cultural climate, his animated representation of human feelings and garment folds were ultimately seen as excessive, unrealistic, and deeply flawed.

According to Jörg Garms' analysis of literary responses to Bernini's art, in the course of the first

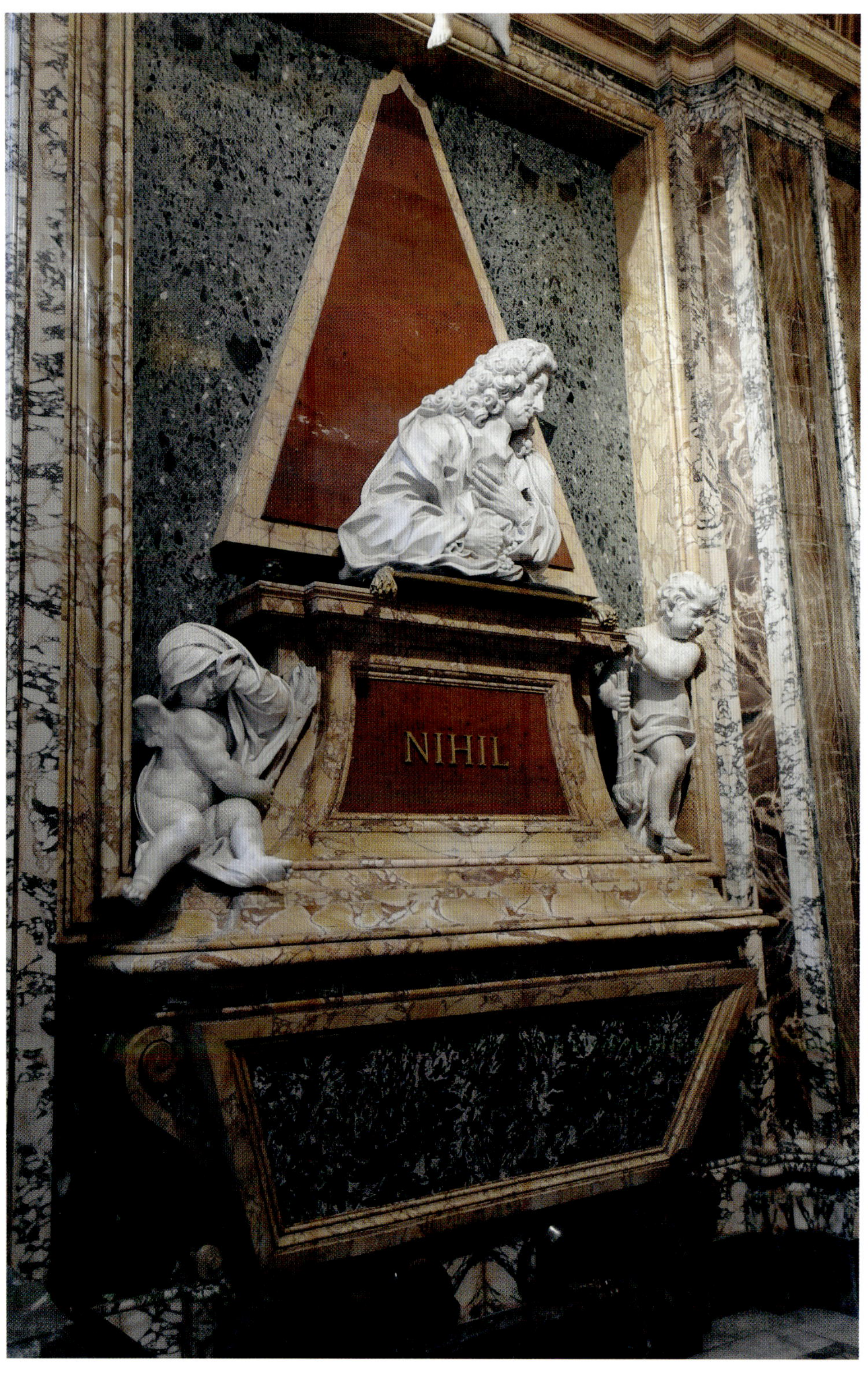

6.42 Giuseppe Mazzuoli, *Tomb of Prince Angelo Altieri*, Albertoni Altieri Chapel, 1710, marble, Santa Maria in Campitelli, Rome

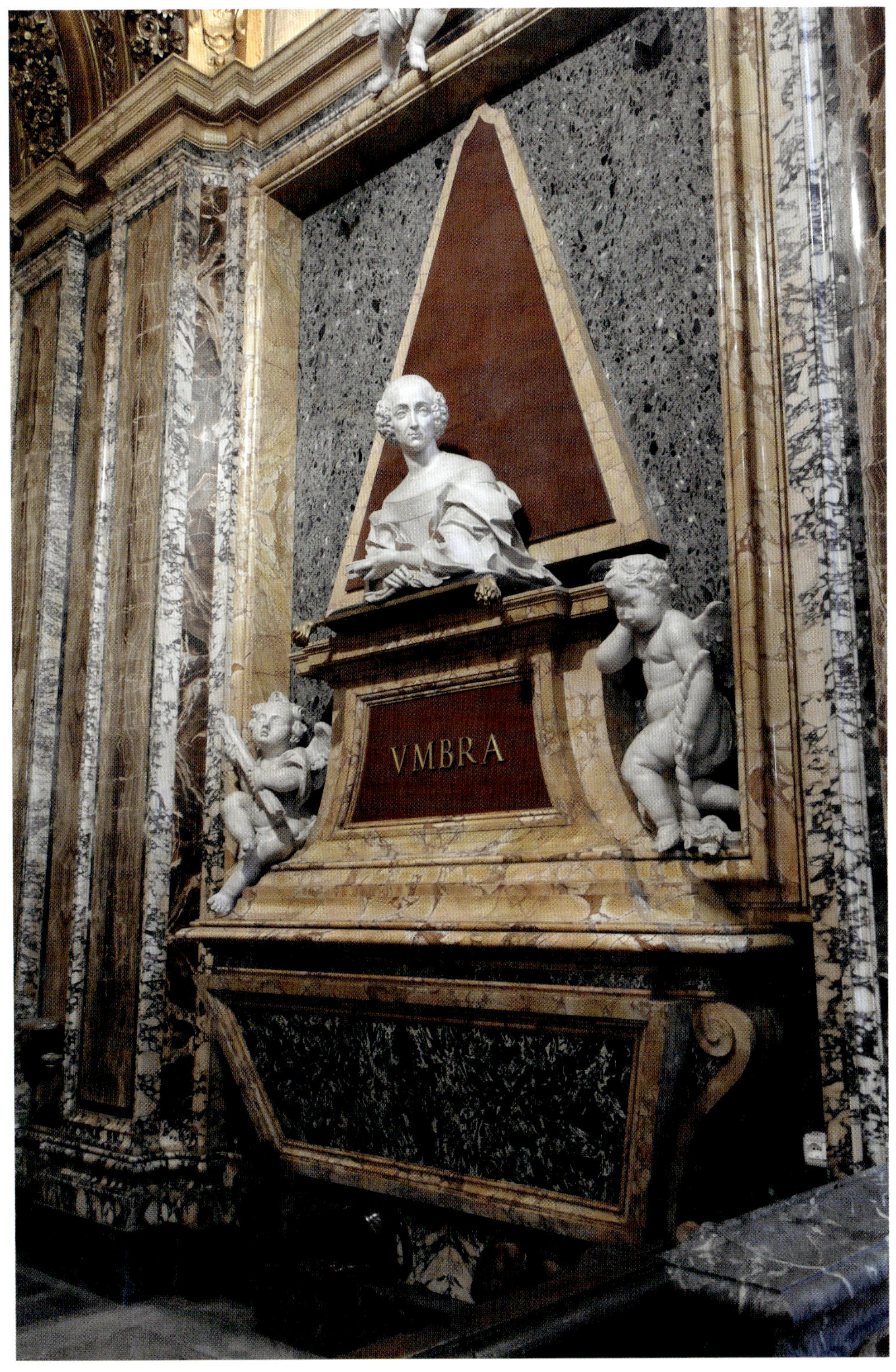

6.43 Giuseppe Mazzuoli, *Tomb of Laura Carpegna Altieri*, 1710, marble, Albertoni Altieri Chapel, Santa Maria in Campitelli, Rome

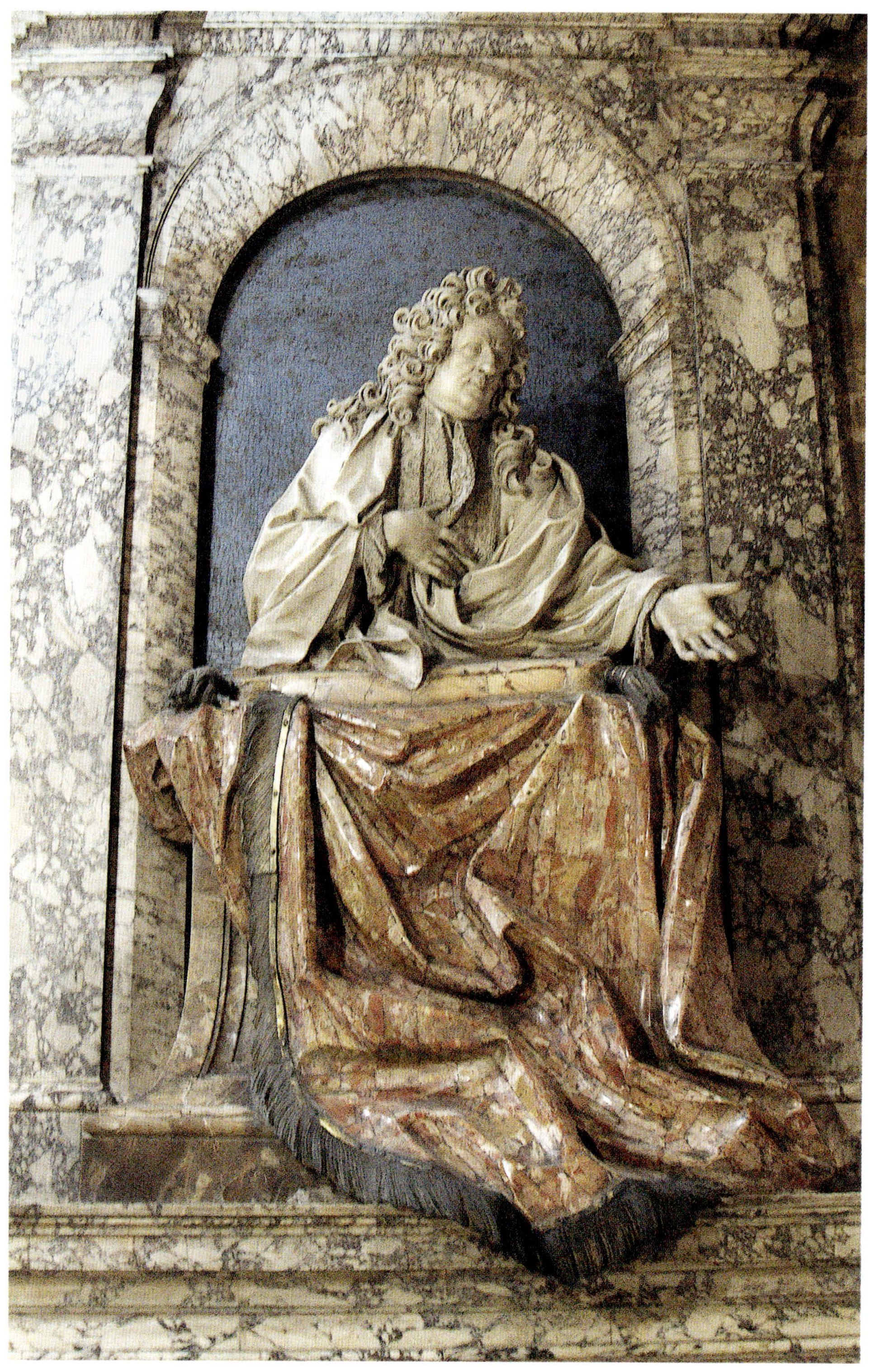

6.44 Bernardino Cametti, *Tomb of Giovanni Muti*, 1725, marble, Muti-Bussi Chapel, San Marcello al Corso, Rome

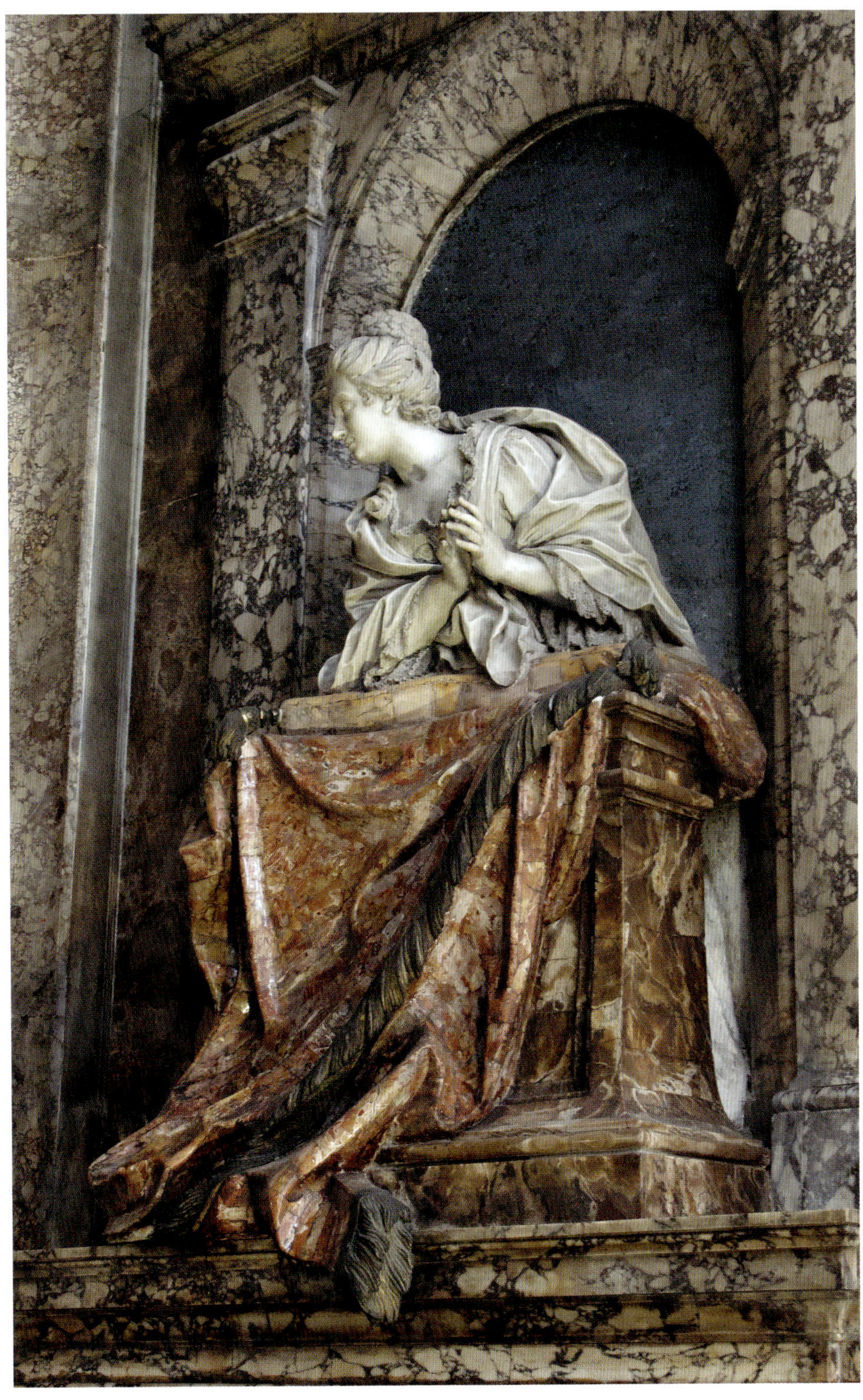

6.45 Bernardino Cametti, *Tomb of Maria Colomba Vicentini*, 1725, marble, Muti-Bussi Chapel, San Marcello al Corso, Rome

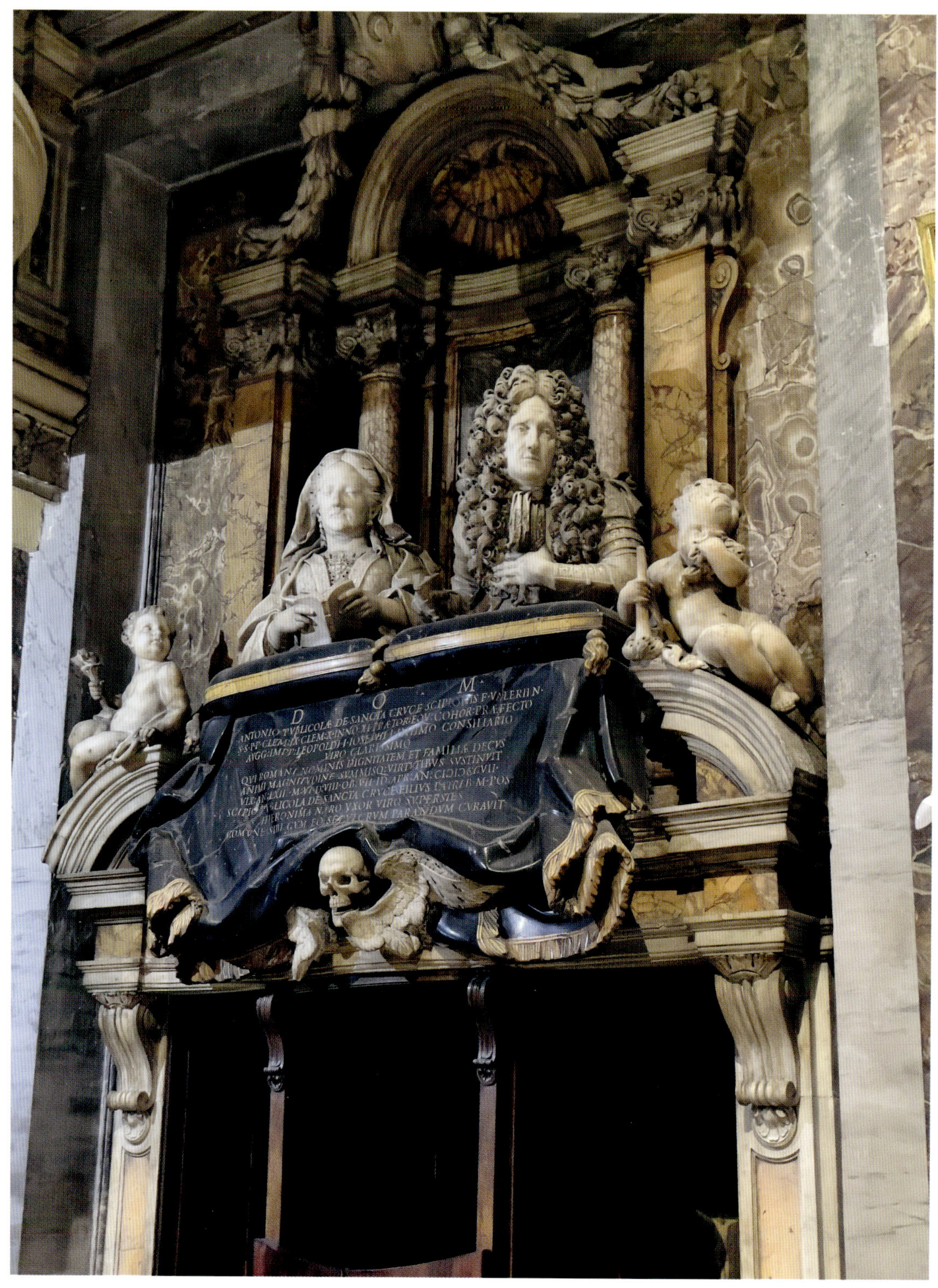

6.46 Lorenzo Ottoni, *Tomb of Antonio and Girolama Publicola*, 1727, marble, Santa Maria in Publicolis, Rome

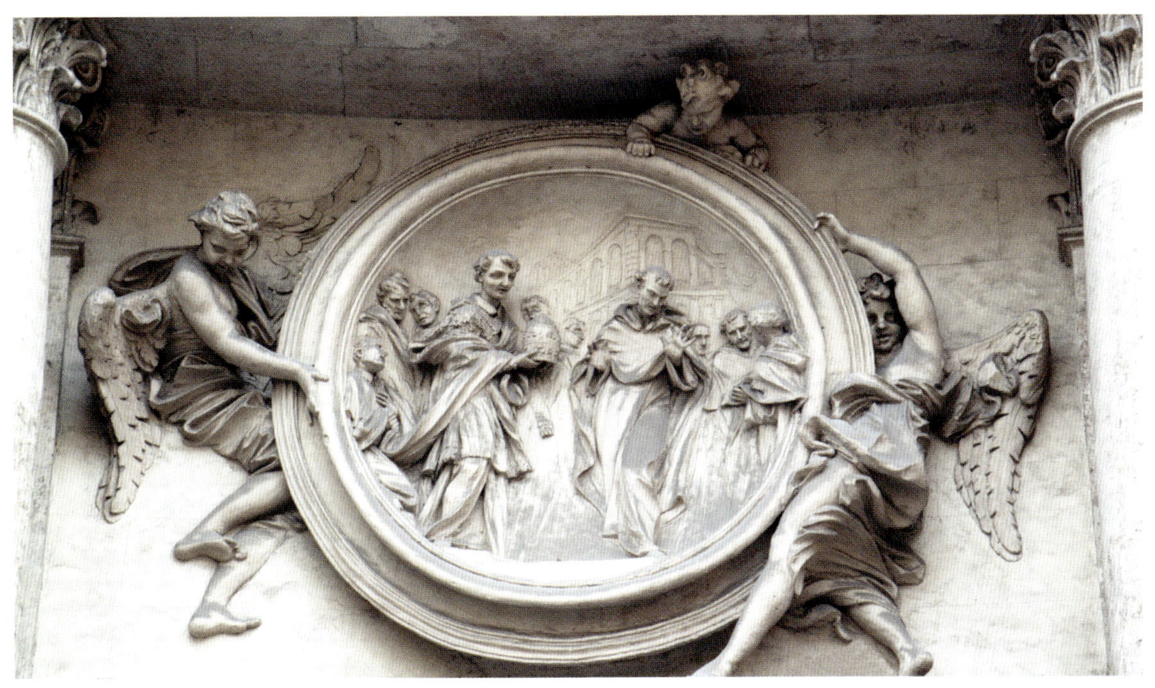

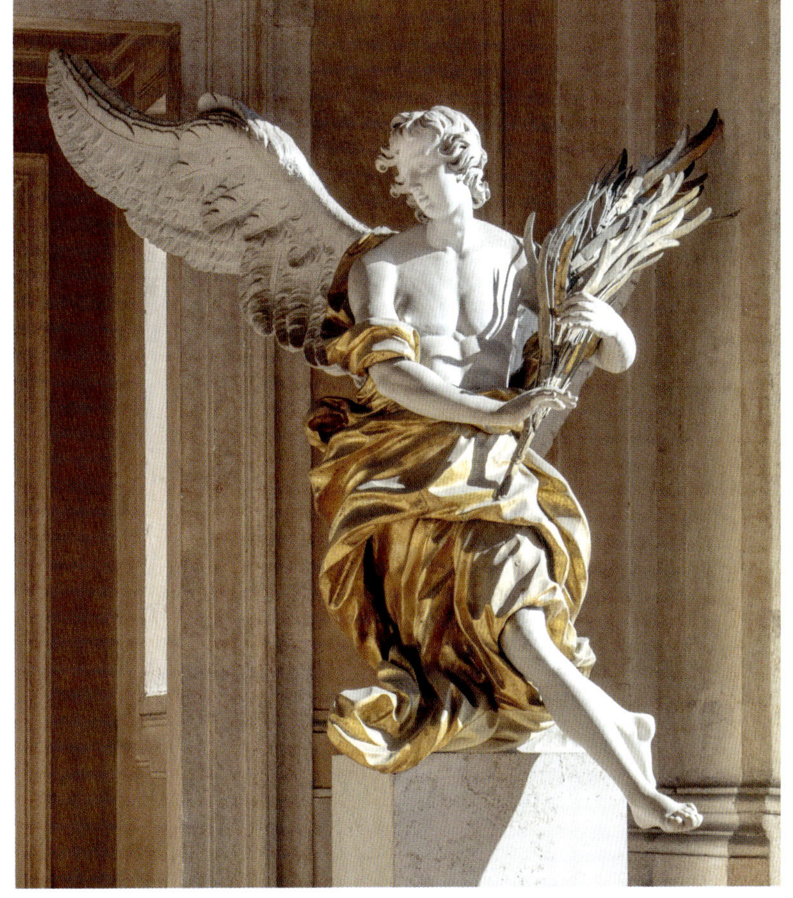

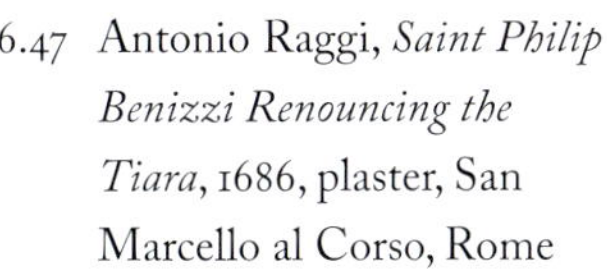

6.47 Antonio Raggi, *Saint Philip Benizzi Renouncing the Tiara*, 1686, plaster, San Marcello al Corso, Rome

6.48 Pietro Bracci, *Angel with Palm Branch*, 1749, marble and gilt plaster, Benediction Loggia, Santa Maria Maggiore, Rome

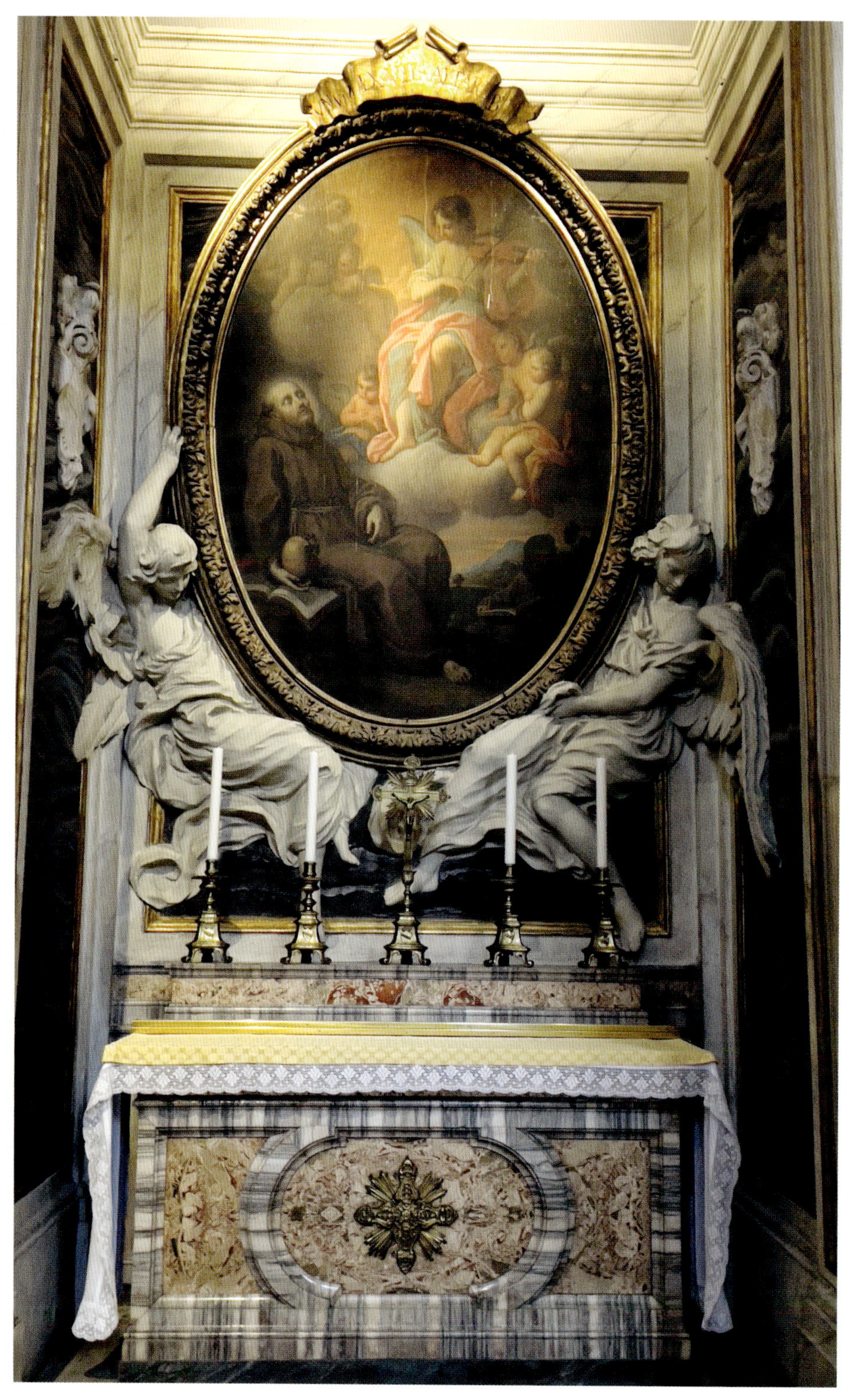

6.49 Collaborators of Ferdinando Fuga, *Angels Holding Ovals*, Altar of Saint Francis, 1746–7, plaster, Santa Maria Maggiore, Rome

third of the eighteenth century there was a gradual shift in emphasis.[111] While previous authors stressed the sculptor's carving skill, in comments of that period writers tended to emphasise the aesthetics. Thus, if in an earlier phase there was an appreciation for Bernini's dexterity, subsequently he was criticised for what was seen as a deviant taste. This later development may be discerned in Charles de Brosses' reaction to the sculptor in his letters written between 1745 and 1755 where, while admiring Bernini's genius and skillfulness, he criticised the sculptor for the over emphatic expressions and treatment of the vestments of his statues.[112] What was becoming increasingly appealing to the cognoscenti was a love for simplicity and the representation of an idealised human form that had been captured, in their view, by classical sculptors. And even before Winckelmann's admiration for Greek sculpture became encapsulated in the dictum 'noble simplicity and quiet grandeur', connoisseurs such as de Brosses had already begun faulting Bernini's statuary for lacking exactly those qualities. Reflecting upon his visit to the Villa Borghese, for example, and comparing Bernini's sculptures with the classical ones housed there, he wrote that 'his affected style was far from the loftiness of the grand style and the noble simplicity of ancient art'.[113]

However, and as discussed above, these aesthetic considerations coexisted with a persisting appreciation for Bernini's art. As with all historical and cultural phenomena, contrasting views about Bernini and his influence on other artists fluidly melded, with no sharp caesura demarcating the end of one era and the beginning of another. Clearly, Bernini's sculptural idiom was bound to become less appealing under the influence of intellectuals such as Johann Winckelmann, whose *Reflections on the Imitation of Greek Works in Painting and Sculpture* (1755) represents a changing tide in the history of European taste.[114] Yet, as Winckelmann's letter to Gian Ludovico Bianconi of July 1758 attests, Bernini was still very popular with the Romans, even as he labels the sculptor a 'guastator del suo mestiere' ('spoiler of his trade').[115] And in his subsequent opus, *History of the Art of Antiquity* (1764), the author repeatedly criticises Bernini for being a bad example for younger artists and having led them into 'swamps and puddles'.[116] Thus, while recognising his artistry, Bernini was branded as an insidious model for younger artists.

Italian critics would follow suit. In *Dell'arte di vedere nelle belle arti del disegno secondo i principi di Sulzer, e di Mengs* (1781), Francesco Milizia venomously labeled Bernini's *Saint Bibiana* 'Without nobility, without beautiful shapes, and poorly dressed . . . She tries to express something, but does not express anything.'[117] Sixteen years later the same author, in *Dizionario delle belle arti del disegno estratto in gran parte dalla enciclopedia metodica* (1797), accused Bernini of being 'the first to introduce license and errors under the pretext of gracefulness' and, having neglected to follow the true models of classical sculpture, 'became the model of many false copyists'.[118] Nevertheless, along with criticism from foreigners such as Füssli (1770) ('[in the *Apollo and Daphne*] Bernini substituted the marvelous for a lack of beauty'),[119] Quatremère de Quincy in the *Encyclopédie méthodique* (1788) (the expression of his statues was affected and their attitudes mannered),[120] August von Schlegel in his *Die Gemälde* (1799) (the gestures and actions of Bernini's sculptures were too theatrical and inopportune)[121] or Karl Ludwig Fernow in *Über den Bildhauer Canova und dessen Werke* (1806) (his garments resemble the frozen, turbulent waves of a sea agitated by a storm, distorted faces, violent actions without cause or purpose),[122] the decisive blow to the reputation of the genius of the Baroque was struck by Leopoldo Cicognara. In his influential *History of Sculpture* (1813–18) Cicognara labeled the sculptor as 'the most dangerous man of his century for the aura that surrounded him' and for being 'unable to sculpt without twisting every part [of the body] deep down to the bones'.[123] As it has been poignantly remarked, Bernini's reputation in the 1800s 'was about to face a long century'.[124]

* * *

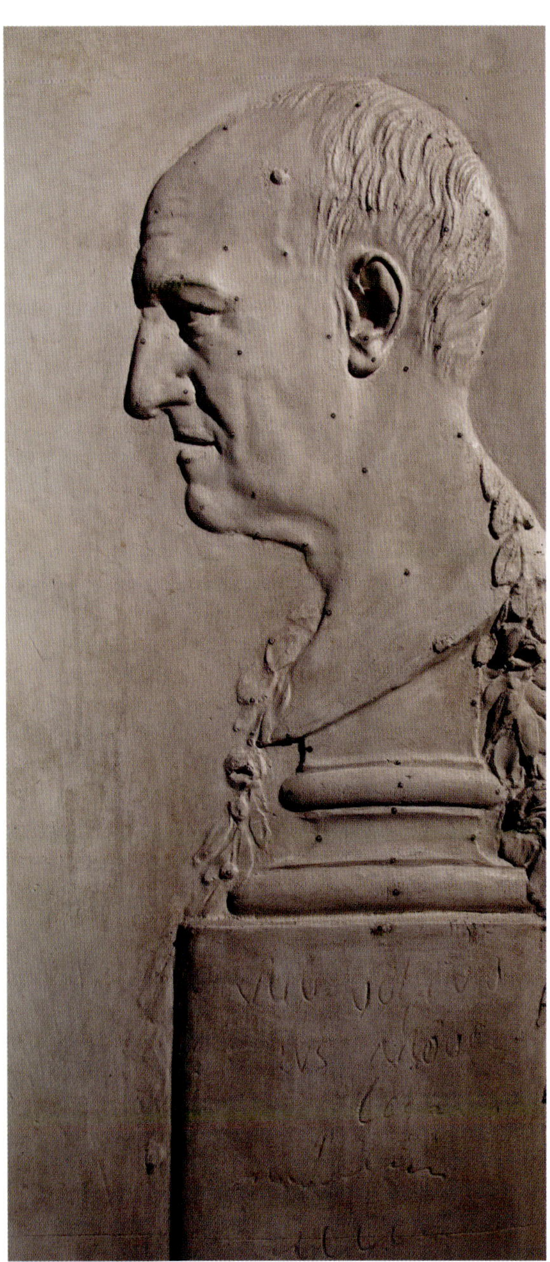

6.50 Antonio Canova, *Portrait of Giovanni Volpato*, detail of the model for the Funerary Monument of Giovanni Volpato, 1803–4, plaster, 160 × 114 × 4 cm (63 × 44 ⅞ × 1 ⅝ in), Accademia di Belle Arti, Ravenna, on loan to the Liceo artistico P.L. Nervi

Antonio Canova (1757–1822) arrived in Rome on 4 November 1779, aged 22.[125] Thanks to the intercession of engraver Giovanni Volpato (fig.6.50), within four years he obtained the major commission for the *Tomb of Clement XIV* in the basilica of Santi Apostoli (1783–7) (fig.6.11), a work that led immediately to a second, major papal assignment: the *Tomb of Clement XIII* in Saint Peter's Basilica (1784–92) (fig.6.51). With these monuments, executed between two painterly landmarks of the Neoclassical era – Anton Rafael Mengs' *Parnassus* in Villa Albani (1761) and Jacques-Louis David's *Oath of the Horatii* (1784) – the young artist made sculpture the most representative art of the new age,[126] a feat comparable to Bernini's who, with the youthful works for Scipione Borghese, had made sculpture the most symbolic medium of Baroque art. Embracing the paradoxical principle that had been voiced just over a decade earlier by Winckelmann – 'the only way for us to become great or, if this be possible, inimitable, is to imitate the ancients'[127] – Canova broke totally away from the art of the preceding century and was immediately acclaimed as the most important sculptor of the age.[128] His impact on contemporary sculpture was so powerful that by the early nineteenth century his achievement would be immortalised by Lord Byron's famous proclamation: 'Europe – the World – has but one Canova.'[129]

About seventeen years after Canova's arrival, on 8 March 1797, Bertel Thorvaldsen (1770–1844) also reached the Eternal City, endowed with comparable talent, vision, and ambition. Just like his Italian counterpart, who had obtained from the Venetian Senate a three-year allowance to continue his studies in Rome, so too had the young Danish artist received from the Royal Academy of Art a grant to travel abroad for as long a period.[130] Through their reinterpretation of classical, primarily Greek, sculpture, the two artists encapsulated and matched the aspirations of those intellectuals and art critics who believed that the artists' primary role was to

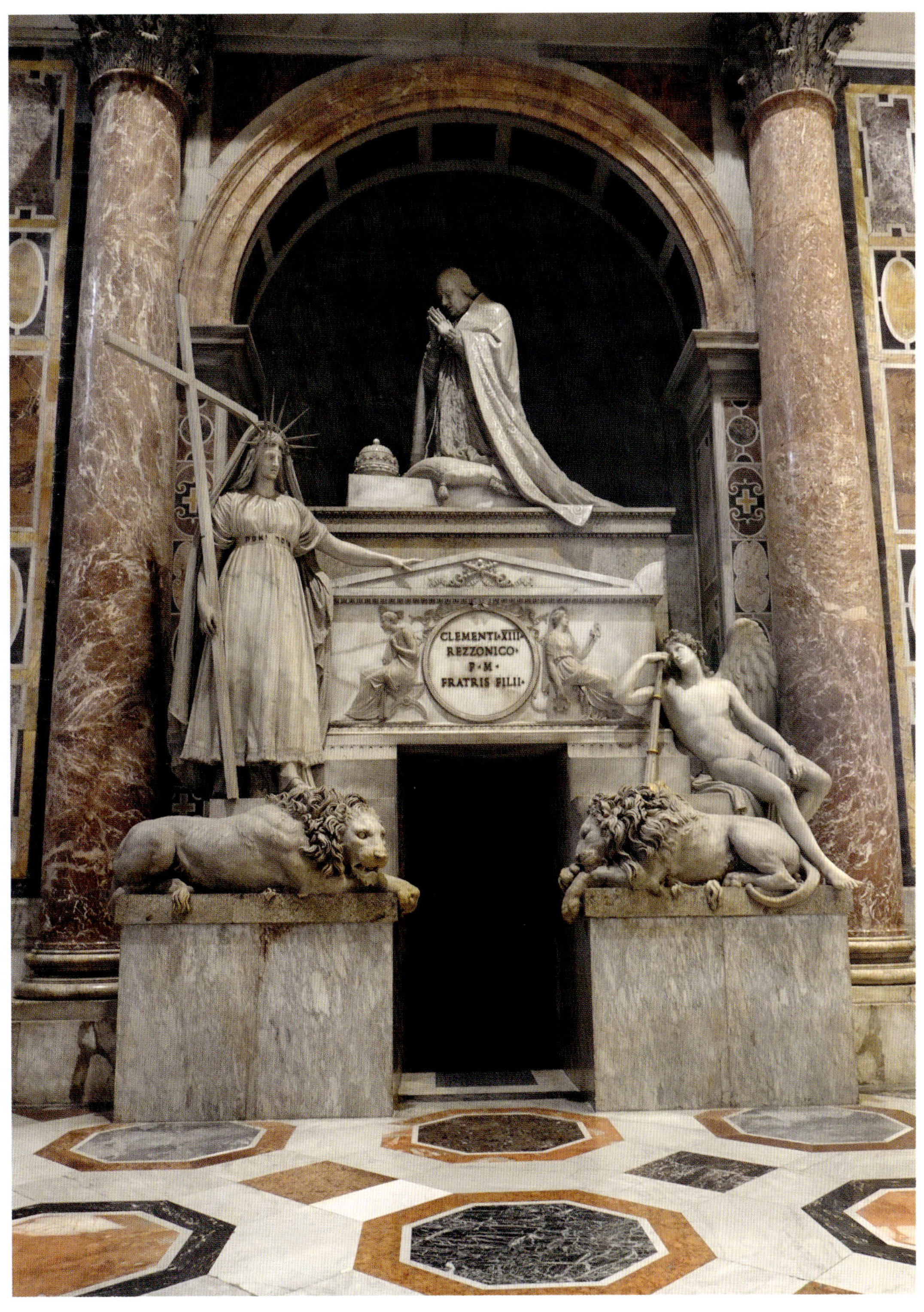

6.51 Antonio Canova, *Tomb of Pope Clement XIII*, 1784–92, marble, Saint Peter's Basilica, Rome

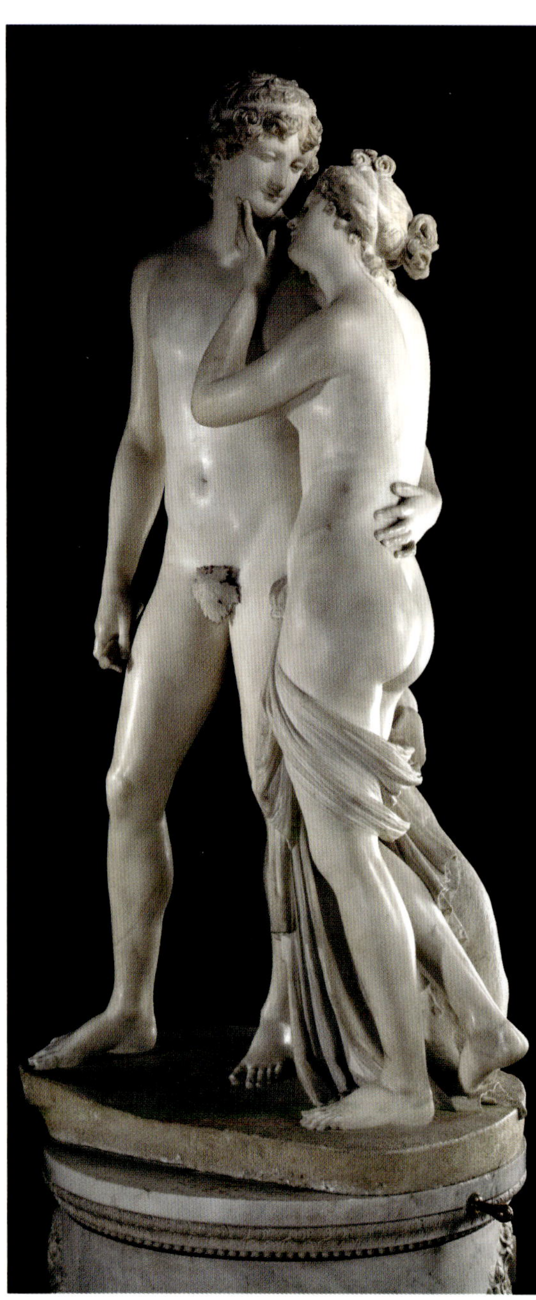

6.52 Antonio Canova, *Venus and Adonis*, 1789–94, marble, 185 × 80 × 60 cm (72 13/16 × 31 ½ × 23 5/8 in), Musée d'art et d'histoire, Ville de Genève. Dépot de la Ville de Genève, 1995

filter the tangible world through their genius and elevate it to an ideal realm.[131] The consummate, highly rarified, tender beauty of Canova's *Venus and Adonis* (1789–94) (fig.6.52), that sparked an emotional response nowadays known as the 'Stendhal syndrome',[132] and the stunning, Olympian, athletic beauty of Thorvaldsen's *Jason with the Golden Fleece* (1803–28) (fig.6.53) are enough to transport even a modern viewer, if not to fainting spells or tears, to boundless admiration. For these artists, as much as Bernini before them, performed true miracles. Their sculptures achieved heights of unparalleled dexterity and poetic imagination that have afforded humanity a view of real or imagined individuals that are truly 'larger than life'.

Describing his visit to the Basilica of Saint John Lateran in 1828, Stendhal judged the above-mentioned twelve statues of the apostles as 'ridiculous'.[133] Stepping off the left aisle into the Corsini Chapel (1732–5) (fig.6.54), where, according to Robert Enggass, one witnesses 'a solution that is at the same time equally distant from the Baroque turmoil of Bernini and the rigid neoclassicism of Canova',[134] Stendhal characterised it as 'the last beautiful chapel produced by the Christian religion'. In the same breath, however, he pithily and disparagingly debunked it by saying 'in short, the chapel lacks nothing except genius in the artists'.[135] Designed by the Florentine architect Alessandro Galilei and executed by some of the most talented artists and craftsmen of the period, despite its opulence, the chapel testifies to the absence of the guiding hand of a superlative artistic genius.[136] Clearly, as is the case with two other chapels that comparably bookend the taste and expressive possibilities of late-sixteenth and early seventeenth-century Roman art – the Sistine and Pauline Chapels in Santa Maria Maggiore – in the Corsini Chapel one may be struck by the individual features of this sumptuous space, but the Gesamtkunstwerk here displayed fails to transport the viewer to the lofty aesthetic planes achieved by Bernini. Indeed, one of this artist's supreme achievements – perhaps his greatest – was his incredible vision and ability to orchestrate dozens of collaborators and assistants to execute his bold, visionary compositions such as Saint Peter's Square, the crossing of Saint Peter's, the *Cathedra Petri*, the *Four Rivers Fountain*, or the Cornaro Chapel.[137] Thus, it is not surprising to learn that for Stendhal, the Corsini Chapel represented the nadir that Roman art had reached in the century between the death of Bernini and the emergence of Canova.[138]

Still, if Bernini's artistry was exceptional and enlightened, his prophetic powers were less so. In talking with his friend Paul Fréart de Chantelou when in Paris, the artist stated that he had to thank his lucky star for the great reputation in which he was held but that, after his death and its ascendancy no longer active, his fame would soon wane.[139] As argued in the foregoing pages, while he was possibly correct about the sidereal influence on his career, he was wrong as to how quickly his notoriety would decline. Nevertheless, as fate would have it, 'what Winckelmann, the classicist doctrinaire, had begun, Ruskin, the medieval revivalist, completed'.[140] It took the efforts of a host of scholars in the twentieth century and the objectivity afforded by the passage of time to rekindle interest and admiration for this prodigious artist. Perhaps, and in spite of his biographers' efforts to cast him in the role of the new Michelangelo, on a spiritual level Bernini did not equal his predecessor.[141] But it is an indisputable fact that, as Leopoldo Cicognara perspicaciously, if disapprovingly, observed, 'Where Bernini did not execute, he directed, and where he did not direct, he influenced' ('Il Bernini dove non fece, diresse, e dove non diresse, influì').[142] It is no hyperbole, rhetorical bombast, or an affront to any great artist who lived before or after him to claim that no one in the history of western art has had a more preponderant imprint on his world and on the physical aspect of his city than the mastermind of the Roman Baroque: Gian Lorenzo Bernini.

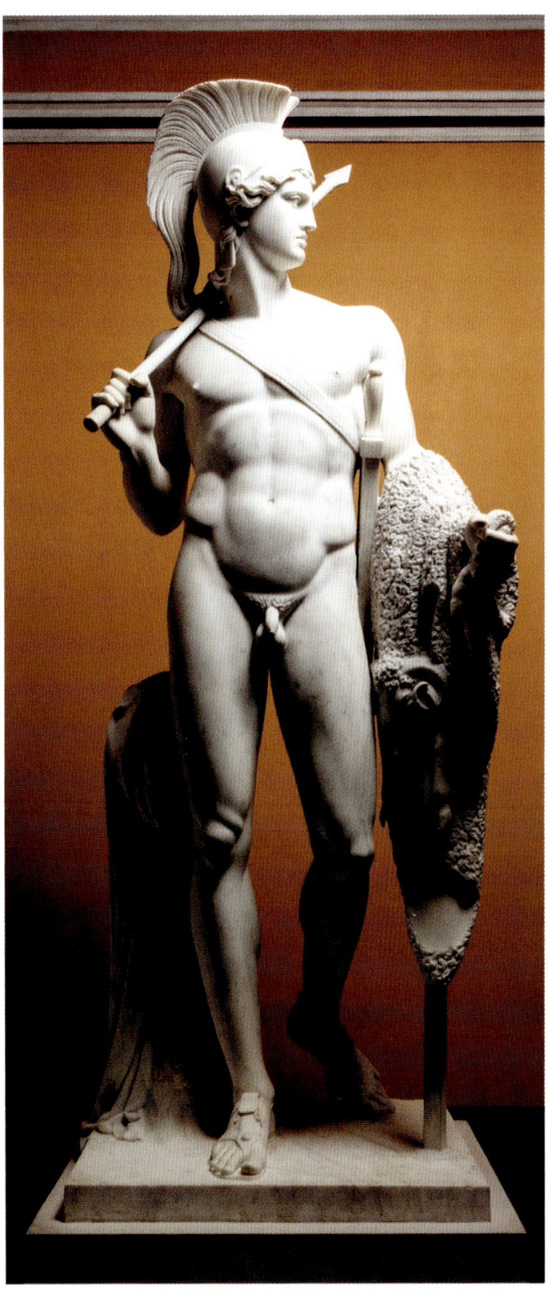

6.53 Bertel Thorvaldsen, *Jason with the Golden Fleece*, 1803–28, marble, height 241 cm (94⅞ in), Thorvaldsen Museum, Copenhagen

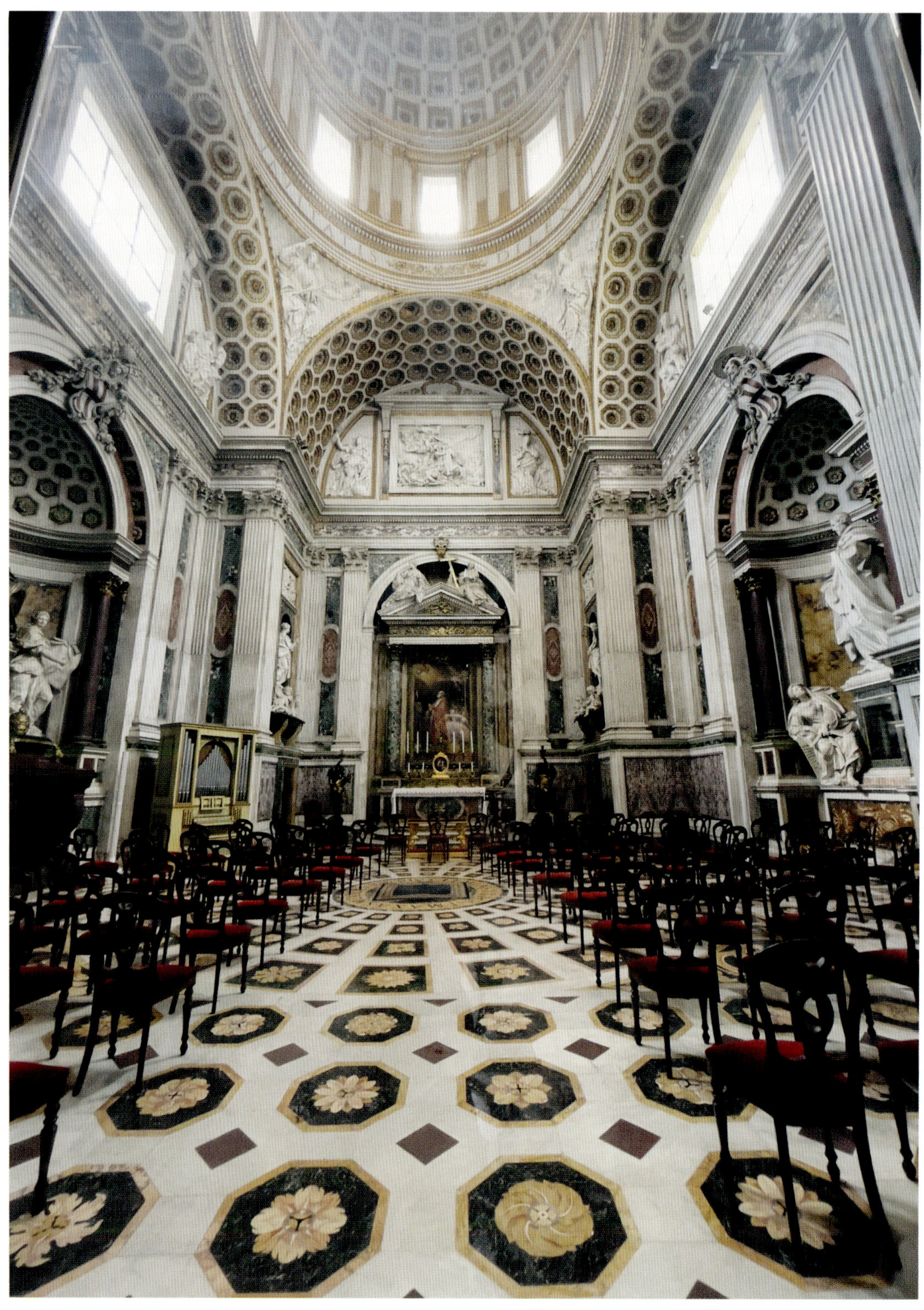

6.54 Alessandro Galilei, Corsini Chapel, 1732–5, Saint John Lateran, Rome

Notes

PREFACE

1 *The Letters of Cassiodorus*, Thomas Hodgkin (ed. and trans.), London, 1886, vol.VII, no.15, p.331: 'This art of statuary the Etruscans are said to have practised first in Italy; posterity has embraced it, and given to the City an artificial population almost equal to its natural one.' Leopoldo Cicognara, *Storia della scultura dal suo risorgimento in Italia fino al secolo di Canova*, 8 vols, Prato, 1824, VI, p.45: 'Un popolo di statue fregiò tutti questi sacri edificj.'

2 It has become normal practice to spell Bernini's first name in the abbreviated form Gian Lorenzo or Gianlorenzo. However, as rightly pointed out by Maurizio Fagiolo dell'Arco, *Berniniana: Novità sul regista del Barocco*, Milan, 2002, pp 50–51, both of his biographers and all his signed documents record the name as 'Gio. Lorenzo'. Thus, to be precise, the correct form of his first name should be Giovan Lorenzo. It is worth noting in this context that, even in his last will and testament, Bernini signed his name as 'Io Giovanni Lorenzo Bernino testatore mano propria.' Strictly speaking, it would be more consonant with the artist's wishes to refer to him as Bernino, not Bernini.

3 Andrea Bacchi and Liliana Barroero (eds), *La riscoperta del Seicento*, Genoa, 2017.

4 The Bibliotheca Hertziana online catalogue, for example, lists well over 2500 entries pertaining to Bernini. For a brief survey of the historiography of seventeenth-century sculpture and relative bibliography, see Steven F. Ostrow and Anthony Colantuono, 'Rome as the Center of Early Modern Sculpture' in *Critical Perspectives on Roman Baroque Sculpture*, Anthony Colantuono and Steven F. Ostrow (eds), University Park, 2014, pp 11–18.

CHAPTER I

1 Giovanni Pietro De' Crescenzi Romani, *Il Nobile Romano, O' Sia Trattato di Nobiltà*, Bologna, 1693, p.3: 'Dare honori a chi n'è indegno è rovinare colui, e screditare lo stesso honore . . . Non può esaltarlo il capriccio del Prencipe, che non gli faccia nemici non solo i Nobili, che posposti si veggono nelle pretese dignità; ma eziandio gl'Ignobili, che di mal occhio rimirano sdegnosi a fare un passo avanti colui, che testè caminava con esso loro del pari.' Translations, unless otherwise stated, are my own.

2 See Anne-Lise Desmas, 'The Birth of a Portrait Sculptor' in *Bernini*, Andrea Bacchi and Anna Coliva (eds), Milan, 2017, p.99, quoting from Cesare D'Onofrio, *Roma vista da Roma*, Rome, 1967, p.283. See also Catherine Hess in *Bernini and the Birth of the Baroque Portrait Sculpture*, Andrea Bacchi, Catherine Hess, and Jennifer Montagu (eds), Los Angeles, 2008, pp 97–9, as well as Tomaso Montanari, 'Due collezionisti alla scoperta dell'Italia' in *Dipinti e sculture dal Musée Jacquemart-André di Parigi*, Andrea Di Lorenzo (ed.), Milan, 2002, pp 117–19, cat.19.

3 See Stanislao Fraschetti, *Il Bernini: la sua vita, la sua opera, il suo tempo*, Milan, 1900, p.32, n.1. Bernini ultimately sculpted four portraits of the pope between the marble and bronze versions. The original portrait is apparently lost. See Desmas, p.99. Also, Tomaso Montanari, 'Il Colore del marmo. I busti di Bernini tra scultura e pittura, ritratto e storia, funzione e stile (1610–1638)' in *I marmi vivi. Bernini e la nascita del*

ritratto barocco, Andrea Bacchi, Tomaso Montanari, Beatrice Paolozzi Strozzi, and Dimitrios Zikos (eds), Florence, 2009, pp 91–2.

4 Fraschetti, p.407: 'Nel Seicento molti artisti vivevano in Roma, divisi virtualmente in due partiti: I fedeli e gli avversari al Bernini, il quale fu quasi sempre l'arbitro delle più importanti iniziative artistiche.'

5 It is not certain whether Paul V's marble portrait now at the Getty Museum was made for the pope himself or his nephew, Cardinal Scipione Borghese. The pope died on 28 January 1621 and documentation of payments to Bernini in June and September of that year for this marble bust do not clarify the matter (although it is more likely that Bernini sculpted it for Scipione). See Anne-Lise Desmas, 'The Birth of a Portrait Sculptor' in *Bernini*, Andrea Bacchi and Anna Coliva (eds), catalogue to the exhibition held at the Galleria Borghese, 1 November 2017 – 4 February 2018, pp 93–102 and pp 114–16. At the other end of Bernini's temporal spectrum, the only 'work' he did for Innocent XI is a caricature of the sickly pope in bed – hardly to be considered a papal commission. Thus, leaving open the possibility that Paul V had commissioned his own portrait, one can assert that the actual number of popes Bernini worked for is seven. For Irving Lavin, Bernini served 'no less than six popes'. See 'Bernini at St. Peter's: *Singularis in Singulis, in Omnibus unicus*' in *St. Peter's in the Vatican*, William Tronzo (ed.), Cambridge, 2005, pp 111–243, here p.111.

6 Giovanni Battista Passeri, *Vite de' pittori, scultori ed architetti che hanno lavorato in Roma morti dal 1641. Fino al 1673*, Rome, 1772, pp 242–3, in the *Life* of Guido Ubaldo Abbatini: 'A quel Dragone custode vigilante degli Orti Esperidi, premeva, che altri non rapisse i pomi d'oro delle grazie Pontificie, e vomitava da per tutto veleno, e sempre seminava spine pungentissime di avversioni per quel sentiero, che conduceva al possesso degli alti favori.' And again, with reference to Abbatini's vault fresco in the Cornaro Chapel, p.246: 'Il Cardinal Cornaro, che ne restò sodisfatto, era di pensiero di non trattarlo male, ma il consiglio di chi ne aveva la sopraintendenza (e Iddio glie lo perdoni) fece che quell'Eminenza gli desse assai meno di quello, che meritava, dicendogli che così lo sodisfaceva a bastanza.' A comparable, 'nasty' Bernini is described, again by Passeri, with reference to his obstructing Giuliano Finelli's career. See Passeri, p.257. Jennifer Montagu, *Alessandro Algardi*, 2 vols, New Haven and London, 1985, I, p.237, n.4, quotes from a lecture given by Ann Sutherland Harris, in which the latter underscored the fact that the opposition to Bernini was due primarily to 'personal jealousy, much of it fully justified, and should not be seen as a sign of clearly defined aesthetic differences'. For an instance of Bernini's support of younger artists, see Steven F. Ostrow, 'Gianlorenzo Bernini, Girolamo Lucenti, and the Statue of Philip IV in Santa Maria Maggiore: Patronage and Politics in Seicento Rome', *The Art Bulletin*, vol.73 (1991), pp 89–118, esp. p.99. See also Jennifer Montagu, 'Bernini Sculptures Not by Bernini' in *Gianlorenzo Bernini: New Aspects of His Art and Thought*, Irving Lavin (ed.), University Park and London, 1985, pp 25–43.

7 On Bernini's portraits, see Maurizio Fagiolo dell'Arco, 'Bernini "regista" del Barocco. Ragioni di una mostra' in *Gian Lorenzo Bernini: Regista del Barocco*, Maria Grazia Bernardini and Maurizio Fagiolo dell'Arco (eds), Geneva and Milan, 1999, pp 19–21. Idem, *Berniniana: Novità sul regista del Barocco*, Milan, 2002, p.39, n.5, points out that Bernini had already been knighted by 18 November 1622, as proven by a document published in Fraschetti, p.32. See also Tomaso Montanari (ed.), *Bernini pittore*, Milan, 2007.

8 For the portrait drawing, see the Biblioteca Marucelliana online reproduction, folio 15r in http://www.maru.firenze.sbn.it/LEONI/index.htm. See also Fagiolo dell'Arco, 'Bernini "regista" del Barocco', p.19.

9 Filippo Baldinucci, *The Life of Bernini*, Catherine Enggass (trans.), Maarten Delbeke, Evonne Levy, and Steven F. Ostrow (eds), University Park, 2006, p.8. Domenico Bernini, *The Life of Gian Lorenzo Bernini by Domenico Bernini*, Franco Mormando (ed. and trans.), University Park, 2011, p.94: 'He [Gian Lorenzo] was raised in the first rudiments of letters with good discipline by Pietro, his father, and by Angelica Galante, his mother, the former born in Florence, the latter in Naples. Pietro had moved from Florence to Naples to satisfy the desire of the viceroy, who wished to make use of his talents as sculptor in the decoration of the Royal Church of San Martino.' For a valuable review of the biographical data concerning both Pietro and Angelica, see Mormando in *The Life*, pp 272–3. For a fundamental essay on Pietro Bernini's early works in Naples, see Hans-Ulrich Kessler, 'Pietro Bernini (1562–1629): Seine Werke in der Certosa di San Martino in Neapel', *Mitteilungen des Kunsthistorischen Institutes in Florenz*, vol.38 (1994), pp 310–36, and the subsequent volume, idem, *Pietro Bernini (1562–1629)*, Munich, 2005.

Pietro was born in 1562 in Sesto di Toscana (today Sesto Fiorentino), worked in Caprarola, near Rome, for Cardinal Alessandro Farnese during the pontificate of Gregory XIII (1572–85), and moved to Naples in 1584. See Fraschetti, p.1. Pietro's family probably moved to Rome in 1606 as he is documented as having accepted his first papal commission at the end of 1606. Kessler, *Pietro Bernini*, p.22: 'Ende 1606 ist Pietro Bernini erstmals dokumentarisch in Rom nachweisbar, wo er am 30. Dezember seinen ersten päpstlichen Auftrag firmierte (Doc. 71, 72).' The contract involved his carving of the *Assumption* marble relief now in the baptistery of Santa Maria Maggiore.

10 Some of the ideas here expressed were presented in a paper read at the conference *Vom Sebeto an die Donau*, Vienna Center for the History of Collecting, Vienna, 9–10 November 2018, with the title 'Naples and Neapolitan Artists Seen Through "Northern" Lenses', subsequently published as Livio Pestilli, 'Napoli e gli artisti napoletani visti attraverso lenti forgiate al "nord"' in *Fortunata Neapolis: Kunst- und Kulturtransfer zwischen Neapel, Wien und Mitteleuropa*, Sebastian Schütze (ed.), Berlin and Boston, 2020, pp 219–35.

11 From the word for belfry, *campanile*, i.e., standing by one's local church as a symbol of regional or national affiliation.

12 On *campanilismo* and nationalism, see the important essay by Charles Dempsey, 'National Expression in Italian Sixteenth-Century Art: Problems of the Past and Present', *Studies in the History of Art*, vol.29 (1991), pp 14–24.

13 Francesco Maria Torrigio, *I sacri trofei romani del trionfante prencipe degli apostoli San Pietro gloriosissimo*, Rome, 1644.

14 See Lisa Pon, 'Michelangelo's First Signature', *Source: Notes in the History of Art*, vol.4 (1996), pp 16–21, as well as Livio Pestilli, 'Michelangelo's Pietà: Lombard Critics and Plinian Sources', *Source: Notes in the History of Art*, vol.19 (2000), pp 21–30.

15 Maarten Delbeke, Evonne Levy, and Steven F. Ostrow, 'Prolegomena to Bernini's Biographies: Critical Essays' in *Bernini's Biographies: Critical Essays*, Maarten Delbeke, Evonne Levy, and Steven F. Ostrow (eds), University Park, 2006, p.70, n.233.

16 For Rossella Pantanella's partial transcription of the document that sanctioned Bernini's Roman citizenship, see Fagiolo dell'Arco, *Berniniana*, Appendix 3 B.9, pp 215–16. See also Mormando in *The Life*, pp 272–3, n.9, who quotes from Fagiolo dell'Arco.

17 At the end of the eighteenth century, Francesco Milizia, *Dizionario delle belle arti del disegno estratto in gran parte dalla Enciclopedia metodica*, 2 vols, Bassano, 1797, I, p.106, considered Bernini a Roman: 'menò in Roma tutta la sua vita che fu di 82 anni, onde si può dir Romano'.

18 Louise Rice, 'The Pre-Mochi Projects for the Veronica Pier in Saint Peter's' in *The Eternal Baroque: Studies in Honour of Jennifer Montagu*, Carolyn H. Miner (ed.), Milan, 2015, pp 175–202, here p.199, n.34: BAV (Biblioteca Apostolica Vaticana), ACSP (Archivio Capitolare di San Pietro), H71, fol. 162v: 'Die 15 Maij finitum fuit tertium modellum sacelli et altaris Sanctissimi Sudarij (inventore Equite Io. Laurentio Bernino ~~Florentino~~ Neapolitano) et collocatum in loculamento ubi est ostiolum quo ascenditur ab Vultum Sanctum (me praesent) hora 22. In quo modello ligneo construendo impensa sunt scuta amplius 140.'

19 Oskar Pollak, *Die Kunsttätigkeit unter Urban VIII: Die Peterskirche in Rom*, Hildesheim and New York, 1981, 5, p.3: 'Die lunae 5. februarij 1629. Fuit Congreg^{o} gen^{lis} . . . De mandatu Sanct^{mi} D~ni N~ri vivae vocis oraculo dictis Ill^{mis} DD. Cardinalibus, ut asseruerunt dato, unanimos, et quam libentissimè admiserunt in Architectum fabricae huius Sacrosanctae Basilicae D. Equitem Joannem Laurentium Berninum Florentinum, cum omnibus et singuli honoribus, privilegijs, esemptionibus, salario, emolumentis, et oneribus solitis, et consuetis.'

20 Archivio di Stato di Roma (ASR), Notai AC 4245, pp 273r. – 275v., 300r.–301v. See also Franco Borsi, Cristina Acidini Luchinat, and Francesco Quinterio, *Gian Lorenzo Bernini. Il testamento, la casa, la raccolta dei beni*, Florence, 1981, p.53.

21 Catherine M. Soussloff, 'Imitatio Buonarroti', *Sixteenth Century Journal*, vol.20 (1989), pp 581–602; Evonne Levy, 'Chapter 2 of Domenico Bernini's *Vita* of His Father: Mimesis' in *Bernini's Biographies*, pp 164–5; Carolina Mangone, *Bernini's Michelangelo*, New Haven and London, 2020.

22 Passeri.

23 Jacob Hess, *Die Künstlerbiographien von Giovanni Battista Passeri*, Leipzig and Vienna, 1934, p.169. Hess compiled the definitive and most complete version of Passeri's *Vite* by complementing the 1772 edition of the biographies with four manuscript versions. The author clarifies in n.3, p.169, that the last six words of the quotation were crossed out in the MS. and not included in the published version. Apparently,

Bernini's efforts to pass himself off as a Florentine were successful in at least one instance. In Nicola Pio's unpublished *Le vite di pittori scultori et architetti* of 1724, the author incorrectly wrote: 'Nacque in Firenze nell'anno 1598'. The manuscript, Cod. ms. Capponi 257 in the Vatican Library, was published by Catherine and Robert Enggass in 1977.

24 Cesare D'Onofrio, *Roma nel Seicento*, Florence, 1969, p.152: 'Al Porta successe Carlo Maderno da Como, qual continuò sin alla morte, che fù nel ponteficato di Urbano VIII *nell'anno della nostra Salute 1621* alli 2 di febraro, e con l'architettura di questo si fece la facciata, il portico, e tutta la fabrica sin alle cappelle di Gregorio XIII e di Clemente VIII e nella facciata ha seguito in gran parte il disegno di Michelangelo Buonaroti. Dopo la morte di Maderno fù ammesso il Cav. Gio. Lorenzo Bernini, fiorentino, come scrive il Baglione; *ma la verità è ch'è nato in Napoli.*' (Italics mine.) Maderno actually died on 30 January 1629. For Bernini's nomination as architect of St. Peter's, see Oskar Pollak, *Die Kunsttätigkeit unter Urban VIII: Die Peterskirche in Rom*, Hildesheim and New York, 1981 [orig. 1931], p.3, Regest 5.

25 Biblioteca Casanatense, Ms. 4984: *ROMA/ORNATA dall'Architettura, Pittura, e Scoltura/Dimostrata/Da Fioravante Martinelli Romano* [*c.*1658–60], p.192. As D'Onofrio indicates, the list of annotations made by Borromini to this manuscript are recorded in Heinrich Thelen, *Francesco Borromini. Die Handzeichnungen*, 3 vols, I, Abteilung. Zeitraum von 1620–32, p.99.

26 Flaminio Vacca, *Memorie di varie antichità trovate in diversi luoghi della città di Roma*, Rome, 1594, published posthumously in Famiano Nardini's *Roma antica*, 1666 and reprinted by Antonio Nibby (ed.), 4 vols, Rome, 1820, IV, here pp 6–7.

27 Passeri, p.430: 'Io non dico, che egli non fosse vanaglorioso, avido di fama, ed inamorato di se stesso, ma questi erano incentivi naturali della patria, che non avrebbe mai potuto staccarsegli da dosso, perche erano ereditarj del clima, e poi ciascheduno è desideroso di applausi.'

28 Maria Elena Ghelli, 'Il Vicerè Marchese del Carpio (1683–1687)', *Archivio storico per le province napoletane*, A. 58 (1933), p.289.

29 Archivio Segreto Vaticano, Segreteria di Stato, 1024, segnatura 129, *Cifre scritte da Mons. Nuncio di Napoli dal Mese di Novem: 1700 fino li 28 Dicemb. 1717*, 14 giugno 1701, 31r–31v.

30 Peter Stenitzer, 'Il Conte Harrach Viceré a Napoli (1728–1733)' in *Settecento Napoletano. Sulle ali dell'aquila imperiale 1707–1734*, Naples, 1994, pp 43–55, especially pp 44 and 50.

31 G. Ceci, 'La Compagnia della Morte in Napoli' *Archivio storico per le provincie napoletane*, vol.38, Naples, 1913, pp 145–62.

32 Bernardo De Dominici, *Vite de' pittori, scultori ed architetti napoletani*, 3 vols, Naples, 1742–5, III, pp 225–6. From here on, BDD. The modern edition of this work, published by Fiorella Scricchia Santoro and Andrea Zezza, 3 vols, Naples, 2008, will be referred to as SSZ.

33 Lady Morgan, *The Life and Times of Salvator Rosa*, 2 vols, London, 1824, I, p.89.

34 According to Christopher Marshall, *Baroque Naples and the Industry of Painting: The World in the Workbench*, New Haven and London, 2016, pp 36–7, Reni was in Naples in 1620 while Domenichino went there in 1630. A comparable aggressive treatment was, supposedly, also reserved for Giuseppe Cesari (i.e., the Cavalier D'Arpino). See BDD, II, p.263, SSZ, I, p.942. For a recent discussion of this 'anti-foreign labour agitation', see Marshall, pp 34–9.

35 Carlo Cesare Malvasia, *Felsina pittrice. Vite de pittori bolognesi*, 2 vols, Bologna, 1678, II, iv, p.34: 'Del Gessi [Reni's assistant] parimenti ebbe pensiero valersi nella Cappella di S. Gennaro a Napoli, conducendolo seco, se ben poi inutilmente; poiche appena ebbe disegnato qualche cartone, e principiato un pò di fresco, che lasciato tutto in quella guisa, se ne fuggì, tornandosene a casa. La cagione di ciò fu il sospetto, che non gli n'avvenisse male da quella gente, da lui creduta poco amica del forestiere, e congiurata (per politica) contro ogni Professore, che de' suoi non fosse.' Ibid., p.332, with regard to Domenichino: 'Applicò dunque al lavoro della famosa Cappella di S. Gennaro in Napoli, detta del Tesoro, non riflettendo alla già manifesta congiura de gli operarii di quella Città, che stretti insieme, e giurati contro ogni straniero, che la grand'opera lor di mano tor volesse, nè posero in spavento, se non in pericolo, l'Arpino prima, poi Guido, e finalmente il Gessi, che animoso anche più degli altri, non ebbe però petto da resistere a gl'insulti, come s'era dato vanto.' On the lingering suspicion that Domenichino might have been poisoned by his antagonists while in Naples, ibid., pp 334–5.

36 Johann Wolfgang von Goethe, *Italian Journey (1786–1788)*, W.H. Auden and E. Mayer (trans.), London and San Francisco, 1982, p.215.

37 Horace, Epode V, v. 43. For Charles VIII, see Atanasio Mozzillo, *Il Napoletano da Boccaccio a Goethe*, Naples, 1995, p.19. For Kircher, see Tara E. Nummedal, 'Kircher's Subterranean World and the Dignity of the Geocosm' in *The Great Art of Knowing: The Baroque Encyclopedia of Athanasius Kircher*, Fiesole, 2001, p.38.

38 Dionigi Atanagi, *De le lettere facete, et piacevoli di diversi grandi huomini, et chiari ingegni, raccolte per M. Dionigi Atanagi*, Venice, 1561, pp 296–7: 'Io pur venni a Napoli gentile, & da bene, il cui sito a me pare maraviglioso, & il piu bello, ch'io vedessi mai, dico il piu bello, ch'io vedessi mai, perche io non ho veduto città, c'habbia dall'un de lati il monte, & dall'altro la batti il mare, come fa questa: & anche per molte altre sue particolarità, che tutte insieme, & ciascuna per se, la fanno parer mirabile. Ma perche dovete sapere, che la natura non vuole, ne si conviene (come disse quella pecora del Petrarca) Per far ricco un, por gli altri in povertate, quando l'hebbe molte delle sue doti piu care concedute, le parve di ristringer la mano, affine che l'altre città non le mandassero loro ambasciatori a dolersi con esso lei di tanta partialità, & propose fra se stessa di dare questo terrestre Paradiso ad habitare a Diavoli, et cosi come haveva proposto, mandò ad effetto.' See also Mozzillo, p.9.

39 Joseph Addison, *Remarks on Several Parts of Italy, &c. In the Years 1701, 1702, 1703*, London, 1767 [orig. 1761], p.129: 'The inhabitants of Naples have been always very notorious for leading a life of laziness and pleasure, which I take to arise partly out of the wonderful plenty of their country, that does not make labour so necessary to them, and partly out of the temper of their climate, that relaxes the fibres of their bodies, and disposes the people to such an idle indolent humour. Whatever it proceeds from, we find they were formerly as famous for it as they are at present.' See also Mozzillo, p.14.

40 See Katia Fiorentino, 'La rivolta di Masaniello del 1647' in *Civiltà del Seicento a Napoli*, 2 vols, Naples, 1984, II, p.43.

41 Mozzillo, p.51.

42 Benjamin Rand, *The Life, Unpublished Letters, and Philosophical Regimen of Anthony, Earl of Shaftesbury*, London, 1900, p.471.

43 That according to outsiders the Neapolitans behaved in a way that 'was all their own' may be gathered from Baldinucci's statement that when Salvator Rosa recited his satires in front of his literary friends 'he accompanied his readings with the most delightful gestures and the most ridiculous grimaces typical of the Neapolitans' ('accompagnando la lettura co' più bei lazzi e colle più ridicolose smorfie al suo modo napoletano'). Filippo Baldinucci, *Notizie dei professori del disegno da Cimabue in qua*, 7 vols, Florence, 1847, V, p.496.

44 Passeri, p.417: 'Li Pittori Napoletani non sono molto dediti ad una lunga applicazione al disegno, ma sogliono prima del tempo dar di mano ai pennelli, e come essi dicono a *pittare*.' Hess, p.386: 'Li Pittori Napolitani non sono molto dediti, per proprio costume, ad una lunga applicazione al disegnare; ma prima del tempo, a dar di mano alli pennelli, et alli colori e come essi dicono a *pintare*.'

45 The hegemonic role of the Tuscan idiom in early modern Europe, be it linguistic or artistic, is also obvious when considering that even a foreigner, such as Dominicus Lampsonius, in his 1564 letter to Vasari about his *Vite* of 1550 – in which Lampsonius upholds the importance of the northern artists' interest in landscape to counter Vasari's emphasis on *istoria* – the Flemish painter and humanist employs the word *depignere*.

46 Addison, p.127.

47 BDD, III, pp 613–14; SSZ, pp 1170–72.

48 The epithet, based on Luca's father's pleading with the young artist to complete his works quickly, initially was used to signify 'Luca hurry up'. Subsequently, given the speed with which he completed his works, it would take on the meaning of 'Luca works quickly'. BDD, III, 396, SSZ, III, 758.

49 BDD, III, 438, SSZ, III, 835.

50 BDD, III, 630, SSZ, III, 1193.

51 ibid.: 'Ma dico, che in Napoli vi è per anche la disgrazia d'esser ignota la perfezione delle misure, e nobiltà di parti dell'ottime antiche statue, che veramente sono di perfettissima erudizione, e necessaria a costituire eccellente un Pittore: ma per contrario dico, che se da' Napoletani si praticasse tal studio restarebbe raffreddato quell fuoco che gli ha fatto partorire opere grandi, e magnifiche: come p[e]r ragion di esempio può vedersi in Luca Giordano.'

52 Giovan Pietro Bellori, *The Lives of the Modern Painters, Sculptors and Architects*, Hellmut Wohl (ed.), Alice Sedgwick Wohl (trans.), Cambridge, 2005, p.263.

53 Passeri, p.434.

54 On Neapolitan drawings, see the many valuable essays in *Le dessin napolitain*, Francesco Solinas and Sebastian Schütze (eds), Rome, 2010.

55 Andrea Zezza, 'De Dominici e il disegno' in *Le dessin napolitain*, p.11. Rossana Muzii, 'Il culto del disegno presso i pittori napoletani del Seicento e del Settecento con la guida di Bernardo De Dominici', in *Le dessin*

napolitain, F. Solinas and S. Schütze (eds), Rome, 2010, pp 15–30.

56 Zezza, pp 9 and 13.

57 ibid., p.9. This critique paraphrases Vincenzo Borghini's criticism of the Florentines who, according to him, had 'buon occhio e cattiva lingua'. See *Dizionario Biografico degli Italiani*, Rome, 1970, vol.12, p.683, under Borghini, Vincenzio Maria.

58 Giorgio Vasari, *Lives of the Painters, Sculptors and Architects*, 2 vols, Gaston du C. de Vere (trans.), New York and Toronto, 1996, I, p.930.

59 Joseph Jérôme Le Français de Lalande, *Voyage d'un François en Italie, fait dans les Années 1765 & 1766*, 8 vols, Venice, 1769. This edition was followed by the second augmented edition *Voyage en Italie, Contenant l'Histoire & les Anecdotes les plus singulieres de l'Italie, & sa description; les Usages, le Gouvernement, le Commerce, la Littérature, les Arts, l'Histoire Naturelle, & les Antiquités; avec des jugemens sur les Ouvrages de Peinture, Sculpture & Architecture, & les Plans de toutes les grandes villes d'Italie*, 8 vols, Paris, 1786.

60 Jean-Jacques Bouchard, *Voyage dans le Royaume de Naples in Œuvres de Jean-Jacques Bouchard in Journal II, Voyage dans le Royaume de Naples. Voyage dans la campagne de Rome*, Emanuele Kanceff (ed.), Turin, 1976, p. 264: 'il n'y a point de race au monde plus presomptueuse et plus vanteuse que cette noblesse, ni plus vaine, estant toute dans l'apparence et l'exterieur.' Ibid., p. 274: 'gens vains et tous entierement dans l'exterieur et l'apparance, dont il sont autant ou plus religieus observateurs que nos plus grands coquets de courtisans françois, ce qui a ruiné toute cette noblesse qui est aujourdhui gue<u>se jusques au dernier point.' Passeri, referring to Rosa's flashy re-entry into Rome with retinue after his successful stay in Florence, states: 'infermità veramente paesana, che la bagianaria di Napoli è unica' (a truly peasant infirmity, as that pompous Neapolitan vainglory is unique'.)

61 Paul Fréart de Chantelou, *Diary of the Cavaliere Bernini's Visit to France*, Anthony Blunt (ed.) George C. Bauer (ann.), Margery Corbett (trans.), Princeton, 1985, p.23; idem, *Journal de voyage du Cavalier Bernin en France*, M. Stanić (ed.), Paris, 2001, p.51. As with all of Chantelou's comments, especially on artistic theory and taste, one must keep in mind that these may be additions to the text that the Frenchman inserted for personal reasons in the social and historical context in which he lived. On the 'editing' process by Chantelou, Steven F. Ostrow, 'Bernini's Voice: From Chantelou's Journal to the Vite', in Delbeke, Levy, and Ostrow (eds), *Bernini' Biographies*, pp 111–41, and Daniela Del Pesco, *Bernini in Francia. Paul de Chantelou e il Journal de voyage du Cavalier Bernini en France*, Naples, 2007, p.11: 'Le parti dedicate a considerazioni su argomenti di teoria dell'arte, le valutazioni di artisti e di opere sembrano attribuibili, invece, ad un'elaborazione più meditata. L'ipotesi che avanziamo è che il *Journal*, pur presentandosi come un diario ideato per scopi privati, per "notre comune étude et pour notre divertissement même" come Paul scrive al fratello [Jean de Fréart] sia stato redatto nella forma che conosciamo per attestare la credibilità culturale di Chantelou in un momento di profonda trasformazione delle attività artistiche in Francia, e riveli le sue ambizioni di svolgere un ruolo nella nuova organizzazione istituzionale voluta da Colbert.' See also Ostrow, 'Gianlorenzo Bernini, Girolamo Lucenti, and the Statue of Philip IV in Santa Maria Maggiore', p.99.

62 Charles-Louis de Secondat Baron de Montesquieu, *The Spirit of the Laws*, 2 vols, London, 1750 [orig. French version published in Geneva in 1749], 'On the laws in their relation to the nature of the climate', I, Book XIV, Ch.2, on 'The Difference of Men in Different Climates'.

63 Montesquieu, p.320.

64 Montesquieu, *The Spirit of the Laws* [Cambridge, Integral], Book XIV, Chapter 2, pp 231–2. See open source: https://archive.org/details/MontesquieuTheSpiritOfLawsCambridgeIntegral/page/n265.

65 ibid., p.232.

66 ibid., p.234.

67 Johann Joachim Winckelmann, *History of the Art of Antiquity*, Harry Francis Mallgrave (trans.), Los Angeles, 2006, p.186.

68 Polybius, *The Histories of Polybius*, 6 vols, W.R. Paton (trans.), London and New York, 1922, V, Book 21, p.351.

69 Anna Maria Rao, 'Conclusion: Why Naples's History Matters' in *A Companion to Early Modern Naples*, Tommaso Astarita (ed.), Leiden and Boston, 2013, p.481. It should not surprise us that, although totally sympathetic towards Italy and all it stood for, even Stendhal in 1828 could look at the 'deep south' and make the following statement: 'We have just spent seventy-five days away from Rome. Perched on mule-back, we have seen that part of Africa that is called Sicily.' Stendhal, *A Roman Journal*, Haakon Chevalier (ed.), New York, 1957, p.244, in an entry for 1 October 1828.

70 Charles-Nicolas Cochin, *Voyage d'Italie, ou recueil de notes sur les ouvrages de peinture et de sculpture qu'on voit dans les principales villes d'Italie*, 3 vols, Paris, 1751. The first printed edition was published in 1756 but it remained more of a resumé of the voyage than a guidebook. The first edition issued for a wider audience saw the light in 1758. See Christian Michel's *Le Voyage d'Italie de Charles-Nicolas Cochin (1758)*, Rome, 1991, pp 1–67.

71 For an assessment of the impact that Cochin's work had on contemporaries and other authors, see Michel, as in n.70.

72 Cochin, *Voyage d'Italie*, I, p.143.

73 ibid., p.177.

74 Lalande, as in n.59.

75 ibid., pp 244–5: 'Mais lorsque je fus aux Chartreux à Naples, je fus agréablement surpris de voir que cet artiste étoit digne d'aller de pair avec les plus grands maître pour la beauté du caractere, du style, du dessin & de l'expression ; il a su réunir les plus grandes beautés de l'art avec l'imitation de la nature, & la noblesse, quand le sujects qu'il a traités l'ont exigé. On en peut juger par les douze prophetes placés dans la nef de l'église, ce sont des chefs-d'œuvre de l'art.'

76 ibid., pp 373–4.

77 Jean-Claude Richard de Saint-Non, *Voyage pittoresque, ou description des royaumes de Naples et de Sicile*, 4 vols, Paris, 1781–6.

78 Walter S. Melion, *Shaping the Netherlandish Canon: Karel van Mander's Schilder-Boeck,* Chicago and London, 1991, pp 150–51. In three letters addressed to Vasari (1565), Titian (1567), and Giulio Clovio (1570) Lampsonius argues in favor of the hegemony of Netherlandish engravers and points out how Vasari's *Vite* fail 'to obtain as history beyond Florence and Rome'.

79 Saint-Non, I, p.109.

80 Among the more recent reminders of this attitude, see Rosemary Sweet, *Cities and the Grand Tour: The British in Italy, c. 1690–1820*, Cambridge, 2012, pp 188–9.

81 John Moore, *A View of Society and Manners in Italy: With Anecdotes Relating to Some Eminent Characters*, 3 vols, London, 1781, II, pp 141–2.

82 Goethe, p.320.

83 ibid., pp 321–2.

84 ibid., pp 322–3.

85 Giulio Cesare Capaccio, *Il Forastiero*, Naples, 1634, p.940: 'Napoli è tutto il mondo.'

86 Goethe, p.191.

87 See Sarah McPhee, *Bernini's Beloved: A Portrait of Costanza Piccolomini*, New Haven and London, 2012, pp 1–2, 44, 149–50. Idem, 'Costanza Bonarelli: Biography Versus Archive' in *Bernini's Biographies*, pp 315–76.

88 For the letter Bernini's mother sent to Cardinal Francesco Barberini asking that he 'rein in' Gian Lorenzo's ire, see McPhee, *Bernini's Beloved*, pp 149–50. The letter was first published by Pio Pecchiai, 'Il Bernini Furioso', *Strenna dei romanisti*, vol.10 (1949), pp 181–2. Bernini's general 'Neapolitan' nature is confirmed by the French diarist Paul Fréart de Chantelou who, in writing to his brother, stated that Bernini's temperament 'is all fire'. Chantelou, *Diary*, p.14.

89 On La Chambre's work, see Tomaso Montanari, 'Pierre Cureau de la Chambre e la prima biografia di Gian Lorenzo Bernini', *Paragone*, vol.24–5 (1999), pp 103–32.

90 Pierre Cureau de la Chambre, *Eloge du Cavalier Bernin*, Paris, 1681, p.25: 'A parler franchement, de tout cela il ne resultoit point une grande & noble physionomie, un bel air de teste; mais dés qu'il ouvroit la bouche, c'estoit un charme que de l'entendre, d'autant plus qu'il accompagnoit tout ce qu'il disoit, de certains gestes merveilleusement expressifs, & qui sont propres aux Napolitains.'

91 Italics mine. Filippo Baldinucci, *Vita del Cavaliere Gio. Lorenzo Bernino, scultore, architetto, e pittore*, Florence, 1682, p.65: 'Soleva dire per ischerzo esser questa avidità di frutte un peccato originale di chi nasceva in Napoli.' Domenico Bernini, *Vita del Cavalier Gio. Bernino*, Rome, 1713, p.177: 'Fù parco di vitto, usando solo una sorte di vivanda nella sua mensa, mà avido di frutti, il cui appetito egli diceva, essere proprietà annessa di chi nasce in Napoli.' Baldinucci, *The Life*, p.72; Domenico Bernini, *The Life*, p.233. Such love for fruit is further confirmed by Chantelou's entry for 10 August 1665, when Bernini asked him to stop by the market 'to see the fruit', as he had been told that there was no garden more beautiful in Paris. Chantelou, *Diary*, p.110.

92 Fiorentino, p.43.

93 ibid. The author quotes from the contemporary 'cronica' written by Alessandro Giraffi, who in turn derived his information from Antonio Paduano's *Ragguaglio del tumulto di Napoli*, Padua, 1648.

94 Peter Burke, *The Historical Anthropology of Early Modern Italy: Essays on Perception and Communication*, Cambridge, 2005 [orig. 1987], p.202.

95 Fiorentino, p.43.

96 Burke, p.191.

97 Chantelou, *Diary*, pp 21–5.

98 ibid., p.23.

99 ibid., pp 21–2.

100 ibid., pp 21–3. On this topic, see Cicero, *Orator*, H.M. Hubbell (trans.), Cambridge, MA, 1962, xi, 36, pp 331–3, and Aristotle, *Poetics*, in *The Complete Works of Aristotle*, 2 vols, Julian Barnes (ed.), Princeton, 1985, 1282[a] 1–23, pp 2034–5. The debate between *disegno* and *colore* went on for quite some time. The 'classic' example advancing the Florentine-Roman bias in favor of *disegno* as opposed to the Venetians' emphasis on *colore* is in Vasari's biography of Titian when, upon seeing Titian's painting of the *Danae* for Cardinal Alessandro Farnese, Michelangelo reportedly stated that 'his colouring and his style pleased him very much but that it was a shame that in Venice they did not learn to draw well from the beginning and that those painters did not pursue their studies with more method'. Giorgio Vasari, *Lives of the Artists*, George Bull (trans.), Harmondsworth, 1979, p.455. Basically, intellectuals claimed that flashy colors attract the incompetent viewer, whereas the educated will focus on *disegno* in both its meanings of *drawing* and *design*. In the seventeenth century the concept was incorporated in Bellori's 'The Idea of the Painter, the Sculptor and the Architect selected from the beauties of nature, superior to Nature', Hellmut Wohl (ed.), Alice Sedgwick Wohl (trans.), Cambridge, 2005, p.61, delivered at the Accademia di San Luca in 1664: 'Since the common people refer everything to the sense of sight, they praise things that are painted from nature because they appreciate beautiful colors, not beautiful forms which they do not understand; they are bored by the refinement and approve of novelty; they disdain reason, follow opinion, and turn away from the truth of art, upon which, as on its proper base, the most noble simulacrum of the Idea stands consecrated.' Most succinctly, the concept was expressed by Benvenuto Cellini who derided those painterly compositions that made use of flashy colors as *ingannacontadini*, that is, peasants' decoy. See Paola Barocchi, *Scritti d'arte del Cinquecento*, 3 vols, Milan and Naples, 1971, I, p.521. Ibid., in the comment at the bottom of the page the author quotes the *Vocabolario della crusca* for the definition of the term: 'Qualunque lavoro d'arte, grossolano, ma molto appariscente, e che perciò alletta e inganna i contadini, ossia le persone rozze e inesperte.' De' Crescenzi Romani, p.185: 'Non mi dispiace tuttavolta la distinzione, che fanno i Dottori tra lo scrivere, e'l copiare, tra il disegnare, e'l dipingere; poiche l'uno è opera più d'ingegno che di mano, l'altra è opra di mano, e, se per arte s'esercita, è sempre vile.'

101 Chantelou, *Diary*, p.23.

102 ibid.

103 On Bernini's opinions, and how some may represent Chantelou's more than the artist's, see Ostrow, 'Bernini's Voice', pp 111–41.

104 For the Spanish Crown's removal of Bernini's monumental bronze sculpture of the *Crucified Christ* and replacement with Domenico Guidi's version, see Tomaso Montanari, 'Bernini per Bernini: Il secondo "Crocifisso" monumentale. Con una digressione su Domenico Guidi', *Prospettiva*, vol.136 (2009), pp 2–25. For a discussion of the two versions of the *Crucified Christ* ascribed to Bernini, see the exhibition catalogue *Bernini*, Andrea Bacchi and Anna Coliva (eds), Città di Castello, 2018, pp 284–9.

105 Baldinucci, *The Life*, p.73.

106 A good example of this mindset is condensed in Bernini's above mentioned answer to the papal nuncio's question as to why some artifacts please immediately, whereas others not so: 'He [Bernini] replied that this difference proceeds from the knowledge or lack of it in the artist; those pictures which are not constructed on correct principles nor based on a groundwork or drawing, which are distinguished only by lovely coloring or an unskilled charm, please only the eye and not the mind, which searching for satisfaction recoils with disgust from works not designed strictly according to good rules and imbued with intelligence and knowledge. Take for example a picture by Barocci, with its beautiful coloring and graceful figures, which may please even the learned at first sight more than a work by Michelangelo. His [Michelangelo's] work may seem rough and disagreeable, so much that one averts the eyes, yet even in the act of turning away and leaving it, one feels that it draws and retains the gaze and after examining it for a little while one is forced to exclaim, "Ah! This really is beautiful"; indeed it fascinates imperceptibly, making it hard to move away and every time it seems more and more lovely. Is not the opposite the case, where the picture is by Barocci or some other painter whose only talent lies in his coloring and his charm of manner, for then the beauty of the painting grows less and less each time one sees it.' See Chantelou, *Diary*, pp 21–2. The *Accademia del Disegno* was founded by Giorgio Vasari in 1563. See Nikolaus

Pevsner, *Academies of Art: Past and Present*, Cambridge, 1940, as well as Zygmunt Waźbiński, *L'Accademia Medicea del Disegno a Firenze nel Cinquecento*, 2 vols, Florence, 1987, and Karen-edis Barzman, *The Florentine Academy and the Early Modern State: The Discipline of Disegno*, Cambridge, 2000.

107 Aristotle, *Poetics*, II, p.2321, 1450b 1–2: 'the most beautiful colours laid on without order will not give one the same pleasure as a simple black-and-white sketch of a portrait'. The preference of drawing over coloring is part of the controversy regarding which of the two aspects is more important in painting and it forms the discriminating element in critical judgment. For Cicero, for example, everyone was innately capable of discerning the good from the bad in art because of an interior aesthetic sense common to all humanity (a sort of subconscious instinct) or '*tacito quodam sensu*' (*De Oratore*, H. Rackham (trans.), Cambridge, 1977, III, I, 195, 6, pp 155–7) and he declares that: 'it is remarkable how little difference there is between the expert and the plain man as critics, though there is a great gap between them as performers'. (Cicero, *Orator*, Cambridge, 1971, xi. 36, p.157: 'Mirabile est, cum plurimum in faciendo intersit inter doctum et rudem, quam non multum differat in iudicando.') Aristotle, on the other hand, claimed that only the educated connoisseur is equipped to judge art. In all professions there are three levels of competency: the ordinary practitioner, the master, and the man educated in the art. For him it is the intellectual who is best placed to sit in judgment on artistic matters. Of these two classical trends it was the latter that was to gain the upper hand by the seventeenth and eighteenth centuries. See also Daniela Del Pesco's 'Bernini a Parigi: disegnare progetti "dal vero"' in *Bernini disegnatore. Nuove prospettive di ricerca*, Sybille Ebert-Schifferer, Tod A. Marder, and Sebastian Schütze (eds), Rome, 2017, p.263, and Livio Pestilli, 'Bellori's "old lady" or: On Informed versus Uninformed Criticism', *Word and Image*, vol.26 (2010), pp 393–9, here, p.395.

108 George C. Bauer in Chantelou, *Diary*, p.22, n.60: 'It has even been suggested, on the authority of this and other passages in the diary, that while in Paris the artist deliberately adapted his views to the classicising ones of his hosts; or alternatively, that such passages owe more to Chantelou than to Bernini. Either conclusion would be overhasty.' Bauer goes on to note that the apparent dichotomy between drawing/design and color is not Bernini's real intent: 'In this passage he is not concerned with arguing the superiority of design (*disegno*) over color (*colore*), though his argument nominally takes that form, but rather with vindicating the autonomous intellectual content of art.' On the other hand, Del Pesco, *Bernini in Francia*, pp 124 and 131, feels that, since Chantelou desired to give greater authority to his text, Bernini's ideas on art were not always related objectively.

109 See below.

110 Although Bernini never envisioned writing a treatise on the arts, one can get a good understanding of his ultimately traditional views from the various comments he made according to his biographers and Chantelou. See Steven F. Ostrow, 'Bernini e il paragone', in Montanari (ed.), *Bernini pittore*, pp 223–33, and idem, '"Appearing to be what they are not": Bernini's Reliefs in Theory and Practice', in *Critical Perspectives on Roman Baroque Sculpture*, A. Colantuono and S.F. Ostrow (eds), University Park, 2014, pp 165–84. For a recap of his opinions, see Irving Lavin, *Bernini and the Unity of the Visual Arts*, 2 vols, New York and London, 1980, I, pp 9–15. Bernini acted as *rettore* (teacher) of the Accademia. Pietro Roccasecca, 'Teaching in the Studio for the "Accademia del Disegno dei pittori, scultori e architetti di Roma" (1594–1636)' in *The Accademia Seminars: The Accademia di San Luca in Rome, c. 1590–1635*, Peter M. Lukehart (ed.), Washington, New Haven and London, 2009, pp 123–59. See also Franco Mormando, Domenico Bernini, *The Life*, p.295, n.7.

111 Chantelou, *Diary*, 5 September, p.168: 'In his Academy in Rome prizes were given by Cardinal Francesco Barberini. Here the prize for the artist who submits the best drawing should be a commission for a picture from it, to be purchased at a liberal sum.' Chantelou, *Journal*, p.156. Tomaso Montanari, *Bernini pittore*, Cinisello Balsamo, 2007, pp 44–5, citing Nikolaus Pevsner, *Le accademie d'arte*, Turin, 1982 [orig. Eng. 1940], pp 82–3. When Nicholas Stone was accepted into Bernini's personal workshop in 1638 he recorded in his diary: '. . . and that he was att his housse I schould be welcome to spend my time with the other of his disciples . . . if I would come to him he would first have practice after some things he had and I should se his manner of workeing and then worke my self; in the meane time (sayes he) I would aduise you as you haue begun to continue in drawing with chalke, beying very necessary'. See Helga Tratz, 'Werkstatt

und Arbeitsweise Berninis', *Römisches Jahrbuch für Kunstgeschichte*, vol.23–24 (1988), pp 395–483, here p.417, quoting from 'The Note-Book and Account Book of Nicholas Stone', Walter Lewis Spiers (ed.), *The Walpole Society*, vol.7 (1918–19), p.170. Tratz, pp 417–18, also quotes from Chantelou's *Journal*, 14 October 1665, when Bernini went to visit Simon François de Tours 'who was delighted to welcome the Cavaliere. He told him that he was one of his pupils, that he had drawn at his school for a long time and had often been chided for the noise he made.' Chantelou, *Diary*, pp 300–301. Simon François frequented Bernini's workshop from 1627 until 1638.

112 Chantelou, *Diary*, 5 July, p.69; idem, *Journal*, pp 51–2. He reiterates the concept on 5 September during his visit to the Royal Academy; idem, *Diary*, p.167; idem, *Journal*, pp 155–6. Interestingly, the minutes of the Académie omit Bernini's advice that students alternate drawing from classical statuary with creative sculpting or painting. *Procès-Verbaux de l'Académie Royale de Peinture et de Sculpture 1648–1792*, Anatole de Montaiglon (ed.), Paris, 1875, t.1, p.290: 'Ledit sieyr Chevalier *Bernin* a confirmé par ses advis les sentimens de la Compagnie touchant l'esducation des Eslèves, assavoir qu'avant d'estudier d'aprèz nature, il faut leur remplire l'esprist des belles hidée de l'Antique.' See also Ostrow, 'Bernini e il paragone', pp 223–33, and idem, "'Appearing to be what they are not'", pp 165–84.

113 Among the many publications, see the collection of essays in *Bernini: Sculpting in Clay*, C.D. Dickerson III, Anthony Sigel, and Ian Wardropper (eds), New Haven and London, 2012; *Material Bernini*, Evonne Levy and Carolina Mangone (eds), London and New York, 2016; *Bernini disegnatore*, Ebert-Schifferer, Marder, and Schütze (eds).

114 Michael Cole, 'What Is a *Bozzetto*' in *Material Bernini*, p.136.

115 For the pertinence of the trope to Bernini's work, see the following essays in *Material Bernini*: Carolina Mangone, 'Bernini scultore pittoresco', pp 69–104; Steven F. Ostrow, 'Bernini's *Bozzetti* and the Trope of Fire', pp 148–68; Tara L. Nadeau, 'The Concept of Bernini's "Calculated Spontaneity": A Critical Reassessment', pp 169–86. See also Steven F. Ostrow's important recap of the scholarship on this topic in "'The Fire of Art"? A Historiography of Bernini's *Bozzetti*' in *Bernini: Sculpting in Clay*, pp 75–85.

116 The term was coined by Irving Lavin in 'Calculated Spontaneity: Bernini and the Terracotta Sketch', *Apollo*, vol.107, no.195 (1978), pp 398–405, reprinted in *Visual Spirit: The Art of Gianlorenzo Bernini*, 2 vols, London, 2007, pp 376–92.

117 Baldinucci, *The Life*, p.72.

118 The term is quoted by Steven F. Ostrow with regard to Anthony Sigel's study of Bernini's clay *bozzetti*, in Ostrow's 'Bernini's *Bozzetti* and the Trope of Fire', p.156.

119 Joachim von Sandrart, *L'Academia Todesca della Architettura, Scultura & Pittura: oder Teutsche Academie der Edlen Bau- Bild- und Mahlerey-Künste*, Nuremberg, 1675, p.200: 'weil dieser erfahrne Künstler (da andere nur ein oder zwey Modellen gemacht) biß in 22. alle 3. Spannen hoch von Wachs mir gezeigt'. Idem, *Academia Nobilissimæ Artis Pictoriæ*, Frankfurt, 1683, p.188: ,'pro quâ statuâ (cum alii unam saltem aut duas;) ipse industriâ maximâ viginti duas plasmaverat è cerâ ideas, quas ipse mihi monstrabat, trium palmorum omnes'.

120 See, again, Ostrow's conclusions in "'The Fire of Art"?', p.85.

121 Chantelou's statements are in sharp contrast with Baldinucci's and Domenico Bernini's praise for the brief time it took Gian Lorenzo to execute the second portrait of Scipione Borghese. If Chantelou's report truly reflects Gian Lorenzo's ideas, then one has to conclude that the biographers, as well as the artist, were inconsistent in their views. The differences of opinion as to whether speed of execution was an indication of mastery or lack of a pondered planning is a recurrent theme in Renaissance and Baroque art. See Nicola Suthor, *Bravura. Virtuosität und Mutwilligkeit in der Malerei der Frühen Neuzeit*, Munich, 2010, especially pp 87–111 and 141–63.

122 Chantelou, *Journal*, in an entry on 9 August, p.110 and p.316, n.1; idem, *Diary*, p.107. See also Del Pesco, *Bernini in Francia*, pp 285–6.

123 ibid. According to George C. Bauer, Chantelou, *Diary*, p.107, n.39, this is probably the painting now in the Musée de Grenoble, listed in Terisio Pignatti, *Veronese*, Venice, 1976, as cat. no. A119.

124 ibid. Brauer, n.40, again citing Pignatti, suggests the painting is probably the one in Augsburg, Städtische Kunstsammlungen, cat. no.116. Also Del Pesco, *Bernini in Francia*, pp 285–6.

125 Chantelou, *Diary*, 2 October, p.246.

126 John Pope-Hennessy, *Raphael: The Wrightsman Lectures*, New York, 1970, p.40.

127 Chantelou, *Diary*, pp 283–4; idem, *Journal*, p.247. Even though Bernini talks of working with *macchie* in large

compositions, certainly the same concept applies to his drawings, especially those executed with a wash.

128 Irving Lavin (ed.), *Drawings by Gianlorenzo Bernini from the Museum der Bildenden Künste Leipzig, German Democratic Republic*, Princeton, 1981, p.4. See n.54.

129 ibid., p.5.

130 ibid., p.4: 'There is no evidence that Bernini ever made complete, highly finished prototypes for his own use in executing a work; indeed, when it came to the final execution, he might even dispense with his preliminary studies altogether.' In a note, Lavin relates this comment especially in relation to the Louis XIV bust. Pamela Gordon and Steven Ostrow, 'Function' in *Drawings by Gianlorenzo Bernini from the Museum der Bildenden Künste*, p.13: 'Bernini relied on visual recollection, and not on the preparatory work, as his guide . . . Exactitude of detail was not necessary in the drawings; it came only in the finished work.'

131 Baldinucci, *Vita*, p.74; Domenico Bernini, *The Life*, p.96 and n.17 on p.274.

132 This, in essence, is how Cigoli felt about the need to imitate Michelangelo's architectural ideas. In an architectural context, Carolina Mangone sums up his ideas similarly: 'emulating Michelangelo by fully understanding the rules before breaking them'. See Mangone, *Bernini's Michelangelo*, p.164.

133 See Dempsey, p.19 on the analogies between the *questione della lingua* and the *questione della lingua visiva*, with relative reference to Bruno Migliorini, *La storia della lingua italiana*, Florence, 1960, p.309.

134 In the famous satirical attack on Bernini during the extemporaneous interpretation of a Carnival comedy in Rome, in which Rosa took on the stock role of Coviello from the *commedia dell'arte* (but with the name Formica), De Dominici points out that it was an easy role for the artist because 'the Neapolitan idiom was natural for him'. BDD, III, p.222. See also Passeri, pp 421–2, and Baldinucci, *Notizie dei professori*, V, p.440.

135 See n.43. On the Neapolitan dialect, see Ferdinando Galiani, *Del Dialetto Napoletano*, Naples, 1779, p.8: 'pare ormai, che parlar Napoletano e buffoneggiare sia una stessa cosa'.

136 See Marshall, p.13.

137 Burke, p.85: 'It is likely, for example, that throughout our period [early modern] most educated people knew at least one dialect and spoke it on occasion . . . but it is hard to see how many women could have been fluent speakers of anything but their local dialect.' Angelica and Pietro both lived in the *rione Carità*. They signed the matrimonial *processo* on 11 January 1587, while the actual *atto* is dated 17 January. She was twelve years old and he twenty-four. When Gian Lorenzo was born in 1598, the seventh child of their union, Angelica was twenty-three years old. See Fagiolo dell'Arco, *Berniniana*, pp 76 and 199–201.

138 For a different interpretation of Bernini's national identity, see Fagiolo dell'Arco, *Berniniana*, p.54.

139 Giambattista Basile, *The Tale of Tales, or Entertainment for the Little Ones*, N.L. Canepa (trans.), Detroit, 2007.

140 idem, *Lo cunto de li cunti*, Michele Rak (ed.), Milan, 1999, p.vii and ff.

141 It is true that in the *Fiera di Farfa* – Bernini's interlude to Cardinal Francesco Barberini's 1639 Carnival spectacle *Chi soffre speri* – and more so in his only extant play, *The Impresario* – Bernini has the Neapolitan servant, Coviello, expressing himself in his southern dialect. However, it is important to note that the protagonist of *The Impresario*, Gratiano (Graziano) alias Bernini – speaks in the Bolognese dialect appropriate to this stock character as derived from the *commedia dell'arte*. For the untitled Italian version and the English translation of this play, see Donald Beecher and Massimo Ciavolella, 'A Comedy by Bernini' in *Gianlorenzo Bernini: New Aspects of His Art and Thought. A Commemorative Volume*, Irving Lavin (ed.), University Park and London, 1985, pp 63–113. The introductory essay and English translation of the play were subsequently published separately in 1994 by Dovehouse Editions Canada. Bernini's linguistic sensitivity is reflected in the diversified mode of expression he assigns to each character. See also Frederick Hammond, 'Bernini and the "Fiera di Farfa"' in *Gianlorenzo Bernini: New Aspects of His Art and Thought*, pp 115–25.

142 Felicita Audisio, 'Lettere e testi teatrali di Bernini: una postilla linguistica' in *Barocco romano e Barocco italiano: il teatro, l'effimero, l'allegoria*, Marcello Fagiolo dell'Arco and Maria Luisa Madonna (eds), Rome, 1985, pp 26–43, here p.32.

143 ibid., p.32: 'La lingua, si può dire, sia un equivalente del comportamento.'

144 Paul Hamilton, 'Hazlitt and the "Kings of Speech"' in *Metaphysical Hazlitt: Bicentenary Essays*, Uttara Natarajan, Tom Paulin, and Duncan Wu (eds), London and New York, 2005, p.69. A similar concept is expressed by Domenico Michelessi in his introduction, 'Memorie intorno alla vita, ed agli scritti del conte Francesco Alagarotti' in *Opere del Conte Algarotti*, 17 vols,

Cremona, 1778, I, p.I: 'Gli uomini sono cotanto inclinati a rassomigliare agli altri uomini, che la nostra vita civile è per l'ordinario retta, e determinata dall'esempio sì fattamente, che noi pieghiamo, e conformiamo le idee, e i sentimenti, e sia gli atti, e la voce, e i segni esteriori del volto all'imitazione di coloro, co' quali viviamo.'

145 See Fraschetti, p.200, where he transcribes part of a 'Canzonetta' written in the Neapolitan idiom by the title 'Le lodi e grandezze della Aguglia e Fontana di Piazza Navona' by Francesco Ascione, a Neapolitan living in Rome: 'Io so' de sto penziere,/Mentre nasciste là nello Sebeto,/Buono scultore sí meglio Poeto.'

CHAPTER 2

1 Ernst Kris and Otto Kurz, *Legend, Myth, and Magic in the Image of the Artist: A Historical Experiment*, New Haven and London, 1979. The volume was originally published in German as *Die Legende vom Künstler: ein geschichtlicher Versuch,* Vienna, 1934.

2 ibid., p.11.

3 Giorgio Vasari, *Le vite de' più eccellenti architetti, pittori, et scultori italiani, da Cimabue insino a' tempi nostri*, Torrentino, Florence, 1550. This first edition was subsequently superseded by the Giunti edition *Le vite dei più eccellenti pittori, scultori e architettori*, Florence, 1568. The bibliography on this subject is extensive. On this approach to biographies, see Paul Barolsky's trilogy *Michelangelo's Nose*, University Park, 1990, *Why Mona Lisa Smiles and Other Tales by Vasari*, University Park, 1991, and *Giotto's Father and the Family of Vasari's Lives*, 1992. See also Patricia Rubin, *Giorgio Vasari: Art and History*, New Haven, 1995.

4 Filippo Baldinucci, *Vita del Cavaliere Gio. Lorenzo Bernino, scultore, architetto, e pittore*, Florence, 1682, published in English as *The Life of Bernini by Filippo Baldinucci*, Catherine Engass (trans.), University Park, 1966, and Domenico Bernini, *Vita del Cavaliere Gio. Lorenzo Bernino*, Rome, 1713, published in English as *The Life of Gian Lorenzo Bernini*, Franco Mormando (ed. and trans.), University Park, 2011.

5 See Catherine Soussloff, 'Critical Topoi in the Sources on the Life of Gianlorenzo Bernini', PhD diss., Bryn Mawr College, 1982; idem, 'Old Age and Old-Age Style in the "Lives" of Artists: Gianlorenzo Bernini', *Art Journal*, vol.46 (1987), pp 115–21; idem, 'Imitatio Buonarroti', *Sixteenth Century Journal*, vol.20 (1989), pp 581–602; idem, 'Lives of Poets and Painters in the Renaissance', *Word and Image*, vol.6 (1990), pp 154–62.

6 Maarten Delbeke, Evonne Levy, and Steven F. Ostrow (eds), *Bernini's Biographies: Critical Essays*, University Park, 2006. This important collection of essays is prefaced by an extensive introductory chapter, 'Prolegomena to the Interdisciplinary Study of Bernini's Biographies', that thoroughly recaps the various phases of Bernini biographical studies while laying the ground for future investigations.

7 On the significance of *omission* in the *Lives* of artists, especially with reference to Bellori's exclusion of Bernini in his work, see Soussloff, 'Imitatio Buonarroti', pp 596–7.

8 Giovan Pietro Bellori, *The Lives of the Modern Painters, Sculptors and Architects*, Hellmut Wohl (ed.), Alice Sedgwick Wohl (trans.), Cambridge, 2005, p.295: 'Although sculpture up to this time lags far behind that of the ancients, with a paltry number of statues deserving of fame . . .' This state of affairs, of course, is also linked to the famous quarrel between the *anciens* and the *modernes*, a topic tangential to the subject here at hand. Sparked by Charles Perrault's long poem 'The Age of Louis the Great' read in the Parisian Academy in 1687 to celebrate the recovery of Louis XIV from an operation – the aim being that of comparing favorably the modern world with that of the ancients – its public delivery was seen by his critics as a denunciation of those classical authors they considered the apex of the classical tradition. See Charles Perrault, *Memoirs of My Life*, Jeanne Morgan Zarucchi (ed. and trans.), Columbia, 1989, pp 1–27. See Sebastian Schütze, '"Liberar questo secolo dall'invidiare gli antichi": Bernini und die "Querelle des Anciens et des Modernes"' in *Docta Manus*, Johannes Myssok, Jürgen Wienerm, and Joachim Poeschke (eds), Munster, 2007, pp 345–58.

9 Donatella Livia Sparti, 'Tecnica e teoria del restauro scultoreo a Roma nel Seicento, con una verifica sulla collezione di Flavio Chigi', *Storia dell'arte*, vol.92 (1998), pp 60–131, here pp 61–2, quoting from Vincenzo Giustiniani, *Discorsi sulle arti e sui mestieri*, Anna Banti (ed.), Florence, 1981, pp 72–3.

10 Donatella Livia Sparti, 'The "Rebirth" of Ancient Sculpture in 17th-Century Rome' in *Bernini*, Andrea Bacchi and Anna Coliva (eds), exh.cat., Galleria Borghese, 1 November 2017 – 4 February 2018, Milan, 2017, p.75, English edition.

11 Jennifer Montagu, *Roman Baroque Sculpture: The Industry of Art*, New Haven and London, 1989, p.151, and Giulia Fusconi, 'La fortuna dei marmi Ludovisi nel Cinquecento e Seicento' in *La collezione Boncompagni*

Ludovisi: Algardi, Bernini e la fortuna dell'antico, Antonio Giuliano (ed.), Venice, 1992, p.23.

12 Montagu, *Roman Baroque Sculpture*, p.151. Idem, *Alessandro Algardi*, 2 vols, New Haven and London, 1985, I, pp 10–11. For the belief that 'many established sculptors who were well into their careers continued to execute restorations', see Anthony Colantuono and Steven F. Ostrow (eds), *Critical Perspectives on Roman Baroque Sculpture*, University Park, 2014, pp 2–3. Giovanni Baglione, *Le vite de' pittori, scultori et architetti dal pontificato di Gregorio XIII fino a tutto quello d'Urbano VIII*, Rome, 1649, p.69, in his life of Egidio della Riviera (Egidio Fiammingo), recorded the opinion that the Florentine painter Lorenzo Lotto was the first person in Rome to charge good sculptors with the task of integrating the missing parts of ancient statuary. On the extensive restoration work done by sculptors during this period, see Peter M. Lukehart, 'Carving Out Lives: The Role of Sculptors in the Early History of the Academy of San Luca', *Studies in the History of Art*, vol.70 (2008), pp 185–217.

13 A case in point, although not for a sculptural task, is related by Domenico Bernini, *The Life*, p.132, who informs us that Cardinal Antonio Barberini, having learned that Bernini had written some plays, 'not only gave his full approval of them but also successfully persuaded the Cavaliere [Bernini] to have them performed on stage . . . Therefore, the Cavaliere, either persuaded or compelled, gave his consent to the production.' For a reflection of this rapport between a powerful patron and Bernini in his only play to have reached us, see Gian Lorenzo Bernini, *The Impresario*, Donald Beecher and Massimo Ciavolella (eds), Ottawa, 1994, p.35. Graziano (*alias* Gian Lorenzo Bernini), in response to Cinzio's communication, asks: 'So this is a command performance for His Highness?' Cinzio then specifies: 'Yes, Sir, he commands it. And he added that, if at first you chose not to understand his princely meaning, I was to tell you plainly: he commands it.'

14 Bellori, *The Lives,* p.296. According to Baglione, p.151, Guglielmo della Porta's integration of the missing lower parts of the legs on the *Farnese Hercules* was deemed comparable to the work of classical sculptors to the point that, when the missing parts were eventually recovered, Michelangelo convinced the Farnese family not to remove della Porta's 'per mostrare con quel rifacimento si degno al mondo, che le opere della scultura moderna potevano stare al paragone de' lavori antichi'.

15 Sparti, 'The "Rebirth" of Ancient Sculpture', p.82, and Stefano Pierguidi's entry '*Marcus Curtius Throwing Himself into the Chasm*' in *Bernini*, Bacchi and Coliva (eds), III.1, pp 84–5. As to the alleged location where the sculpture was found, Flaminio Vacca, *Memorie di varie antichità trovate in diversi luoghi della città di Roma*, Rome, 1594, in Antonio Nibby, *Roma antica di Famiano Nardini*, 1820, IV, p.5: 'Dove è oggi la Chiesa di S. Maria Liberaci dalle pene dell'inferno, vi fu trovato a tempo mio un Curzio a cavallo scolpito in marmo di mezzo rilievo, quale precipitavasi nella voragine, ed oggi si ritrova in Campidoglio nell'ingresso del Palazzo de' Conservatori.'

16 Matthias Winner, 'Ermafrodito' in *Bernini Scultore: La nascita del Barocco in Casa Borghese*, Anna Coliva and Sebastian Schütze (eds), Rome, 1998, p.130. See also Anna Coliva (ed.), *Bernini scultore: la tecnica esecutiva*, Rome, 2002, pp 133–43.

17 ibid.

18 Ovid, *Metamorphoses*, F.J. Miller (trans.), Cambridge, MA, 1916, IV, pp 285–388.

19 Montagu, *Roman Baroque Sculpture*, p.161. François Raguenet, *Le monumens de Rome*, Amsterdam, 1701, pp 32–3. Tobias George Smollett, *Travels Through France and Italy*, 2 vols, London, 1766, II, p.115.

20 Winner, p.130.

21 ibid.

22 ibid., p.131.

23 See Pierguidi in *Bernini*, III.2, p.88.

24 Alessandra Costantini, 'Ares Ludovisi' in *La collezione Boncompagni Ludovisi: Algardi, Bernini e la fortuna dell'antico*, Venice, 1992, pp 74–83. See also Francis Haskell and Nicholas Penny, *Taste and the Antique: The Lure of Classical Sculpture 1500–1900*, New Haven and London, 1981. For the statue's possible identification with Achilles, see Filippo Coarelli's entry 'Ares o Achille?' in *Bernini Scultore*, Coliva and Schütze (eds), pp 134–47. More specifically, on the Mars figure Bernini restored the nose, the right hand, the tip of the thumb and index finger of the left hand, the hilt of the sword, the upper and lower rim of the shield, the right foot, the tip of the left foot toe, and the penis. On the Eros figure he added the head, the left arm with the quiver, the right arm up to the elbow, the right foot with part of the leg, and the tip of the left wing. See Coarelli, 'Ares o Achille?', p.134.

25 Costantini, p.80: 'a Cav.re Bernini scultore per restauratione di una statua antica di Adone e per ogni altro lavoro fatto per il casino di essa vigna fino al 14 corrente.'

26 ibid.

27 ibid.

28 Stanislao Fraschetti, *Il Bernini: la sua vita, la sua opera, il suo tempo*, Milan, 1900, p.96. Giovanni Andrea Borboni, *Delle statue*, Rome, 1661, p.313. See also Rudolph Wittkower, *Gian Lorenzo Bernini: The Sculptor of the Roman Baroque*, London, 1966, p.196, no.27.

29 Oreste Ferrari and Serenita Papaldo, *Le sculture del Seicento a Roma*, Rome, 1999, p.478.

30 Montagu, *Roman Baroque Sculpture*, p.155.

31 Ferrari and Papaldo, p.478.

32 Montagu, *Alessandro Algardi*, p.27: 'Wittkower is no doubt correct in saying that this procedure explains why the head is too small for the body, but it is hard to accept his claim that "this relation, paralleled in the *Longinus* [by Bernini] . . . gives the whole figure a non-classical individuality and virility". On the contrary, fine though Bernini's head is in itself, it throws the whole statue out of proportion, for the rest of the figure is not only too tall, it is also too broad, so that it appears clumsy, an impression which is increased by the lack of coherence between the vivid and decisive look of the upturned head and the vague and imprecise gesture of the outstretched arm.'

33 ibid., p.402, no.123. See also Ferrari and Papaldo, p.478.

34 Sparti, 'Tecnica e teoria del restauro', pp 61, 74, and 109.

35 ibid., p.76.

36 There is also a later tradition that claims Bernini restored the *Barberini Faun* in the Munich Glyptothek, for which, see Wittkower, *Gian Lorenzo Bernini*, p.179, no.11.

37 See n.23.

38 See Paul Fréart de Chantelou, *Journal de voyage du Cavalier Bernin en France*, Paris, 2001, 8 June, p.53; idem, *Diary of the Cavaliere Bernini's Visit to France*, Anthony Blunt (ed.), George C. Bauer (ann.), Margery Corbett (trans.), Princeton, 1985, p.25. Domenico Bernini, *The Life*, pp 101–2: 'Bernini used to say that these two statues contained within them all that which was most perfect in nature without any affectation of art.' See also Tomaso Montanari, 'Gian Lorenzo Bernini e Sforza Pallavicino', *Prospettiva*, vol.87/88 (1997), pp 42–68.

39 Giorgio Vasari, *Lives of the Painters, Sculptors and Architects*, 2 vols, Gaston du C. de Vere (trans.), New York and Toronto, 1996, I, p.805. Idem, *Le vite de' più eccellenti pittori, scultori, e architettori*, Florence, 1568, II, 133: 'E nel vero hanno molta piu' grazia queste anticaglie in questa maniera restaurate che non hanno que' tronchi imperfetti, e le membra senza capo o in altro modo difettose e manche.' See Fondazione Memofonte at http://www.memofonte.it/autori/giorgio-vasari-1511 1574.html

40 Vasari, *Vite*, 1568, II, 224: 'Bramante adunque, desiderando che 'l Sansovino fusse noto a papa Iulio, ordinò di fargli acconciare alcune anticaglie. Onde egli messovi mano, mostrò nel rassettarle tanta grazia e diligenza, che 'l Papa e chiunque le vidde giudicò che non si potesse far meglio.' See Fondazione Memofonte at http://www.memofonte.it/autori/giorgio-vasari-1511-1574.html

41 Benvenuto Cellini, *Autobiography of Benvenuto Cellini*, John Addington Symonds (trans.), Garden City, 1961, p.430, II.69. Idem, *La vita*, Turin, 1973, p.393: 'E se bene e' non si conviene a mme [*sic*] il rattoppare le statue, perché ell'è arte da certi ciabattini, i quali la fanno assai malamente; imperò l'eccellenzia di questo gran maestro mi chiama asservirlo.' The sculpture is now in the Bargello Museum and its actual execution, on a design by Cellini, is probably by Willem de Tredote, who at the time was one of Cellini's studio collaborators. See Michael W. Cole, *Cellini and the Principles of Sculpture*, Cambridge, 2002, p.83 and pp 161–7.

42 On the subordinate role of restorers of ancient statuary, see Wittkower, *Gian Lorenzo Bernini*, p.178, under '11. Restorations of Antique Statues'.

43 'Ne supra crepidam sutor' (literally, 'Shoemaker, do not go beyond the sandal'), or 'Let a shoemaker stick to his last'. See Livio Pestilli, 'Pliny's "Ne Supra Crepidam Sutor": Representing Shoemakers in Italian Art and Society', *Source: Notes in the History of Art*, vol.26 (Spring 2007), pp 10–22.

44 Plato, *Republic*, IV.420b–421a. The memorable Plinian anecdote of Apelles and the Shoemaker is perhaps the best encapsulation of this tradition. See n.43. Also Pliny the Elder, *Natural History*, 10 vols, H. Rackham (trans.), Cambridge, MA, 1984, vol.IX, p.323, XXV.84–85, and Sarah Blake McHam, *Pliny and the Culture of the Italian Renaissance*, New Haven and London, 2013, pp 3 and 29.

45 Horace, *Satires*, I, III.124–30; Juvenal, *Satires*, III.293–94. For Pliny, see n.44.

46 See Michael Grant, *The Emperor Constantine*, London, 1993, p.89.

47 Plutarch, 'Life of Pericles' in *Plutarch's Lives*, Bernadotte Perrin (trans.), Cambridge and London, 1967, III, p.5: 'Labour with one's hands on lowly tasks gives witness, in the toil thus expended on useless things, to one's own indifference to higher things.' See also Galen, *On the Usefulness of the Parts of the Body*, 2 vols, M. Tallmadge

(trans.), Ithaca, 1968, I, p.190: 'Who will deny that the foot is a small ignoble part of an animal?'

48 For examples of paintings relating to shoemakers and cobblers by Giovanni Martino Spanzotti and Defendente Ferrari, Giacomo Ceruti, Giacomo Francesco Cipper ('il Todeschini') and Antonio Cifrondi, see Pestilli, 'Pliny's "Ne Supra Crepidam Sutor"'.

49 Dante Alighieri, *Convivio*, Franca Brambilla Ageno (ed.), Florence, 1995, pp 367–8: 'Bene sono aliquanti folli che credono che per questo vocabulo "nobile" s'intenda "essere da molti nominato e conosciuto," e dicono che viene da uno verbo che sta per conoscere, cioè "nosco". E questo è falsissimo; ché se ciò fosse, quali cose più fossero nomate e conosciute in loro genere, più sarebbero in loro genere nobili: e così la guglia di San Pietro sarebbe la più nobile pietra del mondo; e Asdente, lo calzolaio da Parma, sarebbe più nobile che alcuno suo cittadino . . . E però è falsissimo che "nobile" venga da "conoscere," ma viene da "non-vile"; onde "nobile" è quasi "non vile".'

50 Giovanni Boccaccio, *The Decameron*, G.H. McWilliam (trans.), London, 1995, p.757, X.viii. I have changed McWilliam's translation of the Italian 'più tosto' from 'not to mention' to 'rather than', which is not only more accurate but also gives a clearer understanding of the social paradox and juxtaposition between philosophers and shoemakers that Boccaccio was trying to make. See also Franco Sacchetti, *Il Trecentonovelle*, Florence, 1946 and Turin, 1970, XC, pp 206–8, and *Rime del Burchiello, comentate dal Doni*, Venice, 1553, pp 185–6.

51 Leonardo Fioravanti, *Dello specchio di scientia universale, Libri tre*, Venice, 1564, p.63v: 'Non è stata nel mondo la più bassa arte di quella del calzolaro, & che cio sia il vero, le genti che di essa si servono la portano sotto li piedi, & la calpestano.' Also quoted in Niccolò Tommaseo, *Dizionario della lingua italiana*, 7 vols, Turin, 1916, II, p.1137.

52 As late as 1824, in Filippo Pananti's *La Civetta*, the author has Juno address her unfaithful husband, Jupiter, saying, 'You son of Satan, you've been seen strolling even with two cobblers' wives' ('Figliol di Satanasso, /Fin con le mogli di due ciabattini/Tu sei stato veduto andare a spasso'); F. Pananti, *Opere in versi e in prosa*, 3 vols, Florence, 1824, II, p.25. For images of cobblers working outdoors, see Jan Miel's *Cobbler*, in Giuliano Briganti, Ludovica Trezzani, and Laura Laureati (eds), *I Bamboccianti: pittori della vita quotidiana a Roma nel Seicento*, Rome, 1983, pp 91–132, figs 4.2 and 4.8. See also Mina Gregori, *Giacomo Ceruti*, Monumenta Bergomensia, vol.58, Cinisello Balsamo, 1982, pls 46 and 46a.

53 *Opere di Tommaso Garzoni da Bagnacavallo: La Piazza Universale di tutte le Professioni del Mondo; Cioè La Sinagoga de gli Ignoranti; L'Hospidale de' Pazzi incurabili; & Il Teatro de' varij, & diversi Cervelli Mondani*, Venice, 1617, 'De' Calzolari, O Caligari, et Ciavattini, Discorso CXXXI', p.362: 'E quella differenza fra' calzolari, e ciavattini per conto di precedenza, ch'è fra il magnifico, & il zani de' nostri tempi.' For the 'zani', see Tommaseo, VII, p.1933, under 'Zanni': 'Personaggio ridicolo di commedia detto più communemente Arlecchino; ed è voce bergamasca accorciata dall'intero nome Giovanni, che rappresenta un Servo semplice e goffo bergamasco. Ma va a sparire dall'uso.'

54 Sarah McPhee, 'Bernini's Books', *The Burlington Magazine*, vol.142 (2000), pp 442–8. The library inventory actually pertains to Luigi Bernini's library, but the author argues that Gian Lorenzo's books formed the greater part of the collection. At his death the books were just incorporated in Luigi's, who still lived in Gian Lorenzo's palace on Via della Mercede. For a different opinion, see Mormando, Domenico Bernini, *The Life*, p.265, n.137.

55 Garzoni, pp 362–3. This condescending attitude toward shoemakers and cobblers was to remain a constant in Italian society well into the eighteenth century, as proven by the proclamations made by some of Goldoni's characters in his plays. See, for example, Carlo Goldoni, *Il padre di famiglia*, in *Commedie Scelte*, 4 vols, Livorno, 1819, IV, act I, scene 6, p.98, where Trastullo, Pancrazio's servant, states that '"Lady" is a term used even for a shoemaker's wife' ('Signora, si dice anco alla moglie d'un calzolajo; alla moglie di un mercante bisogna darle qualche cosa di più'); or, as a further example, idem, *Il ventaglio*, in *Commedie*, 3 vols, N. Mangini (ed.), Turin, 1971, III, p.523, where Coronato, the innkeeper, says to Crespin the shoemaker, 'Thank God I am neither a cobbler nor a shoemaker' ('Per grazia del cielo, io non faccio né il ciabattino, né il calzolaro'). See also Giuseppe Baretti, *La frusta letteraria*, 2 vols, L. Piccioni (ed.), Bari, 1932, II, pp 166–70, no.21.

56 *Vocabolario degli Accademici della Crusca*, 11 vols, Florence, 1878, III, p.2: 'Dicesi per dispregi anche di Chi faccia male la propria arte o mestiere, sia per trascurataggine, sia per imperizia.' See also Salvatore Battaglia, *Grande dizionario della lingua italiana*, Turin, 1971, III, p.104: 'Figur[ativo] Chi compie in

modo sciatto il proprio lavoro: artigiano, scrittore artista'; or G. Devoto and G.C. Oli, *Dizionario della lingua italiana*, Florence, 1971, p.471: 'Persona sciatta o incompetente nell'esercizio di un lavoro o di un'arte.' In English as well, 'cobbler' has a comparable perjorative meaning: 'One who mends clumsily, a clumsy workman, a mere botcher.' *The Compact Edition of the Oxford English Dictionary*, 2 vols, Oxford, 1971, I, p.451. See also the standard *OED*, 2nd edn, 20 vols, Oxford, 1989, II, p.561.

57 If there is a rare instance in which the term 'ciabattino/ciabattini' has been employed in seventeenth-century literature on sculpture, I have not been able to locate it.

58 Agostino Mascardi, *Discorsi morali su la Tavola di Cebete Tebano*, Venice, 1627, pp 320–21: 'Ho vedute nella Città di Roma molte botteghe, ch' à prima faccia sembrano di scultori eccellenti; perche nell'entrata vi si veggono de' busti, delle teste, delle braccia, & altre parti rotte di staute antiche; le quali tutto che sieno, o rose dal tempo, o dalla ferocia de' Barbari spezzate, pur non sò come nelle loro honorate reliquie la peritia de gli artefici, da cui furono formate dichiarano. ma rivolgendomi bene intorno, non mi venne mai veduto un pezzo di marmo intero, di cui un simolacro fabricar si potesse; toltane la sola casa del Cavalier Bernino, che nell' età sua giovanile, con lo scarpello sà dar senso di vita alle pietre, meglio, che non fece co'l canto favololso Anfione. M'avvidi poscia della cagione dell'errore; poiche que' miserabili rappezzatori ['cobblers'] di pietre vecchie, abbandonati dall'ingegno, e traditi dall'arte, poveri di disegno, e d'inventione mendichi, logorano l'età loro in rifar un naso all'uso di Tropea; in racconciar ['repair'] un gomito; in attaccar un dito, in somma in rattacconare ['patch'] con marmo nuovo le figure decrepite, con farne riuscire, (come dicevano quei buon'huomini,) un panno tessuto à vergato.' See also Jonathan Unglaub, '"Amorosa Contemplatione": Bernini, Bruni, and the Poetic Vision of Saint Teresa', *The Art Bulletin*, vol.102 (2020), pp 32–63, here p.41 and p.61, n.46.

59 See Elisabetta Di Stefano, *Orfeo Boselli e la 'nobiltà' della scultura*, Palermo, 2002, p.63 at http://www1.unipa.it/~estetica/download/Orfeo_Boselli.pdf

60 Filippo Baldinucci, *Vocabolario Toscano dell'Arte del Disegno*, Florence, 1681, p.131: 'Rabberciare. Rattoppare, aggiuguer pezzi a cose rotte o guaste. E fra' nostri Artefici vale propriamente, per racconciare una cosa malandata affatto, così come si può, e non del tutto.' Ibid., *rapportare* p.132 and *appiccare* p.11 (*rapiccare* or *rappiccare*, p.132) are also synonyms, especially used with reference to the addition of pieces of marble to modern sculptures. See below, n.78 for Francesco da Sangallo's use of this term.

61 Brigitte Bourgeois, '"Secure for Eternity": Assembly Techniques for Large Statuary in the Sixteenth to the Nineteenth Century' in *History of Restoration of Ancient Stone Sculptures*, Janet Burnett Grossman, Jerry Podany, and Marion True (eds), Los Angeles, 2003, pp 149–62.

62 Vasari, *Vite*, I, Ch. IX: 'Del fare i modelli di cera e di terra, e come si vestino e come a proporzione si ringradischino poi nel marmo; come si subbino e si gradinino e pulischino e impomicino e si lustrino e si rendino finiti.' For the full translation of the Introduction, see Louisa S. Maclehose, *Vasari on Technique*, London, 1907. See https://catalog.hathitrust.org/Record/000365730

63 Maclehose, pp 151–2. Vasari, *Vite*, 1568, I, p.35: 'Per che quelli che hanno fretta a lavorare e che bucano il sasso da principio e levano la pietra dinanzi e di dietro risolutamente, non hanno poi luogo dove ritirarsi, bisognandoli; e di qui nascono molti errori che sono nelle statue, ché, per la voglia ch'à l'artefice del vedere le figure tonde fuor del sasso a un tratto, spesso si gli scuopre un errore che non può rimediarvi se non vi si mettono pezzi commessi, come abbiamo visto costumare a molti artefici moderni; il quale rattoppamento è da ciabattini e non da uomini eccellenti o maestri rari, et è cosa vilissima e brutta e di grandissimo biasimo.'

64 Estelle Lingo, *Mochi's Edge and Bernini's Baroque*, London and Turnhout, 2017, pp 19–25 also mentions the theme within a discussion on the *paragone* between painting and sculpture. Ibid., p.180.

65 Pliny the Elder, *Natural History*, 10 vols, D.E. Eichholz (trans.), Cambridge, MA and London, 1971, XXXVI.iv, 34, 36, 37, 41. For a fundamental study of the *Laocoön* and Pliny's reference to the other three works praised for their compositional complexity by using the phrase *ex uno lapide*, see Salvatore Settis, *Laocoonte: fama e stile*, Rome, 1999, here pp 41–50. On the use of the term and the subtle shades of its meaning, see Fabio Barry, *Painting in Stone: Architecture and the Poetics of Marble from Antiquity to the Enlightenment*, New Haven and London, 2020, pp 65–71.

66 Pliny, XXXVI.iv, 37. Irving Lavin, '"*Ex Uno Lapide*": The Renaissance Sculptor's *Tour de Force*' in *Il Cortile delle Statue. Der Statuenhof des Belvedere im Vatikan*, Mainz, 1998, p.194, points out that Diodorus Siculus, Pausanias,

and Herodotus also make reference to works carved *ex uno lapide* with similar admiration.

67 For the extensive impact the Laocoön had throughout the sixteenth century, see Sonia Maffei, 'La fama di Laocoonte nei testi del Cinquecento', in Settis, *Laocoonte: fama e stile*, pp 85–228.

68 Pliny, XXXVI.iv.36–37.

69 Lavin, '"*Ex Uno Lapide*"', p.196.

70 My translation. Giovanni Gaetano Bottari and Stefano Ticozzi, *Raccolta di lettere sulla pittura, scultura ed architettura scritte dai più celebri personaggi dei secoli XV, XVI e XVII*, 8 vols, Milan, 1822, III, pp 474–5. Despite his last name, Galeotto Franciotti Della Rovere was most likely born in Rome. He was the son of Giovanfrancesco Franciotti, a merchant from Lucca, and Luchina Della Rovere, sister of Giuliano – the future Julius II – from whom he adopted his second last name. See http://www.treccani.it/enciclopedia/franciotti-della-rovere-galeotto_%28Dizionario-Biografico%29/

71 Mary B. Hollinshead, 'Extending the Reach of Marble: Struts in Greek and Roman Sculpture', *Memoirs of the American Academy in Rome. Supplementary Volumes*, vol.1 (2002), especially pp 142 and 152. On struts and their presence in Bernini's *Apollo and Daphne*, see Michael Cole, 'Bernini Struts' in *Material Identities*, Joanna Sofaer (ed.), Malden, 2007, pp 55–66. See also the discussion and reassessment of struts in Anna Anguissola, *Supports in Roman Marble Sculpture: Workshop Practice and Modes of Viewing*, Cambridge, 2018.

72 Settis, p.50.

73 Barry, *Painting in Stone*, p.66.

74 McHam, p.216 and pp 219–23.

75 See Lavin, '"*Ex Uno Lapide*"', and McHam. However, it should be noted that even before the actual discovery of the *Laocoön*, when in 1464 the Opera del Duomo of Florence commissioned from Agostino di Duccio the famous 'giant' that was to comprise four marble blocks, people recognised the greater the difficulty and artistic merit of a sculpture carved *ex uno lapide*. In fact, in December 1466 'the operai of the cathedral agreed to increase Agostino's fee for the figure, because now he proposed to execute it from a single block of marble, rather than four'. See Irving Lavin, 'Bozzetti and Modelli: Notes on Sculptural Procedure from the Early Renaissance through Bernini' in *Stil und Überlieferung in der Kunst des Abendlandes. Akten des 21. internationalen Kongresses für Kunstgeschichte in Bonn 1964*, Berlin, 1967, III, p.98. This 'giant' marble block was eventually 'inherited' by Michelangelo who carved his *David* from it.

76 Detlef Heikamp, 'La fontana di Nettuno. La sua storia nel contesto urbano' in *L'acqua, la pietra, il fuoco. Bartolomeo Ammannati scultore*, Beatrice Paolozzi Strozzi and Dimitrios Zikos (eds), Florence, 2011, p.204.

77 Lavin, '"*Ex Uno Lapide*"', p.198. See also Gabriella Capecchi, 'Superare l'antico: il Laocoonte "perfetto"' in *Baccio Bandinelli scultore e maestro 1493–1560*, Detlef Heikamp and Beatrice Paolozzi Strozzi (eds), Florence, 2014, pp 129–55.

78 Francesco da Sangallo in Benedetto Varchi, *Lezzioni nella quale si disputa della maggioranza delle arti* in *Trattati d'arte del Cinquecento fra manierismo e controriforma*, Paola Barocchi (ed.), Bari, 1960–62, I, p.77: 'e talvolta, [these sculptors] pensando fare meglio, con rapiccare de' pezzi al marmo hanno vituperato loro e tolto a l'arte la sua proprietà'.

79 Benedetto Varchi, *Lezzione nella quale si disputa della maggioranza delle arti e qual sia più nobile, la scultura o la pittura*, Florence, 1546, pp 49–50: 'E si vede ancora che i colossi si fanno di pezzi, o per mancamento di materia, come avviene mille volte, o per difetto d'arte, come si vide nell'Ercole di Piazza, quando cadde quel pezzo con gran danno di chi v'era sotto; e le statue antiche si racconciano e si rappezzano tutto 'l giorno.' See the Fondazione Memofonte online edition at http://www.memofonte.it/home/files/pdf/scritti_varchi1.pdf.

See Roberta Bartoli, 'Bandinelli contro tutti. L'artista negli occhi dei contemporanei' in *Baccio Bandinelli scultore e maestro (1493–1560)*, Detlef Heikamp and Beatrice Paolozzi Strozzi (eds), Florence, 2014, pp 36–59. This author, p.57, also cites a 1544 document published by Louis Waldman that corroborates the event: 'nel mentre il Duca Cosimo stava in ringhiera del Palazzo antico della Signoria, cadde dall'Ercole del Bandinelli un pezzo di marmo dalla spalla dritta, che ammazò un contadino'. For a more positive and historically balanced analysis of Bandinelli's *Hercules and Cacus*, see Virginia L. Bush, '"Hercules and Cacus" and Florentine Traditions', *Memoirs of the American Academy in Rome*, vol.35 (1980), pp 163–206, as by the late sixteenth century, in a different historical and political context, 'the statue was better understood and even praised'.

80 Bronzino, in Varchi, *Lezzioni nella quale si disputa della maggioranza delle arti*, in Barocchi (ed.), *Trattati d'arte*

del Cinquecento, I, p.66: 'Or non si fanno i colossi di molti pezzi? Et a quante figure si rifanno i busti e le braccia e quello che manca loro! Senza i tasselli, che si veggiano in dimolte figure, che sono uscite nuove con simili toppe di mano del loro artefice, sì che né in questo consiste l'arte, perché quando una figura sia d'infiniti pezzi, pur che stia bene, non dà noia alla bontà dell'arte.' Pomponius Gauricus, *De sculptura*, Paolo Cutolo (ed.), Naples, 1999 [orig.1504], pp 242–4, takes it for granted that accidents could happen while sculpting marble and 'prescribes' the glue to remedy the problem: 'Se sarà capitato qualche incidente si dovrà applicare come collante il mastice macerato e reso malleabile come la cera; oppure si mescoleranno pece, blu oltremare, cera e una volta riscaldate le superfici da incollare si avvicineranno.' ('Glutinum vero, si quid forte acciderit, mansam masticem atque in cerae modum perdomitam statim adapplicato. Item et sic. Picem, armenium, ceram admisceto et concalefactis admoveto.')

81 Wittkower, *Gian Lorenzo Bernini*, p.6: 'Every Renaissance sculpture is encompassed by the marble block, and the cube of the block constitutes its physical as well as its spiritual limits. The block-shape seemed to impose no limitations on the imagination of the late sixteenth-century Mannerist sculptors. They invented freely, unimpeded by material restrictions. Thus contours of figures were broken up and extremities made to stick out. This new freedom, expressive of a deep spiritual change, led also to multiple viewpoints in sculpture.'

82 Heikamp, p.205: 'Anche il rabberciare è in sé un passo straordinario, che preannuncia l'arte scultorea del secolo successivo, la grande rivoluzione che trova coronamento in Bernini. Rattoppare il marmo significa godere di una molto maggiore libertà d'azione nel creare le forme e le sagome di una statua o di un gruppo.'

83 Raffaello Borghini, *Il Riposo*, Florence, 1584, IV, p.593: 'Poscia havendosi à fare il Nettuno che è nel mezo della ricca fontana di piazza, egli a concorrenza di Benvenuto Cellini, di Vincentio Danti, e di Giambologna fece il modello, & à lui dal Duca Cosimo fu allogata la statua, e tutta l'opera della Fontana. Ma perche il marmo gli riuscì stretto nelle spalle non poté egli sicome disiderava far mostrare alla sua figura attitudine con le braccia alzate; ma fu costretto à farla con gran difficultà, come hoggi si vede.'

84 Heikamp, pp 222 and 235. If one is to believe Vasari, the need to use additional marble blocks to the 'giant' one that had been quarried for what would eventually become the most iconic *ex uno lapide* statue of the Renaissance, Michelangelo's *David*, was what other sculptors had requested had they been selected to make a reasonable work of art out of it. Giorgio Vasari, *La vita di Michelangelo nelle redazioni del 1550 e del 1568*, 5 vols, Paola Barocchi (ed.), Milan and Naples, 1962–72, I, p.19: 'Michelagnolo, quantunque fussi dificile a cavarne una figura intera senza pezzi – al che fare non bastava a quegli altri l'animo di non finirlo senza pezzi, salvo che a lui, e ne aveva avuto desiderio molti anni innanzi – , venuto in Fiorenza tentò di averlo.' ('Although it was difficult to carve out of it [the colossal marble block] a whole figure without [the addition of other marble] pieces – since those other [sculptors] did not have the courage to complete it without [additional marble] pieces, except for him, who had had the desire [to complete it] many years before – , having come to Florence he tried to have it [assigned to himself].' My translation.) To my knowledge, however, no one has addressed the 'breach of faith' in Michelangelo's sustained adherence to the integral unity of his sculptures when it came to his *Risen Christ*. The two pieces he added to form the crossbeam and the very top of the cross created a symbolically justified inclusion of the tool of Christ's sacrifice, but it is an otherwise unrealistic, abbreviated treatment of the same. One would think that this exceptional approach to a sculpture must have deeply troubled the artist, if not his critics. Still, no contemporary documentation or secondary sources exist that refer to this anomaly. See William E. Wallace, *Michelangelo, God's Architect: The Story of his Final Years and Greatest Masterpiece*, Princeton and Oxford, 2019, p.132.

85 Heikamp, p.235.

86 ibid. On the political implications of the Ammannati fountain, see Felicia M. Else, *The Politics of Water in the Art and Festivals of Medici Florence: From Neptune Fountain to Naumachia*, London, 2019.

87 See Oscar Pollak, *Die Kunsttätigkeit unter Urban VIII. Die Peterskirke in Rom*, 2 vols, Vienna, 1981, II, 1649, p.431, and 1718, pp 443–4. See also Lingo, *Mochi's Edge*, p.158.

88 For the *Saint Longinus*, see Wittkower, *Gian Lorenzo Bernini*, pp 196–7. Lingo, *Mochi's Edge*, p.180, following Montagu, *Roman Baroque Sculpture*, p.30, reiterates that Bolgi's *Saint Helen*, Bernini's *Saint Longinus*, and Duquesnoy's *Saint Andrew* were primarily sculpted out of two marble blocks 'with two or more smaller marble

additions on the sides', while Mochi's *Saint Veronica* was executed from only three blocks. See also Louise Rice, 'The Unveiling of Mochi's "Veronica"', *The Burlington Magazine*, vol.156 (2014), p.736, and C.D. Dickerson III and Anthony Sigel, *Bernini: Sculpting in Clay*, C.D. Dickerson III, Anthony Sigel, and Ian Wardropper (eds), New Haven and London, 2012, p.129. Orfeo Boselli, *Osservazioni sulla scultura antica. I manoscritti di Firenze e di Ferrara*, Antonio P. Torresi (ed.), Ferrara, 1994, Capitolo 22, pp 152–3, justifies the use of multiple blocks of marble on large bas-reliefs or statues and refers specifically to Duquesnoy's *Saint Andrew*, Mochi's *Saint Veronica*, and Bernini's *Saint Longinus* to make his point. Phoebe Dent Weil (ed.), *Osservazioni della Scoltura Antica, dai manoscritti Corsini e Doria e altri scritti*, Florence, 1978, dates the Corsini manuscript to circa 1657 and points out that the Doria version, penned in the 1700s, has the date '1650' written on the frontispiece.

89 Lingo, *Mochi's Edge*, p.153, as others before, identifies the four colossal statues in the crossing piers of Saint Peter's as 'where the Renaissance practice of sculpture effectively ended'. As underscored in idem, 'Sculpture, Rupture, and the "Baroque"' in *Art and Reform in the Late Renaissance*, Jesse M. Locker (ed.), New York and London, 2019, pp 33–46, Bernini's break with ancient and Renaissance sculpture was also owed to his 'planned drapery's complete rebellion' in rapport with the body it clothed that led him to establish 'a Baroque stylistics for sculpture' (p.41).

90 Rudolf Wittkower, *Sculpture: Processes and Principles*, Harmondsworth, 1977, p.167.

91 Coliva, pp 17–19. To the *Pluto and Proserpina* he added part of Proserpina's hair at the top of the head; to the *David*, part of the mantle beneath the pouch; to the *Angel with the Crown of Thorns*, a marble insert to the right wing; and a stucco addition to the right wing of the *Angel with the Superscription*. On the *Constantine the Great*, Bernini added a marble piece to the horse's tail. See Mark Weil, *The History and Decoration of the Ponte S. Angelo*, University Park and London, 1974, where the author quotes from an *avviso* of 19 November 1668, p.133, from the Diary of Carlo Cartari: 'Intesi dal Segretario di Monsig.[nor]e Bernini, che quanto prima si porrà in opera la Statua del Constantino, alle Scale del Palazzo Vaticano fatto dal Cavaliero, tutto d'un pezzo, tanto il cavallo, quanto l'huomo, eccetto un pocopezzo di coda del Cavallo, che è aggiunta.' Given all we know about Michelangelo's approach to sculpture, it should be stressed that the 'mortise and tenon' solution for the replacement of the missing left leg of Christ in the Florence *Pietà* is without doubt *not* a solution attributable to Michelangelo himself.

92 Anne-Lise Desmas, 'Why Legros Rather Than Foggini Carved the "St. Bartholomew" for the Lateran: New Documents for the Statue in the Nave', *The Burlington Magazine*, vol.146 (2004), p.799 and *Appendix 3*, p.805, letter dated 6 September 1704: 'Vi è più nelle condizioni di d[etto] mercante che il marmo deve esser tutto d'un pezzo e questo, l'hanno stimato necessario li scultori, p[er]ché hanno veduto che, con il progresso del tempo, le statue nelle commessure fanno del movimento, come attualmente si riconosce nelle statue fatte in S. Pietro.' See also Frank Martin, *Camillo Rusconi: ein Bildhauer des Spätbarock in Rom*, Berlin and Munich, 2019, no. 94, pp 147–8. It should be noted that in another letter, possibly dated between 1704 and 1705 and perhaps by Filippo Patrizi himself, sent to the Archbishop Lorenzo Corsini about the marble needed for the statue of *Saint Bartholomew*, the former seems to imply or expect that the sculptors involved in the Lateran project might be perfectly willing to use additional pieces of marble to complete their statues. See Desmas, p.805, Appendix no. 4 and Martin, no. 106, p.149: 'S'intende ancora nel marmo poterci fare la base aggiunta, e forse un braccio, o qualche pezzo di paneggiamento, o altro che portasse in fuora bisognando p[er] vantaggiarsi di non dover pigliare il marmo più grande, quale crescerebbe di prezzo.'

93 My thanks to Simona Turriziani, Responsabile Archivio Storico della Fabbrica di San Pietro, for informing me that, to date, no 'official' document has emerged that corroborates Filippo Patrizi's claim.

94 Irving Lavin, *Bernini and the Crossing of Saint Peter's*, New York, 1968, p.39: 'In the last analysis, however, the chronological importance of the crossing may lie less in the diversity of the individual elements than in the common bond by which they are related. In Saint Peter's, for the first time, Bernini treats a volume of real space as the site of a dramatic action, in which the observer is involved physically as well as psychologically. The drama takes place in an environment that is not an extension of the real world, but is coextensive with it. And because the statues act as witnesses, the observer is associated with them and hence, inevitably, becomes a participant in the event. In this way, Bernini charged the space with a conceptual and visual unity so powerful that it overcomes every change in plan and disparity of style.'

95 The changed location for the other three statues created some anomalies, such as their averted glances: *Saint Helen*, designed for the niche diagonally across from the *Saint Veronica*, should have been looking towards the *Baldacchino* but now looks towards the transept; *Saint Longinus*, who should have been looking toward the top of the *Baldacchino* towards the planned statue of the *Risen Christ* – which was never executed – now looks away from it. *Saint Andrew*'s gaze, which was the least affected by the diagonal move from the north-west to the south-east pier, was instead penalised because it was conceived as being viewed and approached from the nave. For the changes in the disposition of the statues, see Lavin, *Bernini and the Crossing of Saint Peter's*, especially the diagram on p.24. See also Estelle Lingo, *François Duquesnoy and the Greek Ideal*, New Haven and London, 2007, pp 119–39, for a discussion of the way the statue of *Saint Andrew* was affected by the change.

96 Irving Lavin, *Bernini and the Unity of the Visual Arts*, 2 vols, New York and London, 1980, I, p.21. For peregrinations suffered by three of the four statues before they were installed in the current niches, see Lavin, *Bernini and the Crossing of Saint Peter's*, n.95. The statues of *Saint Andrew* and *Saint Longinus* – like their female counterparts meant to be placed diagonally from each other – according to a decree of 26 April 1638 should have occupied the south-east and the north-west piers, respectively.

97 Coliva and Schütze (eds), *Bernini Scultore: La nascita del Barocco in Casa Borghese*, as in n.16.

98 Lingo, *Mochi's Edge*, p.207.

99 ibid., pp 168–72 for a discussion of this statue.

100 Leopoldo Cicognara, *Storia della scultura dal suo risorgimento in Italia fino al secolo di Canova*, 8 vols, Prato, 1823–4, VI, pp 181–2.

101 Francesco Milizia, *Dell'arte di vedere nelle belle arti del disegno secondo i principii di Sulzer e di Mengs*, Venice, 1823, p.19.

102 Oskar Pollak, *Die Kunsttätigkeit unter Urban VIII. Die Peterskirche in Rom*, New York, 1981 (originally 1931), 1649, p.431, and 1718, p.443.

103 Montagu, *Roman Baroque Sculpture*, p.30. Rice, 'The Unveiling', p.736, and Appendices nos. 7 and 9, p.740. On the number of blocks comprising the *Saint Longinus*, see Wittkower, *Gian Lorenzo Bernini*, p.197. On Duquesnoy's *Saint Andrew*, see Pollak, 1728, p.446, and Marion Boudon-Machuel, *François du Quesnoy 1597–1643*, Paris, 2005, pp 229–35 and 370–72 who, however, specifies that she based her analysis by viewing the statue from the basilica floor. To really be able to account for the total number of blocks used, one would need to stand on a scaffold, closer to the statue – a prospect currently not planned by the Fabbrica di San Pietro. Lingo, *Mochi's Edge*, p.181, reiterates what Boudon-Machuel stated.

104 Lingo, *Mochi's Edge*, p.181, quoting from Marcella Favero, *Francesco Mochi. Un carriera di scultore*, Trent, 2008, p.241, letter of 12 March 1640.

105 Rice, 'The Unveiling', p.739 for the English translation and Appendix 7, p.740, for the original transcription.

106 ibid.

107 On Mochi's 'eccentric' sculptural style later in his career, see Montagu, *Alessandro Algardi*, I, p.120. For a better understanding of Mochi's late style, see Lingo, *Mochi's Edge*.

108 Johann Joachim Winckelmann, *History of the Art in Antiquity*, Harry Francis Mallgrave (trans.), Los Angeles, 2006, p.219: 'In all antiquity, we never find sleeves that are wide and rolled up according to today's manner for shirts, like those *Bernini* gave to Saint Veronica in Saint Peter's in Rome.'

109 See Estelle Lingo, 'Francesco Mochi's Balancing Act and the Prehistory of Bernini's *Four Rivers Fountain*' in *Matters of Weight: Force, Gravity, and Aesthetics in the Early Modern Period*, David Young Kim (ed.), Emsdetten, 2013, pp 129–51.

110 Lingo, *Mochi's Edge*, p.178.

111 On Mochi's use of the garment as a sudarium and the classical source for the nymphs that 'make sails of their garments', see Lingo, *Mochi's Edge*, p.178.

112 For an extensive study of the 'world' of struts, see Anguissola, *Supports in Roman Marble Sculpture*, especially pp 59–83, 159–67, and 188–221. Figural struts, as opposed to plain struts (typically quadrilateral pegs that connect a limb to another part of the statue), were carved to represent an object that was thus more 'camouflaged' and visually better integrated with the overall sculpture. Ibid., p.49: 'Figural supports seem to have represented a meaningful yet marginal phenomenon in Greek freestanding sculpture of the fifth century BC, and the use of non-figural struts remained exceptional. Beginning in the fourth century BC, the work of Praxiteles seems to have initiated a new phase in the development of struts. In a number of types attributed to this prolific Athenian sculptor, supports are integral in the construction of the piece and its visual effect.'

113 Pollak, II, 1754, p.451: 'Inoltre essendosi introdotto il far scopettare le statue ogni settimana l'Oratore [Mochi]

espone al Em[inen]ze VV[ostre] che la sua non ha bisogno di tale diligenza perche essendo finita in tutte le parti la polvere non ha dove attaccarsi, e perche la negligenza e la disgratia potrebbe far cadere scala, ò altro stromento, che gettarsi à terra, braccio, mano, velo, o altra parte.' See also Lingo, *Mochi's Edge*, p.186.

114 Duquesnoy's ability in carving this statue's folds, as well as in his *Saint Susanna*, is highly praised by Bellori, *The Lives*, pp 229–30. In the next century, instead, Cicognara found the folds a bit excessive and voluminous. See Cicognara, VI, p.168.

115 For payments pertaining to the copper cross, see Pollak, II, 1674–1677, pp 435–6. Also, Boudon-Machuel, as in n.103 and Lingo, *Mochi's Edge*, p.181. Boudon-Machuel refers to the cross as having been made of 'bronze ou cuivre', and Lingo, seemingly basing her comment on Boudon-Machuel's study, states that the cross is 'stucco-covered bronze'. The uncertainty about the actual metal used is due to the feminine Latin adjective *aenea* used in three of the four payment entries (Pollak, 1674, 1676, and 1677), which could mean either 'made of bronze' or 'made of copper'. However, the fourth and only payment recorded in Italian (Pollak, 1675) is very specific and leaves no doubt as it specifies that it is 'per conto della croce di Rame'. The many rivets used to shape and hold in place the cylindrical sheets of copper, visible in any good close-up photograph of the cross by *Saint Andrew*'s right hand, for example, are also indisputable proof of the metal used.

116 Duquesnoy was following a design for the statue that had been provided by Bernini. See Lavin, *Bernini and the Crossing of Saint Peter's*, p.20.

117 On the use of pins or rods when joining together two pieces of marble, see Bourgeois, pp 149–78, and Sparti, 'Tecnica e teoria del restauro scultoreo', pp 60–131.

118 Pollak, 56, p.66: 'per haver fatto un ferro per regere il tronco della Croce di S. Andrea.'

119 Orfeo Boselli, *Osservazioni della Scoltura Antica*, Phoebe Dent Weil (ed.), Florence, 1978, devotes the whole third chapter to garments.

120 Irving Lavin describes *Saint Longinus*' stance as one of Bernini's 'most revolutionary conceptions'. See 'Calculated Spontaneity: Bernini and the Terracotta Sketch' in *Visible Spirit: The Art of Gianlorenzo Bernini*, London, 2007, I, p.380, originally published in *Apollo*, vol.107, no.195 (1978), pp 398–405. On the Greek artists' use of the 'heroic diagonal' see Kenneth Clark, *The Nude: A Study in Ideal Form*, Garden City, 1956, p.251. Michael W. Cole, *Ambitious Form: Giambologna, Ammanati, and Danti in Florence*, Princeton and Oxford, 2011, p.103: 'The more dramatically the sculptor liberated an arm or an attribute from the block, the greater the show of virtuosity.'

121 Rudolf Preimesberger, 'Il San Longino del Bernini in San Pietro in Vaticano: dal bozzetto alla statua' in *Bernini a Montecitorio: ciclo di conferenze nel quarto centenario della nascita di Gian Lorenzo Bernini*, Rome, 2001, pp 97–111, here p.108: 'Non è quindi Longino l'eroe della rappresentazione, ma la lancia.' The wooden lance is covered with stucco, creating the illusion that the lance, too, is made of marble. For the payment to the carpenter Giovanni Battista Soria of one *scudo* for the wooden spear, see Pollak, 54, p.62, and 1791, p.457.

122 A similar pin was necessary to successfully anchor the right arm to the Fogg Art Museum terracotta model. See Dickerson III, Sigel, and Wardropper, *Bernini: Sculpting in Clay*, p.126.

123 I here purposely misquote Milan Kundera's title for his famous novel, *The Unbearable Lightness of Being* (Harper & Row, 1984).

CHAPTER 3

1 Filippo Baldinucci, *The Life of Bernini*, Catherine Enggass (trans.), Maarten Delbeke, Evonne Levy, and Steven F. Ostrow (eds), University Park, 2006, p.75.

2 On this anecdote and the importance of paradoxes and witty antitheses for Baldinucci, Cardinal Sforza Pallavicino, and seventeenth-century literary and theological discourse, see Maarten Delbeke, *The Art of Religion: Sforza Pallavicino and Art Theory in Bernini's Rome*, Farnham, London and New York, 2012, pp 63–95.

3 David Summers, *Michelangelo and the Language of Art*, Princeton, 1981, p.64. Giovanni Paolo Lomazzo, *Trattato dell'arte de la pittura*, Milan, 1584, p.485: 'Quantunque però sia sempre più degno di lode che [*sic*] fa le cose sue più accuratamente se ben con maggior tempo, che chi le fa con prestezza & male havendo da porsi avanti à gl'occhi molte parti che'l primo non possiede, onde è scritto d'Apelle, che dicendogli talvolta uno ch'egli haveva fatto in picciolo tempo una gran pittura gli rispose che ciò ben si vedeva, si come anco motteggiò una volta Michel Angelo il suo Vasari.' It should be noted that Lomazzo refers to the Sala dei Cento Giorni by implication, not by specifically mentioning it and citing Michelangelo as having criticised the frescoes by saying 'E si vede'.

4 Giorgio Vasari, *Lives of the Painters, Sculptors and Architects*, 2 vols, Gaston du C. de Vere (trans.), New York and Toronto, 1996, II, p.742. Idem, *Le vite de' più eccellenti pittori scultori e architettori*, 6 vols, Rosanna Bettarini and Paola Barocchi (eds), Florence, 1966–97, VI, pp 116–17: 'Essendogli mostro un disegno e raccomandato un fanciullo che allora imparava a disegnare, scusandolo alcuni che era poco tempo che s'era posto all'arte, rispose: "E' si conosce".'

5 Leon Battista Alberti, *On Painting*, John R. Spencer (trans.), New Haven, 1956, p.97. The quotation is adopted from Summers' translation in *Michelangelo and the Language of Art*, pp 104–5.

6 Plutarch, 'De liberis educandis', in *Plutarch's Moralia*, 14 vols, Frank Cole Babbitt (trans.), London, 1927, I, 7:31. On the subject of 'whether it is better to work quickly or slowly' and Michelangelo's correct attribution of the quip to Plutarch according to Francisco de Hollanda, see his *Diálogos em Roma (1538): Conversations on Art with Michelangelo Buonarroti*, Grazia Dolores Folliero-Metz (ed.), Heidelberg, 1998, pp 114–15: 'It is thus not a fault to be a little slow or even very slow and to spend much time and care on a work if the object be greater perfection; it is only lack of skill that is a defect.'

7 Plutarch, *Lives*, Bernadotte Perrin (trans.), Cambridge, MA, 1916, III, 159, p.41.

8 See particularly Pliny the Elder's *Natural History*, XXV, H. Rackham (trans.), Cambridge, MA and London, 1984, and ibid., XXXVI–VII, D.E. Eichholz (trans.), Cambridge, MA and London, 1971.

9 Christopher Gill, 'The Question of Character-Development: Plutarch and Tacitus', *The Classical Quarterly*, vol.33 (1983), p.472, cites Plutarch's *Aemilius*, 1 (sometimes as preface to *Timoleon*, as in the Loeb edition), as an instance of this approach: 'I began the writing of my "Lives" for the sake of others, but I find that I am continuing the work and delighting in it now for my own sake also, using history as a mirror and endeavouring in a manner to fashion and adorn my life in conformity with the virtues therein depicted.' Plutarch, *Lives, Pericles,* III, p.3: 'But in the exercise of his mind every man, if he pleases, has the natural power to turn himself away in every case, and to change, without the least difficulty, to that object upon which he himself determines. It is meet, therefore, that he pursue what is best, to the end that he may not merely regard it, but also be edified by regarding it.'

10 See Pliny, 1984, XXXV.xxxvi, 64, where the author does not specify the actual identity of the female figure he painted for the Temple of Lacinian Hera and claims the story took place in the town of Agrigento, as well as Cicero, *De inventione*, II, I, 1–3, who maintained the event occurred in Croton. Cicero's version of the story is also related by Dionysius of Halicarnassus. See *De veterum scriptorum censuram* in *Dionysii Halicarnassensis Operum*, Leipzig, 1775, vol.5, p.417, at https://phaidra.cab.unipd.it/detail_object/o:69652

11 Baldinucci, *The Life*, p.77: 'Teneva per favola ciò che si racconta della Venere Crotoniate, cioè che Zeusi la ricavasse dal più bello di diverse fanciulle, togliendo da chi una parte, e da chi un'altra; perchè diceva egli, che un bell'occhio d'una femmina non istà bene sopra un bel viso d'un'altra; così una bella bocca, e vadasi discorrendo.' The exemplum of selective imitation echoes Seneca's analogy of bees that produce their own honey by culling nectar from different flowers. See *The Epistles of Seneca*, Cambridge and London, 1970, vol.V, LXXXIV, 227–81.

12 Tomaso Montanari, 'Gian Lorenzo Bernini e Sforza Pallavicino', *Prospettiva*, vol.87/88 (1997), pp 42–68, esp. p.62, quoting from Pallavicino's *Arte della perfezion cristiana*: 'molte qualità son buone ciascuna per sé, ma non accoppiate fra loro, onde ho udito qualche fino conoscitor della dipintura che 'l mentovato consiglio di Zeusi in Crotone havrebbe potuto indurlo a formare non tanto un viso bellissimo, quanto un mostro'. Said concept, Montanari points out, is also expressed in a letter written twenty years earlier, on 24 November 1646, by Virgilio Malvezzi to his nephew, Sforza Pallavicino. Ibid., n.151, p.68: 'essendo io d'opinione molto contraria ad Aristotile (scusabile in questo caso, come ignorante della pittura), dandomi ad intendere che, per formare un bel volto, chi pigliasse ciascheduna parte d'esso a imitare da diversi oggetti *formarebbe un mostro* e perlomeno una faccia non bella'. Montanari further believes that 'ricondurre a Pallavicino l'origine di alcune delle più importanti idee di Bernini sull'arte mi pare particolarmente economica perché la frequentazione e l'intimità intellettuale, certificate dalla quantità di documenti fin qui esaminati, consentono di non figurarsi Gian Lorenzo sprofondato nella lettura dei tomi del cardinale o di altri, intento ad assimilare le teorie poi a Chantelou e registrate dai biografi'. Ibid., pp 62–3. On the rapport between some of Pallavicino's ideas on art and their adoption by Bernini's biographers, see Delbeke, *The Art of Religion*.

13 Filippo Baldinucci, *The Life of Bernini by Filippo Baldinucci*, Catherine Enggass (trans.), University Park, 1966, pp 11–12. Idem, *Vita del Cavaliere Gio. Lorenzo Bernino, scultore, architetto, e pittore*, Florence, 1682, p.7: 'Anche la Santità di Papa Paolo V. volle di mano di lui il proprio ritratto, dopo il quale ebbe a scolpire quello del Cardin. Scipione Borghese di lui Nipote; e già s'era condotto al fine del bel lavoro, quando portò la disgrazia, che e' si scoprisse un pelo nel marmo, che occupava appunto tutto il più bello della fronte; egli, che animosissimo era, e già aveva fatto una maravigliosa pratica nel maneggiare il marmo, a fine di togliere a se stesso, e molto più al Cardinale la confusione, che era per apportargli una sì fatta novità, fattosi condurre in camera un pezzo di marmo di sufficiente grandezza, e di conosciuta bontà, senza darne notizia a persona, nel corso di quindici notti, che solamente impiegò in quel lungo lavoro, ne condusse un'altro simile, di non punto minor bellezza del primo; poi fattolo portar nel suo studio ben coperto, acciocchè da niuno de' suoi familiari potesse esser veduto, attendeva la venuta del Cardinale a vedere il ritratto finito. Comparso finalmente quel Signore, e veduto il primo ritratto, del quale col darsi il lustro s'era fatto il difetto assai più palese, e più sconcio, a prima vista si turbò in se stesso; ma per non contristare il Bernino dissimulava. Fingeva in tanto il ben'avveduto Artefice di non accorgersi del disgusto del Cardinale, e perchè più grato gli giugnesse il sollievo, ove più grave era stata la passione, il tratteneva in discorsi; quando finalmente gli scoperse l'altro bellissimo ritratto. L'allegrezza, che mostrò quel Prelato nel vedere il secondo ritratto senz'alcun difetto, fece ben conoscere quanto era stato il dolore, ch'egli avea concepito nel rimirare il primo; e piacquegli tanto l'industria, e diligenza, che per non disgustarlo aveva usato il Bernino, che da indi innanzi l'amò sempre con amor tenerissimo. Trovasi oggi l'una, e l'altra Statua nel Palazzo della Villa Borghese, e di sì grande, e sì bella maniera, che lo stesso Bernino, che un giorno vi fu col Card. Antonio Barberino, dopo quarant'anni, nel vederle proruppe in queste parole: *Oh quanto poco profitto ò fatto io nell'arte della Scoltura in un sì lungo corso di anni, mentre io conosco, che da fanciullo maneggiava il marmo in questo modo!*'

14 Filippo Baldinucci, *Vocabolario toscano dell'arte del disegno*, Florence, 1681, p.25 (misnumbered as p.26): 'Camera f.[emminile] Stanza fatta per dormirvi.' Giacomo Devoto and Gian Carlo Oli, *Vocabolario illustrato della lingua italiana*, 2 vols, Milan, 1976, I, 423: 'càmera: s.[ostantivo] f.[emminile] 1. Stanza di dimensioni normali (non corridoio o ripostiglio) e part.[icolarmente] quella destinata al riposo'.

15 See n.13.

16 See Tomaso Montanari's entry for the second bust in the exhibition catalogue, *I marmi vivi. Bernini e la nascita del ritratto barocco*, Andrea Bacchi, Tomaso Montanari, Beatrice Paolozzi Strozzi, and Dimitrios Zikos (eds), Florence, 2009, pp 308–11, esp. p.308: 'Sappiamo che per raggiungere questo straordinario risultato, Bernini intagliò il marmo [of the first portrait] direttamente di fronte al modello, secondo una pratica rarissima e temeraria' – here Montanari uses the word 'modello' to signify the living person – and p.310: 'i marmi non sono, infatti, l'uno la copia dell'altro, ma due derivazioni indipendenti dallo stesso modello, la prima condotta avendo sott'occhio il cardinale, la seconda (se dobbiamo prestar fede alle fonti) tutta realizzata a memoria.' Montanari bases his comments on the letter written by Lelio Guidiccioni to Bernini on 4 June 1633, partially transcribed by Cesare D'Onofrio, *Roma vista da Roma*, Rome, 1967, p.382 ss., subsequently amplified by Philipp Zitzlsperger, *Gianlorenzo Bernini. Die Papst- und Herrscherporträts. Zum Verhältnis von Bildnis und Macht*, Munich, 2002, pp 179–83, Joris van Gastel, *Il marmo spirante: Sculpture and Experience in Seventeenth-Century Rome,* Berlin, 2013, pp 213–21, and finally, Silvia Gattabria's thesis, *Gian Lorenzo Bernini e le arti figurative nel pensiero di Lelio Guidiccioni*, Università degli studi della Tuscia, 2004, pp 77–89, with a complete transcription.

17 It should be noted, however, that at the beginning of the sixteenth century Pomponius Gauricus, *De sculptura*, Paolo Cutolo (ed.), Naples, 1999 [orig. 1504], pp 242–3, with regard to sculpture in general, stated that the making of models prior to sculpting the full-size marble statue was a venerable tradition that contemporary sculptors were not following as much: 'Questa tecnica era un tempo in grandissimo uso: non si modellava pressoché nulla se non con l'abbozzo. Così infatti si rilevano i futuri errori e si eliminano senza danno prima che venga realizzata l'opera e, molto diversamente da quanto pensano questi scultori della nostra epoca, si opera più rapidamente quando si lavora con un modello da riprodurre.' ('Maximo haec olim in usu: nihil fere moliebatur nisi ex proplastice. Ex ea enim et futura deprehenduntur errata et nullo prius quam fiant incommodo castigantur multoque aliter quam isti nostri opinantur ipsa res citius expeditur, proposito

iam exemplari quod imiteris.') On Lelio Guidiccioni's commentary on Bernini's mnemonic powers, see Rudolph Preimesberger, 'Lelio Guidiccioni's Letter to Bernini: A Commentary', *The Sculpture Journal*, vol.20 (2011), pp 207–22, here pp 211–12.

18 Pliny, XXXV.xlv, 156: 'He [Varro] also praises Pasiteles, who said that modelling was the mother of chasing and of bronze statuary and sculpture, and who, although he was eminent in all these arts, never made anything before he had made a clay model.' See also Salvatore Settis, *Laocoonte: fama e stile*, Rome, 1999, p.57.

19 For Algardi's use of a clay model prior to sculpting the ultimately unexecuted marble bust of either Francesco D'Este, Duke of Modena, or his brother, Cardinal Rinaldo d'Este, see Jennifer Montagu, *Alessandro Algardi*, 2 vols, New Haven and London, 1985, I, p.157, and II, n.3, p.259. Edmé Bouchardon's splendid model bust of Clement XII, now in the Fine Arts Museums of San Francisco, took only five days to complete – the head itself was executed in three and a half hours. See Anatole de Montaiglon and Jules Guiffrey (eds), *Correspondance des directeurs de l'Académie de France à Rome avec les Surintendants des Bâtiments*, Paris, 1898, t.VIII, pp 151–2. See n.33.

20 Tomaso Montanari, 'Il colore del marmo. I busti di Bernini tra scultura e pittura, ritratto e storia, funzione e stile' in *I marmi vivi*, pp 71–135, esp. p.128, and p.135, n.127, citing Madeleine Laurain-Portemer, *Études Mazarines*, Paris, 1981, p.205, n.2. For the different processes of sculpting, from antiquity to today, see Peter Rockwell, *Lavorare la pietra*, Rome, 1989, pp 115–36. For the English version, idem, *The Art of Stoneworking: A Reference Guide*, Cambridge, 1993.

21 Daniela Del Pesco, 'La légation de Flavio Chigi à Paris en 1664: mémoires et documents nouveaux (avec quelques observations sur le *Journal de voyage du Cavalier Bernini en France de Paul de Chantelou*', *Mélanges de l'École Française de Rome*, vol.123 (2011), pp 475–512, here p.505: 'Il a travaillé avec grande attache ces deux jours cy au modelle de son buste.' For De' Rossi's letter, see Léon Mirot, *Le Bernin en France: les travaux du Louvre et les statues de Louis XIV*, Paris, 1904, pp 218–19. *Pace* Charles Perrault who, in his *Mémoires*, Paul Lacroix (ed.), Paris, 1878, p.51, claimed the contrary: 'Ne fit point de modele de terre, selon l'usage des autres sculpteurs.'

22 Domenico Bernini, *The Life of Gian Lorenzo Bernini by Domenico Bernini*, Franco Mormando (ed.), University Park, 2011, p.198.

23 'The Note-Book and Account Book of Nicholas Stone', Walter Lewis Spiers (ed.), *The Walpole Society*, vol.7 (1918–19), pp 158–200, here p.170.

24 van Gastel, *Il marmo spirante*, p.217: 'Io non sono mai per dimenticarmi il diletto che m'è toccato dall'intervenire sempre all'opera, vedendo ciascuna mattina Vostra Signoria con leggiadria singulare far sempre mille moti contrarij: discorrer sempre aggiustato sul conto delle cose occorrenti et con le mani andar lontanissimo dal discorso; rannicchiarsi, distendersi, maneggiar le dita sul modello, con la prestezza, et varietà di chi tocca un Arpe; segnar col carbone il marmo in cento luoghi, batter col mazzuolo in cent'altri; batter dico, in una parte e guardar nell'opposta; spinger la mano battendo innanzi, et volger la faccia guardando indietro; vincer le contrarietà, et con animo grande sopirle subito; spezzarglisi il marmo per un pelo in due pezzi quando era già il lavoro condotto; imprender nuovo lavoro in nuovo marmo, et ricondurlo con tanta velocità, che niuno se ne sia accorto; né ciò sia credibile se non si vedessero in essere tutti due.' In the text, I have adopted the English translation published by Joris van Gastel on p.92 up to the word 'instantly', making three changes that seemed more appropriate to me: *prestezza*, translated as 'effortless grace' has been replaced by 'speed'; *contrarietà*, translated as 'contrarieties' has been substituted by 'impediments'; *sopirle* (in the Italian transcription of the text on p.217), translated as 'appeasing' has been replaced by 'solving'.

25 See *Gian Lorenzo Bernini: il testamento, la casa, la raccolta dei beni*, Franco Borsi, Cristina Acidini Luchinat, and Francesco Quinterio (eds), Florence, 1981, p.108. My thanks to Steven F. Ostrow for reminding me of this document.

26 Anthony Sigel, 'Visual Glossary' in *Bernini: Sculpting in Clay*, C.D. Dickerson III, Anthony Sigel, and Ian Wardropper (eds), New Haven and London, 2012, p.96, with reference to the transferal of the measurements from a model to the marble block: 'As many as fifty or more measurements would be used to ensure that the proportions of the larger model were identical to those of the smaller one.'

27 On the sculpting process based on the transferal of points used in early modern Italy, see Rockwell, *Lavorare la pietra*, pp 127–34. My thanks to sculptor Giuseppe Greco Luciani in Carrara for discussing the subject with me on different occasions.

28 See Chapter 2, p.49.

29 For the documents that prove the actual date of execution of the busts, see Stanislao Fraschetti, *Bernini. La sua vita, la sua opera, il suo tempo*, Milan, 1900, pp 107–8, and Howard Hibbard, 'Un nuovo documento sul busto del Cardinale Scipione Borghese del Bernini', *Bollettino d'arte*, IV, vol.46, 1961, pp 101–5. On the two Scipione Borghese portraits, see Sarah McPhee's entry in the exhibition catalogue *Bernini*, Andrea Bacchi and Anna Coliva (eds), Galleria Borghese, Rome, 1 November 2017 – 4 February 2018, pp 240–44; Montanari, *I marmi vivi*, pp 308–11; Catherine Hess's entry in *Bernini and the Birth of Baroque Portrait Sculpture*, Andrea Bacchi, Catherine Hess, and Jennifer Montagu (eds), Los Angeles and Ottawa, 2008, pp 185–9; Anna Coliva, *Bernini scultore: la tecnica esecutiva*, Rome, 2002, pp 217–33; Anna Coliva's entry in *Bernini Scultore: La nascita del Barocco in Casa Borghese*, Anna Coliva and Sebastian Schütze (eds), Rome, 1998, pp 276–89.

30 Domenico Bernini, *The Life*, pp 99–100: 'Cardinal Borghese asked Bernini to do his portrait in marble, and so the artist set himself to work, bringing it to completion in a short period of time. The cardinal himself went to examine the portrait in the studio where Gian Lorenzo usually worked; so much did the work please the cardinal that he ordered it to be polished and finished so that he could have it brought on a specified day to the Apostolic Palace and shown to his uncle, the pope. Bernini obeyed the cardinal's orders, but while they were being carried out, a new and unexpected incident occurred. In finishing the face of the portrait with their pumice-stone, the polishers uncovered a vein in the marble, or, as we say, a "hair," that crossed the entire forehead and noticeably altered the likeness of the sitter. This turn of events greatly troubled the heart of Gian Lorenzo's father, so anxious for his son's success. The studio assistants, well aware that the pope was anxiously awaiting the portrait, strove in vain to eliminate the blemish, which, in fact, was a natural feature of the marble itself.

Amid this great agitation on the part of his father and assistants, Gian Lorenzo arrived upon the scene. Having been apprised of the situation, dauntless he asked for a new block of marble. Eager to transform the very defects of nature into a motive for his own glory, Bernini simply set out to re-create the same portrait in a different block of marble and, except to replenish his energy with a bit of food, did not rest from this labor for the space of three days, when he brought the work to completion. On the appointed day, it was transported before the pontiff. However, from a certain livelier quality of expression in this new version, the cardinal easily recognised that this work was not the same one he had seen some days earlier. It was necessary therefore for Gian Lorenzo to reveal what had transpired; hearing the report, the pope wanted the first portrait brought before him. The amount of praise accorded Gian Lorenzo after the subsequent comparison of the two portraits was simply beyond belief, as was, moreover, the well-merited honor heaped upon the little artist by that illustrious gathering of men.'

31 Ascanio Condivi, *Vita di Michelagnolo Buonarroti*, Giovanni Nencioni (ed.), Florence, 1998, p.13: 'Messesi Michelagnolo a farla in marmo di mezzo rilievo e così la 'mpresa gli succedette, che mi ramenta udirlo dire che, quando la rivede, cognosce quanto torto egli abbia fatto alla natura, a non seguitar prontamente l'arte della scultura, facendo giudicio per quell'opera quanto potesse riuscire.'

32 Among the authors who have done so, see Evonne Levy's considerations in *Bernini's Biographies: Critical Essays*, Maarten Delbeke, Evonne Levy, and Steven F. Ostrow (eds), University Park, 2006, pp 165–71; Tomaso Montanari, *La libertà di Bernini. La sovranità dell'artista e le regole del potere*, Turin, 2016, p.238; Rudolf Wittkower, *Gian Lorenzo Bernini: The Sculptor of the Roman Baroque*, London, 1966, cat.no.31; Franco Mormando, Domenico Bernini, *The Life*, see ns 16–23, pp 280–82.

33 In this context, it is worth remembering that Edmé Bouchardon's splendid clay portrait of Clement XII in preparation for the execution of the marble bust took five days to complete. Montaiglon, *Correspondance*, VIII, pp 151–2, in a letter from director Vleughels to the superintendent D'Antin: 'Le portrait de Sa Sainteté fut commencé, comme je l'ai écrit à V. G., mercredi dernier, et il fut fini dimanche après-midi, ce qui fit admirer le sculpteur, tant pour sa promptitude que pour son habileté, car il n'a été que trois heures et demie à faire la tête. Le Pape est très content, et tous ceux qui l'ont vue; outre que la tête est très ressemblante, elle est d'un très beau travail.' See n.18. For Bouchardon's portrait of Clement XII now in the Legion of Honor, Fine Arts Museums in San Francisco, see https://art.famsf.org/edm%C3%A9-bouchardon/pope-clement-xii-lorenzo-corsini-1730-1740-54899

34 Wittkower, *Gian Lorenzo Bernini*, no.31, pp 199–200.

35 On a concise recap of the chronology of the king's bust, see ibid., no.70, pp 246–7. Paul Fréart de Chantelou, *Journal de voyage du Cavalier Bernin en France*, M. Stanić (ed.), Paris, 2001, p.61, 20 June. Bernini alerted the king that it would be a difficult enterprise that would cause him some hardship since he would have to pose for twenty sessions, two hours at a time. From Chantelou's *Diary* we also learn that, even on a relatively small project such as the portrait of Louix XIV, having learned from other sources that the king wanted the sculptor to make a portrait of himself and the queen (11 June) Bernini asked for some clay to make small clay 'sketches' of the overall composition (11 June); Louis XIV made the official request to have his portrait executed (20 June); drew two portraits of the king, one in profile one frontal (23 June); worked on the clay model of the bust (24 June, 25 June, 27 June, 1 July, 13 July); drew the king during a meeting of his Council without having him pose in a still position (27 June); had the marble block roughed out by an assistant while he was still working on the clay model (6 July) – according to Mattia de' Rossi, Bernini began sculpting on 5 July, see n.39; was working on the marble bust (23 and 31 July); was working on the bust but complains that the block chosen for the portrait was 'marmo cotto' (friable marble) and was, thus, forced to use the drill more than he wished because he feared that with the chisel the marble would crack (4 August); was still working on the bust (11 August); the Venetian ambassador praises the bust in his studio (17 August); Bernini says he needs the king to pose for two more sittings to complete the bust (19 August); worked on eyes and cheeks of sculpture in front of the king (21 August); morning and evening worked on the bust (27 August); was working on the mouth of the sculpture (4 September); admitted the marble turned out better than he thought (7 September); had designed a base for the bust (10 September); Le Brun visited Bernini and saw bust (12 September); asked Chantelou to tell the king to come to studio with two to three collets to see which would come best in marble (12 September); worked on the collet (22 September); tells the king the portrait is finished (5 October); was drawing his bust to make a pedestal for it (12 October). On Bernini's employment of studio hands, assistants, and collaborators, see the valuable study by Helga Tratz, 'Werkstatt und Arbeitsweise Beninis', *Römisches Jahrbuch für Kunstgeschichte*, vol.23–24 (1988), pp 395–483.

36 Pierre-Jean Mariette, *Abecedario*, 6 vols, Paris, 1851–3, I, p.125.

37 ibid.

38 ibid.

39 Hibbard, pp 101–5.

40 Mariette, vol.I, p.126.

41 For the collaborative aspects of sculpting in bronze, see, for example, Michael W. Cole, *Ambitious Form: Giambologna, Ammanati, and Danti in Florence*, Princeton and Oxford, 2011, p.21.

42 Chantelou, *Diary*, 11 June, p.29. Idem, *Journal*, p.56. Thus, despite Perrault's comments to the contrary ('He worked straightaway upon the marble, and did not make a clay model as other sculptors are accustomed to do. Instead, he contended himself with making two or three pastel sketches of the King's profile'), Bernini certainly availed himself of clay models before tackling a marble bust, as other sculptors would. See n.21. See Charles Perrault, *Memoirs of My Life*, Jeanne Morgan Zarucchi (ed. and trans.), Columbia, 1989, p.61.

43 Chantelou, *Diary*, p.39, and idem, *Journal*, p.62. Fraschetti, p.345, n.1, cites from the *Comptes des Bâtiments du Roi* (tom. 1) where the payments for the blocs are recorded.

44 Chantelou, *Diary*, p.53, and idem, *Journal*, p.70. It should be noted that Margery Corbett's translation (*Diary*, p.53) is misleading. It is not that on 6 July 'He began to block out the marble.' Rather, this was a task that a sculptor would normally leave to his assistants: 'Il a commencé à faire ébaucher son marbre.' Mirot, p.66, quoting a letter by Bernini's assistant Mattia de' Rossi, specifies that Bernini actually began work on the marble bust on 5 July.

45 Chantelou, *Diary*, p.60, and idem, *Journal*, p.75.

46 idem, *Diary*, p.60, and idem, *Journal*, p.76.

47 Domenico Bernini, *The Life*, p.200. Idem, *Vita del Cavalier Gio. Lorenzo Bernino*, Rome, 1713, pp 135–6.

48 Jennifer Montagu, *Roman Baroque Sculpture: The Industry of Art*, New Haven and London, 1989, p.106 and p.209, n.13. Idem, 'Bernini Sculptures Not by Bernini' in *Gianlorenzo Bernini: New Aspects of His Art and Thought*, University Park and London, 1985, p.26, p.37, n.13, and p.38, n.7. The author cites as a source for Bernini's use of assistants, and Giuliano Finelli in particular, Jacob Hess, *Die Künstlerbiographien von Giovanni Battista Passeri*, Leipzig and Vienna, 1934, p.247, as well as a letter in the Archivio Spada quoted by Minna Heimbürger Ravalli, *Architettura e arti minori nel barocco italiano: Ricerche nell'archivio Spada*, Florence, 1977, p.77, n.7. Andrea

Bacchi and Catherine Hess, 'Creating a New Likeness: Bernini's Transformation of the Portrait Bust' in *Bernini and the Birth of Baroque Portrait Sculpture*, Los Angeles, 2008, pp 17–18, quoting a 1630 letter from Virgilio Spada writing from Rome to his brother Cardinal Bernardino Spada in Bologna: '[T]he Cavalier Bernino, today a sculptor of great fame, has until now kept at his side a young man so skilled that Bernini's rivals say the latter's credit derives from the former. Indignant that his skill should feed another's fortune and not his own, he left Bernini and set up his own shop, giving himself the opportunity to work and thus demonstrate that he was and is the author of those much-esteemed works: when the subject turned to this young man, Domenichino, the famous painter who a few days ago came to see me, so praised him for proving that the art of sculpture has never had a man who was his equal.' The authors further add: 'There can be no doubt that the "young man so skilled" is none other than Giuliano Finelli, who is documented as working in Gian Lorenzo's workshop from the start of the 1620s.'

49 Mariette, p.127: 'Au rest, je ne prétend pas, par tout ce que je viens d'avancer, rien diminuer de la gloire que mérite si justement le Bernin; mais je pense que ses beaux ouvrages l'ont assez immortalisé, sans qu'il soit besoin, pour le faire paroître encore plus grand, de mêler dans son histoire des faits dénués de toute vraysemblance, et, si j'ose le dire, d'emprunter le langage de la fable.'

50 Ursula Schlegel, 'Bozzetti in Terracotta by Pietro Stefano Monnot', *Boston Museum Bulletin*, vol.72, no.367 (1974), pp 56–68. Similarly, Wittkower, *Gian Lorenzo Bernini*, p.208, with regard to the *Bust of Thomas Baker* at the Victoria and Albert Museum, wrote: 'Those who have studied Bernini's procedure . . . will know that many of his "originals" were to a large extent prepared by assistants and that it is the degree of his touching up that is decisive for the appearance of the work.'

51 Rudolf and Margot Wittkower, *Born Under Saturn: The Character and Conduct of Artists: A Documented History from Antiquity to the French Revolution*, New York and London, 1969, p.271, point out that 'for almost sixty years he maintained the largest studio in Italy and perhaps in Europe'.

52 The ambassador for the d'Este court in Parma, in a communication dated 8 January 1633, also claimed that the pope had commissioned the portrait. Fraschetti, quoting the *Archivio di Stato in Modena – Cancelleria Ducale – Avvisi di Roma*, p.107: 'Il Cavalier Bernini di commissione del Papa, ha fatto in marmo la testa del Cardinal Borghese che le ha donato in ricompensa 500 zecchini et un diamante di 150 scudi.' Catherine Hess, in her catalogue entry in *Bernini and the Birth of Baroque Portrait Sculpture*, p.187, believes it was Urban VIII who either commissioned or allowed Bernini to sculpt the portrait. Montanari, *I marmi vivi*, p.310, underscores that, while the work was paid for by Cardinal Scipione himself, the document published by Fraschetti alludes to the fact that it was executed under the pope's oversight. Sarah McPhee in *Bernini*, Andrea Bacchi and Anna Coliva (eds), Milan, 2017, p.240, believes that the patron was the cardinal himself.

53 John Pope-Hennessy, *Italian High Renaissance and Baroque Sculpture: An Introduction to Italian Sculpture*, New York, 1985, p.124.

54 Evonne Levy's insightful essay, 'Chapter 2 of Domenico Bernini's *Vita* of his Father: Mimesis' in *Bernini's Biographies*, pp 159–80, discusses this leitmotif especially in view of the recurring theme of the *Imitatio Buonarroti* in both Baldinucci's and Domenico Bernini's biographies. See also Catherine Soussloff, 'Imitatio Buonarroti', *Sixteenth Century Journal*, vol.20 (1989), pp 581–602, and, more recently, Carolina Mangone, *Bernini's Michelangelo*, New Haven and London, 2020.

55 Ironically, the second bust also developed a hairline crack in the mozzetta that the Cardinal dons, from the bottom left to top right. See Sarah McPhee's entry in *Bernini*, Andrea Bacchi and Anna Coliva (eds), Milan, 2017, p.244.

56 My thanks to Steven F. Ostrow for pointing out this fact. Here, again, the facts are manipulated in the biographer's process of myth-making so as to increase the readers' admiration for the precociousness of the sculptor. In 1632, when the busts were sculpted, Bernini was thirty-four years old.

57 Coliva, *Bernini Scultore: La nascita del Barocco in Casa Borghese*, p. 288, n.1, specifies that afterwards the bust was polished with acids. See also idem, *Bernini scultore: la tecnica esecutiva*, pp 222–33.

58 Levy, 'Chapter 2 of Domenico Bernini's *Vita*', pp 165–71, points out as much.

59 See n.24.

60 Baldinucci, *The Life*, p.80. Leaving aside the possibility that a human agent might have caused the marble to crack and Gian Lorenzo Bernini's superhuman sculptural skill, the fact that even the second portrait

has a hairline crack from bottom left to top right of his mozzetta tells us something about Bernini's acceptance of marble blocks that were less-than-optimal for his works. Although this incident, in retrospect, could be seen as providential, since Michelangelo had also had his problems with a *pelo* in his first version of the *Risen Christ*, thus reinforcing the idea that Bernini was indeed the new Michelangelo, it does remind one how different the two sculptors were. Anna Coliva, citing H. Kauffmann, *Giovanni Lorenzo Bernini. Die figürlichen Kompositionen*, Berlin, 1970, p.75, rightly points out that Bernini always paid little attention to the selection of the best marble possible and there is no evidence that he ever went to Carrara to choose or 'test' his own blocks, like Michelangelo did. See Anna Coliva's entry in *Bernini Scultore: La nascita del Barocco in Casa Borghese*, p.279. For Michelangelo's first version of the *Risen Christ*, now in the Church of San Vincenzo in Bassano Romano, see William E. Wallace, 'Michelangelo's Risen Christ', *Sixteenth Century Journal*, vol.XXVIII, no.4 (1997), pp 1251–80, and Irene Baldriga, 'The First Version of Michelangelo's Christ for S. Maria sopra Minerva', *The Burlington Magazine*, vol.142 (2000), pp 740–45; Silvia Danesi Squarzina, 'The Bassano "Christ the Redeemer" in the Giustiniani Collection', *The Burlington Magazine*, vol.142 (2000), pp 746–51. On Bernini overcoming 'defects', personal or artistic, see Levy, 'Chapter 2 of Domenico Bernini's *Vita*', p.163.

61 Baldinucci, *The Life*, p.65. Idem, *Vita*, pp 57–8. Domenico Bernini, *The Life*, p.225: 'He boldly undertook the beginnings of this monument, placing it, with the usual liveliness of his genius, in a large niche above the door leading to the church's sacristy. In doing so, he transformed what was originally a handicap into a necessary component of his intended design.' Idem, *Vita*, p.166: 'Ne [Alexander VII's funerary monument] intraprese dunque arditamente i principii, e colla solita vivacità del suo ingegno situòllo in una gran Nicchia sopra la Porta, che conduce dalla Sacrestia alla Chiesa, con far servire il difetto a necessità della sua intenzione.'

62 Chantelou, *Journal*, Friday 9 October, p.239. In relating to Colbert what Bernini had stated, on 19 October, p.272, Chantelou changes the statement slightly by using the verb 'to do' instead of 'to know': 'Chi vuol veder ciò che può un grand'uomo, bisogna metterlo in necessità' ('If you want to see what a great man can do, put him in a difficult position'. Chantelou, *Diary*, p.315).

63 Domenico Bernini, *The Life*, p.100: 'However, from a certain livelier quality of expression in this new version, the cardinal easily recognised that this work was not the same one he had seen some days earlier.' Idem, *Vita*, pp 10–11: 'Fu portata dunque nel giorno stabilito al Pontefice, mà facilmente riconobbe il Cardinale da una certa non sò quale espressione più viva, che quella non era la figura, che alcuni giorni avanti haveva veduto, e necessitato Gio: Lorenzo a Scuoprire il fatto, volle il Papa, che quivi ancora si portasse il primo Ritratto.' See also Levy, 'Chapter 2 of Domenico Bernini's *Vita*', p.170, and Stefano Pierguidi, '"A Certain Livelier Quality of Expression": Bernini's Two Versions of the Bust of Scipione Borghese' in *Multiples in Pre-Modern Art*, Zurich, 2014, pp 229–43.

64 *Pace* John Pope-Hennessy, who stated: 'Where the two busts differ most strikingly is not in the head, but in the lower part, for the sculptor seems to have sensed that in the area of the chest and shoulders the forms were over-animated to the verge of triviality, and since fate offered him a second chance, he decided that they should be restrained and unified. In this sense the second bust constitutes a critique of the first.' For interpretations similar to the one here advanced, see Wittkower, *Gian Lorenzo Bernini*, no. 31, who believed the second portrait 'lacks the animation and vitality of the first one', and Montanari, *I marmi vivi*, p.310: 'E' probabile che lo scultore sia intervenuto in minor grado sul secondo esemplare (che risulta perciò meno mosso e rifinito) per mancanza di tempo, ma anche per contenere i "peli" (cioè le fessure del marmo) che ancora una volta iniziavano a manifestarsi, e che sono evidenti in tutta la mozzetta.' On Bernini's approach to 'copies', see the interesting considerations by Evonne Levy, 'Repeat Performances: Bernini, the Portrait and its Copy' in *Sculpture Journal*, vol.20, no.2 (2011), pp 239–49, here p.247: 'In many ways Bernini's production of portraits, and a few of their copies, is analogous to the process-oriented rather than goal-oriented nature of theatrical performance as defined recently by Tzachi Zamir: "Theatrical repetition (whether rehearsed or performed for an audience) is process-oriented: it is the capacity and the action of living afresh the enacted sequence of events."'

65 Maria Assunta Sorrentino, 'Vicende storico conservative' in *Bernini scultore: La tecnica esecutiva*, Anna Coliva (ed.), Rome, 2002, p.220. See also Pierguidi, '"A Certain Livelier Quality of Expression"', p.237.

66 Domenico Bernini, *The Life*, p.102, makes it a point to emphasise this: 'Thus, as the boy advanced in age, a desire to arrive at the perfection of his art so grew in him that Pietro, his father, was obliged to make the youth sleep in the same room with him in order to prevent Gian Lorenzo from returning to his study during those hours that should be dedicated to the repose of one's body.' The same idea is reiterated with regard to the second portrait of Scipione Borghese: 'Eager to transform the very defects of nature into a motive for his own glory, Bernini simply set out to re-create the same portrait in a different block of marble and, except to replenish his energy with a bit of food, did not rest from this labor for the space of three days, when he brought the work to completion.' Idem, *The Life*, p.99.

67 Ernst Kris and Otto Kurz, *Legend, Myth, and Magic in the Image of the Artist: A Historical Experiment* [orig. *Die Legende vom Künstler: ein geschichtlicher Versuch*, Vienna, 1934], New Haven and London, 1979, p.125.

68 Baldinucci, *The Life*, p.9. The sounding of the Ave Maria occurred half an hour after sunset. See Roberto Colzi, 'Che ora era? Raffronto tra le ore all'italiana e alla francese a Roma', *Studi romani*, vol.43 (1995), pp 93–102, here pp 95–6.

69 For this theme in seventeenth-century art, see Livio Pestilli, '"The Burner of the Midnight Oil": A Caravaggesque Rendition of a Classic *Exemplum*. An Unrecognised Self-portrait by Michael Sweerts?', *Zeitschrift für Kunstgeschichte*, vol.59 (1993), pp 119–33. Certainly, Baldinucci's employment of a 'nocturnal clock' was also a way of implying the secretive and clandestine nature of Bernini's carving of the second bust in the privacy of his room. My thanks to Steven Ostrow for underlining this feature of the anecdote.

70 For a quick consultation of William Wordsworth's poem, see https://www.poetryfoundation.org/poems/45536/ode-intimations-of-immortality-from-recollections-of-early-childhood

71 See Tomaso Montanari, 'Pierre Cureau de la Chambre e la prima biografia di Gian Lorenzo Bernini', *Paragone*, 3rd ser., nos 24–25 (1999), pp 103–32, as well as 'At the Margins of the Historiography of Art: The *Vite* of Bernini Between Autobiography and Apologia' in *Bernini's Biographies*, pp 73–109.

72 Pierre Cureau de la Chambre, *Preface pour servir à l'histoire de la vie et des ouvrages du Cavalier Bernin*, Paris, 1685, p.6. For a convenient, digital access to the text, see the Bibliotheca Hertziana website dlib.biblhertz.it/Ca-BER1921-2810#page/1/mode/2up

73 ibid.

74 ibid., p.6.

75 ibid., pp 6–7.

76 ibid., p.7.

77 ibid., p.8.

78 Baldinucci, *The Life*, pp 9–10. For complementary considerations of the anecdotes pertaining to the drawing for Paul V, the Scipione Borghese busts, and the *Saint Lawrence* statue, see Levy's essay 'Chapter 2 of Domenico Bernini's *Vita*' as in n.54, On the drawings for Paul V, see also Steven Ostrow, 'Bernini's Voice: From Chantelou's *Journal* to the *Vite*' in *Bernini's Biographies*, pp 122–3.

79 Subsequently, in a slightly modified version, Domenico Bernini describes the same initial encounter of Gian Lorenzo with the pope. Domenico Bernini, *The Life*, pp 98–9.

80 Baldinucci, *The Life*, p.10; Domenico Bernini, *The Life*, p.98. That the epithet was not just a literary invention of Bernini's biographers may be gathered by Fulvio Testi's famous letter to Count Francesco Fontana of 29 January 1633, where the Modenese ambassador refers to Bernini as 'quel famosissimo scultore che ha fatto la statua del Papa e la Dafne ch'è nella Vigna di Borghese ch'è il Michelangelo del nostro secolo tanto nel dipignere quanto nello scolpire e che non cede a nissuno degli antichi nell'eccellenza dell'Arte'. See Fraschetti, p.108.

81 Giorgio Vasari, *Lives of the Artists*, George Bull (trans.), Harmondsworth, 1979, pp 64–5. Pliny, XXXV. 81–83, pp 320–23. See Paul Barolsky, *Why Mona Lisa Smiles and Other Tales by Vasari*, University Park, 1991, pp 10–12, and Norman E. Land, 'Apelles and the Origin of Giotto's O', *Source: Notes in the History of Art*, vol.25 (2005), pp 6–9.

82 On Pliny in general, see Sarah Blake McHam, *Pliny and the Artistic Culture of the Italian Renaissance*, New Haven and London, 2013. On Apelles and Protogenes, ibid., p.49.

83 In Vasari's 1550 edition of the *Vite*, Pope Benedict is qualified as the XII. In the 1568 edition, erroneously, as Pope Benedict IX but it was a 'typo', as it should have been Benedict XI (1303–4). On the thorny question as to whether the pope in Vasari's account should be Benedict XI or Benedict XII, see Peter Murray, 'Notes on Some Early Giotto Sources', *Journal of the Warburg and Courtauld Institutes*, vol.16 (1953), pp 58–80.

84 Vasari, pp 64–5, as in n. 81. See also Kris and Kurz, pp 96–7, and Patricia Lee Rubin, *Giorgio Vasari: Art and History*, New Haven and London, 1995, p.309.

85 Kris and Kurz, pp 96–7.

86 Baldinucci, *The Life*, p.12. The sculpture was probably executed for and in collaboration with Cardinal Maffeo Barberini, the future Urban VIII, and eventually purchased by Leone Strozzi for his Roman villa which was subsequently destroyed. It was sculpted just before the *Saint Sebastian*. See Schütze's extensive entry in *Bernini Scultore*: *La nascita del Barocco in Casa Borghese*, pp 67–77.

87 Levy, 'Chapter 2 of Domenico Bernini's *Vita*', pp 172–3.

88 Domenico Bernini, *The Life*, pp 102–103. Mormando's edition of Domenico Bernini's *Life* provides a brief biographical sketch of the artist by Pier Filippo Bernini, the artist's eldest son. The document is preserved in the Bibliothèque Nationale, Paris, Ms. italien, 2084, fols. 132–5. Idem, *The Life*, pp 238–41. In this brief biography, that Mormando calls *The Vita Brevis*, Pietro (or Pier) Filippo writes: 'One night, while he was doing a Saint Sebastian [*sic*] on his grill for Strozzi, not satisfied with his rendering of one of the legs, he lit a fire in order to burn his own leg and observe the effect that it had.' This manuscript was published for the first time in 1844 by Paolo Mazio in the periodical *Il Saggiatore*, and subsequently by Felicita Audisio in 'Lettere e testi teatrali di Bernini: Una postilla linguistica' in *Barocco romano e barocco italiano. Il teatro, l'effimero, l'allegoria*, Marcello Fagiolo dell'Arco and Maria Luisa Madonna (eds), Rome, 1985, pp 26–43.

89 See Heiko Damm, 'Gianlorenzo on the Grill: The Birth of the Artist in his Primo Parto di Devozione' in *Bernini's Biographies*, pp 223–49.

90 On the hagiographic features of artists' biographies, see Carl Goldstein, 'Rhetoric and Art History in the Italian Renaissance and Baroque', *The Art Bulletin*, vol.73 (1991), pp 641–52.

91 For the reference to Horace's *Ars Poetica*, see Schütze, *Bernini Scultore: La nascita del Barocco in Casa Borghese*, p.71, and to Aristotle's *Poetics*, see Domenico Bernini, *The Life*, p.285, n.41.

92 Aristotle, *Poetics* in *The Complete Works of Aristotle*, 2 vols, Jonathan Barnes (ed.), Princeton, 1985, II, 1455a, XVII, 28–33, p.2329.

93 Horace, *Satires, Epistles and Ars Poetica*, H. Rushton Fairclough (trans.), Cambridge and London, 1978, 99–103, pp 458–9.

94 Quintilian, *The Institutio Oratoria*, 4 vols, Harold Edgeworth Butler (trans.), Cambridge, MA and London, 1985, II, Book VI, 26–8, pp 430–33: 'Summa enim, quantum ego quidem sentio, circa movendos adfectus in hoc posita est, ut moveamur ipsi.'

95 Dante Alighieri, *Convivio*, Franca Brambilla Ageno (ed.), Florence, 1995, IV, x, 11: 'Onde nullo dipintore potrebbe porre alcuna figura, se intenzionalmente non si facesse prima tale quale la figura essere dee.' See https://www.danteonline.it/italiano/opere2.asp?idcod=000&idope=2&idliv1=4&idliv2=10&idliv3=1&idlang=OR. For the translation, see https://digitaldante.columbia.edu/text/library/the-convivio/book-04/

96 Antonio Possevino, *Tractatio De Poesi & Pictura ethnica, humana, & fabulosa collata cum vera, honesta, & sacra*, Lyon, 1594, XXVI, p.301: 'Ut igitur funestissimus Christi Redemptoris, ac vitae nostrae Parentis interitus admirationem, & acerbum dolorem in alijs pariat, necesse est, ut in Pictoris animo, insit, unde existat admirationis magnitudo, & impetus doloris erumpat. Si vis enim me flere, prius flendum est stibi ipsi, in quit Poeta.' Federico Borromeo, *Sacred Painting*, Kenneth S. Rothwell, Jr. (trans.), Cambridge, MA and London, 2010, p.47: 'just as an orator's attempt to stir the minds of others is futile if he does not first stir his own, every painter must first arouse some sense of religious devotion in his own mind, or he will not be able to impart to his own works the devotion or a sensibility that one can praise'.

97 See the useful resumé of Domenico Bernini's life and works in Domenico Bernini, *The Life*, pp 4–14.

98 See the introduction to Seneca the Elder, *Declamations*, 2 vols, Michael Winterbottom (trans.), Cambridge and London, 1974, I, pp vii–xxiv.

99 ibid., II, 10:5, pp 448–75. The placement of a painting in the temple of Minerva in which a man – although a slave – is depicted being tortured to death, impaired the prestige of Athens since, as Gallio argues, 'We have always been accounted merciful.' Ibid., pp 13–14.

100 Philip Sohm, 'Caravaggio the Barbarian' in *Caravaggio: Reflections and Refractions*, Lorenzo Pericolo (ed.), Farnham, 2014, p.182.

101 Carlo Dati, *Vite de pittori antichi*, Florence, 1667, pp 44–61 and, with regard to Michelangelo, p.7: 'Seneca Retore nell'argomento della Controv. 34 racconta questa storietta. Il P.[adre] Andrea Schotto nelle note dubita se l'accidente sia vero, o finto per esercizio de i Declamatori. Come assolutamente non ha per vera la voce, che corre del nostro Michelangelo Buonarroti, ch'egli ponesse in croce un'uomo, e lo vi lasciasse morire,

per esprimere al vivo l'imagine del Salvador Crocifisso.' See also Sohm, pp 182–3. For a reading of this anecdote as an example of Michelangelo's 'unrestricted mimesis' ('schrankenlosen Mimesis'), see Andreas Plackinger, *Violenza. Gewalt als Denkfigur im michelangelesken Kunstdiskurs*, Berlin, 2016, pp 190–208. Carlo Cesare Malvasia, *Felsina pittrice. Vite de pittori bolognesi*, Bologna, 1678, p.347.

102 Baldinucci, *The Life*, p.34. Idem, *Vita*, p.29: 'Era necessario, che un'Uomo, qual era il Bernino fusse posto alla coppella delle persecuzioni.'

103 Levy, 'Chapter 2 of Domenico Bernini's *Vita*', pp 172–3, sees in Michelangelo's naturalism in his early painting of *Saint Anthony Beaten by Devils* after Schongauer a link to his identification with Saint Anthony.

104 Domenico Bernini, *The Life*, p.103.

105 Wittkower, *Gian Lorenzo Bernini*, p.13.

106 Chantelou, *Journal*, p.228, 6 October. These words are spoken by Bernini within the context of his comparison between painting (an illusion, a lie) and sculpture (truth).

107 Départments des arts graphiques, Musée du Louvre, Paris, INV 6952, Recto, attributed to Giovanni Francesco Barbieri (i.e., Guercino).

108 Domenico Bernini, *The Life*, p.199: 'Bernini claimed that in posing for an artist completely immobile, a person was never as true to himself as when in motion, for it was then that all those qualities that are his alone and not of another, become evident and give true likeness to a portrait.'

109 Chantelou, *Diary*, 20 June, p.38; idem, *Journal*, p.61.

110 idem, *Journal*, p.65, Sunday 27 June.

111 idem, *Diary,* p.165, idem, *Journal,* p.154, 4 September. Bernini felt that the best time to study the sitter's mouth was when the person was just about to talk or had just finished doing so.

112 idem, *Diary*, pp 88–9 (29 July), 92 (30 July), 115 (12 August); idem, *Journal*, p.96 (29 July), p.98 (30 July), pp 115–16 (12 August).

113 For an extensive analysis of this statue and the collaborative efforts between patron, Urban VIII, and artist, as well as the literary and visual sources that informed the sculpture, see Sebastian Schütze, *Kardinal Maffeo Barberini, später Papst Urban VIII., und die Entstehung des römischen Hochbarock*, Munich, 2007, pp 194–205.

114 Of course, the *affetti* (emotions) had been the focal aspect of Renaissance art theory. See Leon Battista Alberti, *On Painting*, John R. Spencer (trans.), New Haven and London, 1977, p.77: 'The *istoria* will move the soul of the beholder when each man painted there clearly shows the movement of his own soul. It happens in nature that nothing more than herself is found capable of things like herself.' Ibid., also cites Cicero, *De amicitia*, XIV, 50: 'For there is nothing more eager or more greedy than nature for what is like itself.'

115 Bandinucci, *The Life*, p.13.

116 Domenico Bernini, *The Life*, p.106.

117 See Franco Mormando's English translation of Pier Filippo's *The Vita Brevis of Gian Lorenzo Bernini* in Domenico Bernini, *The Life*, pp 237–41.

118 ibid., p.239. For the transcription of the original text, see Audisio, pp 26–44, n.55.

119 On the biblical significance of Bernini's depiction of David with sealed lips, see Irving Lavin, 'The Silence of Bernini's *David*', *Artibus et historiae*, vol. 79 (2019), pp 11–21.

120 Wittkower, *Gian Lorenzo Bernini*, no.17: 'Both [Baldinucci and Domenico Bernini] report that Bernini worked the face before the mirror and that Cardinal Maffeo Barberini on some occasions held it for him. Most likely they heard the story from Bernini himself, and if it is true – and there is no reason why it should not be – it must have happened before 6 August 1623 (Barberini's accession to the papal throne).'

121 As underscored by Lavin, 'The Silence of Bernini's *David*', pp 13 and 17, the *David* was begun on 8 July 1623 and completed by 3 January 1624, while Cardinal Maffeo Barberini was elected pope on 6 August 1623.

122 See Maria Antonietta Visceglia, 'Il cerimoniale come liguaggio politico' in *Cérémonial et rituel à Rome (XVIe–XIXe siècle)*, Collection de l'École française de Rome, Rome, vol.231 (1997), pp 117–76. The hierarchical stratification of papal Rome witnessed a multiplication of distinctive symbols that had not only religious and symbolic meanings, but also represented attributes of honor and power: from the vestments, to the color of the vestments, the use of the rochet by the upper echelon of the curia, the concession of red tassels of a cardinal's hat, the ribbons allowed to decorate their horses, the authority of carrying a parasol (*umbraculum*) and having a second carriage. As for Urban VIII's attention to such symbols, the author discusses the pope's changes to court ceremonials so as to benefit his nephew, Taddeo Barberini, with the conferment on 28 April 1631 of the title of Prefect of Rome. To this end, on 21 March 1632, he reinstated the ritual and consignment of the Golden Rose which, among other privileges, gave Taddeo the right to *precedenza*; a privilege so important

that it engendered a political crisis when the Venetian ambassador, having twice crossed his path, failed to stop his carriage, thus negating him the privilege of *right of way*. Ibid., p.160, the author specifies that this custom, which was initiated out of courtesy, eventually became a symbol of the 'qualità delle persone'. Patricia Waddy, *Seventeenth-Century Roman Palaces: Use and the Art of the Plan*, New York and Cambridge, MA, 1990, Appendix 3, pp 331–41, publishes an incomplete draft of the biography of Taddeo Barberini written by his older brother Francesco where, on p.336, the diplomatic incident with the Venetian ambassador is described. See also *Specchio di Roma barocca: una guida inedita del XVII secolo*, Joseph Connors and Louise Rice (eds), Rome, 1990, p.146, where the anonymous French author of this guide, dated between 1677 and 1681, notes: 'Les cérimonies qui s'observent dans la rencontre de ces carrosses dont les uns s'arrestent par honneur pour laisser passer les autres seroient quelque chose de trop long pour vouloir icy les décrire.'

123 Peter Burke, *The Historical Anthropology of Early Modern Italy: Essays on Perception and Communication*, Cambridge, 2005 [orig. 1987], p.171, citing the Archivio di Stato, Rome, Camerale II, Ceremoniali, busta 2, 'Memoriale delle Cerimonie di Corte' (1685), pp 1–4.

124 Like everyone in Baroque society, Bernini was all too aware of the etiquette relating to meeting and accompanying a visitor and the relative esteem the host demonstrated for the guest by such behavior. Chantelou informs us that while in Paris, Bernini accompanied an important guest, such as Colbert, 'as usual as far as the end of the salle'. That this did not occur when Michel Le Tellier, Minister of State, and M.de Lionne departed after a visit on 12 August 1665, is significant not only because it was an indication of what Bernini thought of the two gentlemen, but also because Chantelou found it worthy of mention: 'Then they left and he did not accompany them out.' See Chantelou, *Diary*, pp 57 and 116; idem, *Journal*, pp 73 and 116. A second instance occurred when the members of the Académie de peinture came to pay homage to Bernini. When it was time for their departure, he failed to accompany them out and his behavior shocked and displeased his visitors. See Mirot, p.64/224. Conversely, according to a letter written by Mattia de' Rossi, Bernini received a welcoming gesture from the queen that, according to those at court, was not shown to either princes or ambassadors, as she went to greet him 'sino l'ultima anticamera accanto la sala' ('all the way to the last antechamber next to the hall'). Ibid., p.46/206. On the highly codified, courtly etiquette Bernini would witness while in Paris, see Del Pesco, 'La légation de Flavio Chigi à Paris en 1664', especially pp 500–501, for even the number of steps taken by the king or the papal legate when accompanying out a guest were a sign of the relative consideration they were held in. When, after the audience of 29 July 1664, the king walked the papal legate, Cardinal Flavio Chigi, to the door of the room, he showed his exceptional respect by 'deigning to take one step outside the royal chamber'. This etiquette applied to women, as well as men. See Waddy, pp 27–8.

125 Francesco Sestini, *Il maestro di camera*, Rome, 1646, p.202: 'sapendo ciascuno il luogo che gli tocca'. See also Marin Olin, 'Diplomatic Performance and the Applied Arts in Seventeenth-Century Europe' in *Performativity and Performance in Baroque Rome*, Peter Gillgren and Mårten Snickare (eds), London and New York, 2012, pp 25–45, and Waddy, pp 1–13, pp 61–2, and Appendix I, pp 325–8: 'Nota dei trattamenti soliti usarsi in Roma verso gli Ambasciatori del Serenissimo Granduca di Toscana, et di quelli, che da loro si usano verso gli altri.'

126 Vasari, *Lives*, p.270.

127 Baldinucci, *The Life*, p.76.

128 Domenico Bernini, *The Life*, p.175.

129 See Alan Thacker, '*Loca Sanctorum*: The Significance of Place in the Study of the Saints' in *Local Saints and Local Churches in the Early Medieval West*, Alan Thacker and Richard Sharpe (eds), Oxford, 2002, p.13. See also Livio Pestilli, *Picturing the Lame in Italian Art from Antiquity to the Modern Era*, London and New York, 2017, pp 35–63.

130 Rudolf and Margot Wittkower, *Born Under Saturn*, p.271. The anecdote is reported by Carlo Ridolfi, *Le meraviglie dell'arte, overo le vite de gl'illustri pittori veneti, e dello stato*, Venice, 1648, p.162.

131 Carlo Cesare Malvasia, *Felsina pittrice. Vite de' pittori bolognesi*, 2 vols, Giampietro Zanotti (ed.), Bologna, 1841 (orig. ed. 1682), II, p.273. Quoted by Tomaso Montanari, 'Bernini e Cristina di Svezia. Alle origini della storiografia berniniana' in *Gian Lorenzo Bernini e i Chigi tra Roma e Siena*, Siena, 1998, p.339, where the author assumes the event to have really taken place since Christina's visit to Guercino's studio, though omitted by Gualdo Priorato in his *Historia della sacra real maestà di Christina Alessandra regina di Svetia*, Rome, 1656, is confirmed by Bonaventura

Bisi's letter to Leopoldo de' Medici on 30 November 1655. But Bisi's comment '[Christina] Ha volsuto prima di partire conoscere il Guerzino da Cento e l'Albano, e con tutti si è mostrata cortesissima' merely corroborates the fact that Christina visited these artists in their studio. He does not, however, refer to the 'tale' that the monarch felt the need to touch Guercino's hand. Montanari returns to this anecdote on p.353 where he reinforces Baldinucci and Domenico Bernini's adherence to the *topos* of the 'divinità e della straordinarietà dell'artista' and the 'pari dignità tra artista e principe' discussed by Kris and Kurz in *Legend, Myth, and Magic in the Image of the Artist*.

132 Giovanni Della Casa, *Galateo*, Ruggiero Romano (ed.), Turin, 1975, XVI, pp 31–2: 'E quantunque il basciare per segno di riverenza si convenga direttamente solo alle reliquie de' santi corpi e delle altre cose sacre, nondimeno, se la tua contrada arà in uso di dire nelle dipartenze: – Signore, io vi bascio la mano –; o: – Io son vostro servidore –; o ancora: – Vostro schiavo in catena –, non dèi esser tu più schifo degli altri, anzi, e partendo e scrivendo, dèi e salutare e accomiatare non come la ragione ma come l'usanza vuole che tu facci, e non come si voleva o si doveva fare ma come si fa: e non dire: – E di che è egli signore? – o: – È costui forse divenuto mio parrocchiano, che io li debba cosí basciar le mani?' Burke, in discussing the seventeenth-century 'repudiation of ritual', misreads this passage by stating: 'his [Della Casa's] particular objection is to the appropriation of religious forms for secular purposes, to kissing the hands of nobles, for example, as if they were the relics of a saint or the consecrated hands of a priest'. All Monsignor Della Casa is advising is to behave according to local customs, even if contrary to one's rational beliefs.

133 See Soussloff, n.54, and, more recently, Mangone, *Bernini's Michelangelo*, for the numerous ways in which Bernini emulated his great predecessor.

134 There are countless examples of this practice but, just to mention two examples by Caravaggio, see his *Self-portrait as Bacchus*, from the painter's early career, and the late *David and Goliath*, both in the Borghese Gallery.

135 See the chronicler Giovanni Cambi, 'Istorie di Giovanni Cambi', in *Delizie degli Eruditi Toscani*, Ildefonso di San Luigi (ed.), Florence, 1785, XXI, p.203: '1504. Del mese di Giugnio 1504. si trasse il Giughante fatto dall'Opera, che lo fecie Michelangniolo [*sic*] Buonaroti Ciptadino Fiorentino, degnio Maestro più che nessuno altro ne' tenpi sua.' Cited initially by Johannes Wilde, 'Michelangelo and Leonardo', *The Burlington Magazine*, vol.95 (1953), pp 65–75, p.70, n.6, and subsequently by Rona Goffen, *Renaissance Rivals: Michelangelo, Raphael, Titian*, New Haven and London, 2002, p.122.

136 Irving Lavin, 'David's Sling and Michelangelo's Bow: A Sign of Freedom' in *Past–Present: Essays on Historicism in Art from Donatello to Picasso*, Berkeley, Los Angeles, and Oxford, 1993, pp 29–61, and Leonard Barkan, *Michelangelo: A Life on Paper*, Princeton and Oxford, 2011, pp 97–126.

137 Barkan, p.115.

138 Lavin, 'David's Sling', pp 33–4.

139 Janie Cole, 'Cultural Clientelism and Brokerage Networks in Early Modern Florence and Rome: New Correspondence between the Barberini and Michelangelo Buonarroti the Younger', *Renaissance Quarterly*, vol.60 (2007), pp 729–88, here pp 734–5.

140 During this time, the two men frequently exchanged ideas about art and artists as the cardinal was a member of the Congregazione della Fabbrica di San Pietro. See Schütze, *Kardinal Maffeo Barberini*, p.158 and pp 228–32. For Michelangelo the Younger's relationship with Maffeo Barberini, see Maria G. Masera, *Michelangelo Buonarroti il Giovane*, Turin, 1941.

141 In the 1622 preface to the *Rime* dedicated to the Cardinal Barberini, Michelangelo the Younger reminded his readers that he had consulted the manuscript versions of the poems in the Vatican Library. See *Rime di Michelagnolo Buonarroti Raccolte da Michelangnolo suo Nipote*, Florence, 1623: 'A i Lettori. Perche diverse rime di Michelagnolo Buonarroti e manuscritte e di stampa vanno attorno poco emendate, si fanno consapevoli i lettori che conferitosi il testo che de' suoi componimenti si conserva nella libreria vaticana, il quale in gran parte è di mano dell'autore, insieme con quanto di essi componimenti si trova appresso li suoi eredi & appresso altri in Firenze, se ne sono scelte le più opportune, e più risolute lezioni.'

142 Elena Lombardi, 'Michelangelo Buonarroti il Giovane e i suoi interessi per l'erudizione e l'araldica', Casa Buonarotti, 2012/01, p.6. The author also claims, p.6, n.22, that Michelangelo the Younger sojourned in Rome so long because, suffering from a problem with his kidneys, he trusted that a stay in a milder climate might help him. See https://www.casabuonarroti.it/

wp-content/uploads/2012/01/Michelangelo-Buonarroti-il-Giovane.pdf

143 Schütze, 'Nettuno' in *Bernini Scultore: La nascita del Barocco in Casa Borghese*, p.173, points out that, after Montalto's death, the commission was taken over by Scipione Borghese.

144 Rudolf Preimesberger, 'David' in Coliva and Schütze (eds), *Bernini Scultore: La nascita del Barocco in Casa Borghese*, p.210, explains that, with his *David*, Michelangelo had begun this process of 'story-telling', that is, with his 'giant' he had 'represented through the medium of sculpture not a "statue", rather a "story"; not David, but the clash between David and the Giant Goliath [who is] present although not visible' ('prima di tutto il "gigante" di Michelangelo di Piazza della Signoria, consiste nell'aver rappresentato nel *medium* della scultura non una "statua", bensì una "storia"; non David, bensì la lotta di David contro il gigante Golia, presente benché non visibile'). For Vasari and Borghini, who 'felt that less can be said about sculpture in the round than about paintings and reliefs', see Thomas Frangenberg, 'The Art of Talking about Sculpture: Vasari, Borghini and Bocchi', *Journal of the Warburg and Courtauld Institutes*, vol.58 (1995), pp 115–31.

145 Horace, *Ars poetica*, in *Satires, Epistles and Ars Poetica*, v. 148–52, pp 462–3: 'Ever he [the poet] hastens to the issue, and hurries his hearer into the story's midst, as if already known, and what he fears he cannot make attractive with his touch he abandons; and so skilfully does he invent, so closely does he blend facts and fiction, that the middle is not discordant with the beginning, nor the end with the middle.' Bernini, of course, had achieved the same concept in other statues such as the *Saint Lawrence*, the *Pluto and Proserpina*, and the *Apollo and Daphne*.

146 Alberti, 1977, p.72: 'Composition is that rule of painting by which the parts of the things seen fit together in the painting. The greatest work of the painter is not a colossus [as it is for the sculptor], but an *istoria*.' Michelangelo claimed that the closer a relief approximated painting, the worse a sculptural work it was. See *Due lezzioni di M. Benedetto Varchi*, Florence, 1549, p.154: 'Io dico, chela pittura mi par piu tenuta buona quanto piu va verso il rilievo, & il rilievo piu tenuto cattivo, quanto piu va verso la pittura.' Bernini shared his opinion in upholding the superiority of sculpture over painting in that the former renders things as in nature, three-dimensionally, while painting gives such an illusion on a two-dimensional surface and is, therefore, a lie. On Bernini's views on relief sculpture, see Steven F. Ostrow, '"Appearing to be what they are not": Bernini's Reliefs in Theory and Practice' in *Critical Perspectives on Roman Baroque Sculpture*, Anthony Colantuono and Steven F. Ostrow (eds), University Park, 2014, pp 164–84.

147 Alberti, p.77: 'The *istoria* will move the soul of the beholder when each man is painted there clearly shows the movement of his own soul . . . These movements of the soul are made known by movements of the body.' This concept was shared by many artists. Leonardo, for one, claimed as much: 'The good painter has to paint two principal things, that is to say, man and the intention of his mind. The first is easy and the second difficult, because the latter has to be represented through gestures and movements of the limbs.' Quoted by Johannes Nathan, 'Drawings and Sketches for Surviving or Documented Paintings' in *Leonardo da Vinci 1452–1519: The Complete Paintings and Drawings*, Frank Zöllner and Johannes Nathan (eds), Cologne, 2007, p.256, citing from Martin Kemp and Margaret Walker, *Leonardo on Painting*, New Haven and London, 1989, paragraph no. 388.

148 Barkan, pp 121–2: 'Indeed, with all the artistic, political, and personal urgencies that this project [the *David*] held for him [Michelangelo], it was imperative for the process of creating the final product to traverse a medium such as language, which, unlike visual art, could not be judged merely by the notion that it provided a transparent representation of reality. It also permits him, short of physical self-portraiture, to insert himself into the picture.'

CHAPTER 4

1 Plutarch, *Lives*, *Pericles*, Bernadotte Perrin (trans.), III, Cambridge, MA, 1916, p.3.

2 ibid., p.5.

3 Plutarch, *Lives*, *Timoleon*, Bernadotte Perrin (trans.), VI, Cambridge, MA, 1918, p.261. See also Christopher Gill, 'The Question of Character-Development: Plutarch and Tacitus', *The Classical Quarterly*, vol.33 (1983), pp 469–87, here p.472.

4 Plutarch, *Lives*, *Pericles*, pp 5–7. For the sake of consistency within my text, in this quotation I have altered the name of Phaedias to Phidias.

5 It should be noted, however, that Plutarch also states in *Cimon*, 4: 'Now Polygnotus was not a mere artisan, and

did not paint the stoa for a contract price, but gratis, out of zeal for the welfare of the city, as the historians relate.' As pointed out by Eva C. Keuls, *Plato and Greek Painting*, Leiden, 1978, p.145: 'the painter is not "banausic" and therefore ideally should not work for pay'. It is also important to note that from Plutarch's statement one gathers that even poets are considered, to some extent, manual executants, despite the oft acclaimed Virgilian 'numine afflatur' (divine inspiration) (*Aeneid*, VI, 50). This is an indication that by the first century AD poets were not considered on a par with philosophers.

6 Lucian, *The Dream, or Lucian's Career*, A.M. Harmon (trans.), Cambridge, MA, 1967, 9, p.223. Ranuccio Bianchi Bandinelli, 'L'artista nell'antichità classica' in *Artisti e artigiani in Grecia. Guida storica e critica*, Filippo Coarelli (ed.), Rome and Bari, 1980 [originally published as 'Zur gesellschaftliche Stellung des bildenden Künstlers in der griechischen Klassik' in *Erlanger Forschungen*, vol.23 (1974), pp 5–25], pp 51–73, here pp 56–7, specifies, however, that Lucian also recognises that in the work of a great artist/artisan there is something that goes beyond the manual activity that achieves a 'poetic' level that moves the soul of the viewer. See Lucian, *The Dream*, 8. Lactantius (*c.*250 – *c.*325), *The Divine Institutes*, II, 2, p.42, who states that Seneca maintained as much: 'Seneca, therefore, rightly says in his moral treatises: They worship the images of the gods, they supplicate them with bended knee, they adore them, they sit or stand beside them through the whole day, they offer to them contributions, they slay victims; and while they value these *images* so highly, they despise the artificers who made them.' See Coarelli, *Artisti e artigiani in Grecia*, p.XIV.

7 Bernhard Schweitzer, 'L'artista figurativo' in Coarelli, *Artisti e artigiani in Grecia*, pp 25–47, here pp 42–3; originally published as 'Der bildende Künstler und der Begriff des Künstlerischen in der Antike' in *Zur Kunst der Antike*, Ausgewälte Schriften, vol.I, Tübigen, 1963, pp 18–40.

8 Aristotle, *Rhetoric*, in *The Complete Works of Aristotle*, 2 vols, Jonathan Barnes (ed.), Princeton, 1985, II, Book I, 9, 30, p.2176. See also Michel Austin, 'Le attività economiche nella Grecia antica' in Coarelli, *Artisti e artigiani in Grecia*, pp 237–49, here pp 242 and 247, orig. published as *Economies et sociétés en Grèce ancienne*, Paris, 1972, pp 22–31 and 125–8. As Austin reminds his readers, pp 242–3, even though this mentality may not reflect the view of people who had to earn their living by their craft, the only real sources we have to judge the classical world come from the hegemonic aristocratic class. For example, there are only very few sources that express any antagonistic views for the fifth century, such as Herodotus.

9 Schweitzer, p.45.

10 Valerius Maximus, *Memorable Doings and Sayings*, 2 vols, D.R. Shackleton Bailey (trans.), Cambridge, MA, 2000, II, 8, 14.6, pp 273–5: 'Glory has sometimes been sought even by men of note from the lowliest materials. For what was C. Fabius about, a citizen of the highest nobility, when he painted the walls in the temple of Welfare which C. Junius Bubulcus had dedicated and inscribed his name thereon?' See Filippo Coarelli, 'Cultura artistica e società' in *Storia di Roma*, 7 vols, Arnaldo Momigliano and Aldo Schiavone (eds), Turin, 1990, II. 1, p.168.

11 Pliny the Elder, *Natural History*, 10 vols, H. Rackham (trans.), Cambridge, MA and London, 1984, XXXV.vii, 20, p.275: 'Next in celebrity [after Fabius Pictor] was a painting by the poet Pacuvius in the temple of Hercules in the Cattle Market. Pacuvius was the son of a sister of Ennius, and he added distinction to the art of painting at Rome by reason of his fame as a playwright. After Pacuvius, painting was not esteemed as handiwork for persons of station.' See Coarelli, 'Cultura artistica e società', p.168. Idem, in *Artisti e artigiani in Grecia*, pp VII–XXX, rightly cautions the reader to be mindful of the cultural and social changes that occurred across various centuries (ideas held in classical Greece were not necessarily similarly upheld in Hellenistic Greece, Republican Rome, or Imperial Rome), who expressed those ideas (philosophers, playwrights, historians), or to ascribe modern ideas to classical texts ('work' in its abstract sense did not exist for the Greeks: what existed for them were specific types of work or, better, trades, i.e., *téchnai*).

12 Danièle Alexandre-Bidon and Didier Lett, *Children in the Middle Ages: Fifth–Fifteenth Centuries*, Jody Gladding (trans.), Notre Dame, 1999, p.38 and n.24, p.143. In fact, even child slavery was condoned for practical reasons. In the sixth century, Cassiodorus (*c.*485 – *c.*495) wrote: 'Slavery is not a result of their captivity but of their freedom: their parents sell them, naturally, because they stand to profit by their servitude. And, in truth, they are, without doubt, better off as slaves, if they are thus transferred from work in the fields to domestic work in the city.' Cassiodorus, *Variorum liber*, 8, 33, Theodor Mommsen (ed.), Berlin,

1894. Jacques Paul Migne, *Patrologia Latina*, Paris, 1865, LXIX, cols. 764: 'Præsto sunt pueri ac puellæ, diverso sexu atque ætate conspicui, quos non facit captivitas esse sub pretio, sed libertas; hos merito parentes vendunt, quoniam de ipsa famulatione proficiunt. Dubium quippe non est, servos posse meliorari, qui de labore agrorum ab urbana servitia transferuntur.'

13 Leonardo da Vinci, *Il trattato della pittura*, Codice Vaticano Urbinate 1270: '32. Differenza tra la pittura e la scultura. Tra la pittura e la scultura non trovo altra differenza, senonché lo scultore conduce le sue opere con maggior fatica di corpo che il pittore, ed il pittore conduce le opere sue con maggior fatica di mente. Provasi così esser vero, conciossiaché lo scultore nel fare la sua opera fa per forza di braccia e di percussione a consumare il marmo, od altra pietra soverchia, ch'eccede la figura che dentro a quella si rinchiude, con esercizio meccanicissimo, accompagnato spesse volte da gran sudore composto di polvere e convertito in fango, con la faccia impastata, e tutto infarinato di polvere di marmo che pare un fornaio, e coperto di minute scaglie, che pare gli sia fioccato addosso; e l'abitazione imbrattata e piena di scaglie, e di polvere di pietre. Il che tutto al contrario avviene al pittore, parlando di pittori e scultori eccellenti; imperocché il pittore con grande agio siede dinanzi alla sua opera ben vestito e muove il lievissimo pennello co' vaghi colori, ed ornato di vestimenti come a lui piace; ed è l'abitazione sua piena di vaghe pitture, e pulita, ed accompagnata spesse volte di musiche, o lettori di varie e belle opere, le quali, senza strepito di martelli od altro rumore misto, sono con gran piacere udite.' Cennini's *Libro dell'arte*, of about 1400, proves that such sartorial considerations were frequently quoted in fifteenth-century Florence: 'And let me tell you that doing a panel is really a gentleman's job, for you may do anything you want to with velvets on your back.' Cennino D'Andrea Cennini, *The Craftsman's Handbook*, Daniel V. Thompson Jr. (trans.), New York, 1960, p.CXLV, p.91. See also Sarah Blake McHam, *Pliny and the Artistic Culture of the Italian Renaissance: The Legacy of the 'Natural History'*, New Haven and London, 2013, p.86.

14 For Lapo da Castiglionchio's translation of Lucian's piece, see David Marsh, *Lucian and the Latins: Humor and Humanism in the Early Renaissance*, Ann Arbor, 1998, p.3. A Latin translation of Lucian's complete works was published in Basel and Saumur in 1619.

15 Lucian, *The Dream*, pp 219–21.

16 ibid., p.221.

17 ibid., p.225.

18 ibid., p.227.

19 ibid.

20 Filippo Baldinucci, *Vita del Cavaliere Gio. Lorenzo Bernino, scultore, architetto, e pittore*, Florence, 1682, p.69: 'Fece anche sempre della medesima grande stima, di che diede aperti segni; in prova di che mi basterà dire, che la prima volta, che la Maestà della Regina di Svezia volle fargli l'onore di andare a vederlo operare nella propria Casa, egli la ricevette con quell'Abito medesimo grosso, e rozzo, col quale soleva lavorare il marmo, che per esser l'Abito dell'Arte stimavalo egli il più degno, con che potesse ricevere quella gran Signora, la quale bella finezza essendo di subito penetrata dal sublime ingegno di quella Maestà, non solo gli accrebbe concetto dello spirito di lui, ma fece sì che ella medesima, in segno pure di stima dell'Arte, volesse toccare l'Abito stesso con le sue proprie mani.'

21 Bernardo De Dominici, *Vite de' pittori, scultori ed architetti napoletani*, 3 vols, Naples, 1742–5, III, p.535: 'All'Ammiraglio Binchs [*sic*] fece ancora alcuni belli rametti ben faticati, e con diligenza dipinti, e per ricevere quel Signore, si fece una veste da camera di tela d'oro, con berrettone lungo consimile, e con fiocco d'oro e allora che quello capitò finse non aver saputo nulla di sua venuta; e ciò fece per l'ofanità di riceverlo in tal modo.'

22 See Livio Pestilli, *Paolo de Matteis: Neapolitan Painting and Cultural History in Baroque Europe*, Farnham, 2013, pp 146–8.

23 Anne de Thoisy-Dallem, 'L'apparat de l'intimité ou la robe de chambre masculine du temps de sa splendeur' in *Habits. Modes et vestiaire masculin des XVIIIe et XIXe siècles*, exh.cat., Toulon, Villa Rosemaine, Serge Liagre (ed.), Toulon, 2013, pp 26–33. See also James Clifton, 'Paolo de Matteis's *Allegory of the End of the War of the Spanish Succession*' in *Fortunata Neapolis: Kunst- und Kulturtransfer zwischen Neapel, Wien und Mitteleuropa*, Sebastian Schütze (ed.), Berlin and Boston, 2020, pp 1–16.

24 ibid. Nicolas de Largillière's portrait of Charles Le Brun (1686) and Pierre Mignard's self-portrait (1696) were both displayed at the French Royal Academy. For these portraits, now at the Louvre, and comments, see Clifton, p.7.

25 Pliny, XXXV, 85.

26 It must be emphasised that in classical Greece slaves, metics, citizens, laborers, and architects were for the most part paid equally in a per diem or piecework manner, as documented for the work on Athens'

Erechtheion. See Coarelli, *Artisti e artigiani in Grecia*, pp xxiii–xxiv.

27 Pliny, XXXV, 120, pp 348–9: 'Another recent painter was Famulus, a dignified and severe but also very florid artist; to him belonged a Minerva who faced the spectator at whatever angle she was looked at. Famulus used to spend only a few hours a day in painting, and also took his work very seriously, as he always wore a toga, even when in the midst of his easels. The Golden House was the prison that contained his productions, and this is why other examples of his work are not extant to any considerable extent.'

28 *The Oxford Classical Dictionary*, N.G.L. Hammond and H.H. Scullard (eds), Oxford, 1970, p.1080.

29 In the eyes of ancient societies, all artists remained *bánausoi*, artisans, craftsmen, laborers. See Jacob Burkhardt, 'I greci e i loro artisti' in *Artisti e artigiani in Grecia*, pp 5–22.

30 Aelian, *Historical Miscellany*, Nigel G. Wilson (trans.), Cambridge, MA, 1997, IX, 11, p.291.

31 Pliny, XXXV, 62–63, pp 307–9.

32 ibid.

33 See Bianchi Bandinelli, p.56.

34 Hans Lauter, 'La posizione sociale dell'artista figurativo nella Grecia classica' in Coarelli, *Artisti e artigiani in Grecia*, p.127, points out that the view Greek society had of artists changed from the time of Alexander the Great and the Diadochi, as they became court artists and their art the object of scientific analysis, such as Polycleitus' *Kanon*.

35 While there is no work that focuses on artists' or craftsmen's garments, there are poems and documents that focus on the way the Lombards dressed in the seventh and eighth centuries, as well as the way individuals dressed *à la mode* in the twelfth and thirteenth centuries. In all cases, garments were seen as the reflection of an attitude that was both cultural and moral. See Maria Luisa Meneghetti, '"Nutz. En ma chamiza": Idéologie et métaphor vestimentaire dans la poésie des troubadours' in *Micrologus, Le corps et sa parure/The Body and its Adornment*, vol.XV, 2007, pp 157–72.

36 Pierre-Alain Mariaux, 'L'habit fait l'artiste? Remarques sur le vêtement de travail (XIIe–XVe siècles)' in *Micrologus, Le corps et sa parure/The Body and its Adornment*, vol.XV, pp 207–18.

37 ibid., pp 209 and 215.

38 On anonymity in the Middle Ages as 'fiction', see Tobias Burg, *Die Signatur: Formen und Funktionen vom Mittelalter bis zum 17. Jahrhundert*, Berlin, 2007, p.14. Heinrich Klotz, 'Formen der Anonymität und des Individualismus in der Kunst des Mittelalters und der Renaissance', *Gesta*, vol.15 (1976), pp 303–12, where the author states that the biblical source of the medieval restraint in boasting authorship is to be found in Saint Paul's letter to the Galatians 6:14, where Paul declares: 'As for me, the only thing I can boast about is the cross of our Lord Jesus Christ, through whom the world is crucified to me, and I to the world.' See also Albert Dietl, *Die Sprache der Signatur: Die mittelalterlichen Künstlerinschriften Italiens*, 4 vols, Berlin, 2009, I, pp 12–13 and ff. See also Enrico Castelnuovo, 'I volti dell'artista medievale: Molte domande, poche risposte', *Annali della Scuola Normale Superiore di Pisa*, vol.4 (2003), pp 3–10, and Peter Cornelius Claussen, *Magistri doctissimi Romani: Die römischen Marmorkünstler del Mittelalters*, Stuttgart, 1987, p.1, who specifies that 'die Künstler Roms, nicht nur die Marmorari, haben ihre Werke im Mittelalter häufig, wahrscheinlich in der Regel, signiert'. Maria Lidova, 'The Artist's Signature in Byzantium: Six Icons by Ioannes Tohabi in Sinai Monastery (11th–12th Century)' in *Opera. Nomina. Historiae*, vol.1 (2009), pp 77–98, discusses the eleventh-century Georgian monk Ioannes Tohabi in the monastery of Saint Catherine in Sinai who not only signed six icons but also included his self-portrait in one of them.

39 See Carl Goldstein, 'Rhetoric and Art History in the Italian Renaissance and Baroque', *The Art Bulletin*, vol.73 (1991), pp 641–52, here p.646.

40 Giorgio Vasari, *Lives of the Painters, Sculptors, and Architects*, 2 vols, Gaston du C. de Vere (trans.), New York and Toronto, 1996, II, pp 418 and 422. See Paul Barolsky, *Why Mona Lisa Smiles and Other Tales by Vasari*, University Park, 1991, pp 29–30.

41 For a comparable understanding of an ostentatious display of garments in thirteenth-century France, see Meneghetti.

42 Vasari, *Lives*, I, p.614.

43 Eugenia Paulicelli, 'Fashion, Gender and Cultural Anxiety in Italian Baroque Literature', *Roman Notes*, vol.50 (2010), pp 35–46, here p.37, quoting John Harvey, *Men in Black*, Chicago, 1995, p.12, says as much: 'In literature . . . "Meanings" of clothes are "constructions" that are organized into narratives.'

44 For Cristofano Gherardi, see Paul Barolsky, *Michelangelo's Nose: A Myth and Its Maker*, University Park and London, 1990, pp 17–18, and idem, *Why Mona*

Lisa Smiles, p.28. For Buffalmacco, idem, *Michelangelo's Nose*, pp 28–9.

45 Giovanni Boccaccio, *The Decameron*, G.H. McWilliam (trans.), London, 1995, VIII, 3, 6 and 9; Franco Sacchetti, *Il Trecentonovelle*, Turin, 1970, CLXI, pp 462–6. Vasari explicitly refers to these two authors in his *Life of Giotto*.

46 Vasari, *Lives*, I, pp 145–6.

47 ibid., II, pp 336–7.

48 ibid., p.338.

49 Barolsky, *Michelangelo's Nose*, p.17.

50 ibid., p.24.

51 Vasari, *Lives*, II, p.740.

52 ibid., p.746.

53 ibid, I, p.201.

54 ibid., pp 226–7.

55 ibid., p.454.

56 ibid., II, p.140.

57 ibid., p.450. Later in life, in 1550, Garofalo became totally blind. Ibid., p.451.

58 Giovan Pietro Bellori, *The Lives of the Modern Painters, Sculptors and Architects*, Hellmut Wohl (ed.), Alice Sedgwick Wohl (trans.), Cambridge, 2005; Giovanni Battista Passeri, *Vite de' pittori, scultori ed architetti che hanno lavorato in Roma morti dal 1641. Fino al 1673*, Rome, 1772; Lione Pascoli, *Vite de' pittori, scultori, ed architetti moderni*, Valentino Martinelli and Alessandro Marabottini (eds), Perugia, 1992. See Joseph Connors' review of Baglione, Passeri, and Pascoli's new editions published between 1992 and 1995 in the *Journal of the Society of Architectural Historians*, vol.57, no.4 (1998), pp 469–71.

59 Passeri, pp 101–2 and 110.

60 ibid., pp 215–16: 'Si trattò sempre con civiltà nel vestire, ma non con maniere vane, e smoderate, rendendosi sempre riguardevole, e degno d'ogni rispetto.' Ibid., p.298: 'Vestì sempre nobilmente, ma con moderatezza, e nel praticarlo si rese grato, desiderabile, amorevole, cortese.'

61 Bellori, *The Lives*, pp 205 and 365.

62 ibid, p.185. See also Norman E. Land, 'Renaissance Ideas About Self-Portrayal', *Source: Notes in the History of Art*, vol.20 (2001), pp 25–7.

63 Bellori, *The Lives*.

64 ibid., pp 185 and 95.

65 ibid., p.95.

66 ibid.

67 ibid.

68 ibid.

69 ibid. On the possible causes of the friction between the brothers, see Hellmut Wohl's comments in Bellori, *The Lives*, p.112, n.130.

70 ibid., p.122.

71 ibid., p.95.

72 Joseph Connors, review of Lione Pascoli, *Vite de' pittori, scultori ed architetti moderni*, Valentino Martinelli and Alessandro Marabottini (eds), Perugia, 1992, in *Journal of the Society of Architectural Historians*, vol.57 (1998), pp 469–71, here p.469.

73 For Pascoli's epithet, see Connors, p.471.

74 Pascoli, p.151: 'Amava estremamente la pulitezza, e vestiva nobilmente.'

75 ibid., p.515: 'Vestiva civilmente, e quasi sempre di nero, e stava sulla biancheria piucchè in altra cosa.'

76 ibid., p.582: 'Vestiva assai civilmente, ed assai civilmente ancora si trattava.'

77 ibid., p.594: 'Vestiva assai civilmente, e per lo più di nero, ed avea genio particolare di trattar colla nobiltà.'

78 ibid., p.679: 'Vestiva assai civilmente, ed assai civilmente si trattava alla mensa.'

79 ibid. For Gimignani, see p.742, for Odazzi, see p.830, and for Mazzuoli, see p.934: 'Vestiva civilmente senza però cercare attillatura, e lindezza . . . Ad ognuno però soggiungeva, che disdicea; perchè dalla maniera del vestire, siccome da qualsivoglia altre esterior portatura a gitto si scorge l'interiore dell'animo, che ne è dispotico regolatore.'

80 ibid., p.854: 'Vestiva nobilmente, ed accompagnando la nobiltà dell'abito con quella del tratto preso si sarebbe da ognuno che non ne avesse avuta notizia per un gran personaggio.'

81 Neither Baglione nor Bellori ascribe this particular trait to Sacchi. Rudolf Wittkower, *Gian Lorenzo Bernini: The Sculptor of the Roman Baroque*, London, 1966, p.236, suggests that Sacchi, who died in 1661, saw the first large model (1660) of the *Cathedra Petri* – which was smaller than the final project – and criticised it as too small. No other source relates this story. Like many other anecdotes, this one, too, is most likely a fabrication Pascoli included to embellish his narrative. If not fabricated altogether, the critique was passed on to Pascoli by word of mouth and omitted in all other sources.

82 Pascoli, p.75: 'Non fu molto amico degli altri professori, criticar solea l'opere di tutti, e le sapeva criticare. Imperocchè conoscendo i valentu'uomini ciocchè essi san fare, conoscono eziando ciocchè si fa bene, o male dagli altri. Trattava pochissimo generalmente con loro,

e niente col Bernini, con cui avea avuto qualche non leggier contrasto. Volle questi nulladimeno invitarlo a veder prima, che si scoprisse la magnifica cattedra da lui fatta in S. Pietro per sentirne il parere; ed ito a prenderlo a casa colla carrozza, andovvi egli in farsetto, in berretta, ed in pianelle; nè vi fu modo, tuttochè avvertito ne fosse, che in altra forma si volesse vestire. Ciò però ei non fece senza misterio; perchè era assai destro, ed accorto, e non operava mai a caso. Ma comecchè generalmente si dicesse, che fosse disprezzo, non si potè saper mai il suo vero fine; perchè ricusò sempre di dirlo.'

83 Rosita Levi Pisetzky, *Storia del costume in Italia*, 5 vols, Milan, 1966, III, p.15.

84 ibid., p.402: 'Vestì sempre si nero, e quasi alla spagnuola, ma con parrucca, e basette.'

85 Passeri, pp 349–50. Levi Pisetzky, III, p.127.

86 Giovanni Baglione, *Le vite de' pittori, scultori et architetti dal pontificato di Gregorio XIII fino a tutto quello d'Urbano VIII*, Rome, 1649, p.147: 'Costui faceva del bell'humore, e voleva andar sempre vestito alla Francese, benche egli non fusse mai stato in Francia, nè sapesse dire una parola di quel linguaggio . . . cosa da ridere di questo humore, che nelle apparenze riponesse gli habiti della virtù.'

87 Paulicelli, p.36. In fact, being a sympathiser of the Spanish nation and having been convinced on one occasion to go about town dressed *alla francese*, Francesco Albani repented having done so since he had repeatedly considered features of the French style 'capricious and variable'. See Carlo Cesare Malvasia, *Felsina pittrice. Vite de pittori bolognesi*, Bologna, 1678, II, p.177: 'Essendo egli [Albani] di affezione Spagnuolo, tanto un giorno aver preso a dire, e a persuaderlo l'accorto Giacinto Campana, che l'avea fatto uscir fuore vestito di nuovo alla Francese a suo dispetto, quando s'era impegnato a mille volte giurare, che mai quelle capricciose ed instabili usanze avria seguito.'

88 Giovanni Sonta Pagnalmino, *Della carrozza da nolo: overo del vestire, & usanze alla Moda*, Milan, 1648, p.5: 'veggo far leggiadra pompa di se stessa una manica di giovinotti di diverse parti d'Europa, vestiti, come hoggidì s'appella, Alla Moda'. For Pagnalmino's real identity, see Levi Pisetzky, III, p.317. Michel de Montaigne also mentions this national divide in his *Journal*. See *The Works of Michael de Montaigne comprising his Essays, Letters, and Journey Through Germany and Italy*, William Hazlitt (trans.), Philadelphia, 1849, p.635.

89 ibid., p.59: 'Dalle due Mode principali, testè avvertite, da quanto si è discorso alla Spagnuola, & alla Francese, mi s'apre il valico a detestare una stranezza, per non dir pazzia, d'alcuni cervelli Italiani, i quali senza veruna occasione, tanto s'affettionano, o dirò meglio, si connaturalizzano con una di queste due nationi, che scordantisi d'essere Italiani.'

90 Levi Pisetzky, III, pp 9–15.

91 *The Book of the Courtier by Count Baldesar Castiglione*, Leonard Eckstein Opdycke (trans.), New York, 1901, p.103.

92 ibid.

93 ibid.

94 Levi Pisetzky, III, p.371. See also Harvey.

95 Harvey, pp 48, 52–6.

96 ibid., p.72.

97 ibid., pp 76–7. Under Philip IV, in 1623, black clothing became official and obligatory for Spanish courtiers. Ibid., p.80.

98 Sisinio Poli was the nephew of Cardinal Fausto Poli whose funerary chapel was designed by Bernini and represents the artist's last architectural project – see Chapter 6, n.9. Their close family ties are proven by the fact that, when in 1639 Bernini married Caterina Tezio in the Church of San Tommaso in Parione, the ceremony was celebrated by Monsignor Gaudenzio Poli, Sisinio's older brother, who, as archbishop of Amelia, had to obtain special dispensation to officiate in this church. Sisinio is credited with having carried out Bernini's ideas as production or stage designer in Ottaviano Castelli's 1641 opera *Genoinda o Innocenza difesa*, even though the playwright himself, in a letter to Cardinal Mazarin, sarcastically mused how Sisinio had 'become a stage designer in a few days'. Frederick Hammond's *Music and Spectacle in Baroque Rome: Barberini Patronage under Urban VIII*, New Haven, 1994, especially pp 242 and 280: 'A questa commedia ha fatte due vedute di lontananza il nipote di monsignor Fausto, già diventato ingegnere di machine sceniche in pochi giorni, e sono l'una il sole cadente del Bernino, quale si predica da tutti all'Eminenza non averci parte nessuna benche visibilmente v'assista, e la seconda veduta della girandola presa da Montecavallo cred[uta] da S. Eminenza per inventione del nipote: alla quale credenza il linguac[ciuto] [Gian Lorenzo Bernini] dice haver cooperato che in dette machine tutta la spesa ha fatta Monsignor Fausto.'

99 See Levi Pisetzky, III, p.134 and pl. 161.

100 Other images of Bernini include the portrait drawing by Ottavio Leoni, from which he derived the print discussed in Chapter 1, the drawn self-portrait of disputed authorship in the Ashmolean Museum (*c.*1630), the incomplete painted portrait in the Prado Museum, also of about 1630, the drawing by a Bernini assistant in the Vatican Library, Carlo Pellegrini's portrait of *Bernini as David* in a Milan private collection, and Giovan Battista Castiglione's canvas of *c.*1634 in the Galleria di Palazzo Bianco in Genoa. For the portraits depicting Bernini, see Tomaso Montanari, *Bernini pittore*, Cinisello Balsamo, 2007; and, for an earlier discussion of the subject, see Maurizio Fagiolo dell'Arco, *Berniniana: Novità sul regista del Barocco*, Milan, 2002, pp 51–4, especially p.53, where the author discusses a portrait of Bernini in a private collection in which he is depicted as an old man. Attributed to Guillaume Courtois (il Borgognone), the painting depicts the artist wearing the usual black garment under a white rabat collar. A portrait drawing, probably executed by one of his assistants, that shows Bernini donning a more casual shirt is at the Istituto Centrale per la Grafica, Rome. See Rita Bernini, 'I disegni di Giovan Lorenzo Bernini nelle collezioni dell'Istituto Centrale per la Grafica: considerazioni sul volume Gualtieri-Corsini' in *Bernini Disegnatore: nuove prospettive di ricerca*, Sybille Ebert-Schifferer, Tod A. Marder, and Sebastian Schütze (eds), Rome, 2017, pp 59–74, here p.64, fig.8.

101 To the right of Gian Lorenzo is a portrait of a youth also depicted as a 'man in black'. For Irving Lavin, 'Bernini at St. Peter's: *Singularis in Singulis, in Omnibus Unicus*' in *St. Peter's in the Vatican*, William Tronzo (ed.), Cambridge, 2005, pp 11–243, here p.139 (fig.149, p.143), this person represents Luigi Bernini, Gian Lorenzo's younger brother, and sees an affinity with the portrait drawing of a young man in Windsor Castle (fig.150, p.143). Montanari, *Bernini pittore*, p.186, fig.26, rejects the identification of the Windsor drawing with Luigi. For the various types of topcoats worn at the time, see Levi Pisetzky, III, pp 139–52 and 351–60.

102 On François Cheron's medal, see Tomaso Montanari's entry, n.13 in *Gian Lorenzo Bernini: Regista del Barocco*, Maria Grazia Bernardini and Maurizio Fagiolo dell'Arco (eds), Geneva and Milan, 1999, pp 302–3. For Leclerc's engraving, see Pierre Cureau de la Chambre's *Eloge du Cavalier Bernin* (originally published in Paris in 1681), along with its *Préface pour servir à l'historire de la vie et des ouvrages du Cavalier Bernin* (originally read at the Académie française in Paris in 1685). The engraving appears at the beginning of both the *Préface* and the *Eloge*. On Cureau de la Chambre's ownership of Bernini's portrait and its encapsulation of the artist's characteristics, see *Eloge*, p.16: 'ce qui est tres-bien remarqué dans un Buste de luy nouvellement arrivé icy, qui est parlant, & comparable à tout ce qu'il y a de plus precieux & de plus achevé en ce genre-la.' From the object file documentation at the Philadelphia Museum of Art, it is clear that Catherine Hess and Andrea Bacchi, in preparation for the 2008 Bernini exhibition at the Getty Museum and National Gallery of Canada, Ottawa, also suspected, correctly in my view, that Leclerc's engraving reproduces the Fioriti bust. Subsequently, in the catalogue that was published in concomitance with the exhibition, the bust was listed among the lost works. See *Bernini and the Birth of Baroque Portrait Sculpture*, Andrea Bacchi, Catherine Hess, and Jennifer Montagu (eds), Los Angeles, 2008, p.296, L24. On the provenance of the bust from a private collection in the Channel Islands and, subsequently, the Victoria and Albert Museum, see Dean Walker, 'A Portrait Bust of Gian Lorenzo Bernini, and Notes from the 'Fifties', *The Sculpture Journal*, vol.4 (2000), pp 65–71. My thanks to curator Jennifer Thompson and departmental assistant Xena Wang for information on the sculpture and its provenance.

103 For a comparable dual approach to self-representation, see Poussin's self-portraits at the Louvre and the British Museum. My thanks to Steven F. Ostrow for pointing out this other example.

104 In a letter dated 17 August 1637, to Francesco I d'Este, Fulvio Testi quotes Bernini as stating that 'his craft is that of the chisel and not of the brush' ('l suo mestiere è dello scalpello, e non del pennello'). See Fulvio Testi, *Lettere*, 3 vols, Maria Luisa Doglio (ed.), Bari, 1967, II, p.742. Also cited by Montanari, *Bernini pittore*, p.63. The portrait of a young artist drawing in the Milan Koelliker collection LK0584 (see Montanari, *Bernini pittore*, p.46, fig.41) for the present writer is neither by Bernini nor does it represent Bernini. For a different assessment, see Delfín Rodríguez Ruiz, 'Gian Lorenzo Bernini, Roma y la Monarquía Hispánicha' in *Bernini: Roma y la Monarquía Hispánica*, Madrid, 2014, p.18, fig.4. Starting at least from November 1630 – by which time Urban VIII had put Bernini in charge of the refurbishing of the crossing of Saint Peter's and of

the *Baldacchino* over Saint Peter's tomb – the sculptor began signing documents as *architetto*. See Oskar Pollak, *Die Kunsttätigkeit unter Urban VIII: Die Peterskirche in Rome*, 2 vols, Hildesheim and New York, 1981, II, 42, p.37.

105 The comment is recorded in ms. ital. 2084, folio 131r at the Paris Bibliothèque Nationale. See George Charles Bauer, 'Bernini in Paris', in *An Architectural Progress in the Renaissance and Baroque: Sojourns In and Out of Italy: Essays in Architectural History Presented to Hellmut Hager on his Sixty-Sixth Birthday*, vol.1, University Park, 1992, pp 308–19, here p.312 and n.35, p.317. For the full Italian transcription of this document that complements the artist's *Vita Brevis* written by his oldest son, Pier Filippo Bernini (see Mormando, *Appendix I*), see Felicita Audisio, 'Lettere e testi teatrali di Bernini: una postilla linguistica' in *Barocco romano e Barocco italiano: il teatro, l'effimero, l'allegoria*, Marcello Fagiolo dell'Arco and Maria Luisa Madonna (eds), Rome, 1985, pp 42–3: 'mentre si facevano i fondamenti [for the *Baldacchino*] per situar le colonne si lavoraveno i suoi piedistalli di marmo per distinguerli dalla materia più nobile, com'è la scarpa dalla calzetta di seta'.

106 Domenico Bernini, *The Life of Gian Lorenzo Bernini*, Franco Mormando (ed. and trans.), University Park, 2011, p.175. Idem, *Vita del Cavalier Gio. Lorenzo Bernino*, Rome, 1713, p.104: 'Seppelo la Regina, & un giorno, mentre meno il Cavaliere si aspettava l'honore di quella visita, con numeroso corteggio venne a trovarlo a sua Casa. Egli, che si trovava appunto allora sul lavoro, la ricevè con quel medesimo habito indosso, che è proprio della professione, e benche agio non gli mancasse di poterselo togliere, e rivestirsi, rispose, a chì ciò fare lo consigliò, *Non avere abito più decoroso per ricevere una Regina, che pretende visitare un Virtuoso, che quello grossolano, e rozzo, che era proprio di quella virtù, che tale appresso il Mondo lo rendeva.* Il che penetrato dal sublime ingegno di quella gran Signora, non solo gli accrebbe concetto, mà in segno ancora di stima volle colle proprie mani toccarlo.'

107 Paul Fréart de Chantelou, *Diary of the Cavaliere Bernini's Visit to France*, Anthony Blunt (ed.), George C. Bauer (ann.), Margery Corbett (trans.), Princeton, 1985, p.169; idem, *Journal de Voyage du Cavalier Bernin en France*, Milovan Stanić (ed.), Paris, 2001, p.157, 6 September: 'Sur cela, il a appelé son homme et lui a demandé sa casaque avec laquelle il travaille et s'est mis à donner quelques coups au linge du petit *Christ* du signor Paolo [Bernini], pendant quoi Mme de La Baume est venue conduite par M. d'Albon, ce qui a fort déplu au Cavalier. Il a néanmoins continué.'

108 The *avviso* is taken from the diary of Carlo Cartari (Archivio di Stato, Rome, *Cartari-Febei*, 73–104). See Mark S. Weil, *The History and Decoration of the Ponte S. Angelo*, University Park and London, 1974, p.133: 'non sdegna di essere veduto lavorare; ma che bisogna farlo avvisare prima che si entra nella Camera terrena, che chiama il suo studio, et è à mano sinistra nel Cortile [of his palace]'. The avviso was previously published by Maria Cristina Dorati Da Empoli, 'Il Bernini e gli angeli di ponte San Angelo nel diario di un contemporaneo', *Commentari*, vol.17 (1966), pp 349–52.

109 See Chapter 5, n.101.

110 Franco Mormando, 'Gian Paolo Oliva: The Forgotten Celebrity of Baroque Rome' in *The Holy Name: Art of the Gesù: Bernini and His Age*, Linda Wolk-Simon (ed.), Philadelphia, 2018, pp 185–221, here p.197. Oliva's comments referred to Bernini's *Constantine*.

111 Donald Beecher and Massimo Ciavolella, 'A Comedy by Bernini' in *Gianlorenzo Bernini: New Aspects of His Art and Thought. A Commemorative Volume*, Irving Lavin (ed.), University Park and London, 1985, pp 63–113, here p.105: 'Signor si. Non guardate che io stia in questo habito; io ho tanta gran volontà d'imparare qualche cosa in questo genere, che per non dar gelosia al signor Gratiano, se bisognasse, volentieri sotto altro habito mi metterei a fare la colla, a dare di gesso, che sò io.' See Chapter 1, n.141.

112 Kristina Herrmann-Fiore, 'Il tema "Labor" nella creazione aritistica del Rinascimento' in *Der Künstler über sich in seinem Werk*, Matthias Winner and Oskar Bätschmann (eds), Weinheim, 1992, 245–92, here p.245. Irving Lavin, 'Bernini's Image of the Sun King' in *Past–Present: Essays on Historicism in Art from Donatello to Picasso*, Berkeley and Los Angeles, 1993, pp 138–200, here p.293, n.62, notes that the *locus classicus* in antiquity for the concept of labor as necessary to achieve glory is in Hesiod's *Works and Days*, lines 289–91, and, citing Rudolf Wittkower, 'The Vicissitudes of a Dynastic Monument: Bernini's Equestrian Statue of Louis XIV' in *Essays in Honor of Erwin Panofsky*, De Artibus Opuscula, vol.40, Millard Meiss (ed.), New York, 1961, p.507f, specifies that 'Bernini's notion of Glory at the apex of the mountain as the reward of virtue depends on a tradition stemming from Petrarch.'

113 Ernst Steinmann, *Die Porträtdarstellungen des Michelangelo*, Leipzig, 1913, p.16 and ff. and Tables 2–6. See also Herrmann-Fiore, pp 248–9. There are four versions of this painting: in Casa Buonarroti, the Louvre, the Biblioteca Ambrosiana, and in a private collection in Genoa.

114 Herrmann-Fiore, pp 252–3.

115 The engraving was published in *Prosopographia, sive virtutum animi, corporis, bonorum et externorum, vitiorum, et affectuum variorum*, *c*.1585–90. Herrmann-Fiore, p.251.

116 See Herrmann-Fiore, p.249 and fig.2. In the background of the print, climbing the Mountain of Virtue, are the personifications of Architecture, Painting, and Sculpture. Sculpture, as the most strenuous of the activities, wears an ox-hide.

117 The portrait in Casa Buonarroti, according to Pina Ragionieri, *Il volto di Michelangelo*, Florence, 2008 (cat.no.50), is mentioned in an inventory of 1684. Thus, one can be quite certain that it had been in the family possession well before Baldinucci wrote his Bernini biography in 1682. For the 'Descrizione della Galleria della Casa Buonarroti fatta nel 1684 o circa da Michelangelo di Leonardo di Buonarroto Buonarroti', see https://www.casabuonarroti.it/strumenti-di-ricerca/descrizione-buonarrotiana/

118 For a recap of the self-portrait and portraits of the artist, see Bernardini and Fagiolo dell'Arco, pp 295–304, and Montanari, *Bernini pittore*.

119 David R. Coffin, 'Pirro Ligorio on the Nobility of the Arts', *Journal of the Warburg and Courtauld Institutes*, vol.27 (1964), pp 191–210, here p.193.

120 *Hamlet* in *The Complete Works of Shakespeare*, Hardin Craig (ed.), Chicago, 1961, Act I, sc. 3, pp 908–9: 'Costly thy habit as thy purse can buy,/But not express'd in fancy; rich, not gaudy;/For the apparel oft proclaims the man.'

121 Filippo Baldinucci, *The Life of Bernini by Filippo Baldinucci*, Catherine Enggass (trans.), University Park, 2006 [orig. 1966], p.10; Domenico Bernini, *The Life*, p.98. See also Catherine Soussloff's 'Imitatio Buonarroti', *Sixteenth Century Journal*, vol.20 (1989), pp 581–602, and more recently the important, full-length study by Carolina Mangone, *Bernini's Michelangelo*, New Haven and London, 2020.

122 Léon Mirot, *Le Bernin en France: les travaux du Louvre et les statues de Louis XIV*, Paris, 1904, p.218, in a letter written by Mattia De' Rossi on 20 June 1665: 'Nella fossa che gira attorno il palazzo dove è la scarpa sotto il piano terreno, vi è un scoglio grande nel quale mostra essere fondato il sud.[detto] palazzo, e sopra detto scoglio dalle parte della porta principale in vece d'adornamento di doi colonne, vi ha fatto due grandi Ercoli, che fingono guardare il palazzo, alli quali il sig. caval. gli da un segnificato e dice Ercole è il rettrato della vertù per mezzo della sua fortezza e fatica, quale risiede su il monte della fatica che è lo scoglio detto di sopra, e dice chi vole risiedere in questa regia, bisognia che passi per mezzo della vertù e della fatica.' Bernini had already conceived of an entrance flanked by two statues of Hercules when in 1650 he designed a palace for Prince Niccolò Ludovisi on the site of Palazzo di Montecitorio. Mattia de' Rossi's painting (before 1655) of the building as envisioned by Bernini is now preserved in Palazzo di Montecitorio. See https://storia.camera.it/montecitorio/stampe-e-dipinti-del-palazzo-montecitorio/palazzo-ludovisi-montecitorio-roma-collezione. See also Anthony Langdon, *A Guide to Baroque Rome: The Palaces*, London, 2015, pp 186–9, and Anthony Blunt, *Guide to Baroque Rome*, London, 1982, pp 186–7. Bernini's equestrian statue of Louis XIV with the king at the summit of the Mountain of Virtue, of course, embodied this very concept. See Lavin, 'Bernini's Image of the Sun King', p.174. On this theme, see also Erwin Panofsky's classic study, *Hercules am Scheidewege, un andere antike Bildstoffe in der neueren Kunst*, Leipzig, 1930. For the full image of the medal, see Chapter 5, fig.5.1.

123 Chantelou, *Journal*, p.195; idem, *Diary*, p.216, 20 September: 'When we got back to the hôtel Mazarin we found Marigny, who had come to see the bust. He paid the Cavaliere a great many compliments and praised the ease with which he worked. He replied by quoting what Michelangelo had said one day to Ammannati, "I shit blood while I work."'

124 Vasari, *Lives*, II, p.697.

125 Baldinucci, *The Life*, p.72.

126 ibid., p.73.

127 I avail myself here of Charles Avery's translation of the Latin quotation in *Bernini: Genius of the Baroque*, London, 1997, p.274.

CHAPTER 5

1 Domenico Bernini, *Vita del cavalier Gio. Lorenzo Bernino*, Rome, 1713, claims that his father's trip began on 29 April. Cecil Gould, *Bernini in France: An Episode in Seventeenth-Century France*, London, 1981, p.1, citing a letter published by Stanislao Fraschetti in *Il Bernini: la sua vita, la sua opera, il suo tempo*, Milan,

1900, p.340, n.2, dated 25 April which reported Bernini was due to leave that day, as well as another by his assistant, Mattia de' Rossi, which states that on 29 April they were in Radicofani, is justifiably surprised by those who insist on quoting Domenico's incorrect date. Franco Mormando (ed.), *The Life of Gian Lorenzo Bernini by Domenico Bernini*, University Park, 2011, p.381, n.1, states that, although the actual date is unknown, he concurs that the journey probably began on 25 April, as stated by Bernini's earlier biographer, Filippo Baldinucci. See Baldinucci, *The Life of Bernini by Filippo Baldinucci*, Catherine Enggass (trans.), University Park, 1966, p.50. For the date of arrival in Paris, see Paul Fréart de Chantelou, *Journal de voyage du Cavalier Benin en France*, Milovan Stanić (ed.), Paris, 2001, pp 42–4.

2 Catherine Hess in her translation of Baldinucci's *Vita*, p.51: 'another of Bernini's pupils in sculpture'. In the Italian edition, p.52: 'suo giovane scultore'. For the correct spelling of Giulio's last name and his French origins, see Alfredo Marchionne Gunter, 'Giovan Lorenzo Bernini e Giulio Cartarè' in *Berniniana: Novità sul regista del Barocco*, Milan, 2002, pp 218–27, and Jacopo Curzietti, 'Sull'origine francese di Giulio Cartarè (1642–1699). Documenti e precisazioni in merito al nucleo familiare dell'ultimo allievo di Gian Lorenzo Bernini', *RIHA Journal*, no.0230, 1 October 2019. For Cartarè's involvement with the Académie de France, see idem, 'Gian Lorenzo Bernini e l'Académie de France à Rome. Una nota documentaria sul ruolo di Giulio Cartarè', *Valori Tattili*, 10/11 (2017–18), pp 45–9.

3 Fraschetti, p.340. Gould, p.20, states that in a dispatch of the papal nuncio, Carlo Roberti de' Vittori, the king sent 20,000 scudi, while Jules Guiffrey, *Comptes des Bâtiments du Roi sous le règne de Louis XIV*, 5 vols, Paris, 1881–8, I, p.61, records 30,000 'livres'.

4 Chantelou, *Journal*, p.9, quoting from Pierre Clément, *Lettres, Instructions et Mémoires de Colbert*, 7 vols, vol.V, *Fortifications, Sciences, Lettres, Beaux-Arts, Bâtiments*, Paris, 1868. Similarly, in a letter from Charles Perrault to Poussin in Rome which, however, was never delivered: 'le plus beau et le plus superbe palais du monde'. *Mémoires de ma vie*, Paris, 1909, pp 55–7. Louis XIV had already tried to entice Bernini to go to Paris in 1662. See Léon Mirot, *Le Bernin en France: les travaux du Louvre et les statues de Louis XIV*, Paris, 1904, pp 23–4, n.3, where he published a letter dated 27 October 1662, in the Bibliothèque Nationale, ms. Ital. 2083, p.175, in which Cardinal Antonio Barberini informs him that the King had a 'gran desiderio di viderla qua, per quel poco tempo tempo che V.[ostra] S.[ignoria] si compiacessi'.

5 On the 'droit de quartier' and a Frenchman's attitude towards the concept, see also *Specchio di Roma Barocca: Una guida inedita del XVII secolo*, Joseph Connors and Louise Rice (eds), Rome, 1990, p.XV. In brief, the French interpreted the right to diplomatic immunity not just for their palace but also for the neighborhood around it.

6 For an account of the events, see Ludwig von Pastor, *The History of the Popes*, 40 vols, London, 1940, XXXI, pp 94–9. See also Daniela Del Pesco, *Bernini in Francia: Paul de Cantelou e il 'Journal de voyage du Cavalier Bernin en France'*, Naples, 2007, pp 11–12, p.19, n.14, and 55, and idem, 'La légation de Flavio Chigi à Paris en 1664: mémoire et documents nouveaux (avec quelques observations sur le *Journal de voyage du cavalier Bernin en France* de Paul de Chantelou)', *Mélanges de l'École Française de Rome*, vol.123 (2011), pp 475–512, here pp 475–6. Mormando, Domenico Bernini, *The Life*, pp 376–7, gives a thoughtful evaluation of the claim of 'a secret papal concession at Pisa allowing the "loan" of Bernini to the French court' and the lack of a viable confirmation of the 'secret' agreement.

7 For Alexander VII's consent to have Bernini leave Rome for Paris, see the brief published in Domenico Bernini, *The Life of Gian Lorenzo Bernini*, Franco Mormando (ed. and trans.), University Park, 2011, p.190 (idem, *Vita*, p.123), and Baldinucci, *The Life*, p.50 (idem, *Vita del Cavaliere Gio. Lorenzo Bernino, scultore, architetto, e pittore*, Florence, 1682, p.44).

8 Already in 1662 Cardinal Barberini reassured Bernini that traveling such distances should not deter him since 'le posso dire per esperienza, che si possono i viaggi far con l'istesso commodo col quale sista [*sic*] in una stanza'. See Mirot, p.175. Bernini was also probably suffering from kidney stones. See Mattia de' Rossi's letter of 1 May 1665, written from Siena where he stated that 'il sig.[nor] cavaliere nostro' felt 'il suo solito dolore di reni'. Mirot, p.39.

9 Baldinucci, *The Life*, p.50. Paul Fréart de Chantelou, *Diary of the Cavaliere Bernini's Visit to France*, Anthony Blunt (ed.), George C. Bauer (ann.), Margery Corbett (trans.), Princeton, 1985, p.73: 'Then he repeated what Father Oliva had said about his journey: "If an angel came and told me that you would die on this journey I should still say: 'Go'."' Idem, *Journal*, p.85: '[Padre Oliva] lui a répété ensuite ce que ce père lui dit au sujet de son

voyage: *Se un Angelo venisse a dirmi che voi dovreste morir in quel viaggio, io direi nondimeno: andatevi.*'

10 Tod Marder, *Bernini and the Art of Architecture*, New York, London, and Paris, 1998, p.281, gives a slightly more positive interpretation of Bernini's visit to France by suggesting that it should perhaps be viewed as 'a diplomatic rather than an architectural embassy, a coda to Cardinal Flavio Chigi's visit and the subsequent Peace of Pisa'.

11 So, reportedly, stated Cardinal Sforza Pallavicino in Baldinucci, *The Life*, p.85. Chantelou, *Diary*, p.149: 'But he owed gratitude to God for making him the first man of the century in his art.' Idem, *Journal*, p.141.

12 See Chantelou, *Diary*, pp 310–11; idem, *Journal*, pp 268–9. George Charles Bauer, 'Bernini in Paris' in *An Architectural Progress in the Renaissance and Baroque: Sojourns In and Out of Italy; Essays in Architectural History Presented to Hellmut Hager on his Sixty-Sixth Birthday*, University Park, 1992, p.315.

13 Bernini became a 'pawn' in the power play between Louis XIV and Alexander VII. Marder, *Bernini and the Art of Architecture*, p.262, aptly claims: 'Bernini had become a trophy-architect. His services and his presence were symbols of power. In this context Alexander VII would concede the loan of his architect's services to the French king even if an Italian project were, by its very origin, doomed from the start.'

14 Georges Bernard Depping (ed.), *Correspondance administrative sous le régne de Louis XIV*, 4 vols, Paris, 1855, IV, p.548: 'il y a de certaines choses où l'architecture italienne ne se peut jamais accommoder avec la nostre.'

15 See, for example, Chantelou, *Diary*, pp 171–2 and 182–3; idem, *Journal*, pp 159–60 and 168–9. See also Marder, *Bernini and the Art of Architecture*, pp 267–8.

16 See Clément, V, p.501, 2 December 1664: 'Il me dit mesme ces paroles, que l'on y avoit fait plus d'observations et trouvé plus de deffauts qui'il ne falloit de pierres pour le bastir, et que quand il en feroit encore un autre, il en arriveroit autant, parce que les architectes de France ne manqueroient jamais de blasmer tout ce qu'il feroit, et avoient intérest de ne mettre pas en œvre le dessin d'un Italien.' See also Depping, pp 548–9, and Bauer, p.311.

17 On 6 September, for example, Bernini criticised the materials and the way Parisian masons built their walls, as compared to the Roman way. Chantelou, *Diary*, p.170; idem, *Journal*, p.158. Three days earlier, when Louis XIV asked if it was true what had been reported to him about Bernini's comment upon seeing the king's apartment ('Non ci sono qui stanze per uomini' or 'There are no rooms here to masculine taste'), Chantelou tried to cover up for the artist by saying that what Bernini had stated was either misunderstood or twisted to denigrate the artist. Chantelou, *Diary*, p.164; idem, *Journal*, p.154. For a list of Bernini's inopportune comments, see Gould, pp 56–9.

18 This is how Bernini expresses his idea to Chantelou, *Journal*, p.237, as to what the Louvre ought to be: 'È ben vero, a-t-il dit, *che le fabbriche sono i ritratti dell'animo dei principi.*' Idem, *Diary*, p.270.

19 Charles Perrault, typically adversarial to Bernini, states as much in his *Memoirs*: 'The Cavaliere paid no attention to detail, thinking only about making great theaters or festival halls, and taking no trouble over all the practicalities, all the constraints and all the arrangements of the necessary apartments, things which are innumerable and which demand a kind of commitment that the Cavaliere Bernini did not and could never have, owing to his quick and lively nature.' See Charles Perrault, *Memoirs of My Life*, Jeanne Morgan Zarucchi (ed. and trans.), Columbia, 1989, p.65. See also Stanić's introduction to Chantelou's *Journal*, pp 5–27, and Marder, *Bernini and the Art of Architecture*, p.265. Oddly enough, in Domenico Bernini's biography of his father the artist is quoted as having said that 'the praiseworthy architect is the one who knows how to combine the beauty of a building with the convenience and comfort afforded to its inhabitants'. See Mormando's comments in Domenico Bernini, *The Life*, p.117 and p.303, n.41, where the author points out as much. In Baldinucci's biography, instead, we are told that in architecture 'the highest merit lay not in making beautiful and commodious buildings, but in being able to make do with little, to make beautiful things out of the inadequate and ill-adapted, to make use of a defect in such a way that if it had not existed one would invent it'. This is not the only instance in which Bernini's reputed statements on art conflict with each other or seem at odds with his artistic practice. See Chapter 1.

20 Clément, pp 245–65.

21 In a letter to Colbert dated 24 June 1664, Benedetti pointed out how Italian and French architects could have learned from each other: 'Per fare dunque un buon misto, sarei di parere, che si dovesse scogliere il migliore dell'una e dell'altra maniera . . .' Mirot, p.179/19. See also Chantelou, *Journal*, p.350. Although this approach might sound as an absurd compromise that would only generate a pastiche, this is what

occurred when planning the *tiburio* (lantern) of the Milan Cathedral. Bramante, who had presided the jury, claimed that 'in less than an hour, by taking from this [project] something and from that [other] something else, we will be able to come up with one that will be just right'. ['Ma ben dico così, che se questi ingegneri volieno quando saremo readunati, li, inante a le V. Mag. in mancho de una hora, togliendo da questo una cosa, e da quella una altra, come ho detto di sopra, porremo fare uno, il quale starà bene.'] See Sabine Frommel, 'Zwischen Geniestreich und kollektiver Leistung: Gian Lorenzo Bernini Entwürfe für den Louvre' in *A Transitory Star: The Late Bernini and his Reception*, Claudia Lehmann and Karen J. Lloyd (eds), Berlin and Boston, 2015, p.91, citing Andres Lepik, *Das Architekturmodell in Italien 1335–1550*, Worms, 1994, p.55, n.72. The same recommendation was given to Brunelleschi after his design for the dome lantern of the Florence Cathedral was accepted in 1436. He was asked by the committee to incorporate 'what seems good and useful in other models and put into his, so that the lantern contain all the perfect parts'. Ibid.

22 Gould, p.12.

23 In a famous passage, Chantelou, *Journal*, pp 268–9, dated 18 October, Bernini unleashes his frustration with Colbert's concern with toilets and conduits. See below and n.30.

24 On 20 June, Bernini showed Louis XIV his new drawings for the Louvre. Flanking the main entrance to the palace, which rested on a mountain represented by a level of roughly hewn stones, Bernini had decided to replace the previous two columns with two giant sculptures of Hercules who seemed to be looking at the palace. The artist explained that their symbolic meaning was that of 'the portrait of virtue [achieved] through his strength and labor, which resides atop of the mountain of labor represented by the abovementioned rocks and said that he who wishes to reside in this royal palace must advance by the means of virtue and labor. This idea and allegory greatly pleased His Majesty, believing it was something grand and wise.' See Mirot, pp 57–8, 217–18, and Bauer, p.314. See Chapter 4, p.123 and n.122.

25 Chantelou, *Journal*, p.22. Bernini was not to be the only one to encounter such difficulties in Paris. Already under Francis I the Parisian guilds had opposed the 'importation' of Italian artists. Nikolaus Pevsner, *Academies of Art: Past and Present*, New York, 1973, p.82.

26 Mirot, p.50/210. See also Fraschetti, pp 354–5, n.2.

27 Sabine Frommel, 'Les projects du Bernin pour le Louvre, tradition italienne contre tradition française' in *Le Bernin et l'Europe*, Paris, 2002, pp 43–76, echoing Guglielmo De Angelis d'Ossat, 'Louis Le Vau, architetto berniniano suo malgrado' in *Gian Lorenzo Bernini e l'architettura europea del Sei–Settecento*, Gianfranco Spagnesi and Maurizio Fagiolo dell'Arco (eds), Rome, 1984, t.2, p.511ff., claims that even though Bernini's project remained on paper, some changes in French architecture would not have taken place without Bernini's presence in Paris. See also Marder, *Bernini and the Art of Architecture*, pp 261–72, and Anthony Blunt's *Postscript* to Chantelou, *Diary*, p.335, as well as Mirot, pp 260–75.

28 The final project is the result of a concerted effort by Louis Le Vau, Claude Perrault, and Charles Lebrun. Gil R. Smith, *Architectural Diplomacy: Rome and Paris in the Late Baroque*, Cambridge, MA and London, 1993, p.9: 'Courting Bernini for the next two years to bring LeVau into line, Colbert was ultimately able to set up a committee of architects more receptive to his dominion.' For a concise, if dated, narrative about the Louvre, Bernini's plans, and the final outcome, see Anthony Blunt, *Art and Architecture in France 1500–1700*, Hong Kong, 1999, pp 218 ff. See also Del Pesco, *Bernini in Francia*, p.65. On Bernini's adoption of some ideas developed in the drawings for the Louvre by Pietro da Cortona and Carlo Rainaldi, see Frommel, 'Zwischen Geniestreich und kollektiver Leistung', pp 71–94.

29 Stanić in Chantelou, *Journal*, pp 22–3. Mirot, p.276, points out how the French architects, led by Perrault, considered the abandonment of Bernini's Louvre project as a victory for their national art. The quotation about French architecture is taken from Voltaire's comments on Mansart's architecture. See Blunt, *Art and Architecture*, p.221. Having been asked for his opinion about two plans to complete the facade of the Duomo of Milan, in 1652 Bernini stressed the importance that, rather than focusing on the beauty of the single parts, the overall impact that an architectural project should have is one of '*meraviglia*' and '*stupore straordinario*'. See Maurizio Fagiolo dell'Arco, *Berniniana: Novità sul regista del Barocco*, Milan, 2002, p.187.

30 Chantelou, *Journal*, pp 268–9. The Italian word *coglione* (literally, testicle) is probably best translated as 'asshole'. In Chantelou's *Diary*, Margery Corbett's translation leaves Chantelou's *couillon* out by simply writing

'c—'. Del Pesco, *Bernini in Francia*, p.452, also records 'coglione' and on p.490, n.275, specifies that on fol. 532 of Chantelou's manuscript the word recorded is 'coüillon'. L. Lalanne's edition simply has the letter 'c'. Morgan Zarucchi, *Memoirs*, p.66, states that Perrault wrote *cocallon*, failing to consult Chantelou's original text and thus, while stating that the word *cocallon* is nowhere to be found in seventeenth-century dictionaries, translates the word as 'boaster'. Gould, p.108, writes 'bugger'.

31 Carlo Vigarani, agent of the Duke of Modena, was one of a number of influential Italians at the French court. Mirot, p.8/168: 'Vigarani, l'agent du duc de Modène à Paris et jadis chargé d'affaires à Rome, habile machiniste, qui montait les pièces à effet pour les fêtes de Versailles.'

32 Fraschetti, p.343: 'Temo grandemente che i grandissimi honori ricevuti al suo arrivo non le habbiano fatto fare una dichiaratione disavantaggiosa per lui, e troppo ardita su la grande fabrica del Louvre, e che per tal strada non habbia dato campo ai malevoli di nuocerlo appresso Sua Maestà havendo detto dal primo giorno, che bisognava abbattere tutto il Louvre se si havesse voluto fare qualche cosa di buono. Questo aggiunto a molte altre cose, sule quali egli ha trovato che dire fatte intendere al Re non le hanno fatto nissun buon servitio, e se poi ha egli cambiato di maniera di parlare vien creduto effetto de buoni avisi di Mr Cobert e non lascia d'essersi fatto gran danno. Haveva bisogno al suo arrivo di un buon consiglio, che non ha havuto, e parlo di cio con sicurezza, perché a Versaglia sò quello che da S. M[a] ne fu detto in presenza di cinquanta gran Signori dopo avermi honorato di domandarmi se lo havevo visto: Il Discorso terminò in dirmi che non voleva che il Bernino vedesse la festa di Versaglia, perchè lo haveva conosciuto in una sola meza hora, che havea parlato seco, per un'huomo prevenuto à non trovar niente in francia [*sic*] di ben fatto.'

33 Del Pesco, *Bernini in Francia*, p.17.

34 Anthony Blunt, *Art and Architecture in France 1500–1700*, London, 1982 [orig. 1953], pp 61–4. Hamish Alexander Drummond Miles, 'The Italians at Fontainebleau', *Journal of the Royal Society of Arts*, vol.119 (1971), pp 851–61. See also *Primatice maître de Fontainebleau*, exh.cat., Musée du Louvre, Paris, 22 September 2004 – 3 January 2005.

35 See Donald A. Rosenthal, *La Grande Manière: Historical and Religious Painting in France 1700–1800*, exh.cat., Memorial Art Gallery of the University of Rochester, 2 May – 26 July 1987, pp 46–51, and Livio Pestilli, *Paolo de Matteis: Neapolitan Painting and Cultural History in Baroque Europe*, Farnham, 2013, p.44.

36 ibid. Even after Bernini's return to Rome from France, one of the reasons why his statue of Louis XIV probably failed to please the patron was 'the professional jealousy of the French artists'. See Tod Marder, *Bernini's Scala Regia at the Vatican Palace*, Cambridge, 1997, p.212.

37 Johann Wolfgang Goethe, *Italian Journey (1786–1788)*, W.H. Auden and Elizabeth Mayer (trans.), San Francisco, 1982, p.147.

38 ibid., p.133. Goethe made a similar remark about Neapolitan art. See Chapter 1.

39 *The Diary of John Evelyn*, E.S. De Beer (ed.), Oxford, 2006, p.180, 18 May 1645: 'when on my Way, turning about to behold this one & yet glorious City, upon an Eminence of Ground I did not without some regret give it my last farewell'. Ibid., p.183.

40 *The Journal of Montaigne's Travels in Italy by Way of Switzerland and Germany in 1580 and 1581*, 3 vols, William George Waters (ed. and trans.), London, 1903, II, pp 163–4.

41 Thomas Dandelet, 'Spanish Conquest and Colonization at the Center of the Old World: The Spanish Nation in Rome, 1555–1625', *The Journal of Modern History*, vol.69 (1997), pp 479–511, here p.486.

42 On the negative impression Montaigne had of Rome's lack of an industrious sector class ('[T]his city has hardly any laborers and men who live by the work of their hands') and how this image of the Roman economy has shaped the dominant historical view until recently, see Renata Ago, 'Rome's Economic Life, 1492–1692' in *A Companion to Early Modern Rome, 1492–1692*, Pamela M. Jones, Barbara Wisch, and Simon Ditchfield (eds), Leiden and Boston, 2019, pp 184–98.

43 Michel de Montaigne, *The Complete Essays*, M.A. Screech (trans.), London and New York, 2003, p.1128.

44 On the concept of *natio/nationes* and its multiple shades of meaning in early modern Italy, see Chur Alexander Koller and Susanne Kubersky-Piredda, *Identità e rappresentazione. Le chiese nazionali a Roma, 1450–1650*, Rome, 2015.

45 On the legal definitions and status of foreigners in relation to the host city, see Irene Fosi, 'The Plural City: Urban Spaces and Foreign Communities' in *A Companion to Early Modern Rome*, pp 169–83, here p.173.

46 Koller and Kubersky-Piredda, *Identità e rappresentazione*, p.9..

47 On the international character of the curial notaries, see Laurie Nussdorfer, 'Notaries and the Accademia

di San Luca, 1590–1630' in *The Accademia Seminars: The Accademia di San Luca in Rome, c. 1590–1635*, Peter M. Lukehart (ed.), New Haven and London, 2009, p.59.

48 Peter Burke, *The Historical Anthropology of Early Modern Italy: Essays on Perception and Communication*, Cambridge, 2005, p.113: 'From the eleventh century, if not before, Italy – or at least, the many towns of the north and centre – was becoming what might reasonably be called a "notarial culture", with a high proportion of notaries in the population.' Nussdorfer, p.59, underscores the fact that, unlike most cities, Rome had civic or Capitoline notaries as well as curial notaries. Many of the foreign notaries worked as Curial notaries on the needs of ecclesiastics. Sixtus V made a radical change when he limited the number of Capitoline notaries to thirty and allowed them to sell their offices, 'thus initiating the process of turning a free and very loosely organized profession into a closed corporation of venal officeholders'.

49 Andreas Rehberg, 'Le comunità "nazionali" e le loro chiese nella documentazione dei notai stranieri (1507–1527)' in *Identità e rappresentazione,* Koller and Kubersky-Piredda (eds), pp 211–31, here p.211, quoting from Jean Lesellier, 'Notaires et archives de la Curie romaine (1507–1627): les notaires français à Rome', *Mélanges d'archéologie et d'histoire*, vol.50 (1933), pp 250–75. During this same period there were 519 Italian notaries, of which only 59 were Roman.

50 Fosi, 'The Plural City', pp 170 and 179.

51 The popes' desire to create seminaries for young clerics coming from parts of Europe threatened by the Reformation was mirrored by their wish to influence the arts and sciences, as well. See Susanne Kubersky-Piredda, 'Chiese nazionali fra rappresentanza politica e Riforma cattolica: Spagna, Francia e Impero a fine Cinquecento' in *Identità e rappresentazione*, pp 17–64, here p.18. Fosi, 'The Plural City', p.182: 'Subsequently, colleges were established for: the Greeks (1577); the English (1579); the Maronites, or Lebanese Christians (1584); the Scots (1600); and the Irish (1628).'

52 For papal efforts to educate young men from other European countries, see Paolo Broggio, 'L'*URBS* e il Mondo: Note sulla presenza degli stranieri nel Collegio Romano e sugli Orizzonti Geografici della "Formazione Romana" tra XVI e XVII secolo', *Rivista di storia della Chiesa in Italia*, vol.56 (2002), pp 81–120. For the Spanish monarchy's 'infiltration' of Roman society, see Dandelet, p.487. The 'Spanish nation' at this time comprised Iberia, the islands of Sardinia, Mallorca, Menorca, and the Indies. Irene Fosi, 'Non solo pellegrini: Francesi a Roma nella prima età moderna. Qualche esempio e osservazione', *Anabases*, vol.5 (2007), pp 137–48, points out how religious conversion or baptism of the offspring of artists' living in Rome was a factor that generated integration between locals and foreigners, as the latter, not infrequently, asked their Italian colleagues to act as godfathers or godmothers to their newly born.

53 On the international character of Rome, starting in the second half of the sixteenth century, and its role as the leading center where artists 'from the four corners of Europe' interacted, see Nicole Dacos, *Les peintres belges à Rome au XVI*[e] *siècle*, Brussels and Rome, 1964, p.63. See also Gilles Montègre, *La Rome des français au temps des lumières: Capitale de l'Antique et carrefour de l'Europe 1769–1791*, Rome, 2011, p.8.

54 Fosi, 'Non solo pellegrini', p.139: 'La cospicua presenza di nomi stranieri nei registi di diverse parrocchie romane è spia di un'integrazione non superficiale e occasionale che si rafforzava con la scansione dei più significativi riti di passaggio. Non sono neppure troppo rari i casi di stranieri che sceglievano padrini e madrine dei loro figli non fra i connazionali, ma piuttosto fra Romani, compagni di lavoro e vicini di casa, quasi per ricevere una sanzione ufficiale della avvenuta integrazione nella città ospite.' Despite this form of integration, Fosi, 'The Plural City', p.180, points out that for foreigners in Rome endogamy was 'the decisive factor in promoting both their integration and their original identity'. See also Christopher Johns, 'The Entrepôt of Europe: Rome in the Eighteenth Century' in *Art in Rome in the Eighteenth Century*, Edgar Peters Bowron and Joseph J. Rishel (eds), Philadelphia, 2000, p.35: 'Understanding these familial and professional networks and not underestimating the power of amity or enmity in Rome's artistic culture are absolutely essential to even a basic comprehension of how things worked. In sum, artists and the art industry (for such it was) occupied an important social and economic niche in Settecento Rome, and the cultural and artistic cosmopolitanism characteristic of the era began at a fundamental personal level.' For a partial list of eighteenth-century international, familial connections in Rome between Italian and foreign artists, see Johns, p.35, and Liliana Barroero and Stefano Susinno, 'Arcadian Rome, Universal Capital of the Arts' in *Art in Rome in the Eighteenth Century*, pp 62–3.

55 See Frits Scholten and Joanna Woodall, 'Netherlandish Artists on the Move' in *Art and Migration: Netherlandish Artists on the Move, 1400–1750*, Frits Scholten, Joanna Woodall, and Dulcia Meijers (eds), Leiden, 2014, pp 6–39.

56 Karel van Mander, *Het Schilder-Boeck*, Amsterdam, 1618 [1617], fol. 140. The *Lives* were incorporated in *The Book of Painters* as part of the six sections that comprise the volume. See also idem, *Le vite degli illustri pittori fiamminghi, olandesi e tedeschi*, Ricardo de Mabro Santos (ed. and trans.), Sant'Oreste, 2000, p.161, who interjects the name of the city 'Roma' in the phrase quoted that is not in the original Dutch edition: 'Visitò l'Italia e raggiunse la scuola universale della pittura – Roma – dove dedicò molto tempo al disegno, perfezionando soprattutto la resa delle figure e dei fabricati.'

57 Patrizia Cavazzini, *Painting as Business in Early Seventeenth-Century Rome*, University Park, 2008, pp 19 and 43, points out that by the end of the sixteenth century foreign artists found the absence of rules that restricted them from operating in Rome one of the attractions that brought them south. An equally important factor was that Netherlandish artists 'sought refuge in Rome from the wars in their country' and found in the Church's artistic enterprises hope for employment. Idem, 'Middle-Class Patronage, Collecting, and the Art Market' in *A Companion to Early Modern Rome, 1492–1692*, pp 412–26, here p.417, states that another reason foreign artists were attracted to Rome was that 'According to Karel van Mander, the city was the only place in Europe where the painters' guild did not bother foreigners.' Strictly speaking, Karel van Mander, *The Lives of the Illustrious Netherlandish and German Painters, from the first edition of the Schilder-Boeck 1603–1604*, 6 vols, Hessel Miedema (ed. and trans.), Doornspijk, 1994–9, 1:265. fol. 251v, states that '*perhaps*' Rome is the only city where foreigners were not bothered by the guilds. *Het Schilder-Boeck*, Amsterdam, 1604, fol. 251v: 'excepting almost only Rome' *('sonder schier alleen te Room')*.

58 Richard E. Spear and Philip Sohm, *Painting for Profit: The Economic Lives of Seventeenth-Century Italian Painters*, New Haven, 2010, p.7.

59 It should be noted that forty-one of the artists mentioned in the ninety-four *Lives* included in van Mander's *Schilder-Boeck* and over 500 Netherlanders in the course of the seventeenth century were 'drawn to warmth'. See *Drawn to Warmth: 17th-Century Dutch Artists in Italy*, Peter Schatforn and Judith Verberne (eds), Zwolle, 2001, here p.22. For the presence of Netherlandish artists in Rome during the seventeenth century, see also Didier Bodart, *Les peintres des Pays-Bas Méridionaux et de la Principauté de Liège à Rome au XVIIème siècle*, Brussels and Rome, 1970, I, pp 10 and 14.

60 Giulio Mancini, *Considerazioni sulla pittura*, 2 vols, A. Marucchi and L. Salerno (eds), Rome, 1956–7, I, p.97. See also Liliana Barroero, '"*Il se rendit en Italie*". Artisti stranieri a Roma nel Seicento', *Roma moderna e contemporanea*, vol.1 (1993), pp 13–34, here p.17: 'franzesi e fiamenghi che vanno e vengono, non li si può dar regola'.

61 Jacques Thuillier, '"Il se rendit en Italie . . .": notes sur le voyage à Rome des artistes français au XVIIe siècle' in *'Il se rendit en Italie'. Études offertes à André Chastel*, Rome, 1987, pp 321–36, esp. pp 331–2.

62 Arjan de Koomen, '"Una cosa non meno maravigliosa che honorata": The Expansion of Netherlandish Sculptors in Sixteenth-Century Europe', *Nederlands Kunsthistorisch Jaarboek*, vol.63 (2013), pp 82–109, here p.95 and pp 99–100. A number of these Flemish, but also French, sculptors became very successful in Rome, such as Jakob Cornelisz Cobaert Fiammingo, Nicolas Cordier, Niccolò (Pippi) d'Arras (Nicolas Mostaert), and Egidio (Gillis van Vliete) della Riviera Fiammingo. See Peter M. Lukehart, 'Carving Out Lives: The Role of Sculptors in the Early History of the Academy of San Luca', *Studies in the History of Art*, vol.70 (2008), pp 185–217.

63 See, for example, Dacos, p.11. According to the same author, p.48, Frans Floris' trip to Venice and his apprenticeship in Tintoretto's atelier marks the end of Rome's monopoly in the formative experience of Netherlandish painters. For a recent assessment of the impact Rome had on the art of a Netherlandish artist, see Edward H. Wouk, *Frans Floris (1519/20–1570): Imagining a Northern Renaissance*, Leiden and Boston, 2018, pp 71–120.

64 de Koomen, p.97.

65 See Walter S. Melion, *Shaping the Netherlandish Canon: Karel Van Mander's Schilder-Boeck*, Chicago, 1991, for van Mander's refusal of the superiority of Italian art to the northern schools of painting.

66 van Mander, *Het Schilder-Boeck*, Haarlem, 1604, fol. 199r. See also idem, *Le vite*, p.113.

67 van Mander, *Het Schilder-Boeck,* fol. 210r, and idem, *Le vite*, p.141. In his *Life of Lucas van Leijden* (*Het Schilder-Boeck* fol. 212r, *Le vite* p.147) van Mander checks Vasari's statements by negating his claim that all the eminent Flemish artists learned their art from Italian

artists and states that Vasari was not well informed on the subject. See Giorgio Vasari, *Le vite de' più eccellenti pittori scultori ed architetti*, Gaetano Milanesi (ed.), Florence, t.V, pp 408–9. See https://archive.org/details/levitedepieccelo7milagoog/page/n415

68 van Mander, *Het Schilder-Boeck*, fol. 215r, and idem, *Le vite*, pp 153–4.

69 Melion, especially pp 143–59.

70 van Mander, *Le vite*, p.173.

71 ibid., p.278.

72 Francisco de Hollanda, *Diálogos em Roma (1538): Conversations on Art with Michelangelo Buonarroti*, Grazia Dolores Folliero-Metz (ed.), Heidelberg, 1998, p.77.

73 ibid.

74 ibid.

75 Wolfgang Drost, in his Introduction to the *Diálogos em Roma (1538): Conversations on Art with Michelangelo Buonarroti*, p.12, cites Carlo Aru's doubts in his 'I Dialoghi romani di Francisco de Hollanda', *L'Arte*, vol.XXXI (1928), pp 117–28, and quotes Carl Justi's comparable comments as recorded by Hans Tietze.

76 Edgar Wind, 'Shaftesbury as a Patron of Art', *Journal of the Warburg Institute*, vol.2 (1938), pp 185–8, here p.187.

77 *Critical Perspectives on Roman Baroque Sculpture*, Anthony Colantuono and Steven F. Ostrow (eds), University Park, 2014, p.8.

78 Smith, p.221.

79 Tomaso Montanari, 'Bellori e la politica artistica di Luigi XIV' in *L'idéal classique: les échanges artistiques entre Rome et Paris au temps de Bellori (1640–1700)*, Olivier Bonfait and Anne-Lise Desmas (ed.), Paris, 2002, pp 117–38, here p.122: 'Bellori aveva finalmente compreso che la politica culturale transalpina aveva subito una mutazione genetica, e che dall'età della copia e della traduzione si era passati ad un'imperialistica appropriazione, ad una sottrazione di identità storica. In altri termini, che Errard non si trovava a Roma solo (e cito parole delle due lettere) "per l'amore delle cose antiche" ma anche per "impoverire la città [. . .] di memorie così pretiose".'

80 Smith, p.221.

81 Charles Perrault, *Le Siècle de Louis le Grand. Poeme par M. Perrault de l'Académie Françoise*, Paris, 1687, and idem, *Paralelle des anciens et des modernes*, Paris, 1688–97. See the editor and translator Jeanne Morgan Zarucchi's introduction to Perrault, *Memoirs of My Life*, pp 13–16. The panegyric was written on the occasion of Louis XIV's recovery from a fistula operation. Perrault's intention was to flatter both the king and his contemporaries, comparing favorably modern to ancient societies. The poem generated the controversy, as his critics saw it as an affront to the classical literary tradition, and propelled Perrault in the position of spokesman of the Moderns. For reflections of this pan-European debate in the Italian artistic scene and Bernini's role in showing how modern sculpture had surpassed classical statuary, see Sebastian Schütze, 'Bernini und die *Querelle des Anciens et des Modernes*' in *Docta Manus: Studien zur italienischen Skulptur für Joachim Poeschke*, Johannes Myssok and Jürgen Wiener (eds), Munster, 2007, pp 346–58.

82 Giuseppe Ghezzi, *Il centesimo dell'anno M.DC.XCV celebrato in Roma dall'Accademia del Disegno*, Rome, 1696. For Ghezzi's role in reclaiming Rome's leading role in modern art vis-à-vis French claims to artistic and cultural hegemony, and upholding Bernini as the highest representative of modern art, see Stefania Ventra, *L'Accademia di San Luca nella Roma del secondo Seicento. Artisti, opere, strategie culturali*, Florence, 2019, especially pp 133–60, here p.156; idem, '"*coll'Arte ha mostrato il nostro Secolo superiore*": Giuseppe Ghezzi, l'Accademia di San Luca e Bernini come vessillo del primato di Roma moderna', *Studi di storia dell'arte*, vol.28 (2017), pp 194–200. Tomaso Montanari, 'Introduction' in Giovan Pietro Bellori, *The Lives of the Modern Painters, Sculptors and Architects*, Hellmut Wohl (ed.), Alice Sedgwick Wohl (trans.), Cambridge, 2005, p.28: 'Here, in my opinion, is the true essence of the political function of the *Lives*: it lies in keeping the dialogue with Paris open, indeed very open, but for the purpose of forcefully reminding the French that Rome always remained the archetype to refer to, not the goal to surpass.'

83 Perrault, *Memoirs of My Life*, p.56. See also Anatole de Montaiglon and Jules Guiffrey (eds), *Correspondance des directeurs de l'Académie à Rome avec les Surintendants des Bâtiments* [hereafter Montaiglon, *Correspondance*], 17 vols, Paris, 1887, I, p.1.

84 Paul Zanker, *The Power of Images in the Age of Augustus*, Ann Arbor, 1990. See also Peter Burke, *The Fabrication of Louis XIV*, New Haven and London, 1992.

85 This is exactly what Carlo Dati underscores in his *Vite de pittori antichi*, Florence, 1667, in his dedication of his volume to Louis XIV, as he compares this monarch's virtues to those of Alexander the Great.

86 Perrault, *Memoirs of My Life*, pp 56–7.

87 ibid., p.57.

88 See Connors and Rice, p.70. The 'perpetual secretary' of the Parisian Académie Royale, Nicolas Guerin, in his *Description de l'Académie Royale des Arts de Peinture et de Sculpture*, Paris, 1715, p.254, reiterates the concept. From among those artists who received a prize for their artistic excellence were to be chosen those young artists who were then sent to Rome as 'pensionnaires' of the king, and his liberality allowed them to 'dessiner d'après les plus excellens Ouvrages de cette Ville si celebre, & même de les copier, est le plus grand de tous les avantages pour se perfectionner dans la pratique'.

89 In a letter to Le Nôtre dated 2 August 1679, citing from a previous missive sent to Colbert by the French architect, then in Rome. See Montaiglon, *Correspondance*, I, p.85, no. 148.

90 ibid., XVIII, published by Paul Cornu in 1912, formed the index to this *magnum opus*.

91 ibid., I, p.341. On Rome's incomparable wealth of artistic treasures, ibid., 20 June 1692, p.290: 'Certainement Rome est si pleine de tant de belles choses que je ne craindreay pas de dire que, dans tout le reste du Monde, il n'y a rien de comparable au Vatican tout seul, le prenant dans toute son estendue.' Ibid., 22 April 1693, p.381.

92 ibid., 13 September 1689, p.188: 'les Italiens, qui sont beaucoup plus meffiants que le reste du Monde.'

93 ibid., 7 May 1686, p.156: 'Je ne croy pas qu'il y ait des gens dans le monde plus intraitables que le gens de ce pays dans des occasions où ils croient que l'on ne sauroit se passer d'eux.'

94 ibid., 6 January 1693, p.347: 'il n'y a point de lieu au Monde où les François soient moins aymés.' Charles Poerson, instead, believed they were equally envious as individuals of other nationalities: 'Les Italiens ne son pas plus envieux que les autres Nations.' ibid., IV, 23 May 1712, p.98. As a corrective to this view, however, even though Charles Poerson described Italy as a 'proud and jealous' nation (ibid., IV, 11 July 1711, p.3), the Duke D'Antin reminded him that Italians were no more, no less than other nationalities (ibid., 23 May 1712, p.98).

95 ibid., 29 July 1692, p.304: 'J'ay remarqué encore que les Peintres et Sculpteurs Italiens négligent fort l'anatomie, jusqu'à la mépriser et la blasmer même indirectement, parce qu'ils l'ignorent et qu'ils son naturellement fort paresseux.'

96 ibid., IV, 7 July 1712, p.129: 'mais, généralement parlant, la frequentation oisive et vicieuse des Italiens les amolit et leur fait bientôt perdre cette ardeur si necessaire dans les Beaux-arts.'

97 ibid., IV, 14 August 1714, p.327: 'J'ai déja touché, Monseigneur, 3,000 livres, ainsi que votre Grandeur me l'a commandé par sa lettre du 2 de juillet, ce qui m'a été d'un grand et utile scours pour faire travailler aus apprests de l'embarquement des caisses, sans quoi j'aurois eu de la peine à faire agir les Italiens, qui sont extremement pauvres et paresseux.'

98 ibid., II, 3 June 1698, p.400.

99 ibid., IV, 23 April 1715, p.392: 'Aussi a-t-il [Monsieur Amelot] charmé tout le monde de Rome, qui naturellement ne loue pas bien volontiers les Estrangers.' On Poerson's contempt for Italian artists, with the exception of Maratta, see Olivier Michel, 'Charles-François Poerson' in *L'idéal classique: Les échanges artistiques entre Rome et Paris au temps de Bellori (1640–1700)*, Olivier Bonfait and Anne-Lise Desmas (eds), Paris, 2002, p.192. Joachim von Sandrart, *L'Academia Todesca della Architectura, Scultura & Pittura oder Teutsche Academie der Edlen Bau-, Bild- und Mahlerey Künste*, 2 vols, Nuremberg, 1675, I, t.2, Book 3, XXIV, p.348: 'Damit nun dieser gute Künstler sich auch in Marmorstein zu arbeiten berühmt machen möchte weil die Italiäner sonderlich von ihm ausgaben daß er damit nicht umzugehen wuste und nur in Erden Wachs und Bein gut wäre bildete er aus einem schönen weißen Marmorstein einen stehenden *Cupido*, der einen Bogen schneidet in Lebens-Grösse worvon es allda viel Redens gegeben welchen aber doch die Italiänische Bildhauer nicht loben wolten sondern etliche Jahr lang veracht und unterdruckt hielten daß niemand diesen zukauffen begehrte bis daß endlich.' See also Andrea Bacchi, 'Bernini e gli scultori del suo tempo' in *Aus aller Herren Länder: Die Künstler der Teutschen Academie von Joachim von Sandrart*, Turnhout, 2015, p.148: 'gli scultori italiani non vollero lodare, anzi per alcuni anni continuarono a disprezzarlo e affossarlo [nei giudizi], tanto che nessuno lo (the *Cupid*) volle comprare.'

100 The foundry was part of the complex labeled '*le fornace per la fabrica di S. Pietro*', which is where the kilns were located in Greuter's map of Rome here reproduced. The church of Santa Marta is indicated by the number 213. Much of the *Cathedra Petri*, including the two *Latin Fathers of the Church* erected in the apse of Saint Peter's, were cast in this foundry. There was a second one, the 'Fonderia apostolica in Borgo', also known as the 'Fonderia del Belvedere', located near the church of Sant'Anna, indicated in the open area north of the obelisk in Greuter's map, just above the letter A. This latter one is where the bronze sections of the

Solomonic columns for the *Baldacchino* were cast. See Helga Tratz, 'Werkstatt und Arbeitsweise Berninis', *Römisches Jahrbuch für Kunstgeschichte*, vol.23–24 (1988), pp 397–483, here pp 425–6, and Oskar Pollak, *Die Kunsttätigkeit unter Urban VIII: Die Peterskirke in Rom*, Hildesheim and New York, 1981, 1098, 1104, p.337. The first instance in which the 'Fonderia apostolica in Borgo' is clearly labeled '*la fonderia*' occurs in Francesco De Paoli's map of 1623. The structure is further depicted without an indication of its function in Giovanni Blaeu's map of 1663 and Giovanni Battista Falda's edition of 1676. It is then clearly designated as the '*Fonderia de Cannoni*' in Giovanni Battista Nolli's map of 1748. It last appears designated as 'Fonderia' in the 1891 map published by the Istituto Cartografico Italiano. In the 1929 map of the Stato della Città del Vaticano, in its location one finds the 'Posta' and its adjacent 'Pal[azzo] Belvedere' buildings. For Greuter, and De Paoli, see *Le piante di Roma*, 3 vols, Amato Pietro Frutaz (ed.), Rome, 1962, II, Pls. 291 and 303. Ibid., III, Pl. 342 for Blaeu, Pl. 361 for Falda, Pl. 412 for Nolli, Pl. 550 for the Istituto Cartografico Italiano, and Pl. 597 for the Stato della Città del Vaticano map.

101 Montaiglon, *Correspondance*, I, 25 March 1692, p.268: 'Il y a, derrière l'eglise de Saint-Pierre, un hastelier où le Cavalier *Bernin* a fait la statue équestre du Roy.' Domenico Bernini, *The Life*, p.211: 'For the convenience of being close to Saint Peter's, Bernini worked on the statue [of Louis XIV] in a large studio near that same temple and there, for the space of twelve years, one could witness a concourse of the finest aristocracy not only of Rome but of all Europe as well.' For the vicissitudes regarding this chapel, see Cristiano Giometti, 'Il modello del *Battesimo* di Domenico Guidi e proposte per una committenza Albani a Guidi e Ottoni' in *Sculture romane del Settecento, III: La professione dello scultore*, Rome, 2003, pp 51–65, and idem, *Domenico Guidi 1625–1701: Uno scultore barocco di fama europea*, Rome, 2010, pp 94–7.

102 Montaiglon, *Correspondance*, I, 9 February 1694, pp 455–63. It should be noted that La Teulière and Théodon did not see eye to eye, as La Teulière accused Théodon of having tried to poison him. See also Robert Enggass, *Early Eighteenth-Century Sculpture in Rome*, 2 vols, University Park and London, 1976, I, p.63.

103 Montaiglon, *Correspondance*, I, 23 September 1692, p.325: 'l'on donneroit à chaque Sculpteur un lieu pour travailler auprès de St-Pierre; de manière que le Sr *Theodon* en aura toujours un comme les autres, quand *Domenico Guidi* voudroit avoir le sien, comme il le prétend.'

104 For the *avviso* and a discussion of the commission, see Stefano Pierguidi, *Pittura di marmo. Storia e fortuna delle pale d'altare a rilievo nella Roma di Bernini*, Florence, 2017, p.238, quoting from Ermete Rossi, 'Roma ignorata', *Roma*, XX, 1942, p.375, and ibid., XXI, 1943, pp 60–61. On the 'nationality' of both Ottoni and Lucenti, see Pellegrino Antonio Orlandi, *Abecedario pittorico*, Venice, 1753, pp 305 and 347, respectively.

105 Enggass, vol.I, p.65: 'Hà S. Sta ordinato che si fermi in Roma Monsù Teudon scultore dei gli migliori che hoggi habbiamo quale già si era preparato per andarsene in francia e scapare da Roma, ondi si suppone che NS. voglia impiegarlo in qualche opera . . .' Capitoline Archives, Cred. 14, vol.10, fols 92v and 93r.

106 Montaiglon, *Correspondance*, VIII, 9 November 1730, pp 156–7: 'J'ai fait un modèle pour l'ornement de la fontaine de Trève à Rome, à laquelle le Pape veut faire travailler. Si j'ay le bonheur d'être préféré au concours où je vai être exposé avec mes confrères et que Votre Grandeur me permette d'exécuter ce grand ouvrage, je tâcherai de m'y fair honneur; sinon, je me rendrai à Paris pour y travailler sous ses ordres, auxquels je serai toujours très soumis.'

107 Dom Calmet, *Bibliothèque lorraine, ou Histoire des hommes illustres*, Nancy, 1751, pp 8–20.

108 ibid., p.10. John Pinto, *The Trevi Fountain*, New Haven and London, 1986, p.98, referring to a letter from Edmé Bouchardon of 3 September 1731, describing events that occurred five months earlier, mentions 'thirty different models exhibited in the Quirinal Palace'.

109 Calmet, pp 10–11: 'Les Romains voyant que cet Ouvrage étoit tombé à un étranger, inspirerent au Pape de faire faire la Façade du Portail de saint Jean de Latran, préférablement à cette Fontaine; ce qui fut exécuté. Le Pape fit faire aussi dans cette même Eglise une Chapelle ornée de Sculptures & de Tombeaux pour sa Famille; Adam y composa un bas-relief qu'il exécuta en marbre, représentant S. André Corcini [i.e., Corsini], lorsqu'il refuse l'Episcopat, & la sainte Vierge qu lui apparoît pour le lui faire accepter. Cet oubrage fut trouvé si bien, qu'Adam fut reçu en consequence Academicien de l'Académie de S. Luc de Rome, le 8. Septembre 1732.'

110 Anne-Lise Desmas, *Le ciseau et la tiare: les sculpteurs dans la Rome des papes 1724–1758*, Rome, 2012, p.316:

'Mais il est possible de constater d'emblée que l'enchaînement des faits tel que Calmet l'écrivit ne correspond pas à la réalité. Le projet d'un nouveau portique occidental au Latran ne put interférer sur celui de la fontaine de Trevi: l'organisation des deux chantiers fut préparée au cours du même été 1732. En outre, Adam ne fut pas élu académicien le 8 septembre 1732 mais le 19 novembre suivant; or à cette date, le pape avait déjà signé depuis deux mois le chirographe qui officialisait son choix de l'architecte Nicola Salvi pour la construction de la fontaine.'

111 ibid.

112 ibid., p.317.

113 ibid. Montaiglon, *Correspondance*, VIII, 4 January 1731, p.172: 'les architects veulent être les maîtres de tout'.

114 On Algardi's creative powers, see Jennifer Montagu, *Alessandro Algardi*, 2 vols, New Haven and London, 1985.

115 See Giometti, 'Il modello del *Battesimo* di Domenico Guidi', and idem, *Domenico Guidi 1625–1701*. See also Allan Braham and Hellmut Hager, *Carlo Fontana: The Drawings at Windsor Castle*, London and Bradford, 1977, p.44: 'It was to the architect Carlo Fontana, and not to a sculptor, that Innocent XII entrusted the overall design [of the Baptismal Chapel].'

116 On the Lateran project, see Michael Conforti, *The Lateran Apostles*, 2 vols, PhD diss., Harvard University, Cambridge, MA, 1977; idem, 'Planning the Lateran Apostles' in *Studies in Italian Art and Architecture, 15th through 18th Centuries*, Henry A. Millon (ed.), Rome, 1980, pp 243–55, and Frederick Den Broeder, 'The Lateran Apostles: The Major Sculpture Commission in Eighteenth-century Rome', *Apollo*, vol.85 (1967), pp 360–65.

117 Jennifer Montagu, *Roman Baroque Sculpture: The Industry of Art*, New Haven and London, 1989, p.77: 'According to tradition theory, Painting, Sculpture and Architecture were three sisters, all born of *Disegno*, a word which encompasses both drawing in the limited sense, and design, in the sense of invention. Ideally, this might be so, but in practice very few sculptors appear to have been able to draw, and while this need not, of course, prevent them from designing, working out their ideas in clay, or even in atrociously bad drawings, more often it meant that they were content to work on designs provided for them by other artists, whether painters or architects.' Idem, *Alessandro Algardi*, p.115. For a cautionary reminder not to overemphasise the assumption that architects and painters dictated what sculptors had to execute, see Michael Conforti, 'Pierre Legros and the Rôle of Sculptors as Designers in Late Baroque Rome', *The Burlington Magazine*, vol.119 (1977), pp 556–61.

118 For the 'twinning' of the two academies, see Anatole de Montaiglon (ed.), *Procès-Verbaux de l'Académie Royale de peinture et de sculpture*, 10 vols, Paris, 1878, II, pp 68, 77–8. See also Lukehart (ed.), *The Accademia Seminars*; Oliver Michel, 'I pittori francesi e i concorsi dell'Accademia di San Luca nel XVII secolo' in *I disegni di figura nell'Archivio Storico dell'Accademia di San Luca*, 3 vols, Angela Cipriani and Enrico Valeriani (eds), Rome, 1988–1991, vol. I, p.8; Enggass, vol.I, pp 24–7; and Smith, pp 17–25.

119 Enggass, vol.I, p.27.

120 ibid.

121 ibid. Charles Poerson, writing to D'Antin on 30 May 1711, announces that, because of Carlo Maratta's old age – at the time he was 89 years old – and his inability to tend to the many responsibilities incumbent upon the Principe of the Accademia di San Luca, members of the institution asked him to serve as 'Vice-Prince'. Given the Italians' renowned conceit, Poerson seemed shocked by it, stating 'il paroit assez surprenant que Messieurs les Italiens veuillent bien se soumettre à la conduite d'un François'. See Montaiglon, *Correspondance*, III, p.474. Subsequently, on 11 July, he soberly acknowledges that the reason he was chosen for said post was not because of his merit, but rather, because he represented the French crown. See Montaiglon, *Correspondance*, IV, p.3.

122 Domenico Guidi's appointment as rector of the Académie in Rome is acknowledged by the Académie Royale on 24 July 1676. See Montaiglon, *Procès-Verbaux de l'Académie Royale*, II, pp 89–90. For Servandoni's acceptance into the Académie Royale, see ibid., V, pp 83–4. For the model Francesco Calciono, who is recorded in the minutes of the Académie from 1674 through 1685, when he is accorded an additional 50 *livres* to the initial pension of 350 *livres* in consideration of the long-standing services he provided, see ibid., II, pp 39, 65, 108, 110, 118, and 307.

123 The foreign *principi* were: Paul Brill, 1620–21; Simon Vouet, 1624–7; Charles Errard, 1672 and 1678, Charles LeBrun, 1676–7, Charles Poerson, 1715–18 and 1721–2; Jean-François de Troy, 1744–5; Francisco Preciado de la Vega, 1764–6 and 1777–8; Anton Raphael Mengs, 1771–2. See Matteo Lafranconi, 'Da Vouet a Poussin: La

comunità artistica francese nell'Accademia di San Luca' in Bonfait and Desmas (eds), *L'ideal classique*, pp 211–22.

124 Michel, 'I pittori francesi', p.7. Of these foreign members of the Accademia, sixteen in 1664 and twenty-two in 1675 were French. See also Angela Cipriani, 'Presenze francesi all'Accademia di San Luca: 1664–1675' in Bonfait and Desmas (eds), *L'idéal classique*, pp 223–8.

125 Giovanni Battista Passeri, *Vite de' pittori, scultori ed architetti che hanno lavorato in Roma morti dal 1641. Fino al 1673*, Rome, 1772, p.172, in the biography of the still unidentified Flemish artist Vincenzo Armanno: 'Non conversava volentieri, che co' suoi compatriotti, ed oltramontani, avendo com'è il solito delle genti straniere poco genio con quelli d'Italia, stando sempre in sospetto, di essere ingannato.'

126 Montaiglon, *Correspondance*, I, 1 January 1692, p.247: 'Un pays où l'artifice et le manège tiennent lieu de mérite et de raison.'

127 Montaiglon, *Correspondance*, VIII, 16 October 1732, p.380: 'selon la coutume de ce païs, l'architecte étoit choisi avant que d'entrer en concurrence.'

128 Pio Pecchiai, *Il Gesù di Roma*, Rome, 1952, p.176. Among the many participants, whose names are all listed by Pecchiai, there were twelve Italian and seven foreign sculptors. Carlo Mauro Bonacina, the Jesuit who was put in charge of the whole project, inflates the number of workers to 500. Archivium Romanum Societatis Iesu, Rom 140, fol 18r: 'E pure tra Scultori, Fonditori, ed altri, montavano gli Operaj al numero di cinquecento; e ben lo mostra il brieve tempo, in cui l'Opera fu compiuta; da che cominciata il 1695. fù al publico aperta il di 10 ottobre del 1699. quando per comune avviso degli intendenti non meno di 25 ò 30 anni vi abbisognavano, seguendo il modo di operare consueto à praticarsi quì in Roma.' Enggass, p.131: 'more than a hundred men, all told.' See also Evonne Levy, *Propaganda and the Jesuit Baroque*, Berkeley, Los Angeles, and London, 2004, p.87. Levy's comments are based on Padre Carlo Mauro Bonacina's *Memoria*, dated 15 February 1706. On the Chapel of Saint Ignatius, see also Bernhard Kerber, *Andrea Pozzo*, Berlin and New York, 1971, pp 140–86.

129 Enggass, I, p.26.

130 ibid., p.65. See n.99 above.

131 Giovanni Bottari and Stefano Ticozzi, *Raccolta di lettere sulla pittura, scultura ed architettura scritte dai più celebri personaggi dei secoli XV, XVI e XVII*, 8 vols, Milan, 1822, II, pp 315–16.

132 ibid.

133 Francesco Saverio Baldinucci, *Vite di Artisti dei secoli XVII–*XVIII, Anna Matteoli (ed.), Rome, 1975, pp 91–2: 'Circa all'anno 1695, coll'occasione che fabbricavasi la ricca Cappella di Sant'Ignazio della Compagnia di Gesù di Roma, voleva con molto giudizio il Padre Pozzo, architetto della medesima, valersi dell'arte e perizia del nostro Rusconi – che sempre stimò un valoroso scultore – nel fare uno de' gruppi laterali che in essa presentemente si vedono. Ma dominando assai in quel tempo la nazione francese, ricca di potenza e d'alte protezioni, fu levata al Rusconi questa bella occasione di farsi compitamente conoscere per quello che era, e fu data a due professori di detta nazione: l'uno Monsù Legrò e l'altro Monsù Teodone. Dispiacque molto al Padre Pozzi quest'accidente; ma con tutto ciò, dovendosi fare ancora le statue de' due grand'Angioli, alti dodici palmi, che restano situati sopra una porta di detta Cappella *in cornu Epistolae*, diedene l'incumbenza al nostro Cammillo: il quale, con tutto lo studio e applicazione, li terminò. E collocate al luogo loro, fu tale la stima e la lode che ne riportarono dagli intendenti, che fu detto da alcuni non solo esser di gran lunga migliori de' predetti gruppi fatti dai francesi, ma eziandio che considerata la nobile e gentile aria delle teste, la leggiadria e spirito dell'attitudini, e la proprietà del panneggiamento, potevano dirsi – per ischerzo – i più bell'Angioli che si fussero mai fatti vedere per Roma.' To this viewer, Monnot's angels above the altar are qualitatively superior to any of the other four angels in the chapel. See also Stephanie Walker, *The Sculptor Pietro Stefano Monnot in Rome, 1695–1713*, 2 vols, PhD diss., New York University, 1994, I, pp 80–81.

134 Montaiglon, *Correspondance*, II, no. 650, pp 173–6, 15 November 1695. *Pensionnaires* at the academy were supposed to work only for the king.

135 ibid. La Teulière had to inform the Superintendent, Villacerf, in Paris and justify himself for not having been aware of what was taking place under his watch. For Villacerf's reply, see document no. 656, pp 183–4, 5 December 1695.

136 ibid., no. 650, p.173: 'Il [Le Gros] me dit, pour toute raison, que le P. Jésuite, qui conduisoit l'ouvrage, lui avoit défendu très expressément d'en parle à personne, quoique dans la conversation il y eût échappé de me dire que le Sr *Dorigni*, Graveur François, avoit mesnagé cette affaire.'

137 ibid.: 'Plusieurs personnes ont produit des modelles pour les groupes. Celuy deu Sr *Legros* a esté le plus généralement approuvé, tout le monde en ignorant

l'autheur, la pluspart croyant que c'estoit un Sculpteur Génois.'

138 Lione Pascoli, *Vite de' pittori, scultori, ed architetti moderni*, Valentino Martinelli and Alessandro Marabottini (ed.), Perugia, 1992, p.360. All Lione Pascoli records is that 'At this time the splendid Chapel of St. Ignatius at the Gesù was being decorated with statues, low-reliefs, and multi-figural groups, and the best masters worked on these sculptures. Camillo was given the task of sculpting two angels. He executed them diligently and, having been placed under the organ of the same chapel, he received the praise of all of Rome, and the particular protection of cardinal Albani, who was the worthy successor of Innocent XII.'

139 Alessandro Marabottini, 'Introduzione' in Pascoli, p.21.

140 ibid., 'Ma da altre biografie, come quella del Rusconi, del Luti, dell'Odazi, apprendiamo come il Pascoli li frequentasse e fosse con loro in rapporti più di amico che di committente. Così possiamo essere ben certi che in tutti questi casi ebbe notizie dirette e sicure, nei limiti in cui si può dar fiducia alla memoria non sempre precisa degli artisti.'

141 Archivium Romanum Societatis Iesu, Rom 140, fol. 20r. See also Enggass, I, p.133.

142 Pecchiai, *Il Gesù di Roma*, p.180. The twelve sculptors were all invited to view the models at the same time and each one of them had to vote for the one they considered the best, excepting their own. Legros received the most votes, followed by Michel Maille and Giovanni Francesco Guarnieri (or Guarneri). See also Enggass, p.133, and Levy, *Propaganda and the Jesuit Baroque*, pp 101–2 and n.107, p.274.

143 Archivium Romanum Societatis Iesu, Rom 140, fol. 22r: 'Alla voce, che'l maggior premio era toccato à Monsù le Gros, la numerosa squadra de' giovani Francesi che l'aspettava alzò un altissimo grido co'l Viva Viva Monsù Le Gros. Scendeva egli allor giù per la scala con in mano il sacchetto delli cento scudi in tante piastre, che scuoteva per farle sentire: ma giunto appena al Cancello di detta scala, che mette nel piano, la Gioventù Francese affollatasegli lì attorno, e levatolo di peso, il portarono come in trionfo, rinuovando tratto tratto il Viva. Lo strepito straordinario, che faceano, nello girar per le strade, chiamava il popolo, il quale dimandava che cosa volesse dirsi quella novità. Monsu le Gros dopo l'onor ricevuto dal suo talento, volle farlo alla sua generosità, regalando non solo i Compagni nazionali, ma molti amici, tutti eccellenti Virtuosi con un solenne, e splendido convito; di cui troppo uscirei da termini del mio proposito, se togliessi à narrar la galloria, le bizzarrie innocenti, le invenzioni spiritose, in cui diede quella vivace, ed ingegnosa Gioventù, per accrescere gli applausi, ed iñalzar [*sic*] le glorie del suo Maestro.'

144 Bonacina himself relates the controversy that arose when he and Pozzo were chosen to head the project of the chapel of Saint Ignatius: 'As soon as it was known [that Pozzo and Bonacina had been assigned the chapel project], almost as if from the sound of a trumpet, everyone took to arms. You cannot believe how much raving went on in every circle, in every corner, and not only by our own but also amongst the lay community, disapproving openly that a work of such engagement and such expectation and expense should be managed by a Pozzo and a Bonacina, that is two brothers of low rank and born foreigners.' See Levy, *Propaganda and the Jesuit Baroque*, p.97.

145 ibid., p.107.

146 ibid., p.101.

147 Ironically, however, according to Pierre-Jean Mariette, Legros' demise was caused by his own envy of Rusconi's subsequent success: 'He returned to Rome where he died in 1719. If he was sickened by the Académie de Paris [that refused to accept him as a member simply on the merit of the reputation he had achieved in Rome], he was even more upset by the honors Camillo Rusconi received for the sculptures which that skillful sculptor executed at St. John Lateran. He had expected, at the very least, to share [the accolades] with him and that would have been appropriate; but, to his disadvantage, he was a foreigner and had not curried favor with Carlo Maratta [. . .] it is believed the grief brought him to the end of his days.' See Pierre-Jean Mariette, *Abecedario*, 6 vols, Paris, 1854–6, III, p.120.

148 Montaiglon, *Correspondance*, IV, p.231, dated 29 July 1713: '. . . le *Sr Legros*, qui est, de l'aveu des Italiens, le plus habile Sculpteur qui soit dans l'Italie.'

149 ibid., VIII, p.233, dated 9 August 1731: 'Tout le monde est content du portrait du Pape que *Bouchardon* a fini; il faut qu'il soit véritablement bien, puisque les Italiens y donnent leurs applaudissemens.'

150 Johns, p.19. The exhibition was held in the Philadelphia Museum of Art, 16 March – 28 May and at the Museum of Fine Arts, Houston, 25 June – 27 September. See n.25.

151 Dean Walker, 'An Introduction to Sculpture in Rome in the Eighteenth Century' in Bowron and Rishel (eds), *Art in Rome in the Eighteenth Century*, p.214.

152 On the lack of political unity in Italy, which, however, was supplemented by the cultural and linguistic commonality of the different Italian regions, see Charles Dempsey, 'National Expression in Italian Sixteenth-Century Art: Problems of the Past and Present', *Studies in the History of Art*, vol.29 (1991), pp 14–24.

153 Thuillier, '"Il se rendit en Italie . . .', p.323, n.2.

154 Abbé de Fontenai, *Dictionnaire des Artistes, ou notice historique et raisonnée des Architectes, Peintres, Graveurs, Sculpteurs, Musiciens, Acteurs & Danseurs; Imprimeurs, Horlogers & Méchaniciens*, 2 vols, Paris, 1776. See Montaiglon, *Correspondance*, XIII, no. 6823, p.271.

155 Fontenai: 'De même que les anciens Romains alloient à Athènes qui étoit le centre de l'éloquence et de la philosophie, de même *Le Brun* pensa que, de nos jours, les François devoient aller à Rome pour y étudier les beaux-arts. C'est en effet dans cette ville que les ouvrages des anciens Grecs, des *Michel-Anges*, des *Raphaëls*, des *Dominiquins*, donnent des leçons muettes, bien supérieures à toutes celles que pouvoient donner de vive voix les plus grands maîtres moderns.'

156 Francesco Algarotti, *Saggio sopra l'Accademia di Francia che è in Roma*, Livorno, 1763, pp 11–14. The French edition was published six years later as *Essai sur la peinture, et sur l'Académie de France, établie à Rome*, M. Pingeron, Capitaine d'Artillerie & Ingénieur au service de Pologne (trans.), Paris, 1769, pp 261–336.

157 Hugh Honour, *Neo-classicism*, Harmondsworth, 1968, p.14.

158 On the evolving awareness of the differences between Greek and Roman sculptures from the sixteenth through the seventeenth centuries, see Estelle Lingo, 'The Greek Manner and a Christian "Canon": François Duquesnoy's "Saint Susanna"', *The Art Bulletin*, vol.84 (2002), pp 65–93, and idem, *François Duquesnoy and the Greek Ideal*, New Haven, 2007.

159 Montègre, p.1, citing Saint-Évremond, *Œvress Mêlées*, London, 1705, t. II, p.196.

160 ibid.

161 See Françoise Waquet, *Le Modèle français et l'Italie savante. Conscience de soi et perception de l'autre dans la République des Lettres (1660–1750)*, Rome, 1989. For the roots of this French reaction to 'all things Italian', see especially pp 255–90. On the tug-of-war, see also Dietrich Erben, *Paris und Rom. Die staatlich gelenkten Kunstbeziehungen unter Ludwig XIV*, Berlin, 2004, and Ingo Herklotz, 'Ecfrasi e scultura a Roma all'ombra di Luigi XIV: Una nuova fonte per Domenico Guidi' in *Gli allievi di Algardi. Opere, geografia, temi della scultura in Italia nella seconda metà del Seicento*, Andrea Bacchi, Alessandro Nova, and Lucia Simonato (eds), Milan, 2019, pp 29–53.

162 *Correspondance inédite du Comte de Caylus avec le P. Paciaudi, Théatin (1757–1765)*, Charles Nisard (ed.), I, Paris, 1877, p.244, n.3, quoting from Voltaire's correspondence edited by Beuchot, t.XII, p.541: 'Étalez moins votre abondance,/Votre origine et vos honneurs;/Il ne sied pas aux grands seigneurs/De se vanter de leur naissance./L'Italie instruisit la France;/Mais, par un reproche indiscret,/Nous serions forcés à regret/A manquer de reconnaissance./Dès longtemps sortis de l'enfance,/Nous avons quitté les genoux/D'une nourrice en décadence/Dont le lait n'est plus fait pour nous./Nous pourrions devenir jaloux/Quand vous parlez notre langage;/Puisqu'il est embelli par vous,/Cessez donc de lui faire outrage./L'égalité contente un sage./Terminons ainsi le procès;/Quand on est égal aux Français,/Ce n'est pas un mauvais partage.' For Deodati de' Tovazzi, writer and translator, see the *Enciclopedia Treccani* http://www.treccani.it/enciclopedia/immagine-dell-italiano_%28Enciclopedia-dell%27Italiano%29/

163 Waquet, p.53.

164 ibid., p.290.

165 ibid., p.97, quoting from Francesco Algarotti's letter of 10 July 1743 to Querini.

166 Jean-Baptiste de Boyer (Marquis d'Argens), *Reflexions critiques sur les différentes écoles de peinture*, Paris, 1752. See also Christian Michel, *Le voyage d'Italie de Charles-Nicolas Cochin (1758)*, Rome, 1991, p.57, and Waquet, p.294.

167 Jean-Baptiste de Boyer d'Argens, pp 20–21: 'Les Étrangers, & surtout les Ialiens, se figurent que, parce que nous envoyons quelques-uns de nos jeunes gens téudier [*sic*] à Rome, ils sont en droit de soutenir, que l'on ne peut devenir grand Peintre que chez eux, puisque nous allons, nous qui prétendons être leur rivaux, apprendre notre métier dans leur Pais. Ce raisonnement pouvoit être fort bon il y a soixante & dix ans; mais il n'a aucun fondement aujourd'hui.'

168 ibid., p.23: 'Il y a une raison sans replique, pour prouver que nos Peintres n'ont point besoin d'aller chercher ailleurs la perfection de leur Art. Nos meilleurs Artistes, à l'exception de deux ou trois, ne furent point à Rome; le Sueur, Jouvenet, Fontaine, de Troie, Rigaud, Largiliere, Caze, ne sortirent point de Paris . . . Il faut donc convenir qu'on peut être un très-grand Peintre, sans devoir rien aux Italiens.'

169 Waquet, p.1, citing from Vittorio Di Tocco, *Ideali d'indipendenza in Italia durante la preponderanza spagnuola*, Messina, 1926, p.276. For Cellini's quotation, see *The Life of Benvenuto Cellini*, 2 vols, John Addington Symonds (trans.), London, 1888, I, p.200.
170 Montègre, p.15.
171 ibid.
172 Johns, p.20, asserts that Rome remained 'the cynosure of eighteenth-century European cultural life'.
173 Montaiglon, *Correspondance*, XVII, p.361, 14 April 1802: 'Pourquoi le peintre le plus célèbre en Europe, dans le dernier siècle, se trouve-t-il être un Allemand, M. *Mengs*? Pourquoi le sculpteur le plus célèbre, vivant, est-il un Vénitien, M. *Canova*? . . . Je sai qu'on soutient à Paris que nous avons eu, pendant le dernier siècle, d'aussi bons peintre que *Mengs*; mais le reste de l'Europe ne juge pas ainsi. Il en est de même à l'égard de *Canova*.' François Cacault, minister of the French Republic to the Holy See, was the person who saw the closure of the Académie de France in Rome in 1793.
174 Bellori, *The Lives*, p.76, in the *Life* of Annibale Carracci.
175 Domenico Bernini, *Vita*, p.80: 'Roma qualche volta travede, mà non giammai perde la vista, con inferire, Esser una Città, in cui tal volta vien contrariata dall'invidia la virtù, ma non mai oppressa.'

CHAPTER 6

1 Paul Fréart de Chantelou, *Journal de voyage du Cavalier Bernin en France*, Milovan Stanić (ed.), Paris, 2001, p.286. Idem, *Diary of the Cavaliere Bernini's Visit to France*, Anthony Blunt (ed.), George C. Bauer (ann.), Margery Corbett (trans.), Princeton, 1985, p.342. Cecil Gould, *Bernini in France: An Episode in Seventeenth-Century History*, London, 1981, p.114 and p.147, n.129, claims that Bernini had arrived in Rome by 3 December, giving as his source *Journal du Voyage du Cavalier Bernin en France*, Ludovic Lalanne (ed.), Paris, 1885, pp 260–61, where Bernini's 8 December letter is transcribed. This source does not mention the actual date of Bernini's arrival in Rome.
2 Léon Mirot, *Le Bernin en France: les travaux du Louvre et les statues de Louis XIV*, Paris, 1904, pp 273–4; Gould, pp 116–17.
3 Mirot, p.276. Queen Christina of Sweden, in a letter written from Hamburg on 1 September, denounced the idea as absolutely false.
4 On the Louis XIV statue, see Rudolf Wittkower, 'The Vicissitudes of a Dynastic Monument: Bernini's Equestrian Statue of Louis XIV', in *Essays in Honor of Erwin Panofsky*, De Artibus Opuscula, vol.40, Millard Meiss (ed.) New York, 1961, pp 497–531; Robert W. Berger, 'Bernini's Louis XIV Equestrian: A Closer Examination of Its Fortunes at Versailles', *The Art Bulletin*, vol.63 (1981), pp 232–48; Guy Walton, 'Bernini's Equestrian Louis XIV', *The Art Bulletin*, vol.64 (1982), pp 319–20.
5 Mirot, p.277; Gould, pp 124–6. We first hear of Colbert's desire to have Bernini sculpt an equestrian statue of the king in Chantelou's entry in his *Journal* of 13 August 1665. Chantelou, *Journal*, p.114; idem, *Diary*, p.118. See also, Colbert's letter of 15 July 1667 to ambassador Duke de Chaulnes in Rome in Anatole de Montaiglon and Jules Guiffrey (eds), *Correspondance des directeurs de l'Académie de France à Rome avec les Surintendants des Bâtiments*, 17 vols, Paris, 1887–1908 [hereafter Montaiglon, *Correspondance*], I, p.14, no. 21.
6 Mirot, p.277.
7 Wittkower, 'The Vicissitudes of a Dynastic Monument', p.512.
8 On the sequence of events pertaining to the statue of Louis XIV, see Gould, 127–9, and Stanislao Fraschetti, *Il Bernini: La sua vita, la sua opera, il suo tempo*, Milan, 1900, pp 361–3. See also Karen J. Lloyd, 'All the King's Horses: Bernini's Equestrian Statues between Paris and Rome' in *A Transitory Star: The Late Bernini and his Reception*, Claudia Lehmann and Karen J. Lloyd (eds), Berlin, 2015, pp 117–33. After the face of the king was altered by Girardon to represent the mythological figure of Marcus Curtius, the statue was initially diverted to the Versailles gardens, by the Swiss Basin, and it is now located indoors in the Musée National du Château, Versailles et de Trianon.
9 Cardinal Fausto Poli's fortunes were intimately connected with Urban VIII's favoritism. He became 'sottomaestro' of the papal household (1623). In this role he also oversaw the architectural projects revolving around the Vatican and the Basilica of Saint Peter's – that is, in the very years that Bernini was put in charge of the papal projects – mediated with artists, and had a say in defining their compensation. He was subsequently made Archpriest of the Basilica of Saint Peter's (1626), papal majordomo (1629), Archbishop of Amasia (1633), and Cardinal of S. Crisogono (1643). Finally, in May 1644, Fausto was proclaimed Bishop of Orvieto. In his testament, the cardinal

requested that his body be eventually translated to S. Crisogono and that Sisinio, his only heir, commission a funerary monument according to his wishes ('con quella memoria che parerà al d.[etto] mio erede'). See Chapter 4, n.98. For Fausto and Gaudenzio Poli, see Giovanna Sapori, 'Profilo di Fausto Poli "sovrintendente alle arti" nella casa Barberini', *Rivista dell'istituto nazionale d'archeologia e storia dell'arte*, vol.61 (2006 [2011]), pp 196–7, and idem, 'Collezioni di centro, collezionisti di periferia', in *Geografia del collezionismo: Italia e Francia tra il XVI e il XVIII secolo*, Olivier Bonfait, Michel Hochmann, Luigi Spezzaferro, and Bruno Toscano (eds), Rome, 2001, pp 41–59. See also Giovanna Curcio, 'Il maggiordomo e l'architetto (1624–1629): tracce per una storia dei palazzi vaticani' in *I Barberini e la cultura europea del Seicento*, Rome, 2007, pp 521–46. For the Poli Chapel, see Livio Pestilli, 'Bernini e collaboratori nella cappella Poli (dell'Angelo Custode, o del Santissimo Sacramento) a San Crisogono in Trastevere: precisazioni storiche ed artistiche', *21: Inquiries into Art, History, and the Visual*, vol.1 (2021), pp 77–134. See https://doi.org/10.11588/xxi.2021.1.79016. On Giulio Cartari (Cartarè) see Chapter 5, n.2. As Jennifer Montagu observed in 'Bernini Sculptures Not by Bernini' in *Gianlorenzo Bernini: New Aspects of His Art and Thought. A Commemorative Volume*, University Park and London, 1985, p.26: 'Cartari appears to have had considerable skill as a marble carver, but to have lacked the capacity to make any name for himself as a creative artist.'

10 On Bernini's home in Via della Mercede, see Francesco Quinterio, 'La casa del Bernini' in *Gian Lorenzo Bernini. Il testamento, la casa, la raccolta dei beni*, Franco Borsi, Cristina Acidini Luchinat, and Francesco Quinterio (eds), Florence, 1981, pp 13–37 and pp 87–102. For a quick overview of Bernini's four homes in Rome, see the article by Claudio Rendina (5 June 2011) in the daily *La Repubblica*: http://ricerca.repubblica.it/repubblica/archivio/repubblica/2011/06/05/bernini-le-sue-case-le-quattro-residenze.html

11 Domenico Bernini, *The Life of Gian Lorenzo Bernini by Domenico Bernini*, Franco Mormando (ed. and trans.), University Park, 2011, p.232.

12 Filippo Baldinucci, *The Life of Bernini*, Catherine Enggass (trans.), Maarten Delbeke, Evonne Levy, and Steven F. Ostrow (eds), University Park, 2006, p.88.

13 Domenico Bernini, *The Life*, p.232.

14 Baldinucci, *The Life*, p.70.

15 Domenico Bernini, *The Life*, p.232.

16 ibid. Baldinucci, *The Life*, p.70, states that Bernini died 'at about midnight', nine days away from his eighty-second birthday. The notary who opened Bernini's will stated that the artist's death occurred 'hora 6 circiter', that is, at about the sixth hour after sunset, as per the Italian way of dividing the day, which started at sunset. See Franco Mormando's comments in Domenico Bernini, *The Life*, p.421, n.19, as well as Roberto Colzi's 'Che ora era? Raffronto tra le ore all'italiana e alla francese a Roma', *Studi romani*, vol.43 (1995), pp 93–102.

17 Antonino Bertolotti, *Archivio storico artistico archeologico e letterario della città e provincia di Roma*, Fabio Gori (ed.), Spoleto, 1878–9, vol.III, p.305.

18 ibid.

19 Mormando, in Domenico Bernini, *The Life*, p.423.

20 Baldinucci, *The Life*, p.71.

21 Borsi, Acidini Luchinat, and Quinterio, p.60: 'Il mio corpo voglio che sia seppellito nella sacrosanta basilica di S. Maria Maggiore, dove oltr'havere la sepoltura di casa mia, servirà a monsignor Pietro Filippo mio figlio canonico della medema [*sic*] basilica per una quotidiana memoria di raccordarsi dell'anima mia, li funerali rimetto ad arbitrio dell'infrascritti miei heredi alli quali raccordo, ch'a' poveri defunti sono più necessarii li suffragi di messe et orationi che di apparenze dell'esequie.' Mormando, in Domenico Bernini, *The Life*, p.423, nicely translates 'poveri defunti' as 'the poor souls of the deceased', but Bernini's Italian is more nuanced. 'Poveri defunti' implies not only compassion for the deceased but also a regret for the loss of life. Thus 'unfortunate' or 'unlucky' is closer to the biographer's intentions.

22 Baldinucci, *The Life*, p.72; Domenico Bernini, *The Life*, p.233.

23 Domenico Bernini, *The Life*, p.233.

24 See Fraschetti, p.106, and Mormando, in Domenico Bernini, *The Life*, p.423, n.29. The image here published reflects the current aspect of the marble plaque, with the family crest being just about totally eroded. A photograph available online still shows what appears to be a base made of ashlar upon which there is a column with a sphere at its summit. See https://www.walksinrome.com/blog/berninis-tomb-santa-maria-maggiore-rome. The photo was taken on 19 March 2006 by Ebacherdom.

25 Mormando, in Domenico Bernini, *The Life*, p.423, specifies that the inscription dates to after 1746, when Pope Benedict XIV granted the status of nobility to the

artist's family. It is worth repeating that Gian Lorenzo Bernini himself had been knighted by Gregory XV in 1621 with the Order of Christ. See Baldinucci, *The Life*, p.14, and Domenico Bernini, *The Life*, p.109.

26 Romolo Artioli and Benedetto Carpineta, 'La ricerca della tomba di Gian Lorenzo Bernini', *Atti del III congresso nazionale di studi romani*, C. Galassi Paluzzi (ed.), Bologna, 1935, vol.II, pp 321–4.

27 *Bernini in Vaticano: Braccio di Carlo Magno maggio - luglio 1981*, Anna Gramiccia (ed.), Rome, 1981, p.310, cat. no. 329. Mormando, in Domenico Bernini, *The Life*, p.423, n.29. Artioli and Carpineta, p.322: 'Venne constatata l'esistenza di 6 casse metalliche, in condizioni relativamente buone, con le relative iscrizioni, indicanti salme della famiglia Bernini, tumulate dal 1840 al 1870, e per di più l'esistenza di un mucchio di materiali, senza traccia di metalli, costituito da avanzi di casse di legno e resti di ossa alcune conservate, altre polverizzate, senza alcun segno d'individuazione fra cui si trovò l'impugnaura dorata di uno spadino cavalleresco.' From the *Libro dei morti seppelliti nella basilica*, it was determined that 40 persons had been buried in the Bernini family sepulcher. It should be noted that in 1807 some laborers working for the Basilica of S. Maria Maggiore stole lead coffins for the value of the material itself, but, supposedly, the theft affected only the tombs belonging to the Sciarra, Cesarini, and Rospigliosi families, as well as those of the church Canons. Nevertheless, Bernini's lead coffin could have been stolen by the French soldiers who, between 1790 and 1815, desecrated many Roman churches. See Artioli and Carpineta, p.323. The period during which the French troops caused the greatest damage to a number of churches was between 1798 and 1799.

28 Giulia Fusconi, *Disegni decorativi del barocco romano*, Rome, 1986, pp 16–18. Fraschetti, p.257. Tomaso Montanari, 'Bernini e Cristina di Svezia. Alle origini della storiografia berniniana' in *Gian Lorenzo Bernini e i Chigi tra Roma e Siena*, Paola Barocchi (ed.), Cinisello Balsamo, 1998, pp 328–477, here p.390, suggests that, had Bernini succeeded in completing his project for a new apse of the Basilica of Santa Maria Maggiore, where he might have created a sepulcher for Clement IX, he would also have had the possibility of building himself a less modest monument than the current one. See also Montanari's entry in Maria Grazia Bernardini and Maurizio Fagiolo dell'Arco (eds), *Gian Lorenzo Bernini: Regista del Barocco*, Geneva and Milan, 1999, pp 450–51, n.229.

29 Neither Fame nor Virtue as described by Ripa match exactly what Gimignani has sketched. See Cesare Ripa, *Iconologia*, Venice, 1669, pp 192 and 672–4.

30 Istituto Centrale per la Grafica, Inv. FC. 127531r. The drawing, black pencil on beige paper, measures 22.5 × 17.2 cm. If I am correct in seeing the figure of a reclining woman looking up towards Bernini's bust, with a child on either side of her and, possibly but rather illegibly, a third one between her and the cartouche, it might be a personification of *Caritas*. However, while such a personification would make sense in a papal monument, its presence in a sepulcher for an artist is difficult to justify. Perhaps, this figure is *Mater Natura*. If this were her identity, then she would represent a disconsolate Nature who, paraphrasing Bembo's distich on Raphael's tomb, could be thought as saying: 'While Bernini was alive, she feared of being conquered and, when dying, she feared dying herself.' Ursula Fisher Pace (private communication) and Montanari, *Gian Lorenzo Bernini: Regista del Barocco*, pp 450–51, instead see three putti in the lower part of the drawing. Fraschetti, p.257, on the other hand – who was the first to publish the drawing – saw in the winged figure crowning Bernini's bust a 'simbolico personaggio alato, forse il Tempo', and in the lower part of the monument only two putti ('due putti agitati in atto di dolore ed uno piangente, che recano un cartoccio su cui si legge il nome del Bernini').

31 For the sepulcher and the documentation related to it, see Montanari, 'Bernini e Cristina di Svezia', also Bernardini and Fagiolo dell'Arco, pp 450–51, n.229, and Sergej Androsov, catalogue entry, in ibid., p.451, n.230. For Bernini's last will and testament as well as an inventory of his belongings, see Borsi, Acidini Luchinat, and Quinterio, p.105: '*Nel cortile del Palazzo*, dove habitano l'illustrissimi Signori figli, et heredi della b.[eata] m.[emoria] del Signor Cavaliere Giovanni Lorenzo Bernino, vi sono le seguenti robbe. Una statua più grande del naturale, che rappresenta una fama, la quale hoggi si ritrova nella bottega di Mastro Giacomo Bertioli scarpellino al'incontro S. Maria in Via, per non esserci luogo in casa.'

32 Montanari, 'Bernini e Cristina di Svezia', p.390. Fraschetti, p.379, n.1, published a letter from the State Archives in Modena in which it is stated that it was the pope himself who had chosen as his final resting place the Basilica of Santa Maria Maggiore. Clement IX, like his predecessor, Alexander VII, probably began thinking of his final tomb soon after he became pope. On this topic as well as the excessive cost that

the new apse project would have represented for the papal coffers and the Rospigliosi family, see Sebastiano Roberto, *Gianlorenzo Bernini e Clemente IX Rospigliosi. Arte e architettura a Roma e in Toscana nel Seicento*, Rome, 2004, pp 261–87.

33 Montanari, 'Bernini e Cristina di Svezia', p.390, and Roberto, pp 264–5.

34 Roberto, p.269.

35 Tomaso Montanari, 'Gian Lorenzo Bernini e Sforza Pallavicino', *Prospettiva*, vol.87/88 (1997), p.55. Sforza Pallavicino died in 1667 and the tombstone, designed by Mattia de' Rossi, had to receive Bernini's approval. On Pallavicino, see especially Maarten Delbeke, *The Art of Religion: Sforza Pallavicino and Art Theory in Bernini's Rome*, Farnham, 2012, especially pp 97–133, where the proper commemoration of an individual is believed to be that provided by men of letters rather than by artists.

36 Plutarch's *Lives*, Bernadotte Perrin (trans.), London, 1914, I, xix, p.359: 'And to those who expressed their amazement that many men of no fame had statues, while he had none, he used to say: "I would rather have men ask why I have no statue, than why I have one." In short, he thought a good citizen should not even allow himself to be praised, unless such praise was beneficial to the commonwealth.'

37 Giovanni Antonio Borboni, *Delle Statue*, Rome, 1661, p.336: 'Hor se non solamente non si puo biasimare; ma è capace di merito infinito, chi ammette le Statue con haver nell'animo i fini lodati; che lodi, e che meriti si guadagnerà mai, chi le haverà per eccesso di humiltà ricusate? Scrisse Pauolo ai Corinthi, *Qui matrimonio iungit Virginem suam, benè facit, & qui non iungit, melius facit*. Così dirò io a mio proposito. Chi s'è sposato coll'immortalità del suo nome in qualche Statua, ha fatto bene; ma chi se è voluto in cio mantener Celibe, ha fatto meglio.' On Borboni's ideas on the superiority of the written word in commemorating individuals worthy of a public statue, see also Delbeke, *The Art of Religion*, pp 108–12.

38 The idea that words outlast sculpture in time and space may have been influenced by Pindar's *Nemean Odes* (the Aldine *editio princeps* was published in Venice in 1513) that Bernini's son, Pier Filippo, would likely have known. At the beginning of the fifth Nemean Pindar writes: 'I am not a sculptor, so as to fashion stationary/ statue that stand on their same base./Rather, on board every ship/and in every boat, sweet song,/go forth from Aegina and spread the news that/Lampon's mighty son Pytheas/has won the crown for the pancratium in Nemea's games,/not yet showing on his cheeks late summer,/the mother of the grape's soft bloom.' See Pindar, *Olympian Odes, Pythian Odes*, 2 vols, William H. Race (ed. and trans.), Cambridge, MA, 1997, II, pp 38 and 49. See Maria Pavlou, 'Pindar "Nemean" 5: Real and Poetic Statues', *Phoenix*, vol.64 (2010), pp 1–17. See also Delbeke, *The Art of Religion*, as in n.35.

39 See, especially, Tomaso Montanari, 'At the Margins of the Historiography of Art: The *Vite* of Bernini Between Autobiography and Apologia' in *Bernini's Biographies: Critical Essays*, Maarten Delbeke, Evonne Levy, and Steven F. Ostrow (eds), University Park, 2006, pp 73–109, and idem, 'Bernini and Christina of Sweden' in *Art History in the Age of Bellori: Scholarship and Cultural Politics in Seventeenth-Century Rome*, Janis Bell and Thomas Willette (eds), New York, 2002, pp 94–126.

40 Montanari, 'Bernini e Cristina di Svezia', p.391.

41 Sergej Androsov, n.230.

42 Montanari, 'Bernini e Cristina di Svezia', p.399, fig.51.

43 Jacopo Curzietti, '"Con disegno del Cavalier Bernino". Giulio Cartari e la decorazione della cappella Poli in S. Crisogono a Roma', *Storia dell'arte*, 120 (2008), pp 41–58, here p.44. Sergej Androsov, n.230, suggested that the sculptor of the Gaudenzio Poli portrait (at the time still unknown) might be the same artist who sculpted Bernini's terracotta portrait.

44 Montagu, 'Bernini Sculptures Not by Bernini', p.25: 'These sculptors [Bernini's assistants], many of whom have been virtually forgotten by the history of art, were responsible for the realization of many of the master's conceptions and for the creation of much of what we see today as constituting the fabric of Baroque Rome.'

45 Giovan Pietro Bellori, *The Lives of the Modern Painters, Sculptors and Architects*, Hellmut Wohl (ed.), Alice Sedgwick Wohl (trans.), Cambridge, 2005. For the Italian edition, see Giovan Pietro Bellori, *Le vite de' pittori, scultori e architetti moderni*, Evelina Borea (ed.), Turin, 1976.

46 Bellori, *The Lives*, p.49.

47 The *Lives* of Guido Reni, Andrea Sacchi, and Carlo Maratta (or Maratti) remained in manuscript form only to be published in 1942 by Michelangelo Piacentini. See Bellori, *Le vite*, p.vii. The six Italian painters are Annibale and Agostino Carracci, Barocci, Caravaggio, Domenichino, and Lanfranco. The architect is Domenico Fontana and the sculptor Alessandro Algardi. The foreign painters' biographies included are those of Rubens, Van Dyck, and Poussin. François Duquesnoy completes the list as the only foreign sculptor.

48 Bellori, *The Lives*, p.51, n.4.

49 For the exact number of popes for whom Bernini worked see Chapter 1, n.5.

50 Montanari, 'Bernini e Cristina di Svezia', p.378. Although the letter among the papers relating to Bernini in the Bibliothèque Nationale in Paris bears no signature, Montanari has found an identical copy of it in the Biblioteca Angelica signed by 'Decio cardinal Azzolino'. Ibid., pp 378–9.

51 On the genesis of Baldinucci and Domenico Bernini's biographies of Gianlorenzo Bernini, see Montanari, 'At the Margins of the Historiography of Art', pp 73–109; idem, 'Bernini e Cristina di Svezia', pp 385–425.

52 For a valuable historical contextualisation of Bellori and his *Lives*, see Tomaso Montanari's introduction to Bellori, *The Lives,* pp 1–39, and Giovanni Previtali, 'Introduzione', in Bellori, *Le vite*, pp IX–LX.

53 See Bruce Boucher, *Italian Baroque Sculpture*, London, 1998, p.203. Ann Sutherland Harris plausibly endorsed Boucher's view in *Seventeenth-Century Art and Architecture*, London, 2005, p.113. See also Dean Walker, 'An Introduction to Sculpture in Rome in the Eighteenth Century' in *Art in Rome in the Eighteenth Century*, London, 2000, p.212. On the other hand, Julius S. Held and Donald Posner, *17th and 18th Century Art*, New York, 1971, p.355, claimed 'his [Bernini's] work remained the main influence on Italian sculpture far into the next century'. For a corrective view on this subject, see Livio Pestilli, 'On Bernini's Reputed Unpopularity in Late Baroque Rome', *Artibus et historiae*, vol.63 (2011), pp 119–42.

54 For these two sculptors, see Estelle Lingo's *François Duquesnoy and the Greek Ideal*, New Haven, 2007, and Jennifer Montagu, *Alessandro Algardi,* 2 vols, New Haven and London, 1985.

55 Gould, pp 134–40, in discussing the impact on other artists, notes 'Bernini's influence on French students at the Rome academy lasted until well into the eighteenth century' and reminds his readers that in the 1720s and 1730s, 'when Rome itself was experiencing a revival of interest in Bernini, half a century after his death, there was a corresponding resurgence of his influence among young French sculptors who were *pensionnaires* at the Rome academy', singling out especially artists such as Bouchardon, Michel-Ange Slodtz, and, most of all, Lambert-Sigisbert Adam.

56 On the subject of draping and folds in sixteenth- and seventeenth-century sculpture, see Estelle Lingo, *Mochi's Edge and Bernini's Baroque*, London and Turnhout, pp 47–101 and pp 204–5. Bernini's exaggerated treatment of the garments, especially in his late years – such as the *Angel with the Crown of Thorns* and *Angel with the Superscription* designed for the Castel Sant'Angelo bridge but now in the Church of Sant'Andrea delle Fratte – where the folds hardly bear any relationship to the body beneath them, was far removed from classical ideals. See below.

57 Lingo, *Mochi's Edge*, pp 47–101, esp. pp 49 and 68.

58 Baldinucci, *The Life*, p.75; idem, *Vita del cavaliere Gio. Lorenzo Bernino, scultore, architetto, e pittore*, Florence, 1682 p.68; Domenico Bernini, *Vita del cavaliere Gio. Lorenzo Bernino*, Rome, 1713, p.149.

59 Baldinucci, *The Life*, pp 74–5.

60 Quoted by Tomaso Montanari, 'Creating an Eye for Models: The Role of Bernini' in *Bernini: Sculpting in Clay*, C.D. Dickerson III, Anthony Sigel, and Ian Wardropper (eds), New Haven and London, 2012, p.63.

61 Montaiglon, *Correspondance,* IX, p.445.

62 ibid., p.469.

63 ibid., X, p.434: 'qui est un de ses plus beaux morceaux'. Vandières approves the execution of the cast on 19 February 1753, ibid., p.438, which is finally received by Natoire three years later, by 22 September 1756, ibid., p.159.

64 ibid., XII, p.119, 16 July 1766, letter from Natoire to Marigny: 'Un de nos sculpteur [*sic*], nommé *Oudon*, a entrepris de faire deux statues pour l'église des Chartreux de Rome; le Père procureur général françois de cette maison, connoissan ce jeune artist, me parla de son proget et du dessain qu'il avoit de se servir du s[r] *Oudon*; j'approuvay beaucoup son idée en l'assurent du mérite du sujet dont il fesoit choix; de sorte que le jeune sculpteur a mis la main à l'œuvre et a fait un très bon modelle qu'il exécute actuelement en grand. Je crois que cette occasion luy sera d'un très gran avantage pour son avancement; l'une de ses figures représantante *saint Bruno*, fondateur de cet ordre, et l'autre *saint Jean-Baptiste*, leur partron.' Ibid., note 1, the editor specifies: 'Le *saint Bruno* fut seul exécuté et excita, comme on sait, une admiration générale.'

65 ibid., XIII, p.398.

66 ibid., XIV, p.222.

67 ibid., p.235. Even after the Académie de France ceased to exist on 13 January 1793 (ibid., XVII, p.i and ff), we hear of the survival of Bernini's plaster cast in an inventory of 1 August 1796, listing all of the items that had belonged to said institution. Ibid., XVI, p.439. The Académie was re-founded in 1804.

68 M. Valery, *Historical, Literary, and Artistical Travels in Italy: A Complete and Methodical Guide for Travellers and Artists*, C.E. Clifton (trans.), Paris, 1839, p.540, French edition: *Voyages Historiques et Littéraires en Italie, pendant les années 1826, 1827 et 1828*, Paris, 1833, t. IV, p.97.

69 See the preface by Fabrizio Clerici to *I disegni di figura nell'Archivio Storico dell'Accademia di San Luca*, 3 vols, Angela Cipriani and Enrico Valeriani (eds), Rome, 1988, I. See also Pestilli, 'On Bernini's Reputed Unpopularity in Late Baroque Rome', as well as Andrea Bacchi and Anne-Lise Desmas, 'The Fortunes of Bernini in 18th-Century Sculpture' in *Bernini*, Andrea Bacchi and Anna Coliva (eds), catalogue to the exhibition held at the Galleria Borghese, 1 November 2017 – 4 February 2018, pp 333–48.

70 Cipriani and Valeriani, I, p.121, drawing A.94, p.129, by an anonymous artist.

71 ibid., I, p.135 and p.145, drawings A.110 by G.A. Martinez, A.111 by F. Evangelista, and A.112 by R. De Rossi. The reference to 'il profeta Daniele' instead of 'Habakkuk' on p.135 is an error (oral communication by Angela Cipriani).

72 ibid., I, pp 148–50 and 157, drawings A.121 by R. Ricci and A.122 by an anonymous draftsman.

73 See n.53 and Chapter 5, n.116.

74 Cipriani and Valeriani, II, p.72 and pp 85–6, drawings A.201 by G.B Puccetti, A.202 by G.B. Vannini, A.203 by an anonymous artist.

75 ibid., pp 119–20 and 126–7, drawings A.243 by P.L. Bossio, A.244, A.245a, and A.245b all by anonymous artists. In both of these contests Maratta was also one of the judges.

76 ibid., p.192.

77 ibid., p.199, drawings A.353 by G. Giacoboni, A.353 by P. Silvestri, A.354 by B. Schiaccioni, A.355 by F. Nati, A.356 by L. Bianchini, A.357 by G. Paladino. See also p.238.

78 ibid., III, p.101 and p.212 for *Saint Bibiana*. Ibid, p.99, A.499 by F. Cornachi, A.501 by P. Camporese, A.503 by A. Nahl for the *Apollo Belvedere*. Johann Joachim Winckelmann, *History of the Art of Antiquity*, Harry Francis Mallgrave (trans.), Los Angeles, 2006, p.334. Tobias George Smollett, *Travels Through France and Italy*, 2 vols, London, 1766, II, p.150.

79 Charles de Brosses, *Lettres Familières sur l'Italie*, 2 vols, Paris, 1931, II, p.162: 'Le fameux baldaquin [. . .] n'a pas besoin que j'en fasse ici l'éloge: son mérite est assez connu; c'est le plus beau jet de fonte qu'il y ait au monde.'

80 Giuseppe Pavanello, 'Canova/Roma' in *Canova. Eterna bellezza*, Giuseppe Pavanello (ed.), Cinisello Balsamo, 2019, pp 18–43, here p.18: 'lavorato con tanta delicatezza che sembra imposibile [*sic*], vi sono le Foglie di aloro di meraviglioso lavoro, bello è ancora il nudo che non credevo tanto'. Pavanello quotes from Antonio Canova, *Scritti*, 2 vols, Hugh Honour and Paolo Mariuz (eds), Rome, 2007, I, pp 144–5 and 155.

81 Edgar Peters Bowron, in *Art in Rome in the Eighteenth Century*, Edgar Peters Bowron and Joseph J. Rishel (eds), Philadelphia, 2000, p.426.

82 The 'twin' churches of Santa Maria di Montesanto and Santa Maria dei Miracoli in Piazza del Popolo, as well as the church of Sant'Agnese and Palazzo Ludovisi, were only partially designed by Bernini. In the Louvre painting of the same theme (1759), among the pictures within the picture Panini also includes the *Tomb of Urban VIII*, the *Cathedra Petri*, the *Ecstasy of Saint Teresa*, and *Habakkuk and the Angel*.

83 When in 1998 Claudio Strinati asked Maurizio Fagiolo dell'Arco to get involved with the planning of the exhibition *Gian Lorenzo Bernini: Regista del Barocco*, that would be held at Palazzo Venezia between 21 May and 16 September 1999, the latter's immediate response, tellingly, was 'Ma una mostra del Bernini esiste già: si chiama Roma' ['But a Bernini exhibition already exists: it's called Rome']. See Maurizio Fagiolo dell'Arco, *Berniniana: Novità sul regista del Barocco*, Milan, 2002, p.11.

84 Leo Bruhns, 'Das Motiv der ewigen Anbetung in der römischen Grabplastik des 16., 17., und 18. Jahrhunderts', *Römisches Jahrbuch für Kunstgeschichte*, vol.IV (1940), pp 253–432.

85 John Shearman, 'The Chigi Chapel in S. Maria del Popolo', *Journal of the Warburg and Courtauld Institutes*, vol.24 (1961), pp 129–60, esp. pp 133–4.

86 ibid., p.135. For Athanasius Kircher's interpretation of the obelisk's spreading form as indicative of God's divine light as it reaches the world, and the obelisk-like form such *lux* takes in a couple of diagrams, see Fabio Barry, 'Im-material Bernini' in *Material Bernini*, Evonne Ley and Carolina Mangone (eds), London and New York, 2016, pp 39–67, esp. pp 51–3. Idem, *Painting in Stone: Architecture and the Poetics of Marble from Antiquity to the Enlightenment*, New Haven and London, 2020, pp 321–2. See also 'Fioravante Martinelli: Roma Ricercata Nel suo sito & nella scuola di tutti gli Antiquarij, e dedicata All'Em. mo e Rev.mo Sig.re Cardinal Chigi, Roma 1658' in Christina Strunck, 'Bellori und Bernini Rezipieren

Raphael: Unbekannte Dokumente zur Cappella Chigi in Santa Maria del Popolo', *Marburger Jahrbuch für Kunstwissenschaft*, vol.30 (2003), pp 131–82, here p.180.

87 Shearman, p.130. The first to 'return' the attribution of the Chigi sepulcher to Raphael was Domenico Gnoli, 'La Sepoltura d'Agostino Chigi nella chiesa di S. Maria del Popolo in Roma', *Archivio storico dell'arte*, vol.2 (1889), pp 317–26.

88 Rudolf Wittkower, *Gian Lorenzo Bernini: The Sculptor of the Roman Baroque*, London, 1966 [orig. 1955], p.232. On the various phases of decoration and restoration of the Chigi Chapel, the various interpretations of the documentation available, some of the issues that still remain unclear, and a recap of the relevant bibliography, see Nicole Riegel, 'Die Chigi-Kapelle in Santa Maria del Popolo: eine kritische Revision', *Marburger Jahrbuch für Kunstwissenschaft*, vol.30 (2003), pp 93–130, and Strunck, 'Bellori und Bernini Rezipieren Raphael'. For a succinct recapitulation of the decorative phases, see Christina Strunck, 'Cappella Chigi in Santa Maria del Popolo' in *Rom: Meisterwerke der Baukunst von der Antike bis heute; Festgabe für Elisabeth Kieven*, Christina Strunck (ed.), Petersberg, 2007, pp 223–5.

89 The bronze globe imitated the one that capped the top of the obelisk which would eventually be moved to Saint Peter's Square and that legend claimed contained the ashes of Julius Caesar. See Shearman, p.133.

90 On Agostino's bronze portrait, that was never put in place, see Francesco Petrucci's entry in Bernardini and Fagiolo dell'Arco (eds), no. 73, pp 355–6, quoting Gnoli, p.319. On the second bronze relief designated for the decoration of Agostino's sarcophagus, see Enzo Bentivoglio, 'La Cappella Chigi: l'immagine ritrovata del secondo pannello bronzeo del monumento di Agostino, gli inediti precedenti artistici del mosaicista Luigi (da Pace) veneziano ed altre considerazioni' in *Raffaello a Roma*, Rome, 1986, pp 309–14. The third panel was never cast.

91 Shearman, p.132; Gnoli, p.322; Strunck, 'Bellori und Bernini Rezipieren Raphael', p.135.

92 Shearman, p.132. On the different marbles employed and their metaphorical meaning, see Barry, *Painting in Stone*, p.322. It was during the initial phase of the renovation of the chapel (1652–4) that the lower part took on a different iconographic program. See Strunck, 'Bellori und Bernini Rezipieren Raphael', p.134.

93 Filippo Titi, *Studio di pittura, scultura, et architettura, nelle chiese di Roma*, Rome, 1674, p.425. See Shearman, p.135, n.36.

94 Filippo Titi, *Ammaestramento utile, e curioso di pittura scoltura et architettura nelle chiese di Roma*, Rome, 1686, p.361, and idem, *Descrizione delle pitture, sculture e architetture esposte al pubblico in Rome*, 2 vols, Rome, 1763, II, p.391. Francesco Posterla, *Roma sacra, e moderna*, Rome, 1725, p.272.

95 Shearman, p.135, n.36. One of Bernini's important collaborators, Ludovico Gimignani, adopted the idea in his design for the tomb of Agostino Favoriti (1685) executed by the sculptor Filippo Carcani in Santa Maria Maggiore, and also incorporated it in a drawing for a planned tomb of Queen Christina of Sweden. See Ursula V. Fisher Pace, 'Contributo alla storia del monumento funebre di Cristina' in *Cristina di Svezia e Roma*, Stockholm, 1999, pp 81–96, here pp 83–5.

96 Gnoli, p.324, states that the pyramidal design was subsequently much 'abused' so as to obfuscate the originality of Agostino's tomb. The author of Caprara's monument remains anonymous. For his military role, see Walter Buchowiecki, *Handbuch der Kirchen Roms*, 2 vols, Vienna, 1970, II, p.261.

97 Bruhns.

98 ibid., p.270: 'Die Idee der ewigen Andacht hat sich wahrhaft großartig verkörpert: der verseinerte Erzbischof fordert durch alle Jahrhunderte die Gläubigen auf, gleich ihm die Knie zu beugen und den Schutzpatron der Stadt zu verehren.'

99 Anthony Blunt, *Guide to Baroque Rome*, New York, 1982, p.108, and Montagu, I, p.165. For an important study of the development of portraiture in Rome, see Steven F. Ostrow, '"Sculptors Pursue Likeness": The Typology and Function of Seventeenth-Century Portrait Sculpture in Rome' in *Bernini and the Birth of Baroque Portrait Sculpture*, Andrea Bacchi, Catherine Hess, and Jennifer Montagu (eds), Los Angeles, 2008, pp 65–83.

100 Baldinucci, *Vita*, p.67: 'È concetto molto universale, ch'egli sia stato il primo, che abbia tentato di unire l'Architettura con la Scultura, e Pittura in tal modo, che di tutte si facesse un bel composto.' Idem, *The Life*, p.74: 'The opinion is widespread that Bernini was the first to attempt to unite architecture with sculpture and painting in such a manner that together they make a beautiful whole.' Irving Lavin, *Bernini and the Unity of the Visual Arts*, New York, 1980, called it 'the unity of the visual arts'. For two articles that shed light on the use and meaning of the term in Baldinucci and Domenico Bernini, see Tomaso Montanari, 'Il "bel composto": nota filologica su un nodo della storiografia berniniana', *Studi secenteschi*, vol.46 (2005), pp 195–210,

and Maarten Delbeke, 'Gianlorenzo Bernini's *Bel Composto*: The Unification of Life and Works in Biography and Historiography' in *Bernini's Biographies*, pp 251–74. See also Maarten Delbeke's chapter, 'The Composite Work' in *The Art of Religion*, pp 135–72.

101 Anthony Blunt, *Artistic Theory in Italy 1450–1660*, Oxford, 1980, p.133: 'They [Church authorities] set about making religion more accessible, not by giving it a more rational foundation as the Protestants had done, but by making it appeal to the emotions.'

102 Bruhns, pp 334–5.

103 ibid., p.338: 'Bernini, der sich auf dem Theater ebenso zu Hause fühlte wie am Zeichentisch oder auf dem Bauplatz oder in der Bildhauerwekstatt, hat hier alle Künste, die er beherrschte, auf einmal augeboten, sie aber auch auf allzu engem Schauplatz in ein Gedränge gegeneinandergebracht. Die Wand, die sich nach vorne preßt und zu einer Wunderbühne-aufplatzt; der Himmelsbote, der herabgeschwebt ist, um eine hingegebene Nonne in eine überirdische Verzücking dahinsinken zu lassen; die Versinnlichung des Übersinnlichen, die Festhaltung des Verschwebenden – sind in dem Altar der hl. Therese gewiß so überzeugend gestaltet, daß die Kunstgeschichte aller Zeiten kaum etwas Ebenbürtiges aufweist.' Also see the fundamental comments on the Cornaro Chapel in Lavin's *Bernini and the Unity of the Visual Arts*.

104 See Blunt, *Guide to Baroque Rome*, p.47 and, especially, Ostrow, '"Sculptors Pursue Likeness"', pp 69–75.

105 The Albertoni Altieri Chapel was decorated by Sebastiano Cipriani (1710), with the altarpiece representing the *Blessed Ludovica Albertoni* by Lorenzo Ottoni (1702–8), Giuseppe Passeri's vault fresco of the *Assumption of the Virgin*, and the striking portraits of Laura Carpegna Altieri by Giacomo Antonio Lavaggi and Prince Angelo Altieri by Giuseppe Mazzuoli (1709). The Muti-Bussi Chapel was designed by Francesco Ferrari, with memorials of Giovanni Muti and his wife Maria Colomba Vicentini by Bernardino Cametti (1725).

106 See n.56.

107 On the two Bernini statues in Sant'Andrea delle Fratte, originally meant to be placed on the Ponte Sant'Angelo but considered too precious by Clement IX who wanted to send them to his hometown of Pistoia, see Mark Weil, *The History and Decoration of the Ponte S. Angelo*, University Park and London, 1974, esp. p.33: 'Bernini's statues of the *Angels Carrying the Superscription and the Crown of Thorns* were not sent to Pistoia but remained in the sculptor's house until March 1729, when Prospero Bernini, the son of Paolo Bernini, donated them to the Church of S. Andrea delle Fratte.' The reason for the change in plans was that the pope died in 1679 and the statues remained in Bernini's studio.

108 'Essi dunque non hebbero altra mira, ne altro fine, o intenzione, che di vestir l'ignudo col mostrarlo; coprirlo per manifestarlo.' See Orfeo Boselli, *Osservazioni della scoltura antica*, Phoebe Dent Weil (ed.), Florence, 1978, *Ms. Corsini, f. 75*.

109 Pietro Bracci, in his diary, explicitly tells us of his looking at Bernini's high altar for Saint Peter's for inspiration when he designed the *Assumption and Glory of Angels* for the high altar of the Cathedral of Naples and, by implication, Bernini's *Tomb of Alexander VII* when he designed the Maria Clementina Sobieska, as it was similarly placed above a doorway. See Elisabeth Kieven, 'Pietro Bracci, Sculptor', in *Pietro Bracci and Eighteenth-Century Rome*, Elisabeth Kieven and John Pinto (eds), University Park, 2001, pp 9–24, here p.18.

110 Federico Bellini, 'L'interno della basilica liberiana nel rifacimento di Ferdinando Fuga', *Palladio. Rivista di storia dell'architettura e restauro*, vol.15 (1995), pp 49–62, esp. p.52. See also Anne-Lise Desmas, *Le ciseau et la tiare: les sculpteurs dans la Rome des papes 1724–1758*, Rome, 2012, pp 159–61. As the possible author of fig.45, Desmas refers to the same sculptors (Giovanni Ledous, Giuseppe Claus, or Pietro Pacilli). See her plate 37b. See also, Elisabeth Kieven, *Ferdinando Fuga. Architettura romana del Settecento: I disegni di architettura dalle collezioni del Gabinetto Nazionale delle Stampe. Il Settecento*, Rome, 1988, pp 61–3, cat. 50–51. For Fuga's autograph plan in the Istituto Nazionale d'Archeologia e Storia dell'Arte (Biblioteca di archeologia e storia dell'arte), *Coll. Lanciani*, Roma, XI.46.II.4 accession number 31809, see the online reproduction in the Stanford Digital Repository at https://purl.stanford.edu/fk079qq7773. According to Michael Erwee, *The Churches of Rome, 1527–1870*, 2 vols, London, 2014, I, p.391, the stucco angels are by Pietro Pacilli, Giuseppe Vans, and Jean Le Doux (the same sculptors indicated by Desmas). Idem, II, p.216, notes 44–50, cites as his source the Archivio Segreto Vaticano.

111 Jörg Garms, 'Le Bernin dans la literature européenne d'Ancien Regime' in *Le Bernin et l'Europe: Du baroque triumphant à l'âge romantique*, Paris, 2002, p.132.

112 De Brosses, *Lettres Familières sur l'Italie*.

113 Charles de Brosses, *Le président de Brosses en Italie: lettres familières écrites d'Italie en 1739 et 1740*, 2 vols, Paris, 1858, II, p.50: 'Le Bernin excelle dans les ouvrages où il faut de la mollesse et de la délicatesse. Mais son goût maniéré est bien loin de la fierté, du grand goût et de la simplicité de l'antique.'

114 Garms, p.145. Johann Joachim Winckelmann, *Reflections on the Imitation of Greek Works in Painting and Sculpture*, Elfriede Heyer and Roger C. Norton (trans.), La Salle, IL, 1987.

115 Johann Joachim Winckelmann, *Lettere italiane*, Milan, 1961, p.310: 'The Romans don't think at all. A statue of *Charity* by Bernini is all they care for.'

116 idem, *History of the Art of Antiquity*, p.193.

117 Francesco Milizia, *Dell'arte di vedere nelle belle arti del disegno secondo i principi di Sulzer, e di Mengs*, Genoa, 1786 (orig. 1781), p.10.

118 idem, *Dizionario delle belle arti del disegno estratto in gran parte dalla enciclopedia metodica*, 2 vols, Bassano, 1797, I, pp 106–7: 'Egli ful il primo a introdurre licenza e scorrezioni sotto pretesto di grazia . . . e per aver negletto i veri modelli dell'arte, egli servì di modello a tanti falsi copisti.'

119 For these foreign critics of Bernini's style, see Lucia Simonato, *Bernini scultore. Il difficile dialogo con la modernità*, Milan, 2018, pp 33–72. For Füssli's comments, see Giovanni Bottari and Stefano Ticozzi, *Raccolta di lettere sulla pittura, scultura ed architettura scritte dai più celebri personaggi dei secoli XV, XVI e XVII*, 8 vols, Milan, 1757–1825, VI, p.288.

120 *Encyclopédie methodique*, 1788–1825, I, p.277, under '*Bernin*' quoted by Simonato, pp 35 and 252, n.94.

121 *Athenaeum 1798–1800. Tutti i fascicoli della rivista di August Wilhelm Schlegel e Friedrich Schlegel*, G. Cusatelli (ed.), E. Agazzi and D. Mazza (trans.), Milan, 2009, p.321, quoted by Simonato, pp 33 and 252, n.86.

122 Cited by Simonato, p.29 and p.252, n.76. Carl Ludwig Fernow, *Über den Bildhauer Canova und dessen Werke*, Zurich, 1806, p.67.

123 Milizia, *Dizionario*, I, pp 106–7: 'Finì il Bernini col non poter più accorgersi dell'immensa sua bizzarria nel comporre, e non pose più mano alla scultura senza torcere ogni parte, persino dove sono le ossa.'

124 Simonato, p.40: 'Un po' ammanierato, un po' novello Caravaggio, Gian Lorenzo si apprestava ad affrontare un lungo secolo.'

125 Elena Lissoni, 'Cronologia' in the exhibition catalogue to *Canova Thorvaldsen. La nascita della scultura moderna*, Stefano Grandesso and Fernando Mazzocca (eds), Milan, 2019, pp 392–4. The information pertaining to Canova and Thorvaldsen is derived primarily from the catalogues to the two splendid exhibitions that opened in Milan and Rome in the fall of 2019. See also Giuseppe Pavanello (ed.), *Canova: Eterna Bellezza*, Cinisello Balsamo, 2019.

126 Fernando Mazzocca, 'Antonio Canova. "Una felice rivoluzione nelle arti"', in *Canova Thorvaldsen*, pp 19-30, here p.21.

127 Winckelmann, *Reflections*, p.5.

128 Lissoni, 'Cronologia', p.392.

129 Lord George Gordon Byron, *The Poetical Works of Lord Byron*, Thomas Moore *et alia* (ed.), New York, 1852, p.52, in a letter from Venice to John Hobhouse dated 2 January 1818.

130 Canova became highly acclaimed in 1779 after he exhibited his *Dedalus and Icarus* at the Fiera della 'Sensa' in Venice. With the money he earned he undertook his longed-for trip to Rome, where he was hosted by the Venetian ambassador, Girolamo Zulian, in Palazzo Venezia. See Lissoni, 'Cronologia', p.392, and Mazzocca, 'Antonio Canova. "Una felice rivoluzione nelle arti"', pp 19–30. Thorvaldsen received the Major Gold Medal and the accompanying grant from the Academy in 1793 but could not depart for Rome until 1796 because the institution could only afford one scholarship at a time. Thus, Thorvaldsen had to wait until the previously subsidised artist returned to Denmark. Bjarne Jørnæs, *The Sculptor Bertel Thorvaldsen*, Copenhagen, 2011, p.21.

131 On what constituted the 'Greek ideal' in the seventeenth century, on how 'subtle contour' became a defining feature of Greek sculpture, and on how it contributed to the rise of Neoclassicism in the eighteenth century, see Lingo, *François Duquesnoy and the Greek Ideal.*

132 Stendhal, *A Roman Journal*, Haakon Chevalier (trans.), New York, 1957, 16 June 1828, p.187: 'At first sight, and without any metaphysical reasoning, a statue of Canova's moves a young Italian woman to tears. Less than a week ago Giulia V . . . was obliged to hide her tears behind her veil. Madame Lamberti had taken her to see Canova's *Farewell of Venus and Adonis*; and on our way we were speaking of quite other things – and very gayly, as it happened.' The first and most significant incident that characterises what we now define as the 'Stendhal syndrome', however, describes the author's own reaction to the

monuments and works of art he saw in Florence, in the church of Santa Croce: 'My soul, affected by the very notion of being in Florence, and by the proximity of those great men whose tombs I had just beheld, was already in a state of trance. Absorbed in the contemplation of *sublime beauty*, I could, as it were, feel the stuff of it beneath my fingertips. I had attained to that supreme degree of sensibility where the *divine intimations* of art merge with the impassioned sensuality of emotions. As I emerged from the porch of *Santa Croce*, I was seized with a fierce palpitation of the heart (that same symptom which, in Berlin, is referred to as an *attack of nerves*); the well-spring of life was dried up within me, and I walked in constant fear of falling to the ground.' Stendhal, *Rome, Naples and Florence*, John Calder (trans.), London, 1959, p.302.

133 Stendhal, *A Roman Journal*, 5 July 1828, p.227.

134 Robert Enggass, *Early Eighteenth-Century Sculpture in Rome*, 2 vols, University Park and London, 1976, I, p.16.

135 Stendhal, *A Roman Journal*, p.228. On the Corsini Chapel, Vernon Hyde Minor, *Baroque Visual Rhetoric*, Toronto, 2016, pp 177–207, here p.177, quotes the *Diario di Roma* where Francesco Valesio comments that it 'has not met the satisfaction of all, being judged too precious and dry [*venendo riputata minuta e secca*]'. On the other hand, British visitors were especially interested in the Corsini Chapel, with Philip Yorke describing it as 'one of the most perfect pieces of modern architecture'. See Elisabeth Kieven, 'An Italian Architect in London: The Case of Alessandro Galilei (1691–1732)', *Architectural History*, vol.51 (2008), pp 1–31, here p.25.

136 Enggass, pp 15–19. Vernon Hyde Minor, *Passive Tranquillity: The Sculpture of Filippo Della Valle*, Philadelphia, 1997, pp 29–43.

137 Quite appropriately he has been defined as the 'director' of the Baroque. See Bernardini and Fagiolo dell'Arco.

138 Stendhal, *A Roman Journal*, p.228.

139 Chantelou, *Diary*, 23 July, pp 74–5: 'Our conversation then turned to his own works – the *David*, the *Proserpine*, the *Daphne* – M. de Ménars repeated the epigram of Urban VIII and praised the works of the Cavaliere above those of antiquity. He replied with great modesty that he owed all his reputation to his star which caused him to be famous in his lifetime, that when he died its ascendancy would no longer be active and his reputation would decline or fail very suddenly.' Chantelou, *Journal*, p.86.

140 Wittkower, *Gian Lorenzo Bernini*, p.1.

141 For a similar evaluation, see John Pope-Hennessy, *Italian High Renaissance and Baroque Sculpture: An Introduction to Italian Sculpture*, New York, 1985, p.106: 'Bernini did not become a Michelangelo – his talent was more facile, and his spiritual horizon was more limited – but he grew up to exercise a greater influence on the art of his own time than any other sculptor had exercised before.'

142 Leopoldo Cicognara, *Storia della scultura dal suo risorgimento in Italia fino al secolo di Canova*, 8 vols, Prato, 1823–4, VI, p.45.

Bibliography

Addison, J., *Remarks on Several Parts of Italy, &c. In the Years 1701, 1702, 1703*, London, 1767

Aelian, *Historical Miscellany*, Wilson, N.G. (trans.), Cambridge, MA, 1997

Ago, R., 'Rome's Economic Life, 1492–1692', in *A Companion to Early Modern Rome, 1492–1692*, Jones, P.M., Wisch, B., and Ditchfield, S. (eds), Leiden and Boston, 2019, pp 184–98

Alberti, L.B., *On Painting*, Spencer, J.R. (trans.), New Haven, 1956

Alexandre-Bidon, D., and Lett, D., *Children in the Middle Ages: Fifth–Fifteenth Centuries*, Gladding, J. (trans.), Notre Dame, 1999

Algarotti, F., *Saggio sopra l'Accademia di Francia che è in Roma*, Livorno, 1763

Algarotti, F., *Essai sur la peinture, et sur l'Académie de France, établie à Rome*, Pingeron, M. (trans.), Paris, 1769, pp 261–336

Androsov, S., catalogue entry in *Gian Lorenzo Bernini: Regista del Barocco*, Bernardini, M.G., and Fagiolo dell'Arco, M. (eds), Geneva and Milan, 1999, p.451, n.230

Anguissola, A., *Supports in Roman Marble Sculpture: Workshop Practice and Modes of Viewing*, Cambridge, 2018

Argens, J-B. de Boyer d', *Reflexions critiques sur les différentes écoles de peinture*, Paris, 1752

Aristotle, *Poetics* in *The Complete Works of Aristotle*, 2 vols, Barnes, J. (ed.), Princeton, 1985

Artioli, R., and Carpineta, B., 'La ricerca della tomba di Gian Lorenzo Bernini', *Atti del III congresso nazionale di studi romani*, Galassi Paluzzi, C. (ed.), Bologna, 1935, vol.II, pp 321–4

Aru, C., 'I Dialoghi romani di Francisco de Hollanda', *L'Arte*, vol.XXXI (1928), pp 117–28

Atanagi, D., *De le lettere facete, et piacevoli di diversi grandi huomini, et chiari ingegni, raccolte per M. Dionigi Atanagi*, Venice, 1561

Athenaeum 1798–1800. Tutti i fascicoli della rivista di August Wilhelm Schlegel e Friedrich Schlegel, Cusatelli, G. (ed.), Agazzi, E., and Mazza, D. (trans.), Milan, 2009

Audisio, F., 'Lettere e testi teatrali di Bernini: una postilla linguistica', in *Barocco romano e Barocco italiano: il teatro, l'effimero, l'allegoria*, Fagiolo dell'Arco, M., and Madonna, M.L. (eds), Rome, 1985, pp 26–43

Austin, M., 'Le attività economiche nella Grecia antica', in *Artisti e artigiani in Grecia: Guida storica e critica*, Coarelli, F. (ed.), Rome and Bari, 1980, pp 237–49, orig. published as *Economies et sociétés en Grèce ancienne*, Paris, 1972, pp 22–31 and 125–8

Avery, C., *Bernini: Genius of the Baroque*, London, 1997

Bacchi, A., 'Bernini e gli scultori del suo tempo', in *Aus aller Herren Länder: Die Künstler der Teutschen Academie von Joachim von Sandrart*, Turnhout, 2015

Bacchi, A., and Barroero, L. (eds), *La riscoperta del Seicento*, Genoa, 2017

Bacchi, A., and Coliva, A. (eds), *Bernini*, Milan, 2017

Bacchi, A., and Desmas, A-L., 'The Fortunes of Bernini in 18th-Century Sculpture', in *Bernini*, Bacchi, A., and Coliva, A. (eds), Milan, 2017, pp 333–48

Bacchi, A., and Hess, C., 'Creating a New Likeness: Bernini's Transformation of the Portrait Bust', in *Bernini and the Birth of Baroque Portrait Sculpture*, Los Angeles, 2008, pp 1–43

Bacchi, A., Hess, C., and Montagu, J. (eds), *Bernini and the Birth of Baroque Portrait Sculpture*, Los Angeles, 2008

Bacchi, A., Montanari, T., Paolozzi Strozzi, B., and Zikos, D. (eds), *I marmi vivi. Bernini e la nascita del ritratto barocco*, exh.cat., Florence, 2009

Baglione, G., *Le vite de' pittori, scultori et architetti dal pontificato di Gregorio XIII fino a tutto quello d'Urbano VIII*, Rome, 1649

Baldinucci, F., *Vocabolario Toscano dell'Arte del Disegno*, Florence, 1681

Baldinucci, F., *Vita del Cavaliere Gio. Lorenzo Bernino, scultore, architetto, e pittore*, Florence, 1682

Baldinucci, F., *Notizie dei professori del disegno da Cimabue in qua*, 7 vols, Florence, 1847

Baldinucci, F., *The Life of Bernini by Filippo Baldinucci*, Engass, C. (trans.), University Park, 1966

Baldinucci, F.S., *Vite di Artisti dei secoli XVII–XVIII*, Matteoli, A. (ed.), Rome, 1975

Baldinucci, F., *The Life of Bernini*, Engass, C. (trans.), Delbeke, M., Levy, E., and Ostrow, S.F. (eds), University Park, 2006

Baldriga, I., 'The First Version of Michelangelo's Christ for S. Maria sopra Minerva', *The Burlington Magazine*, vol.142 (2000), pp 740–45

Baretti, G., *La frusta letteraria*, 2 vols, Piccioni, L. (ed.), Bari, 1932

Barkan, L., *Michelangelo: A Life on Paper*, Princeton and Oxford, 2011

Barocchi, P. (ed.), *Trattati d'arte del Cinquecento fra manierismo e controriforma*, Bari, 1960–1962

Barocchi, P., *Scritti d'arte del Cinquecento*, 3 vols, Milan and Naples, 1971

Barolsky, P., *Michelangelo's Nose*, University Park, 1990

Barolsky, P., *Why Mona Lisa Smiles and Other Tales by Vasari*, University Park, 1991

Barolsky, P., *Giotto's Father and the Family of Vasari's Lives*, University Park, 1992

Barroero, L., '"*Il se rendit en Italie*". Artisti stranieri a Roma nel Seicento', *Roma moderna e contemporanea*, vol.I (1993), pp 13–34

Barroero, L., and Susinno, S., 'Arcadian Rome, Universal Capital of the Arts', in *Art in Rome in the Eighteenth Century*, Bowron, E.P., and Rishel, J.J. (eds), Philadelphia, 2000, pp 47–75

Barry, F., 'Im-material Bernini', in *Material Bernini*, Ley, E., and Mangone, C. (eds), London and New York, 2016, pp 39–67

Barry, F., *Painting in Stone: Architecture and the Poetics of Marble from Antiquity to the Enlightenment*, New Haven and London, 2020

Bartoli, R., 'Bandinelli contro tutti. L'artista negli occhi dei contemporanei', in *Baccio Bandinelli scultore e maestro (1493–1560)*, Heikamp, D., and Paolozzi Strozzi, B. (eds), Florence, 2014

Barzman, K-e., *The Florentine Academy and the Early Modern State: The Discipline of Disegno*, Cambridge, 2000

Basile, G., *Lo cunto de li cunti*, Rak, M. (ed.), Milan, 1999

Basile, G., *The Tale of Tales, or Entertainment for the Little Ones*, Canepa, N.L. (trans.), Detroit, 2007

Battaglia, S., *Grande dizionario della lingua italiana*, Turin, 1971

Bauer, G.C., 'Bernini in Paris', in *An Architectural Progress in the Renaissance and Baroque: Sojourns In and Out of Italy: Essays in Architectural History Presented to Hellmut Hager on his Sixty-Sixth Birthday*, University Park, 1992, vol.1, pp 308–19

Beecher, D., and Ciavolella, M., 'A Comedy by Bernini', in *Gianlorenzo Bernini: New Aspects of His Art and Thought: A Commemorative Volume*, Lavin, I. (ed.), University Park and London, 1985, pp 63–113

Bellini, F., 'L'interno della basilica liberiana nel rifacimento di Ferdinando Fuga', *Palladio. Rivista di storia dell'architettura e del restauro*, vol.15 (1995), pp 49–62

Bellori, G.P., *Le vite de' pittori, scultori e architetti moderni*, Evelina Borea (ed.), Turin, 1976

Bellori, G.P., 'The Idea of the Painter, the Sculptor and the Architect selected from the beauties of nature, superior to Nature', in *The Lives of the Modern Painters, Sculptors and Architects*, Wohl, H. (ed.), Sedgwick Wohl, A. (trans.), Cambridge, 2005

Bellori, G.P., *The Lives of the Modern Painters, Sculptors and Architects*, Wohl, H. (ed.), Sedgwick Wohl, A. (trans.), Cambridge, 2005

Bentivoglio, E., 'La Cappella Chigi: l'immagine ritrovata del secondo pannello bronzeo del monumento di Agostino, gli inediti precedenti artistici del mosaicista Luigi (da Pace) veneziano ed altre considerazioni', in *Raffaelllo a Roma*, Rome, 1986, pp 309–14

Berger, R.W., 'Bernini's Louis XIV Equestrian: A Closer Examination of Its Fortunes at Versailles', *The Art Bulletin*, vol.63 (1981), pp 232–48

Bernardini, M.G., and Fagiolo dell'Arco, M. (eds), *Gian Lorenzo Bernini: Regista del Barocco*, Geneva and Milan, 1999

Bernini, D., *Vita del Cavalier Gio. Lorenzo Bernino*, Rome, 1713

Bernini, D., *The Life of Gian Lorenzo Bernini by Domenico Bernini*, Mormando, F. (ed. and trans.), University Park, 2011

Bernini, G.L., *The Impresario*, Beecher, D., and Ciavolella, M. (eds), Ottawa, 1994

Bernini, P.F., 'The Vita Brevis of Gian Lorenzo Bernini', in *The Life of Gian Lorenzo Bernini by Domenico Bernini*, Mormando, F. (ed. and trans.), University Park, 2011, pp 237–41

Bernini, R., 'I disegni di Giovan Lorenzo Bernini nelle collezioni dell'Istituto Centrale per la Grafica: considerazioni sul volume Gualtieri-Corsini', in *Bernini Disegnatore: nuove prospettive di ricerca*, Ebert-Schifferer, S., Marder, T.A., and Schütze, S. (eds), Rome, 2017

Bertolotti, A., *Archivio storico artistico archeologico e letterario della città e provincia di Roma*, Gori, F. (ed.), Spoleto, 1878–1879, vol.III, p.305

Bianchi Bandinelli, R., 'L'artista nell'antichità classica', in *Artisti e artigiani in Grecia: Guida storica e critica*, Coarelli, F. (ed.), Rome and Bari, 1980

Blunt, A., *Artistic Theory in Italy 1450–1660*, Oxford, 1980

Blunt, A., *Guide to Baroque Rome*, New York and London, 1982

Blunt, A., *Art and Architecture in France 1500–1700*, London, 1982 and Hong Kong, 1999

Boccaccio, G., *The Decameron*, McWilliam, G.H. (trans. with Introduction), London, 1995

Bodart, D., *Les peintres des Pays-Bas Méridionaux et de la Principauté de Liège à Rome au XVIIeme siècle*, Brussels and Rome, 1970

Borboni, G.A., *Delle Statue*, Rome, 1661

Borghini, R., *Il Riposo*, Florence, 1584

Borromeo, F., *Sacred Painting*, Rothwell, Jr., K.S. (trans.), Cambridge, MA and London, 2010

Borsi, F., Acidini Luchinat, C., and Quinterio, F., *Gian Lorenzo Bernini. Il testamento, la casa, la raccolta dei beni*, Florence, 1981

Boselli, O., *Osservazioni della scoltura antica*, Dent Weil, P. (ed.), Florence, 1978

Boselli, O., *Osservazioni sulla scultura antica. I manoscritti di Firenze e di Ferrara*, Torresi, A.P. (ed.), Ferrara, 1994

Bottari, G.G., and Ticozzi, S., *Raccolta di lettere sulla pittura, scultura ed architettura scritte dai più celebri personaggi dei secoli XV, XVI e XVII*, 8 vols, Milan, 1822

Bouchard, J-J., *Voyage dans le Royaume de Naples in Œuvres de Jean-Jacques Bouchard in Journal II, Voyage dans le Royaume de Naples. Voyage dans la campagne de Rome,* Emanuele Kanceff (ed.), Turin, 1976

Boucher, B., *Italian Baroque Sculpture*, London, 1998

Boudon-Machuel, M., *François du Quesnoy 1597–1643*, Paris, 2005, pp 229–35 and pp 370–72

Bourgeois, B., '"Secure for Eternity": Assembly Techniques for Large Statuary in the Sixteenth to the Nineteenth Century', in *History of Restoration of Ancient Stone Sculptures*, Grossman, J.B., Podany, J., and True, M. (eds), Los Angeles, 2003

Bowron, E.P., and Rishel, J.J. (eds), *Art in Rome in the Eighteenth Century*, Philadelphia, 2000

Braham, A., and Hager, H. *Carlo Fontana: The Drawings at Windsor Castle*, London and Bradford, 1977

Briganti, G., Trezzani, L., and Laureati, L. (eds), *I Bamboccianti: pittori della vita quotidiana a Roma nel Seicento*, Rome, 1983

Broggio, P., 'L'*URBS* e il Mondo: Note sulla presenza degli stranieri nel Collegio Romano e sugli Orizzonti Geografici della "Formazione Romana" tra XVI e XVII secolo', *Rivista di storia della Chiesa in Italia*, vol.56 (2002), pp 81–120

Bruhns, L., 'Das Motiv der ewigen Anbetung in der römischen Grabplastik des 16., 17., und 18. Jahrhunderts', *Römisches Jahrbuch für Kunstgeschichte*, vol.IV (1940), pp 253–432

Buchowiecki, W., *Handbuch der Kirchen Roms*, 2 vols, Vienna, 1970, II, p.261

Burg, T., *Die Signatur: Formen und Funktionen vom Mittelalter bis zum 17. Jahrhundert*, Berlin, 2007

Burke, P., *The Fabrication of Louis XIV*, New Haven and London, 1992

Burke, P., *The Historical Anthropology of Early Modern Italy: Essays on Perception and Communication*, Cambridge, 2005

Burkhardt, J., 'I greci e i loro artisti', in *Artisti e artigiani in Grecia: Guida storica e critica*, Coarelli, F. (ed.), Rome and Bari, 1980, pp 5–22

Bush, V.L., '"Hercules and Cacus" and Florentine Traditions', *Memoirs of the American Academy in Rome*, vol.35 (1980), pp 163–206

Byron, G.G., Lord, *The Poetical Works of Lord Byron*, Moore, T. *et al.* (ed.), New York, 1852

Calmet, D., *Bibliothèque lorraine, ou Histoire des hommes illustres*, Nancy, 1751

Cambi, G., 'Istorie di Giovanni Cambi', in *Delizie degli Eruditi Toscani*, San Luigi, I. di (ed.), Florence, 1785

Canova, A., *Scritti*, 2 vols, Honour, H., and Mariuz, P. (eds), Rome, 2007

Capaccio, G.C., *Il Forastiero*, Naples, 1634

Capecchi, G., 'Superare l'antico: il Laocoonte "perfetto"', in *Baccio Bandinelli scultore e maestro 1493–1560*, Heikamp, D., and Paolozzi Strozzi, B. (eds), Florence, 2014

Cassiodorus, *The Letters of Cassiodorus*, Hodgkin, T. (ed. and trans.), London, 1886

Cassiodorus, *Variorum liber*, 8, 33, Mommsen, T. (ed.), Berlin, 1894

Castelnuovo, E., 'I volti dell'artista medievale: Molte domande, poche risposte', *Annali della Scuola Normale Superiore di Pisa*, vol.4 (2003), pp 3–10

Castiglione, B. Count, *The Book of the Courtier by Count Baldesar Castiglione* (1528), Eckstein Opdycke, L. (trans.), New York, 1901

Cavazzini, P., *Painting as Business in Early Seventeenth-Century Rome*, University Park, 2008

Cavazzini, P., 'Middle-Class Patronage, Collecting, and the Art Market', in *A Companion to Early Modern Rome, 1492–1692*, Jones, P.M., Wisch, B., and Ditchfield, S. (eds), Leiden and Boston, 2019, pp 412–26

Ceci, G., 'La Compagnia della Morte in Napoli', *Archivio storico per le provincie napoletane*, vol.38, Naples, 1913, pp 145–62

Cellini, B., *The Life of Benvenuto Cellini*, 2 vols, Symonds, J.A. (trans.), London, 1888

Cellini, B., *Autobiography of Benvenuto Cellini*, Symonds, J.A. (trans.), Garden City, 1961

Cellini, B., *La vita*, Turin, 1973

Cennini, C., *The Craftsman's Handbook*, Thompson Jr., D.V. (trans.), New York, 1960

Chantelou, P.F. de, *Diary of the Cavaliere Bernini's Visit to France*, Corbett, M. (trans.), Princeton, 1985

Chantelou, P.F. de, *Journal de voyage du Cavalier Bernin en France*, Stanić, M. (ed.), Paris, 2001

Cicero, *Orator*, Hubbell, H.M. (trans.), Cambridge, MA, 1962

Cicero, *De Oratore*, Rackham, H. (trans.), Cambridge, MA, 1977

Cicognara, L., *Storia della scultura dal suo risorgimento in Italia fino al secolo di Canova*, 8 vols, Prato, 1823–1824

Cipriani, A., and Valeriani, E. (eds), *I disegni di figura nell'Archivio Storico dell'Accademia di San Luca*, 3 vols, Rome, 1988

Cipriani, A., 'Presenze francesi all'Accademia di San Luca: 1664–1675', in *L'idéal classique: Les échanges artistiques entre Rome et Paris au temps de Bellori (1640–1700)*, Bonfait, O., and Desmas, A-L. (eds), Paris, 2002, pp 223–8

Clark, K., *The Nude: A Study in Ideal Form*, Garden City, 1956

Claussen, P.C., *Magistri doctissimi Romani: Die römischen Marmorkünstler del Mittelalters*, Stuttgart, 1987

Clément, P., *Lettres, instructions et mémoires de Colbert*, 7 vols, Paris, 1868

Clerici, F., *I disegni di figura nell'Archivio Storico dell'Accademia di San Luca*, 3 vols, Cipriani, A., and Valeriani, E. (eds), Rome, 1988

Clifton, J., 'Paolo de Matteis's *Allegory of the End of the War of the Spanish Succession*', in *Fortunata Neapolis: Kunst- und Kulturtransfer zwischen Neapel, Wien und Mitteleuropa*, Schütze, S. (ed.), Berlin and Boston, 2020, pp 1–16

Coarelli, F. (ed.), *Artisti e artigiani in Grecia: Guida storica e critica*, Rome and Bari, 1980 [originally published as 'Zur gesellschaftliche Stellung des bildenden Künstlers in der griechischen Klassik', in *Erlanger Forschungen*, vol.23 (1974)]

Coarelli, F., 'Cultura artistica e società', in *Storia di Roma*, Momigliano, A., and Schiavone, A. (eds), 7 vols, Turin, 1990

Cochin, C-N., *Voyage d'Italie, ou recueil de notes sur les ouvrages de peinture et de sculpture qu'on voit dans les principales villes d'Italie*, 3 vols, Paris, 1751

Coffin, D.R., 'Pirro Ligorio on the Nobility of the Arts', *Journal of the Warburg and Courtauld Institutes*, vol.27 (1964), pp 191–210

Colantuono, A., and Ostrow, S.F. (eds), *Critical Perspectives on Roman Baroque Sculpture*, University Park, 2014

Cole, J., 'Cultural Clientelism and Brokerage Networks in Early Modern Florence and Rome: New Correspondence between the Barberini and Michelangelo Buonarroti the Younger', *Renaissance Quarterly*, vol.60 (2007), pp 729–88

Cole, M.W., *Cellini and the Principles of Sculpture*, Cambridge, 2002

Cole, M.W., 'Bernini Struts', in *Material Identities*, Sofaer, J. (ed.), Malden, 2007

Cole, M.W., *Ambitious Form: Giambologna, Ammanati, and Danti in Florence*, Princeton and Oxford, 2011

Cole, M.W., 'What Is a Bozzetto', in *Material Bernini*, Levy, E., and Mangone, C. (eds), London and New York, 2016, pp 123–45

Coliva, A., and Schütze, S. (eds), *Bernini Scultore: La nascita del Barocco in Casa Borghese*, Rome, 1998

Coliva, A. (ed.), *Bernini scultore: La tecnica esecutiva*, Rome, 2002

Colzi, R. 'Che ora era? Raffronto tra le ore all'italiana e alla francese a Roma', *Studi romani*, vol.43 (1995), pp 93–102

Condivi, A., *Vita di Michelagnolo Buonarroti*, Giovanni Nencioni (ed.), Florence, 1998

Conforti, M., 'The Lateran Apostles', PhD diss., Harvard University, Cambridge, MA, 1977

Conforti, M., 'Pierre Legros and the Rôle of Sculptors as Designers in Late Baroque Rome', *The Burlington Magazine*, vol.119 (1977), pp 556–61

Conforti, M., 'Planning the Lateran Apostles', in *Studies in Italian Art and Architecture, 15th through 18th Centuries*, Millon, H.A. (ed.), Rome, 1980, pp 243–55

Connors, J., 'Review of Lione Pascoli, *Vite de' pittori, scultori ed architetti moderni*, Martinelli, V., and Marabottini, A. (eds), Perugia, 1992', *Journal of the Society of Architectural Historians*, vol.57 (1998), pp 469–71

Connors, J. and Rice, L. (eds), *Specchio di Roma barocca: una guida inedita del XVII secolo*, Rome, 1990

Costantini, A., 'Ares Ludovisi', in *La collezione Boncompagni Ludovisi: Algardi, Bernini e la fortuna dell'antico*, Venice, 1992

Curcio, G., 'Il maggiordomo e l'architetto (1624–1629): tracce per una storia dei palazzi vaticani', in *I Barberini e la cultura europea del Seicento*, Rome, 2007, pp 521–46

Cureau de la Chambre, P., *Eloge du Cavalier Bernin*, Paris, 1681

Cureau de la Chambre, P., *Preface pour servir à l'histoire de la vie et des ouvrages du Cavalier Bernin*, Paris, 1685

Curzietti, J, '"Con disegno del Cavalier Bernino". Giulio Cartari e la decorazione della cappella Poli in S. Crisogono a Roma', *Storia dell'arte*, 120 (2008), pp 41-58

Curzietti, J., 'Gian Lorenzo Bernini e l'Académie de France à Rome. Una nota documentaria sul ruolo di Giulio Cartarè', *Valori Tattili*, vol.10/11 (2017–2018), pp 45–9

Curzietti, J., 'Sull'origine francese di Giulio Cartarè (1642–1699). Documenti e precisazioni in merito al nucleo familiare dell'ultimo allievo di Gian Lorenzo Bernini', *RIHA Journal*, no.0230, 1 October 2019

Dacos, N., *Les peintres belges à Rome au XVIe siècle*, Brussels and Rome, 1964

Damm, H. 'Gianlorenzo on the Grill: The Birth of the Artist in his Primo Parto di Devozione', in *Bernini's Biographies: Critical Essays*, Delbeke, M., Levy, E., and Ostrow, S.F. (eds), University Park, 2006, pp 223–49

Dandelet, T., 'Spanish Conquest and Colonization at the Center of the Old World: The Spanish Nation in Rome, 1555–1625', *The Journal of Modern History*, vol.69 (1997), pp 479–511

Danesi Squarzina, S., 'The Bassano "Christ the Redeemer" in the Giustiniani Collection', *The Burlington Magazine*, vol.142 (2000), pp 746–51

Dante Alighieri, *Convivio*, Brambilla Ageno, F. (ed.), Florence, 1995

Dati, C., *Vite de pittori antichi*, Florence, 1667

De Angelis d'Ossat, G., 'Louis Le Vau, architetto berniniano suo malgrado', in *Gian Lorenzo Bernini e l'architettura europea del Sei-Settecento*, Spagnesi, G., and Fagiolo dell'Arco, M. (eds), Rome, 1984

De Brosses, C., *Le président de Brosses en Italie: lettres familières écrites d'Italie en 1739 et 1740*, 2 vols, Paris, 1858

De Brosses, C., *Lettres Familières sur l'Italie*, 2 vols, Paris, 1931

De' Crescenzi Romani, G.P., *Il Nobile Romano, O' Sia Trattato di Nobiltà*, Bologna, 1693

De Dominici, B., *Vite de' pittori, scultori ed architetti napoletani*, 3 vols, Naples, 1742–1745

De Dominici, B., *Vite de' pittori, scultori ed architetti napoletani*, 3 vols, Scricchia Santoro, F. and Zezza, A. (eds), Naples, 2003–2008

D'Onofrio, C., *Roma vista da Roma*, Rome, 1967

D'Onofrio, C., *Roma nel Seicento*, Florence, 1969

Del Pesco, D., *Bernini in Francia. Paul de Chantelou e il Journal de voyage du Cavalier Bernini en France*, Naples, 2007

Del Pesco, D., 'La légation de Flavio Chigi à Paris en 1664: mémoires et documents nouveaux (avec quelques observations sur le *Journal de voyage du cavalier Bernin en France* de Paul de Chantelou)', *Mélanges de l'École Française de Rome*, vol.123 (2011), pp 475–512

Del Pesco, D., 'Bernini a Parigi: disegnare progetti "dal vero"', in *Bernini disegnatore. Nuove prospettive di ricerca*, Ebert-Schifferer, S., Marder, T.A., and Schütze, S. (eds), Rome, 2017

Delbeke, M., Levy, E., and Ostrow, S.F. (eds), *Bernini's Biographies: Critical Essays*, University Park, 2006

Delbeke, M., 'Gianlorenzo Bernini's *Bel Composto*: The Unification of Life and Works in Biography and Historiography', in *Bernini's Biographies: Critical Essays*, Delbeke, M., Levy, E., and Ostrow, S.F. (eds), University Park, 2006, pp 251–74

Delbeke, M., *The Art of Religion: Sforza Pallavicino and Art Theory in Bernini's Rome*, Farnham, 2012

Delbeke, M., Levy, E., and Ostrow, S.F., 'Prolegomena to Bernini's Biographies: Critical Essays', in *Bernini's Biographies: Critical Essays*, Delbeke, M., Levy, E., and Ostrow, S.F. (eds), University Park, 2006, pp 1–72

Della Casa, G., *Galateo*, Romano, R. (ed.), Turin, 1975

Dempsey, C., 'National Expression in Italian Sixteenth-Century Art: Problems of the Past and Present', *Studies in the History of Art*, vol.29 (1991), pp 14–24

Den Broeder, F., 'The Lateran Apostles: The Major Sculpture Commission in Eighteenth-Century Rome', *Apollo*, vol.85 (1967), pp 360–65

Dent Weil, P. (ed.), *Osservazioni della Scoltura Antica, dai manoscritti Corsini e Doria e altri scritti*, Florence, 1978

Depping, G.B. (ed.), *Correspondance administrative sous le régne de Louis XIV*, 4 vols, Paris, 1855

Desmas, A-L., 'Why Legros Rather Than Foggini Carved the "St. Bartholomew" for the Lateran: New Documents for the Statue in the Nave', *The Burlington Magazine*, vol.146 (2004), pp 796–908

Desmas, A-L., *Le ciseau et la tiare: les sculpteurs dans la Rome des papes 1724–1758*, Rome, 2012

Desmas, A-L., 'The Birth of a Portrait Sculptor', in *Bernini*, Bacchi, A. and Coliva, A. (eds), Milan, 2017

Devoto, G., and Oli, G.C., *Dizionario della lingua italiana*, Florence, 1971

Dickerson III, C.D., Sigel, A., and Wardropper, I. (eds), *Bernini: Sculpting in Clay*, New Haven and London, 2012

Dietl, A., *Die Sprache der Signatur: Die mittelalterlichen Künstlerinschriften Italiens*, 4 vols, Berlin, 2009

Di Lorenzo, A., *Dipinti e sculture dal Musée Jacquemart-André di Parigi*, Milan, 2002

Di Stefano, E., *Orfeo Boselli e la 'nobiltà' della scultura*, Palermo, 2002

Di Tocco, V., *Ideali d'indipendenza in Italia durante la preponderanza spagnuola*, Messina, 1926

Dorati Da Empoli, M.C., 'Il Bernini e gli angeli di ponte San Angelo nel diario di un contemporaneo', in *Commentari*, vol.17 (1966), pp 349–52

Ebert-Schifferer, S., Marder, T.A., and Schütze, S. (eds), *Bernini disegnatore. Nuove prospettive di ricerca*, Rome, 2017

Else, F.M., *The Politics of Water in the Art and Festivals of Medici Florence: From Neptune Fountain to Naumachia*, London, 2019

Enggass, R., *Early Eighteenth-Century Sculpture in Rome*, 2 vols, University Park and London, 1976

Erben, D., *Paris und Rom. Die staatlich gelenkten Kunstbeziehungen unter Ludwig XIV*, Berlin, 2004

Erwee, M., *The Churches of Rome, 1527–1870*, 2 vols, London, 2014

Evelyn, J., *The Diary of John Evelyn*, De Beer, E.S. (ed.), Oxford, 2006

Fagiolo dell'Arco, M., 'Bernini "regista" del Barocco. Ragioni di una mostra', in *Gian Lorenzo Bernini: Regista del Barocco*, Bernardini, M.G. and Fagiolo dell'Arco, M. (eds), Geneva and Milan, 1999, pp 19–21

Fagiolo dell'Arco, M., *Berniniana: Novità sul regista del Barocco*, Milan, 2002

Favero, M., *Francesco Mochi: Un carriera di scultore*, Trent, 2008

Fernow, C.L., *Über den Bildhauer Canova und dessen Werke*, Zurich, 1806

Ferrari, O., and Papaldo, S., *Le sculture del Seicento a Roma*, Rome, 1999

Fioravanti, L., *Dello specchio di scientia universale, Libri tre*, Venice, 1564

Fiorentino, K., 'La rivolta di Masaniello del 1647', in *Civiltà del Seicento a Napoli*, 2 vols, Naples, 1984

Fisher Pace, U.V., 'Contributo alla storia del monumento funebre di Cristina', in *Cristina di Svezia e Roma*, Stockholm, 1999, pp 81–96

Fontenai, A. de, *Dictionnaire des Artistes, ou notice historique et raisonnée des Architectes, Peintres, Graveurs, Sculpteurs, Musiciens, Acteurs & Danseurs; Imprimeurs, Horlogers & Méchaniciens*, 2 vols, Paris, 1776

Fosi, I., 'Non solo pellegrini: Francesi a Roma nella prima età moderna. Qualche esempio e osservazione', *Anabases*, vol.5 (2007), pp 137–48

Fosi, I., 'The Plural City: Urban Spaces and Foreign Communities', in *A Companion to Early Modern Rome, 1492–1692*, Jones, P.M., Wisch, B., and Ditchfield, S. (eds), Leiden and Boston, 2019, pp 169–183

Frangenberg, T., 'The Art of Talking about Sculpture: Vasari, Borghini and Bocchi', *Journal of the Warburg and Courtauld Institutes*, vol.58 (1995), pp 115–31

Fraschetti, S., *Il Bernini: la sua vita, la sua opera, il suo tempo*, Milan, 1900

Frommel, S., 'Les projects du Bernin pour le Louvre, tradition italienne contre tradition française', in *Le Bernin et l'Europe*, Paris, 2002

Frommel, S. 'Zwischen Geniestreich und kollektiver Leistung: Gian Lorenzo Bernini Entwürfe für den Louvre', in *A Transitory Star: The Late Bernini and his Reception*, Lehmann, C., and Lloyd, K.J. (eds), Berlin and Boston, 2015

Frutaz, A.P. (ed.), *Le piante di Roma*, 3 vols, Rome, 1962

Fulvio Testi, *Lettere*, 3 vols, Doglio, M.L. (ed.), Bari, 1967

Fusconi, G., *Disegni decorativi del barocco romano*, Rome, 1986, pp 16–18

Fusconi, G., 'La fortuna dei marmi Ludovisi nel Cinquecento e Seicento', in *La collezione Boncompagni Ludovisi: Algardi, Bernini e la fortuna dell'antico*, Giuliano, A. (ed.), Venice, 1992

Galen, *On the Usefulness of the Parts of the Body*, 2 vols, Tallmadge, M. (trans.), Ithaca, 1968

Galiani, F., *Del Dialetto Napoletano*, Naples, 1779

Garms, J., 'Le Bernin dans la literature européenne d'Ancien Regime', in *Le Bernin et l'Europe: Du baroque triumphant à l'âge romantique*, Paris, 2002

Garzoni da Bagnacavallo, T., *La Piazza Universale di tutte le Professioni del Mondo; Cioè La Sinagoga de gli Ignoranti; L'Hospidale de' Pazzi incurabili; & Il Teatro de' varij, & diversi Cervelli Mondani*, Venice, 1617

Gastel, J. van, *Il marmo spirante: Sculpture and Experience in Seventeenth-Century Rome*, Berlin, 2013

Gattabria, S., *Gian Lorenzo Bernini e le arti figurative nel pensiero di Lelio Guidiccioni*, tesi di laurea Università degli studi della Tuscia, 2003–2004

Gauricus, P., *De sculptura*, Cutolo, P. (ed.), Naples, 1999

Ghelli, M.E., 'Il Vicerè Marchese del Carpio (1683–1687)', *Archivio storico per le province napoletane*, A.58, 1933, p.289

Ghezzi, G., *Il centesimo dell'anno M.DC.XCV celebrato in Roma dall'Accademia del Disegno*, Rome, 1696

Gill, C., 'The Question of Character-Development: Plutarch and Tacitus', *The Classical Quarterly*, vol.33 (1983), pp 469–87

Giometti, C., 'Il modello del *Battesimo* di Domenico Guidi e proposte per una committenza Albani a Guidi e Ottoni', in *Sculture romane del Settecento, III: La professione dello scultore*, Rome, 2003, pp 51–65

Giometti, C., *Domenico Guidi 1625–1701: Uno scultore barocco di fama europea*, Rome, 2010

Giustiniani, V., *Discorsi sulle arti e sui mestieri*, Banti, A. (ed.), Florence, 1981

Gnoli, D., 'La sepoltura d'Agostino Chigi nella chiesa di S. Maria del Popolo in Roma', *Archivio storico dell'arte*, vol.2 (1889), pp 317–26

Goethe, J.W., *Italian Journey (1786–1788)*, Auden, W.H., and Mayer, E. (trans.), London and San Francisco, 1982

Goffen, R., *Renaissance Rivals: Michelangelo, Raphael, Titian*, New Haven and London, 2002

Goldoni, C., *Il padre di famiglia*, in *Commedie Scelte*, 4 vols, Livorno, 1819

Goldoni, C., *Il ventaglio*, in *Commedie*, 3 vols, Mangini, N. (ed.), Turin, 1971

Goldstein, C., 'Rhetoric and Art History in the Italian Renaissance and Baroque', *The Art Bulletin*, vol.73 (1991), pp 641–52

Gordon, P., and Ostrow, S.F., 'Function', in *Drawings by Gianlorenzo Bernini from the Museum der Bildenden Künste Leipzig, German Democratic Republic*, Lavin, I. (ed.), Princeton, 1981, pp 7–16

Gould, C., *Bernini in France: An Episode in Seventeenth-Century History*, London, 1981

Gramiccia, A. (ed.), *Bernini in Vaticano: Braccio di Carlo Magno maggio - luglio 1981*, Rome, 1981, cat. no. 329.

Grant, M., *The Emperor Constantine*, London, 1993

Gregori, M., *Giacomo Ceruti*, Monumenta Bergomensia, vol.58, Cinisello Balsamo, 1982

Guerin, N., *Description de l'Académie Royale des Arts de Peinture et de Sculpture*, Paris, 1715

Guiffrey, J., *Comptes des Bâtiments du Roi sous le règne de Louis XIV*, 5 vols, Paris, 1881–1888

Hamilton, P., 'Hazlitt and the "Kings of Speech"', in *Metaphysical Hazlitt: Bicentenary Essays*, Natarajan, U., Paulin, T., and Wu, D. (eds), London and New York, 2005

Hammond, F., 'Bernini and the "Fiera di Farfa"', in *Gianlorenzo Bernini: New Aspects of His Art and Thought*, Lavin, I. (ed.), University Park and London, 1985, pp 115–25

Hammond, F., *Music and Spectacle in Baroque Rome: Barberini Patronage under Urban VIII*, New Haven, 1994

Harvey, J., *Men in Black*, Chicago, 1995

Haskell, F., and Penny, N., *Taste and the Antique: The Lure of Classical Sculpture 1500–1900*, New Haven and London, 1981

Heikamp, D., 'La fontana di Nettuno. La sua storia nel contesto urbano', in *L'acqua, la pietra, il fuoco. Bartolomeo Ammannati scultore*, Paolozzi Strozzi, B., and Zikos, D. (eds), Florence, 2011

Heimbürger Ravalli, M., *Architettura e arti minori nel barocco italiano: Ricerche nell'archivio Spada*, Florence, 1977

Held, J.S., and Posner, D., *17th and 18th Century Art*, New York, 1971

Herklotz, I., 'Ecfrasi e scultura a Roma all'ombra di Luigi XIV: Una nuova fonte per Domenico Guidi', in *Gli allievi di Algardi. Opere, geografia, temi della scultura in Italia nella seconda metà del Seicento*, Bacchi, A., Nova, A., and Simonato, L. (eds), Milan, 2019, pp 29–53

Herrmann-Fiore, K., 'Il tema "Labor" nella creazione aritistica del Rinascimento', in *Der Künstler über sich in seinem Werk*, Winner, M., and Bätschmann, O. (eds), Weinheim, 1992, pp 245–92

Hess, J., *Die Künstlerbiographien von Giovanni Battista Passeri*, Leipzig and Vienna, 1934

Hibbard, H., 'Un nuovo documento sul busto del Cardinale Scipione Borghese del Bernini', *Bollettino d'arte*, 4th series, vol.46 (1961), pp 101–5

Hollanda, F. de, *Diálogos em Roma (1538): Conversations on Art with Michelangelo Buonarroti*, Folliero-Metz, G.D. (ed.), Heidelberg, 1998

Hollinshead, M.B., 'Extending the Reach of Marble: Struts in Greek and Roman Sculpture', *Memoirs of the American Academy in Rome. Supplementary Volumes*, vol.1 (2002)

Honour, H., *Neo-classicism*, Harmondsworth, 1968

Horace, *Satires, Epistles and Ars Poetica*, Rushton Fairclough, H. (trans.), Cambridge and London, 1978

Johns, C., 'The Entrepôt of Europe: Rome in the Eighteenth Century', in *Art in Rome in the Eighteenth Century*, Bowron, E.P., and Rishel, J.J. (eds), Philadelphia, 2000, pp 17–45

Jones, P.M., Wisch, B., and Ditchfield, S. (eds), *A Companion to Early Modern Rome, 1492–1692*, Leiden and Boston, 2019

Jørnæs, B., *The Sculptor Bertel Thorvaldsen*, Copenhagen, 2011

Kauffmann, H., *Giovanni Lorenzo Bernini. Die figürlichen Kompositionen*, Berlin, 1970

Kemp, M., and Walker, M., *Leonardo on Painting*, New Haven and London, 1989

Kerber, B., *Andrea Pozzo*, Berlin and New York, 1971

Kessler, H-U., 'Pietro Bernini (1562–1629): Seine Werke in der Certosa di San Martino in Neapel', *Mitteilungen des Kunsthistorischen Institutes in Florenz*, vol.38 (1994), pp 310–36

Kessler, H-U., *Pietro Bernini (1562–1629)*, Munich, 2005

Keuls, E.C., *Plato and Greek Painting*, Leiden, 1978

Kieven, E., *Ferdinando Fuga. Architettura romana del Settecento: I disegni di architettura dalle collezioni del Gabinetto Nazionale delle Stampe. Il Settecento*, Rome, 1988, pp 61–3

Kieven, E., 'Pietro Bracci, Sculptor', in *Pietro Bracci and Eighteenth-Century Rome*, Kieven, E., and Pinto, J. (eds), University Park, 2001, pp 9–24

Kieven, E., 'An Italian Architect in London: The Case of Alessandro Galilei (1691–1732)', *Architectural History*, vol.51 (2008), pp 1–31

Klotz, H., 'Formen der Anonymität und des Individualismus in der Kunst des Mittelalters und der Renaissance', *Gesta*, vol.15 (1976), pp 303–12

Koller, C.A., and Kubersky-Piredda, S., *Identità e rappresentazione. Le chiese nazionali a Roma, 1450–1650*, Rome, 2015

Koomen, A. de, '"Una cosa non meno maravigliosa che honorata": The Expansion of Netherlandish Sculptors in Sixteenth-Century Europe', *Nederlands Kunsthistorisch Jaarboek*, vol.63 (2013), pp 82–109

Kris, E., and Kurz, O., *Legend, Myth, and Magic in the Image of the Artist: A Historical Experiment*, New Haven and London, 1979

Kubersky-Piredda, S. 'Chiese nazionali fra rappresentanza politica e Riforma cattolica: Spagna, Francia e Impero a fine Cinquecento', in *Identità e rappresentazione: Le chiese nazionali a Roma, 1450–1650*, Koller, A., and Kubersky-Piredda, S. (eds), Rome, 2015, pp 17–64

Kundera, M., *The Unbearable Lightness of Being*, Harper & Row, 1984

Lafranconi, M., 'Da Vouet a Poussin: La comunità artistica francese nell'Accademia di San Luca', in *L'ideal classique: Les échanges artistiques entre Rome et Paris au temps de Bellori (1640–1700)*, Bonfait, O., and Desmas, A-L. (eds), Paris, 2002, pp 211–22

Lalande, J.J., *Voyage d'un François en Italie, fait dans les Années 1765 & 1766*, 8 vols, Venice, 1769

Land, N.E., 'Renaissance Ideas About Self-Portrayal', *Source: Notes in the History of Art*, vol.20 (2001), pp 25–7

Land, N.E., 'Apelles and the Origin of Giotto's O', *Source: Notes in the History of Art*, vol.25 (2005), pp 6–9

Langdon, A., *A Guide to Baroque Rome: The Palaces*, London, 2015

Laurain-Portemer, M., *Études Mazarines*, Paris, 1981

Lauter, H., 'La posizione socile dell'artista figurativo nella Grecia classica', in *Artisti e artigiani in Grecia: Guida storica e critica*, Coarelli, F. (ed.), Rome and Bari, 1980

Lavin, I., 'Bozzetti and Modelli: Notes on Sculptural Procedure from the Early Renaissance through Bernini', in *Stil und Überlieferung in der Kunst des Abendlandes. Akten des 21. internationalen Kongresses für Kunstgeschichte in Bonn 1964*, Berlin, 1967

Lavin, I., *Bernini and the Crossing of Saint Peter's*, New York, 1968

Lavin, I., 'Calculated Spontaneity: Bernini and the Terracotta Sketch', *Apollo*, vol.107, no.195 (1978), pp 398–405

Lavin, I., *Bernini and the Unity of the Visual Arts*, 2 vols, New York and London, 1980

Lavin, I. (ed.), *Drawings by Gianlorenzo Bernini from the Museum der Bildenden Künste Leipzig, German Democratic Republic*, Princeton, 1981

Lavin I. (ed.), *Gianlorenzo Bernini: New Aspects of His Art and Thought*, University Park and London, 1985

Lavin, I., 'Bernini's Image of the Sun King', in *Past–Present: Essays on Historicism in Art from Donatello to Picasso*, Berkeley, Los Angeles and Oxford, 1993, pp 138–200

Lavin, I., 'David's Sling and Michelangelo's Bow: A Sign of Freedom', in *Past–Present: Essays on Historicism in Art from Donatello to Picasso*, Berkeley, Los Angeles and Oxford, 1993

Lavin, I., '"*Ex Uno Lapide*": The Renaissance Sculptor's *Tour de Force*', in *Il Cortile delle Statue. Der Statuenhof des Belvedere im Vatikan*, Mainz, 1998

Lavin, I., 'Bernini at St. Peter's: *Singularis in Singulis, in Omnibus Unicus*', in *St. Peter's in the Vatican*, Tronzo, W. (ed.), Cambridge, 2005

Lavin, I., *Visible Spirit: The Art of Gianlorenzo Bernini*, 2 vols, London, 2007

Lavin, I., 'The Silence of Bernini's *David*', *Artibus et historiae*, vol.79 (2019), pp 11–21

Leonardo da Vinci, *Il trattato della pittura*, Codice Vaticano Urbinate 1270

Lepik, A., *Das Architekturmodell in Italien 1335–1550*, Worms, 1994

Lesellier, J., 'Notaires et archives de la Curie romaine (1507–1627): les notaires français à Rome', *Mélanges d'archéologie et d'histoire*, vol.50 (1933), pp 250–75

Levi Pisetzky, R., *Storia del costume in Italia*, 5 vols, Milan, 1964–1969

Levy, E., *Propaganda and the Jesuit Baroque*, Berkeley, Los Angeles and London, 2004

Levy, E., 'Chapter 2 of Domenico Bernini's *Vita* of His Father: Mimesis', in *Bernini's Biographies: Critical Essays*, Delbeke, M., Levy, E., and Ostrow, S.F. (eds), University Park, 2006, pp 164–5

Levy, E., 'Repeat Performances: Bernini, the Portrait and its Copy', in *Sculpture Journal*, vol.20, no.2 (2011), pp 239–49

Levy, E., and Mangone, C. (eds), *Material Bernini*, London and New York, 2016

Lidova, M., 'The Artist's Signature in Byzantium: Six Icons by Ioannes Tohabi in Sinai Monastery (11th–12th Century)', in *Opera. Nomina. Historiae*, vol.1 (2009), pp 77–98

Lingo, E., 'The Greek Manner and a Christian "Canon": François Duquesnoy's "Saint Susanna"', *The Art Bulletin*, vol.84 (2002), pp 65–93

Lingo, E., *François Duquesnoy and the Greek Ideal*, New Haven and London, 2007

Lingo, E., 'Francesco Mochi's Balancing Act and the Prehistory of Bernini's *Four Rivers Fountain*', in *Matters of Weight: Force, Gravity, and Aesthetics in the Early Modern Period*, Young Kim, D. (ed.), Emsdetten, 2013

Lingo, E., *Mochi's Edge and Bernini's Baroque*, London and Turnhout, 2017

Lingo, E., 'Sculpture, Rupture, and the "Baroque"', in *Art and Reform in the Late Renaissance*, Locker, J.M. (ed.), New York and London, 2019, pp 33–46

Lissoni, E., 'Cronologia', in *Canova Thorvaldsen. La nascita della scultura moderna*, Grandesso, S., and Mazzocca, F. (eds), Milan, 2019, pp 392–4

Lloyd, K.J., 'All the King's Horses: Bernini's Equestrian Statues between Paris and Rome', in *A Transitory Star: The Late Bernini and his Reception*, Lehmann, C., and Lloyd, K.J. (eds), Berlin, 2015, pp 117–33

Lomazzo, G.P., *Trattato dell'arte de la pittura*, Milan, 1584

Lombardi, E., 'Michelangelo Buonarroti il Giovane e i suoi interessi per l'erudizione e l'araldica', Casa Buonarotti, 2012/01

Lucian, *The Dream, or Lucian's Career*, Harmon, A.M. (trans.), Cambridge, MA, 1967

Lukehart, P.M., 'Carving Out Lives: The Role of Sculptors in the Early History of the Academy of San Luca', *Studies in the History of Art*, vol.70 (2008), pp 185–217

Lukehart, P.M. (ed.), *The Accademia Seminars: The Accademia di San Luca in Rome, c. 1590–1635*, New Haven, 2009

Maclehose, L.S., *Vasari on Technique*, London, 1907

Maffei, S., 'La fama di Laocoonte nei testi del Cinquecento', in Settis, S., *Laocoonte: fama e stile*, Rome, 1999

Mancini, G., *Considerazioni sulla pittura*, 2 vols, Marucchi, A., and Salerno, L. (eds), Rome, 1956–1957

Mander, K. van, *Het Schilder-Boeck*, Haarlem, 1604 and Amsterdam, 1618

Mander, K. van, *The Lives of the Illustrious Netherlandish and German Painters, from the First Edition of the Schilder-Boeck 1603–1604*, 6 vols, Miedema, H. (ed. and trans.), Doornspijk, 1994–1999

Mander, K. van, *Le vite degli illustri pittori fiamminghi, olandesi e tedeschi*, Mabro Santos, R. de (ed. and trans.), Sant'Oreste, 2000

Mangone, C., 'Bernini scultore pittoresco', in *Material Bernini*, Levy, E., and Mangone, C. (eds), London and New York, 2016, pp 69–104

Mangone, C., *Bernini's Michelangelo*, New Haven and London, 2020

Marchionne Gunter, A., 'Giovan Lorenzo Bernini e Giulio Cartarè', in *Berniniana: Novità sul regista del Barocco*, Milan, 2002, pp 218–21

Marder, T., *Bernini's Scala Regia at the Vatican Palace*, Cambridge, 1997

Marder, T., *Bernini and the Art of Architecture*, New York London and Paris, 1998

Mariaux, P-A., 'L'habit fait l'artiste? Remarques sur le vêtement de travail (XIIe–XVe siècles)', in *Micrologus, Le corps et sa parure / The Body and its Adornment*, XV, pp 207–18

Mariette, P-J., *Abecedario*, 6 vols, Paris, 1854–6

Marsh, D., *Lucian and the Latins: Humor and Humanism in the Early Renaissance*, Ann Arbor, 1998

Marshall, C., *Baroque Naples and the Industry of Painting: The World in the Workbench*, New Haven and London, 2016

Martin, F., *Camillo Rusconi: ein Bildhauer des Spätbarock in Rom*, Berlin and Munich, 2019

Mascardi, A., *Discorsi morali su la Tavola di Cebete Tebano*, Venice, 1627

Masera, M.G., *Michelangelo Buonarroti il Giovane*, Turin, 1941

Mazzocca, F., 'Antonio Canova. "Una felice rivoluzione nelle arti"', in *Canova Thorvaldsen. La nascita della scultura moderna*, Grandesso, S., and Mazzocca, F. (eds), Milan, 2019, pp 19–30

McHam, S.B., *Pliny and the Artistic Culture of the Italian Renaissance*, New Haven and London, 2013

McPhee, S., 'Bernini's Books', *The Burlington Magazine*, vol.142 (2000), pp 442–8

McPhee, S., 'Costanza Bonarelli: Biography Versus Archive', in *Bernini's Biographies: Critical Essays*, Delbeke, M., Levy, E., and Ostrow, S.F. (eds), University Park, 2006, pp 315–76

McPhee, S., *Bernini's Beloved: A Portrait of Costanza Piccolomini*, New Haven and London, 2012

Melion, W.S., *Shaping the Netherlandish Canon: Karel van Mander's Schilder-Boeck*, Chicago and London, 1991

Meneghetti, M.L., '"Nutz. En ma chamiza": Idéologie et métaphor vestimentaire dans la poésie des troubadours', in *Micrologus, Le corps et sa parure / The Body and its Adornment*, vol.XV, 2007, pp 157–72

Michel, C., *Le voyage d'Italie de Charles-Nicolas Cochin (1758)*, Rome, 1991

Michel, O., 'I pittori francesi e i concorsi dell'Accademia di San Luca nel XVII secolo', in *I disegni di figura nell'Archivio Storico dell'Accademia di San Luca*, 3 vols, Cipriani, A., and Valeriani, E. (eds), Rome, 1988–1991

Michel, O., 'Charles-François Poerson', in *L'idéal classique: Les échanges artistiques entre Rome et Paris au temps de Bellori (1640–1700)*, Bonfait, O., and Desmas, A-L. (eds), Paris, 2002

Michelessi, D., 'Memorie intorno alla vita, ed agli scritti del conte Francesco Algarotti', in *Opere del Conte Algarotti*, 17 vols, Cremona, 1778

Migliorini, B., *La storia della lingua italiana*, Florence, 1960

Migne, J.P., *Patrologia Latina*, Paris, 1865, LXIX, cols. 764

Miles, H.A.D., 'The Italians at Fontainebleau', *Journal of the Royal Society of Arts*, vol.119 (1971), pp 851–61

Milizia, F., *Dell'arte di vedere nelle belle arti del disegno secondo i principi di Sulzer, e di Mengs*, Genoa, 1786 and Venice, 1823

Milizia, F., *Dizionario delle belle arti del disegno estratto in gran parte dalla enciclopedia metodica*, 2 vols, Bassano, 1797

Miner, C.H. (ed.), *The Eternal Baroque: Studies in Honour of Jennifer Montagu*, Milan, 2015

Minor, V.H., *Passive Tranquillity: The Sculpture of Filippo Della Valle*, Philadelphia, 1997

Minor, V.H., *Baroque Visual Rhetoric*, Toronto, 2016

Mirot, L., *Le Bernin en France: les travaux du Louvre et les statues de Louis XIV*, Paris, 1904

Montagu, J., *Alessandro Algardi*, 2 vols, New Haven and London, 1985

Montagu, J., 'Bernini Sculptures Not by Bernini', in *Gianlorenzo Bernini: New Aspects of His Art and Thought. A Commemorative Volume*, University Park and London, 1985, pp 25–61

Montagu, J., *Roman Baroque Sculpture: The Industry of Art*, New Haven and London, 1989

Montaiglon, A. de (ed.), *Procès-Verbaux de l'Académie Royale de peinture et de sculpture*, 10 vols, Paris, 1875–1892

Montaiglon, A. de, and Guiffrey, J. (eds), *Correspondance des directeurs de l'Académie de France à Rome avec les Surintendants des Bâtiments*, 17 vols, Paris, 1887–1908

Montaigne, M. de, *The Works of Michael de Montaigne comprising his Essays, Letters, and Journey Through Germany and Italy*, Hazlitt, W. (trans.), Philadelphia, 1849

Montaigne, M. de, *The Journal of Montaigne's Travels in Italy by Way of Switzerland and Germany in 1580 and 1581*, 3 vols, Waters, R.G. (ed. and trans.), London, 1903

Montaigne, M. de, *The Complete Essays*, Screech, M.A. (trans.), London and New York, 2003

Montanari, T., 'Bernini e Cristina di Svezia. Alle origini della storiografia berniniana', in *Gian Lorenzo Bernini e i Chigi tra Roma e Siena*, Barocchi, P. (ed.), Cinisello Balsamo, 1998

Montanari, T., 'Gian Lorenzo Bernini e Sforza Pallavicino', *Prospettiva*, vol.87/88 (1997), pp 42–68

Montanari, T., 'Pierre Cureau de la Chambre e la prima biografia di Gian Lorenzo Bernini', *Paragone*, vol.24–25 (1999), pp 103–32

Montanari, T., 'Bellori e la politica artistica di Luigi XIV', in *L'idéal classique: les échanges artistiques entre Rome et Paris au temps de Bellori (1640–1700)*, Bonfait, O., and Desmas, A-L. (eds), Paris, 2002, pp 117–38

Montanari, T., 'Bernini and Christina of Sweden', in *Art History in the Age of Bellori: Scholarship and Cultural Politics in Seventeenth-Century Rome*, Bell, J., and Willette, T. (eds), New York, 2002, pp 94–126

Montanari, T., 'Due collezionisti alla scoperta dell'Italia', in *Dipinti e sculture dal Musée Jacquemart-André di Parigi*, Di Lorenzo, A. (ed.), Milan, 2002, pp 117–19

Montanari, T., 'Il "bel composto": nota filologica su un nodo della storiografia berniniana', *Studi secenteschi*, vol.46 (2005), pp 195–210

Montanari, T., 'At the Margins of the Historiography of Art: The *Vite* of Bernini Between Autobiography and Apologia', in *Bernini's Biographies: Critical Essays*, Delbeke, M., Levy, E., and Ostrow, S.F. (eds), University Park, 2006, pp 73–109

Montanari, T., *Bernini pittore*, Cinisello Balsamo, 2007

Montanari, T., 'Bernini per Bernini: Il secondo "Crocifisso" monumentale. Con una digressione su Domenico Guidi', *Prospettiva*, vol.136 (2009), pp 2–25

Montanari, T., 'Il colore del marmo. I busti di Bernini tra scultura e pittura, ritratto e storia, funzione e stile (1610–1638)', in *I marmi vivi. Bernini e la nascita del ritratto barocco*, Bacchi, A., Montanari, T., Paolozzi Strozzi, B., and Zikos, D. (eds), Florence, 2009, pp 71–135

Montanari, T., 'Creating an Eye for Models: The Role of Bernini', in *Bernini: Sculpting in Clay*, Dickerson, III, C.D., Sigel, A., and Wardropper, I. (eds), New Haven and London, 2012

Montanari, T., *La libertà di Bernini. La sovranità dell'artista e le regole del potere*, Turin, 2016

Montègre, G., *La Rome des français au temps des lumières: Capitale de l'Antique et carrefour de l'Europe 1769–1791*, Rome, 2011

Montesquieu, C-L. de Secondat Baron de, *The Spirit of the Laws*, 2 vols, London, 1750

Moore, J., *A View of Society and Manners in Italy: With Anecdotes Relating to Some Eminent Characters*, 3 vols, London, 1781

Morgan, L., *The Life and Times of Salvator Rosa*, 2 vols, London, 1824

Morgan Zarucchi, J., 'Introduction to Charles Perrault', in *Memoirs of My Life*, Columbia, 1989, pp 1–27

Mormando, F., 'Gian Paolo Oliva: The Forgotten Celebrity of Baroque Rome', in *The Holy Name: Art of the Gesù: Bernini and His Age*, Wolk-Simon, L. (ed.), Philadelphia, 2018

Mozzillo, A., *Il Napoletano da Boccaccio a Goethe*, Naples, 1995

Murray, P., 'Notes on Some Early Giotto Sources', *Journal of the Warburg and Courtauld Institutes*, vol.16 (1953), pp 58–80

Muzii, R., 'Il culto del disegno presso i pittori napoletani del Seicento e del Settecento con la guida di Bernardo De Dominici', in *Le dessin napolitain*, Solinas, F., and Schütze, S. (eds), Rome, 2010, pp 15–30

Nadeau, T.L., 'The Concept of Bernini's "Calculated Spontaneity": A Critical Reassessment', in *Material Bernini*, Levy, E., and Mangone, C. (eds), London and New York, 2016, pp 169–86

Nathan, J., 'Drawings and Sketches for Surviving or Documented Paintings', in *Leonardo da Vinci 1452–1519: The Complete Paintings and Drawings*, Zöllner, F., and Nathan, J. (eds), Cologne, 2007

Nisard, C. (ed.), *Correspondance inédite du Comte de Caylus avec le P. Paciaudi, Théatin (1757–1765)*, vol.I, Paris, 1877

Nummedal, T.E., 'Kircher's Subterranean World and the Dignity of the Geocosm', in *The Great Art of Knowing: The Baroque Encyclopedia of Athanasius Kircher*, Fiesole, 2001

Nussdorfer, L., 'Notaries and the Accademia di San Luca, 1590–1630', in *The Accademia Seminars: The Accademia di San Luca in Rome, c. 1590–1635*, Lukehart, P.M. (ed.), New Haven and London, 2009

Olin, M., 'Diplomatic Performance and the Applied Arts in Seventeenth-Century Europe', in *Performativity and Performance in Baroque Rome*, Gillgren, P., and Snickare, M. (eds), London and New York, 2012

Orlandi, P.A., *Abecedario pittorico*, Venice, 1753

Ostrow, S.F., 'Gianlorenzo Bernini, Girolamo Lucenti, and the Statue of Philip IV in Santa Maria Maggiore: Patronage and Politics in Seicento Rome', *The Art Bulletin*, vol.73 (1991), pp 89–118

Ostrow, S.F., 'Bernini's Voice: From Chantelou's Journal to the Vite', in *Bernini's Biographies: Critical Essays*, Delbeke, M., Levy, E., and Ostrow, S.F. (eds), University Park, 2006, pp 111–41

Ostrow, S.F., 'Bernini e il paragone', in *Bernini pittore*, Montanari, T. (ed.), Milan, 2007, pp 223–33

Ostrow, S.F., '"Sculptors Pursue Likeness": The Typology and Function of Seventeenth-Century Portrait Sculpture in Rome', in *Bernini and the Birth of Baroque Portrait Sculpture*, Bacchi, A., Hess, C., and Montagu, J. (eds), Los Angeles, 2008, pp 65–83

Ostrow, S.F., '"The Fire of Art"? A Historiography of Bernini's Bozzetti', in *Bernini: Sculpting in Clay*, Dickerson III, C.D., Sigel, A., and Wardropper, I. (eds), New Haven and London, 2012, pp 75–85

Ostrow, S.F., '"Appearing to be what they are not": Bernini's Reliefs in Theory and Practice', in *Critical Perspectives on Roman Baroque Sculpture*, Colantuono, A., and Ostrow, S.F. (eds), University Park, 2014, pp 165–84

Ostrow, S.F., 'Bernini's *Bozzetti* and the Trope of Fire', in *Material Bernini*, Levy, E., and Mangone, C. (eds), London and New York, 2016

Ostrow, S.F., and Colantuono, A., 'Rome as the Center of Early Modern Sculpture', in *Critical Perspectives on Roman Baroque Sculpture*, Colantuono, A., and Ostrow, S.F. (eds), University Park, 2014, pp 11–18

Ovid, *Metamorphoses*, Miller, F.J. (trans.), Cambridge, MA, 1916

Paduano, A., *Ragguaglio del tumulto di Napoli*, Padua, 1648

Pagnalmino, G.S., *Della carrozza da nolo: overo del vestire, & usanze alla Moda*, Milan, 1648

Pananti, F., *Opere in versi e in prosa*, 3 vols, Florence, 1824

Panofsky, E., *Hercules am Scheidewege, un andere antike Bildstoffe in der neueren Kunst*, Leipzig, 1930

Pascoli, L., *Vite de' pittori, scultori, ed architetti moderni*, Martinelli, V., and Marabottini, A. (eds), Perugia, 1992

Passeri, G.B., *Vite de' pittori, scultori ed architetti che hanno lavorato in Roma morti dal 1641. Fino al 1673*, Rome, 1772

Pastor, L. von, *The History of the Popes*, 40 vols, London, 1940, vol.XXXI, pp 94–9

Paulicelli, E., 'Fashion, Gender and Cultural Anxiety in Italian Baroque Literature', *Roman Notes*, vol.50 (2010), pp 35–46

Pavanello, G. (ed.), *Canova: Eterna Bellezza*, Cinisello Balsamo, 2019

Pavanello, G., 'Canova/Roma', in *Canova: Eterna Bellezza*, Pavanello, G. (ed.), Cinisello Balsamo, 2019, pp 18–43

Pavlou, M., 'Pindar "Nemean" 5: Real and Poetic Statues', *Phoenix*, vol.64 (2010), pp 1–17

Pecchiai, P., 'Il Bernini Furioso', *Strenna dei romanisti*, vol.10 (1949), pp 181–2

Pecchiai, P., *Il Gesù di Roma*, Rome, 1952

Perrault, C., *Le Siècle de Louis le Grand. Poeme par M. Perrault de l'Académie Françoise*, Paris, 1687

Perrault, C., *Parallelle des anciens et des modernes*, Paris, 1688–1697

Perrault, C., *Mémoires*, Lacroix, P. (ed.), Paris, 1878

Perrault, C., *Mémoires de ma vie*, Paris, 1909

Perrault, C., *Memoirs of My Life*, Jeanne Morgan Zarucchi (ed. and trans.), Columbia, 1989, pp 1–27

Pestilli, L., '"The Burner of the Midnight Oil": A Caravaggesque Rendition of a Classic *Exemplum*. An Unrecognized Self-portrait by Michael Sweerts?', *Zeitschrift für Kunstgeschichte*, vol.59 (1993), pp 119–33

Pestilli, L., 'Michelangelo's Pietà: Lombard Critics and Plinian Sources', *Source: Notes in the History of Art*, vol.19 (2000), pp 21–30

Pestilli, L., 'Pliny's "Ne Supra Crepidam Sutor": Representing Shoemakers in Italian Art and Society,' *Source: Notes in the History of Art*, vol.26 (Spring 2007), pp 10–22

Pestilli, L., 'Bellori's "old lady" or: On Informed versus Uninformed Criticism', *Word & Image*, vol.26 (2010), pp 393–9

Pestilli, L., 'On Bernini's Reputed Unpopularity in Late Baroque Rome', *Artibus et historiae*, vol.63 (2011), pp 119–42

Pestilli, L., *Paolo de Matteis: Neapolitan Painting and Cultural History in Baroque Europe*, Farnham, 2013

Pestilli, L., *Picturing the Lame in Italian Art from Antiquity to the Modern Era*, London and New York, 2017

Pestilli, L., 'Napoli e gli artisti napoletani visti attraverso lenti forgiate al "nord"', in *Fortunata Neapolis: Kunst- und Kulturtransfer zwischen Neapel, Wien und Mitteleuropa*, Schütze, S. (ed.), Berlin and Boston, 2020, pp 219–35

Pestilli, L., 'Bernini e collaboratori nella cappella Poli (*dell'Angelo Custode, o del Santissimo Sacramento*) a San Crisogono in Trastevere: precisazioni storiche ed artistiche', *21: Inquiries into Art, History, and the Visual*, vol.1 (2021), pp 77–134

Pevsner, N., *Academies of Art: Past and Present*, Cambridge, 1940 and New York, 1973

Pevsner, N., *Le accademie d'arte*, Turin, 1982

Pierguidi, S., '"A Certain Livelier Quality of Expression": Bernini's Two Versions of the Bust of Scipione Borghese', in *Multiples in Pre-Modern Art*, Zurich, 2014, pp 229–43

Pierguidi, S., '*Marcus Curtius Throwing Himself into the Chasm*', in *Bernini*, Bacchi, A., and Coliva, A. (eds), *Bernini*, Città di Castello, 2017

Pierguidi, S., *Pittura di marmo. Storia e fortuna delle pale d'altare a rilievo nella Roma di Bernini*, Florence, 2017

Pignatti, T., *Veronese*, Venice, 1976

Pindar, *Olympian Odes, Pythian Odes*, 2 vols, Race, W.H. (ed. and trans.), Cambridge, MA, 1997

Pinto, J., *The Trevi Fountain*, New Haven and London, 1986

Plackinger, A., *Violenza. Gewalt als Denkfigur im michelangelesken Kunstdiskurs*, Berlin, 2016

Pliny the Elder, *Natural History*, 10 vols, Eichholz, D.E. (trans.), Cambridge, MA and London, 1971

Pliny the Elder, *Natural History*, 10 vols, Rackham, H. (trans.), Cambridge, MA and London, 1984

Plutarch, *Lives*, *Marcus Cato*, Perrin B. (trans.), London, 1914

Plutarch, *Lives*, *Pericles*, Perrin, B. (trans.), Cambridge, MA, 1916

Plutarch, *Lives*, *Timoleon*, Perrin, B. (trans.), Cambridge, MA, 1918

Plutarch, *Moralia*, 14 vols, Babbitt, F.C. (trans.), London, 1927

Pollak, O., *Die Kunsttätigkeit unter Urban VIII: Die Peterskirke in Rom*, Vienna, Hildesheim and New York, 1981

Polybius, *The Histories of Polybius*, 6 vols, Paton, W.R. (trans.), London and New York, 1922

Pon, L., 'Michelangelo's First Signature', *Source: Notes in the History of Art*, vol.4 (1996), pp 16–21

Pope-Hennessy, J., *Raphael: The Wrightsman Lectures*, New York, 1970

Pope-Hennessy, J., *Italian High Renaissance and Baroque Sculpture: An Introduction to Italian Sculpture*, New York, 1985

Possevino, A., *Tractatio De Poesi & Pictura ethnica, humana, & fabulosa collata cum vera, honesta, & sacra*, Lyon, 1594

Posterla, F., *Roma sacra, e moderna*, Rome, 1725

Preimesberger, R., 'Il San Longino del Bernini in San Pietro in Vaticano: dal bozzetto alla statua', in *Bernini a Montecitorio: ciclo di conferenze nel quarto centenario della nascita di Gian Lorenzo Bernini*, Rome, 2001, pp 97–111

Preimesberger, R., 'Lelio Guidiccioni's Letter to Bernini: A Commentary', *The Sculpture Journal*, vol.20 (2011), pp 207–22

Primatice maître de Fontainebleau, exh.cat., Musée du Louvre, Paris, 22 September 2004–3 January 2005

Priorato, G., *Historia della sacra real maestà di Christina Alessandra regina di Svetia*, Rome, 1656

Quinterio, F., 'La casa del Bernini', in *Gian Lorenzo Bernini. Il testamento, la casa, la raccolta dei beni*, Borsi, F., Acidini Luchinat, C., and Quinterio, F. (eds), Florence, 1981, pp 13–37

Quintilian, *The Institutio Oratoria*, 4 vols, Butler, H.E. (trans.), Cambridge, MA and London, 1985

Ragionieri, P., *Il volto di Michelangelo*, Florence, 2008

Raguenet, F., *Le monumens de Rome*, Amsterdam, 1701

Rand, B., *The Life, Unpublished Letters, and Philosophical Regimen of Anthony, Earl of Shaftesbury*, London, 1900

Rao, A.M., 'Conclusion: Why Naples's History Matters', in *A Companion to Early Modern Naples*, Astarita, T. (ed.), Leiden and Boston, 2013

Rehberg, A., 'Le comunità "nazionali" e le loro chiese nella documentazione dei notai stranieri (1507–1527)', in *Identità e rappresentazione: le chiese nazionali a Roma, 1450–1650*, Koller, A., and Kubersky-Piredda, S. (eds), Rome, 2015, pp 211–31

Rice, L., 'The Unveiling of Mochi's "Veronica"', *The Burlington Magazine*, vol.156 (2014), pp 735–40

Rice, L., 'The Pre-Mochi Projects for the Veronica Pier in Saint Peter's', in *The Eternal Baroque: Studies in Honour of Jennifer Montagu*, Miner, C.H. (ed.), Milan, 2015, pp 175–202

Ridolfi, C., *Le meraviglie dell'arte, overo le vite de gl'illustri pittori veneti, e dello stato*, Venice, 1648

Riegel, N., 'Die Chigi-Kapelle in Santa Maria del Popolo: eine kritische Revision', *Marburger Jahrbuch für Kunstwissenschaft*, vol.30 (2003), pp 93–130

Rime del Burchiello, comentate dal Doni, Venice, 1553

Rime di Michelagnolo Buonarroti Raccolte da Michelangnolo suo Nipote, Florence, 1623

Ripa, C., *Iconologia*, Venice, 1669

Roberto, S., *Gianlorenzo Bernini e Clemente IX Rospigliosi. Arte e architettura a Roma e in Toscana nel Seicento*, Rome, 2004, pp 261–87

Roccasecca, P., 'Teaching in the Studio for the "Accademia del Disegno dei pittori, scultori e architetti di Roma" (1594–1636)', in *The Accademia Seminars: The Accademia di San Luca in Rome, c. 1590–1635*, Lukehart, P.M. (ed.), Washington, New Haven and London, 2009, pp 123–59

Rockwell, P., *Lavorare la pietra*, Rome, 1989

Rockwell, P., *The Art of Stoneworking: A Reference Guide*, Cambridge, 1993

Rodríguez Ruiz, D., 'Gian Lorenzo Bernini, Roma y la Monarquía Hispánicha', in *Bernini: Roma y la Monarquía Hispánica*, Madrid, 2014

Rosenthal, D.A., *La Grande Manière: Historical and Religious Painting in France 1700–1800*, exh.cat., Memorial Art Gallery of the University of Rochester, 2 May–26 July 1987, pp 46–51

Rubin, P.L., *Giorgio Vasari: Art and History*, New Haven and London, 1995

Sacchetti, F., *Il Trecentonovelle*, Florence, 1946 and Turin, 1970

Saint-Non, J-C-R. de, *Voyage pittoresque, ou description des royaumes de Naples et de Sicile*, 4 vols, Paris, 1781–1786

Sandrart, J. von, *L'Academia Todesca della Architettura, Scultura & Pittura: oder Teutsche Academie der Edlen Bau- Bild- und Mahlerey-Künste*, Nuremberg, 1675

Sandrart, J. von, *Academia Nobilissimæ Artis Pictoriæ*, Frankfurt, 1683

Sapori, G., 'Collezioni di centro, collezionisti di periferia', in *Geografia del collezionismo: Italia e Francia tra il XVI e il XVIII secolo*, Bonfait, O., Hochmann, M., Spezzaferro, L., and Toscano, B. (eds), Rome, 2001, pp 41–59

Sapori, G., 'Profilo di Fausto Poli "sovrintendente alle arti" nella casa Barberini', *Rivista dell'istituto nazionale d'archeologia e storia dell'arte*, vol.61 (2006 [2011]), pp 196–7

Schatforn, P., and Verberne, J. (eds), *Drawn to Warmth: 17th-Century Dutch Artists in Italy*, Zwolle, 2001

Schlegel, U., 'Bozzetti in Terracotta by Pietro Stefano Monnot', *Boston Museum Bulletin*, vol.72, no.367 (1974), pp 56–68

Scholten, F., and Woodall, J., 'Netherlandish Artists on the Move', in *Art and Migration: Netherlandish Artists on the Move, 1400–1750*, Scholten, F., Woodall, J., and Meijers, D. (eds), Leiden, 2014, pp 6–39

Schütze, S., *Kardinal Maffeo Barberini, später Papst Urban VIII., und die Entstehung des römischen Hochbarock*, Munich, 2007, pp 194–205

Schütze, S., '"Liberar questo secolo dall'invidiare gli antichi": Bernini und die "Querelle des Anciens et des Modernes"', in *Docta Manus: Studien zur italienischen Skulptur für Joachim Poeschke*, Myssok, J., Wienerm, J., and Poeschke, J. (eds), Munster, 2007, pp 345–58

Schütze, S. (ed.), *Fortunata Neapolis: Kunst- und Kulturtransfer zwischen Neapel, Wien und Mitteleuropa*, Berlin and Boston, 2020

Schweitzer, B., 'L'artista figurativo', in *Artisti e artigiani in Grecia. Guida storica e critica*, Coarelli, F. (ed.), Rome and Bari, 1980, pp 25–47

Seneca, *The Epistles of Seneca*, Cambridge and London, 1970

Seneca the Elder, *Declamations*, 2 vols, Winterbottom, M. (trans.), Cambridge and London, 1974

Sestini, F., *Il maestro di camera*, Rome, 1646

Settis, S., *Laocoonte: fama e stile*, Rome, 1999

Shakespeare, W., *The Complete Works of Shakespeare*, Craig, H. (ed.), Chicago, 1961

Shearman, J., 'The Chigi Chapel in S. Maria del Popolo', *Journal of the Warburg and Courtauld Institutes*, vol.24 (1961), pp 129–60, esp. pp 133–4

Sigel, A., 'Visual Glossary', in *Bernini: Sculpting in Clay*, Dickerson III, C.D., Sigel, A., and Wardropper, I. (eds), New Haven and London, 2012

Simonato, L., *Bernini scultore. Il difficile dialogo con la modernità*, Milan, 2018

Smith, G.R., *Architectural Diplomacy: Rome and Paris in the Late Baroque*, Cambridge, MA and London, 1993

Smollett, T.G., *Travels Through France and Italy*, 2 vols, London, 1766

Sohm, P., 'Caravaggio the Barbarian', in *Caravaggio: Reflections and Refractions*, Pericolo, L. (ed.), Farnham, 2014

Solinas, F., and Schütze, S. (eds), *Le dessin napolitain*, Rome, 2010

Sorrentino, M.A., 'Vicende storico conservative', in *Bernini scultore: La tecnica esecutiva*, Coliva, A. (ed.), Rome, 2002, p.220

Soussloff, C., 'Critical Topoi in the Sources on the Life of Gianlorenzo Bernini', PhD diss., Bryn Mawr College, 1982

Soussloff, C., 'Old Age and Old-Age Style in "Lives" of Artists: Gianlorenzo Bernini', *Art Journal*, vol.46 (1987), pp 115–21

Soussloff, C., 'Imitatio Buonarroti', *Sixteenth Century Journal*, vol.20 (1989), pp 581–602

Soussloff, C., 'Lives of Poets and Painters in the Renaissance', *Word and Image*, vol.6 (1990), pp 154–62

Sparti, D.L., 'Tecnica e teoria del restauro scultoreo a Roma nel Seicento, con una verifica sulla collezione di Flavio Chigi', *Storia dell'arte*, vol.92 (1998), pp 60–131

Sparti, D.L., 'The "Rebirth" of Ancient Sculpture in 17th-Century Rome', in *Bernini*, Bacchi, A. and Coliva, A. (eds), exh.cat., Galleria Borghese, 1 November 2017–4 February 2018, Milan, 2017

Spear, R.E., and Sohm, P., *Painting for Profit: The Economic Lives of Seventeenth-Century Italian Painters*, New Haven, 2010

Speirs, W.L., 'The Note-Book and Account Book of Nicholas Stone', *The Walpole Society*, vol.7 (1918–19), pp 158–200

Steinmann, E., *Die Porträtdarstellungen des Michelangelo*, Leipzig, 1913

Stendhal, *A Roman Journal*, Chevalier, H. (trans.), New York, 1957

Stendhal, *Rome, Naples and Florence*, Calder, J. (trans.), London, 1959

Stenitzer, P., 'Il Conte Harrach Viceré a Napoli (1728–1733)', in *Settecento Napoletano. Sulle ali dell'aquila imperiale 1707–1734*, Naples, 1994, pp 43–55

Strunck, C., 'Bellori und Bernini Rezipieren Raphael: Unbekannte Dokumente zur Cappella Chigi in Santa Maria del Popolo', *Marburger Jahrbuch für Kunstwissenschaft*, vol.30 (2003), pp 131–82

Strunck, C., 'Cappella Chigi in Santa Maria del Popolo', in *Rom: Meisterwerke der Baukunst von der Antike bis heute; Festgabe für Elisabeth Kieven*, Strunck, C. (ed.), Petersberg, 2007, pp 223–5

Summers, D., *Michelangelo and the Language of Art*, Princeton, 1981

Sutherland Harris, A., *Seventeenth-Century Art and Architecture*, London, 2005

Suthor, N., *Bravura. Virtuosität und Mutwilligkeit in der Malerei der Frühen Neuzeit*, Munich, 2010

Sweet, R., *Cities and the Grand Tour: The British in Italy, c.1690–1820*, Cambridge, 2012

Thacker, A., '*Loca Sanctorum*: The Significance of Place in the Study of the Saints', in *Local Saints and Local Churches in the Early Medieval West*, Thacker, A., and Sharpe, R. (eds), Oxford, 2002

Thoisy-Dallem, A. de, 'L'apparat de l'intimité ou la robe de chambre masculine du temps de sa splendeur', in *Habits. Modes et vestiaire masculin des XVIIIe et XIXe siècles*, exh. cat., Toulon, Villa Rosemaine, Liagre, S. (ed.), Toulon, 2013, pp 26–33

Thuillier, J., '"Il se rendit en Italie…": notes sur le voyage à Rome des artistes français au XVIIe siècle', in *'Il se rendit en Italie'. Études offertes à André Chastel*, Rome, 1987, pp 321–36

Titi, F., *Studio di pittura, scultura, et architettura, nelle chiese di Roma*, Rome, 1674

Titi, F., *Ammaestramento utile, e curioso di pittura scoltura et architettura nelle chiese di Roma*, Rome, 1686

Titi, F., *Descrizione delle pitture, sculture e architetture esposte al pubblico in Roma*, 2 vols, Rome, 1763

Tommaseo, N., *Dizionario della lingua italiana*, 7 vols, Turin, 1916

Torrigio, F.M., *I sacri trofei romani del trionfante prencipe degli apostoli San Pietro gloriosissimo*, Rome, 1644

Tratz, H., 'Werkstatt und Arbeitsweise Berninis', *Römisches Jahrbuch für Kunstgeschichte*, vol.23–24 (1988), pp 395–483

Unglaub, J., '"Amorosa Contemplatione": Bernini, Bruni, and the Poetic Vision of Saint Teresa', *The Art Bulletin*, vol.102 (2020), pp 32–63

Vacca, F., *Memorie di varie antichità trovate in diversi luoghi della città di Roma*, Rome, 1594, in Nardini, F., *Roma antica*, 1666, reprinted by Nibby, A. (ed.), 4 vols, Rome, 1820

Valerius Maximus, *Memorable Doings and Sayings*, 2 vols, Shackleton Bailey, D.R. (trans.), Cambridge, MA, 2000

Valery, M., *Historical, Literary, and Artistical Travels in Italy: A Complete and Methodical Guide for Travellers and Artists*, Clifton, C.E. (trans.), Paris, 1839

Varchi, B., *Due lezzioni di M. Benedetto Varchi*, Florence, 1549

Varchi, B., *Lezzioni nella quale si disputa della maggioranza delle arti e qual sia più nobile, la scultura o la pittura*, in *Trattati d'arte del Cinquecento fra manierismo e controriforma*, 3 vols, Barocchi, P. (ed.), Bari, 1960–1962

Vasari, G., *Le vite de' più eccellenti architetti, pittori, et scultori italiani, da Cimabue insino a' tempi nostri*, Florence, 1550 and 1568

Vasari, G., *La vita di Michelangelo nelle redazioni del 1550 e del 1568*, 5 vols, Barocchi, P. (ed.), Milan and Naples, 1962–1972

Vasari, G., *Le vite de' più eccellenti pittori scultori e architettori*, 6 vols, Bettarini, R., and Barocchi, P. (eds), Florence, 1966–1997

Vasari, G., *Lives of the Artists*, Bull, G. (trans.), Harmondsworth, 1979

Vasari, G., *Lives of the Painters, Sculptors and Architects*, 2 vols, Gaston du C. de Vere (trans.), New York and Toronto, 1996

Ventra, S., '"*coll'Arte ha mostrato il nostro Secolo superiore*": Giuseppe Ghezzi, l'Accademia di San Luca e Bernini come vessillo del primato di Roma moderna', *Studi di storia dell'arte*, vol.28 (2017), pp 194–200

Ventra, S., *L'Accademia di San Luca nella Roma del secondo Seicento. Artisti, opere, strategie culturali*, Florence, 2019

Visceglia, M.A., 'Il cerimoniale come liguaggio politico', in *Cérémonial et rituel à Rome (XVIe–XIXe siècle)*, Collection de l'École française de Rome, Rome, vol.231 (1997), pp 117–76

Vocabolario degli Accademici della Crusca, 11 vols, Florence, 1878

Waddy, P., *Seventeenth-Century Roman Palaces: Use and the Art of the Plan*, New York and Cambridge, MA, 1990

Walker, D., 'A Portrait Bust of Gian Lorenzo Bernini, and Notes from the 'Fifties', *The Sculpture Journal*, vol.4 (2000), pp 65–71

Walker, D., 'An Introduction to Sculpture in Rome in the Eighteenth Century', in *Art in Rome in the Eighteenth Century*, Bowron, E.P., and Rishel, J.J. (eds), Philadelphia, 2000, pp 211–23

Walker, S., *The Sculptor Pietro Stefano Monnot in Rome, 1695–1713*, 2 vols, PhD diss., New York University, 1994

Wallace, W.E., 'Michelangelo's Risen Christ', *Sixteenth Century Journal*, vol.XXVIII, no.4 (1997), pp 1251–80

Wallace, W.E., *Michelangelo, God's Architect: The Story of his Final Years and Greatest Masterpiece*, Princeton and Oxford, 2019

Walton, G., 'Bernini's Equestrian Louis XIV', *The Art Bulletin*, vol.64 (1982), pp 319–20

Waquet, F., *Le Modèle français et l'Italie savante. Conscience de soi et perception de l'autre dans la République des Lettres (1660–1750)*, Rome, 1989

Waźbiński, Z., *L'Accademia Medicea del Disegno a Firenze nel Cinquecento*, 2 vols, Florence, 1987

Weil, M.S., *The History and Decoration of the Ponte S. Angelo*, University Park and London, 1974

Wilde, J., 'Michelangelo and Leonardo', *The Burlington Magazine*, vol.95 (1953), pp 65–75

Winckelmann, J.J., *Lettere italiane*, Milan, 1961

Winckelmann, J.J., *Reflections on the Imitation of Greek Works in Painting and Sculpture*, Heyer, E., and Norton, R.C. (trans.), La Salle, IL, 1987

Winckelmann, J.J., *History of the Art of Antiquity*, Mallgrave, H.F. (trans.), Los Angeles, 2006

Wind, E., 'Shaftesbury as a Patron of Art', *Journal of the Warburg Institute*, vol.2 (1938), pp 185–8

Winner, M., 'Ermafrodito', in *Bernini scultore. La nascita del Barocco in Casa Borghese*, Coliva, A., and Schütze, S. (eds), Rome, 1998

Wittkower, R., 'The Vicissitudes of a Dynastic Monument: Bernini's Equestrian Statue of Louis XIV', in *Essays in Honor of Erwin Panofsky*, De Artibus Opuscula, vol.40, Meiss, M. (ed.), New York, 1961, pp 497–531

Wittkower, R., *Gian Lorenzo Bernini: The Sculptor of the Roman Baroque*, London, 1966

Wittkower, R., *Sculpture: Processes and Principles*, Harmondsworth, 1977

Wittkower, R., and Wittkower, M., *Born Under Saturn: The Character and Conduct of Artists: A Documented History from Antiquity to the French Revolution*, New York and London, 1969

Wouk, E.H., *Frans Floris (1519/20–1570): Imagining a Northern Renaissance*, Leiden and Boston, 2018

Zanker, P., *The Power of Images in the Age of Augustus*, Ann Arbor, 1990

Zezza, A., 'De Dominici e il disegno', in *Le dessin napolitain*, Solinas, F., and Schütze, S. (eds), Rome, 2010, pp 7–14

Zitzlsperger, P., *Gianlorenzo Bernini. Die Papst-und Herrscherporträts. Zum Verhältnis von Bildnis und Macht*, Munich, 2002, pp 179–83

Zöllner, F., and Nathan, J., *Leonardo da Vinci 1452–1519: The Complete Paintings and Drawings*, Cologne, 2007

Picture Credits

1.1 © Studio Sébert Photographes; 1.2 Royal Collection Trust/© Her Majesty Queen Elizabeth II 2021; 1.3 © Author; 1.4 Public domain; 1.5 © Author. Per gentile concessione della Fabbrica di San Pietro in Vaticano; 1.6 © Author; 1.7 © Author; 1.8 © Author; 1.9 © Author; 1.10 National Gallery of Victoria, Melbourne; 1.11 © Author; 1.12 © Gabinetto Fotografico delle Gallerie degli Uffizi; 1.13 © 2021. Photograph Scala, Florence/bpk, Bildagentur für Kunst, Kultur und Geschichte, Berlin; 1.14 Royal Collection Trust/© Her Majesty Queen Elizabeth II 2021; 1.15 © Roma, Istituto centrale per la grafica, per gentile concessione del Ministero della cultura; 1.16 Harvard Art Museum/Fogg Museum; 1.17 Kimbell Art Museum, Fort Worth, Texas; 1.18 © Author; 1.19 Public domain; 1.20 Royal Collection Trust/© Her Majesty Queen Elizabeth II 2021; 1.21 © 2021. Photograph Scala, Florence/bpk, Bildagentur für Kunst, Kultur und Geschichte, Berlin; 1.22 Royal Collection Trust/© Her Majesty Queen Elizabeth II 2021; 1.23 © Roma, Istituto centrale per la grafica, per gentile concessione del Ministero della cultura; 1.24 © Gabinetto Fotografico delle Gallerie degli Uffizi; 1.25 © The Albertina Museum, Vienna; 1.26 © Princeton University Museum; 1.27 © Trustees of the British Museum; 2.1 © George Tatge for Alinari. Per concessione del Ministero per i Beni e le Attività Culturali/Archivi Alinari, Florence; 2.2 © RMN-Grand Palais (musée du Louvre)/Hervé Lewandowski; 2.3 © Luciano Romano. Courtesy of Borghese Gallery, Rome; 2.4 © Luciano Romano. Courtesy of Borghese Gallery, Rome; 2.5 © Author; 2.6 © Author; 2.7 © Luciano Romano. Courtesy of Borghese Gallery, Rome; 2.8 © Author; 2.9 Public domain; 2.10 © Author; 2.11 © Raffaello Bencini/Archivi Alinari, Florence; 2.12 © Author; 2.13 © Scala, Firenze – per concessione del Ministero Beni e Attività Culturali e del Turismo; 2.14 © Peter Vallance/Alamy Stock Photo; 2.15 © Rufus46, CC BY-SA 3.0; 2.16 © I, Sailko, CC-BY SA 3.0; 2.17 © Author. Per gentile concessione della Fabbrica di San Pietro in Vaticano; 2.18 © Author. Per gentile concessione della Fabbrica di San Pietro in Vaticano; 2.19 © Author. Per gentile concessione della Fabbrica di San Pietro in Vaticano; 2.20 © Author. Per gentile concessione della Fabbrica di San Pietro in Vaticano; 2.21 © Author; 2.22 Jennifer Montagu; 2.23 © Author. Per gentile concessione della Fabbrica di San Pietro in Vaticano; 2.24 © Author. Per gentile concessione della Fabbrica di San Pietro in Vaticano; 2.25 © Author. Per gentile concessione della Fabbrica di San Pietro in Vaticano; 2.26 © Author. Per gentile concessione della Fabbrica di San Pietro in Vaticano; 2.27 © Author. Per gentile concessione della Fabbrica di San Pietro in Vaticano; 2.28 © Author. Per gentile concessione della Fabbrica di San Pietro in Vaticano; 2.29 © Author. Per gentile concessione della Fabbrica di San Pietro in Vaticano; 2.30 © Author. Per gentile concessione della Fabbrica di San Pietro in Vaticano; 2.31 © Author. Per gentile concessione della Fabbrica di San Pietro in Vaticano; 3.1 © Luciano Romano. Courtesy of Borghese Gallery, Rome; 3.2 © Luciano Romano. Courtesy of Borghese Gallery, Rome; 3.3 © Luciano Romano. Courtesy of Borghese Gallery, Rome; 3.4 © Victoria and Albert Museum, London; 3.5 © RMN-Grand Palais (Château de Versailles)/Gérard Blot; 3.6 © Luciano Romano. Courtesy of Borghese Gallery, Rome; 3.7 © Author. Per gentile concessione della Fabbrica di San Pietro in Vaticano; 3.8 © J. Paul Getty Museum, Los Angeles; 3.9 Public domain; 3.10 © 2021. Photograph Scala, Florence; 3.11 © RMN-Grand Palais (musée du Louvre)/Michel Urtado; 3.12 © The Morgan Library & Museum, New York; 3.13 ©

Luciano Romano. Courtesy of Borghese Gallery, Rome; 3.14 © RMN-Grand Palais (musée du Louvre) / Thierry Le Mage; 4.1 © Author; 4.2 Public domain; 4.3 © Fine Art Images / Archivi Alinari, Florence; 4.4 © Raffaello Bencini / Archivi Alinari, Florence; 4.5 © Per concessione del Ministero per i Beni e le Attività Culturali / Alinari Archives, Florence; 4.6 © Author. Per gentile concessione della Fabbrica di San Pietro in Vaticano; 4.7 Public domain; 4.8 © Per concessione del Ministero per i Beni e le Attività Culturali / Alinari Archives, Florence; 4.9 © The Morgan Library & Museum, New York; 4.10 © Kunsthalle Bremen. Photo: Marcus Meyer, ARTOTHEK, Bremen; 4.11 © Mauro Magliani per Alinari. Per concessione del Ministero per i Beni e le Attività Culturali / Archivi Alinari, Florence; 4.12 © Musée Fabre de Montpellier Méditerranée Métropole – Photographie Frédéric Jaulmes; 4.13 Public domain; 4.14 © Artothek / Archivi Alinari, Florence; 4.15 © Mauro Magliani for Alinari. Per concessione del Ministero per i Beni e le Attività Culturali / Archivi Alinari, Florence; 4.16 Royal Collection Trust / © Her Majesty Queen Elizabeth II 2021; 4.17 © Antonia Reeve; 4.18 Public domain; 4.19 © Per gentile concessione della Fabbrica di San Pietro in Vaticano; 4.20 © Metropolitan Museum of Art, New York; 4.21 Public domain; 4.22 © Schuler Auktionen; 4.23 © Allen Memorial Art Museum, Oberlin College, Ohio; 4.24 © RMN-Grand Palais (musée du Louvre) / Thierry Le Mage; 4.25 © 2021. Photograph Scala, Florence; 4.26 © Creative Commons CC0 1.0 Universal Public Domain Dedication; 4.27 © Metropolitan Museum of Art, New York; 4.28 © Trustees of the British Museum; 4.29 © Trustees of the British Museum; 4.30 © Metropolitan Museum of Art, New York; 5.1 © Trustees of the British Museum; 5.2 Public domain; 5.3 © Creative Commons – CC by NC; 5.4 © Metropolitan Museum of Art, New York; 5.5 © Biblioteca Nazionale Centrale 'Vittorio Emanuele II'; 5.6 © Author; 5.7 © Author; 5.8 © Author; 5.9 © Author; 5.10 © Author; 5.11 Public domain; 6.1 © RMN-Grand Palais (Château de Versailles) / Gérard Blot; 6.2 © Daniele Martini; 6.3 © Daniele Martini; 6.4 © Adam Eastland / Alamy Stock Photo; 6.5 © Author; 6.6 © Governatorato SCV – Direzione dei Musei per gentile concessione del Capitolo della Basilica Papale di Santa Maria Maggiore; 6.7 © Roma, Istituto centrale per la grafica, per gentile concessione del Ministero della cultura; 6.8 Public domain; 6.9 © 2021. Photograph Scala, Florence / bpk, Bildagentur für Künst, Kultur und Geschchte, Berlin; 6.10 © The State Hermitage Museum. Photograph by Leonard Kheifets, Alexander Koksharov; 6.11 © Author; 6.12 © Daniele Martini; 6.13 © Author; 6.14 © Author; 6.15 © Author; 6.16 © Author; 6.17 © Author; 6.18 © Author; 6.19 © Author; 6.20 © Author. Per gentile concessione della Fabbrica di San Pietro in Vaticano; 6.21 © 2021 Museum of Fine Arts, Boston; 6.22 © Allen Phillips / Wadsworth Atheneum; 6.23 © 2021 Museum of Fine Arts, Boston; 6.24 © Author; 6.25 © Author; 6.26 © Gabinetto Fotografico delle Gallerie degli Uffizi; 6.27 © Author; 6.28 © Author; 6.29 © Author; 6.30 © Author; 6.31 © Author; 6.32 © Author; 6.33 © Author; 6.34 © Peter1936F, CC BY-SA 4.0; 6.35 © Photograph Scala, Florence / Fondo Edifici di Culto – Ministero dell'Interno; 6.36 © Steven Zucker; 6.37 © Photograph Scala, Florence / Fondo Edifici di Culto – Ministero dell'Interno; 6.38 © Author; 6.39 © Author; 6.40 © Author; 6.41 © Author; 6.42 © Author; 6.43 © Author; 6.44 © Author; 6.45 © Author; 6.46 © Author; 6.47 © Author; 6.48 © Author; 6.49 © Author; 6.50 © Author; 6.51 © Author. Per gentile concessione della Fabbrica di San Pietro in Vaticano; 6.52 © Musée d'art et d'histoire, Ville de Genève, Bettina Jacot-Descombes / Flora Bevilacqua; 6.53 © CC0 in the public domain; 6.54 © Author

Index